Stefan Alkier and Annette Weissenrieder (Eds.)
Miracles Revisited

Studies of the Bible and Its Reception

Edited by
Dale C. Allison, Jr., Volker Leppin, Choon-Leong Seow, Barry Dov Walfish, Eric Ziolkowski

Volume 2

Miracles Revisited

New Testament Miracle Stories and their Concepts of Reality

Edited by
Stefan Alkier and Annette Weissenrieder

DE GRUYTER

ISBN 978-3-11-048792-3
e-ISBN 978-3-11-029637-2
ISSN 2195-450X

Library of Congress Cataloging-in-Publication Data
A CIP catalog record for this book has been applied for at the Library of Congress.

Bibliographic information published by the Deutsche Nationalbibliothek
The Deutsche Nationalbibliothek lists this publication in the Deutsche Nationalbibliografie; detailed bibliographic data are available in the Internet at http://dnb.dnb.de.

Logo: Martin Zech
Printing: Hubert & Co. GmbH & Co. KG, Göttingen
♾ Printed on acid-free paper
Printed in Germany

www.degruyter.com

Table of Contents

Stefan Alkier, Annette Weissenrieder

Preface

> Es kommt alles wieder, auch die Wunder, grade die Wunder. Sie haben ihre Gesetze.
>
> Kurt Tucholsky 1927

Through the study of miracles, the contributors in this volume show how unique perspectives to the history of antiquity are made possible with many consequences: as the first argument, miracles allow us to establish new directions in the debate about concepts of reality in antiquity and beyond. Since David Hume if not earlier, the interpretation of miracle stories has been dominated in the West by the binary distinction of fact vs. fiction. Even in the latest research this modern opposition is accepted as self-evident. The resulting ontology continues to underly the form-critical study of New Testament miracle stories, leading to interpretive nuances that presuppose the distinction of fact vs. fiction but have no basis in either the texts in question or their concepts of reality. Thus many scholars distinguish between stories with a historical basis and therefore a claim to facticity (e.g. healings interpreted in terms of psychosomatic therapies, or exorcisms in terms of social therapy) and stories invented out of whole cloth as fictional expressions of childlike desires (e.g. miraculous gifts or favors).

In order to overcome an impediment to research presented by this opposition of terms, between fact and fiction, supernatural and natural events, the authors in this volume ask about the changing use of miraculous events in religious as well as secular systems of thought and knowledge.

In the second argument, miracles allow us to thematize and historicize the social constitution, assumptions of normality and boundaries in and between epistemic systems. Reality and epistemology were not first disputed in modernity, but scathing criticism of miracles and sympathizing skepticism appeared in close proximity to each other already in antiquity, for example in *De morbo sacro* of the *Corpus Hippocraticum*. And in the third argument, miracles allow us to substantiate anew already-illuminated theoretical issues.

In addition, there is a recent debate in New Testament studies which introduces Ecology. At the same time, we should not allow miracles to follow the predominance of form criticism, which dominated the debate not only in New Testament. Not only did it lead to confining the miracle-discourse to the question of historicity, but a restriction to individual pericopes accompanied this, so that the macro-texts were neglected. The authors of this volume not only inquire into the macro-context more strongly than has been customary in research, but also expand the miracle-discourse to genres such as letters, histories, and apocalypses, while some authors exceed the boundaries between visual and textual sources. In order to do justice to these extraordinary perspectives, which occur alongside the interface of epistemic systems, we sought an interdisciplinary conversation that goes beyond the limits of antiquity to identify further traces.

The greater part of the published studies date back to discussions at a conference on 'Healing Stories and Concepts of Reality from Antiquity to the Middle Ages' at San Francisco Theological Seminary, November 16–18, 2011. The conference was designed collectively by Annette Weissenrieder and Stefan Alkier and made possible through the cooperation of San Francisco Theological Seminary and the Fachbereich Evangelische Theologie at the Goethe University, Frankfurt am Main. We also thank the association of friends and benefactors of the Goethe University for their generous support. Specifically, we thank the vice-president of the Goethe University, Prof. Dr. Rainer Klump, who made it possible for the students of the Goethe University to attend the conference.

We hold the opinion that interdisciplinary discourse opened new perspectives during the conference in a delightful way and with the addition of the conference-papers in the present volume this can be introduced now to international miracle research. We thank Lukas Walker, the doctoral students Phil Erwin, Thomas Soden, Katy Valentine, Michael Rydryck and Prof. Polly Coote for helpful support in proofreading. A special word of thanks goes to Alena Schulz and Michael Rydryck (Fachbereich Evangelische Theologie, Goethe University, Frankfurt am Main) for their invaluable assistance in preparing the index. In addition, we thank the editors for the acceptance of our volume in the new series, which will support the *Encyclopedia of the Bible and Its Reception* (EBR). Thanks also to the staff of De Gruyter Verlag, first and foremost Dr. Albrecht Döhnert, for the same friendly as well as professional collaboration.

Stefan Alkier and Annette Weissenrieder, July 2012

I Rereading New Testament Miracle Stories

Stefan Alkier

"For nothing will be impossible with God" (Luke 1:37)

The Reality of "The Feeding the Five Thousand" (Luke 9:10–17) in the Universe of Discourse of Luke's Gospel

1 Fact – Fiction – Friction

It is not always easy to classify a text as a miracle story. A short semantical analysis of Luke 9:10–17 cannot fail to notice that this text does not contain any of the terminology one commonly finds in miracle stories. Not only are terms like δυνάμεις (*dynameis*), ἔργον (*ergon*), παράδοξον (*paradoxon*), σημεῖον *(semeion)*, τέρας *(teras)*, θαῦμα (*thauma*) missing, but the text also fails to narrate the kinds of common reactions we find in other New Testament miracle stories. Despite the fact that there are more than 5,000 men on the scene, nobody wonders about the feeding of so many with only five loaves and two fish. Nobody praises God or his prophet, nobody gets frightened, nobody is beside themselves, nobody gets wild, and nobody even remarks: "We have seen strange things today" (Luke 5:26b).

Most modern exegetes have not been astonished either. They are used to asking: "How can we explain what *really* could have happened?" No one seems to have a problem with the deficient form of this miracle story. Why are exegetes so sure that the feeding of 5,000 is a miracle story? Why have they so easily classified this text as a miracle story in spite of the semantic, pragmatic and syntactical problems noted above?

The text confronts the readers with the obvious discrepancy between only five loaves and two fish in the hands of the disciples of Jesus and the large crowd of men that were fed with them. The text narrates that 5,000 men were fed with 5 loaves and two fish and that 12 baskets of broken pieces of bread were left over. The text does not, however, say frankly how this was done. With this implicit question the author directs the reader to find the right answer by remembering what he has already read in Luke's Gospel and what he will find by continuing to read. This is a way of reading that follows the strategies of the text itself. In some reception theories the reader who is in tune with these strategies is called the implied reader (Wolfgang Iser[1]). Other theorists talk about the model or the ideal reader (Umberto Eco[2]).

But real readers have a choice among very different readings, and following the strategies of the text is not the way most often chosen by real flesh and blood readers. Since the form-critical method taught exegetes to ignore the syntactical, semantic and pragmatic network between the micro- and the macro text, the common practice has been to isolate the stories and to explain the miraculous in the light of the concept of reality that the real reader finds convincing.

Since historical-critical exegetes decided to criticize the biblical texts in light of the empirical conception of reality that can be constructed in terms of cause and effect and analogy and repetition, they became more and more convinced that miracle stories are a product of religious fiction. Such fiction uses the miraculous as a code to express something that, by definition, is not miraculous but real. For David Friedrich Strauß,[3] the reality of the miracle story is the idea. For Rudolf Bultmann,[4] the self-understanding of existence formed the reality of the account. For Elisabeth Schüssler Fiorenza,[5] Christian propaganda stands at the center. For Gerd Theißen[6] – who has transformed good old demythologizing into psychotherapy – the desires of the poor and depressed are the reality behind the miracle story.

There is, however, a significant difference between Bultmann's hermeneutical concept of demythologizing and Gerd Theißen's psychological transformation of this program. Bultmann's concept was created in opposition to the explanations of rationalism. Theißen's approach tries to combine the two.

---

1 Cf. Wolfgang Iser, *Der implizite Leser: Kommunikationsformen des Romans von Bunyan bis Beckett* (Munich 1972); Hannelore Link, *Rezeptionsforschung: Eine Einführung in Methoden und Probleme* (2nd ed.; Stuttgart et al. 1976).

2 Umberto Eco, *The Role of the Reader: Explorations in the Semiotics of Texts* (Bloomington, Ind. 1979).

3 Cf. David Friedrich Strauss, *Das Leben Jesu* vol. 1 (Tübingen 1835), 75.

4 Cf. Rudolf Bultmann, *Jesus Christus und die Mythologie*, in: id., *Glauben und Verstehen* vol. 4 (4th ed.; Tübingen 1984), 141–89, esp. 146. Cf. Konrad Hammann, *Rudolf Bultmann: Eine Biographie* (2nd rev. ed.; Tübingen 2009).

5 Cf. Elisabeth Schüssler Fiorenza, *Miracles, Mission, and Apologetics*, introduction to *Aspects of Religious Propaganda in Judaism and Early Christianity,* by id. (University of Notre Dame Center for the Study of Judaism and Christianity in Antiquity 2; Notre Dame, Ind. 1976), 2.

6 Cf. Gerd Theißen, *Urchristliche Wundergeschichten: Ein Beitrag zur formgeschichtlichen Erforschung der synoptischen Evangelien* (StNT 8; Gütersloh 1974), 44.

Rationalism, from H. E. G. Paulus[7] up to Theißen, often appeals to a trick or a forgery. In Theißen's, *The Shadow of the Galilean (Der Schatten des Galiläers)*, rich women support Jesus. Johanna, one of these wealthy women, explains: "When I or others send him (Jesus) food, bread, fish or fruits and my servants suddenly get it out, for the crowd it seems to be a miracle. These poor people have never seen that much food at one time. Thus, if one desires it, for that person a real miracle happens."[8]

In this explanation of the "miracle," the 5000 were poor people who did not notice the rich women and their servants. Their conclusion is, therefore, that Jesus himself and not the rich women fed them by a miracle. But this rationalistic explanation of what "really" happened pays a high price for its demythologizing of the miracle stories. Jesus is no longer a miracle worker and he becomes not a shaman – as some contemporary scholars like to say about Jesus[9] – but a charlatan who lets the people think of him in ways that are not true. Moreover, Jesus has effectively stolen the thanks from those to whom it should have been given – the wealthy women. Theißen's genre of "gift miracles"[10] with its rationalistic explanation of how Jesus' miracles occurred, leave a bad taste in one's mouth.

The common problem of the rationalist hermeneutic and other such attempts to explain miracles is that they fail to read the microtext carefully. Specifically, they fail to read the particular account together with its meaning generating relations to other parts of the macro text. They bring their concept of reality to the isolated miracle stories because, from David Hume[11] to Gerd Theißen, they are

---

7 Cf. Heinrich Eberhard Gottlob Paulus, *Philologisch-kritischer und historischer Kommentar über die drei ersten Evangelien, in welchem der griechische Text, nach einer Recognition der Varianten, Interpunctionen und Abschnitte, durch Einleitungen, Inhaltsanzeigen und ununterbrochene Scholien als Grundlage der Geschichte des Urchristenthums synoptisch und chronologisch bearbeitet ist*, 3 vols. (Lübeck 1800–1802).

8 Cf. Gerd Theißen, *Der Schatten des Galiläers: Historische Jesusforschung in erzählender Form* (13th ed.; Gütersloh 1993), 168: "Wenn ich oder andere ihm Lebensmittel schicken, Brote, Fische und Früchte, und meine Leute holen sie plötzlich heraus, dann erscheint es der Menge wie ein Wunder. Diese armen Leute haben oft noch nie so viel Lebensmittel auf einmal gesehen. Wenn man so will, geschieht auch tatsächlich ein Wunder." Cf. also the English version Gerd Theißen, *The Shadow of the Galilean: The Quest of the Historical Jesus in Narrative Form* (updated ed.; Augsburg, Minn. 2007).

9 Cf. Bernd Kollmann, *Neutestamentliche Wundergeschichten: Biblisch-theologische Zugänge und Impulse für die Praxis* (Stuttgart et al. 2002), 22; Bernd Kollmann, *Jesus und die Christen als Wundertäter* (FRLANT 170; Göttingen 1996).

10 Cf. Theißen, *Urchristliche Wundergeschichten*, 111 ff.

11 David Hume, *Enquiries Concerning Human Understanding and Concerning the Principals of Morals* (repr. from the 1777 edition and Analytical Index by L. A. Selby-Bigge, 3rd rev. ed. With notes by P. H. Nidditch; Oxford 1975), 109–31.

convinced that miracle stories are an expression of an irrational, childish state of humanity. The investigation of New Testament miracle stories in the tradition of the historical-critical paradigm, therefore, depends on a binary logic that understands the miraculous of the miracle stories merely as religious fiction. Most important are the oppositions of fact and fiction and rational/irrational. The miraculous of the miracle stories belongs in this paradigm to the irrational and fictional.[12]

A semiotic-critical point of view provides an alternative to this binary way of thinking. To put the point briefly, my proposal is that the miraculous of the miracles is better understood in terms of a third way: The miraculous is neither fact nor fiction, but *friction*. The miraculous represents a break in the binary logic of the everyday experience. It is an aspect of reality that resists all the worldly explanations that cannot think something really new, truly contingent, creatively creative.[13]

What the miraculous is depends on the conscious and unconscious concepts of reality that always work in the background when we talk about miracles. Or, to put it the other way round: When we talk about miracles, we always talk about reality. What we call a miracle is not the same as what biblical texts call δυνάμεις (*dynameis*), παράδοξον (*paradoxon*), σημεῖα καὶ τέρατα *(semeia kai terata)*, and so on. I hope to elucidate a frictional concept – or concepts – of miracles by becoming a disciple of the biblical texts. If we take miracles as utterances of other experiences, other ways of thinking and world views, they could help us see what

---

12 Gerd Theißen, *Urchristliche Wundergeschichten*, 42: “Nun ist das ganze Urchristentum Zeichen eines tiefgreifenden Wandels, in dem sich die antike Kultur einem ‘neuen’ Irrationalismus zuwandte”; and 45: “Natürlich hat es wunderhafte Phänomene gegeben: unwahrscheinliche Heilungen und Wundercharismatiker. Aber erst durch symbolische Steigerungen wurden diese wunderhaften Phänomene in ein paradoxes handeln göttlicher Wesen verwandelt. Vergleichbare symbolische Steigerungen der Realität charakterisieren aber das ganze Neue Testament.”

13 This concept of the miraculous as friction does not only work in theology, but in philosophy and the arts, too: Cf. André Michels, *Zwei Rationalismen? Zur epistemischen Bedeutung des Wunders*, in *Wunder: Kunst, Wissenschaft und Religion vom 4. Jahrhundert bis zur Gegenwart, Katalog zur Ausstellung der Deichtorhallen Hamburg und der Siemens Stiftung, kuratiert von der Praxis für Ausstellungen und Theorie* (ed. Daniel Tyradellis, Beate Hentschel, and Dirk Luckow; Hamburg 2011), 249: “Wunder nennen wir ein Ereignis, das rational (noch) nicht erklärbar ist. Von den Religionen als Zeichen Gottes verstanden und gedeutet, weist es auf einen Bruch in der Rationalität, die Grenzen der rationalen Erklärbarkeit hin. Diese können zwar immer wieder verschoben werden, wie es sich im Laufe der Jahrhunderte gezeigt hat, bleiben aber letztlich unaufhebbar. ‘Wunder’ wäre demnach der Name für diesen unaufhebbaren Rest, für das Reale, das dem Rationalen, so spitzfindig, ausgeklügelt oder perfide seine Mittel auch sein mögen, Widerstand leistet.”

we do not see with our common sense explanations. I want to read the biblical texts as depictions of other worlds that I do not know.[14] To aid in this task I shall use two interwoven methodological concepts: Charles Sanders Peirce's idea of a "universe of discourse" and Umberto Eco's notion of an "Encyclopedia".

2 The Semiotic Concepts of the Universe of Discourse and the Encyclopedia[15]

Signs are not reducible to formal relational entities. A sign functions only through its use in sign connections such as conversations, texts, pictures, buildings, traffic laws, television broadcasts, pop concerts, scientific congresses, and so forth. These relevant sign connections, however, constitute an entire given culture, which is therefore to be understood not as monadic and monological, but rather as relational and dialogical. Cultures are based on the communally conventionalized, creative, and often contradictory use of signs. Cultures are connections of signs.

A sign thus requires at least two relationships in order to function: it must belong to a currently perceptible sign structure and, at the same time, to a culture as the whole of its virtual sign connections. In dependence upon and through a modification of Peirce's conceptuality, I shall call the concretely perceptible sign connection the "universe of discourse." With Umberto Eco I refer to this all-embracing cultural sign relation as the "Encyclopedia."

2.1 The Universe of Discourse

Semiotic grammar works out a formal sign model that describes which components must be combined so that a sign process in general, *semiosis*, can come about. It makes possible the explanation of which formal conditions a sign must fulfill and to which type of sign (more precisely, type of signs) it belongs (more precisely, can belong). It says nothing, however, about the communicative conditions of the use of signs. This task falls to semiotic rhetoric.

---

14 Cf. Stefan Alkier and Bernhard Dressler, "Wundergeschichten als fremde Welten lesen lernen," in *Religion zeigen: Religionspädagogik und Semiotik* (ed. B. Dressler and M. Meyer-Blanck; Münster 1998), 163–87.

15 Cf. Stefan Alkier, "New Testament Studies on the Basis of Categorical Semiotics," in *Reading the Bible Intertextually* (ed. R. B. Hays, L. Huizenga, and S. Alkier; Waco, Tex. 2009), 223–48.

Within this formulation of the question, Peirce's concept of the universe of discourse plays a fundamental role. James Jakób Liska defines it aptly: "The universe of discourse is what an utterer and interpreter must share so that communication can result."[16]

The concept of the universe of discourse does not develop out of the hermeneutic tradition or from a new text theory, nor did Peirce bring it to expression in the framework of his semiotic thought. It belongs much more to the discussion of logic in the nineteenth century. Boole formulated it in 1857 as follows: "In every discourse, whether the mind is now concerned with its own thoughts or the individual is communicating with another, there is an assumed or explicit border, inside of which the objects of its use are enclosed ... this universe of discourse is in the strictest sense the last *object* of the discourse."[17] Helmut Pape comments aptly: "The concept of the universe of discourse is used to solve the semantic problem of a suitably limited connection to the object [Gegenstandsbezug]."[18]

Peirce develops the logic of "Existential Graphs" in the framework of his semiotic philosophy. It concerns "a new conception of the relationship of reality, experience, and logic."[19] Later he comments: "The semantic conception of the EG [Existential Graph] is the idea that every logic must be related to a type of situation or universe of discourse. A given sign can consequently only function as a sign if it is ordered to a world – to the universe of discourse of the sign connection and context [Zeichenzusammenhang] – inside of whose conditions it can generate meanings."[20]

This foundational idea can be formulated for the concerns of every science. The universe of discourse of a given sign connection is then the world that this sign-connection establishes and assumes, so that what is told by or claimed by the sign-connection can plausibly function. *Alice in Wonderland* refers to a different world than the nature reports that the television program *Wonderful World* shows, and the latter would lose its credibility if it were to show marvellous creatures that we naturally are ready to accept and indeed expect in Alice's wonderland.

---

16 James Jakób Liszka, *A General Introduction to the Semeiotic of Charles Sanders Peirce* (Indiana and Bloomington, Ind. 1996), 92.

17 G. Boole, *An Investigation into the Laws of Thought*, 1857, 42, quote in: Charles S. Peirce, *Semiotische Schriften* vol. 3 (1906–13) (trans. and ed. C. Kloesel and H. Pape; Frankfurt a. M. 1993), 46.

18 Helmut Pape, introduction to *Semiotische Schriften* vol. 3 (1906–13), by C. S. Peirce (trans. C. Kloesel and H. Pape; Frankfurt a. M. 1993), 7–74, here: 49.

19 Ibid, 15.

20 Ibid, 22.

The communicative problem of the universe of discourse consists, however, precisely in the fact that there are different worlds with different laws and we must indicate in every act of expression that to which our statements relate. On this point we assume the common knowledge of the respectively indicated world between us and our conversation partner, and we must do that in order to be able to say more than one sentence a day.

The act of reference to a commonly recognized world belongs to the economy of human sign usage. The theory of the universe of discourse limits the validity of statements to a defined realm; it designates the scope of statements.

2.2 The Encyclopedia

The concept of the universe of discourse is always related to a concrete sign connection and context, be it a text, an archaeological site, a picture, or a coin. In contrast, the encyclopedia, which is necessarily virtual and impossible to grasp fully, due to its complexity, encompasses the conventionalized knowledge of a given society and thus breaches the boundaries of individual sign relations by virtue of the concept of the universe of discourse. Each act of sign production and sign reception must be related to at least one encyclopedia of culturally conventionalized knowledge.

Human communication functions with the use of many media and, at the same time, makes use of different sign systems. We speak, sing, paint, dance, form objects and design clothing, hairstyles, buildings, objects, and public and private spaces. No one communicates only in texts; no text functions without a connection to other sign systems. An encyclopedia consists not only of linguistic knowledge, but also of the knowledge of forms of address, norms of behavior, technical and practical knowledge, and so forth. The differences of cultural encyclopedias should not be obscured by the forces of increasing standardization in Western and North American culture. To see this, one need only imagine a German going for coffee and biscuits in Norway for the first time without the encyclopedic information that one has coffee and biscuits in Norway in the late evening and not in the afternoon as in Germany.

Whatever applies for the contemporaneity of various cultures is true in a compounded and amplified manner for the diversity of world knowledge in cultures that are not contemporaneous. The world of early Christianity is not our world, and it is to its enduring credit that historical-critical research has drawn attention to this irreducible difference. But the world of early Christianity, like any other world, does not consist only of texts and linguistic signs. The sign processes that have relevance in various ways for the preaching of Jesus, the composition of

New Testament writings, and the process of canonization must also be considered in working out an early Christian encyclopedia. They can only be considered, however, in so far as there are present remnants in our current time that can take on a sign function. To this, however, belong not only the texts that have come down to us but also the remnants of material culture. These sign complexes must be explored in the light of their respective universes of discourse with the appropriate diligence and care. Viewing these universes of discourse together enables the approximate concretization of a virtual encyclopedia of early Christianity.[21]

With that, the entries into the virtual encyclopedia of early Christianity are to be understood as cultural semantic units that can be provided with various indices – for example space and time – in order to take into account in an appropriate manner the diversity, but also the inconsistency, of this encyclopedia. It is thus not a question of an onthology of origin that could digest everything that falls under the name of early Christianity into a homogenous early Christian stew. It is rather a question of taking into account in an appropriate manner the complexity, heterogeneity, inconsistency, and diversity of early Christian sign production and reception.

The early Christian encyclopedia records not only early Christian sign production, but also its reception. It does not ask the question, "What is genuinely Christian?" Rather, it asks: "What is relevant for early Christianity?" For this kind of encyclopedic research, social-scientific and cultural-anthropological investigations are of decisive importance.

Just as relevant, however, is the question of the arrangement of space in cities and villages in which early Christian sign-production took place, even if these spaces were not arranged by Christians. Relevant also are questions concerning the technology for work and tools for agriculture and fishing. These culture-specific pieces of knowledge should be regarded and formulated as semantic segments of early Christian worlds of significance, which commonly provide a sound basis for the interpretation of individual sign complexes, be they texts, coins, pictures, or archaeological sites. Therefore, semiotic exegesis demands interdisciplinary cooperation in all areas of research that expands our knowledge of the (early) Christian encyclopedia.

It will be necessary not only to study the encyclopedia(s) of early Christianity, but also those of their recipients and of our own time. In this way, the important

---

21 Cf. Stefan Alkier and Jürgen Zangenberg, "Zeichen aus Text und Stein: Ein semiotisches Konzept zur Verhältnisbestimmung von Archäologie und Exegese," in *Zeichen aus Text und Stein: Studien auf dem Weg zu einer Archäologie des Neuen Testaments* (TANZ 42; Tübingen and Basel 2003), 21–62.

insight of historical criticism regarding the differences between "world views" can be more precisely described and more effectively used for the interpretation of texts. One can then largely avoid applying fallacious, anachronistic assumptions concerning reality from one's own encyclopedia to early Christian texts, as often happens with the interpretation of miracles.[22]

3 A Reading of Luke 9:10–17 in the Universe of Discourse of Luke's Gospel

The story about the feeding of the 5,000 (Luke 9,10–17)[23] is part of the Gospel of Luke, and as such it participates in the universe of discourse of Luke's Gospel. Because of this fact, the question of the plausibility of feeding 5,000 men is not to be explained by an appeal to modern or rationalistic assumptions that come from outside of the text. Its plausibility is instead a function of the story's relationship to other parts of the macro text in which it occurs (i.e., the Gospel of Luke as a whole).

The microtext (Luke 9:10–17) begins with Luke 9:10a: "On their return". This opening comment marks the following text as a sequel to all that has already been narrated in the Gospel of Luke. Without knowledge of Luke 1:1–9:9 it is not possible to understand the scene in Luke 9:10–17. And, as we will see, the theological plausibility of the miracle in 9:10–17 depends upon reading the Gospel to its end.

With regard to the hermeneutics of what we are used to classifying as "miracle stories," we can learn that it makes little sense to cut the miracle stories out of their macro texts – here, the Gospel of Luke – because full meaning, plausibility and conclusiveness of the micro text can only be generated in relation to other parts of the macro text. To put the matter differently, a miracle story without its context is underdetermined.

---

22 Cf. Stefan Alkier, "Wen wundert Was? Einblicke in die Wunderauslegung von der Aufklärung bis zur Gegenwart," *ZNT 7/Themenheft Wunder und Magie* (2001): 2–15.

23 Cf. Ulrich Busse, *Die Wunder des Propheten Jesus: Die Rezepzion, Komposition und Interpretation der Wundertradition im Evangelium des Lukas* (Stuttgart 1979), 232–48; A. J. Farrer, "Loaves and Thousands," in *Journal of Theological Studies*, N.S. 4 (1953): 1–14; Richard H. Hiers and Charles A. Kennedy, "The Bread and Fish Eucharist In the Gospels and Early Christian Art," in *Perspectives in Religious Studies* 3 (1976): 21–48; Bas Van Iersel, "Die wunderbare Speisung und das Abendmahl in der synoptischen Tradition (Mk VI 35–44 par.,VIII 1–20 par.)," *Novum Testamentum* 7 (1964): 167–94; Michael Pettem, "Le premier récit de la multiplication des pains et le problème synoptique," in *Studies in Religion/Sciences Religieuses* 14 (1985): 73–83.

The opening of 9:10–17 hints at what has happened before. The very formulation of the text presupposes readers who know what has been narrated in 1:1–9:9. Readers who want to understand the feeding story must know who the apostles who have returned are and what they have done. Luke 9:10 informs us that the deeds of these individuals must have been extraordinary because they tell Jesus "what great things they have done" (ὅσα ἐποίησαν / *hosa epoiesan*). We find the needed information in 9:1–6. In these verses we notice and understand the emphasis implicit in the syntagma ὅσα ἐποίησαν (*hosa epoiesan*): "Jesus called the twelve together and gave them power (δύναμις / *dynamis*) and authority (ἐξουσία/ *exousia*) over all demons and to cure diseases, and he sent them out to proclaim the kingdom of God and to heal." Luke 9:6 testifies that the apostles have done what Jesus told them and enabled them to do. Importantly, these deeds are the kinds of things that he has already done before chapter 9 and that he will continue to do in the feeding story: "to proclaim the kingdom and to heal with δύναμις (*dynamis*) and ἐξουσία (*exousia*)." No wonder, then, that the returning apostles immediately tell Jesus that they themselves have done the same kinds of great things that they have seen Jesus doing. By relating 9:1–6 to 9:10 we notice that the expression ὅσα ἐποίησαν (*hosa epoiesan*) as miracle terminology. The same expression – ὅσα ἐποίησεν (*hosa epoiesen*) – describes the glorious thing that Jesus did to the Gerasene demoniac in 8:39.

Jesus reacts in 9:10b. His reaction indicates that he believes what the apostles have told him. He himself knows that it takes a lot of effort to act with δύναμις (*dynamis*) and ἐξουσία (*exousia*) (cf. 6:18; 8:46). This is why he wants his returning apostles to rest just as he himself rests after he has done great things (cf. 5:16; 9:18). But as so often is the case the crowd disturbs their rest and silence and Jesus must again assume the role of teacher and healer until the end of the day (cf. 9:11–12a).

But what have the apostles done the whole day? Did they rest? It seems so because in v. 12b they are strong enough to begin to act again: "the twelve came to him and said, 'Send the crowd away, so that they may go into the surrounding villages and countryside, to lodge and get provisions; for we are here in a deserted place'."

Jesus did not call them or ask them to give him advice. They decided by themselves that Jesus needed advice because in their eyes he is not doing what the situation demands. They reverse the teacher/disciple relationship and begin speaking to him in the position of the teacher. They address Jesus as a disciple who does not really know what he is doing. They tell him how things are and what he should now be doing.

Jesus responds with a counteraction. With his ἐξουσία (*exousia*) / authority as the real teacher he gives the upstart miracle workers an order: "You give them something to eat!" (9:13a). The emphasis in this sentence rests on "YOU." Jesus denies the authority of his apostles to give him advice and declares with this emphatic YOU that they must do and will do what he, the real source of authority, wants them do.

The tension between the ἐξουσία (*exousia*) of the apostles and that of Jesus does not come to an end here because the apostles do not accept the authority of Jesus. They calculate with the rational logic of limited resources and human possibilities. Their answer to Jesus' order is pure irony. They want to make Jesus understand that the order he has given is not rational but absurd. What Jesus has commanded stands against everything a sane mind knows. They ignore their own previous frictional experiences of δύναμις (*dynamis*) and ἐξουσία (*exousia)* and even their experiences of the δύναμις (*dynamis*) and ἐξουσία (*exousia)* of Jesus, their teacher: "We have no more than five loaves and two fish – unless we go and buy food for all these people" (9:13b). The narrator adds: "For there were about five thousand men." (9:14).

The irony of the apostle's answer does not only result from the statements about the lateness of the day and the problem of organizing such a great amount of food, it also stems from the immense costs involved with feeding 5,000 men. Careful readers of Luke's Gospel know that at this point in the story the apostles have no money. Moreover, such readers know that the apostles know that Jesus knows that they have no money on hand. It was after all Jesus' own order in 9:3: "He said to them: Take nothing on your journey, no staff, no bag, neither bread, nor money."

But Jesus ignores the ignorance and irony of the apostles and continues his program of making them disciples again, people who accept his ἐξουσία (*exousia*) / authority and the frictional possibilities of divine power. To accomplish this he gives them a new order: "Make them sit down in groups of about fifty each." Because the story up to this point shows that the disciples do not want to do what their teacher says, the narrator declares: "They did so and made them all sit down." (9:14b–15a). Now the ignorant miracle workers are acting as disciples again.

Now that Jesus has won the battle of authority on earth he contacts the divine power in heaven: "And taking the five loaves and two fish, he looked up to heaven, and blessed and broke them, and gave them to the disciples to set before the crowd." (9:16).

By obeying Jesus the disciples are enabled to follow his first order and give the crowd something to eat. They give them the five loaves and two fish, but now these few items have been changed. When Jesus looks into heaven and blesses the bread from the earth and fish from the sea, heaven and earth are brought together. The materiality of bread and fish has become an effective sign of all the dimensions of God's creativity. In Luke this creative activity does not function as pure symbolism, but in a very materialistic way: "And all ate and were filled. What was left over was gathered up, twelve baskets of broken pieces." (9:17)

Importantly, the abundance of the blessed and broken bread and fish is not only a sign of the eschatological dimension of the feeding story or of the Lord's Supper. The twelve baskets are also an ironical answer to the ignorant irony of the miracle working apostles who could not follow the logic of God's powerful creativity because they were bounded by the rational logic of supply and demand. The twelve baskets mean that from the five loaves and two fish each one of them has now received his own basket.[24]

4 Jesus is not a Shaman or: How the Feeding of the 5000 Worked according to the Gospel of Luke

Why is the story of feeding the 5,000 in the Gospel of Luke not merely a nice fairytale? Why is the story so prone to be misunderstood by us in terms of Gerd Theißen's category of "Geschenkwunder"? We find the answer in Luke's Gospel itself: Luke did not want to tell fairytales like the one about Jesus the charlatan and his rich women that one can read about in Theißens *The Shadow of the Galilean*. Luke wanted to be a historian (cf. Luke 1:1–4). As an ancient historian his Gospel provides an answer concerning the plausibility of the feeding stories when we take him at his word and follow his "orderly account."

Careful readers notice that 9:17 fulfills what Mary sang in 1:53: "He has filled the hungry", and what Jesus prophesied in 6:21: "Blessed are you who are hungry now, for you shall be satisfied". The plausibility of these fulfillments comes from God's presence in the story of the Gospel of Luke, especially as this presence is represented in Jesus: "Jesus himself symbolizes God's presence among the people because he is so closely identified with the father (10:21–22)."[25]

---

24 Bas van Iersel, "Die wunderbare Speisung und das Abendmahl," 190ff, notices the relation of the feeding story to Lord's supper and the importance of the functionality of the term "twelve." He does not, however, see the irony in the text.

25 Carl Holladay, *A Critical Introduction to the New Testament: Interpreting the Message and Meaning of Jesus Christ* (Nashville, Tenn. 2005), 180. Cf. also C. Kavin Rowe, *Early Narrative Christology: The Lord in the Gospel of Luke* (BZNW 139; Berlin and New York 2006).

But God's presence[26] does not appear for the first time in the narrative of Luke's gospel, but in Luke's own reflection on what he thought he had to do as an historian. Thus he sets out to retell a story that others before him have already told. Nevertheless, he takes his own work to be necessary because all his predecessors have missed the true order of the events. And yet, despite his critique, Luke admits that they have actually given a narrative of the events in question. His contribution consists in his desire to add to and to retell the true order of the events of the story. These events as presented in the gospel did not happen as a result of human action and will, but as the fulfilment of God's intentions just as they were already foretold in the Holy Scriptures of Israel. Luke's prologue presents God not only by using the *passivum divinum* in v. 1:1b – "the things that have been fulfilled among us" –; but also by arguing that God is the true author of the events that Luke transforms into written signs. Luke's 'correct' version of the gospel therefore narrates what God did. Luke presents the story in his Gospel as the narrative about the things God did "among us" (1:1) and every sign in the Gospel has to be read from this perspective.

God is not only one character among others in the narrative. His acts and deeds do not only function as the content of the written story, they are also the dynamic object[27] which motivates not only the whole work of Luke, but every shorter

26 Cf. Stefan Alkier, "Ways of Presence and Modes of Absence in the Gospel of Luke – Or: How Scripture works," in *The Presence and Absence of God: Claremont Studies in the Philosophy of Religion* (ed. Ingolf U. Dalferth; Religion in Philosophy and Theology 42; Tübingen 2009), 41–55.
27 Charles Sanders Peirce, "Sundry Logical Conceptions," in *The Essential Peirce* vol. 2 (ed. by the Peirce Edition Project; Bloomington and Indianapolis, Ind. 1998) 272f., defines the sign triad as follows: "A Sign or Representamen, is a First which stands in such a genuine triadic relation to a Second, called its object, as to be capable of determining a Third, called its Interpretant, to assume the same triadic relation to its object in which it stands itself to the same Object." The sign represents the object *in one respect*. No sign is able to represent its object in every respect or capacity. It always takes a certain point of view. Peirce called the object that is represented in the sign triad through the choice of a special respect the *immediate* object. The immediate object has its place inside of the sign triad and indeed only inside this triad. The *dynamic* object, on the other hand, is the object that motivates the generation of a sign and of which the immediate object represents only some respect. The connection between the dynamic and the immediate object is given through the *ground* of the dynamic object. To speak of the *respect* of the immediate object thus means that the dynamic object cannot entirely be represented by the sign, but rather only with a view to a characteristic quality, which it shares with other objects. The generation of meaning is thus understood as a sign process that is motivated and driven by a dynamic object and that forms from the outset a first interpretant, which perceives something as a sign of this dynamic object. Furthermore, by means of this sign and on the basis of a ground postulated between both the dynamic and the immediate object, the interpretant brings in a certain aspect of the dynamic object as an immediate object in the sign relation, to be differentiated ontologically from the dynamic object.

narrative of "the things that have been fulfilled among us." In the act of narrating the one gospel story, Luke presents his Gospel as a truthful and proven sign of the presence of God.

In v. 1:26 God appears as an active character within the narrative: "In the sixth month the angel Gabriel was sent from God to a city of Galilee named Nazareth." The readers are already acquainted with the angel Gabriel as an agent or mediator of God from the first episode. Here, however, Luke explicitly emphasizes that what happens now is the explicit idea and will of God.

The angel visits Mary, the virgin, and the very first words he tells her clearly link Mary with God: "Greetings, O favored one, the Lord is with you." (1:28b). Mary becomes afraid, but, unlike Zechariah, she starts thinking about the meaning of the words of the angel. Gabriel declares: "Do not be afraid, Mary, for you have found favor with God. And behold, you will conceive in your womb and bear a son, and you shall call his name Jesus. He will be great and will be called the Son of the Most High. And the Lord God will give to him the throne of his father David and he will reign over the house of Jacob forever, and of his kingdom there will be no end" (1:30b–33).

The virgin birth is an intertextual link to the prophecy of Isaiah. Luke does not use the name of Immanuel as Matthew does when quoting Isa 7:14 (cf. Matt 1:23), but like Matthew he combines the virgin birth with the arrival of the messiah. The virgin birth indicates that God himself is the father of Jesus. Jesus is the son of God in a singular way, a way that no other creature was or ever will be.

Mary asks (just like, presumably, the reader): "How will this be, since I am a virgin?" (1:34). The angel explains this miracle: "The Holy Spirit will come upon you, and the power of the Most High will overshadow you. Therefore, the child to be born will be called holy – the Son of God. And behold, your relative Elizabeth in her old age has also conceived a son, and this is the sixth month with her who was called barren. For nothing will be impossible with God." (1:35–36). The pious and trustful answer of Mary is: "Behold, I am the servant of the Lord; let it be to me according to your word" (1:38).

God is not only the all-knowing author of the "events that have been accomplished among us" (1:1), but the actor who makes things happen that human beings cannot do. It is his creative power that makes the pregnancy of the elderly Elizabeth happen and it is the power of his own Holy Spirit that causes the pregnancy of the virgin and the feeding of the 5,000.

John and Jesus come into being as bodily signs of the creative power of God. Both act as characters that present the power of God continuously. Both are connected with God through his Holy Spirit, but with a considerable difference – John is identified as the precursor (cf. 3:4–6), while Jesus is the messiah himself. John is filled with the Holy Spirit, "even from his mother's womb", and yet, he has a flesh-

and-blood father named Zechariah (cf. 1:5–25). The miracle, which is explained by the power of God, worked the same way as was done for Abraham and Sarah.

In contrast to John, and all other human beings, Jesus has no fleshly father: God's own creative power causes Mary's pregnancy. He becomes the Son of God like no other before or after him. In the universe of the discourse of the Gospel of Luke, he is not only *a* son of god, but he is *the* Son of God. Because of this fact, he not only represents God as a symbol, he is the fleshly presence of God. Or, as the Gospel of John puts it: "And the Word became flesh and dwelt among us, and we have seen his glory, glory as of the Son from the Father, full of grace and truth." (John 1:14). Perhaps John read Matthew and Luke and omitted the virgin birth (probably because of its repercussions of Greek and Roman myths concerning the sexual affairs of the gods with human women). Regardless, the idea of the presence of God in Jesus is the same. Jesus of Nazareth presents God not only in his words and deeds, but also in his flesh.[28]

In Luke 11 Jesus teaches his disciples how to communicate with this powerful and creative God. They can talk to him like a child talks to his parents: "Father, hallowed be your name. Your Kingdom come. Give us each day our daily bread" (11:2f.). The feeding of the 5,000 story proclaims that God fulfilled this petition of Jesus. The love, power and creativity of his father is not restricted in the boundaries of human competence. His frictional δύναμις *(dynamis)* transcends the possibilities of daily human life. The hermeneutical and theological key in the universe of discourse of Luke's Gospel is the recognition that God is a God who communicates with his creation. Luke presents a God who can be asked for all the necessities of life precisely because he has the will, knowledge, freedom and power to do what he wants. After the narration of the Lord's prayer, we read in chapter 11: "So I say to you: Ask, and it will be given you; search and you will find; knock and the door will be opened to you." And if we read further, we even find a specific reference to fish: "Is there anyone among you who, if your child asks for a fish, will give a snake instead of a fish?" (11:11)

In the first appearance story in Luke's Gospel (24:13–33), Luke narrates the episode of the two apostles on the road to Emmaus: "While they were talking and discussing together, Jesus himself drew near and went with them. But their eyes were kept from recognizing him." (24:15–16). The *passivum divinum* implies that they did not identify him because God kept their eyes shut. The implicit logic is:

28 I agree with Hartwig Thyen who reads the Gospel of John as an intertextual commentary and correction of the Synoptics. Cf. Thyen, *Das Johannesevangelium* (HNT 6; Tübingen 2005). This commentary is the most important work about John written in German since that of Rudolf Bultmann. It should be translated into English.

Jesus' resurrected body looks (according to Luke) just the same as the earthly body of Jesus before his crucifixion. For that reason the resurrected body in the Emmaus-episode does not function as a proof for the resurrection, because God does not seem to want to use this apparent proof.

What does the resurrected Jesus do in this scene? He walks with them, he talks to them and he teaches them like he did before his death: "And beginning with Moses and all the Prophets, he interpreted to them in all the Scriptures the things concerning himself." (24:27). He opens the Scriptures because without them it is impossible to understand the story of the gospel as "the things that have been accomplished among us" (1:1). The Scriptures are the necessary hermeneutical key for understanding that God has been present even on the cross and his power is the reason for the empty tomb. Only God possesses the omnipotent creative power that is necessary to resurrect Jesus, the crucified one.

The two apostles on the road to Emmaus do not believe in the resurrection of the crucified one, because they did not yet see him (cf. 24:24c). Jesus criticizes them for that: "O foolish ones, and slow of heart to believe all that the prophets have spoken! Was it not necessary that the Christ should suffer these things and enter into his glory?" (24:25).

The pragmatic message of Luke, therefore, is that it is not necessary to see the body of the resurrected crucified to believe, but it is necessary to know and to understand the Holy Scriptures of Israel with regard to the story of Jesus Christ. In the Gospel of John we find something like a commentary on Jesus' critique in the Emmaus episode: "Blessed are those who have not seen and yet have believed" (John 21:29b).

Reading the Scriptures as the word of God with regard to the story of Jesus Christ opens the reader's heart to the story of God, the story of the presence of God in all history, in the present and in the future, and especially his presence in Jesus. Thus we read in John 10:22: "All things have been handed over to me by my father, and no one knows who the Son is except the Father, or who the Father is except the Son and anyone to whom the Son chooses to reveal him."[29] But the two on the road to Emmaus do not and cannot understand until Jesus "took the bread and blessed it and broke it and gave it to them" (24:30b), just as he had done in Luke 9:16 and 22:19. "And their eyes were opened,[30] and they recognized him. And he vanished from their sight." (24:31).

---

29 Cf. John 10:30: "I and the Father are one." Cf. H. Thyen, *Das Johannesevangelium* (HNT 6; Tübingen 2005), 499–500.

30 Cf. Richard B. Hays, "Intertextuality, Narrative, and the Problem of Unity of the Biblical Canon," in *Kanon und Intertextualität* (ed. Stefan Alkier and Richard B. Hays; Kleine Schriften des Fachbereichs Evangelische Theologie der Goethe-Universität Frankfurt/Main 1; Frankfurt a. M. 2010), 53–70, here: 68.

5 Some Guidelines for a Theological Interpretation of the Feeding Story

Theological interpretations of biblical texts are never reducible to historical or scientific knowledge. Much more is in view here, particularly regarding the significance of exegesis for the formation of present and future practices.

In general, modern interpretations of the feeding story have understood it as an invitation to share with others. This is nice, and it does at least ensure that the story serves to motivate some kind of pragmatic action on the part of modern readers. But the reduction of this story to an ethic of sharing fails to comprehend the theological dimensions of the account. These dimensions largely depend upon a theology of a responsive God whom one can thank, and to whom one can direct petitions not only, for example, concerning the salvation of one's own soul, but also for the provision of one's daily bread, and even for bread to be provided for the many.

One can even say more broadly that the symbolic, and so also the ethical function of the narratives that the restrictive code of modern, Western theology invokes when it lumps them together under the vague umbrella term "miracles" will itself only work if, in the context of the original universe of discourse of the biblical texts, the accounts were experienced and received as events that happened.

The interpretive horizon of the feeding of the 5,000 story cannot be adequately examined through the lens of a rationalist hermeneutic. Rather, one needs a theological hermeneutic that considers the intertextual connections among texts that focus on the God of Israel as the God who is merciful, just, and who desires to communicate with his creatures.[31] That means interpreting, in particular, through Old Testament texts and through other passages in the New Testament. Also, however, one must consider other texts from the wider collection of

31 The Feeding Story triggers several intertextual associations with Old Testament texts. The Exodus narrative provides a plausible context for recognizing God's miraculous ability to provide food. In that story God gave the Israelites who had fled from Egypt not only his word, but also an abundance of food so that all the people were satisfied (cf. Exod 16:1–36). Even the reference to the 5,000 being divided into groups of fifty probably alludes to the Exodus tradition (cf. Exod 18:21–26) and helps one understand that the 5,000 are being presented as God's people. The Psalms also recall the fact that God is one who supplies provisions when they remember the Exodus account (cf. Ps 78:21–29). The notion that God is the miraculous giver of food also occurs in the collection of stories in the Elijah and Elisha traditions (cf. 1 Kgs 17:8–16; 2 Kgs 4:42–44). Cf. Richard B. Hays, "Intertextuality, Narrative, and the Problem of Unity of the Biblical Canon," 53–70.

Jewish and Christian writings. Whoever desires to become a disciple of the Jesus of the feeding story must turn and in complete trust ask of God for his own bread and for bread to be provided for others. This is all the more necessary when one's options are, by the world's reckoning, limited.

This is not to say that one can anticipate miracles because, as God's friction, they defy what is feasible and calculable. In precisely this, however, they limit the totalitarian claims of causal explanations of reality, explanations that always lead to an exploitive ideology of what is possible.

The request made in faith can, in any case, be misunderstood when it is employed as a substitute for concrete political action. In this way such a request can itself devolve into another exercise in a cynical use of power that reinforces the unjust structures that are already in place. The actual material needs of those who are suffering and in want can thereby be shifted to God. This problem is, unfortunately, one of which the Christian church is perennially guilty.

Every individual act of thanksgiving and every individual request addressed to God transcends the boundaries of daily experience. It gets the potential to break open the self-contained character of common sense experience and politics. These frictional experiences generate an awareness of the possibility of new, genuinely contingent expectations, expectations that do not perpetuate shoddy substitutes for political action, but can instead motivate and orient our individual and our political life.

Michael Rydryck

Miracles of Judgment in Luke-Acts

In one of his works on form criticism Klaus Berger states the following concerning so called miracle-stories in biblical writings[1]: "Miracle / miracle-story is no kind of genre, but a modern description of an ancient concept of reality" [MR].[2]This statement is part of a growing consensus. Its implications have been elaborated by Stefan Alkier for the exegesis of the New Testament and by Peter Müller for biblical pedagogy. For an analysis of miracles of judgment in Luke-Acts, Berger's statement has two important consequences: first, it shows the impossibility of identifying miracle-like phenomena of judgment by methods of form criticism. Second, it directs the analyzing focus to the concepts of reality in the examined texts. In my paper I will follow these two lines of interpretation in at least two ways: After a short reflection on the character of miracles in biblical texts in general, I will outline some aspects of a hermeneutics of miracles based upon an extrabiblical example taken from popular culture and interpreted in patterns of theological exegesis. Second, I will focus on miracles of judgment in Luke-Acts as often underrated or even ignored miracle-like phenomena. Touching the *communis opinio* on miracles (of judgment) in Luke-Acts, I will apply the hermeneutics of miracles outlined before on specific phenomena in Luke-Acts, which could be interpreted as miracles of judgment.

It is commonplace in New Testament studies that the phenomenon "miracle" poses also a difficult terminological problem[3]: there is neither a standard terminology, nor is every related phenomenon *expressis verbis* called "miracle." The terms θαῦμα, δυνάμεις, 'έργον, παράδοξον, σημεῖον and τέρας are, especially in Luke-Acts, used with reference to healings and exorcisms. Each of these terms emphasize different aspects of powerful phenomena and are actually far from referring to the same.

Nevertheless all these terms have one thing in common: they all express experiences on the limits of that reality, which one is daily used to. They are taking place on the borderline of human possibilities. Also, they point to powerful phenomena, which occur in the passing and marking of the limits of different spaces of possibilities, power or perception.

---

1 All translations from German texts are given by the author [MR].

2 Klaus Berger, *Formen und Gattungen im Neuen Testament* (Tübingen: Francke, 2005), 362.

3 Cf. Stefan Alkier, "Wunder. III. Neues Testament. IV. Kirchengeschichtlich," *RGG*[4] 8: 1719–25.

These liminal phenomena would be misinterpreted if defined/understood in modern ontological categories, since there is no strict distinction between "immanent" and "transcendent" in ancient/biblical texts in general. In biblical texts for example there is only one reality with different spaces of possibility, power and perception, but also with different spheres of knowledge, time and existence. It is therefore necessary to be aware of this dynamic and multi-dimensional concept of reality while analyzing biblical texts.[4]

By focusing on a phenomenon of popular culture I was able to outline some aspects of a hermeneutics of liminality based on studies of New Testament and Practical Theology scholars:miracles often appear strange – they cause confusion and/or amazement. Take for example the owls in the first of the Harry Potter novels[5]: the owls are invading the apparently "normal" world of the Dursleys.[6] As messengers with letters from the mysterious and repressed world of "witchcraft and wizardry," they contact Harry, the orphaned son of the Potter family. The suppression and burning of the letters only increase number and ambition of the owls. They are relentless in their mission. The effect of this incredible event on the Dursleys gradually progresses from anger to panic. To Harry, however, the owls seem promising and their message is highly attractive. Finally, the Dursleys have to surrender to the terrifying power of the world to which Harry now belongs, which is betwixt and between their "normal" reality.

It is a miracle, isn't it? The owls are transients. They pass the border from the world of witchcraft and wizardry to the everyday life of a British suburb. And, by passing through it, they are marking the existence of this special border.[7] In the words of Henning Luther: "Along the frontier to the Other, the Unknown, to the moment unfamiliar and strange it is possible to perceive, that that which exists is not all that exists" [MR].[8]The owls are part of the communication between different spaces of reality. They are messengers that make the border temporarily passable and perceptible. The effects of this passing and marking vary greatly: For

---

4 For the theological implications of this thought cf. Henning Luther, *Religion und Alltag* (Stuttgart: Radius 1992), 47 f.

5 Cf. for the following Joanne K. Rowling, *Harry Potter and the Philosopher's Stone* (London: Bloomsbury 2010), 28–48.

6 For the tension between concepts of reality and the appearance of normality see Stefan Neuhaus, *Märchen* (Tübingen: Francke 2005), 347 f.

7 That the Harry Potter novels deal with contrasting concepts of reality outlines Neuhaus, *Märchen*, 345–52. Cf. also the thoughts concerning liminality and the perception of everyday life in Luther, *Religion und Alltag*, 46–48, 215–17.

8 Luther, *Religion und Alltag*, 54.

some it may be disturbing, terrifying or at least without meaning, for others it is fascinating – an expressive, meaningful promise.[9]

Only due to the liminality of frontiers, in the combination of marking and passing through them, in causing fascination and fear, the appearance of the owls is a miracle. Miracles are paradoxical phenomena – they are full of power and meaning in opposition to an apparently "normal" certainty, to social conventions and to the commonly known. To be clear, paradoxical does not necessarily mean incomprehensible. Miracles are always part of a communication, a dialogue, between different spaces of reality.[10] If not, they remain one-dimensional curiosities – maybe strange or incredible but definitely without meaning to those who experience them. In this way, miracles are inter-dimensional or interliminal phenomena. They occur in the passing and marking of limits between spaces of possibility and power making dialogue possible and difference perceptible.

Because of their setting in a frontier-area, miracles are ambiguous and collide with the certainties of everyday life, which makes them paradoxical. They are communicative and meaningful acts, which makes them plausible. And they happen beyond the limits of our control, unrejectably and effectively, which makes them powerful. Therefore, a phenomenology of miracles has to be a paradoxy of power.

Miracles gain plausibility in a specific semiotic context, i.e. the universe of discourse.[11] Within the universe of discourse, powerful and interliminal phenomena may be plausible as miracles – initially distinct from the extratextual question of the matters of fact.[12] Any attempt at a hermeneutics of miracles which does not recognize this specific semiotic context and instead operates with so-called common or apparently self-evident categories of reality is bound to fail, since miracles are paradoxical and plausible in their specific contexts and concepts of reality.

These concepts of reality, arranged for example within the universe of discourse of a text, have to be related with the conventionalized knowledge of an

9 For the hermeneutical implications see Karl-Heinrich Bieritz, "Zeichen und Wunder" in *Zeichen und Wunder* (ed. Werner Ritter and Michaela Albrecht; BTSP 31; Göttingen: Vandenhoeck und Ruprecht 2007), 290–312.

10 See Bieritz, *Zeichen und Wunder*, 301–4.

11 See Stefan Alkier, *Neues Testament* (Tübingen: Francke 2010), 146–48.

12 See Stefan Alkier and Bernhard Dressler, "Wundergeschichten als fremde Welten lesen lernen: Didaktische Überlegungen zu Mk 4:35–41," in *Religion zeigen. Religionspädagogik und Semiotik* (ed. Bernhard Dressler and Michael Meyer-Blanck; Veröffentlichungen des Religionspädagogischen Instituts Loccum 4; Münster: Lit 2003), 163–87.

epoch or culture, i.e. a specific encyclopedia. Only then, the matters of fact and possibility can be interpreted accurately. Due to the close relation of a specific universe of discourse and a valid encyclopedia the question of "miracle" implies the question of validity and plausibility of the concepts and meanings of reality in general.[13] But, plausibility does not guarantee relevance. Only the experience of the powerful paradox, the unrejectable, effective, and ambiguous mystery makes miracles meaningful to a potential percipient.[14]

Otherwise miracles could easily be trivialized or misinterpreted. If, for example, a miracle-like phenomenon is not perceived as powerful and meaningful but as absurd or illusory, it loses its character as a genuine, powerful paradox. But, more fundamentally, this seems to be the problem of a one-dimensional wonder,[15] i.e. a miraculous phenomenon which occurs not in marking and passing the limits of different spaces but has its setting on only one side of the frontier. Let us have a second look at the owls: as transients the owls are part of a miracle – their appearance is powerful, paradoxical, and ambiguous. What if the owls were no longer messengers but appeared exclusively in one or the other world? A glance back at the scene referred to in the beginning is instructive: in the beginning of the novel as well as its cinematic adaptation the owls appear for the first time in the British suburb. They come in great numbers and cause a lot of attention. Nevertheless their appearance remains without meaning to the spectators – a curious spectacle of nature.[16] The frontier is neither passed nor is it perceivable.

On the other side of the frontier, in the world of witchcraft and wizardry, the owls are far from appearing peculiar. They are normal and expected, mostly reliable postal workers – not unlike carrier pigeons. The owls carry news and parcels without being transients in the outlined sense. They belong to everyday life and therefore do not cause amazement or fear in this context.[17]

Beyond the liminality of the frontier, the one-dimensional wonder loses its miracle-like character. On one side owls are wild animals, while on the other they are part of the service sector. A one-dimensional wonder, if recognized, remains without meaning. Such a phenomenon has lost its possibility of perceiving the

13 Cf. the fundamental study of Stefan Alkier, *Wunder und Wirklichkeit in den Briefen des Apostels Paulus: Ein exegetischer Beitrag zu einem Wunderverständnis jenseits von Entmythologisierung und Rehistorisierung* (WUNT 134; Tübingen: Mohr Siebeck 2001).

14 Cf. Bieritz, *Zeichen und Wunder*, 295–97.

15 The problem in its contradictory character is raised by Bieritz, *Zeichen und Wunder*, 291f, 301.

16 Cf. Rowling, *Harry Potter and the Philosopher's Stone*, 10–12.

17 Cf. for example Rowling, *Harry Potter and the Philosopher's Stone*, 149 f., 181.

paradoxical fascination of liminality and its power to shape any concept of reality: “The one world within the limits easily becomes the only reality” [MR][18].

Miracles instead are effective and powerful on the limits of different spaces of reality and power. This specific characteristic makes them a focal point of theological interest, not only in regard to biblical texts. For Christian theology, miracles in their liminality reveal one kind of nexus between the divine and the human dimension of reality. Miracle-like phenomena include hermeneutic dynamics with regard to questions of possibilities and concepts of reality on the borderline betwixt and between different spaces.[19] The perception of miracles therefore may cause frustration, alteration, or even creation of theological concepts of reality.

At this point it is necessary to turn to the mainstream of exegetical opinion about miracles in Luke-Acts. Gerd Theißen writes concerning miracles (of judgment): “Modern and ancient people put more emphasis on the fear of punishment than on the increase of appreciation by imposing rules. It is therefore much more remarkable that in the New Testament miracles of judgment are nearly missing” [MR].[20] More recently, Theißen has regarded solely healing and exorcism stories done by Jesus as reliable examples of miracles in the New Testament.[21] This perspective includes many unsolved difficulties, but still represents the main discourse in German (miracles) scholarship.

Theißen’s point of view is also important for the exegesis of Luke-Acts in particular. Miracles in Luke-Acts for many scholars seem to be recognizable through the methods of form-criticism. Luke has a special preference for healing and exorcism stories, which are, in general, comprehensible in modern medical or psychological categories. Jesus seems to be the charismatic healer par excellence, familiar to Hellenistic culture in which the texts were written.

Other miracle-like phenomena in this perspective are legends or superstition. Miracles of judgment only occur in Acts and are told to impose rules or to help

18 Luther, *Religion und Alltag*, 46.

19 It is necessary to say, that miracles do not have to be curious or extraordinary in an emphatic sense. Miracle-like phenomena can also happen on the frontiers of every-day life: “Experiences of frontiers are not limited to dramatic and exceptional situations, but run through every-day life itself.” (Luther, *Religion und Alltag*, 217).

20 Gerd Theißen, *Urchristliche Wundergeschichten: Ein Beitrag zur formgeschichtlichen Erforschung der synoptischen Evangelien* (StNT 8; Gütersloh: Gütersloher Verlagshaus 1987), 117.

21 See Gerd Theißen, “Die Wunder Jesu: Historische, psychologische und theologische Aspekte,” in *Zeichen und Wunder (*ed. Werner Ritter and Michaela Albrecht; BTSP 31; Göttingen: Vandenhoeck und Ruprecht 2007), 30–52.

the reader come to terms with emotions like wrath, feelings of inferiority, and the like.

At the beginning of this essay I referred to the impossibility to generate a hermeneutics of miracles based on form-criticism, because it assumes what it attempts to prove by extrapolating a pattern and then identifying only such texts as miracles which fit that pattern. In fact, "miracle of judgment" is not a category given by the biblical texts.

Why the focus on healing and exorcism stories? Concerning Luke-Acts, there can be no doubt that these kinds of stories are an important part of Luke's theology. But considering only this aspect, generates a false picture of God acting in Luke-Acts. To complete the picture of Luke's theology, it is therefore necessary to emphasize God's wrath as well as his mercy, his power to heal as well as his power to judge. Or like it is said in chapter one of Luke's Gospel (Luke 1:51–53):

"He has shown strength with his arm; he has scattered the proud in the thoughts of their hearts. He has brought down the powerful from their thrones, and lifted up the lowly; he has filled the hungry with good things, and sent the rich away empty."[22]

Luke-Acts tells the story of God who imposes his eschatological rule. He acts through persons like John the Baptist, Jesus, Peter, and Paul. But God also acts by sending angels or without mediation. On the one hand, God acts through preaching, healing, and exorcising demons. On the other hand, he enacts his rule by announcing and working miracles of judgment, punishing the proud and freeing the captured. The holy God shapes his reign by acts of power. Thus, the divine dimension of possibility and power comes in contact with the human dimension. In other words, the boundary between the divine and the human spaces of reality is crossed and marked by God. Contact with God causes opponents of God, or the unholy, to vanish (or perish). This means demons, diseases, and persons such as Herod who failed to give glory to God (see Acts 12:20–24). God's reign, as pictured in Luke-Acts, is not harmless but full of potency.

In Luke 1:5–25 the first miracle of judgment occurs when an angel appears before Zechariah who is serves the Jerusalem temple. Zechariah's reaction appears formulaic in light of the intertexts of Gen 15 and 1 Sam 1. First, Zechariah asks for a sign to confirm himself. By asking this way, Zechariah indicates that he is unaware of the eschatological nature of the appearance. He underestimates the ambiguous power of the holy presence. The announcing angel works the requested sign as a punishing one because of Zechariah's lack of belief: Zechariah

22 All quotes from biblical texts are taken from the Fully Revised and Updated Harper Collins Study Bible.

falls silent until the foretold birth of his son (Luke 1:18–20). Some scholars interpret this revocation of voice as a psychosomatic consequence of the experienced epiphany. Such interpretation(s) join(s) the long tradition of rationalistic hermeneutics of miracles, which (problematically) transfers the modern encyclopedia to the ancient texts.

Remaining within the discourse of Luke-Acts, the meaning of Zechariah's muteness seems quite different: the revocation of Zechariah's voice is contextualized by the border-crossing epiphany in the temple of God and the appearance of a holy presence in front of a human being. In this context, the punishing sign as well as the promised birth mark the border between human and divine spaces of possibility. The presence of the holy God is creative and injuring at the same time. Zechariah's lack of belief vanishes with his voice and the birth of John the Baptist gives shape to the imminence of the reign of God.

In this story, borders are crossed and marked in different ways: the spatial border between divine and human spaces is represented by the appearance near the altar in the temple of God, i.e. a place which by definition is intended for border-crossing communication. The different limits of divine and human possibilities are marked by the muteness of Zechariah and the promised birth of his son. Furthermore there are limits of time, which are crossed in multiple ways: the histories of Abraham and Samuel are experienced again by the characters in the context of Luke's Gospel. The promise of John the Baptist's birth and the interpretation of his life in Zechariah's first speech after regaining his voice point simultaneously to the past and the future: John is both the returning Elijah and the prophet of the eschatological time. God passes the limits of linear time by combining future, past, and present in the inauguration of his eschatological reign.

The imminence of the reign of God is characterized in Luke-Acts as restitution and judgment. Luke 13:1–9 shows that the divine judgment has yet to begin. Two miracles of judgment are combined with an interpreting parable:

The scene is opened by a group of people coming to Jesus who report to him that Pilate has killed a great number of Galilaeans. Obviously, they interpret this event as a divine judgment for the sins these Galilaeans must have done. Jesus does not refute this interpretation. Moreover, he extends the interpretation to a universal threat of judgment for all those who do not repent. He likewise refers to the fall of the tower in Siloam and interprets this event as divine judgment. Death seems to be the consequence of sin and sin has to vanish in the presence of the divine/God. The narrative function of Jesus is not to limit the consequences of God's wrath. On the contrary, Jesus predicts wrath without limits in the time to come, if the people do not repent. The event horizon to the divine judgment has already passed and was marked by the events referred to in this scene.

The following parable affirms and supplements the theology presented in the preceding scene. Jesus tells a parable which interprets the preceding events in the context of the eschatological judgment – alluding to the sermon of repentance of John the Baptist in Luke 3, showing an intertextual relation to Jer 8:13 with synoptic parallels in Mark 11 and Matt 21. The message of Luke 13:1–5 is modified in such a way that there remains a final period for repentance, to avoid the eschatological wrath of God.

Luke 13:1–9 shows the liminal character of miracle-like phenomena. A massacre and the collapse of the tower in Siloam could be interpreted in human categories as cruel acts of Roman oppression or as terrible accidents. Also, the lack of fruit on a fig tree is not necessarily an extraordinary event. Only when contextualized in the theological or, more precisely, eschatological setting of Luke-Acts do these events acquire the specific meaning of miracles of judgment. The final frontier of God's eschatological judgment appears to be crossed and thus appeals to the reader to bring fruits worthy of repentance. One-dimensional, i.e. rationalistic, interpretations of the events would be inadequate in Luke's perspective. To modern readers, this point of view may seem offensive and difficult to accept. However, such an offense cannot be solved theologically by ignoring or misinterpreting texts like these to paint a picture of Jesus and God that is easier to accept.[23] Miracles of judgment are an important part of the universe of discourse shaped in Luke-Acts and are to be interpreted within that context. How this interpretation fits into a specific encyclopedia is another question, which cannot be answered by exegesis alone.

At the beginning of the book of Acts a miracle of judgment occurs, which is not often recognized as such: the death of Judas (Acts 1:15–20):

> In those days Peter stood up among the believers (together the crowd numbered about one hundred twenty persons) and said, "Friends, the scripture had to be fulfilled, which the Holy Spirit through David foretold concerning Judas, who became a guide for those who arrested Jesus – for he was numbered among us and was allotted his share in this ministry." (Now this man acquired a field with the reward of his wickedness; and falling headlong, he burst open in the middle and all his bowels gushed out. This became known to all the residents of Jerusalem, so that the field was called in their language Hakeldama, that is, Field of Blood.) "For it is written in the book of Psalms, 'Let his homestead become desolate, and let there be no one to live in it'; and 'Let another take his position of overseer.'

23 For such political and, in part, offending issues concerning miracles cf. the paper of James Noel in this book.

In the perspective of form-criticism this text is not a miracle but a legend, a text of minor theological relevance. By looking at the text as part of the universe of discourse of Luke-Acts its character as that of an act of judgment seems obvious. The death of Judas is presented as fulfilling scripture by referring to intertexts from the Book of Psalms. The reference to the Holy Ghost, who spoke through David, and the verb δεῖ, as indication for a divine act, characterize the betrayal and death of Judas as some kind of necessity. The limits of time are abrogated in this event because David predicted the events that are fulfilled in God's imminent reign.

Acts 1:18 states that Judas has fallen and consequently his body burst asunder, expelling his bowels. Interpreted simply as a horrific demise, this event would be conceivable within the context of everyday life. But, contextualized by the Holy Scriptures of Israel it becomes transparent as a divine act of judgment. Borders are marked and crossed in different ways, such as the abrogated limits of time and the intertextual interplay cited above. Judas is forced to pass the final frontier of human existence. His death marks the limit that is set to those who stand against God. The consequence of their way of acting is death – a most familiar thought from the Psalms. From the perspective of the reader, the death of Judas appeals to the recognition of the eschatological judgment of God as the final limit of every human decision.

Acts 9:1–9 tells the repentance of Saul-Paul caused by an epiphany. Saul falls blind as a result of the appearance. Some scholars interpret this blindness in a rationalistic way as a physical consequence caused by the intense light. But let us have a closer look: in the beginning Saul is characterized as a persecutor. While he is on his way to persecute the Christians in Damascus he has a vision and audition of Jesus. The voice of Jesus accuses Saul (Acts 9:4): "He fell to the ground and heard a voice saying to him, "Saul, Saul, why do you persecute me?" The question contains an accusation; the persecutor is called such by his victim. Saul loses all his power; he falls to the earth and is struck with blindness. He reacts with trembling and astonishment and shows respect to the powerful other, calling him "Kyrios." Like Jacob at the river Jabbok, Saul asks for the identity of the appearing other and finds out that it is Jesus. Without explaining his reasons, the Kyrios-Jesus gives orders to Saul. In the end of the scene, verse 9, Saul shows his repentance: he does not eat or drink for the time of his blindness.

The event has a pedagogical character without being called punishment or judgment *expressis verbis*. Saul's own power is taken only to be restored afterward by Jesus. The persecutor vanishes and becomes the chosen vessel of God's mission. Saul is brought to his limits by losing his own abilities. In an act of recreation he is empowered through the power of the divine other. The power of taking and giving shows the superiority of God and his messiah. The border between the human and the divine dimension of possibility is crossed in at least two ways: one, the miracle of judgment makes Saul powerless; two, the empowerment as a chosen vessel makes Saul more powerful than before. Both acts are beyond human possibility. Furthermore, the events mark a biographical frontier: the persecutor of Christ becomes the vessel of Christ; his former life is finally past and his new life is a recreation of God.

The list of miracles of judgment in Luke-Acts could easily be extended. Texts like Acts 5:1–11; Acts 12:19–24 or Acts 13:6–12 are not the only but surely the most prominent ones. I hope that it became clear, that miracles of judgment are an important part of Luke's narration and theology. They are complementary to healings, exorcisms, and stories of liberation. Restoration and judgment are closely connected in God's action to impose his eschatological reign. Miracles occur on the frontier between the divine and the human dimension of possibility. They are powerful phenomena of liminality expressing the character of God's imminent reign as pictured in Luke-Acts.

Philip Erwin

Epiphany Reconsidered: A parallel reading of Acts 9:1–9 and *Iliad* 188–224a

1 Introduction

The epiphany of Jesus to Saul on the Damascus road in Acts 9:1–9 inaugurates a shift both in Saul's character and in the overall narrative of Acts. Prior to this scene Saul had entered the narrative only briefly at the periphery of the stoning of Stephen (Acts 7:58) and as a persecutor of the *ekklesia* (Acts 8:3). From chapter nine forward, Saul (later to be known as Paul; Acts 13:9) emerges from a peripheral role as persecutor to a central role as one who proclaims the message of Jesus Christ. Given these dramatic shifts, most commentators interpret this scene as Saul's conversion or prophetic call.[1] Specifically, the categories of conversion/call are often generated by comparing Saul's epiphanic experience to those of prophets, e.g. Moses (Exod 3:3; 19:16–20); Isaiah (Isa 49); and Jeremiah (Jer 1);[2] gentiles/idolaters who convert to "Judaism," e.g. Aseneth (*Joseph and Aseneth* 14);[3] Heliodorus (2 Macc 3:22ff.); and the epiphany of Isis to Lucius in Apuleius'

1 Some interpreters, following Krister Stendahl, classify this scene as a prophetic "commissioning" or "call": Krister Stendahl, "Paul Among Jews and Gentiles," in *Paul Among Jews and Gentiles and Other Essays* (Philadelphia: Fortress Press, 1976), 7–23; Ernst Haenchen, *The Acts of the Apostles: A Commentary* (trans. R. McL. Wilson et. al.; Philadelphia: The Westminster Press, 1971), 322; Luke Timothy Johnson, *The Acts of the Apostles*, Sacra Pagina (Collegeville, Minn.: Liturgical Press, 1992), 166–69; Beverly Roberts Gaventa, *The Acts of the Apostles* (Nashville: Abingdon Press, 2003), 146–56; Richard I. Pervo, *Acts: A Commentary* (Hermeneia; Minneapolis: Fortress Press, 2009), 230–44, see especially 236. Others, even of more recent vintage, maintain that this scene is comparable to other religious conversions of antiquity and is thus classifiable as a conversion: Christoph Burchard, *Der Dreizehnte Zeuge: Traditions- und kompositionsgeschichtliche Untersuchungen zu Lukas' Darstellung der Frühzeit des Paulus* (Göttingen: Vandenhoeck & Ruprecht, 1970), 59–88; James D.G. Dunn, *The Acts of the Apostles* (Valley Forge, PA: Trinity Press International, 1996), 117–25; Charles H. Talbert, "Conversion in the Acts of the Apostles: Ancient Auditors' Perceptions," in *Reading Luke-Acts in its Mediterranean Milieu* (Leiden: Brill, 2003), 135–48; Ben Witherington III, *The Acts of the Apostles: A Socio-Rhetorical Commentary* (Grand Rapids, Mi.: William B. Eerdmans Publishing Company, 1998), 302–20, see especially 303–4.

2 See Stendahl, "Paul Among Jews and Gentiles," 8–11; Johnson, *The Acts of the Apostles*, 163–64.

3 See Burchard, *Dreizehnte Zeuge*, 55–88.

Metamorphoses 11.3 ff.[4] Despite the variation in date, language, and social context of these epiphanic accounts, one may observe a common, for lack of a better term, "religious"[5] orientation in each account. From the prophets to Lucius, each

4 Jason Lamoreaux reads Acts 9:1–19 in light of *Joseph and Aseneth* and Apuleius' *Metamorphosis*, using Victor Turner's model of ritual process and Social Identity Theory. See Jason Lamoreaux, "Social Identity, Boundary Breaking, and Ritual: Saul's Recruitment on the Road to Damascus." *Biblical Theology Bulletin: A Journal of Bible and Theology* 38 (2008): 122–35, see particularly 127–32.

5 The terms "religious" and "conversion" require provisional definitions. First, I understand "religious" primarily in terms of ritualistic patterns of behavior associated with a divine figure. Ritual itself is a difficult term to define; however, for the sake of brevity, I understand ritual here, apropos a divine figure, simply as acts that signify devotion. To define what I mean (to critique) concerning conversion is best expressed by the oft-cited Arthur Darby Nock: participating in various cults "led to an acceptance of new worships as useful supplements and not as substitutes, and they did not involve the taking of a new way of life in place of the old. This we may call adhesion in contradistinction to conversion. By conversion we mean the reorientation of the soul of an individual, his deliberate turning from indifference or from an earlier form of piety to another, a turning which implies a consciousness that a great change is involved, that the old was wrong and the new is right." A.D. Nock, *Conversion: The Old and the New in Religion from Alexander the Great to Augustine of Hippo* (London: Oxford University Press, 1933), 7. I should also acknowledge two critiques of Nock that influence my thinking. First, Ramsay MacMullen raises the point that Nock defines "religion" too narrowly in terms of doctrine and thus must understand conversion as shaped by doctrine or, as MacMullen puts it, "verbal orthodoxy"; that is, MacMullen believes other types of non-verbal/doctrinal practices can form an ethically normative way of life (MacMullen, 76). Second, Zeba Crook critiques both Nock and MacMullen on similar grounds, locating them both within a "psychological scale" of interpretation. Crook's critique is the common social-scientific one: "We cannot assume that such different beings experience life and emotions in similar ways. And if they do not experience life and emotions in similar ways, we should not imagine that psychology, which (allegedly) can help us understand our own lives, will be a helpful or illuminating way to understand their lives. For example, behaviour in the ancient world was governed *externally*, by honour and shame, more than it was governed *internally*, by guilt" (Crook, 51; emphasis his). One wonders how Crook would interpret Achilles' deliberation κατὰ φρένα καὶ κατὰ θυμόν (*Il.* 1.193), the "gall [χόλος], which makes a man grow angry for all his great mind, that gall of anger that swarms like smoke inside of a man's heart" (*Il.* 1.108–110; Richmond Lattimore's translation), or Saul's ἐμπνέων ἀπειλῆς καὶ φόνου (Acts 9:1). The options for understanding so-called ancient religion and conversion seem extreme: people approach religious practice either "psychologically" or "socially"; conversion is either "internal" or "external"; or, at the very least, is more one than the other. While I cannot develop a coherent proposal here, I suggest that such alternatives fall well short of addressing the complex accounts of Saul's and Achilles' epiphanies. In a sense, the experiences or behaviors are neither psychological nor social; rather, they exist on a plane of discourse (in narrative/literature) that such categories obfuscate – my simple provisional definitions may (unintentionally) illustrate this point. Ramsay MacMullen, "Conversion: A Historian's View." *The Second Century: A Journal of Early Christian Studies* 5:2 (Summer 1985/1986): 67–81; Zeba Crook, *Reconceptualising*

epiphany has the effect of transforming one's fidelity to a particular deity – whether by opening a prophetic channel or by an exchange of one set of practices/beliefs/religion for another.

Contrary to this classification regarding Acts 9:1–9, Homeric epiphany functions primarily as a narrative device to associate and direct human action with divine will. These associations and directions do not, however, develop cultic devotion of characters to particular gods or goddesses, nor do they require total loyalty or obedience to divine will. This alternative function of epiphany in the *Iliad* led me to consider its potential for generating insights on the epiphany of Saul, which avoids the tendency to fit it into categories of conversion or call. In the following essay I expand on this point, reading Acts 9:1–9 in parallel with perhaps the most famous of Homer's epiphanies, Athena's epiphany to Achilles in *Iliad* 1.188–224. In light of this parallel reading I contend that Saul's epiphany in Acts 9:1–9 functions to prevent Saul's imminent violent action by introducing alternative motivating factors that (re)direct his subsequent actions.

2 Reading the Epiphanies of Saul and Achilles in Parallel

Saul's epiphanic experience parallels other epiphanies insofar as he is visited by a heavenly figure, receives instruction, and, subsequent to that instruction, determines to alter his course of action, particularly in relation to the heavenly figure represented in/by the visitation. In light of current interpretative tendencies it seems reasonable to question the extent to which one must/may classify an epiphany of a heavenly figure as religious in orientation.[6] Given the range of epiphanies consulted by interpreters, one would think that epiphanies in the ancient world always have a religious function – i.e. to solicit worship or honoring of a particular god or heavenly figure. This is not the case for Homer. In *Iliad* 1.188 ff. Athena appears to Achilles in order to prevent him from killing Agamemnon in a fit of rage. Athena does not solicit worship neither for her-

---

Conversion: Patronage, Loyalty, and Conversion in the Religions of the Ancient Mediterranean (Berlin: Walter de Gruyter, 2004), 24–27, 49–52; Homer, *The Iliad* (trans. Richmond Lattimore; Chicago: University of Chicago Press, 1951), 378.

6 Gerd Theißen classifies epiphany, in its broad sense, as a theme of miracle stories, concluding that "epiphany is to myth as anecdote is to biography: it can be a part of a myth, but is complete in itself." Gerd Theißen, *Miracle Stories of the Early Christian Tradition* (trans. Francis McDonagh; Edinburgh: T&T Clark Ltd., 1983), 98.

self, nor for Hera by whom she was sent. At a superficial level of observation, *Iliad* 1.188 ff. and Acts 9:1–9 correspond in terms of the visitation of a divine/heavenly figure and the purpose of that visitation, i.e. to prevent an act of violence. By reading Acts 9:1–9 and *Iliad* 1.188 ff. in parallel I intend not to make a case for literary imitation, source, or a classification of form.[7] Instead, I attempt to read these scenes as independent accounts with similar content and motifs which enhance modern interpretation of epiphanic accounts in ancient contexts.

2.1 *Iliad* 1.188–94a and Acts 9:1–2

The specter of violence frames both Achilles' and Saul's epiphanic episodes. In the former account, Homer describes Achilles' reaction to insults of Agamemnon as he considers whether or not to kill him:

> Thus he (Agamemnon) spoke. And grief came upon the son of Peleus and [the] heart within his hairy chest pondered in two directions: (190) whether he should unsheathe his sharp sword from the side of [his] thigh, displace the men, and slay the son of Atreus, or cease [his] anger and restrain [his] spirit. While he was considering these things in [his] mind and in [his] heart, he began to draw [his] large sword from [its] scabbard ... (*Iliad* 1.188–94a).[8]

Violence appears imminent. Achilles issues no threat or warning of his attack and, despite his apparent dilemma, Achilles begins to act almost reflexively by drawing his sword before he makes a decision on what to do. Moreover, Achilles' deliberation occurs "in [his] mind and in [his] heart" (κατὰ φρένα καὶ κατὰ θυμόν) and is thereby concealed from Agamemnon and others around him. This concealment of Achilles' violent intention prevents any preemptive attempt of Agamemnon or his companions to sway or prevent Achilles from acting out in violence. This heightens the exigency of the situation so that only a god could intervene at this moment.

7 Dennis R. MacDonald's work on Homeric imitation in Acts serves as the example of such an approach. Interestingly, MacDonald does not identify/argue for Acts 9:1–9 as a Homeric imitation/parallel. For a summary of his method see, Dennis R. MacDonald, *Does the New Testament Imitate Homer? Four Cases from the Acts of the Apostles* (New Haven, Conn.: Yale University Press, 2003), 1–15.

8 From this point forward references to the *Iliad* will be abbreviated *Il.* Translations of the Greek text are mine unless otherwise noted. For Greek text see Homer, *The Iliad*, vol. 1 (trans. A.T. Murray (Cambridge, Mass.: Harvard University Press, 1924), 16 and 18.

Acts 9:1 introduces a similar situation. Saul seeks legal sanction to carry out acts of violence against the disciples:

> And Saul, still breathing (ἐμπνέων)[9] of a threat and murder with respect to the disciples of the Lord, went to the high priest [and] requested letters to the synagogues in Damascus, so that if he found some who were [a part] of the way, both men and women, he would bring [them] bound to Jerusalem (Acts 9:1–2).

The imminence of Saul's violence is delayed by (a) the legal process of securing letters and (b) the distance between himself and the disciples. While Saul's apparent relationship to authorities who, in the context of this narrative, hold sanction over life and death intensifies the threat of violence, his intentions obtain less potential than Achilles' whose target stands nearby. This lack of proximity also ensures that Saul's violent intentions are concealed from the disciples. Here interpreters often mistakenly associate ἐμπνέων with speech so that Saul would appear to be publicizing his violent intentions.[10] Besides the semantic limitation of understanding ἐμπνέων as an expressive or speech-related term, such an understanding arbitrarily diminishes the exigency of the situation. The possibility of threats reaching the disciples before Saul receives official sanction leaves open the possibility that the disciples could avoid persecution. Both Saul and Achilles pose real and present danger. Their ability to achieve the violence they intend is intensified by their access to instruments of murder; for Saul it is the sanction of the chief priest while for Achilles it is his own sword. In each case, the

---

9 According to *LSJ* ἐμπνέω with a genitive may be translated either "breathe of ..." or "be laden with ..." I have chosen the translation "breathing" to maintain the primary meaning associated with physical breathing; however, as I will argue, this verbal idea is dissimilar to modern associations of breathe, i.e. exhale, with speech. And, in this case, breathing is best not understood in terms of inspiration, though that is within its semantic range; cf. T. Muraoka, "ἐμπνέω," in *A Greek-English Lexicon of the Septuagint* (Louvain: Peeters, 2009), 228: "'to breath of' + gen., 'παν ἐμπνέονωῆς' Job 10:40"; almost every LXX reference cited here pertains to breathing as in "breathing breath" or "breathing life," etc.

10 Luke Timothy Johnson comments that 9:1–2 are a continuation of 8:1–3. While the scenes seem thematically and, perhaps, narratively connected by way of ἔτι, Saul seems to be pursuing new threat(s) and murder in a new city, Damascus. Other than assuming that the "breathing of a threat and murder" against disciples in Damascus is part of a public campaign or that breathing itself suggests something expressive, I do not find links between 8:1–3 and 9:1ff. in the text which would suggest they are part of the same campaign. Beverly Gaventa interprets Saul's request of letters from the chief priest to be the "specific form" of his "fearsome breath." Richard I. Pervo excludes 9:1–2 from his comments for no apparent reason. See Johnson, *The Acts of the Apostles*, 162; Gaventa, *The Acts of the Apostles*, 148; Pervo, *Acts: A Commentary*, 240.

potential aggressors have the intent, opportunity, and means to act violently against unwitting victims. The privacy of their intentions suggests strongly that divine intervention stands as the only means by which concealed potential violence may be thwarted.

2.2 *Iliad* 1.194b–218 and Acts 9:3–8a

The appearance of Athena interrupts Achilles' anticipated act of violence as she temporarily restrains him and attempts to persuade him to attack Agamemnon with words instead of his sword:

> But Athena came (195) from heaven; for Hera the white-armed goddess sent her forth, loving and caring for both [of them] equally in [her] heart. And [Athena] stood behind [him], and grabbed the son of Peleus by [his] golden hair, showing herself to him alone; and not one of the others saw [her]. And Achilles was astounded, turned around, and immediately he recognized (200) Pallas Athena; and [her] eyes flashed terribly; and speaking with winged words he spoke to [her]: "Why, then, have you come daughter of Zeus who bears the aegis? Is it so that you might see the outrageous behavior of Agamemnon son of Atreus? No, I will tell you, and I think also this will be brought to completion: (205) by such acts of extreme arrogance he shall quickly lose [his] life." And then Athena the owl-eyed goddess said to [him], "I came from heaven to cease your rage, in the hope that you will obey, for the white-armed goddess Hera sent me forth, loving and caring for both [of you] equally in [her] heart. (210) But come now, cease strife, do not draw [your] sword with [your] hand; rather, then, reproach him with words, [speaking] as it will be. For thus I will speak out, and truly this will be fulfilled, and at that time three-times as many prizes will be brought to you on account of his outrageous behavior; but you [must] restrain [yourself], and obey us!" (215) And answering swift-footed Achilles spoke to [her]: "It is fitting indeed, goddess, to obey the word of you two even while I am extremely angry in my heart, so that [it will be] better. If anyone obeys the gods, they certainly listen to him (*Il.* 194b–218).

Athena's appearance is a direct response to Achilles' inner thoughts, intentions, and subtle gesture, which remained concealed from others and generated no other reaction. Homer describes Athena's epiphany in pictorial/visual terms, emphasizing her location/position: "came from heaven" (194b–195); "stood behind [Achilles]" (197); physical features (eyes): "her eyes flashed terribly" (200); "Athena who bears the aegis" (203) and "owl-eyed Athena" (206); and actions: "grabbed the son of Peleus by his golden hair" (197); "showing herself" (197); speech (206). The immediacy with which Athena arrives and appears from heaven transcends the physical limitations of space and time and, as the subsequent narrative indicates, creates an alternative space wherein divine/human discourse may take place without anyone else's knowledge or even the passage of time. Despite this transcendence of physicality, Athena indicates her presence through physical contact and appearance; that is, she has distinct physical features. Athena's eyes flash, mesmerize Achilles, and likely inspire the epithet "owl-eyed Athena."[11] The flashing owl-like appearance of her eyes and the presence of her shield establish a visual profile that makes her instantly recognizable. The visual composition of the scene places Athena on the same plane as Achilles, i.e. she stands behind and not above/over him, unlike Jesus in relation to Saul, who fell to the ground. By taking a position behind Achilles and pulling his hair Athena shows the capacity to coerce through physical contact. Despite this, Athena does not achieve her principle aim – to stop Achilles from killing Agamemnon – by force. While the grabbing of Achilles' hair immediately prevents him from carrying out his violent intention, it fails to prevent Achilles from following through in the future; in fact, Achilles' sword remains drawn until after Athena departs (219)!

Athena's opposition is expressed in speech, though Achilles initiates the discourse by asking her to explain her presence. Her subsequent response (*Il.* 207–214) models the very strategy Athena wishes Achilles to use: resolve his dispute/anger through speech rather than through an act of violence. By restraining her own hand from injuring Achilles or disarming him, Athena demonstrates proper persuasive practice: Athena states her wish and purpose but makes the fulfillment of her charge contingent upon Achilles' cooperation. Additionally, she offers material motivation to persuade Achilles. The promise of "three-times as many prizes" adds weight to the option of self-restraint. So, if he ignores their counsel he will not only dishonor the will of the goddesses but also forfeit his prizes. The proper decision seems obvious, but herein lies a significant point: Athena's rhetorical approach has made room for Achilles to make a decision by and for his own benefit. At this point, he may choose to disregard the goddesses' counsel and kill Agamemnon, or limit his attack to words. Achilles does decide to stay his anger (*Il.* 1.215–218), but also presents a rationale which diverges from the original. Initially, Achilles' dilemma hinged on whether or not to act upon the anger within him; however, after receiving the counsel of Hera through Athena, Achilles' decision now centers on whether or not to obey the gods. Achilles' anger then stands as an alternative to the will of the gods. There is no longer a single fac-

11 This particular case of owl-eyed Athena is notable. While it is also translated as "flashing-eyed" (e.g., A.T. Murray, *Iliad*, 17), γλαυκῶπις, like Hera's epithet βοῶπις ("cow-eyed"), is meant to accentuate the features of the eyes as Simon Pulleyn puts it, "Homer presumably means that their eyes possessed characteristics of each animal: uncannily bright, watchful and piercing in the case of the owl, large and brown in the case of the cow." See Simon Pulleyn, *Homer: Iliad Book One* (Oxford: Oxford University Press, 2000), 184.

tor motivating Achilles' decision, yet it remains his decision to make.[12] The process thus becomes more complex and involves external and internal motivations. Interestingly, Achilles' subsequent decision is a compromise: he decides not to kill Agamemnon while maintaining his anger against him contra Athena's request. Achilles' partial compliance underlines his autonomy to make a decision without the full approval of the goddesses.

The appearance of an engulfing light from heaven initiates Saul's famous Damascus-road epiphany:

> And it happened on the journey [as] he approached Damascus, and suddenly a light from heaven shone around him and [after] falling onto the ground he heard a voice speaking to him: "Saul, Saul, why do you persecute me?" And Saul said: "Who are you, Lord?" And [the voice] replied: "I am Jesus whom you persecute; but stand up, go into the city, and it will be told to you what it is you must do." And the men travelling with him stood speechless, having heard the voice but having observed nothing. And Saul arose from the ground, but opening his eyes he saw nothing (Acts 9:3–8a).

In this case, the light is accompanied and identified by a voice – the speaker is seen neither by Saul nor his companions and is not described by the author/narrator. Φωνή rather than φῶς constitutes the heavenly Jesus' presence. Φῶς here functions not as a distinctive physical feature of Jesus by which one might recognize him; instead, φῶς is an instrument of disruption which, perhaps, causes Saul to fall to the ground (9:3). Φῶς in this situation may have physicality, or what one might call force. The function of the light, regardless of whether or not it causes Saul's fall, is to disrupt a potential act of violence against those whom Jesus wishes to protect. This disruption of violence constitutes one of the more striking parallels between *Il.* 188–224 and Acts 9:1–9: in both epiphanic scenes the one who receives the vision is interrupted and temporarily prevented from carrying out an act of violence. In Acts 9:3 this interruption is achieved without physical contact; a point which may emphasize the power of speech all-the-more. In *Il.* 1.197 this occurs through Athena's pulling of Achilles' hair, which diverts his attention from his murderous intentions to her flashing eyes. Correlation of the voice to a body seems instrumental in *Il.* 1.197; however, no such correlation occurs in Acts 9:3. This omission places emphasis on the speech made by the disembodied voice of Jesus. Only through the speech itself does Saul come to know the identity of the speaker. In addition to the self-identification, the speaker provides

---

12 Richard Gaskin argues persuasively that the intervention of Athena here "does not derogate from the individual's autonomy or responsibility for the action." Richard Gaskin, "Do Homeric Heroes Make Real Decisions?" *The Classical Quarterly* 40:1 (1990): 6.

a tacit sense of disapproval of his intended (and perhaps former; see Acts 8:1–3) actions, and vague instruction to enter the city (presumably Damascus) and await further instruction.

All intended effects of the speech are deferred; the speaker never indicates the objective of the speech, which may only be inferred from context and, perhaps, Saul's subsequent storyline. Abruptly the voice stops. Jesus makes no exit. Much in the way Achilles initially fails to notice Athena's departure, it is not clear when or if anyone saw/noticed the light recede. After the voice stops speaking, Saul's travel companions "stand speechless, having heard the voice but having observed nothing" (Acts 9:7). The desire to contrast their experience with Saul's finds little satisfaction in the text, since the narrator never indicates what Saul saw, except that after rising from the ground he was unable to see.[13] While it is unclear in what way the others witnessed or experienced the epiphany, it is clear that the epiphany, and the message within it, was targeted at Saul.

2.3 *Iliad* 1.219–224a and Acts 9:8b–9

Achilles' compromise – to attack Agamemnon with words instead of his sword while maintaining his anger – shows a shift in his reasoning:

> He spoke and held [his] heavy hand over [the] silver hilt, and thrust [the] large sword back into [its] scabbard, and did not disobey Athena's speech.
>
> But she had gone back to Olympus into the house of the aegis-bearing Zeus with the other gods. But the Son of Peleus again spoke to the Son of Atreus with harsh words, and did not in any way cease [his] anger (*Il.* 218–224a).

By maintaining his anger, Achilles recognizes that the goddesses' request requires a modification of his final decision and action but not an amendment of his inner feelings. Athena intervenes (primarily) to change actions and introduce alternative

---

13 One minor point of distinction worth noting is the author's use of different verbs of sight – βλέπω for Paul and θεάομαι for his travel companions. The former, βλέπω, refers primarily to one's visual acuity, i.e. one's sense of sight. The latter, θεάομαι, refers more specifically to an act of observation or spectation; related to the term θέατρον, "spectacle." While I am not sure whether these word choices indicate a substantial difference in the characters' visual traits/abilities, or simply suggest a different type of action – i.e. Paul and his companions have the same capacity to see but act differently – it seems reasonable to assume that these different terms do indeed retain different meanings. I prefer to render these verbs as simply different types of seeing, where Paul's ability to see is in question and his companions' apparent confusion leads them to inspect their surroundings.

motivations that shape the decision-making process; neither she nor Hera force Achilles to adjust his inner feelings even though those feelings might influence his actions. While this indeed contradicts the literal instructions of Hera, Achilles' compromise seems a satisfactory response, since Homer states: οὔδ' ἀπίθησε μύθῳ 'Αθηναίης. Another feature of this phrase merits comment: speech and persuasion triumph over anger and violence. Athena's speech persuades Achilles to choose an alternative course of action. Indeed the very terms ἀπίθησε and μύθῳ demonstrate the persuasive aspect of Athena's intervention. Here I suggest that Athena's persuasive tactic presents (or reestablishes) a model for settling disputes between comrades; that is, to reserve violent confrontation for one's enemies.

After Achilles confirms his obedience in word and action, Homer indicates that Athena had already departed. The reader learns of this only after it has happened. Much like the disappearance of the light and the stoppage of the voice in Acts 9:7, Athena disappears abruptly. During his response to Athena, Achilles seems unaware of her departure yet Homer fails to indicate whether Achilles addressed an absent goddess. Given the gravity of the situation, it seems odd that Achilles is left alone to make a final decision.

The close of the epiphany scene in Acts 9:8b–9 directs attention to Saul's blindness by explicating its severity, duration, and listing apparent side-effects: "And while leading him by the hand they entered into Damascus. And for three days he was unable to see and neither ate nor drank" (Acts 9:8b–9). This elaboration of Saul's blindness heightens the intensity of his aural experience – while he cannot see, he heard the voice of Jesus speaking from heaven. After witnessing the bright light, hearing the heavenly voice, feeling the sudden impact of falling, and engaging in curious, perhaps fearful, inquisition of the voice ("Who are you, Lord?"), Saul stands silent, lacking in visual orientation, and no longer hearing the voice. The journey to Damascus has lost momentum as Saul's companions move deliberately to guide him by the hand. For three subsequent days in Damascus, Saul neither eats nor drinks nor regains his sight. This reinforces the dullness of Saul's senses and suggests that he is helpless, unable even to eat or drink.[14] Moreover, Saul's physical condition alters his course of action with the result that he does not carry out an act (or acts) of violence against the disciples in Damascus. Blindness limits the range of Saul's potential action in a way far more severe than in the case of Achilles, who receives a mere tug on his hair. Achilles is left with his sword still drawn, and without any physical impairment that would

14 There is no indication that this is a fast – the author uses the term νηστεύω elsewhere (e.g. Acts 13:2), but does not do so here. Instead, the author uses the more generic terms ἔφαγεν and ἔπιεν with a negative correlative construction.

prevent him from acting out in violence. On the contrary, Saul's condition limits the possible range of deviance from Jesus' directive; here, motivation is produced through a physical change and not simply through persuasion. This is still not coercion, to the extent that Saul remains capable of travelling in any direction, but non-compliance would, for all he knows, leave him blind!

3 Parallel Aspects of Epiphany

From the above parallel reading, I have identified two significant common features of the epiphanies. First, each epiphany occurs at what Fritz Graf terms a "crisis situation,"[15] which, in these two cases, pertains to a potential act of violence. Second, the appearance of each divine figure initiated the recognition of the percipient, though in different ways and under different circumstances. Following Daniel Turkeltaub's categories of divine recognition in Homeric (primarily Iliad) epiphanies, I classify Acts 9:1–9 as verbal recognition and *Il.* 188–224 as visual recognition.[16] These two epiphanies compare in a few interesting ways; however, each aspect of epiphany identified here is provisional – neither de- nor pre-scriptive – and may be developed only through careful delineation between, and interpretation of, each scene within its own narrative context.

3.1 Prevention of Violence

The account of Jesus' epiphany to Saul in Acts 9:1–9 draws attention to the prevention of violence in two ways: (1) Saul is described as one who intends to murder "the disciples of the Lord" (9:1), though these intentions remain concealed; (2) Jesus self-identifies as the object of persecution, suggesting that this imminent persecution is the reason for his appearance. The author characterizes Saul as the persecutor and Jesus as the persecuted (Acts 8:1–3; 9:1–2, 5). Several commentators notice that ἔτι in 9:1 establishes a narrative link between 9:1ff. and 8:1–3 –

15 Fritz Graf explains "crisis situation" in terms of dire circumstances which may only be rectified through divine assistance. See Fritz Graf, "Epiphany," *Brill's New Pauly: Encyclopedia of the Ancient World 4 (Cyr-Epy)*: 1122.

16 Here I am following Daniel Turkeltaub's categories of divine recognition, which I will elaborate in a later section. See Daniel Turkeltaub, "Perceiving Iliadic Gods," in *Harvard Studies in Classical Philology* 103 (2007): 56.

the only prior place in the narrative where Saul appears.[17] Saul persecuted disciples in Jerusalem and Samaria and now expands his effort to Damascus, drawing on the paradigm of expansion established in Acts 1:8. This boundary transgression, even at the level of geography, intensifies Saul's evil motivations – especially in light of the fact that he obtains legal authority to pursue them – since the distance alone between Jerusalem and Damascus is treated as another venue, not an obstacle, for his murderous intentions.

Having noted that the concealment of these intense motives necessitates an epiphanic intervention, it is necessary to address how exactly this epiphany functions to prevent violence. The characterization of Saul in 8:1–3 and description of his intentions create an expectation that whoever might oppose him identifies with the objects of his persecution. When Jesus enters the scene, the author makes this association explicit and thus presents Jesus as an obstacle, an opposing force intent on preventing, or at least stalling, Saul's attack. Acts 22 preserves this feature of the epiphany in the first of Paul's retellings,[18] giving no other explanation of Jesus' presence other than to identify himself as the one persecuted (22:5) and attempt to alter Saul's course of action (22:10–11). The second retelling in Acts 26:12–23 complicates the matter: Saul claims to have been given an explanation of Jesus' appearance, which is to send him to the gentiles. Another wrinkle in Acts 26 is its lack of any reference to Ananias. Paul condenses the story into a single scene with a single, not coordinating, epiphany of Jesus. While the progressively more drastic amendments of the initial vision presents numerous problems for a coherent account of 'what actually happened,' my interpretation remains, for the most part, unchanged: Jesus' presence preserves its primary function as an obstacle to Saul's murderous pursuit of the disciples of Jesus. Each account identifies Saul as the persecutor and Jesus as the persecuted.[19]

---

17 See Ernst Haenchen, *The Acts of the Apostles: A Commentary*, 319; Luke Timothy Johnson, *The Acts of the Apostles*, 162; Ben Witherington III, *The Acts of the Apostles: A Socio-Rhetorical Commentary*, 302. Richard Pervo notes this yet excludes vv. 1–2 from his comments. See Pervo, *Acts: A Commentary*, 240.

18 While Paul does, in a sense, retell his epiphanic experience (as Saul) on the road to Damascus, it is important to note that this is not simply an alternative account, nor is it just his own interpretation; rather, the retelling constitutes part of Paul's first apology speech; a self-defense designed to present evidence of his innocence with respect to a criminal charge. It is thus in a specific litigious rhetorical context that one must interpret Paul's "retelling."

19 Beverly Gaventa argues that this entire scene "is primarily a story about the reversal of an enemy" (65). I agree to the extent that this is the final result of the scene; that is, once Saul visits Ananias his role as persecutor ends. My lone hesitation with Gaventa's argument is the tendency to externalize Saul's experience to some sort of shift in social title or status, i.e. from enemy to friend, outsider to insider. I wonder if Gaventa would make the same argument if, instead of visit-

The manner of this prevention of violence here in Acts 9:1–9 resembles what Albin Lesky terms the operation of "göttliche und menschliche Motivation": in Homer, gods intervene at moments where mortals require guidance in decision-making.[20] This need for guidance varies in degree from situation to situation, but always stands in tension with both divine will and fate.[21] Here, without artificially imposing this motif on Acts, I contend that Jesus' terse instruction, and the lack of a threat or coercive determination to direct Saul's action(s), suggests that Saul was not disqualified from determining his own course of action. Like Athena, Jesus does not stay on the scene long enough to confirm Saul's actual subsequent destination and/or actions. The so-called divine versus human motivation here is evident in Saul's blindness, which occurred either during or after, but not before, Jesus' epiphany. The precise cause of the blindness and its purpose remain unclear in Acts 9, whereas 22:11 identifies the light as the cause. In either case, the effect remains instrumental in Saul's subsequent travel, since his companions lead him by the hand into Damascus. Also, this blindness provides an additional reason to visit Ananias; in fact, at this point, it is the only known (possible) motivating factor one could derive from the text. Saul's obedience to the voice's instruction follows his own decision and is not driven by force.

Athena's intervention functions in a slightly different way to prevent an act of violence: she persuades Achilles by appealing to his desire for prizes, the spoils of war, and even contributes to an ongoing deliberation. Homer states the precise motive behind Athena's intervention: "I have come from heaven to stop your anger, with the hope that you would obey (πίθηαι); and the white-armed goddess sent me forth, loving and caring for both of you equally" (*Il.* 207–209). Hera's mutual concern for Agamemnon and Achilles establishes the desired outcome that neither Achilles nor Agamemnon be harmed. With this in mind, the rationale for Athena's persuasive tactic becomes all the more clear: coercing Achilles, by direct physical force, would cause him harm, contrary to Hera's wishes, but persuading him with words prevents Achilles immediate act of violence without harming him

---

ing Ananias, receiving his sight, and being baptized, Saul walked blindly back home or wandered in the desert. In such cases Saul would no longer pose a threat to the disciples, but his identity would also no longer be framed in relation to them. In this way, I think Gaventa's categories force us to think of the epiphany itself as demanding a status change where I believe it only functions to prevent the act of violence and widen the range of Saul's potential actions. See Beverly Gaventa, *From Darkness to Light: Aspects of Conversion in New Testament* (Philadelphia: Fortress Press, 1986), 65f.

20 Albin Lesky, *Göttliche und menschliche Motivation im homerischen Epos* (Heidelberg: C. Winter, 1961), 1.

21 Ibid., 12ff.

and establishes a model for Achilles to implement in his subsequent conflicts with Agamemnon.

While such mutual concern does not appear in Acts 9:1–9, the tactic of persuasion is nonetheless similar: Jesus gives an instruction with the hope that Saul will follow it, but does nothing further to *guarantee* compliance. This is not to suggest that Saul's blinding is not part of his motivation to follow Jesus' instruction. On the contrary, Saul's blindness provides significant impetus. The blindness is a result of the epiphanic experience and thus suggests that following the instructions will restore his sight. What I wish to emphasize here, however, is (1) that Saul maintains the capacity to disobey the instruction and (2) that Jesus remains distant and at no point coerces Saul through physical force to comply with his instruction.[22] The potential consequences of disobedience remain entirely unknown, but such a course of action does not seem appealing in the least. Saul may return home or travel to another city; the narrative does not exclude this possibility, though such options are not explicitly considered. Speech and blindness work to persuade Saul to obey, but Jesus himself does not force the issue; that is, it is not Saul, but his travel companions who lead him by the hand to Damascus. On this point, I understand interruption, distance, and deferral as key narrative components, both in communicating the motive of the divine figure and raising new narrative possibilities – what Bernard Dietrich refers to (with reference to Homeric epiphany) as the expansion of the human's range of potential action.[23]

---

22 Daniel Marguerat reads Jesus' force differently: "The reversal of Saul on the road to Damascus appears then as a stroke of divine force ... I have said: a stroke of divine force. The Risen [Jesus] stopped Saul on his path of persecution, throws him to the ground and dispossessed him of his will and his status of subject ... Now, Paul is led: he will be told (passive Divine) what to do. [Le retournement de Saul sur la route de Damas apparaît dès lors comme un coup de force divin ... Je disais: coup de force divin. Le Ressuscité arrête Saul sur son chemin de persécution, le jette à terre et le dépossède de son vouloir et de son état de sujet ... Désormais, Paul est conduit: il te sera dit (passif divin) ce qui est à faire]." The ellipses leave out no development of these notions of "divine force." In the former case, Marguerat discusses the relationship between Paul's letters and Acts, noticing only that the forceful intervention establishes the story as a focal point for both authors (Paul and, presumably, Luke). Interpreting Marguerat, I think he has produced an interesting distinction – even though he does not develop it – between types of forces acting on Saul. Here, Marguerat suggests that speech is associated with a passive force, while Jesus' presence constitutes an active, more potent, force. If this is what Marguerat intends, then I agree. See Daniel Marguerat, "L'image de Paul dans Actes des Apôtres," in *Les Actes des Apôtres: Histoire, récit, théologie* (Paris: Les Editions du Cerf, 2005), 136–37.

23 B.C. Dietrich introduces this narrative technique of "extending the range of human action" as part of his claim that Homeric epiphanies do not develop a kind of theology or systematic pattern of divine/human interaction. The function of the epiphany for Dietrich is thus almost strictly narratival. See B.C. Dietrich, "Divine Epiphanies in Homer," *Numen* 30/1 (July 1983): 62.

3.2 Divine Recognition: Modes and Circumstances

In his analysis of epiphanies in the *Iliad*, Daniel Turkeltaub identifies five types of divine recognition (i.e. how the god is recognized): (1) post-factum recognition; (2) verbal recognition; (3) aural recognition (mortal recognizes god's voice); (4) visual recognition; (5) unspecified recognition.[24] According to Turkeltaub, these types indicate the percipient's status in relation to the divine. At the onset, however, Turkeltaub points out that recognition of the gods occurs only to select individuals, not to common folk.[25] Recognition of a god's presence suggests in the very act, i.e. without being qualified by any particular mode of recognition, that the individual serves a special purpose or maintains a close relationship to the gods beyond cultic devotion. The particular mode of recognition, then, indicates the degree of proximity between the percipient and the divine figure. Turkeltaub defines this relationship as an ascending hierarchy of proximity from post-factum (the lowest) to unspecified (the highest).[26] Post-factum and verbal recognition constitute modes of recognition, which, Turkeltaub contends, require no special intimate knowledge of the particular divine figure; rather, they operate by means of deduction in the former and explicit self-identification in the latter.[27] The three higher modes operate through pre-existing knowledge of specific traits of the god – voice, appearance, or the unspecified force of their presence. Unspecified recognition suggests the highest degree of intimacy with the god, since the percipient expends no energy or time to identify the god or goddess.

In the case of Achilles' recognition of Athena, Achilles immediately recognizes Athena by her appearance. While it is unclear in the text whose eyes are flashing – δεινὼ δέ οἱ ὄσσε φάανθεν (*Il.* 200) – it is reasonable to understand the flashing eyes as an index of Athena's epithetic "owl-eyes."[28] Regardless of whose

24 Turkeltaub excludes from his analysis appearances of gods in situations where they remain unrecognized or are said to influence actions but do not disclose or signify their presence. See Daniel Turkeltaub, "Perceiving Iliadic Gods," *Harvard Studies in Classical Philology* 103 (2007): 55–56. With respect to New Testament epiphany, Gerd Theißen understands such cases of unrecognized divine action as "partial epiphany," where miraculous effects are evident though the "person" performing them is not. Theißen, *Miracle Stories*, 94.

25 Ibid., 52.

26 Ibid., 56.

27 Ibid.

28 Turkeltaub argues that the "terribly flashing eyes" belong to Achilles, not Athena. See Daniel Turkeltaub, "The Syntax and Semantics of Homeric Glowing Eyes: 'Iliad' 1.200," *The American Journal of Philology* 126/2 (Summer, 2005): 157–86, see especially 174 ff. Pulleyn notes the lack of a conclusive position on to whom to attribute the flashing eyes, though his translation associates them with Athena (83). Simon Pulleyn, *Iliad: Book One*, 179–80.

eyes flash, Athena's general lack of concealment or disguise highlights the significance of Achilles' visual recognition and thereby his close relationship to the goddess. Turkeltaub states a similar position: "Athena's manifestation to him [Achilles] alone of the Achaeans in the first book may distinguish him as closer to the gods than his fellow heroes, but her appearance behind him simultaneously raises doubts about the completeness of his perceptions."[29] While I am in general agreement with Turkeltaub's interpretation, I would emphasize that Athena's position behind Achilles does not conceal her from his notice; rather, it serves to grab his attention by placing her in a perfect spot to yank his hair. Of course, this delays Achilles' recognition, but does little to conceal or disguise her appearance.

Achilles' ability to recognize the goddess is, as Turkeltaub puts it, circularly related to his association to her: "The close association he [Achilles] shares with the gods explains his ability to perceive them and is in turn justified by that ability."[30] The care and concern of the goddesses are sincere even though they are used to manipulate the course of human actions in accordance with Hera's interests. To pursue these interests, Hera requires Achilles' cooperation, not his worship nor even his strict adherence to their counsel. Their relationship is provisional and neither permanent nor exclusive. Achilles need not function as the representative of the goddesses in human affairs nor as their adherent who offers them votives, sacrifices, etc. in exchange for their assistance. On the contrary, Turkeltaub takes Athena's phrase αι̋ κε πίθηαι ("with the hope that you would obey," *Il.* 207) to be a sign of respect to Achilles and "implies that he alone has the ability to refuse their instructions;"[31] moreover, "when he follows Athena's instructions not to kill Agamemnon, he does so not because she compels him, but because he realizes that if he performs this 'favor' for Athena, she will heed his future requests: he tells her 'χρὴ μὲν σφωΐτερόν γε, θεά, ἔπος εἰρύσσασθαι καὶ μάλα περ θυμῷ κεχολωμένον· ὣς γὰρ ἄμεινον.'"[32] In this scene Achilles receives the promise of gifts, i.e. an offering of appeasement, not the goddess! Epiphany, as this scene illustrates, need not solicit or elicit the religious/cultic devotion of the percipient to the visiting divine figure.

Saul's recognition of Jesus differs substantially from Achilles' in terms of both mode and circumstance. In terms of mode, Saul recognizes Jesus only on the basis of an explicit verbal self-identification: "I am Jesus whom you perse-

29 Daniel Turkeltaub, "Perceiving Iliadic Gods," *HSCP* 103 (2007): 74.
30 Ibid., 72.
31 Ibid., 70.
32 Ibid., 70 (footnote 66).

cute" (Acts 9:3). The author also explicitly indicates Saul's lack of recognition of the voice calling his name: "Who are you, Lord?" This locates the recognition squarely within the verbal category. What this suggests about Saul's status in relation to Jesus, the heavenly figure of the epiphany, is a lack of proximity or closeness. Saul knows too little about Jesus to recognize his voice or his very presence. Because of this, Saul seems more restricted in his ability to dialogue with Jesus. Ananias, on the other hand, converses with Jesus and even questions his instructions (Acts 9:13). Open deliberation is lacking in Saul's exchange with Jesus – the instructions are either obeyed or disobeyed there is no room for compromise.

Saul's uncompromised obedience bears rhetorical significance in Acts 26 where Paul emphasizes his obedience: Paul states that after his experience on the road "I was not disobedient to the heavenly vision, rather I declared to those in Damascus first and Jerusalem, and the entire countryside of Judea and [then] to the gentiles to repent and turn to God" (Acts 26:19–20). Although Acts 26 presents an altogether new synthetic account of the vision, the importance of obedience seems clear enough in 9:1–17: if Saul does not follow the instruction he likely would not have his sight restored or the protection of Jesus as suggested in 26:17. Accordingly, the obedience of the vision correlates the experience of recognition to the subsequent relationship with Jesus. Saul's verbal recognition of Jesus in 9:5, which is underscored by his subsequent blindness, establishes a relationship between himself and Jesus wherein Saul's agency is subordinate to Jesus', though not entirely negated. Jesus' words carry a force such that Saul's obedience implies only that he has chosen to follow an order rather than join in a deliberation. Saul's later citation of the words of Jesus as the motivating force behind his actions establishes proximity and distantiation between himself (as percipient and follower) and Jesus (as an authority and heavenly figure). In 26:19, Paul conflates the verbal and visual experiences, thus closing the gap in his recognition, which required Jesus to announce himself. Saul now interacts with Jesus visually and follows his commands on the basis of the relationship that such a visual recognition might imply. So, 26:19 presents a nuance to the experience of 9:5 (as recounted in 26:14): whereas Saul may have initially needed an explicit verbal self-identification from Jesus, he can now attach those words to a visual encounter of Jesus that was previously not possible. Acts 26:19 thus represents a progression in Saul's, now Paul's, relation to Jesus, yet maintains a subordination of will and agency.

Paul's ἀπολογία illustrates the subordination of his will and agency. Instead of taking partial responsibility (or credit) for his actions, Paul makes a Socratean kind of appeal that his actions are not driven by his will alone, but with the assistance of a heavenly figure whom he now knows by voice and vision (Acts 26:22; cf.

Apology, 31). Again, Lesky's argument pertaining to divine and human motivation provides clarity: the god and the mortal share in the decision-making process even though the god may issue an order or plan, and the mortal carries it out.[33] Lesky summarizes the point well in his interpretation of *Il.* 5.671–676 where Athena changes Odysseus' mind, albeit without an epiphany:

> In the fifth Song of the *Iliad*, Odysseus sets about (671), whether he should pursue the wounded Sarpedon, or turn against the mass of the Lycians. As in some other cases, a god accesses human deliberation and brings about the decision. So it is called for here, too, that Athena turned the courage of Odysseus against the Lycians. But she is not acting by herself, but by Odysseus ... Thus, acting upon Odysseus, Athena proves to be an executive helper in making a determination to which she is also subordinated.[34]

Although Lesky does not address the relationship between divine and human motivation in an epiphany, his assessment of divine/human interaction in thought/decision-making and action relates conditions similar to those in epiphanies. Athena and Achilles both contribute to the decision-making process and thereby jointly shape the subsequent course of action. Saul subordinates himself to the agency of Jesus, but in no way vacates his role in either the decision-making process or subsequent action. Verbal recognition in the case of Saul's epiphany places him in a subordinate position to Jesus, but nonetheless initiates a unique relationship, which validates his subsequent actions.

4 A Comment on Classification

Classifications of Saul's epiphanic experience as "call" or "conversion" tend to obscure the immediate function of the epiphany – to prevent an act of violence. Moreover, Saul's subsequent actions are understood as the primary means of classification: for example, Saul's subsequent prophetic career establishes the function of the epiphany as a prophetic call. Restricting classification to the features of the epiphany itself raises the possibility of classifying it in phenomeno-

---

33 Albin Lesky, *Göttliche und menschliche Motivation im homerischen Epos*, 16–17.

34 My translation of the German text: "Im 5. Gesange der Ilias überlegt Odysseus (671), ob er den verwundeten Sarpedon verfolgen oder sich gegen die Masse der Lykier wenden solle. Wie in einigen anderen Fallen greift eine Gottheit in das menschliche Überlegen ein und führt die Entscheidung herbei. So heißt es denn auch hier, daß Athene den Mut des Odysseus gegen die Lykier wandte. Aber sie handelt nicht aus eigenem, sondern durch Odysseus ... So erweist sich die auf Odysseus wirkende Athene als vollziehende Helferin einer Bestimmung, der auch sie unterworfen ist." Albin Lesky, *Göttliche und menschliche Motivation im homerischen Epos*, 17.

logical terms – e.g. as "miracle" or "wonder" – rather than strictly "religious" or social ones. The difficulty with these particular phenomenological categories is evident in Gerd Theißen's comment that "any miracle can be regarded as an epiphany."[35] In this way, the category of miracle is not a feature of epiphany so much as epiphany is a feature of a miracle; the very idea of miracle assumes some kind of divine presence or agency. With respect to "wonder," Verity Platt observes that "in the vocabulary of archaic Greek experience, an epiphany functions as the ultimate form of *thauma*, a 'wonder,' in which divine presence, or *eidos*, is asserted in profoundly physical terms and experienced phenomenologically as sensory extravaganza."[36] While a similar term (θάμβησεν) accompanies Achilles' experience (*Il.* 1.199), such is not the case in Acts 9:1–9. Despite a lack of "wonder," Saul does experience what Platt terms "sensory extravaganza" to the extent that he loses his sight. In this way, Saul's epiphanic experience is primarily a sense experience. The impairment of Saul's vision could be understood both phenomenologically – as an effect of divine presence – and functionally – as the interruption of his (potentially) violent course of action.

5 Conclusion

Reading Acts 9:1–9 in parallel with *Il.* 1.188–224a brings aspects of divine intervention and motivation to the surface of Jesus' epiphany to Saul. As these aspects of epiphany come into sharper focus it becomes clearer how Saul's epiphanic experience functioned in the subsequent narrative, particularly in Paul's apologetic speeches. The relationship between Saul's initial experience, and his later interpretation of that experience, help underline the problems with interpreting 9:1–9 as initiating a prophetic call or conversion. The initial experience leaves much undetermined: Saul receives no message, no mission, no audience or target of a mission or message, and no solicitation of worship, honor, or loyalty. What occurs to Saul directly in Acts 9:1–9 resembles those aspects of epiphany at the fore of *Il.* 1.188–224a: Saul is prevented from acting out in violence and his will and agency is motivated by different means and toward an alternative course of action.

---

35 Theißen, *Miracle Stories*, 94.

36 Verity Platt, *Facing the Gods: Epiphany and Representation in Graeco-Roman Art, Literature and Religion* (Cambridge: Cambridge University Press, 2011), 56.

Select Bibliography

Ancient Authors

Homer, *The Iliad*, vol. 1. Edited and translated by A.T. Murray. Cambridge, Mass.: Harvard University Press, 1924.

Modern Authors

Burchard, Christoph. *Der dreizehnte Zeuge: Traditions- und kompositionsgeschichtliche Untersuchungen zu Lukas' Darstellung der Frühzeit des Paulus*. Göttingen: Vandenhoeck & Ruprecht, 1970.

Crook, Zeba. *Reconceptualising Conversion: Patronage, Loyalty, and Conversion in the Religions of the Ancient Mediterranean*. Berlin: Walter de Gruyter, 2004.

Dietrich, B.C. "Divine Epiphanies in Homer." *Numen* 30/1 (1983): 53–79.

Dunn, James D.G. *The Acts of the Apostles*. Valley Forge, Pa.: Trinity Press International, 1996.

Gaskin, Richard. "Do Homeric Heroes Make Real Decisions?" *The Classical Quarterly* 40/1 (1990): 1–13.

Gaventa, Beverly Roberts. *The Acts of the Apostles*. Nashville: Abingdon Press, 2003.

–. *From Darkness to Light: Aspects of Conversion in New Testament*. Philadelphia: Fortress Press, 1986.

Graf, Fritz. "Epiphany." *Brill's New Pauly: Encyclopedia of the Ancient World* vol. 4 *(Cyr-Epy)*. Edited by Hubert Cancik, Helmut Schneider, et. al. Leiden: Brill Publishing, 2004, 1121–23.

Haenchen, Ernst. *The Acts of the Apostles: A Commentary*. Translated by R. McL. Wilson et. al. Philadelphia: The Westminster Press, 1971.

Johnson, Luke Timothy. *The Acts of the Apostles. Sacra Pagina*. Collegeville, Minn.: Liturgical Press, 1992.

Lamoreaux, Jason. "Social Identity, Boundary Breaking, and Ritual: Saul's Recruitment on the Road to Damascus," *Biblical Theology Bulletin: A Journal of Bible and Theology* 38 (2008): 122–35.

Lesky, Albin. *Göttliche und menschliche Motivation im homerischen Epos*. Heidelberg: C. Winter, 1961.

MacDonald, Dennis R. *Does the New Testament Imitate Homer? Four Cases from the Acts of the Apostles*. New Haven, Conn.: Yale University Press, 2003.

MacMullen, Ramsay. "Conversion: A Historian's View." *The Second Century: A Journal of Early Christian Studies* 5/2 (1985/1986): 67–81.

Marguerat, Daniel. "L'image de Paul dans Actes des Apôtres." In *Les Actes des Apôtres: Histoire, récit, théologie*. Paris: Les Éditions du Cerf, 2005, 136–37.

Metzger, Bruce. *A Textual Commentary on the Greek New Testament*, 2nd edition. New York: United Bible Societies, 1994. Repr., 2000.

Nock, A.D. *Conversion: The Old and the New in Religion from Alexander the Great to Augustine of Hippo*. London: Oxford University Press, 1933.

Pervo, Richard I. *Acts: A Commentary, Hermeneia*. Minneapolis: Fortress Press, 2009.

Platt, Verity. *Facing the Gods: Epiphany and Representation in Graeco-Roman Art, Literature and Religion*. Cambridge: Cambridge University Press, 2011.

Pulleyn, Simon. *Homer: Iliad Book One*. Oxford: Oxford University Press, 2000.

Stendahl, Krister. "Paul Among Jews and Gentiles." In *Paul Among Jews and Gentiles and Other Essays*. Philadelphia: Fortress Press, 1976, 1–77.

Talbert, Charles H. "Conversion in the Acts of the Apostles: Ancient Auditors' Perceptions." In *Reading Luke-Acts in its Mediterranean Milieu*. Leiden: Brill, 2003, 135–48.

Theißen, Gerd. *Miracle Stories of the Early Christian Tradition*. Translated by Francis McDonagh. Edinburgh: T&T Clark Ltd., 1983.

Turkeltaub, Daniel. "Perceiving Iliadic Gods," *Harvard Studies in Classical Philology* 103 (2007): 51–81.

–. "The Syntax and Semantics of Homeric Glowing Eyes: 'Iliad' 1.200." *The American Journal of Philology* 126/2 (2005): 157–86.

Witherington III, Ben. *The Acts of the Apostles: A Socio-Rhetorical Commentary*. Grand Rapids, Mi.: William B. Eerdmans Publishing Company, 1998.

Elaine M. Wainwright

Of Dogs and Women: Ethology and Gender in Ancient Healing

The Canaanite Woman's Story – Matt 15:21–28

There is a tension for many scholars who interpret New Testament healing stories between the 'story' or text to which we have a certain level of accessibility, and the 'reality' which is not so easily accessible to us, indeed is perhaps much less accessible than we like to think as scholars. In the symposium which preceded and led to this collection of essays, the convenors/editors, Stefan Alkier and Annette Weissenrieder, nuanced this tension by reference to the ancients' 'concepts of reality' rather than the reality itself; but the tension between 'reality' and 'concepts of reality' remained and remains in this collection's search for "new perspectives on New Testament miracle stories."

My imagination was captured by the tensive space that this collection opens up; its attention to 'concepts of reality' enabled me to bring a gender perspective, since gender is a key aspect of our concepts of reality and one that is so often neglected. It also allows me to consider healing within the first century health care system, particularly those aspects of such a system that are encoded in the Matthean narrative, as such a systemic approach gives access to 'concepts of reality.'[1] The story of the Canaanite woman and her spirit possessed daughter in Matt 15:21–28 seemed fertile ground for such an exploration as gender plays a significant role in this story. An aspect of the story and its 'concepts of reality,' or contribution to the health care system that has not been as extensively explored as that of gender, is the reference to 'dogs' in that Matthean text and its relation to healing in a first-century health care system.

I propose, therefore, in this paper, to turn first to the story of the Canaanite woman and her spirit-possessed daughter as told within the Matthean narrative [the narrative or inner texture of the text]. This will enable me to address how we might name this story-type (will we name it 'miracle story'?) and how it might have been named in this first-century document. I will then turn attention to the ancient ethology that uses a comparative referent to 'dogs' to characterize the Ca-

1 For an analysis of healing within a first-century health care system, see Hector Avalos, *Health Care and the Rise of Christianity* (Peabody: Hendrickson, 1999), and John J. Pilch, *Healing in the New Testament: Insights from Medical and Mediterranean Anthropology* (Minneapolis: Fortress, 2000).

naanite woman and her daughter, attentive here to the socio-cultural – or what I would prefer to call the ecological – texture of the narrative, in which materiality and sociality are woven into the text. Gender will be a central analytic category across these two areas of analysis. I will conclude by returning to the question of miracle/healing stories and the concepts of reality that they evoke, in order to draw out emphases and possible conclusions, especially in relation to the central theme of this volume.

The Inner or Narrative Texture

A Healing Textualized

The focus story for this paper, that of the casting out of a demon from a spirit-possessed young woman, does not stand alone but rather functions within a unique narrative, that of the Gospel of Matthew. It draws much of its meaning, therefore, from the way in which it functions in that context, just as parallel stories of healing by Asclepius did not function alone but among the *iamata* on the walls of the *abaton* of the Asclepeion of Epidaurus.[2]

Significant attention has been given to the careful structuring of the Matthean narrative generally and the unique place of Matt 15:21–28 within such structuring. Janice Capel Anderson and I have both drawn attention to the placement of Matt 15:21–28 at the axis point of a chiastic structure within a chiastic structure.[3] Both recognize that the story of 15:21–28, within the context of the discussion of the tradition of the Elders (15:1–20), is framed by feeding stories, which in their turn are linked to summary accounts of the healing of many (14:13–36 and 15:29–38/39) [See Diagram 1 below].

The healing that is narrated in 15:21–28 takes meaning from, and gives meaning to, the carefully structured narrative element of 14:13–15:39 (or to 16:12). It is, on the other hand, an isolated story of healing in this part of the narrative, since the majority of Matthean healing stories are gathered together in typical Matthean

2 See, for instance, Lynn R. LiDonnici, *The Epidaurian Miracle Inscriptions: Text, Translation and Commentary* (Texts and Translations 36/Graeco-Roman Religion 11; Atlanta: Scholars, 1995).

3 Janice Capel Anderson, "Double and Triple Stories, the Implied Reader, and Redundancy in Matthew," *Semeia* 31 (1985): 71–90, and *Matthew's Narrative Web: Over, and Over, and Over Again* (JSNTSS 91; Sheffield: Sheffield Academic Press, 1994), 175–91; and Elaine M. Wainwright, *Towards a Feminist Critical Reading of the Gospel According to Matthew* (BZNW 60; New York: Walter de Gruyter, 1991), 100–102.

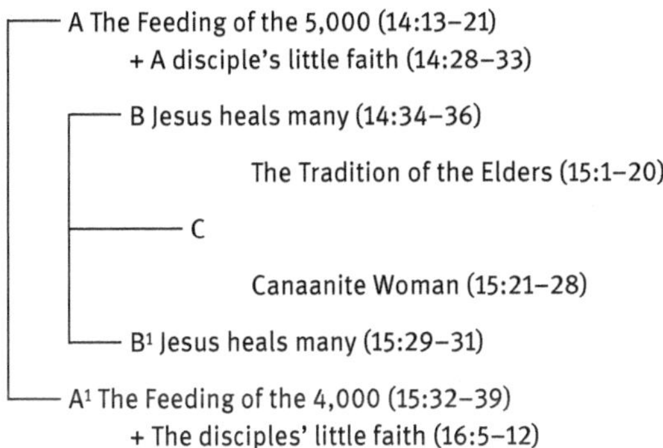

Diagram 1: Framing of Matt 15:21–28[4]

fashion in Matt 8–9. These stories, together with the teachings of Matt 5–7, are intended to demonstrate the threefold ministry of Jesus according to the frame around them in the summary verses of 4:23 and 9:35: *Jesus went throughout Galilee/all the cities and villages, teaching in their synagogues and proclaiming the good news of the kingdom and curing/healing every disease and every sickness among the people.* Together these three activities – teaching, preaching, and healing – characterize Jesus' proclamation of a *basileia* of the heavens in the Gospel of Matthew (see 4:17), or, as I have already noted, "[t]he Matthean health care system is intimately connected to the religious system characterized by preaching and teaching in this narrative."[5] Within this system, as Matt 4:24 notes in expanding 4:23, "those afflicted with various diseases and pains" are described as "demoniacs, epileptics and paralytics". Demon possession belongs with other diseases within the Matthean health care system.

If we turn to the language used to speak healing in the Matthean narratives of healing, we find that the verb ἰάομαι is used to describe the healed daughter in Matt 15:28. The use of this verb is tantalizing in the Matthean narrative as the reader/hearer is much more attuned to θεραπεύω, which dominates the Matthean storytelling. It is used sixteen times in Matthew, and almost always in summary verses (4:23.24; 8:7.16; 9:35; 10:1.8; 12:10.15.22; 14:14; 15:30; 17:16.18; 19:2; 21:14) as compared to five in Mark.[6] Initially I thought that it was the language of the frame around 15:21–28 (14:34–36 and 15:29–31 are both summary verses of Jesus' healing

4 See Wainwright, *Towards a Feminist Critical Reading*, 100.

5 Elaine M. Wainwright, *Women Healing/Healing Women: The Genderization of Healing in Early Christianity* (London: Equinox, 2006), 140.

6 Wainwright, *Women Healing/Healing Women*, 142–43.

ministry). Closer observation, however, demonstrates that while the summary verse 14:14, which opens the chiastic section, uses Θεραθεύω, 14:36, the more immediate frame, describes Jesus' healing of many with the word διεσώθησαν while 15:30 returns to ἐθεράπευσεν. The use of διεσώθησαν at 14:36 may not, however, undermine claims of the Matthean use of Θεραθεύω to describe the healing power of Jesus, as the use of σώζω seems to retain the expression used in Mark – namely that anyone who touches the hem of Jesus' garment will be saved (cf. Mark 6:56); it may have been a well-know phrase and hence not easily altered. The Matthean narrative seems, therefore, to be constructing Jesus as a healer through the use of θεραπεύω.

In the LXX this verb carries connotations of treatment for illness and more generally service, as demonstrated by the careful analysis of vocabulary by Louise Wells (Tob 12:3 but cf 6:9, 1Ez 1:4; Jdt 11:17).[7] Ἰάομαι, on the other hand, was used predominantly in the LXX to refer to divine healing (Tob 12:14; Pss 6:2; 30:2; 41:4 and passim; Wis 16:10; Sir 38:9). It was also the designation given to Asclepius in the *iamata*.[8] The predominant use of θεραπεύω in the Gospel of Matthew seems, therefore, to reflect the emic perspective or 'concepts of reality' of the Matthean storyteller and community, and distinguishes Jesus as healer in Matthew's gospel from divine healers – whether the God of the LXX or Asclepius and Hygieia in the Asklepia. Healing is intimately linked to preaching and teaching and is the work of Jesus, the one in whom God is with God's people (1:23). Of interest in this regard also is that the word δύναμις, referring to deeds of power, is not used positively as a description of Jesus' preaching, teaching or healing except in situations of conflict or of rejection: see 7:22; 11:20, 23; 13:54, 58; and 14:2. Hence it is not able to shed light on the Matthean understanding of Jesus' healings.

Turning again to Matt 15:21–28, in v. 28, the language of transformation or therapeutic change – to use the terminology of the medical anthropologist Arthur Kleinman[9] – is not θεραπεύω. This is not surprising, in that θεραπεύω is not generally used in Matthew for the description of a therapeutic change except in 12:22. The therapeutic change is normally described in terminology of reversal, e.g. the leper is cleansed (8:3), the fever leaves Peter's mother-in-law (8:15), and the daughter of the leader of the synagogue who has just died is raised up (9:25). In Matt 15:28, however, the daughter is healed/ἰάθη, using the language of ἰάομαι.

---

7 Louise Wells, *The Greek Language of Healing from Homer to New Testament Times* (BZNW 83; Berlin: Walter de Gruyter, 1998), 103–19.

8 See LiDonnici, *The Epidaurian Miracle Inscriptions*, 84–131.

9 Arthur Kleinman, *Patients and Healers in the Context of Culture: An Exploration of the Borderland between Anthropology, Medicine, and Psychiatry* (Berkeley: University of California Press, 1995), 303–10.

It is difficult to know the import of the particular language of healing in this narrative. I wish to suggest two possibilities. The first is that apart from a direct citation from the LXX (Is 6:10) at Matt 13:15, in which ἰάομαι designates divine healing, the only other two uses of the verb are in Matt 8:8 and 13: once on the lips of the Capernaum centurion who asks healing for his *pais*, and the second on the lips of Jesus who proclaims the *pais* healed, as does the narrator in relation to the Canaanite woman's daughter in Matt 15:28. Gender does not seem to distinguish recipients of Jesus' healing under the banner of language of ἰάομαι, as those healed are male and female. What does distinguish the two recipients from others healed in Matthew seems to be their ethnicity; but as this paper proceeds, this will be called into question as a distinguishing feature of Matt 15:21–28 and hence I am cautious at this point in claiming ethnicity as the distinguishing aspect in the use of ἰάομαι.[10]

If ethnicity is being evoked in this text, in the world of the centurion and the woman of the coast of Tyre and Sidon, ἰάομαι together with the more prominent ὑγιής that is absent from the gospel, designates divine healing.[11] Is this language then intended to recount Jesus' healings as claims of divinity or of divine agent, and if so, do they redound onto the language of θεραπεύω with a similar claim? The evidence seems to me to be very slim at this point and it is only as the stories were told and retold in the process of rendering the deviant Jesus prominent[12] that they acquired greater significance, in both associating Jesus with divinity and recognizing the stories as 'miracle,' language which we have seen is absent from the Matthean health care system.[13]

---

10 It is not known for sure that the centurion's *pais* is non-Jewish as indeed the ethnicity of the centurion himself is not transparent. The name and the level of authority accorded to the centurion would suggest, however, that he was Roman or of ethnic origin other than Jewish as his position would suggest authority over the Jewish population at the time of the writing of the Gospel of Matthew. This, however, does not indicate the ethnicity of his *pais*. See T. R. Hobbs, "Soldiers in the Gospels: A Neglected Agent," in *Social Scientific Models for Interpreting the Bible: Essays by the Context Group in Honor of Bruce J. Malina* (ed. John J. Pilch; Biblical Interpretation Series 53; Atlanta: Society of Biblical Literature, 2001), 328–48, and Theodore W. Jennings and Tat-Siong Benny Liew, "Mistaken Identities but Model Faith: Rereading the Centurion, the Chap, and the Christ in Matthew 8:5–13," *JBL* 123/3 (2004): 467–94, esp. 475–76.

11 Wells, *Language of Healing*, 33–36.

12 See Jerome H. Neyrey and Bruce J. Malina, *Calling Jesus Names: The Social Value of Labels in Matthew* (Foundations and Facets; Sonoma: Polebridge, 1988) for a much more thorough social scientific explanation of the process of rendering one called deviant by others as a prominent byway of storytelling in the person's community of acceptance and recognition.

13 See in this regard Barry L. Blackburn, "The Miracles of Jesus," in *The Cambridge Companion to Miracles* (ed. Graham H. Twelftree; Cambridge: Cambridge University Press, 2011), 113–30.

B Gender textualized

In turning to an investigation of the gendering of the text of Matt 15:21–28, one notes that vv. 22 and 28b could be said to form the frame around the narrative, v. 21 functioning as the connector. In both verses (22b and 28b), there is a reference to the daughter (ἡ θυγάτηρ) and her state before and after the encounter between her mother and Jesus. In v. 22, the woman begins her encounter with Jesus, crying out to him about the condition of her daughter. In 28a, Jesus ends the encounter with a granting of what the woman wishes (θέλεις). In between there is a vigorous verbal interchange between Jesus and the woman who is named as Canaanite. The text, therefore, is significantly gendered and turns readers' attention to the gendering of healing.

Verse 21 sets the scene as much in the context of the movement of and in the Matthean narrative as a whole, as for this explicit story of healing. It begins with reference to Jesus going away from 'there' (ὁρίων ἐκείνων), 'there' being a reference back to 'the land at Gennesaret' (14:34) or 'that region' (14:35). Narratively, it is to that region that the Pharisees and Scribes from Jerusalem come; where Jesus calls the people to him (15:10) and where his disciples come to him (15:12). It is from this region, therefore that Jesus goes out when he withdraws (ἀνεχώρησεν) to the region of Tyre and Sidon.

The verb ἀνεχωρέω is a significant verb in the movement of the Matthean narrative. It can simply mean 'to depart' or 'to go away from' a place or region. In Matthew's gospel, however, it most often carries connotations of fleeing or escaping from some threat. The *magoi* flee to their own country after their encounter with Herod (2:12) and Joseph flees with the 'child and his mother' to Egypt (2:13), and on his return he flees Judea for Galilee (2:22). While Jesus may not be the subject of the verb in the Infancy Narrative, flight characterizes his story from its beginnings. The adult Jesus himself first flees or withdraws from Judea, the area from which he was taken by Joseph as an infant (4:12; cf. 2:22), and as in that previous flight, he goes to Galilee. This movement opens the way for his "teaching in their synagogues, preaching the gospel of the kingdom and healing every disease" (4:23). Flight from one situation opens the way for Jesus to heal. Jesus demands withdrawal of the mourners in 9:24 who were obstructing his ministry, so that he can proceed to heal the young woman who had just died (9:18). Jesus withdraws again in 12:15 after the Pharisees make plans to destroy him, and this withdrawal also makes way in the same verse for Jesus' healing of the many who follow him in his withdrawal (12:15b). John's death at the hands of Herod Antipas is further impetus for Jesus to withdraw again (14:13), but the crowds still follow him and he "healed their sick" (14:14). It is controversy with the Pharisees and scribes who come from Jerusalem that leads to Jesus' final withdrawal in 15:21. This time it is more radical, into, or at least toward, the district of Tyre and Sidon (15:21). It is a withdrawal outside the boundaries of Galilee and Judea in which all his ministry has taken place up to this point in the narrative and it seems, therefore, to be more heavily weighted, although the threat in 15:1–20 is not articulated as strongly as in 12:14, nor does it seem to carry a threat to Jesus' own life as in some earlier withdrawals. The reader who had already noted the link between Jesus' withdrawal/flight and his continuing to heal would not be surprised that in this withdrawal, Jesus is immediately faced with a woman whose daughter is demon-possessed.

In this tensive situation of Jesus being outside the boundaries in which his ministry has taken place, a new element enters the narrative: namely, Jesus being confronted by a woman from the region of Tyre and Sidon who is designated 'Canaanite.' A reader attentive to the gendering of this narrative could, like Jesus, be confounded not only by this woman's presence in front of Jesus but by her crying out to him: "have mercy on me, *Kyrios*, son of David, my daughter is severely demon-possessed" (15:22). This is the first time in the Matthean narrative that a woman's voice has been heard (the woman with the haemorrhage speaks only to herself – 9:21). And this Canaanite woman cries out aloud in the public arena, and except for her description of her daughter's condition, her words parallel those of the two blind men who likewise called out to Jesus (9:27). The extraordinary difference in Jesus' response confronts the reader/hearer. In response to the cry of the blind men, Jesus initiates a conversation that leads to their healing (9:28–30). He is silent, however, in the face of the cry of the Canaanite women (15:23a), leaving space for the disciples to request Jesus to send her away (15:23b) and for he himself to affirm their response with his claim of being sent only to the lost sheep of the house of Israel (15:24). It is only the woman's placing of herself at Jesus' feet (15:25a – προσεκύνει) that facilitates the on-going encounter, which becomes a challenge/riposte interchange resulting finally in the woman's daughter being healed (vv. 25–28).

At the level of the narrative, it seems clear that this story is significantly genderized but there are also other factors functioning as well to shape meaning. In previous healings involving women, Jesus takes the initiative in relation to the healing of Peter's mother-in-law (8:14–15), and he responds positively to the woman with the haemorrhage who has reached out and touched his garment to effect her healing (9:20–22). In this story, when Jesus silently ignores the woman's request for healing for her daughter, the woman engages in a challenging interchange with Jesus in a way which would have shocked listeners to the Matthean narrative, as we shall see in more detail below when we consider gender within the socio-cultural texture of the text. The different responses to these various women suggest not only that gender features in Jesus' healing ministry in the

Matthean narrative, but also that gender needs to be considered in tandem with other socio-cultural features in the ecological texture of the text.

Before leaving the textual analysis, let me explore more fully what was simply noted above, namely the words of the woman's request for healing, part of which parallels the cry of two blind men (9:27 and 20:30). In the first story of the healing of two blind men, their request is simply ἐλέησον ἡμᾶς, υἱὸς Δαυίδ, whereas in the second there is textual variation in relation to the inclusion and placement of κύριε in the request.[14] These variations do not significantly impact our exploration of the story of the Canaanite woman's daughter, as the significance lies in the fact that her cry represents the developing theologizing in the Matthean community being placed on the lips of this woman. If we leave aside the designation κύριε, which can be a form of respectful as much as a theologized address, the woman's naming of Jesus as ὑιὸς Δαυίδ raises questions, in relation to both her ethnicity and gender, and in relation to healing. Both Lidija Novakovic and Dennis Duling demonstrate convincingly that the title 'Son of David' is a therapeutic one in the Gospel of Matthew, rendering Jesus as prophetic healer.[15] The Canaanite woman is the only female supplicant to address Jesus with such a significant title, thus challenging or indeed shifting gender boundaries. On the other hand, her use of these titles raises a question which will be addressed further below, namely whether she is designated as 'outsider/foreigner' by the name 'Canaanite' or whether it has implications that extend the way 'ethnic' has been understood in relation to this text. These issues will be explored further as we turn now to the socio-cultural and material textures of this text.

---

14 See discussion in Bruce M. Metzger, *A Textual Commentary on the Greek New Testament* (London: United Bible Societies, 1975), 53–54; W. D. Davies and Dale C. Allison, *The Gospel According to Saint Matthew* (ICC 111; Edinburgh: T & T Clark, 1997), 107; and Donald A. Hagner, *Matthew 14–28* (Word Biblical Commentary 33B; Nashville: Thomas Nelson, 1995), 585.

15 Lidija Novakovic, *Messiah and Healer of the Sick: A Study of Jesus as the Son of David in the Gospel of Matthew* (WUNT 2/170; Tübingen: Mohr Siebeck, 2003), and Dennis C. Duling, "Matthew's Plurisignificant 'Son of David' in Social Science Perspective: Kinship, Kingship, Magic, and Miracle," *BTB* 22/3 (1992): 99–116.

The Ecological Texture: healing socialized and materialized

As indicated above, healing functions not only textually, but I would claim that the socio-cultural and material aspects of healing are encoded in or pushed up into the text, giving it an 'ecological' texture that holds these aspects together in a complex web, like that of functioning eco-systems.[16] I want to take up two of these aspects – the socio-cultural categories of gender and ethnicity, and the evoked materiality of human bodies and dogs – in order to further explore the telling of healing stories and the concepts of reality they textualize and/or evoke. Since these features interactively permeate this healing story, I will allow them likewise to permeate my exploration.

This story shares with other healing narratives a focus on bodies, one that I think we so often miss in our day. It is initially the bodily movement of Jesus, ἐξελθὼν ἐκεῖθεν ὁ Ἰησοῦς ἀνεχώρησεν εἰς τὰ μέρη Τύρου καὶ Σιδῶνος, that brings Jesus into the region of Tyre and Sidon from which the γυνὴ Χαναναία ἀπὸ τῶν ὁρίων ἐκείνων goes out, so that these two bodies – gendered bodies – meet on the border which the text evokes. The dominant action of these bodies in this narrative is, however, that of speaking – there are seven references to speech undertaken or denied (vv. 22, 23, 24, 25, 26, 27, 28), and voice is distributed almost evenly, the woman speaking three times and Jesus four. There is no other healing narrative in the gospels in which a women (or, indeed, any supplicant) seeking healing engages the healer in what can only be characterized as a debate or public challenge/riposte, in the language of the social scientists. As such, it is actively reconstructing gender in its very telling.[17] Could it be that healing stories functioned not only in terms of the restoration of human bodies, but also of the socio-cultural, the ecological, contexts in which they were and are told?

The opening cry of the Canaanite woman introduces into the narrative the shadowy figure of her daughter, only spoken about in the text, whose body is severely demon-possessed (κακῶς δαιμονίζεται): two women not embedded in a

16 Kate Rigby, "Earth, World, Text: On the (im)possibility of Ecopoiesis," *New Literary History* 35/3 (2004): 427–42, explores the way Heidegger proposes that Earth pushes up into a text and she relates this to an ecopoiesis.

17 Wendy J. Cotter, *The Christ of the Miracle Stories: Portrait through Encounter* (Grand Rapids: Baker, 2010), 144–46, cites Plutarch (*Mor. 139C),* in which Plutarch instructs the "good wife" to be most conspicuous when she is with her husband, and to stay at home and hide herself when he is not there. Other texts she cites build on this to indicate the proper conduct demanded of a woman in public.

patriarchal family are locked together by the demon possession of the daughter, a phenomenon that is given no further explanation in the narrative. Wendy Cotter has observed in her extensive study of the sources for the New Testament healing stories in Greco-Roman antiquity that "no one meaning can be presumed for the term 'daimon,' but rather, the context dictates its intended significance."[18] The language of the New Testament, and Matthew's gospel as part of this, give expression to a world view or a cosmology that developed during the prior three centuries, in which angels/good spirits and demons/unclean or evil spirits play a crucial role, "midway between gods and men," according to Plutarch.[19] This world view functioned interactively with health-care systems; with political, socio-economic and cultural factors; and with apocalyptic and other worldviews and perspectives within the varied contexts of the first century from which the gospels arose. In Matthew's gospel it functions as a general descriptor of socio-cultural disruption borne on the bodies of human characters, functioning generally in summary passages as does the verb θεραπεύω (4:24; 8:16), but also with reference to individuals (8:28.33; 9:32; 12:22 and in 15:22). We learn nothing more about the Canaanite woman and her daughter and the disruption in their lives which caused what is named as demon possession.

As this story is recounted within the Matthean context, Jesus stands as obstacle to the woman's request through the bodily mode of speech. He ignores her, οὐκ ἀπεκρίθη αὐτῇ λόγον (v. 23), emphasizing his failure to speak the simple word 'Go' to this demon, as he did in 8:32 to those who possessed the two Gadarenes. When he does speak in v. 24, it is to speak the word of the tradition, of chosenness (not being sent *except* [εἰ μή]).[20] The attentive reader hears Jesus' statement as just that, 'tradition' that makes void the word of God, in light of Jesus' challenge to the Pharisees and scribes in the previous narrative segment 15:6–9: "For the sake of your tradition, you make void the word of God" – a struggle being negotiated by the Matthean community which leaves traces in the text.

Mark D. Nanos presents a very nuanced argument in relation to what the 'tradition' might have been that supported Jesus' seeming exclusion of the

18 Wendy Cotter, *Miracles in Greco-Roman Antiquity: A Sourcebook for the Study of New Testament Miracle Stories* (London: Routledge, 1999), 76.

19 Plutarch, *De Defectu Oraculorum* 415A as cited in Cotter, *Miracles in Greco-Roman Antiquity*, 77.

20 See Leticia Guardiolia-Saenz, "Borderless Women and Borderless Texts: A Cultural Reading of Matthew 15:21–28," *Semeia* 78 (1988): 69–81, who identifies the category of 'chosenness.'

woman from his ministry.[21] He wants to challenge the general Jew/Gentile understanding of tradition that has been claimed for the Matthean narrative, especially as an interpretation of Jesus' reference to the "lost sheep of the House of Israel" (15:24). In doing so, he questions whether the woman would have understood herself as a legitimate descendant of the dispersed Northern tribes. On the other hand, he asks: does she disrupt Jesus' understanding of his ministry to the Northern tribes with claims as to an awaited king/messiah from the house of David (see her cry at v. 22)? The final possibility that Nanos canvasses is that more generally accepted, namely that the woman's designation with the despised term 'Canaanite' denies her access to the healing intended for members of the "house of Israel" (v. 24). Nanos summarizes his long and thorough explorations thus:

> ... it is not clear that Gentiles per se are analogized with dogs in this metaphor. She is a Canaanite, a perhaps affectionately appreciated, or alternatively especially despised neighbor who looks to a future Davidic dynasty, and also one who is a woman.[22]

There is a range of socio-religious and cultural traditions which Jesus may be evoking in v. 24 which seeks to interpret the 'word of God' but which may be rendering it void, denying healing to a woman and her daughter in need, for the sake of tradition. This narrative emphasizes that healing may have been understood within the Matthean community as intimately bound up with political and sociocultural traditions or concepts of reality in its first century context, as well as the healing of bodies, thus pointing to the complexity of its health care system.

I wish to turn now to the second 'word' of Jesus evoked by the Canaanite mother's refusal to go away without her daughter being freed from her demon possession: it is not καλόν/'good or rightly ordered,' says Jesus, to take the bread from the children and to throw it to 'the dogs.' It is here that echoes of ancient ethology, whereby connections are made regarding the character of the human from that of an animal, might be heard in this text. Such an insight was brought to light by Alan Cadwallader in his 2008 book *Beyond the Word of a Woman: Recovering the Bodies of the Syrophoenecian Women*.[23] In v. 26, Jesus equates the granting of healing to the young girl, whose mother is outsider or challenging marginal one to the house of Israel, with throwing bread to dogs. He associates the woman whose request he has constantly thwarted and her daughter with the

---

21 Mark D. Nanos, "Paul's Reversal of Jews Calling Gentiles 'Dogs' (Philippians 3:2): 1600 Years of an Ideological Tale Wagging an Exegetical Dog?" *Biblical Interpretation* 17 (2009): 469–72.

22 Nanos, "Paul's Reversal," 473.

23 See in this regard Alan Cadwallader, *Beyond the Word of a Woman: Recovering the Bodies of the Syrophoenecian Women* (Adelaide: ATF Press, 2008), 9–13.

dog [*kunarion*], commonly understood as a slur. I will turn now to a brief consideration of dogs in antiquity in order to assist our understanding of this ethological referent and the turn that the Canaanite woman gives to it.

Perhaps one of the clearest examples of ancient ethology is seen in Plato's *Republic*: "Is not the noble youth very like a well-bred dog in respect of guarding and watching" (Rep 2.375a); or the dog as a true philosopher, "one who shows a true love of wisdom" distinguishing "a friendly from a hostile aspect by nothing save his apprehension of the one and his failure to recognize the other" (Rep 2.376b).[24] Such comparisons became commonplace as a way of passing on wisdom, so that Seneca could say that "we give children proverbs – what the Greeks call *chriai* – to learn off by heart, since a childish mind which cannot yet comprehend anything more can nevertheless grasp such proverbs" (Sen Ep 33.7).[25] There is no evidence that I know of which suggests that the words of Jesus existed prior to his use of them in proverbial form, even though scholars have speculated that this may have been so. Jesus himself as teacher may, however, have couched his words in proverbial form. The materiality of the body of dogs which pushes up into this text therefore requires further investigation.

Homer's account of Odysseus's dog Argos, awaiting Odysseus' return from the Trojan War before dying (Homer, *Odyssey*, 17),[26] speaks to the fact that dogs had long been tamed and were often loved and loving companions to their owners.[27] A frieze from a marble sarcophagus of a dog beneath a child's deathbed demonstrates the common feature of the relationship between both children and adults and their dogs.[28] There are also additional reliefs in which dogs are de-

---

24 Plato, *Republic,* cited from Gregory R. Crane, ed., *Perseus Digital Library*, http://www.perseus.tufts.edu/hopper/, accessed 15 March, 2012.

25 I am indebted for this reference to Alan H. Cadwallader, "When a Woman is a Dog: Ancient and Modern Ethology meet the Syrophoenician Women," *The Bible and Critical Theory* 1.4 (2005). http://www.relegere.org/index.php/bct/. Accessed 11 March, 2011.

26 "As they were talking, a dog that had been lying asleep raised his head and pricked up his ears. This was Argos, whom Odysseus had bred before setting out for Troy. ... As soon as he saw Odysseus standing there, he dropped his ears and wagged his tail, but he could not get close to this master [and] Argos passed into the darkness of death, now that he had seen his master once more after 20 years."

27 See Jarrett A. Lobell and Eric A. Powell, "More than Man's Best Friend," *Archaeology* 63/5 (2010): 26–35.

28 *SEG* XXXIX 1283 ... "K..T.ON (after playing (games with) pleasing Stephanos they were crying, Having suddenly wasted away to death he li[es] here; This is (the) grave of a perished dog Stephanos, Rodope wept for this (dog) and buried him as a man, I am Stephanos (the) dog and I (have) Rodope (as my owner), she built (the) grave." Accessed in J. R. Harrison, "Every Dog has its Day," in *New Documents Illustrating Early Christianity* vol. 10 (ed. S. R. Llewelyn and J. R. Harrison; Grand Rapids: Eerdmans, forthcoming), 110.

picted as being present at the dinner table and children offering food to pet dogs.[29] Harrison has noted that the "loyalty of dogs to their master is depicted on funereal stelai by the stereotype of the animal looking intently at its owner."[30] This is evident in at least two stele. The first is Mhnodotos, a freeman, Μηνόδοτος ἥρως χρη[στος] παροδεῖταις χαίρειν,[31] and the second is Mousa, *IATPEINH/Physician*, on whose tombstone are two small dogs looking intently up at her, or as Firalti and Robert suggest, at the scroll she holds in her left hand.[32] Her stele of the 1st BCE/CE is a significant one beyond the scope of this paper, as it is the first we have available on which the female healer is designated as *IATPEINH* rather than *IATPOΣ*. The significance of the two small dogs seems, however, to have escaped the interpretation of scholars.

Let me follow up further here on the possible link between the two dogs at Mousa's feet, and the words of Jesus to the Canaanite woman – namely, dogs as healing agents. Evidence for this is minimal and scattered not only geographically but also chronologically. It seems that the dog was companion to the ancient Sumerian healing goddess Gula, and figurines and images of dogs characterized her sanctuaries.[33] Archaeologists are mystified by Lawrence Stager's discovery of hundreds of dogs buried at Ashkelon, raising the question as to whether the dog was a sacred animal used in healing rituals along the Phoenician coast, of which Tyre and Sidon are a part. In a recent article, Geoffrey David Miller critiques Stager's hypothesis but argues, as does Nanos, against the popular claim that dogs were held as contemptible in Israelite society.[34] Indeed Nanos would claim that the use of 'dog' as a slur on the Gentiles cannot be demonstrated at all within Judaism up to the first century. Returning to the relationship of dogs to healing, there is further evidence that the dogs in the Epidaurus Asklepium licked children to effect a cure.[35]

29 Harrison, "Every Dog has its Day," 112.

30 Harrison, "Every Dog has its Day," 111.

31 W. H. Buckler and W. M. Calder, eds, *Monumenta Asiae Minoris Antiqua* vol. 6 (Monuments and Documents from Phrygia and Caria; Manchester: Manchester University Press, 1939), #27, p. 12. It acknowledges Mhnodotos, a freeman wishing him greetings and a good passing.

32 Nezih Firatli, *Les steles funéraires de Byzance Gréco-Romaine, avec l'edition et l'index commenté par Louis Robert* (trans. A.N. Rollas; Paris: Librairie Adrien Maisonneuve, 1964), 96–97, Plate 139, Planche 35.

33 Johanna Stuckey, "'Going to the Dogs': Healing Goddesses of Mesopotamia," *MatriFocus* 5/2 (2006): 1–7.

34 Geoffrey David Miller, "Attitude toward Dogs in Ancient Israel: A Reassessment," *JSOT* 32/4 (2008): 487–500.

35 See J. M. C. Toynbee, *Animals in Roman Life and Art* (London: Thames, 1985), 123.

Returning to Matt 15:21–28, and in particular, vv. 26 and 27, we see Jesus, who has been engaged as therapeutic healer, address the Canaanite woman with a colloquial saying which contrasts the bread of children and that thrown to dogs. It is not dogs which are denigrated, but rather a comparison is made between children and dogs at the table. The woman, however, draws into the texture of the narrative a wisdom that was perhaps familiar, with images of dogs being fed by children from their table, of being loved, and being associated with healing. Her words enable Jesus to negotiate his struggle to determine the 'word of God' and 'human tradition' in his encounter with this woman and the demon possession of her daughter. He recognizes the great faith of the woman (v. 28) as not only what she desires (θέλεις), but what God desires (see 6:10; 7:21; 26:42 and passim). Her faith, expressed as desire for healing; as urgent need; as refusal to go away without the healing she has requested; and as a courage which shifted Jesus' understanding of his own power, is affirmed in this narrative. As a result of her faith, her daughter is healed instantly. Transformation has taken place in the encounter, drawing the woman's daughter into its ambit. There is no reference to the demon leaving the daughter, as is usual in descriptions of therapeutic change, just the word ἰάθη. Her healing functions with those of the two sets of blind men, of the centurion's *pais*, of Peter's mother-in-law, the woman with the haemorrhage, the ruler's daughter and many others, as demonstrative of the *basileia* of the heavens that Jesus preaches and teaches.

Conclusion

This healing story, while it continues the storyline of Jesus as healer, bringing in the *basileia* of the heavens, extends healing to include the socio-cultural stigmas borne on the gendered bodies of the two females in this narrative and the demon-possessed body of the daughter, but not without the struggle of challenge and riposte. Such healing is not brought about by the male healer's action and or words but rather by the woman whose bodily presence and speech continues to confront and challenge Jesus, her faith thereby shifting gender categories and extending the provenance of the bread for the children of the house of Israel. It can be shared socio-politically and socio-culturally. The woman brings about this shift as she extends Jesus' cultural metaphors to make them more inclusive, as both she and Jesus engage ethological metaphors. Healing happens therefore at the levels of materiality and sociality. Bread and healing are a thread through this section of the Matthean narrative, issuing in a new inclusive practice – can it become a 'tradition' that is in keeping with and not contrary to the 'word of God'? It seems that the story functions, within a complex health care system, to speak of healing as indicative of the *basileia* of the heavens, in a way that can extend cultural codes of exclusion, of traditioning, of labeling as much as it can of bodies. A change in one affects a change in the others, and in this particular story, it is Jesus himself who experiences this healing as much as does the Canaanite woman's daughter. This story suggests, therefore, that healing, and telling stories of healing, functioned in diverse ways in ancient concepts of reality, especially when these are placed within a first-century and Matthean understanding of their health care system.

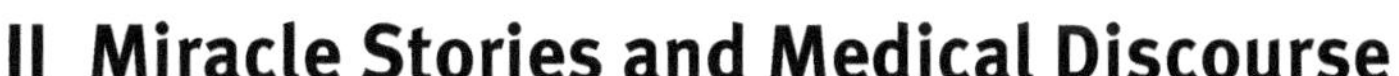

II Miracle Stories and Medical Discourse

Annette Weissenrieder

Stories Just Under the Skin: *lepra* in the Gospel of Luke

Paul Valéry,[1] a famous French Philosopher, presents skin as the "most substantial," "most important," and "deepest" part of a person. This view constructs the human being as an ectodermic creature whose actual depth is paradoxically contained in its surface. To the extent that a person operates as a social being, this surface could also reflect deeper social dimensions. Many New Testament scholars refer in their analysis implicitly or explicitly to Mary Douglas and her concept of purity and taboo.[2] In Douglas's work, the body represents a model that can be applied to "every closed system" in that its limitations symbolize all possible limitations that are threatened or unsafe.[3] Thus, the body can also be understood to be a symbol of society.[4] Starting from this theoretical background, scholars define skin (*chrōs/derma) as the final border of the body,* which is threatened by diseases of the skin especially *lepra*. The interpretation of the bodily border can be extended one step further to represent the border of Jewish society, which would be threatened by the illness of *lepra*. According to Douglas's analysis, the Jewish society would interpret *lepra* as a cause of impurity since it attacks and destroys a clearly defined structural border.[5]

---

1 Paul Valery, *Oeuvres. La Pleiade II: L'Idee fixe ou deux hommes à la mer* (Paris: coll. Bibliothèque de la Pléiade, 1960), 215 ff.

2 In Pilch's essay *Leprosy – A Test Case*, 49 ff., he adopts large portions of his first essay under the summarizing dictum "The Interpretive Strategy." ("Selecting an appropriate Model: Leprosy – A Test Case," in *Healing in the New Testament: Insights from Medical and Mediterranean Anthropology* [ed. id.; Minneapolis: Fortress, 2000] 38–54).

3 Mary Douglas (*Purity and Danger: An Analysis of Concepts of Pollution and Taboo* [New York: Routledge Classics, 2002]), 124: "The body is a model which can stand for any bounded system. Its boundaries can represent any boundaries which are threatened or precarious. The body is a complex structure. The functions of its different parts and their relation afford a source of symbols for other complex structures. We cannot possibly interpret rituals concerning excreta, breast milk, saliva and the rest unless we are prepared to see in the body a symbol of society, and to see the powers and dangers credited to social structure reproduced in small on the human body."

4 Douglas, *Purity and Danger*, 125 equates the problem of the openings of the body with the problem of the political-structural and cultural unity of a minority, as in the case of Israel. The unity can only be preserved if clearly defined structural boundaries exist that may not be crossed.

5 "Four kinds of social pollution seem worth distinguishing. The first is danger pressing on external boundaries; the second, danger from transgressing the internal lines of the system; the third, danger in the margins of the lines. The fourth is danger from internal contradiction, when

In the New Testament the illness *lepra* appears frequently, especially in the Gospel of Luke [Luke 4:27; 5:12–16; 7:22; 17:11–19]. This is surprising considering the pagan readers of the gospel of Luke, who would not be familiar with the context of Leviticus 13, or focused on the terms lepra, cleansing and priests (λέπρα – καθαρίζειν – ἱερεύς; *lepra, katharizein, hiereus*) and therefore on ritualistic aspects.

Luke 17:11–19 recounts a meeting between Jesus and ten sick lepers. In New Testament scholarship *lepra* is seen as a harmless skin disease with primarily ritualistic consequences. Once Jesus has "seen" the ten men, he sends them to the priests. On their way there, they experience healing and one, a stranger, or other, ἀλλογενής *allogenēs*, and Samaritan, comes back. This seems to suggest a dichotomous analysis of the text: The thanklessness and lack of faith of the nine (Jews?) and the gratefulness and belief of the Samaritan.

In what follows I aim to show in a first part that skin in ancient times was not interpreted as a limiting boundary of the body. The second part is dedicated to the illness construct of *lepra* in New Testament texts and its context, of which ancient medicine and texts of Qumran are an important part. Here I want to show that the distinction of "natural" and "supernatural" healing sometimes even intervenes in ancient medical texts. And finally I aim to show that the illness narratives sketched out in New Testament are often sprinkled with insights of ancient society and politics. The illness construct of *lepra* in Luke is not focused on its ritualistic dimension but connected with a special geographical and historical perspective which was well-known in the first century C.E.

1 The Body Construct of "Skin"

In his dissertation on *Rabelais* written 1942, Mikhail Bakhtin traced the process by which the notion of body that he calls "grotesque body" disappeared in Renaissance. What does a grotesque body mean? The material bodily principle is the concept of grotesque realism.[6] "In grotesque realism," Bakhtin says, "the bodily element is deeply positive. It is presented [...] as something universal, representing all the people. As such it is opposed to severance from the material and bodily roots of the world; it makes no pretense to renunciation of the earthy, or independence of the earth and the body."[7] And he further explains his notion

some of the basic postulates are denied by other basic postulates, so that at certain points the system seems to be at war with itself." Douglas, *Purity and Danger*, 123f.

6 Mikhail Bakhtin, *Rabelais and His World* (trans. Helene Iswolsky; Bloomington: Indiana University Press, 1984), 18.

7 Bakhtin, *Rabelais and His World*, 19.

of a "grotesque body" writing, "Contrary to modern canons, the grotesque body is not separated from the rest of the world. It is not a closed, completed unit; it is unfinished, outgrows itself, transgresses its own limits. The stress is laid on those parts of the body that are open to the outside world, that is, the parts through the world enters the body or emerges from it, or through which the body itself goes out to meet the world. This means that the emphasis is on the apertures or convexities, or on various ramifications and offshoots: the open mouth, the genital organs, the breasts, the phallus, the potbelly, the nose. The body discloses its essence as a principle of growth which exceeds its own limits only in copulation, pregnancy, childbirth, the throes of death, eating, drinking, or defecation. This is the ever unfinished, ever creating body, the link in the chain of genetic development, or more correctly speaking, two links shown at the point where they enter into each other. This especially strikes the eye in archaic grotesque."[8] With his image of a grotesque body, Bakhtin questions not only the body construct of his time but also the notion of the skin as the final border of the body. Can this also be said for Greco-Roman antiquity? In what follows I focus on ancient medical texts from the fifth century B.C.E. to the first century C.E.

The surface of the body in antiquity can be understood to be a porous structure that is a place of unfathomable metamorphoses. In the Hippocratic treatise *Art* we read: "In those persons in whom the skin is stretched, and parched and hard, the disease terminates without sweats; but in those in whom the skin is loose and rare, it terminates with sweats."[9] Hidden beneath the surface of the body is a multitude of diverse "fluxes" that are in constant motion and can also continually change their form. The inside of the body comes out and mingles with the world.[10] Therefore we read in the Hippocratic treatise *De alimento*, "Differ-

---

8 Bakhtin, *Rabelais and His World*, 26.

9 CH *Art*. 71 (Translation: Smith).

10 See also Gal. *De Naturalibus Facultatibus* "But why do I mention the situation of the bladder, peritoneum, and thorax? For surely, when the vapours have passed through the coats of the stomach and intestines, it is in the space between these and the peritoneum that they will collect and become liquefied (just as in dropsical subjects it is in this region that most of the water gathers). Otherwise the vapours must necessarily pass straight forward through everything which in any way comes in contact with them, and will never come to a standstill. But, if this be assumed, then they will traverse not merely the peritoneum but also the epigastrium, and will become dispersed into the surrounding air; otherwise they will certainly collect under the skin." (Translation: Brock) See Annette Weissenrieder, "Medical Texts and Authors," in *Embodying New Testament Anthropology in Context* (ed. A. Weissenrieder and T. Martin); chap. 3 explains that is *De Naturalibus Facultatibus* one of Galen's most important books dealing with the functions of various organs (Gal. chap. 9 ff.). Here Galen expresses the idea that the unity of the organism is governed by "nature," which with its *dynamis* lies in the province of physiology, Galen

ences of diseases depend on nutriment, on breath, on heat, on blood, on phlegm, on bile, on humours, on flesh, on fat, on vein, on artery, on sinew, muscle, membrane, bone, brain, spinal marrow, mouth, tongue, oesophagus, stomach, bowels, midriff, peritoneum, liver, spleen, kidneys, bladder, womb, skin. All these things both as a whole and severally. Their greatness great and not great."[11] The bodily fluids in question are blood, pus, liquid from wounds, phlegm, lethal discharges,[12] water,[13] or menstrual bleeding. All these "fluxes" have a functional resemblance. Accordingly, ancient physicians did not distinguish between normal and pathological excretions. In the seventh book "On the Epidemics," the author describes secretions that occur through the arteries, ligaments, bones, tendons, or skin. "They are the best when they go down from the disease, like varicose veins, heaviness of the loins. [...] Also swellings under the skin which push out, for example scrofulous tumors and suppurations like ulcers, and similar eruptions, or peeling skin, loss of hair, *leprous skin*, scaly skin, or the like. All abscesses occurring in a mass, not gradually, and the others that have been described are bad if inappropriate for the compass of the disease [...]."[14]

The "fluxes" are classified exclusively according to their effectiveness for the body and according to their material manifestation, but not according to their pathological manifestation. They were determined to be pathological only through the duration of an illness or as evidence of a severe illness. Healing excretions from the body were either initiated by the body itself or controlled by a physician through the use of various medications.

In addition to the diverse orifices of the body,[15] the skin as a whole is considered a possible point of exit, since it can open or be opened at any point. In the minds of the ancient authors, the skin is permeable from the inside in order to

---

makes physiology also a large part of physics in an attempt to biologize physics (in this sense he is using the term very differently than we do). The most important characteristic of nature is its τεχνή, its creativity: The living being is a creative artist. This treatise is also very valuable in understanding the humoral doctrine.

11 CH *Alim.* 25 (Translation: Jones).

12 Cf. CH *Epid.* VII 35. The books contained in *De morbus popularibus I–VII* (*Epid.*) are characterized by the fact that they were compiled at the *sickbed*. The texts seem to have been originally intended for educational purposes. Morbidity and mortality are the focal points of these writings. The seventh book in particular contains a collection of accounts of illnesses, which often end fatally. See A. Weissenrieder, "Medical Texts and Authors," chap. 3.

13 Cf. CH *Epid.* VI 5. *Epid.* II, IV and VI contain the private notes of a traveling doctor from the early 4th cent. B.C.E. See for further thoughts Weissenrieder, "Medical Texts and Authors," chap. 3.

14 CH *Epid.* II 1.7. (Translation: Smith)

15 According to ancient concepts, the eyes, ears, nose, mouth, loins, breasts, navel, anus, and vaginal opening are all considered possible orifices of the body.

transport "impurities" outward.[16] The authors make a distinction among pores, which can be expanded into openings by heating,[17] allowing various fluids to be secreted; secretions under the skin[18] that can exit through sores; discolorations of the skin,[19] which indicate different illnesses of the spleen or liver; and peeling of the skin due to dryness, particularly on the head.[20]

The medical historian Walter Schönfeld points out that the skin can therefore be interpreted as a "therapeutic organ."[21] According to the theory of the pathology of the humors, the skin phenomena mentioned here are not initially considered to be independent illnesses, but rather, they may be interpreted as signs of internal disorders. The duration of an illness and the escalation of a skin ailment can change the interpretation of the phenomena as a therapeutic evacuation as related to particular illnesses. After all, the inside of the body and internal disorders remain invisible and to a certain degree, unknown. Speculations about the inside are possible only through signs that appear on the skin or through significant discharging "fluxes."

---

16 See Gal. *De Sanitate Tuenda* VI 218–19 K. where Galen says that the pores of the skin through which "superfluities are transmitted." Galen defines health in terms of a correct mixture of basic qualities, uniformity of material, and the proper combination and composition of these. As damaging agents, Galen names unavoidable things such as age (a receding of physical substance) as well as faulty nourishment. If not mentioned otherwise I am referring to Kühn's edition on Galen, abbreviated with K.: *Galen (inklusive des Werks von Pseudo-Galen). Opera Omnia*, 22 vol. (ed. Carolus Gottlob Kühn; Leipzig: C. Knobloch, 1821–33 = Hildesheim, 1964–65).

See *Galen. A translation of Galen's Hygiene (De Sanitate Tuenda)* (ed. Montraville Green with introduction by Sigerist; Springfield: Thomas, 1951); Georg Wöhrle, *Studien zur Theorie der antiken Gesundheitslehre* (Hermes Einzelschriften 56; Stuttgart: Steiner, 1990), 213–48. Cf. also *De Tremor, Palpatione, Convulsion et Rigore* VII 616 K.: "We do not posit masses and pores as elements of the body, nor do we declare that heat comes from motion or friction or some other cause; rather, we suppose the whole body breathing and flowing together, the heat not acquired nor subsequent to the generation of the animal, but itself first and original and innate. This is nothing other than the nature and soul of life, so that you would not be wrong thinking heat to be a self-moving and constantly moving substance."

17 For example, fever, CH *Epid.* VI 5.15 or hot water baths, CH *Liquor.* 6.

18 Ichorous fluids under the skin, CH *Epid.* II 1.6; streams of salt under the skin, CH *Epid.* I 10.7; bile under the skin, CH *Affect.* 32.6. The text CH *De Affectionibus* is intended for a lay audience; accordingly, it deals primarily with therapy, while etiology is clearly kept in the background. See Weissenrieder, "Medical texts and authors," chap. 3.

19 CH *Epid.* I 10.7.

20 CH *Morb.* II 7.

21 Walter Schönfeld, "Die Haut als Ausgang der Behandlung, Verhütung und Erkennung fernörtlicher Leiden: Eine geschichtliche Studie," *Sudhoffs Archiv* 36 (1943): 43–89, here 71 points out that, in terms of medical understanding, the skin did not lose its function as a therapeutic organ until the mid-19th century.

To summarize at this point: The starting point for this brief analysis of skin was the question of whether it was understood by the ancients as a linear border to the body.[22] The different passages indicate that the skin was thought of rather as a porous tissue that opened outward from the inside. The skin was fragile and it was a boundary, but it was not meant to demarcate the body against the outside world and vice versa. It was above all a surface on which the inside revealed itself.[23]

2 The Illness Construct of *lepra* in Antiquity

Leprosy in today's sense of the word is a chronic infectious illness,[24] which is marked by a loss of sensitivity that occurs due to the breakdown of the peripheral nerves, pain perception and finally, loss of various sections of the limbs, primarily toes and fingers. This description is not consistent with Greek sources on λέπρα – *lepra* or Hebrew sources on *sara'ath.*

Λέπρα in the ancient medical texts is evaluated either as a therapeutic evacuation through the skin for an internal disorder – and therefore as a sign in the skin that can be interpreted semiotically – or as a prolonged skin ailment.[25]

22 Cf. also Claudia Benthien, *Haut: Literaturgeschichte, Körperbilder, Grenzdiskurse* (Hamburg: Rohwolt, 1999), 49f., which explains that the skin was not always interpreted as a linear border. Rather, this interpretation has only existed since the Renaissance, triggered by the history of humoral anatomy. Benthien describes the "old body canon" as follows: "Diese Grenzen verlaufen sowohl zwischen Körper und Welt als auch zwischen den einzelnen Körpern wesentlich undifferenzierter und offener als im neuen Körperkanon: Bereits an der Grenze des einzelnen Körpers zeigt sich das Vermischt und Verwobensein mit der Welt, indem vorstehende Körperteile (beispielsweise Nase oder Bauch) als in die Welt ragend verstanden werden und indem das Körperinnere aus dem Leib heraustritt, sich mit der Welt vermischt."

23 Barbara Duden, *Geschichte unter der Haut: Ein Eisenacher Arzt und seine Patientinnen um 1730* (Stuttgart: Klett Cotta, 1991) 144, which actually makes this determination in reference to texts from around 1730. However, the descriptions of the functions of the skin are comparable to ancient perceptions, making these statements quite fitting vis-à-vis the Hippocratic descriptions. A change in the basic axioms concerning skin is not seen until the middle of the 18th century.

24 The leprosy bacillus was first described by Hansen in 1868 or 1874. For this reason, leprosy is also called Hansen's disease.

25 For δέρμα *derma* – skin in CH see e.g. *Epid.* II 1.10.7; II 3.16.3; *Epid.* IV 11.4; *Epid.* V 9.2; 26.4; 97.4; *Epid.* VI 3.11.4; VI 6.5.7; *Epid.* VII 35.4; 35.12; *Coac.* 2.209; *LocHom.* 13.22, 10.35, 21.12; *Carn.* 9.18; 15.6; 17.7; 9.19; 15.5; *Aphor.* 5.20; 5.22; *Vict.* II 64.3; 64 22; 66.31; *Haemor.* 4.9; *Humor.* 4.8; 5.13. For chrōs – skin in CH see *Humid* 1.5; 1.16; 1.27; 1.32–33; 4.8–10; 6.6; *Fract.* 21.13; 25.5; 30.33; *Morb.* 1.22.6. Cf. Hans-Josef Kühn and Ulrich Fleischer, *Index Hippocraticus, cui elaborando interfuerunt sodales Thesauri Linguae Graecae Hamburgensis. Curas postremas adhibuerunt K. Alpers, A. Anastassiou, D. Irmer, V. Schmidt* (Göttingen: Vandenhoeck & Ruprecht, 1989).

One view affirms λέπρα – *lepra* as caused by the influence of harmful environmental factors on the body, particularly the impact of dry, hot climates.[26] Medical texts claim a strong correlation between the south and north winds or between dryness and moisture in relation to the illness λέπρα. Some passages also mention the effects of a hot, dry east wind. In chapter 3 of *De aere aquis locis*, the author devotes a special discussion to the effects of warm winds[27] on a city and its inhabitants. Wounds in people who live in areas that are exposed to cold winds, he says, become easily infected and develop into malignant ulcers.[28] In men, "diarrhea, chills combined with fever [...] many forms of eczema and λέπρα"[29] can all be consequences of climatic changes. Thus the geographical localization of the story seems important.

Another view suggests that the illness λέπρα – *lepra* is interpreted as the result of an inadequate balance of bodily fluids. According to these theory, the human body functions by means of a balance of fluids, usually comprised of four substances. If they are in proper balance with one another, the person is healthy. Conversely, illness is explained as an excess or lack of one of these fluids. Some texts argue that a congestion of blood in the arteries leads to a disturbance in the

---

26 For *lepra* in CH see *Epid.* V 9.3; *Morb.* I 3.18; *Affect.* 35.1; *Alim.* 20.1; 17.2; *Epid.* II 5.24; I 7.9; *Aphor.* 3.20.4; *Humor.* 17.5, 20.4; *Prorr.* 2.43; *Liquor.* 4.5.

Galen writes *De Morborum Differentiis* VI 846 K.: "[...] the differentiation of diseases happens also to be twofold in that sometimes, in fact, the *homoiomeric* bodies are changed in their qualities alone, whereas sometimes a certain substance flows into them, which has the qualities spoken of. Certainly the second form, bringing about a swelling around the bodies, is obvious to all doctors. For the *erysipelata*, inflammatory swellings (*phlegmonai*), swellings (*oidemata*), tumours (*phumata*), glandular swellings (*phugethla*), scrofulous swellings (*choirades*), *elephantiases*, *psorai*, *leprai*, *alphoi* and indurations (*skirroi*) are of this class, and can escape no one. The diseases arising in a dyscrasia of the qualities themselves alone are harder to detect, unless at this time a major turning aside of the part towards what is contrary to nature occurs. Under these circumstances it will be readily known by everyone that when heat prevails in the whole body it is termed fever, although sometimes it is also clearly manifest in the parts." And he brings this view further in saying, "For in this symptom the sensation is of superfluities associated with itching alone, in that one cannot give a name to these in any other way unless one wishes to speak of something alkaline or salty or sharp, for such is their nature. It is possible to learn about these from things that are external, like the sea anemone, [...] For itching occurs in those who do not wash, or are filthy, or have indigestion, or who eat unwholesome foods, and far more certainly in those with psora and lepra, because the humour is more copious and thicker in such conditions." VII 197 K. (Translation: Johnston)

27 The relationship between warm wind and *lepra* will be discussed in detail later.

28 CH *Aer.* 4. In *Aer.* 4, these statements are applied only to the people who live in warm areas.

29 CH *Aer.* 3. Basic for the following: Weissenrieder, Images, chap. 6.

"circulation of the blood." Other texts speak of a "disturbance in the circulation of the blood" as a cause, which then leads to the mixing of fluids and finally to secretion in the form of a sore. Thus, an issue of blood is interpreted as a therapeutic evacuation for the illness λέπρα *lepra*.

Can we therefore conclude that λέπρα *lepra* is a harmless skin secretion and that it has a primary ritualistic meaning which Jesus than overcomes?

Let us have a closer look at one passage: *De alimento* (On nutriment) interprets the cause of illness as an imbalance of body fluids. Here leprosy appears at first sight as a harmless skin disease. "Ulceration, blood, pus, lymph, lepra, [...] white leprosy, sometimes harm and sometimes help, and sometimes neither harm nor help." The gloss in one of the Manuscript M delivering the text might be of help: Harm means if the illness takes its way in the depth as well as in the surface of the body. Neither harm nor help result from the cited skin diseases if they remain merely in the surface. In *De Morborum Differentiis* Galen explains this further in saying: "Some of the excesses are in the whole class contrary to nature, like helminthes and ascarides, a stone in the bladder, a chalazion in the eye, a cataract *hypochyma*, a pus, warts. Cysts, fatty swellings *atheromata*, sebaceous swellings *steatomata*, *alphoi*, *leprai*, *leukai*, chalkstones in joints *(poroi)* and all these things found in abscesses (*apostemata*). That we shall call as many of these as primarily hinder function, diseases, as with cataract, and call those that don't, causes of diseases is clear to everyone."[30]

Therefore, we encounter the idea that λέπρα – *lepra* rids the body of harmful materials; it is a *therapeutic evacuation,* which nevertheless could be brought on by a fatally progressing illness, or at any rate could indicate a severe internal illness. This idea is based on the belief that the skin is one of the openings in the body through which harmful bodily substances can flow out just as they would otherwise exit through another part of the body. No distinction is made between normal and pathological secretions.

When we compare Jewish texts from the 1st century B.C.E. on with these medical texts, we can find both etiological meanings, the theory of environmental factors, and in part the theory of bodily fluids, in the Jewish texts.[31] A particularly

30 Gal. *De Morborum Differentiis* VI.863 K. (Translation: Johnston)

31 J.M. Baumgarten, "The 4Q Zadokite Fragments on the Skin Disease," *JJS* 41 (1990): 153–65, here 163: "Healing is indicated by the return of the blood, apparently identified with the spirit of life, to the arteries where it 'moves up and down'. The identification of the blood with the spirit of life would seem to be more in harmony with the biblical perspective (Gen 9:3–4 and Lev 17:10–14)."

informative source is the so-called 4Q fragment on skin ailments:[32] It has been preserved in the Damascus document,[33] which deals with the diagnosis of *sara'ath* by a priest.[34] The text postulates a connection between *sara'ath* and *ruach*, air.[35] This is then associated with medical knowledge and regulations re-

---

32 Johann Maier, *Die Qumran Essener* (Munich: UTB, 1995), names 4Q 269, Frg.7; 4Q 269, Frg. 8; 4Q 273, Frg. 1.ii.2–11; 4Q 272 Frg. I.1(1).9–20 and 4Q 272 Frg. I. Ii.1–18.

The translation follows Eibert Tigchelaar with some changes (his presentation for a symposium in Leiden on the Holy Spirit; Leiden 2011). My changes are based to the ancient medical knowledge on the distinction between "arteries" and "blood vessels."

בבוא הרוח ואחזה בגיד ושב הדם למעלה ולמטה והגיד

When the breath-spirit comes and takes hold of the vessel (blood vessel?), making the blood recede upwards and downwards, and the vessel [...]

וראה הכוהן ביום השביעי

והנה מלא הגיד דם ורוח החיים עולה ויורדח והבשר צמח

נרפא ה[שאח ? ונעלמה ?]ה ספחה

The priest shall examine (him) on the seventh day,

and if the (*blood*) *vessel is filled with blood and the breath-spirit of life pulsates up and down* and the flesh has grown, (then) the swelling?] is healed, [and hidden? is] the scab

ומשפט נחק הראש והזקן [ו] ראה הכוהן והנה באה הרוח בראש או בזקן באוחזה בגיד ובב[שר אשר] מתחת

השער והפך מראה לדק צוהב

And the rule for the scall of the head or the beard [ ]

and the priest shall examine (him), and if the spirit-breath has entered the head or the beard, taking hold of the (blood) vessels, and the fl[esh, which] is underneath the hair, turning its appearance to fine yellowish [...]

And the priest shall order that they shave the head, but not the scalp, in order that the priest may count the dead and live hair, and see whether any has been added from the live to the dead during the seven days, in which case he is unclean, while if none had been added from the live to the dead, and the (blood) vessel is filled with blood (והגיד נמלא דם), and the breath of life pulsates up and down in it (ורוח החיים עולה ויורדח בו), the malady is healed. This is the rule of the law of *ṣara'ath* (skin disease) for the sons of Aaron to separate the ones [afflicted by *ṣara'ath*]."

33 The dating of the fragment is based on the most important handwriting in 4Q 266, which is classified by M. Davis and J.M. Baumgarten, "Cave IV, V, VI Fragments," in *The Dead Sea Scrolls II: Damascus Document, War Scroll, and Related Documents* (ed. J.H. Charlesworth; Tübingen/Louisville: Westminster, 1995), 59–79, here 59, as follows: "The writing is in a semi-cursive Hasmonean hand which in cross paleographic sequence may be dated to the first half of the first century B.C.E."

34 It is interesting that the section on skin ailments, particularly on lepra, does not appear in the texts of the Cairo Genizah.

35 Here, the exact translation is disputed: Cf. Baumgarten, *The 4Q Zadokite Fragments on Skin Disease*, 153–65; Geza Vermes, "Qumran Corner: Preliminary Remarks on Unpublished Fragments of the Community Rule from Qumran Cave 4," *JJS* 42 (1991): 250–59, here 250–55; E. Qimron, "Notes on the 4Q Zadokite Fragment on Skin Disease," *JJS* 42 (1991): 256–59 and

garding impurity and purity. The author puts forward the following explanation, which can be compared to some of the texts of the *Corpus Hippocraticum* and of Galen: If *ruach*, air, enters a person's arteries, making it impossible for the blood to "rise and fall" regularly, this can have various consequences. If the air supply, and consequently the circulation of the blood are disturbed, this will initially produce a swelling or a light spot. The author of the 4Q fragment then considers this point on the skin to be a dead spot, since ruach and blood no longer "rise and fall." *Ruach* is responsible for obstructing the movement of blood, but it also reestablishes a normal flow of blood.

A similar interpretation but chronologically later can be found in Leviticus Rabbah 15, in a Jewish medical book Sepher-ha-Rephu'ot and in the Kitab al Tabbakh which is an exegetical tract of the Pentateuch in the 11th century.

Thus, we see comparability between the phenomena of λέπρα – *lepra* in secular and Jewish (medical texts), although the Jewish literature emphasizes the imbalance of bodily fluids and the disturbance of blood circulation.

One could object that *lepra* simply represents a humble illness and that it is particularly questionable whether ancient medical texts would have been known in Palestine so that we therefore must focus on Leviticus as the main comparable history-of-religion background, because it is here where we find the combination of terms: *lepra*, cleansing and priests.

So it is essential to note that we can verify besides the ritual and social implications also medical implications in Leviticus 13. The *medical implications* in Lev 13 are supported, on the one hand, by the description given for *sara'ath, lepra*: Lev 13 establishes a close connection to diverse sores (ἕλκός *helkos*; *schechi*)[36] and describes around twenty pathological changes in the skin like white skin,[37] an

Michael Wohlers, "AUSSÄTZIGE REINIGT (MT 10,8): Aussatz in antiker Medizin, Judentum und frühem Christentum," in *Text und Geschichte: Facetten theologischen Arbeitens aus dem Freundes- und Schülerkreis, FS D. Lührmann* (ed. S. Maser/E. Schlarb; MThS 50; Marburg 1999), 300 f.

36 For ἑλκός see Gal. *De Symptomatum Causis* VI.6: "It is appropriate to consider in all such cases what is primary and per se, and not through another intermediary, the cause of final result, not what is called *prokatarchontic* or *prokatarktic*, which Hippocrates saw fit to remind us of many times in other places and in saying: "It is sometimes the case in *tetanus* without a wound *helkos*, in a well-conditioned young man during the middle of the summer, that a pouring on of copious cold brings about a restoration of heat, and heat relieves these things."

37 Λεύκη, skin disease, so called from the color, *leukē*. See Gal. VI.863 in conjunction with alphoi and leprai as well as other conditions exemplifying excess as something that may damage function. See CH *Coac* 5.502.3; *Prorr* 43.1 und 5.

eating sore,[38] swelling,[39] ulceration,[40] or raw flesh, which are all well known in ancient medical texts.[41]

However, not only are the skin lesions described in the medical and Old Testament texts with identical adjectives such as elated, deepening, scaly, wetting or even as raw flesh, but also both texts describe in a similar way the meaning of the 7-day period of quarantine for the formation of new skin.[42] And as in Leviticus,

38 Καρκινός and eating sore or ulcer, cancer; used in relation to a superficial abnormality in VI. 874 K. and attributed to black bile VI.875. CH *Epid* II 6.22.2; *Epid.* V 20.8; *Aphor.* 6.38.1; *Vict.* 2. 48. 28; *Mul.* II 133; *Prorr.* 2.11; *Nat.Mul.* 90.1; *Mul.* I 91.12; *Mul.* II 192; 133.20; *Prorr.* 2.13.

39 Οἴδημα, swelling; Galen classifies it as a dyscrasia of homoiomeric bodies due to inflowing material VI. 849 K.

40 Regarding ulceration see the Hippocratic treatise *De ulceribus*. Researchers refer to this treatise as the "Small Surgery" of the *Corpus Hippocraticum*; it primarily deals with the surgical and pharmacological treatment of injuries.

41 Regarding ἅιμορροΐ see VII. 82 K. and earlier examples in C.C. Mettler, *History of Medicine* (Philadelphia: Blakiston Company, 1947), 806.

For ἀλφός see LSJ that gives "dull-white leprosy, esp. on face". It is classified by Galen in VI.849 K. among dyscrasias of homoiomeric bodies "due to a substance in from without" (p.51). See CH *Affect.* 35.1; *Alim.* 20.2; *Aphor.* 3.20; *Epid.* 2. 5.24; 1.7; *Humor.* 20.4; *Liquor.* 4.5.

῎Αμθραξ, a carbuncle or pustule, linked with φλεγμονή, ἐρυσίπελας ἕρπης as disease that give rise to another disease i.e. fever (VI.860 K.).

'Απόστημα abscess, listed with diseases in which an excess causes disturbance of function (VI.863 Kühn). "Sometimes, when the internal surface within the cavity itself is ulcerated and the ulcerated parts coalesce with each other, destruction of the natural conformation occurs. Sometimes, there is a growing up of flesh or some other unnatural excrescence, or induration exists, or inflammation, or an abscess occurs in the actual bodies of the organs, and then when an unnatural swelling occupies the cavity within, narrowing occurs." (VII. 4 K.; Translation: Johnston).

Ἐλεφαντίασις , which is not elephantiasis in the present sense but probably leprosy; see Mirko D. Grmek, *Diseases in the Ancient Greek World* (transl. M. Muellner and L. Muellner; Baltimore and London 1989), 168–76 (= Les maladies à l'aube de la civilisation occidentale: recherches sur la réalité pathologique dans le monde grec préhistorique archaïque et classique [Paris, 1986]); Galen classifies it among the dyscrasias of homoiomeric bodies due a substance flowing from without (VI. 849 K.)

Πύον, discharge from a sore, pus; a disease in which excess causes disturbance of function VI. 863.

42 Gal. *Definitiones Medicae* XIX. 384–85 K.: "Those who are not in a condition 'in accord with nature' for they have gone beyond 'balance' but neither are they contrary to nature for they are mot hindered with respect to functions. Such a thing that is "non-natural" is neither contrary to nature, nor in accord with nature, nor natural. Examples are those having *leuke*, *leprous warts*, warts and the like. For these are not in accord to nature as they are outside what accords with nature, but nor are they contrary to nature for they do not hinder the functions that accord with nature."

central medical texts mention ὁράω when they refer precise investigation of the skin, here by a priest and there by a physician.[43] The term used for seeing means a survey and classification of physical details. The term for seeing, ὁράω, comes close to touching and immediate recognizing and is especially connected in ancient medicine with perception and often translated as mindful seeing. That *sara'ath* was not only interpreted in the context of purity and impurity is also evident in several Old Testament passages which speak of a healing[44] ἰάομαι or of the restoration of the skin.[45] Both terms are used in ancient medical texts and in Luke 17:11–19.

The *social implications* come to the fore in some texts in Old Testament which detail exclusion from the community, resulting in socio-local isolation, and precautions to avoid the contamination of other people. However, the physician Caelius Aurelianus mentions a similar exclusion of sick people in a final comment regarding the illness of elephantiasis: "Others recommend further that in any city which has never before been plagued by this illness, one should kill a sick person if he is a stranger (peregrinus). A citizen, however, should be banished to a quite distant place or made to stay in cold regions in the interior of the country, away from all people, and be brought back (only) when his health is shown to be better, so that other citizens may not be harmed through contact with this illness."[46] In this text, Aurelianus refers to the practice of various physicians, who – as is also reported in the Jewish sources – argued in favor of the exclusion of the sick person from the community.

The aspects I have examined so far have revealed similarities between the biblical texts and the medical texts. However, one term seems to resist such a comparison: καθαρίζειν *katharizein*, cleansing.[47] This term, which appears next to *sara'ath* or λέπρα *lepra* in Lev 13 (LXX), has served in exegesis to confirm the

---

43 Regarding ὁράω in Lev 13:3, 5, 6, 7, 8, 10, 13, 14, 14, 15, 25 and more often.

See for the term ὁράω in CH *Morb.Sacr.* 1.12; *Carn.* 9.19; 19.44; 17.10; 17.1; *Intern.* 17.10; *Mul.* 2.139, 165.2, 163.2, 168.3; *DieJud.* 3.8; 3.17; 3.31; 3.26; 3.16; *Ars.* 11.9; 11.34; 12.13; 11.7; *LocHom.* 3.17; 13.38; 13.44; *Nat.Hom.* 1.6; *Vict.* 3.71.15; *Vict.* 4. 86. 14; 4.91.1; 90.2; 89.115; 90.4; 90.49 ect.

44 For *rph* – healing, see "the plague of λέπρα be healed in the leper" in Lev. 14:3, and "Lord, not this! Heal her [Miriam] [from the λέπρα], I pray!" in Num 12:13 LXX.

45 2 Kgs 5:10,14 "your flesh will be restored and you will be clean; and his flesh was restored so that it was like a little child's, and he was clean."

46 Cael. Aur. TP IV,I,13: "Item alii aegrotum in ea ciuitate, quae numquam fuerit isto morbo uexata, si fuerit peregrinus, caedendum (Drabkin: cludendum) probant, ciuem uero longius exulare aut locis mediterraneis et frigidis consistere ab hominibus separatum, ex inde reuocari, si meliorem receperit ualetudinem, quo possint ceteri ciues nulla istius passionis contagione sauciari." (Translation: Drabkin)

47 See for the topic of purity also Epictet 4.40.

understanding of those texts that reinforce a ritualistic interpretation of the act of cleansing. However, in the *Corpus Hippocraticum* especially in the tract *De ulceribus*, καθαρίζειν *katharizein* refers to healing of ulcers, sores and leprosy in a purely physiological sense.[48]

Behind the interpretation as a cleansing story, which is widespread in the exegeses, is the implication that λέπρα – *lepra* is a harmless skin secretion. But in the context of ancient medical theory, the dominant assumption is that secretions in the skin can signal internal processes. No distinction is made here between normal and pathological secretions. Of primary interest is the question of the effect and material manifestation of the secretions. The evaluation of a secretion as "harmless" – as one frequently sees in today's exegeses – is not consistent with ancient medicine. There we even encounter reports that λέπρα – *lepra* could also be experienced as a severe illness or a plague. The interpretation of the story as a cleansing narrative also points to a second assumption: that of the primarily ritualistic meaning of the illness λέπρα – *lepra*. According to this assumption, the illness construct of λέπρα – *lepra* should be analyzed above all in terms of the categories of purity and impurity. The use of ἰάομαι – *iaomai* in Luke 17:15 and of καθαρίζειν – *katharizein* in ritualistic as well as medical contexts in antiquity speak against this point of view.

3 Early Christianity and Ancient "Rational" Medicine

I aimed to show that regarding illness and healing early Christianity must be related to its context, of which ancient medicine, healing cults and Jewish interpretation of sickness are an important part. Early Christianity not only searched for its own point of view in this process of differentiation, but also related the point of

48 Nevertheless, it is doubtful whether we must make a distinction between the religious and the profane, medical use of καθαρίζειν: In syntactic regard no difference in the use of the word "clean" is apparent. As in the Old Testament texts we also find in the *Corpus Hippocraticum* the construction with the double accusative (the object which is cleaned and the thing which is removed by the cleaning; see καθῆραι τὴν κεφαλὴν φλέγμα; καὶ ἢν δέῃ αὐτὴν αἷμα καθῆραι CH *Aff.* 2 (VI 210 L.); 25 (VI 236 L.); cf. also *Steril.* 240 (VIII 454 L.) and *Mul.* II 134 (VIII 304 L.). Just as in Old Testament texts a simple accusative can be found next to the double accusative which belongs to the object, that is cleaned [CH αὐτόν; τὸ σῶμα CH *Int.* 6 (VII 182 L.); *Mul.* II 47 (VIII 106 L.] or to the object which is removed by the cleansing as for example blood. One may interpret a semantic parallel in the image of the origin of illnesses by miasmata; particularly *De ventibus* from the Hippocratic Corpus may be interpreted in this direction.

view to its theological principles. The first point in question is how early Christians could have access to ancient medical ideas:

The *Corpus Hippocraticum* is of fundamental importance to the history of ancient medicine, given the transition from an *oral to a written tradition* in these texts. From the fifth century B.C.E. on, medical knowledge, previously handed down by word of mouth alone, was recorded in writing. Recently scholars have taken special notice of the question of how medical knowledge was transmitted in antiquity, in other words which literary genres were related, and which, and in what manner, technical concepts were introduced in order to lead the audience, listeners and readers, to certain conclusions. Two examples of this line of investigation can be found in a collection of essays, *Vermittlung und Tradierung von Wissen in der griechischen Literatur*[49] and *Gattungen wissenschaftlicher Literatur in der Antike*.[50]

The issue of the transition from an oral tradition to a written one, however, is more complex than it seems upon a first, merely cursory examination of the Hippocratic Corpus. But why is the question of oral transmission of medical theories so crucial? The sources show that medical-philosophical cases and theories were often discussed orally and in *public lectures*, and were sometimes written down only after a lengthy transmission process. A *certain uniformity* of medical-philosophical theories can be seen in the lectures of *Anonymus Londiensis*, and we have reports of these lectures from laypeople such as Xenophon, who writes in his pedagogical novel about the education of Kyros: “For people are continually talking about unhealthful localities and localities that are healthful; and you may find clear witnesses to either in the physique and complexion of the inhabitants; and in the second place, it is not enough to have regard to the localities only, but tell me what means you adopt to keep well yourself.”[51] Thus the author of the Hippocratic treatise *De affectionibus* addresses explicitly in his *prooemium* the “intelligent lay person,” whom he wishes to enable to help himself in case of illness. Likewise the speech *De flatibus*, which we now have in the form of a treatise, is addressed to the lay person with the knowledge of the basic principles of natural philosophy. From the author of *De natura hominis* we learn of the public’s reaction to various teachings; he describes not without sarcasm how the

49 *Vermittlung und Tradierung von Wissen in der griechischen Literatur* (ed. Wolfgang Kullmann and Jochen Althoff; Script Oralia 21; Tübingen: G. Narr Verlag, 1993).

50 *Gattungen wissenschaftlicher Literatur*, (Script Oralia 95, Reihe A, Altertumswissenschaftliche Reihe 22; ed. Wolfgang Kullmann, Jochen Althoff and Markus Asper; Tübingen, Gunter Narr Verlag, 1998).

51 Xenophon *Institutio Cyri* I 6,16 ff. (Translation: Miller)

audience gives its assent first to one, then to another speaker.[52] In addition, Volker Langholf has demonstrated that even given their diversity, medical theories of the different schools were *in practice* consistent, especially in terms of their knowledge of dietetics.[53] Every lay person confronted with a physical problem, or having an interest in medicine, could at that time find pertinent reading material easily, take part in the many lectures, or find assistance at the market square.

By means of the texts of the *Corpus Hippocraticum*, medicine became a "science" that is written and handed down, with experiences that could be passed on. The existing texts cover a variety of types of texts, subjects, and theories – for example, prognostic, dietary, and therapeutic writings, as well as an ethnographic treatise.[54] Basic to the Hippocratic writings is the theme or assertion that medicine is an art. As such, the achievements and boundaries of medical activity are closely drawn. The major task of the doctor consists in always being aware of these boundaries and in subordinating his own ego to the interests of the ill human being. Medical knowledge is based, primarily, in experience. This enables the healer to assess the prospective natural history of an illness. The task of the doctor is to support the person in his or her fight against the illness, which he defeats by means of practices derived from precise observation. This is also the reason, for example, why questions of the anatomy of the person or of the function of the brain or the muscles hardly were mentioned. The focus was on the healing of illnesses and not on reasons for the occurrence of illness.

A few treatises refer explicitly to oral tradition,[55] for example *De vetere medicina*, which refers to all those "who have attempted to speak or to write on medicine and who have assumed for themselves a postulate as a basis for their

---

52 CH *De Natura Homine* 1 (VI 32.2–34.7 Littré); see also *Hippocrate: La Nature de l'homme* (ed. Jacques Jouanna; Corpus Medicorum Graecorum I,1,2; Berlin: Akademie Verlag, 1975), 222–25 and 235.

53 Volker Langholf, "Über die Kompatibilität einiger binärer und quaternärer Theorien," in *Hippocratica: Éditions du Centre national de la recherche scientifique (Colloques internationaux)* (ed. Mirko D. Grmek; Paris: Belles Lettres, 1980), 333–46.

54 *CH Aer.* 12–14.

55 See for the following *Hippocrate: Des vents – De l'art* (ed. and transl. Jacques Jouanna; Budé V,1, Paris: Les Belles Lettres, 2003), 10–24 and 169ff.; cf. also Kollesch, "Zur Mündlichkeit hippokratischer Schriften," in *Tratados hipocrãticos* (Estudios acerca de su contenido, forma e influencia; Actas del VIIe Colloque International Hippocratique [Madrid, 24–29 de septiembre de 1990], ed. J. A. Lopez Ferez, Madrid 1992), 335–42.

discussion."[56] In *De natura hominis* we read that the treatise is addressed to an audience which is "used to listening to people who speak about the nature of man beyond what is relevant for medicine."[57] We also know of treatises that appear to respond directly as if to questions from an audience, as in this passage from *De morbis* I: "Anyone who wishes to ask correctly about healing, and, on being asked, to reply correctly, must consider the following. [...] When you have considered these questions, you must pay careful attention in discussions, and when someone makes an error in one of these points [...] then you must catch him there and attack him in your rebuttal."[58]

The interface of orality with written text becomes especially clear when we consider the gynecological writings of the Hippocratic Corpus. *De natura muliebri* and *De muliebribus* especially contain long lists of prescriptions and recommended procedures reflecting traditional knowledge gathered over the course of generations.

With some treatises, however, the written character is evident, as for example *De morbis popularibus* VI 8.7, which mentions information, "derived from the small writing-tablet." According to Langholf,[59] this allows us to assume that some chapters of the *Epidemics* can be traced back to written notes first recorded on writing tablets. This would also explain why in this book of the *Epidemics* there are many passages of the same length.

Differences between the treatises can be traced back to the existence of several authors or to the very different time periods in which a treatise was written (think especially of *De hebdomadibus – On the Seven* which is dated to the first century C.E., while other treatises are dated to the 4th century B.C.E.), as well as to different intended audiences (lay people or specialists).

It has been shown therefore that some cases given as examples in the *Epidemics* of the Hippocratic Corpus can only be understood when interpreted as a

---

56 CH *De vetere medicina* 1.1 (I 570 Littré). Cf. van der Eijk, "Medicine and Philosophy in Classical Antiquity," and *Hippocrates: On Ancient Medicine. Transl. with introd. and commentary* (ed. Mark John Schiefsky; Leiden and Boston: Brill, 2005), 35f.

57 CH *De natura homine* 1 (VI 32 Littré). Later on the author says: "The best way to realize this is to be present at their debates. Given the same debaters and the same audience, the same man never wins in a discussion three times in succession, but now one is victor, now another, now he happens to have the most glib tongue in the face of the crowd. Yet it is right that a man who claims correct knowledge about the facts should maintain his own argument victorious always, if his knowledge be knowledge of reality and if he set it forth correctly. But in my opinion such men by their lack of understanding overthrow themselves in the words of their very discussions, and establish the theory of Melissus" (VI 34 Littré; translation: Jones).

58 CH *De morbis* I 1 (VI 140–42 Littré; translation: Potter).

59 Volker Langholf, "Beobachtungen zur Struktur einiger Traktate des 'Corpus Hippocraticum'," *Sudhoffs Archiv* 73 (1989): 64–77.

doctor's private notes. Likewise, the treatises *De flatibus* (*On Breaths*) and *De arte* (*On the Arts of Medicine*) can be better comprehended when they are read as advertising texts designed to attract patients on the "medical marketplace."[60] Both treatises show that the Hippocratics not only had to distinguish themselves from magicians and temple healers, but also had to establish themselves in opposition to intellectual healers who offered healing informed by their philosophy. One thing is clear: "rational" medicine in antiquity was accessible to all people of different levels of education. Therefore, this is no upper-class phenomenon. This brings us to the second aspect in question, the religious aspect:

"Rational"[61] medicine is widespread, above all, in the *Corpus Hippocraticum* and in later works by medical theorists such as Herophilus or Galen,[62] who brought physical and scientific legality to the fore. Therefore it is obvious that one cannot assume a religious foundation for medicine. Different methodical attempts such as the doctrine of the microcosm/macrocosm or the doctrine of the bodily fluids confirm the purely rational background of medicine. There are several possible reasons to reject this one-sided interpretation:

For one, it is striking that in the *Corpus Hippocraticum* an entire treatise is dedicated to the phenomenon of dreaming which then becomes the reason and preparation for the medical doctor's diagnoses (*De victu* IV): the dreaming soul gives information about the state of the body. Thus the treatise begins as follows: "Anyone who has a correct understanding of the signs that occur in sleep will discover that they have great significance for everything."[63] This statement occurs within the context of the author's explanation that dreams have great significance not just as "signs" and "indicators" of the body, but that they should also be understood and valued as divine prophecies of the future. A belief in the divine

---

60 Nutton, "Healers in the Medical Market Place: Towards a Social History of Greek and Roman Medicine," in *Medicine in society: Historical essays* (ed. A. Wear; Cambridge: Cambridge University Press, 1992), 15–58.

61 Cf. on the relationship between 'rational' medicine and New Testament A. Weissenrieder, *Images of Illness in the Gospel of Luke: Insights of Ancient Medical Texts* (WUNT 2/164; Mohr Siebeck: Tübingen, 2003), chapter 2; eadem, "Theory and Practice in Ancient Medicine and Philosophy," in *Embodying New Testament Anthropology in Context: A Sourcebook*, chap. 2. Cf. also eadem & Gregor Etzelmüller, "Christentum und Medizin: Welche Kopplungen sind lebensförderlich?" in *Religion und Krankheit* (ed. G. Etzelmüller and A. Weissenrieder; Darmstadt: WBG, 2010), 1–34; and Annette Weissenrieder and Gregor Etzelmüller, "Christlicher Glaube und Medizin: Stationen einer Beziehung – Christian Beliefs and Medicine: Stations of Relationship," *DMW* 132 (2007): 2747–53.

62 Cf. also Teun Tieleman, *Galen and Chrysippus on the Soul: Argument and Refutation in the "De placitis," Books II–III* (Philosophia Antiqua 58; Leiden: Brill, 1996) and idem, "Religion and Therapy in Galen," in *Religion und Krankheit* (Darmstadt: Wissenschaftliche Buchgesellschaft), 83–95.

63 CH *De victu* IV 86 (VI 640 Littré).

origin of dreams and their prophetic power was widespread in antiquity and was common even in intellectual circles.[64] With it the Hippocratic tradition takes up a method which we know especially from the practice of healing cults.[65] And it is worth noting that the Hippocratics are mindful of prayers to the gods: "They should have brought them [the patients] to the sanctuaries, with sacrifices and prayers, in supplication to the gods."[66]

In addition, closeness is testified also to the so-called *Hippocratic Oath (Ius)*. There it says:[67] "I swear by Apollo Physician, by Asclepius, by Health, by Panacea and by all the gods and goddesses, making them my witnesses that I will carry out, according to my ability and judgment, this oath and this indenture."[68] With the oath the Hippocratic tradition is aligned with the healing god Apollo who is named at the same time in numerous other sources as the "father" of the Asclepiads who autherizes the decisions made by the doctors.[69]

But Hippocrates swears his oath not only by Apollo, but also by Asclepius, who was known as the healing god.[70] A number of healing temples (*Asklepieion*) are known to us from this time. The healing qualities are reflected in the image

---

64 See Philipp van der Eijk, *Aristoteles: De insomniis. De divination per somnum, übersetzt und erläutert* (Aristoteles: Werke in deutscher Übersetzung 14,3; Berlin: Akademie Verlag, 1994), 102–32.

65 L. Edelstein & E. Edelstein, *Asclepius: Collection and interpretation of the testimonies* (Baltimore: John Hopkins, 1994 = 1998).

66 CH *De morbo sacro* 4 (VI. 362 Littré).

67 The treatise goes back to the opening of the training center of the Asclepiads for a broader stratum of society and led to the fact that the medical tradition of Cos could be continued by establishing it on wide base. The social context at the beginning of the oath shows that with this opening, however, the privileges of the family of Asclepiads were also in question. It is a question discussed in the literature repeatedly: whether the oath is really to be attributed to the doctor's school founded by Hippocrates, like Karl Deichgräber, *Der hippokratische Eid: Griechischer und deutscher Text des Eides mit einem Essay über das alte Dokument. Text griechisch und deutsch* (4th ed.; Stuttgart: Hippokrates Verlag, 1983), 48 f.; Jutta Kollesch and Georg Hartwig, "Der hippokratische Eid: Zur Entstehung der antiken medizinischen Deontologie," *Philologus* 122 (1978): 253–63, 253–326 suppose.

Some remarks refer to possible medical topics in antiquity: thus the ban is meant to ensure social security against suicide by poison being made possible by pharmacists and doctors who prepared highly efficient poisons (Theophrastus *Historia Plantarum* IX 16,8); on the subject of abortion there are references to so-called abortion *uvulae* which are not mentioned, indeed, otherwise, in the *Corpus Hippocraticum*. However, other *abortativa* are mentioned (see *De muliebribus* I 68 and *Superfetatione* 27); the fear of impotence of the men shows the ban of the stone cut (only at this point skillful men are mentioned in the CH). Besides, the reference of the healing cults points to the question of the coupling of healing cult with rational medicine.

68 CH *Iusiurandum* 1 (Translation, LCL 1: Jones).

69 See Plato *Phaedo* 270 c; CH *Epistulae* 2.17–24 (IX 314.1–8 Littré).

70 Cf. Ovid *Met.* XV, 637–40.658–62.66–679.736–44; Pausanias II,27,2.

constellation: Asclepius's help and healing of human suffering is indicated in several ways: he touches the sick, conversations are signaled by the attentive posture of his body, which expresses a direct connection to the sick. The snake that bites the patient also indicates help and healing of human suffering.

The doctor Herophilus also mentions medicine or drugs as "the hands of the gods" which we know for example from Plutarch[71] and Galen.[72] This is especially striking because Celsus says that Herophilus among others' did not treat any kind of disease without drugs.[73] Therefore we can say that religious interpretations of illness and scientific-medical knowledge seem not necessarily to have been perceived in antiquity as being in competition.

Nevertheless, this picture of the coupling of rational medicine with the healing cults of its time requires a correction: in the *Corpus Hippocraticum* are found two treatises that touch on the question of whether one should attribute certain illnesses to a divine origin: the treatises *Airs, Waters, Places* and *On Sacred Disease* have already been mentioned.[74] Both determine that there is no illness with sacred or even divine origin, because everything is produced according to the laws of nature – or at least according to the law of the illness. Thus the author opens the text *On the Sacred Disease* as follows: "I am about to discuss the disease called 'sacred.' It is not, in my opinion, any more divine or more sacred than other diseases, but has a natural cause, and its supposed divine origin is due to men's inexperience, and to their wonder at its peculiar character."[75] It is in this context that we also find polemical statements against magicians and charlatans; he also argues against the illness being understood as demonic possession or as an unpredictable, sudden and divine effect on a human being, both of which the author challenges, since he does not allow here for the possibility of divine influence. In this respect he remains solidly grounded in rational medicine. The divinity alone, not the illness, is

71 Plut. *Quaestiones symposiacae* 4.1.3 (*Moralia* 663 b-c).

72 Gal. *De Compositione Medicamentorum Secundum Locos* 6.8 (XII 965 f. Kühn).

73 Cel. *Medicina 5, prohoem.* 1 (*CML* 1, 190 Marx)

74 CH *De morbo sacro* 1; Littré VI, 356–64. The writing is characterized by an effort to grasp "epileptic phenomena" scientifically. The purpose is to detach the illness from its religious connotation. Therefore, the author uses the term "sacred illness" only controversially at the beginning and the end of the writing. Instead the author writes "this illness / suffering," however, not epilepsy. *Epilēpsis* means merely the single attack and is not a name of an illness. Within the CH there is a close correspondence between *De morbo sacro* and *De aere aquis locis*. Thus the writing may go back to Hippocrates, who Galen denies is the author of *De aere aquis locis*.

75 CH *De morbo sacro* 1.1 (Translation: Jones); cf. Philip van der Eijk, "The theology of the Hippocratic treatise On the Sacred Disease," in *Medicine and Philosophy in Classical Antiquity: Doctors and Philosophers on Nature, Soul, Health and Disease* (ed. idem; Cambridge: Cambridge University Press, 2005).

surrounded by cleanness and holiness. For this sole reason, a divinity can by no means be the cause of an illness. This evaluation occurs only when there is a lack of interpretation or an absence of meaning: "Being at a loss, and having no treatment that would help, they concealed and sheltered themselves behind the divine and called this disease sacred in order that their utter ignorance might not be manifest."[76] The lack of interpretation is combined with the second factor, namely the question of guilt. The author writes: "Accordingly I hold that those who attempt in this manner to cure these diseases cannot consider them either sacred or divine; for when they are removed by such purifications and by such treatment as this, there is nothing to prevent the production of attacks in men by devices that are similar. If so, something human is to blame, and not a godhead."[77]

This human guilt is interpreted in the course of the treatise as an inherited illness.[78] If the *Corpus Hippocraticum* is taken at face value, it is exclusively the nature of an illness which is examined in order to interpret an illness. The so-called rational medicine of antiquity is therefore ambivalent concerning its religious foundation. Its religious self-image is supported by the Hippocratic Oath. This religious foundation has its basis in the healing cults of Apollo and Asclepius, for one thing stands out: temple medicine and the temple cult of Asclepius are nowhere called into question. Therefore we can see that the distinction used today between "natural" and "supernatural" interpretive contexts or fact vs. fiction that is assigned to medicine vs. miracle stories was not enforced consistently in ancient times.

4 The Illness Construct Lepra in Luke 17

What does the construct of skin and illness construct of λέπρα – *lepra* as demonstrated from the perspective of ancient medical and Jewish texts, have to do with the healing of the ten lepers in Luke 17? The connection would be provided if we could show that the theory presented by exegetes according to which the illness *lepra* symbolizes a threat to social and religious borders that Jesus overcomes is questionable. It is true that, with fragile regularity, the author of the Gospel of Luke does introduce premises that represent fluctuating borders – such as the geographic classification "between Samaria and Galilee", the notion of *allogenēs* as the other or the paradoxical integration (or disintegration) structure with regard to

76 CH *De morbo sacro* 1 (Littré VI 354.15 ff.; Translation: Jones)
77 CH *De morbo sacro* 3.1 (Littré VI; Translation: Jones).
78 CH *De morbo sacro* 5.1.

the "lepers." These premises have one thing in common: They point to codifications of political, ritualistic, and social provenance, which have a historical basis.

First of all it is striking, that in Luke 17:11–19 Luke introduces premises that are equivocal and ambiguous: The geographic classification of the narrative remains strangely vague. Both the geographic statement of Jesus' route "between Samaria and Galilee" and the description of the location of his meeting with the "lepers" are unclear. Whether Jesus encounters the ten "lepers" at the edge of the village or as he is entering it – that is, in the village – is left open by the text. Ἐισερχόμενος *eiserchomenos* could imply that Jesus met the ten "lepers" "as he already entered into a certain village." This means that the ten men would be in the village, staying farther away. Or εἰσερχόμενος *eiserchomenos* means that Jesus met the ten leprous men "as he is going to enter into the village" which probably means that Jesus was at the edge of the village and met the ten "lepers" outside the village boundary. The question of who is inside or outside seems ambiguous.

Unclear is also the geographic statement of Jesus' route "between Samaria and Galilee." In the Gospel of Luke his journey brings him through Samaria and not – as in Mark – through Judea and Peraea.[79] This route taken by Jesus in Luke 9:51ff is mentioned several times in contemporary literature and the Old Testament.[80] The road which led through Samaria connected the region Galilee with Judea by the shortest route. If we can trust Josephus's records, then Jesus takes a route which has been taken by pilgrims and travelers.[81] The pilgrims could have

---

79 With the Infinitive ἐν τῷ πορεύσθαι *en tō poreusthai* "in making his way" (see also 9:51) and the following διήρχετο *diērcheto* verse 11 has more the character of a report; it is καὶ ἐγένετο *kai egeneto* that suggests the beginning of a new narrative; see also François Bovon, *Das Evangelium nach Lukas: 3. Teilband Lk 15,1–19,27* (EKK III/3; *Neukirchen:* Neukirchener Verlag, 2001), 145.

80 Jos. *Ant.* 20.118; *Bell.* 2.232; *Vit.* 241.145.268–70. 317ff; Judg 21:19; 1 Kgs 12; 2 Kgs 10; Jer 41:4–6; see also Beitzel, "Roads and Highways-Peroman," *ABD* 5: 780.

81 The parallels and changes between Jos. *Antiquitates* and *De Bellum Judaicum* are noteworthy with regard to the conflict between Jews and Samaritans. Whether one can suppose that Josephus had at hand more information later on when he wrote the *Antiquitates*, is uncertain. Hjelm, *The Samaritans and Early Judaism*, 223 doubt this. See especially the following changes:

Bell. 2.232: "Next came an engagement συμβολή between the Galilaeans and the Samaritans. For at a village called Gema, which lies in the Great Plain of Samaria, while many Judeans were going up for the festival a certain Galilean was taken and killed." Translations with changes: Steve Mason.

Ant. 20.118: "Samaritans had hatred ὄχθρα against the Jews πρὸς Ιουδαίους."

Bell. 2.233: "Cumanus, however, put the pleas of these men in second place to the affairs at hand and sent the pleaders, unsuccessful."

Ant. 20.119: Cumanus "having been bribed by the Samaritans, neglected to avenge them."

Bell. 2.236: Now Cumanus took from Caesarea one wing of calvary, which was called 'Sebastene,' and marched out to provide assistance to those who were being ravaged; of Eleazar's group

been completed this journey in three days.[82] Recent studies[83] have shown that the text probably refers to a special region, the Jezreel Valley. According to F.M. Abel and G. Dalmann, the Jezreel Valley represents an independent area that extended the municipal area of Scythopolis westward all the way to the plain of Ptolemais. In Abel's opinion, the Jezreel Valley can be considered an independent region that divides Galilee from Samaria. When Jesus leaves to return to Jerusalem via a region between Samaria and Galilee, this certainly is not merely geographic information, but a signification of the differences between Jerusalem as the heir of Davidic traditions, Samaria as the heir of the Mosaic tradition, and finally Galilee, from where these traditions are given a new orientation.

he arrested many, but killed most." Cumanus burned down the villages, took with him from Caesarea a troop of cavalry known as Sebastenians and set off to the assistance of the victims of these ravages.

Ant. 20.122: Cumanus, after the Jews had taken action and had burned and plundered many villages of the Samaritans, went out with soldiers from Sebaste and marched out against the Jews.

Bell. 2.245–46: "Now in Rome, when Caesar had given a hearing to Cumanus and the Samarians – Agrippa was also there, contending vehemently for the Judeans seeing that many of the powerful were standing in support of Cumanus – he passed judgment against the Samarians and ordered that the three most powerful be done away with, whereas he exiled Cumanus."

Ant. 20.135: Cumanus and the Samaritans were met and that they would have won the case if not the Emperor's wife Agrippina had persuaded Caesar Claudius to make a hearing and 'punish the instigators of the revolt'. This hearing convinced Claudius 'that the Samaritans were the first to move in stirring up trouble'. They were accordingly put to death, and the officials Cumanus and Celer disgraced.

It is doubtful whether Jews and Samaritans are otherwise mostly neutrally- or even friendly-disposed, because the evaluating tone is clearly missing in *De Bellum Judaicum.* It is significant that in *De Bellum Judaicum* the Galileans are shown comparably with the Samaritans; they are both under Roman threat. Josephus refers to the "rashness of the Samaritans," noting that "the success of the Romans made them ridiculously conceited of their own feebleness, and they were eagerly contemplating the prospect of the revolt." Josephus is also using Samareitai instead of Samareis, when he describes in *De Bellum Judaicum*, that "Such was the catastrophe which overlook the Samaritans." See also *Ant.* 17.69; 18.30; 290.118, where the Samareitai are described in a rather polemical tone (see Egger, *Josephus Flavius*, 247–50). See therefore Safrai, *Wallfahrt*, 137–40.

82 Mason, *Josephus: Jewish War*, 189.

83 Martina Böhm, *Samarien und die Samaritai bei Lukas: Eine Studie zum religionshistorischen Hintergrund der lukanischen Samarientexte und zu deren topographischen Verhaftung* (WUNT II/111; Tübingen: Mohr Siebeck, 1999), 273f. says: "In der Lage des unbekannten Dorfes in der 'großen Ebene' wird wohl auch der Schlüssel für die Ortsbestimmung bei Lukas liegen. Diese Ebene bildet einen weiten Zwischenraum zwischen Galiläa und Samaria, der auch durch Bergland auf beiden Seiten umgrenzt ist. Wenn Jesus in der Richtung nach Jerusalem auf ihr wanderte, konnte das ein 'Durchziehen mitten zwischen Samarien und Galiläa' heißen."

The Jezreel Valley is exposed to the dreaded east wind as well as to the south wind, both of which – according to ancient evidence – are responsible, above all, for skin illnesses of widely varying provenance. As previously documented, the medical understanding of that time saw a correlation between the east wind and a higher incidence of λέπρα *lepra* infections: the climatic condition of the hot east wind is reflected in the human body and causes "λέπρα *lepra*," brought on by the drying out of the skin. Taking this into consideration, we should perhaps not interpret the Lucan author's choice of a geographical location in connection with λέπρα *lepra* as coincidental. Thus, the statement of location "between Samaria and Galilee" could indicate a signification of all the differences between Samaria, Jerusalem, and Galilee; it indicates unfavorable climatic conditions with regard to the illness λέπρα *lepra*, but also has a political message:[84]

If one adopts the reference to the Jezreel Valley as the geographical context for the story in Luke 17, then two passages in Josephus *Bell.* 2.466; 477–80 and *Ant.* 14.205–7 are of interest. These texts state that both Jews and Samaritans lived in this valley. Josephus reports on this coexistence within the context of the murdering of Jews by Jews. Josephus, at least, reports extensively about this region, without scrimping on examples of bloody incidents. And it is surely worth noting that he describes this conflict as a plague.[85] Thus it makes sense to analyze both

84 See B. Becking, *The Fall of Samaria: An Historical and Archaeological Study* (Leiden: E.J. Brill, 1992); I. Hjelm, *Jerusalem's Rise to Sovereignty in Ancient Tradition and History: Zion and Gerizim in Competition* (London: T&T Clark International, 2004).

85 Compare, for example, Josephus *Bell.* 2,466: "Thus far the Jews had been faced with aliens only, but when they invaded Scythopolis they found their own nation in arms against them." Questions of ethnicity and relation to Israelite's tribes are important for Josephus. See L. Feldman, "Josephus' attitude toward the Samaritans: A Study of Ambivalence," in *Studies in hellenistic Judaism* (ed. idem; AGJU 40; Leiden: E.J. Brill, 1996), 114–36 and Hjelm, *Samaritans and Early Judaism*, 104–15; in the biblical and the Samaritan tradition, Abraham was the first who raised the Altar in Shechem and in the Samaritan tradition we find Joshua building a cult place on the summit of Mt Gerizim; cf. T.L. Thornton, "Anti-Samaritan Exegesis Reflected in Josephus' Retelling of Deuteronomy, Joshua and Judges," *JTS* 47 (1996): 125–30; the centrality of the temple in Jerusalem became the main issue and this is especially true for the time after its destruction by the Romans 70 C.E. See Hjelm, *Samaritans and Early Judaism*, 226–38; and eadem, "Cult Centralization as a Device of Cult Control," *SJOT* 13/2 (1999): 298–309; eadem, "Mt. Gerazim and Samaritans in Recent Research," in *Samaritans: Past and Present* (Berlin: De Gruyter, 2010); see also Alan David Crown, "The Samaritans as an Exemplar of Jewish-Christian Relations," in *Proceedings of the fifth International congress of the Societe d'études Samaritanes* (ed. Shehadeh and Tawa; Paris: S.N. Librairie Orientaliste Paul Geuthner, 2006), 183–94. For a positive appreciation of Josephus' being objective see R. Egger, *Josephus Flavius und die Samaritaner: Eine terminologische Untersuchung zur Identitätserklärung der Samaritaner* (NTOA 4; Fribourg: Vandenhoeck & Ruprecht, 1986).

aspects – illness and conflict – at the same time. More than almost any other behavior, violence – with its sense of inevitability and its destructive potential – has been closely associated with the imagery of an infectious illness. Infection creates victims, and violence sets off a chain reaction. Violence and illness can both be identified with impurity in societies, so both are to be counteracted with ritual efforts. Thus violence within the social body becomes the agent of an infectious logic, and it develops a virus-like power that can only be conquered through immunization strategies and by isolating those who are ill. Sybille Krämer assumes that the epidemic spread of illness and violence can be disrupted by the rite of sacrifice.[86] In this sense, the sacrificial victim suspends the transmission of illness and violence. The coexistence of Samaritans and Jews seems to have been normal for this region. This geographical region was well-known for its pluralistic religious attitude. The fact that the author mentions more than one priest here, making no explicit distinction between Jewish and Samaritan priests, confirms this view.[87]

---

86 Sybille Krämer, *Medium, Bote, Übertragung: Kleine Metaphysik der Medialität* (Frankfurt a. M.: Suhrkamp, 2008).

87 At this point I would like to note again the concept of the border which we came across concerning skin, town and living together of Samaritans and Jews in the region of the Jezreel Valley: One of the most central definitions of a "border" is found in the Greek philosopher Anaximander, "[Grund der seienden Dinge ist das Grenzenlose. Woraus aber das Entstehen ist den seienden Dingen, in das hinein geschieht auch ihr Vergehen] nach der Notwendigkeit; denn sie geben einander Recht und Buße für die Ungerechtigkeit nach der Ordnung der Zeit." [H. Diels/ W. Kranz, *Die Fragmente der Vorsokratiker* vol. 1 (Zürich and Berlin: Weidmann, 1964), 89.] In antiquity this definition was of central importance: Theophrastus, a student of Aristotle, has quoted this citation; and also the Platonic Simplicius has taken over this view in his commentary on Aristotle. Though Anaximander speaks of the border, the foundation of the "things that are" needs to be free of regulation of a border, which is why he speaks of ἀπειρόν *apeiron*, the boundless. On the one hand *apeiron* can mean being without borders; on the other hand even boundlessness is a regulation and thus a qualitative limitation. This means: While Anaximander speaks of the boundless, he is confronted with the limitations. Therefore, border is an idea which cannot be articulated very easily in the ancient world. It is noteworthy that there seems to be no uniform idea for the border in antiquity: different concepts can refer to different borders as for example πέρας, ὀρός, φράγμα oder μεθόριον. From the beginning the terms reflect the dichotomy: being bound and boundless. In the Hellenism this tendency intensifies as the divine perfection could now be defined as unlimited and be connected with the idea of infinity. Merio Scattola, mentions in her paper "Die Grenze der Neuzeit: Ihr Begriff in der juristischen und politischen Literatur der Antike und Frühmoderne," [in *Die Grenze: Begriff und Inszenierung* (ed. Markus Bauer and Thomas Rahn; Berlin: Akademie Verlag, 1997), 37–72] that the term *fines* is a private-law term that does not include the border of two states. *Fines* connotes more a part of a region that is bordered. The term *regio* is a political term. It refers to the contentious jurisdiction of the Emperor. *Pomerium* refers to the border of a religious region.

This result brings us to our second central point: It is significant for the religious-political context of the story, which among other things sets the standard for the judgment of ἀλλογενής – *allogenēs*. The word ἀλλογενής – *allogenēs* is a *hapax legomenon* in the New Testament, and is normally translated as "originating from another people, foreign to the land"[88] or "foreign-born, foreign."[89] This connotation suggests a clear basis for an interpretation that is founded on a national ethnic interpretation. In contrast to the single use of ἀλλογενής – *allogenēs* in the New Testament, we encounter this term more frequently in the Septuagint. In these instances, ἀλλογενής – *allogenēs* indicates Israelites "except for Aaron and his sons" – that is, those who are not called; people who do not belong to the clan[90] – or it has the meaning "non-Levite"[91] and indicates lay people, non-clergy, or even proselytes. Here, ἀλλογενής – *allogenēs* stands for those outside the holy group, "for whom a certain area is forbidden territory or for whom the precisely performed acts are forbidden."[92] We can summarize the findings as follows: ἀλλογενής – *allogenēs* is a multi-faceted term in the Septuagint, and it changes according to the situation in which it is used. Its specific meaning is determined by the immediate context.

The single Samaritan is being introduced in the text as a believing Samaritan who follows the Torah and not as a "Gentile" Samaritan.[93] Here, the focus is not on the experience of difference in the sense of someone standing outside his own (ritual) community with the connotation of a stranger. Had the ritualistic separation and a different understanding of the healing of *lepra* been relevant here, the author would have provided a more detailed commentary on Lev 13f. or on Samaria and the Samaritans. The lack of such commentary then means that the author interpreted impurity and cleansing as a common experience. In this context, the

---

88 Bauer, *Art.* ἀλλογενής, 152.

89 Büchsel, *Art.* ἀλλογενής, 266f.; Bovon, *Lukas 3*, 145: "Ausländer"; Hans Klein, *Das Lukasevangelium* (KEK; 10th ed.; Göttingen: Vandenhoeck & Ruprecht, 2006), "Fremder";

90 Cf. Gesenius, *Handwörterbuch*, 205.

91 Num 1:51.

92 Cf. Snijders, *Art.* זור/זר, 561; ἀλλογενής appears one other time in Sir 45:13, with the meaning "non-Aaronite."

93 For a general introduction to the Samaritan literature see J.A. Montgomery, *The Samaritans: The earliest Jewish Sect: Their History, Theology and Literature* (Philadelphia: John Winston, 1907 = reprint New York: Ktav, 1968); J. Zangenberg, *Samareia: Antike Quellen zur Geschichte und Kultur der Samaritaner in deutscher Übersetzung (TANZ 15; Tübingen: Francke, 1994) 180–229;* Alan David Crown, *Samaritan Scribes and Manuscripts* (Texts and Studies in Ancient Judaism 80; Tübingen: Mohr Siebeck, 2001), 1–39; B. Tsedaka, *The History of the Samaritans Due to Their Own sources: From Joshua to the Year 2000 AD* (Holon: Institute of Samaritan Studies Press, 2004).

Samaritan is not acknowledged as an outsider or identified as such. This may also be explained by the geographic context in which the coexistence of Jews and Samaritans was taken for granted and which the author described from a perspective based on local conceptions of the milieu. It is only his "different" behavior that marks the one man as "other." In my opinion, a translation of ἀλλογενής – *allogenēs* as "*the one who is different*"[94] is reasonable. If, however, ritual was not the separating factor in the world of Luke 17:11–19, what factor characterizes the being different?

Within the Gospel of Luke, the author uses various passages to acquaint us with the narrative in Luke 17:11–19 and anticipate its account. We can therefore assume that this story was of such great importance to the Lukan author that he wanted to continuously build up to its account. All of the stories that have the healing of "leprosy" as their theme share a narrative core – the cleansing of leprosy by Jesus – which is then given different emphases in the individual stories (Luke 4:27; 5:12–16, and 7:22). This includes the healing of a stranger in Luke 4:27, which is linked to 2 Kgs 5 through the connection with Naaman and which, like the Old Testament pretext, focuses on the ethnic difference between Jews and non-Jews. In Luke 5:12–16, the author introduces the semantic opposition between divine reality and human reality into the text, leading to a subtle recodification of the image of healings of lepra: Familiar vocabulary from the context of purity and impurity is placed in a new context. Then, in Luke 7:22, the author sets up a special form of the semantics of seeing.[95] If these three texts are taken as a template, the story of the healing of lepers would only be required to report the request for cleansing or healing. This is exactly what occurs in Luke 17:11–13. The narrative core of the healing story ends here. The redundancy of this narrative core and its increasing degree of detail make the readers prepared for this ending. Following the account of the healing, the reader would expect a confirmation of the cleansing or healing and the end of the story.

In the discourse of the Lucan gospel on the subject of "lepra," the one leper's seeing could indicate healing, since the man takes over the function of a priest, who could confirm purity through observation. In Lev 13f., seeing cleansed skin is the task of the priests. The previously "leprous" person is only considered pure after making an offering. In Luke 17:15, the "leper" confirms his healing himself, as it were, and completes his "cleansing" not by making an offering (it was

94 In English, the translation, "the other" or "the outsider" requires a classification of its opposite, which is not present in Luke 17:11–19, as we will see below.

95 Ἰδών *idōn* means "gesehen habend – having seen; as he saw." For seeing cf. Luke 10:33 the good Samaritan and Luke 15:20, the father of the lost son.

because he saw, not because he had been confirmed to be clean)[96], but by praising God. This is described with the term ἰάομαι – *iaomai*. This reversion to the vocabulary typical for healing in the Gospel of Luke leads some exegetes to postulate a qualitative difference from καθαρίζειν *katharizein*. However, Lev 14:3 and Num 12:13 both also speak of a healing and not a cleansing, which refutes this idea.[97] This point of view solidifies when one takes into consideration the medical texts that speak of the cleansing (καθαρίζειν *katharizein*) of sores in connection with the healing of *lepra*.

The leper's seeing does not refer to a process of seeing that is available to everyone. This is made clear in the passage immediately following the story about the "coming of the kingdom of God." Here, the not-seeing and the inability to observe the kingdom of God are placed in contradiction to the leper's seeing, and the denial of the signs is contrasted with the ability to see the healing. Verses 15–19 introduce the consequence of the act of seeing, namely, a new form of worship, with the healed man falling down on his face, giving praise to god and giving thanks.[98] It is remarkable that only here in the NT is thanks given to Jesus. Here the author takes up a motif from Luke 22:16 and 19, where it says, that Jesus is sharing the cup and bread in the Last Supper in giving thanks. Is it possible that the second part of this story is referring to a special form of worship, which neither happens on the Mount Gerazim nor in the Temple of Jerusalem, but in a geographic region where Jews and Samaritans lived together?

Prevalent among New Testament scholars today is the notion that New Testament passages often enhance their self-perception by contrasting themselves with the so-called other, the circumcised, the sick, Jews, Gauls, and Samaritans, fre-

---

96 See also Alfred Plummer, *Gospel According to St. Luke* (ICC; fifth ed.; Edinburgh: T&T Clark, 1981), 404; D, 892 and 1424 and some ancient versions read "was cleansed" instead of "was healed."

97 This analysis also has consequences for the division of the text: We could no longer distinguish two independent parts, verses 11–14 and 15–19, which could then be interpreted as cleansing and gratitude. Even if verses 11–14 do correspond to the narrative core of a healing of lepra, this core is broken by the semantics of seeing. Thus, there are no longer two themes that characterize the narrative, but rather, one central theme: the seeing of divine reality.

98 See a different interpretation by Ingrid Hjelm, *The Samaritans and Early Judaism: A Literary Analysis* (JSTOT 303; Sheffield: Sheffield Academic Press, 2000), 117f who writes: "The good Samaritan's act, set in contrast to the priest and the Levite, who might have loved God but had forgotten to be a neighbor, is not more reflective of pro-Samaritanism than the Samaritan leper's return 'to praise God' (Luke 17.15–16). The primary function of these stories is to illustrate the stubbornness of the Jews, and, using the most fitting comparable group, the form the strongest accusation."

quently through hostile stereotypes. For Luke 17:11–19 this is even more enforced in the scholarship: in analyzing the similarities between Leviticus 13f. and ancient medical texts regarding their understanding of the semiotics of the illness *lepra* as well as its social consequences one could see that it is not only the Jewish society which felt attacked through skin diseases but that this idea is known in antiquity. Although societies could felt threatened through skin diseases, skin is in ancient times is not defined as the final border of a body and therefore cannot represent the border of a society. In using the illness *lepra* and not negotiating the ritualistic aspect connected with this illness, the Gospel of Luke expressed admiration for the Samaritans. The illness *lepra* is not seen here as a boundary marker that focuses on the otherness as exclusion but rather as a sign that represents fluctuating borders, like the place where Jesus encounters the ten lepers, the geographical region between Samaria and Galilee, or the understanding of *allogēnes*. The main focus of the story is the different way of seeing which initiated healing and honoring God.

Teun Tieleman

Miracle and Natural Cause in Galen

I Preamble

On many occasions throughout his voluminous writings Galen of Pergamum (A.D. 129–c.213) tells us about therapies he performed upon a wide variety of patients.[1] In his autobiographical showpiece *On Prognosis* we find a greater concentration of such reports, all of which are neat specimens of vivid storytelling. Galen uses them to illustrate a particular point about clinical medicine or to demonstrate his skills as a practitioner or to do both at once. All of them reveal his strong commitment to the notion of medicine as an art or expertise (τέχνη) involving the correct employment of both reason (λόγος) and experience (ἐμπειρία). He firmly rejected suggestions – made by the admiring public as well as professional rivals – that he succeeded through magic, incantations or other non-medical means. If people were amazed, this was only due to their ignorance of the art.[2] In adopting this attitude Galen positioned himself in the tradition of Greek "rational" medicine, which starts with the theories and practices recorded in the oldest treatises of the Hippocratic corpus. But as some of these treatises already indicate, it is wrong to think in terms of a clear-cut division between secular and religious medicine. Galen too combined his science with a religious outlook, attributing a special role to the healing god Asclepius, whose main cultic centre was in Galen's native town Pergamum. Asclepius not only intervened directly at crucial moments in Galen's life and career but more specifically in his decisions as a practicing physician.

In what follows I will consider his work with a view to answering a few related questions: exactly which role do religious beliefs play in it? How does Galen justify them in the context of his philosophy and science? Can we can speak of "miraculous" cures, with respect to Galen and, if so, in which sense? My argument is

---

1 On the reports from the perspective of Galen's patients and their social background see H.F.J. Horstmanshoff, "Galen and His Patients," in *Ancient Medicine in its Socio-Cultural Context* vol. 1 (ed. Ph. J. Van der Eijk, H.F.J. Horstmanshoff and P.H. Schrijvers; Amsterdam – Atlanta, GA, 1995), 83–100.

2 This is the point of the story about Galen's correct prediction of the course taken by Eudemus' illness recounted at *Progn.* 3, pp. 82–86 Nutton: see *infra*, pp. 111–112. Cf. also *Temp.* III, I p. 658 K. (what seems a wonder or marvel (θαῦμα) is not astonishing once one knows the cause) and *infra*, n.10

structured as follows. I will first take a closer look at what may be called the cosmological context of Galen's practice of medicine, viz. his view of the natural world and the place occupied in it by the divine, including the contrast drawn by Galen between his position and Jewish and Christian beliefs (II). As we shall see, the notion of divine creation is also relevant to that of therapy (III). Next I will study a few relevant passages where Asclepius intervenes in Galen's life and clinical practice (IV) before presenting a few conclusions (V).

II The Cosmological Context

Galen studied philosophy before he turned to the study of medicine; from then onwards he combined the two fields. In his *The Best Doctor is also a Philosopher* he explains how they cohere in terms of the three main parts of philosophy, viz. natural philosophy, logic and ethics, all three of which the accomplished doctor should have mastered. In his far more ambitious *On the Doctrines of Hippocrates and Plato* (in 9 books) he projects into the past a tradition of good philosophy-cum-medicine with Hippocrates and Plato as its fountain-heads – an exegetical tour de force designed to demonstrate that the two authorities of its title were not only right but also in basic agreement about the most important matters. In his admiration for Plato Galen reflects the growing appeal of Platonism in the second century, a development that appears to have started in his native Asia Minor in particular. But he did not adhere to Platonism or any other philosophical school, preferring to adopt an independent position which could accommodate viewpoints of different philosophical provenance. At the same time there are issues upon which Galen refrains from pronouncing because he takes them to be insoluble for lack of empirical evidence. Taking a stand on any of them is the hallmark of dogmatist speculation. It is precisely issues of the speculative kind on which the schools have formulated their distinctive doctrines and which keep them divided. As Galen likes to point out, these same issues are also useless for moral or scientific progress. The adherents of the warring schools, however, would sooner betray their country than abandon the dogmas of their own school. Theirs is a sectarian attitude, marked by reliance on authority instead of scientific demonstration and the open-minded study of nature.[3] So Galen declares himself to be an ad-

3 On Galen's attitude to authority it is still worth reading R. Walzer, *Galen on Jews and Christians* (Oxford: Clarendon Press, 1949). For Galen the reference to authority counts as a rhetorical form of arguing see T. Tieleman, *Galen and Chrysippus on the Soul: Argument and Refutation in the* De Placitis *Books II–III* (Leiden: Brill, 1996), 12–22.

herent of what he calls the "school of nature." This attitude sets him apart from most philosophers of his day. As Michael Frede has plausibly argued, it was his bid to overcome the division between the *medical* sects, and in particular the Rationalists and the Empiricists, that inspired his position on philosophical issues in the first place. It led him to work out a methodology in which reason and experience work in concert and in such as way as to leave no room for dogmatist speculation with its characteristic reliance upon authority.[4]

Galen continued explaining his views, or his reluctance to adopt any views on certain issues, until the end of his life. One of his last treatises, *On My Own Opinions*, whose full Greek text has only recently been discovered, is specifically devoted to stating with which views he wants his name to be associated and with which he does not. In the second chapter he summarizes his theological views in a way that is directly relevant to our purposes:

> (1) I declare that I do not know whether the universe is created and whether there is anything outside it or nothing. And since I say that I have no knowledge about things of this kind, it is also obvious that I have no knowledge of what the Maker (δημιουργόν) of everything in the universe is like, whether he is corporeal or incorporeal, and of the place where he resides. So I also declare that I am in doubt about the gods, as Protagoras said,[5] and that I do not know what their substance is like. But I do know that they exist from their acts since the anatomy of all living beings is their work, as is everything they foretell through significant utterances[6] or signs or dreams. The god who is revered in my hometown Pergamum [scil. Asclepius] revealed his power and providence in many ways but in particular by once curing me of a disease. At sea I experienced not only the power but also the providence of Dioscuri. But I believe that it is by no means harmful for humans if they are ignorant of the substance of the gods. I have decided to honour them in accordance with old custom and with Socrates' advice to follow the orders of Apollo.[7] So much for my attitude in religious matters (*On My Own Opinions* ch. 2 Boudon-Pietrobelli).

The first sentence refers to physical issues on which the schools were divided, viz. the question whether the cosmos is eternal or has a beginning and the issue of the extra-cosmic void.[8] These are issues of the insoluble, interminable kind. As Galen

---

4 M. Frede, "On Galen's Epistemology," in *Galen: Problems and Prospects* (ed. V. Nutton; London: ICS, 1981), 279–98.

5 Protagoras Fr. B 4 Diels-Kranz. Note that the reference is imprecise: Protagoras states that he does not know whether the gods exist or not.

6 I.e. things accidentally said by people.

7 Cf. Xenophon, *Mem.* 4. 3. 16; 1.3.1.

8 Plato (or at least the Platonist school) and Aristotle held that there was nothing outside the cosmos; Epicurureanism and Stoicism that outside the cosmos there was an infinite void (with one source attributing to the Stoic Posidonius the postulate of a finite cosmic void): see Aet. II, 9. On the eternity of the cosmos (on which the Platonists were divided among themselves, see in text).

tells us in the second sentence, the nature of God also belongs to them. The reference to the divine "Artisan" or "Maker" (or "Demiurge", δημιουργός) here unmistakably recalls the Platonic *Timaeus*. Platonists and others were divided over the question whether the account of creation expounded there was to be taken literally or as a didactic device for expounding the structure and eternal processes of the cosmos. (The very idea of God deciding at some point to create the world was problematic, although Plato does include an explanation, viz. that the good God wanted others to share in his goodness, being, quite unlike the gods of traditional mythology, devoid of envy: *Tim.* 29e.) For our present purposes it is worth noting that Galen can speak of a divine creator regardless of the issue whether the cosmos has a beginning or not. Seen in this light, creation, then, can also refer to God's steering and sustaining the cosmos, to his acting as its moving cause.

There are two things Galen believes he can affirm about the gods: (1) that they exist; (2) that they care for the world including us humans. Their existence can directly be inferred from what they effect, viz. the wonderful design displayed by living beings and the interventions in human lives of the types mentioned. Clearly these things satisfy the requirement of empirical verifiability so that Galen feels able to take a stand on them. The providence of the gods is accepted on the same basis. Galen recalls his personal experience of the life-saving assistance he once received from Asclepius and, on one perilous occasion at sea, from the Dioscuri: two points that are fairly traditional and common. In a typical turn he implies that it is useful to know that the gods exist and are provident in contrast with knowing what their substance would be like. What we can know is also what we need to know, another sign of divine providence. Galen draws the conclusion – an intellectually respectable one anticipated by Socrates – that he conforms to ancestral custom (in his case, it appears, the cult of Asclepius in particular) and will revere God in the best way available to him. What this will be like in Galen's case is hinted at a little earlier on, by the reference to the anatomy of living beings. In a famous passage from *On the Use of Parts*, he presents the practice of dissection, whose results are expounded in this treatise, as constituting "true piety," since it reveals God's wondrous works. As such, it is superior to offering rich sacrifices in the traditional manner.[9] Penetrating the recesses of nature will present the anatomist and his audience with many occasions for wonderment and awe. But this results precisely from gaining insight into nature's rationality, not from accepting things as mysteries.[10] The rationality of Creation and its Maker is expressed first of

9 *UP* III, p. 237 Kühn.

10 Thus Galen uses the term *thauma* (θαῦμα, "wonder," "marvel") not for things that defy causal explanation but that inspire awe and admiration for Nature's (or the Demiurge's) clever arrange-

all in its purposefulness. We may note that Galen employs a version of what in our time has come to be called the "argument from design."

Another point in this passage deserves our attention. Galen passes without comment – in fact, one might say, rather abruptly – from the notion of a divine Creator to references to a plurality of gods, among whom one is especially dear to him, Asclepius. It would be rash to conclude that he is incoherent on this point, or that something might be wrong with the text. In fact, what we have here is a rather typical instance of the compatibility of the idea of an all-encompassing deity with his many manifestations, which lend themselves to interpretation in terms of the traditional polytheistic pantheon, witness here Galen's reference to Asclepius, the Dioscuri, Apollo and traditional religion. In fact, Plato too had encouraged such a reconciliation. In the *Timaeus*, the Demiurge, having created the world, entrusts the "lesser gods" of the Homeric pantheon with the task of fashioning living beings to populate it (*Tim.* 40d–41d). Here, then, the lesser gods act as instruments or agents of the supreme god.

Asclepius had special significance for Galen, not only because he was his ancestral god, the one connected to his family and native city, but presumably also because of the importance assumed by Asclepius' cult in Galen's day, which even led to his occasionally becoming identified with Zeus.[11] Considered in this light, Asclepius comes to stand for the supreme deity in his healing and life-dispensing capacity.[12]

God's providence manifests itself in His creation of the world as an on the whole beautiful and purposeful construct. This worldview is very much indebted to the Platonic *Timaeus*. It had been endorsed and enriched by Aristotle and the Stoics, who too explained the world as an artifact and God, or Nature, as artistic, or artisan-like. Galen, then, has the backing of a broad and respectable coalition. All the more forcefully he rejects the view that the world is the result of material and fortuitous factors only, held by the Epicureans or other atomists such as the medical scientist Asclepiades of Bithynia (*flor.* first half of the first century B.C.). To the wonderful design tradition Galen brings his expertise as an anatomist. Here he admires and continues the approach taken by Aristotle in his *On the Parts*

---

ments. This response, then, typically follows from acquiring knowledge, in particular about the facts revealed through dissection: a nice example is *UP* IV, p. 248 Kühn; cf. also *De ut. diss.* II, p. 898 Kühn, *UP* III, pp. 41, 154, 696, 698–99, 875, IV p. 198, 301, 361 Kühn.

11 On Galen's devotion to Asclepius see H. Schlange-Schöningen, *Die römische Gesellschaft bei Galen. Biographie und Sozialgeschichte* (Berlin/New York: De Gruyter, 2003), 223–35, esp. 223–24; V. Nutton, *Ancient Medicine* (London: Routledge, 2004), 279–80. V. Boudon, "Galien et le sacre," *Bull Ass. G. Budé* 1988, (*Lettres d'Humanité* XLVII): 327–337).

12 For the evidence and further discussion see Schlange-Schöningen, *Römische Gesellschaft bei Galen*, 74–75

of Animals,[13] in particular in the vast work we have just mentioned – the *On the Use of Parts*. The following passage deals with what we call miracles in the sense of interventions by which God suspends the laws of nature. Although it is rather long, it is worth quoting in full. Having referred to the wonderful design displayed by the eyelashes, which do not grow as opposed to the hair on other parts, Galen continues:

> (2) Has then our Demiurge commanded only these hairs [scil. of the eyelashes] to preserve always the same length and do they preserve it as they have been ordered because they fear their master's command, or reverence the God who gave this order, or themselves believe it better to do this? Is not this Moses' way of treating Nature and is it not superior to that of Epicurus? The best way, of course, is to follow neither of these but to maintain like Moses the principle of the Demiurge as the principle (or cause, ἀρχήν) of generation of all created things, while adding the material principle to it. For our Demiurge created it to preserve a constant length because this was better. When he had decided that he should make it of such a kind [i.e. of constant length and number], he set under part of it a hard body as a kind of cartilage,[14] and under another part a hard skin attached to the cartilage through the eyebrows. It was, then, certainly not sufficient merely to will their becoming thus; for had he wished to make a man out of a stone in an instant, it would not have been possible for him either. It is precisely this point in which our own opinion and that of Plato and the other Greeks who follow the right method in science differ from the position taken by Moses. For the latter it seems enough to say that God simply willed the arrangement of matter and instantaneously it was arranged; for he believes everything to be possible with God, even should he wish to make a bull or a horse out of ashes. We however do not hold this; we say that certain things are impossible by nature and that God does not attempt such things at all but that he chooses the best out of the possibilities of becoming (*On the Usefulness of Parts* XI, ch. 14 = Vol. II, pp. 158–60 Helmreich; translation Walzer's, modified).

It is impossible, within the limited compass of this paper, to do full justice to this rich passage. Among other things, it makes clear in a very intriguing manner the contrast between Galen's Greek philosophical outlook on the one hand and Jewish-Christian beliefs concerning God's creative power on the other.[15] The Mosaic account of creation as narrated in the first chapter of *Genesis* is superior to Epi-

---

13 See P. Moraux, "Galen and Aristotle's *De partibus animalium*," in *Aristotle on Nature and Living Things: Philosophical and Historical Studies Presented to David Balme on his Seventieth Birthday* (ed. A. Gotthelf; Pittsburgh: Mathesis, 1985), 327–43.

14 I.e. the tarsus.

15 See T. Tieleman, "Galen and Genesis," in *The Creation of Heaven and Earth: Re-interpretations of Genesis I in the Context of Judaism, Ancient Philosophy, Christianity, and Modern Physics* (ed. George H. van Kooten; Themes in Biblical Narrative 8; Leiden/Boston: Brill, 2005), 125–45; cf. Also Schlange-Schöningen, *Römische Gesellschaft bei Galen*, 235–51, Gero, S., "Galen on Christians: A Reappraisal of the Arabic Evidence," *Orientalia christiana periodica* 56 (1990): 371–411.

cureanism because it adds the efficient cause (viz. God) to the material one. Moses, however, treats the kind of material used by God as irrelevant; for him, "everything is possible with God," who therefore can create everything out of anything. This is something Galen cannot accept. In line with Plato's teaching in the *Timaeus*, God does select the best of the possibilities, from which his providence and wisdom emerge.[16] But he is constrained by what is impossible by nature. The material out of which God has to create the world, sets limits to, and thus reveals the nature of, His power. This fact is revealed by all instances of imperfection in a world of prevalent beauty and design. The other side of this model is that given that God has selected the best of possibilities he cannot and will not diverge from them, which explains the regularity of natural processes, viz. the cosmos as orderly arrangement.

What we may call a therapeutic application of this principle is found in the following passage:

> (3) Some constitutions are right from birth so weak that they cannot reach the age of sixty even if Asclepius himself were to attend them (*On the Preservation of Health* 1, 12, 15 = *CMG* V, 4, 2, p. 29; K. VI, 63).

Here the divine healer cannot overrule the limitations posed by his weak human material, so to speak. This is of course a matter not of creating a human being but rather of restoring a creature to health, i.e. its original or optimal condition, which normally would make a longer lifespan possible. Although Galen does not draw here a distinction between his and the Jewish-Christian position in these matters, one need only to think of the references to it in the passage from *On the Use of Parts* to realize the difference concerning "miraculous" healings too. But in fact, there is another passage from an Arabic source, where Galen does seem to refer to Christian miracle stories:

> (4) Most people are unable to follow any demonstrative argument consecutively; hence they need parables,[17] and benefit from them – and he [*scil.* Galen] understands by parables tales of rewards and punishments in a future life – just as now we see the people called Christians drawing their faith from parables [and miracles], and yet sometimes acting in the same way [as those who philosophize]. For their contempt of death [and of its sequel] is patent to us every day, and likewise their restraint in cohabitation. For they include men but

---

16 Thus the mythical Centaur represents an unviable assemblage of body parts and so cannot exist: *UP* III, 169–74. Cf. *PHP* III, 8, 33 (approvingly quoting what Plato's Socrates says about mythical creatures, *Phaedr.* 229d3–e4).

17 On Walzer's translation of Arabic *rumūz* as "parabels" cf. Gero, "Galen on Christians," 403–5, who prefers "signs," "indications," i.e. σημεῖα.

> also women who refrain from cohabiting all through their lives; and they number also individuals who, in self-discipline and self-control in matters of food and drink, and in their keen pursuit of justice, have attained a pitch not inferior to that of genuine philosophers (from the *Summary of Plato's Republic*, as quoted by Abu'l-Fida', *Universal Chronicle*, p. 108 Fleischer. Transl. Walzer 1949).

If the attribution to his *Summary of Plato's Republic* is correct,[18] Galen may have made his observations on Christian steadfastness in the face of death in the section dealing with the eschatological myth of Er, which concludes Plato's entire work. This too is a story about the afterlife, where rewards and punishments await the souls of the deceased. In this context Galen may have wanted to explain Plato's choice of ending the work with a myth or even have discussed his use of myths in general. At any rate, it is clear that his point is the strong impact made by such stories on certain people. This is exemplified by the contempt of death, and by virtues such as moderation, shown by Christians. But he in no way believes that their stories could be true. These are the kinds of stories they are expected to accept without proof, that is to say, on the authority of those who compose them, such as Moses in the case of *Genesis*. For people incapable of scientific reasoning this does not, however, diminish their morally improving effect.

III Therapy as (Re-)Creation

One might assume that the theme of intelligent design running through Galen's *On the Use of Parts* sits uncomfortably with what he must have constantly experienced in treating patients – nature failing. Seen in this light, anatomy and therapy seem to be two worlds far apart. But it would be wrong to suppose that Galen's attitude is somehow curiously divided. Even in the passage from *On the Use of Parts* we quoted (Text 2; and cf. Text 3) there is enough to be fairly confident along what lines Galen would have responded to the problem of evil, or imperfection. He never claimed the world to be perfect but only to be the best possible one. Indeed, the imperfections show God's power to be limited. It is either constrained by a factor specified by philosophical tradition (excepting again Epicureanism) as matter, or at any rate stops at some point exerting its influence (as Plotinus was to argue not long afterwards). Plato in the *Timaeus* presents the first alternative,

---

18 Gero, "Galen on Christians," 400–402, proposes the summary of the *Phaedo* instead on the grounds that this dialogies deals with the immortality of the soul whereas a summary of the *Republic*, which is a "blueprint for an ideal society," is a less likely source. The testimony, however, does fit the myth of Er rather well.

with a Demiurge who in his goodness works hard to subdue a pre-existing "errant cause" that contains irregular motions and resists his bid to bring form and order to it (*Tim.* 47e–63a). The *Timaeus* also contains a section on diseases, to which Galen devoted a separate commentary (and this was by no means the only time he wrote on this Platonic dialogue).[19] As our Text (1) suggests, Galen probably saw God's creative activity not only as the unique event by which the cosmos got started but as an ongoing process; in fact, as we have noticed, he allowed for the possibility that only the latter was the case. God, then, continues imposing order on things in the sensible world. His influence is manifested in its orderly functioning including, one may assume, the lives of animals and humans: their generation, birth and growth.[20] It is fair assumption that Galen, given his general outlook, could also regard the healing process in living beings, which is the restoration of normal functioning, as a manifestation of God's sustaining, providential role. In so far as a human doctor assists in the process, it becomes possible to see him as an instrument or extension of God's providential care. In fact, this notion is encouraged by Plato's insistence in the *Timaeus* that the orderly cosmic processes are there for us to emulate in our own lives. That Galen tended to see himself as a divine instrument and his therapy as an extension of God's healing influence is also suggested by a passage where he approvingly cites two statements made by the great Alexandrian medical scientist and practitioner Herophilus of Chalcedon (first half of the 3rd century B.C.): (1) Drugs alone are *per se* nothing if they do not have someone (i.e. a good doctor) to employ them correctly; (2) drugs are just like the hands of the gods, for "they [scil. drugs] effect great things if they have as their utiizer a person who is trained in the rationalist method and, along with this, is also intelligent by nature."[21] Both statements, then, Galen emphasizes, are true at once.

19 Galeni in Platonis Timaeum commentarii fragmenta collegit disposuit explicavit Henricus Otto Schroder. (Corpus Med. Gr., Suppl. 1.), xxviii + 112. Leipzig: Teubner, 1934.

20 Cf. also the reconstruction of Galen's theology in M. Frede, "Galen's Theology," in *Galien et la philosophie*, Entretiens sur l'antiquité classique XLIX (ed. J. Barnes & J. Jouanna; Vandoeuvres/Genève: Fondation Hardt, 2003), 73–129.

21 Galen, *De comp. med. sec. locos* XII, 966, l. 14 Kühn = Herophilus T 249 von Staden; transl. of ll. 14–16 von Staden's, modified. On what this passage tells us about Herophilus' conception of medicine see Von Staden, *Herophilus*, 400.

IV Galen and Asclepius: Providence and the Individual

As we have noticed, Galen combines the idea of an all-encompassing divine Creator with a plurality of gods such as Asclepius, with whom he claims to have a special relation. By the same token he reconciles Platonic philosophical religion with traditional religion. In this section I will focus on Asclepius' role in Galen's own life and, through him, that of his patients. I start with Galen's reference to the cure performed upon him by Asclepius (see Text 1). There are two more passages in his work that inform us about it. The first records how Galen obtained permission from Marcus Aurelius to be exempted from joining the military campaign the Emperor was preparing against the Germans. Galen had only recently been added to the team of court-physicians but he succeeded in achieving his aim:

> (5) [The Emperor] occupied himself with the campaign against the Germans, considering it of the utmost importance that I should accompany him. But he let himself be persuaded to release me when I told him that the opposite had been ordained by my ancestral god, Asclepius, whose servant (θεραπευτής) I had declared myself ever since the day he saved me from a fatal disease, viz. an abcess. Out of reverence for the god he ordered me to wait for his return ... (*On My Own Books* XIX, pp. 18–19 K = *SM* II, p. 99).

Galen is then entrusted with the care of the Emperor's son Commodus (one wonders which was worse). Not everyone was as impressed by Galen's plea as the Emperor was: charges of cowardice appear to have been levelled against him by professional rivals. At any rate, the appeal to Asclepius' cure seems to refer to the same event as that mentioned in text (1). In addition, we have here a striking labeling by Galen of himself as the god's servant. Although it is tempting to take this to refer to some official function, perhaps back home in Pergamum, it cannot be established exactly which one is meant if this were the case.

The second passage relating to the same cure by Asclepius runs as follows:

> (6) I was led by two clear dreams I received to the artery between the thumb and index finger of my right hand and I let the blood flow until it stopped of itself, just as the dreams had ordered ... (*How to Cure People Through Bloodletting* 23, XI p. 314 K.).

Asclepius, then, intervened to point out to Galen the exact spot where to make an incision for bloodletting. The cure as such is in line with Galenic medicine. Galen made contact with the god by receiving a dream from him. Although Galen accepted other forms of divination such as those mentioned in Text (1), the dream seems to have been most important to him. He typically insists that the received dreams were clear, that is to say, they did not require any explanation by an expert. Moreover, the dreams appear to be unsolicited. Thus Asclepius also caused Galen to embark upon a medical career by sending dreams to his father:

> (7) When I was sixteen, my father was prompted by clear dreams to make me study medicine alongside philosophy (*On the Order of My Books* 4, *SM* p.88). [Eudemus] had also heard that when my father was introducing me to philosophy, he had been commanded by unambiguous dreams to educate me thoroughly in medicine, not just as a hobby (*On Prognosis* 2, 12 Nutton).

Elsewhere I have studied more passages where Galen is prompted by dreams to choose a particular form of treatment or even in one case to describe the anatomy of the eye, about which he was much in doubt. I submitted that there appears to have been a psychological need on his part to have the god's backing in making some of his decisions. Further, the steps suggested by Asclepius conform to Galenic medicine.[22] At same time, Galen refrains from criticizing the counter-intuitive type of prescriptions obtained from Asclepius in the context of temple medicine. Here his attitude is rather of the conciliatory kind:

> (8) Another wealthy man, this one not a native but from the interior of Thrace came to Pergamum because a dream had prompted him to do so. A dream appeared to him, the god prescribing that he should drink every day of the drug produced from the vipers and should anoint the body from the outside. The disease [i.e. elephantiasis] after a few days turned into leprosy; and this disease, in turn, was cured [scil. by Galen and other doctors] by the drugs the god commanded (*Outline of Empiricism* 10, p.78 Deichgräber; cf. *Simpl. med. temp. et fac.* 11, 1,1, XII, pp. 313ff. K.).

Here we see Galen accepting what the god tells in the dreams he sends to one of his patients. Again there is nothing outlandish in the prescriptions from the point of view of Galenic medicine. The technique of converting an incurable disease into a curable is also part of it. Compare the following passage about a slanderous suggestion made by one of Galen's rivals, Antigenes:

> (9) Antigenes [...] was annoyed with Eudemus for saying that I rightly deserved not merely praise but admiration from everyone, and he slanderously maintained that my prognoses derived not from medicine but from divination. When some people asked him what sort of divination he meant, he sometimes said that it came from observing the flight of birds, sometimes from sacrifices, sometimes from chance happenings or from consulting horoscopes ... (*On Prognosis* 3.6–7, p.84.1–10 Nutton; translation Nutton's, slightly modified).

22 T. Tieleman, "Religion and Therapy in Galen," in *Religion und Krankheit* (ed. G. Etzelmüller and A. Weissenrieder; Darmstadt: Wissenschaftliche Buchgesellschaft, 2010), 88–92.

Here, as in the immediate context, Galen insists that his successful cure of Eudemus was due to his medical expertise only. His objection to the suggestion of divination made by Antigenes is not that he rejects it in all its forms and under all circumstances. He accepts dreams, premonitions and signs as means of foretelling the future: he does not deny their occasional effectiveness (see also Text 1).[23] What he does reject is an exclusive reliance upon them and their use for the wrong purposes. What Antigenes said was slanderous because it implied that Galen exclusively relied upon divination.

V Conclusion

What the quotations in the previous section show us is Galen's belief in providential care on the individual level as distinguished from that operating on the cosmic level (including also the level of species), which was at issue in sections 1 and 2. But what the passages in all sections have in common is that god(s) and nature belong to one and the same continuous reality, in which universal rules obtain. God does not go against Nature because he does not go against his own creation, i.e. against himself. His actions agree with or indeed even form part of the natural causes studied and explained by natural philosophy and the Galenic system of medicine based upon it. Thus we are dealing with a re-educated Asclepius whose interventions are quite in keeping with Galenic medicine. By the same token the significant dreams he sends in regard to individual cases are not miraculous in the sense of interrupting the natural course of things. They do not come from another, "supra-natural" realm where a completely different set of laws or principles prevails. Rather they come from a higher level of the same continuum. As such, they are manifestations of the divine power extending downwards to human minds receptive to them. For Galen, the experience of something amazing signifies ignorance of its true causes on the part of the person who experiences it. For those who, on the basis of the art of medicine, do know, the astonishment has been replaced by admiration.[24]

---

23 See Nutton's good comments *ad loc.* (on pp. 169–71 of his commentary). Galen even went so far as writing a (lost) eight volume treatise against the Methodist physician Asclepiades, who believed that to predict the future was the job of a prophet not a doctor: see *De nat. fac.* I, 12: *Scr. Min.* III, 121,24–122,3 Helmr. = II, p. 29,7–11 K.

24 I'd like to thank Annette Weissenrieder and Stefan Alkier most warmly for inviting me to participate in their conference on miracle stories and concepts of reality, which proved a highly stimulating experience.

Bibliography

Boudon, V. *Galien et le sacré*, in *Bull. Ass. Guillaume Budé* 4/1988 (Lettres d'Humanité XLVII): 327–37.

Boudon-Millot, V. & A. Pietrobelli, eds. "Galien ressuscité: Édition princeps du texte grec du *de propriis placitis*," *Revue des Études Grecques* 118 (2005): 168–213.

Edelstein, J. & L. Edelstein. *Asclepius: A Collection and Interpretation of the Testimonies* vols. I and II (New York 1975).

Frede, M. "On Galen's Epistemology," in *Galen: Problems and Prospects.* Edited by V. Nutton. London: ICS, 1981, 279–98.

–. "Galen's Theology," in *Galien et la philosophie.* Edited by J. Barnes & J. Jouanna; Entretiens sur l'antiquité classique XLIX. Vandoeuvres/Genève: Fondation Hardt, 2003, 73–129.

Gero, S., "Galen on Christians: A Reappraisal of the Arabic Evidence." *Orientalia christiana periodica* 56 (1990): 371–411.

Grant, R.M. *Miracle and Natural Law in Graeco-Roman and Early Christian Thought.* Amsterdam: North-Holland Pub. Co, 1952.

Horstmanshoff, H.F.J. "Galen and His Patients," in *Ancient Medicine in its Socio-Cultural Context* vol. 1. Edited by Ph. J. Van der Eijk, H.F.J. Horstmanshoff and P.H. Schrijvers. Amsterdam/Atlanta, GA: Rodopi Bv Editions, 1995, 83–100.

Kudlien, F. "Galen's Religious Belief," in *Galen: Problems and Prospects. A Collection of Papers submitted at the 1979 Cambridge Conference.* Edited by V. Nutton. London: Institue of Classical Studies, 1981, 117–30.

Moraux, P. "Galen and Aristotle's *De partibus animalium*," in *Aristotle on Nature and Living Things: Philosophical and Historical Studies Presented to David Balme on his Seventieth Birthday.* Edited by A. Gotthelf; Pittsburgh: Mathesis, 1985.

–. *Ancient Medicine.* London: Routledge, 2004.

Nutton, V. *Galen On Prognosis. Ed., transl. and comm. CMG* V 8,1. Berlin: Akademie-Verlag, 1979.

Schlange-Schöningen, H., *Die römische Gesellschaft bei Galen.* Berlin: De Gruyter, 2003.

Strohmaier, G., "Galen als Vertreter der Gebildetenreligion seiner Zeit" in *Neue Beiträge zur Geschichte der alten Welt. Band II: Römisches Reich.* Edited by E.C. Welskopf. Berlin: Akademie-Verlag, 1965, 375–80.

Tieleman, T. *Galen and Chrysippus on the Soul: Argument and Refutation in the* De Placitis *Books II–III.* Leiden: Brill, 1996.

–. "Galen and Genesis" in *The Creation of Heaven and Earth: Re-interpretations of Genesis I in the Context of Judaism, Ancient Philosophy, Christianity, and Modern Physics.* Edited by G.H. van Kooten. Leiden/Boston: Brill, 2005, 125–45.

–. "Religion and Therapy in Galen," in *Religion und Krankheit.* Edited by A. Weissenrieder and G. Etzelmüller. Darmstadt: Wissenschaftliche Buchgesellschaft, 2010, 83–96.

Von Staden, H. *Herophilus: The Art of Medicine in Early Alexandria.* Cambridge: CUP, 1985.

Walzer, R., *Galen on Jews and Christians.* Oxford: Clarendon Press, 1949.

Christopher Ocker

The Physiology of Spirit in the Reformation: Medical Consensus and Protestant Theologians

Behind a miracle is the movement of an invisible hand. But how is this agency imagined? To the historian, the agent, its mechanisms, and its environment are always relative, never absolute: miracles change over time and mean different things to different people. At the time of the Reformation, this matrix of agency, mechanism, and environment could be observed in spirits.

People diagnosed spirits in the Reformation between 1529 and 1535, when a German conflict between Luther and the papacy grew into a European controversy over traditional religion. The controversy forced them to assess their neighbors' demeanor, not just doctrines, and they made judgements about spirits. Consider this example.

Around mid-morning on 22 February 1534, the feast of *cathedra Petri*, in the city of Orléans, the Franciscan Roland Bressin walked into the novices' dormitory of his cloister, where monks had gathered, listening to strange noises.[1] Bressin thought they heard a spirit. So the ghost was questioned. A friar, Guillaume Falleau, bound it by oath to tell whether it belonged to a woman buried in the church, one knock for yes. There was a loud knock. Further questioning determined that this was the spirit of Louise de Mareua, wife of a reeve of Orléans, François de Saint-Mesmin. Louise had been recently buried in the Franciscan church. Her spirit now claimed to be in hell, having died in mortal sin as a Lutheran heretic. The prior came and posed more questions, same results. The Franciscan provincial minister, Jean Colimant, came and posed more questions, same results again. Another friar, Pierre d'Arras, took a turn and managed to get the spirit to confirm some Catholic orthodoxies: the existence of purgatory and the effective intercessions of saints bidden by prayer. On the feast day of the See of Peter, the Franciscans worried about concealed Lutherans.

It is hard to know just why the friars were so worried in the winter of 1534. Lutheran sympathizers, such as those known to John Calvin studying law at Orléans

---

1 Nicolas Balzamo, "Fausse apparitions et vraie supercherie: l'affaire des Cordeliers d'Orléans (1534–1535)," *Bibliotheque d'Humanisme et Renaissance* 73 (2011): 481–96. For the feastday, Hermann Grotefend, *Zeitrechnung des deutschen Mittelalters und der Neuzeit*, 2 vols., vol. 2 in 2 parts (Hannover: Hahn, 1891–98), 2/2:38.

a year earlier, may have been ready, or almost ready, to publicize their views, because eight months later, in October, pamphlets denouncing the mass distributed at Paris in the "Placards Affair" were simultaneously distributed at Rouen, Blois, Tours, and also Orléans, marking an intimidating moment in the advance of Lutheran sentiment.[2] The Placards Affair encouraged a hesitant king and court to persecute heresy, which had been brewing in Paris and other cities since 1531. Persecution was demanded by the papal bull of Clement VII, recorded by Parlement on 19 December 1533, even while the royal court was pursuing an anti-Habsburg alliance between German Protestants, the French and English crowns, and the pope, a blunt reminder of how obscure Protestant and Catholic lines were, not just in England but in France and the Holy Roman Empire, as well.[3] A Protestant church was only organized at Orléans in 1557.[4]

Bressin and d'Arras had written up their interrogations in protocols. Suspicions may have first been raised when the banging spectacle could not be repeated for clergy and townsfolk in the following days, but the whole business became urgent when the provincial minister, Jean Colimant, announcing the papal bull of Pope Clement VII that admonished King Francis I to supress heresy, decided to tell the story of Louise's ghost and tarnish her memory in a Sunday ser-

2 Balzamo, "Fausses apparitions," 495–496. Jonathan A. Reid, *King's Sister – Queen of Dissent: Marguerite of Navarre (1492–1549) and Her Evangelical Network*, 2 vols. (Leiden: E.J. Brill, 2009), 555 (evangelical activity at Orléans and Calvin's connection to it). Bruce Gordon, *John Calvin* (New Haven: Yale, 2009), 41. Jean Delumeau and Thierry Wanegffelen, *Naissance et affirmation de la Réforme* (Paris: Presses universitaires de France, 1997), 83. Lucien Febvre, *The Problem of Unbelief in the Sixteenth Century* (trans. Beatrice Gottlieb; Cambridge, Ma.: Harvard University Press, 1982), 131–46 and passim.

3 Balzamo, "Fausses apparitions," 495 n. 58. The most important heresy inquests at this time took place in Toulouse, the Vaudois, Alençon, and Paris. Presumably, Protestants in France are likely to have been most active in these towns. Reid, *King's Sister*, 2:383–435, 436–46 (the prospect of a French, German-Protestant, English, papal alliance against the Habsburgs). Marc Venard notes that Francis I's religious policy correlated with his foreign policy. The religious policy was more liberal when the king was at war with Charles I and more orthodox when he and the Habsburgs were at peace, as now. Marc Venard, "La Carte du Christianism éclaté en France et aux Pays-Bas," in *Histoire du Christianisme* 14 vols. (ed. J.-M. Mayeur et al.; Paris: Desclée, 1990–2001), 8:403–74, here 407 n. 7. For England, Peter Marshall, *Religious Identities in Henry VIII's England* (Abingdon: Ashgate Publishing Group, 2006). For Germany in the 1530's, Christopher Ocker, "Between the Old Faith and the New: Spiritual Loss in Reformation Germany," in *Enduring Loss in Early Modern Germany* (ed. Lynn Tatlock; Leiden: E.J. Brill, 2010), 231–58. For the late development of interdependent Lutheran-Catholic identities, Ocker, "The German Reformation and Medieval Thought and Culture," 13–46.

4 Delumeau and Wanegffelen, *Naissance*, 149.

mon at the beginning of March.[5] The woman's shocked husband immediately lodged a complaint at the royal court in Paris, alleging that the Franciscans perpetrated false apparitions. His wife, the widower claimed, died as she lived, a good Catholic.

A high-level commission was sent to town, led by a president of the Chamber of Inquests and the first master of the Chamber of Requests, asking questions. They could not reproduce the spirit's knocking, either. They reviewed the Franciscan protocols, and interrogated friars one by one.[6] Eventually a novice broke down, Pierre de Halcourt, claiming to have posed as the spirit by hitting rafters in the church with a piece of wood, upon instructions from Friars Roland Bressin, Pierre d'Arras, and Jean Colimant. They, with other members of the monastery, were jailed. Even so, the three principals insisted on their innocence. Pierre d'Arras may have hoped to exploit the orthodox fury ignited in reaction to the Placards Affair in October. He managed to bring a list of nine propositions before Paris' faculty of theology on 31 December 1534. Three weeks later, the Sorbonne pronounced. Sure, souls after death can appear to people on earth, they agreed, communicating audibly or through signs, and spirits could be abjured to answer questions, as the Franciscans had done according to standard procedures. Yet the theologians withheld judgement on recent events at Orléans. In Paris, royal magistrates found the Franciscans guilty, ordering the friars to perform a solemn procession through Orléans with bare heads and burning torches in their hands, from their cloister to St. Hilary's, Louise de Mareau's parish church, where they would sing an office for Louise's soul, confess their crimes, and beg God's pardon and the forgiveness of Louise's husband and children. Nine of the accused friars were condemned to two years imprisonment. The fraud was later immortalized in the Lutheran Johann Sleidan's history, using a report from John Calvin, whose own efforts to disabuse French Protestants of their emotional bonds to the dead had limited success in the sixteenth century.[7] Louise's spirit and her family were

5 Balzamo, "Fausse apparitions," 186 n. 20. Paul de Felice, *La tragédie des Cordeliers d'Orléans (1534–1535)* (Orleans: Herluison, 1887), 48–50 for the papal bull.

6 For these courts in the structure of royal courts, Diane Claire Margolf, *Religion and Royal Justice in Early Modern France: The Paris Chambre de l'Edit, 1598–1665* (Kirksville, MO: Truman State, 2003), 37.

7 CO 10:39–42 no. 22. Johannes Sleidanus, *De statu religionis et reipublicae Carolo V. Caesare commentarii*, liber ix (1534), (Frankfurt am Main: Petrus Fabricius, 1568), 176–77. In addition to Balzamo in note 1 above, Alexandra Kess, *Johann Sleidan and the Protestant Vision of History* (Aldershot: Ashgate, 2008), 16–17, 108. On Calvin and ghosts, consider Natalie Zemon Davis, "Ghosts, Kin, and Progeny: Some Featuers of Family Life in Early Modern France," *Daedalus* 1'06 (1977): 87–114, here 95–96. Similarly, belief in ghosts continued after the Reformation in Germany and Scandinavia, even as the genres of ghost tales were adapted to communicate a Lutheran

avenged, and this allegation of mendicant fraud entered the Protestant ledger of Catholic transgressions.

In all this, learned men presupposed the reality of spirits separated from bodies, whatever their view of this particular ghost. In so doing they presupposed a physiology of spirit.

Consider another example. Five years earlier, on 9 February 1529, there were riots in Basel.[8] They culminated months and years of growing tension in the city around evangelical preaching, and they forced the city's council to eliminate all monasteries within the town's walls. The council soon reorganized churches, church services, church properties, and the clergy. This was a dramatic reformation.

The upheaval drove away Desiderius Erasmus, who lived and worked in Basel for the past eight years. Two months after the unrest, Erasmus relocated to Freiburg, where he kept distancing himself from Luther and his followers.[9] He published and reissued several works that repudiated the relationships implied and alleged between him and evangelical radicals.[10]

---

morality. Jürgen Beyer, "On the Transformation of Apparition Stories in Scandinavia and Germany, 1350–1700," *Folklore* 110 (1999): 29–47.

8 Hans R. Guggisberg, *Basel in the Sixteenth Century* (St. Louis: Center for Reformation Research, 1982), 25. Lee Palmer Wandel, *Voracious Idols and Violent Hands: Iconoclasm in Reformation Zurich, Strasbourg, and Basel* (Cambridge: Cambridge University Press, 1995), 149–89. In general, Berndt Hamm, *Bürgertum und Glaube: Konturen der städtischen Reformation* (Göttingen: Vandenoeck und Ruprecht, 1996); Christopher Ocker, *Church Robbers and Reformers in Germany, 1525–1547* (Leiden: E.J. Brill, 2006), 57–58, 75–78, 95–100, 156–61 and the literature noted there.

9 But the question of the intellectual relationship of Erasmus and Luther's followers is reopened by Greta Grace Kroeker, *Erasmus in the Footsteps of Paul* (Toronto: University of Toronto Press, 2011), 133–44 and passim.

10 These works included a collection of his letters published in his former town, the eighth and longest collection published thus far. It included many letters criticizing evangelical rebellions everywhere. The collection appeared in late August/early September 1529, with 400 previously unpublished letters, almost all of which came from 1522–29, and many of which were very critical of the situation in Switzerland and South Germany, especially Strasbourg, and critical of the events of 1525–26 (which led to the publication of the *Detectio praestigiarum*, a work intended to distance himself from the views of Zwingli and Konrad Pellikan on the eucharist, and from his earlier, as he would now have it, experimental criticisms of bodily presence), and critical of recent events in Basel. *Opus epistolarum Desiderii Erasmi Roterdami* 12 vols. (ed. P.S. Allen, H.M. Allen and H.W. Garrod; Oxford: Clarendon Press, 1906–58), 1:596. Erasmus also republished the *Detectio praestigiarum*, first published in 1526; trans. Garth Tissol, ed. James D. Tracy, *Collected Works of Erasmus* (hereafter CWE), 86 vols. (Toronto: University of Toronto Press, 1974–present), 78:147–205, ed. C. Augustij, *Opera omnia Desiderii Erasmo Roterdami* (hereafter ODE), 9 parts, numerous volumes (Amsterdam-Oxford: North-Holland Publishing Company, 1969–2003), 9/1(for *ordinis noni, tomus primus*): 211–62.

These works included a pamphlet called the *Epistola contra pseudo-evangelicos*. The pamphlet rebutted the rebels' claim to act as defenders of the gospel.[11] In it, Erasmus described his personal experience of evangelicals, whose preachers controlled most of Basel's parish churches since late 1525:

> I never entered their churches, but I saw them returning from assembly as though blown-up by foul spirit, all their faces bearing an amazing anger and ferocity. Apart from an old man, there weren't any who courteously offered me or any decent men the respect we'd show anyone at all! But I suppose the soldiers depart from the general's assembly cheered on to the battle and [he lapses into Greek with a Homeric phrase][12] to the θοῦριν ἀλκήν, to the strong shield. Who ever saw in their assemblies anyone pouring out tears for their sins, beating the breast or groaning? Indeed, a great part is consumed by ripping to pieces the life of priests, and if they tell the truth, there are those who in their sermons frequently incite seditions rather than piety.[13]

11 Erasmus, *Epistola contra Pseudo evangelicos*, ed. C. Augustijn, ODE 9/1:introduction 265–81, text 283–309, trans. Garth Tissol, CWE 78:207–53. Erasmus' more immediate purpose was to correct false impressions created by bootleg editions of another one of his books, the *Apologia adversus monachos quosdam Hispanos*, an acidic attack on monasticism and traditional religion. He left Basel in April 1529. He wrote the *Epistola contra pseudeuangelicos* in late October/early November 1529, soon after receiving a letter from Geldenhouwer complaining of his poverty and asking for a recommendation as professor of poetry. Erasmus sent him a ms copy of the *Epistola*, noting his intention to publish it. The book appeared in Freiburg at the turn of the New Year and was soon published again in Cologne.

12 E.g. *Illiad*, 112, 164, 313, 527, 566, 718.

13 For the parish churches, Guggisberg, *Basel in the Sixteenth Century*, 24. Erasmus, *Epsitola contra Pseudo evangelicos*, 292: "Excussae sunt e templis statuae, sed quid refert quum nihilo secius in animo colantur idola viciorum? Nec video quo consilio quidam tanto studio demoliti sint imagines nisi ut esset conspirationis symbolum. Interim obtenditur horrendum idololatriae crimen. Sed quis nunc est tam lapis ut putet lapidibus ac lignis inesse sensum? Et si qui tales sint, quantulum erat negocii docere populum imagines ad hoc tantum repertas, ut imperitis memoriam adiuuent? Excussae sunt preces solemnes, sed iam plurimi sunt qui nihil prorsus orant, quum frequens puraque oratio sit sacrificium maxime proprium christianis. Abrogata est missa, sed quid illi successit sacratius? Non enim iam confero ritus cum ritibus, inductos cum relictis. Nunquam illorum ecclesias sum ingressus, sed aliquando vidi redeuntes a concione veluti malo spiritu afflatos, vultibus omnium iracundiam ac ferociam miram prae se ferentibus, neque quisquam erat omnium qui mihi viris aliquot honestis comitato deferret honores quem exhibemus quibuslibet, praeter unum seniculum. Sic opinor discedunt milites a concione ducis, ad praelium et ad θοῦριν αλκήν exhortati. Quis unquam vidit in illorum concionibus quenquam pro peccatis suis fundentem lacrymas, tundentem pectus aut ingemiscentem? Iam quanta pars ibi consumitur in laceranda sacerdotum vita ac, si verum narrant, frequenter in iis sermonibus qui magis faciunt ad seditiones quam ad pietatem. Abrogata est confessio, sed interim ne Deo quidem confitentur plurimi. Abiectus est cum ieiuniis ciborum delectus, sed interim grauiter indulgetur crapulae, et ita quidam effugerunt iudaismum ut coeperint esse Epicuraei. Protritae sunt

Thinking back over the events that led to a transformation of a city's religious topography, Erasmus diagnosed the effects of sermons on people's faces. He saw evidence of foul *spiritus*. The body's gestures, facial expressions, and tears were traces of spirit acting in human flesh, prompted by a soul informed by the senses.[14] Embedded in Erasmus' polemic is a physiology of spirit.

The ghost of Orléans, who was too ready to take sides in a doctrinal controversy that had not quite started, and this scandalized scholar both remind the student of the history of religion in Europe to think broadly about familiar themes. It hardly needs mentioning that spirit, the Holy Spirit, to be exact, is a familiar Reformation problem. It was an element of doctrinal controversy, embedded in debates over the justification of sinners before God, the nature and effects of divine grace, the inspiration of believers, and the authority of the church.[15] These debates, in turn, were obviously definitive all across Europe: their outcomes established the difference between new Protestant "confessions" and a Catholic identity increasingly reliant on a concept of papal authority, the cult of the saints, and an expanded, modified, and increasingly laicized set of mystical and ritual practices.[16] Yet as important as they were, do theological debates adequately tell us what spirit was, or why, in everyday life, it mattered? Not really.

We must be sure of our subject. What spirit means to us is not what it meant to them. To take a modern-western example, in the famously religious United States, people tend to relegate the spiritual to the immaterial and poetic, where it refers to "inspiration, creativity, the mysterious, the sacred, and the mystical"; "our interiors, our subjective life, as contrasted to the objective domain of ma-

---

ceremoniae, sed nihil accessit spiritui, imo multum decessit meo quidem iudicio." My translation varies slightly with Garth Tissol's in CWE 78:218–53.

14 Erasmus published his translation of Plutarch's *De cohibenda iracundia* in 1525. It gives an account of the effects of anger on the soul and behavior. Ed. by A.J. Koster, *Opera omnia Desiderii Erasmo Roterodami*, ordinis quarti, tomus secundus (Amsterdam/Oxford: North-Holland Publishing Company, 1977), 261–86.

15 Consider Stanley Burgess, *The Holy Spirit: Medieval Roman Catholic and Reformation Traditions* (Peabody, Ma.: Hendrickson, 1997), 141–218; Alois Haas, *Der Kampf um den Heiligen Geist: Luther und die Schwärmer* (Freiburg: Universitätsverlag, 1997), 1–48; Pekka Kärkkäinen, *Luthers trinitarische Theologie des Heiligen Geistes* (Mainz: Peter von Zabern, 2005), 113–94 and passim.

16 Marc R. Forster, *Catholic Germany from the Reformation to the Enlightenment* (New York: Palgrave, 2007), 35–84. Adriano Prosperi, *Tribunali della coscienza: inquisitori, confessori, missionari* (Turin: Einaudi, 1996). Adriano Prosperi, "La confessione e il foro della coscienza," in *Il concilio di Trento e il moderno* (ed. Paolo Prodi and Wolfgang Reinhard; Bologna: il Mulino, 1996), 225–54. Peter Burschel, "'Imitatio sanctorum'. Ovvero: quanto era moderno il cielo dei santi post tridentino?," in *Il concilio di Trento e il moderno*, 309–33. Christopher Ocker, "The German Reformation and Medieval Thought and Culture," *History Compass* 10 (2012): 13–46, here 16–17 (http://onlinelibrary.wiley.com/doi/10.1111/j.1478-0542.2011. 00816.x/abstract).

terial events and objects."[17] Our religion is not their religion. In "knowledge societies" today religion is "functionally differentiated" from other spheres of reality and social practice.[18] It symbolically and collectively represents subjective experiences of transcendence, but has nothing to do with the physics of material bodies. It generates ultimate meaning, but has nothing to do with muscular motion in animals. It provides norms to the social body and symbolic content to human identity and existence, but does not form the state. It may even produce a paradoxical union of immanence and transcendence in religious communication, but does not define the human psyche.[19]

In late medieval and early modern Europe, spirit was almost always seen as a physical entity. This is enormously important. Early modern Europe was, as Rudolf Schlögl points out, an *Anwesenheitsgesellschaft*, "a society of presence,"

---

17 In evidence of how pervasive this specialized function of a generalized religious attitude is, American academics seem hardly less prone than their students to describe themselves as "spiritual." 81% of 40,670 faculty in 421 colleges interviewed in 2004 and 2005 described themselves as "spiritual," and 70% of these would also call themselves "religious." "Spirituality in Higher Education: Students' Search for Meaning and Purpose," (http://spirituality.ucla.edu/docs/reports/Spiritual_Life_College_Students_Full_Report.pdf) and "Spirituality and the Professoriate: A National Study of Faculty Beliefs, Attitudes, and Behaviors," Higher Education Research Institute, Graduate School of Education and Information Studies, University of California, Los Angeles (http://www.spirituality.ucla.edu/results/spirit_professoriate.pdf, accessed 10 March 2008). The word also reflects the predominantly undogmatic approach of most Americans to religion. "U.S. Religious Landscape Survey," The Pew Forum on Religion and Public Life, June 2008 (Washington, D.C.: Pew Research Center, 2008), 3–20. If these studies represent "popular" definitions at play among students and professors, the popular is almost identical with an academic definition of spirituality. Sandra M. Schneiders, "Approaches to the Study of Christian Spirituality," in *The Blackwell Companion to Christian Spirituality* (ed. Arthur G. Holder; Oxford: Blackwell, 2005), 15–33, here 16–19.

18 Knowledge societies are characterized by global, digitized communication networks, freedom of expression, and a heavy dependence on education, with schools in the United States, the UK, Germany, France, and Australia exercising the strongest international influence. *Towards Knowledge Societies* (Paris: United Nations Educational, Scientific and Cultural Organization, 2005), 95 and passim.

19 Thomas Luckmann, "Transformations of Religion and Morality in Modern Europe," *Social compass* 50 (2003): 275–85, here 277. Parsons, *The Evolution of Societies* (ed. Jackson Toby; Englewood Cliff: Prentice-Hall, 1977), 125–40, 193–94. Robert Bellah, *Beyond Belief: Essays on Religion in a Post-Traditionalist World* (San Francisco: Harper, 1970), 21. Niklas Luhmann, *Die Religion der Gesellschaft* (Frankfurt: Suhrkamp, 2000), 77. Such convictions are sometimes contrasted with "theology," but in fact, some theologians have long embraced the idea that religious truth must be, in one way or another, contrasted with institutional religion, for example, Richard Rothe (1799–1867), the "dialectical theologians" who promoted a "religionless Christianity" (Dietrich Bonhoeffer, Paul Tillich), and even death-of-God theologians and promoters in the 1960's and beyond (Gabriel Vahanian, Thomas J.J. Altizer, John A.T. Robinson, Harvey Cox, Mark C. Taylor).

highly reliant on face-to-face communications, which involve the manipulation of gestures and stagings as well as talk. It was much less reliant on bureaucratized institutions or virtual media, unlike "knowledge societies" today.[20] In it, the distinctions between the religious, the aesthetic, the scientific, and the political were blurry and far more fluid than they are in knowledge societies. In early modern Europe, where *spiritus* was also a physical presence, social effectiveness depended in part on a person's ability to perceive and evaluate spirit.

So Erasmus took facial expressions and manners as evidence of spirit. It goes beyond the appraisal of ghosts, because ghosts are traces of a body-spirit continum. To cite another example from still elsewhere, in England, an anonymous participant in the trial of John Firth, who was burned to death in London on 4 July 1533, wondered that this 24-year old sacramentarian heretic was "willyng vs to truste herein the spyryt whych nowe in the ende of the worlde, god hath raysed in his yonge breste to rebuke the worlde," in spite of "the iudgement of the hole worlde" and contrary to 1500 years' Catholic belief. The author (probably Stephen Gardiner, bishop of Winchester) returns his reader again and again to Frith's spirit, the ghost of Luther in Frith,[21] while his open letter displayed the tribunal's

20 Rudolf Schlögl, *Die Stadt in der europäischen Vormoderne: Ein Sozialsystem der Anwesenheitsgesellschaft in der Transformation* (Constance: University of Constance Sonderforschungsbereich 485, 2007), 10–11 and passim. Norbert Haag, "Zum Verhältnis von Religion und Politik im konfessionellen Zeitalter – system- und diskurstheoretische Überlegungen am Beispiel der Lutherischen Erneuerung in Württemberg und Hessen," *Archiv für Reformationsgeschichte* 88 (1997): 166–98.

21 Germen Gardynare, *A letter of a yonge gentylman named mayster Germen Gardynare, wryten to a frend of his, wherin men may se the demeanour [and] heresy of Ioh[a]n Fryth late burned, [and] also the dyspycyo[n]s [and] reasonynge vpon the same, had betwene the same mayster Germen and hym* (London: W. Rastell, 1534), ff. 3r, 5v–6r, 6v, 9r–9v, and passim (for the effort to restore him to orthodoxy). See also Gardynare, *A Letter*, ff. 7v–8r, 12v, 13v–14r, 16v–17r, 28r–29v, 30r–v, 35r. For Frith and this complex time, Diarmaid MacCulloch, *Thomas Cranmer* (New Haven: Yale University Press), 100–102. Christopher Haigh, *English Reformations: Religion, Poltics, and Society under the Tudors* (Oxford: Clarendon, 1993), 66–67, 112–20 for Henry's ecclesiastical policy in these years. A.G. Dickens emphasized that Frith did not deny purgatory and transsubstantiation, for which he was tried, but insisted that no particular position on these doctrines was necessary for salvation. In this Dickens saw a "Henrician forerunner" of "the liberal elements in later Anglican thought." A.G. Dickens, *The English Reformation* (2nd ed.; University Park: Pennsylvania State Press, 1989), 101, 204. Also Thomas Betteridge, *Literature and Politics in the English Reformation* (Manchester: Manchester University Press, 2004), 31–33. Frith was immortalized by John Foxe, *Acts and Monuments*, (1563), book 3, 553–67; (1570), book 8, 1212–19; (1576), book 8, 1028–33; (1583), 1055–61. John Foxe's *The Acts and Monuments Online*, www.johnfoxe.org (accessed 31 May 2012). Foxe also published Frith's writings together with the works of Tyndale and Robert Barnes in 1573. John N. King, *English Reformation Literature: The Tudor Origins of Protestant Tradition* (Princeton: Princeton University Press, 1983), 430.

extraordinary patience in the face of the heretic's true nature – that "men may se" his "demeanour and heresy" as the title announces. The word "demeanour" points us, as Erasmus had pointed us, to the evidence of spirit acting in flesh, as we will see. To be sure, this was not the central point of the campaign against Frith's budding reputation as a reforming martyr, nor was Erasmus' perturbation at rude sermon-goers the central proof of his opposition to "false evangelicals." It is nevertheless a *revealing* ancillary point, if we recognize that spirit and ghosts are not merely metaphors but things, and spirit-knowledge belonged to a social aptitude, the application of expert knowledge of spirits.

In this essay I would like to explore a rudimentary facet of this expert knowledge at the time of the Reformation, which helps account for the extension of a spiritual discourse across regions among people like Erasmus, Cranmer, Gardiner, theologians of the Sorbonne, Calvin, Sleidan, and their audiences. I wish to describe tacit agreements about the nature of spirit in medical and theological literature on the example of a select number of important scholars. I do not mean to privilege literature and learning in shaping early modern culture, any more than I would want to divorce learning from culture, but I do assume that this literature reflects a kind of indigenous science that knew critically and reproduced commonplace assumptions about the self in the world. These commonplace assumptions, I will explain, were unsettled by anatomical discoveries and Platonic speculation in the second and third quarters of the sixteenth century, during a crucial phase of the Reformation and unrelated to the religious controversy. But, I will argue, these speculations failed to undermine a basic presupposition of physical continuity between God and bodily spirit before the end of the sixteenth century. To be sure, there were religious activists who experimented with strong distinctions between the physical and the spiritual in the crucial 1530's, most famously Caspar Schwenckfeld and Sebastian Franck, but their views were rejected by the majority of learned people. Theological critics of traditional religion, such as the heretical physician Michael Servetus and the Lutheran Philip Melanchthon, embraced a late medieval-Renaissance consensus about a physical continuum between God and the biological self, and I will survey their positions. So too did Martin Luther and John Calvin, although Calvin's rhetorical method in theology could seem to effect a functional differentation of religious from natural-philosophical (and medical) discourse. This fact, I will claim, points us to the ambivalent position of the Reformation in European cultural change, a position evident in the peculiar "spirituality" I am trying to describe here.

1 A General Consensus about Spirit

"Spirit" was many things: a substance in the human body, one's inextinguishable, death-defying selfhood, or even God. The Latin *spiritus*, like its vernacular relatives and their cognates in classical Greek and biblical Hebrew, πνεῦμα and רוח, included air and air-like things, a fact especially relevant to biblical humanists like Erasmus, Calvin, Servetus, or Melanchthon. Thomas Elyot documented this semantic plasticity. One-time ambassador of King Henry VIII to the court of Emperor Charles V, he retired from royal service when the king divorced Catherine of Aragon, then devoted himself to translating and writing compendia of ancient Latin and Greek books at exactly this time, the mid-1530's. His works included a dictionary with these entries (italics mine):

> Aer et alactis, alacre, quycke of *spirite*, wytte, lusty of courage, mery, and he that lyueth in hope: proprely he that is in a meane betwene glad and sorte. Somtime it betokeneth a man redy and willing, therof commeth Alacritas, redynes or promptnes of wyll. also feruentnes of mynde.[22]
>
> Animans, idem quod animal, sauynge that it is more larger. For it maye sygnyfye all thynge that hath *spirite*, as welle in heuen, as on erthe.[23]
>
> Antiperistasis is that thinge, wherby where heate commeth colde is expelled, where colde is, heate is expelled: by this, well water in the wynter time is warme, for as moche as the hygh partes of the ayre beinge colde, the heate withdraweth him to the lowest partes. like wise in the body of man the *spirite* is kepte in more feruente by the outwarde colde, by the ioynt conscent & tolleration of al partes of the body.[24]
>
> Genius, an aungell [angel]. Amonge the Paynims [pagans] some supposed it to be the *spirite* of a man. Some dydde put two gouernours of the sowle, a good and an euyll, Bonus genius, & malus genius, whyche neuer departed from vs. sometyme it is taken for nature it selfe, or dilectation meued by nature.[25]
>
> Incubus, a *spyrite*, whiche assumynge the fourme of a man, medleth with womenne. Also that whiche is called the mare, wherwith men be oppressed in their slepe.[26]
>
> Larua, a *spyrite*, whiche apperethe in the nyght time. Some do call it a hegge, some a goblyn. Also a masker, or he that weareth a visour. it is sometyme taken for the same visour.[27]

---

22 Thomas Elyot, *The dictionary of syr Thomas Eliot knyght* (London: Thomas Berthelet, 1538), s.v. aer. For Elyot and this text, David Swain, "'Not lernyd in physicke': Thomas Elyot, the Medical Humanists, and Vernacular Medical Literature," in *Renaissance Historicisms: Essays in Honour of Arthur F. Kinney* (ed. James M. Dutcher and Anne Lake Prescott; Danvers, Ma.: Rosemont Publishing, 2008), 54–68.
23 Elyot, *The dictionary*, s.v. animans.
24 Elyot, *The dictionary*, s.v. antiperistasis
25 Elyot, *The dictionary*, s.v. genius.
26 Elyot, *The dictionary*, s.v. incubus.
27 Elyot, *The dictionary*, s.v. larva.

Phitonicus, & Phitonica, he or she, whyche hath a *spirite* within theym, that gyueth aunswere of thinges to come.[28]

Plumbeus homo, a lumpyshe man withoute courage or *spirite*.[29]

Pneuma, atis, *spirite* or wynd or breth.[30]

Spiritus, spirite, brethe, wynde.[31]

Spirituale, & spiritale, idem quod spiritus.[32]

Rhetorical-biblical, medical, and scholastic-theological modes of discourse overlap in this term.

Tacit to all these meanings was a consensus about spirit bearing the natural philosophical and medical authority of Aristotle and Galen. The consensus had been mediated from antiquity through the Middle Ages by Avicenna, by Averroes, by other Arabic commentators, and by three hundred years of Latin exposition. In the sixteenth century, growing interest in Galen increased the awareness of a classical-scholastic consensus and intensified the realism of Galenic perspectives for many if not most readers. In the second quarter of the sixteenth century, the crucial phase of the religious controversy, when the German conflict over Luther and the papacy became a European debate over traditional religion, Galen's accessible manual *Peri kraxeos* (*De temperamentibus*) was available in Gerard of Cremona's medieval Latin and in Thomas Linacre's humanistic translation (1521, 1527). Linacre's version was republished with the second Greek edition of Galen's works, produced at Basel (1538).[33] The first Greek edition had been published at

28 Elyot, *The dictionary*, s.v. phitonicus.

29 Elyot, *The dictionary*, s.v. plumbeus homo.

30 Elyot, *The dictionary*, s.v. pneuma.

31 Elyot, *The dictionary*, s.v. spiritus.

32 Elyot, *The dictionary*, s.v. spirituale et spiritale.

33 Clara Domingues, "L'aménagement du continent galénique à la Renaissance: les éditions grecques et latines des oeuvres complètes de Galien et leur organisation des traités," in *Lire les médecins grecs à la Renaissance: Aux origines de l'édition médicale* (ed. Véronique Boudon-Millot and Guy Cobolet; Paris: De Boccard, 2004), 163–86, here 163–66. Richard J. Durling, ed., *Burgundio of Pisa's Translation of Galen's Peri Kraseon "De Complexionibus"* (Berlin: De Gruyter, 1976), vii, points out that of the four medieval translations of *Peri Kraxeos* available (three from Arabic, one from Greek), Gerard of Cremona's was used in the early editions of Galen's works. Galen, *Opera*, 2 vols. (Venice: Diomedes Bonardus, 1490), where *De temperamentis* may be found in volume 2. In the Venice 1525 and Basel 1538 editions of the Latin *Opera*, *De temperamentis* may be found in volume 1. *Galeni opera omnia graeca* (Venice: A. Asolanus, 1525). *Galeni opera omnia* ed. A. Cratander, J. Hervagius, J. Bebel (Basel: Thomas Platter, 1538). Galen, *De temperamentis*, trans. Thomas Linacre (Paris: S. Sylvius, 1527, first published Cambridge: J. Siberch, 1521). Linacre's translation was republished nine times before 1550. Galen also discussed the production and basic distinction of pneuma (vital and psychic) in other newly available works. In *De placitis Hippocratis et Platoni*, book 7, he presented his physiology of spirit as the answer to deficiencies in earlier Greek theories.

Venice by Aldo Manuzio (1525).[34] A Galen revival had begun.[35] That Galen and medieval commentary still continued to merge in the medieval-scholastic manner at the time of the Reformation is suggested by English vernacular translations of medieval standbys, such as Arnold of Villanova and Guy de Chauliac, and by accessible humanistic renditions of Galen's pneumatology found in handbooks, such as Thomas Elyot's *Castle of Health*, which was published sixteen times between 1539 and 1610.[36] In Germany, as elsewhere, there stood alongside a rapidly growing vernacular pharmacology, recently studied by Mechthild Habermann, a growing number of Latin medical handbooks, such as the compendium of Galen's *Peri kraxeos* attributed to John of Neuhaus but probably written by John of Paris, the early fourteenth-century theologian, which was published at the end of the fifteenth century.[37] There were editions of the *Articella*, a collection of base texts for medieval scholastic medical commentary, and new works, such as the humanist Johannes Winter of Andernach's translation of Pseudo-Galen's *Medicus*, published with the Greek, and his own fresh composition, a compendium, by which he endeavored to condense Galenic doctrine because it is relevant for "every kind of person" (Andreas Vesalius' first publication was a revision of

---

This was first edited by Asulanus and published in Venice 1525, in the Aldine edition of Galen's works. Galen, *De placitis Hippocratis et Platoni* 3 vols. (ed. with trans. and commentary by Phillip de Lacy; Berlin: Akademie-Verlag, 1984), 1:21, 2:429–79. (Ps.-) Galen, *Definitiones rerum medicarum siue Anagraphe omnium rerum, uerae medicinae, atque adeo omnibus humanarum artium studiosis perutiles*, trans. Johannes Winter von Andernach (Cologne: Johann Gymnicus, 1529).

34 *Galeni opera omnia graeca* (Venice: A. Asolanus, 1525).

35 Of the nineteen Latin editions of Galen's complete works published during the Renaissance, only seven were produced before 1540. Domingues, "L'aménagement, 163–68.

36 Arnaldus de Villanova, *Here is a newe boke, called the defence of age, and recouery of youth, translated out of the famous clarke and ryght experte medycyne Arnold de Noua Uilla, very profytable for all men to knowe* (London: Robert Wyer, 1540), A.ii recto, Bii recto-Bii verso. Guy de Chauliac, *The questyonary of cyrurgyens with the formulary of lytell Guydo in cyrurgie, with the spectacles of cyrurgyens newly added, with the fourth boke of the Terapentyke [sic], or methode curatyfe of Claude Galyen prynce of physyciens, with a synguler treaty of the cure of vlceres, newely enprynted at London, by me Robert wyer, and be for to sell in Poules Churcheyarde, at the sygne of Judyth* (London: Robert Wyer, 1542), Eii recto (on the *rete mirabile*), Giv verso-Hi recto (on the structure of the heart and its function in the production of spirit). Thomas Elyot, *The castel of helth gathered and made by Syr Thomas Elyot knyghte, out of the chiefe authors of physyke, wherby euery manne may knowe the state of his owne body, the preseruatio[n] of helthe, and how to instructe welle his physytion in syckenes that he be not deceyued* (London: Thomas Berthelet, 1539), ff. 10v, 52r–52v. I base the claim about editions from those included in Early English Books Online (http://eebo.chadwyck.com/home).

37 Mechthild Habermann, *Deutsche Fachtexte der frühen Neuzeit: Naturkundlich-medizinische Wissensvermittlung im Spannungsfeld von Latein und Volkssprache* (Berlin: De Gruyter, 2002), 7–223. Johannes de Nova Domo, *Tractatus de complexionibus* (Leipzig: Landsberg, 1495), ff. 1–8.

this text).[38] Finally, published medical disputations, such as Philip Michael Novenianus' Leipzig disputation on the temperaments in 1534, communicated the rudiments of the physiology of spirit.[39]

There was a consensus about spirit and soul. Galen said spirit was a substance linking the emotional, deliberative soul to the moveable body. The soul, it had been held in late medieval and early modern Europe, was the sum total of abstract powers (growth, mobility, reason, and will) that make something alive, "the form of a physical body having living energy," said Aristotle's *On the Soul*. According to Michael Scot's twelfth-century Latin translation, soul is *substantia secundum quod est forma corporis naturalis habentis vitam in potentia*, the substantial form of a body having potency of life.[40] To be a substance, said Aristotle, was simply to be something actual, the realization of some potential thing: οὐσία ἐντελέχεια, "substance is actuality." The soul, said Michael Scot, represents the living body as a finished product, *ista substantia est perfectio*, "that substance is the completeness of the body"; or, as the Dominican William of Moer-

---

38 For the *Articella*, Paul Oskar Kristellar, "Bartholomaeus, Musandinus and Maurus of Salerno and Other Early Commentators of the 'Articella', with a Tentative List of Texts and Manuscripts," in *Studies in Renaissance Thought and Letters* 4 vols. (Rome: Edizioni di storia e letteratura, 1956–1996), 3:403–30. πνεῦμα appears in the *Medicus*, where it is discussed in connection wtih the humors. Galen, *Medicorum schola hoc est Claudii Galeni Isagoge sive medicus eiusdem definitionum medicinalium liber* (ed. Siegfried Singkehler and trans. Johann Winter von Andernach; Basil: Thomas Platter, 1537), 219–21. Joannes Guinterius Andernacus, *Anatomicarum institutionum ex Galeni sententia libri iiii per Ioannem Guinterium Andernacum medicum* (Basel: Robert Winter, June 1539) Preface sig. a2 recto-verso (the preface is only numbered by signatures, while the remainder is numbered by signatures and pages; I will refer to signatures for the preface and pages for the main text): "Accommodaui itaque me in hoc commentario ad minorum ingenia, cum doctrinae compendio, tum uero maxime ordine, et administrationis modo: quem omnes Recentiores omiserunt. praeterquam quod multa falso, omnia barbare conscripserint. Vnde factum est, ut ipsius Anatomae cognitio non tantum medicis ac philosophis necessaria, sed etiam omni hominum generi et honesta, et pulchra, hactenus neglecta iacuerit." For his account of Galen on animal spirit, Ibid., 190–91. Alfred Rupert Hall, *The Scientific Revolution, 1500–1800* (Boston: Beacon, 1960), 44. For the *Articella* in the Renaissance, Paul Oskar Kristellar, "Bartholomaeus, Musandinus and Maurus of Salerno and Other Early Commentators of the 'Articella', with a Tentative List of Texts and Manuscripts," *Studies in Renaissance Thought and Letters* 3:403–30.

39 Philipp Michael Novenianus, *De temperamentis sive complexionibus ac indicationibus curativis decreta* (Leipzig: Melchior Lotter, 1534), ff. 1–24.

40 Aristotle, *De Anima* ii.1, 412a19–20, Aristotle, *De anima* (ed. W.D. Ross; Oxford: Clarendon, 1956), 26. I have the translation of Michael Scotus from the Latin commentary of Averroes. Averroes, *Commentarium magnum in Aristotelis de anima libros* (ed. Stuart Crawford; Cambridge, MA: Medieval Academy of America, 1953), 134. *Aristotle's De Anima in the Version of William of Moerbeke and the Commentary of St. Thomas Aquinas* (trans. Kenelm Foster and Silvester Humphries; New Haven: Yale, 1951), 163.

beke said in another medieval translation, soul is the body's actuality or "act."[41] A fulfillment of corporeal destiny, the soul survived humanistic doubts about scholastic definitions.[42] Even in a de-ontologized view, such as Philip Melanchthon's, the soul was an ἐνδελέχεια, a persistent entity, and *itio ad formam*, on the way to form, not *forma corporis* as such.[43] This rendered the body all the more important, yet Melanchthon, like his medieval predecessors, still stressed the completion of human life in the soul-body continuum.

In the living, ensouled body, spirit was a physical fuel, and it formed the rarefied stuff through which the soul emotionally and morally inflected a body comprised of complex mixtures of the four humors.[44] The heart, liver, and brain produced, injected, accumulated, and dispersed the body's vaporous spirit-fuel.[45]

---

41 Aristotle, *De Anima* ii.1, 411a20–21.

42 Albertus Magnus described *spiritus* as a medium between body and soul, and the Council of Vienne (1311/1312) insisted that soul was form of the body, but not an unmediated form. Thomas Aquinas, by contrast, argued that the soul needs no medium. Boyd H. Hill, Jr., "The Grain and the Spirit in Mediaeval Anatomy," *Speculum* 40 (1965): 63–73, here 64–70.

43 Salatowsky, *De Anima*, 103.

44 Sascha Salatowsky, *De Anima: Die Rezeption der aristotelischen Psychologie im 16. und 17. Jahrhundert* (Amsterdam: B.R. Grüner, 2006), 106–12 offers an excellent survey of *pneuma/spiritus* in Aristotle and Galen. Christine Göttler, "Vapours and Veils: The Edge of the Unseen," in *Spirits Unseen: The Representation of Subtle Bodies in Early Modern European Culture* (ed. Christine Göttler and Wolfgang Neuber; Leiden: Brill, 2007), xv–xxvii, stresses the variety of descriptions of spirit and includes a review of early modern pictorial representations of it. A new library, that of the Genevan Academy, had little by way of medieval commentary, Aristotle and commentaries on the entire *Organon* are well represented, including commentaries on *De anima*, *De natura animalium*, and *De partibus animalium*; Pietro Pomponazzi's *De naturalium effectuum causis sive de instantationibus*, the Basel 1538 Greek edition of Galen's works; and Dioscorides *De medica materia* with the commentary of Andreas Matthiolus. Alexandre Ganoczy, *La bibliothèque de l'Académie de Calvin* (Geneva: Droz, 1969), 117–33 and nos. 286, 290, 311, 314, 315, 335. For the soul as a moral-emotional locus of personality and for Aristotle's ongoing influence, Jill Kraye, "Moral Philosophy," CHRP: 303–86, esp. 364, explains that most philosophers rejected Epicureanism, relied heavily on Cicero and Seneca for information about Epicureans; leaned toward Stoicism but opted for the Aristotelian view that virtue involves a balance of reason and emotion. For an introduction to ancient and early modern views of emotion, Amy M. Schmitter, "Ancient, Medieval and Renaissance Theories of the Emotions," *Stanford Encyclopedia of Philosophy* (http://plato.stanford.edu/entries/emotions-17th18th/, accessed 6 February 2008). Timothy Hampton, "Strange Alteration: Physiology and Psychology from Galen to Rabelais," in *Reading the Early Modern Passions: Essays in the Cultural History of Emotion* (ed. Gail Kern Paster, Katherine Rowe and Mary Floyd-Wilson; Philadelphia: University of Pennsylvania Press, 2004), 272–93, describes the relationship between emotional and physical change, mostly with reference to French Renaissance literature.

45 "spiritus est subtilis uapor ex sangine expressus, uirtute cordis incensus, ut sit uelut flammula, suppeditans uim in exercendis actionibus." Melanchthon, *Commentarius de anima* (Wittenberg: Peter Seitz, 1540), f. 134r (=sig. R6r), and on bodily "spirits" in general, ff. 134r–36r (=sig.

Most scholars followed Galen, dividing *spiritus* into 'vital' and 'animal' phases, 'vital' in its liver-phase and 'animal' in its heart-phase, in order to distinguish between the animating substance common to all living things (which according to some accounts included metals) and that version of the force unique to animals, a physical analogue to the distinction between vegetative and animal soul (a third phase of nervous spirit was sometimes added; the medieval and Renaissance nomenclature, it should be noted, did vary).[46] *Spiritus* was also sometimes likened to the substance of the heavenly empireum, the uppermost sphere of the Ptolemaic cosmos, where *spiritus*-based life forms, such as angels and saints, have their most natural home.[47] For those who leaned toward Aristotle's sharp distinction between perfect cosmic and changeable sublunary spheres, spirit was stuff moving between both and connecting them.

Because spirit formed a nexus between the body and the sustained capacities or "faculties" that constitute the soul-substance of a body, those faculties could affect the body's spirit and vice versa. Willpower, a faculty of a human soul, could influence the production and flow of *spiritus*. The body's physical condition could constrict or improve the spiritual current, while the force or weakness of the current could rebound onto the soul's actions, such as thinking or exercising willpower. The body's temperaments, the physical proportions of the four humors (blood, yellow bile, black bile, and phlegm), the proportions of which caused health or illness and impinged on personality and emotions, also affected the efficiency and flow of spirit and hence the actions of both body and soul. Finally, the passions, the soul's reactions of attraction or repulsion to its perception of real and imagined stimuli, affected, and were affected by, the body's temperaments and spirit.[48] In short, due to the physical role of *spiritus*,

---

R6r-R8r). The commentary is put in its context and summarized by Sachiko Kusukawa, *The Transformation of Natural Philosophy* (Cambridge University Press, 1995), 75–123. Salatowsky, *De Anima*, 105–31 summarizes Melanchthon's treatment of spirit. Commentarius *de anima* (Wittenberg: Peter Seitz, 1540), ff. 136r–77v (=sig. R8r-Z1v) treats the physical basis of the soul's operations, by following Galen's account of venous, arterial, and nervous systems, and by including a thorough discussion of human anatomy, the humors and temperaments, the powers of the soul in general (where he also discusses dreams and vision, and then Galen's three interior senses of common sense, cognition, and memory). Ibid, ff. 117v–97v (= sig. Z1v-b5v) treats the passions.

46 Jürgen Helm, "Die 'spiritus' in der medizinischen Tradition und in Melanchthons *Liber de anima*," in *Melanchthon und die Naturwissenschaften seiner Zeit* (Sigmaringen: Jan Thorbecke, 1998), 219–37, here 221–26.

47 Aristotle, *De generatione animalium* ii.3, 736b29–737a1. Spirit and ether are distinct but similar elements in Aristotle. Salatowsky, *De Anima*, 108–9.

48 Consider Melanchthon's *De anima* commentary of 1540 and Juan Luis Vives' *De anima et vita*, which both recognized the overlap between Galen's medical description of the passions and Aris-

the human animal was known as a "spiritual" being in a particular, comprehensive sense.

An observer could see right through the traces of spirit on the body to the condition of the essence of the self, the soul – its passions, virtues, and vices. But spiritual diagnosis was complex. For example, tears were generally thought to be heated humors spilling out of an over-excited brain through the eyes. The heat that caused this came from a surge of *spiritus*. Any number of external or subjective things could cause this surge. The quick-drying effect of smoke could excite a sudden compensatory reaction in the body – an external cause. Internally, "passions" of the soul, such as happiness, love, envy, shame, joy, or compassion, for oneself, for one's companions, or even for Mary and Christ, could also prompt an upsurge of spirit.[49] Sadness was particularly dangerous. *Tristitia* or *dolor* was "a motion by which the heart, as though beaten, is constricted, pressed, choked, trembles, and droops with a sharp feeling of sorrow. Gradually, when sadness is not driven away, the force (*virtus*) of the heart is impaired and put down, the heart itself dries up and is consumed, the generation of spirits falters, and at last its life-forces having been released, the person perishes. Sadness is a savage evil ...," explained the melancholic Philip Melanchthon.[50] Tears might occur in reaction to sorrow but not as a mere expression of it. In fact, weeping could remedy a potential collapse of animal spirit and the dangerous contraction of the heart.[51] Crying was good. It showed the soul's engagement with its circumstances, not its retreat or defeat.

In sum, a medical consensus said spirit was the fuel of the living body and a medium between soul and flesh. Spirit was also a physical entity, possibly akin to cosmic substance, and could exist apart from a corporeal host as a spiritual body.

totle's "psychological" one, trying, in effect, to coordinate Galen and Aristotle. Vives, *The Passions of the Soul: the Third Book of De anima et vita* (trans. Carlos G. Noreña; Lewiston: Edwin Mellen, 1990). Melanchthon in note 45 above. Vives, throughout book three of *De anima et vita*, observed repeatedly that a passion was not a reaction to an external stimulus but to a *perception* of a stimulus.

49 Galen, *De temperamentis libri tres* (trans. Thomas Linacre; Paris: S. Sylvius, 1527), f. 86r–86v. Vives, *De anima et vita*, iii.19, *The Passions of the Soul: the Third Book of De anima et vita*, 96.

50 Melanchthon, *Commentarius de anima* (1540), f. 180r (= sig. Z 4). See also ibid, f. 186r (= sig. Aa 2), where he explains the heart's attraction of tough bile from the spleen. Similarly, Thomas Aquinas, ST 1a2ae qq. 35–39; Guillaume Budé, *De transitu Hellenismi ad Christianismum. Le passage de l'hellénisme au Christianisme* (trans. M. Lebel; Sherbrooke: Éditions Paulines, 1973), liber iii, 207. John Calvin, in one of few commentaries on Seneca's *De clementia* produced in the first half of the sixteenth century, likewise described happiness as an expansion of the mind and mental disturbance as shrinkage. *Calvin's Commentary on Seneca's De clementia* (ed. introduced, trans., annotated Ford Lewis Battles and André Malan Hugo; Leiden: E.J. Brill, 1969), 66–67.

51 Aquinas, ST 1a2ae q. 38 a. 2.

2 Challenges and Spiritual Reality

In the sixteenth century, the consensus over the physiology of spirit was challenged at two points. This seems to have had the paradoxical consequence of underscoring the fundamental reality of *spiritus*, a physical entity accepted by materialists and spiritualizing Platonists alike.

First, Galen had argued that air is processed by the lungs, which turn air and vaporized humors into a pneumatic (πνευματώδης) substance and pass it on to the heart.[52] The heart converts this substance into vital pneuma/spirit. Nothing medieval scholars had found in their cadavers seemed to contradict this.[53] But Galen also argued that vital spirit is processed further through a *rete mirabile*, a complex network of arteries that was supposed to extend through the neck into the head, slowing the passage of vital pneuma to allow its necessary refinement, so that it may pass into the choroid plexuses of the brain, which finish the production of psychic pneuma.[54] This plexus exists in some animals, but, unknown to Galen, it cannot be found in humans. The existence of a *rete mirabile* was also presupposed by medieval Arabic and Latin medicine. The first to point to its absence was Berengario da Carpi, in dissections performed in 1521 (published in 1523).[55] Rather than question the refinement of *spiritus* in flesh, those scholars who followed Berengario, and they were few, simply reassigned the functions of the *rete mirabile* to other structures, for example, the innermost membrane covering the brain (the *pia mater*, so Berengario himself). Other critics of Galen's errors, such as Andreas Vesalius, included a description of the phantom *rete mirabile* in his *Tabulae anatomicae sex* (1538), then marvelled at his earlier piety when he later questioned the structure in the first edition of his *Fabrica humanae corporis* (1543).[56]

---

52 Galen, *De placitis Hippocratis et Platonis* 445.27–447.30, quoted by Julius Rocca, "Galen and Greek Neuroscience (Notes Towards a Preliminary Study)," *Early Science and Medicine* 3 (1998): 216–40, here 218, from De Lacy's translation.

53 David C. Lindberg, *The Beginnings of Western Science* (2nd ed.; Chicago: University of Chicago, 2007), 345–47.

54 Galen, however, seems to have also believed that air could pass from the nose to the choroid plexuses of the anterior ventricles of the brain, forming another potential channel for the production of psychic pneuma. Julius Rocca, "Galen and Greek Neuroscience (Notes Towards a Preliminary Study," *Early Science and Medicine* 3 (1998): 216–40.

55 Berengaria da Carpi, *Isagogae breues, perlucidae ac uberrimae, in anatomiam humani corporis a communi medicorum academia usitatam* (Bologna: Benedict Hector, 1523), the images of which are available on-line: http://www.nlm.nih.gov/exhibition/historicalanatomies/berengario_biblio.html (accessed 7 November 2011).

56 Julius Rocca, "Galen and Greek Neuroscience (Notes Toward a Preliminary Survey)," *Early Science and Medicine* 3 (1998): 216–40.

Still, anatomists continued to accept the existence of the *rete mirabile* for the next 250 years.[57]

The second challenge to Galen's anatomy of spirit had to do with the principal organ that was supposed to produce it, the heart. Galen had argued that blood enters the heart at the right ventricle, then passes from the right to the left ventricle through the partition separating the ventricles, which he wrongly believed to be porous. Andreas Vesalius, in the *Fabrica* of 1543, questioned this claim.[58] Realdo Colombo, sometime associate of Vesalius in the famous anatomical school of Padua (and of Michelangelo in Rome), argued on the basis of dissections performed soon after, but only published in the year of Colombo's death (1559), that blood from the right ventricle passes to the lungs, where it is enriched with air, then passes to the right ventricle. Michael Servetus, physician to the bishop of Vienne, was aware of the new anatomical discovery, whether through his own dissections or through knowledge of Vesalius and Colombo is unknown. In his *Christianissimi restitutio* of 1553, Servetus coordinated this pulmonary circulation of blood, an improved view of the body's spirit-refining mechanisms, with theology (more on this in a moment). Neither of these discoveries, the non-existent *rete mirabile* and pulmonary circulation, undermined belief in the existence or function of *spiritus* in the body, not even among those few at mid-century willing to abandon Galen.

Rather, *spiritus* was ready to assume the position of soul as the substantial form, the ultimate actuality, of the human person – spirit in the physical, embodied sense. For example, Giovanni Argenterio (d. 1572) criticized Galen's division of *spiritus* into liver, heart, and brain varieties, insisting that a singular spirit produced by the heart accounts for the heat and life of animal bodies.[59] Bernardino

---

57 Sebastian Pranghofer studies the persistence of the *rete mirabile* by examining the relation of anatomical images to the "rhetoric and narrative strategies" used "to negotiate truth" in early modern medicine. Pranghofer, "'It Could be Seen More Clearly in Unreasonable Animals than in Humans' The Representation of the Rete Mirabile in Early Modern Anatomy," *Medical History* 53 (2009): 561–86. See also Sachiko Kusukawa, "The Uses of Pictures in the Formation of Learned Knowledge: the cases of Leonhard Fuchs and Andreas Vesalius," in *Transmitting Knowledge: Words, Images, and Instruments in Early Modern Europe* (ed. Sachiko Kusukawa and Ian MacLean; Oxford University Press, 2006), 73–96.

58 Andreas Vesalius, *De Humani Corporis Fabrica*, i.12 (trans. Daniel H. Garrison, Malcolm H. Hast, electronic edition (http://vesalius.northwestern.edu/index.html, accessed 3 November 2011), n. 28 of book 1, chapter 12. Charles Donald O'Malley, *Michael Servetus: A Translation of His Geographical, Medical and Astrological Writings with Introductions and Notes* (Philadelphia: American Philosophical Society, 1953), 198.

59 Siraisi, "Giovanni Argenterio," 166–75. Giovanni Argenterio, *De somno et vigilia libri duo, in quibus continentur duae tractationes de calido natiuo et de spiritibus* (Florence: Laurentius Torentinus, 1556), 276–77 (contra the association of spirit with the heavens), 280–312.

Telesio (d. 1588), an opponent of metaphysical explanations in medicine and the most important member of a line of medical professors emerging from the mid-sixteenth century to criticize Aristotle, Arabic medicine, and Galen's physiology, retained *spiritus* (which he believed is a substance derived from semen and analogous to nervous spirit in Galen) as the animating material of the body, eliminating any separate animating substance, such as soul, to account for vegetative, animal, and rational powers.[60] Again, spirit survived, and both traditionalists and innovators questioned not its existence but the distinction of spirit and soul. They meant to improve the physiology of pneuma. In the traditional view, a particular animal "spirituality" bound the human being to the stuff out of which God, angels, spheres, luminous stars and planets on celestial spheres, minerals, plants, and animals were made. In the clock-work universe of Telesio, spirit was a substance mediating the warmth of the sun to earthen, animal flesh.[61] To be sure, fissures in a God-nature continuum are detectable in Argenterio and Telesio. Argenterio specifically ridiculed the idea that bodily spirit is linked to air and celestial or any other substance apart from soul (agreeing with theologians, however, that *spiritus* is akin to the substance of angels).[62] Telesio saw the soul as purely an animal phenomenon. Yet it took decades for such naturalistic convictions to seep into the mainstream of the natural philosophy of spirit, inspiring not only the empiricism of Gassendi, Bacon, and Hobbes but also, Michaela Boenke argues, the dualism of Descartes.[63]

Platonic speculation further underscored the connections between bodily spirit and the universe. Perhaps encouraged by Pico della Mirandola's (d. 1494) identification of all forms of spirit with divine spirit, Marsiglio Ficino's (d. 1499) theory of cosmic spirits linked the unifying celestial substance to breath, while he connected human flesh not to the terrestrial air and life-forms that use air, but to a substance in terrestrial minerals that also permeates the celestial

60 Bernardino Telesio, *De rerum natura* (Naples: Horatius Saluianus, 1586), 177–228. Bernardino Telesio, *Quod animal universum ab unica animae substantia gubernatur* in Bernardino Telesio, *Varii de naturalibus rebus libelli*, ed. Luigi De Franco (Florence: La Nuova Italia, 1981), 203–7 for the production of spirit in the brain. For an introduction to Telesio, Michaela Boenke, "Bernardino Telesio," *Stanford Encyclopedia of Philosophy*, http://plato.stanford.edu/entries/telesio/, accessed 26 June 2012. For a complete exposition, Michaela Boenke, *Körper, Spritus, Geist* (Munich: Wilhelm Fink, 2005), 120–70. Telesio based his system on the reduction of all matter to principles of warmth and cold generated by sun and earth (a concept he learned from Gerolamo Cardano, d. 1576). Spirit causes the warmth of living bodies, a point of very general agreement with medical tradition. Boenke, *Körper, Spiritus, Geist*, 128.

61 Telesio, *De rerum natura*, book v, chapter 1, 177.

62 Argenterio, *De somno*, 277–79.

63 Boenke, *Körper, Spritus, Geist*, 257–58.

spheres.[64] Apart from the boost this kind of thinking provided to alchemy and astrology, it also encouraged the well known quasi-medical theological speculations of an eclectic thinker like Jean Fernel.

Fernel, appointed professor of medicine at the university of Paris in 1534, developed what in Padua's famous faculty was later called "some more recent doctrine."[65] Nancy Siraisi might call it "counter-commentary," the work of a scholar breaking free of the Galenic commentary tradition.[66] Reacting to the materialistic interpretation of Galen by Nicolò Leoniceno, a contemporary humanist physician in Ferrara, he tried to synthesize Aristotle, Galen, Cicero, and, as he said, "all the philosophers and poets" on Platonic principles in his book *On the Hidden Causes of Things* (Paris 1548),

> The spirit of nature is what all the philosophers and poets celebrate, which Plato called the world soul and Galen called "the intellect drawn from higher bodies," which Aristotle, speaking about the world, more clearly expressed with this definition: "spirit is called a certain substance, animated and fertile, moving around both in plants and in animals and through everything." This, diffused and spread far and wide, contains everything, nourishes everything, conveying the vital spirit of the world and its own nature with it, getting under each and every thing and making it alive. Concerning this, the prince of Latin philosophy, Cicero, considering the order and constancy of things, most wisely said, "all the parts of the world could not be harmonious unless they were contained by one divine and continuous spirit." In these few words, the spirit, both present and divine, of Greek philosophers is comprehended for us to copy.[67]

And so spirit, "the vector and seat of the soul and all the faculties" (*animi omniumque facultatum vector propriaque sedes*),[68] is the foundation of the soul (such that the soul is immediate to the body), is the heat of the body and a vestige in the body of a supra-elementary fire, is an embodied ether, and is divine.[69] It exercises,

---

64 Marsilio Ficino, *The Books on Life*, iii.3–6 (ed. and trans. Carol V. Kaske and John R. Clarkj; Binghamton: Center for Medieval and Early Renaissance Studies, 1989), 255–75.

65 So said Allessandro Massaria at Padua in 1587. Nancy Siraisi, "Giovanni Argenterio and Sixteenth-Century Medical Innovation: Between Princely Patronage and Academic Controversy," *Osiris* 2nd series, 6 (1990): 161–80, here 161.

66 Hiro Hirai, "Alter Galenus: Jean Fernel et son interprétation platonico-chrétienne de Galien," *Early Science and Medicine* 10 (2005): 1–35, here 32–33. Siraisi, "Giovanni Argenterio," 172.

67 Jean Fernel, *De abditis*, II.vii.107, quoted in Hirai, "Alter Galenus," 23–24 n. 52. My English translation of the Latin differs slightly from his French.

68 Fernel, *De abditis*, II.vii.107. Hirai, "Alter Galenus," 24 n. 54, who also notes a parallel of this idea in Ficino.

69 Hirai, "Alter Galenus," 25–28. On the association of pneuma with divine ether, see also Aristotle, *De generatione animalium* ii.3, 736b29–737a1. They are distinct but similar elements in Aristotle. Salatowsky, *De Anima*, 108–9. This ether has nothing to do with the modern "ether"

explains Hiro Hirai, a "trans-natural," divine function in the exercise of vegetative power (procreation, nutrition and growth), animal power (mobility and sensation), and rational power (intellect and will).[70]

These doctrines of Fernel were somewhat eccentric, but in the face of a mid-century learned consensus over spirit, with its evident interest in unifying cosmic and organic realms, so too was Telesio's naturalistic doctrine. Fernel, in the 1530's, articulated his version of a general conviction of the existence of a physical continuum between nature and the divine. Tellingly, on the *existence* of bodily spirit, both the Platonizer and the materialist agreed.

3 Dualism

If a conviction of continuity between God and animal nature was commonplace among scholars in the 1530's and tacit to their "spirituality" (of course, this continuity was held to be strongest between the rational God and rational, God-like animals, that is, human beings), one might expect most of them to have rejected strong dualisms between body and spirit, and they did. The two best known dualists of the 1530's and 1540's were Germans and intellectual outsiders, the lapsed priest Sebastian Franck and the Silesian count Caspar Schwenckfeld. They were heretics by papal standards on the usual Protestant counts, but the Protestant Schmalkald League also condemned them as "spiritualists" in the spring of 1540, concluding a ten-year campaign by Martin Bucer of Strasbourg, Martin Frecht, the Ulm preacher, and Wittenberg's Philip Melanchthon against them. Their influence, scattered in a few tentative enclaves, inspired later dualisms at the end of the century and in the next, propogated, for example, in the writings of the shoemaker-philosopher Jakob Boehme, the German mystics Valentin Weigel and Johann Arndt, Dutch Familists, and English Antinomians.[71] But at mid-century their

(actually diethyl ether, a common anesthetic), the chemistry of which evolved out of the early modern production of an oleum vitrioli dulce (according to Valerius Cordus, died 1544) or spiritus vitrioli (Paracelsus, died 1541) in the reaction of sulphuric acid and ethyl alchohol (producing diethylsulfate). The name ether was applied to the result of a much improved chemical process in the early eighteenth century by F. Hoffman. See Claus Priesner, "Spiritus aethereus – Formation of Ether and Theories on Etherification from Vilerius Cordus to Alexander Williamson," *Ambix* 33 no. 2–3 (1986): 129–52.

70 Hirai, "Alter Galenus," 28–31.

71 J. Emmet McLaughlin, *Caspar Schwenckfeld Reluctant Radical: His Life to 1540* (New Haven: Yale, 1986), 200–224. J. Emmet McLaughlin, "Spiritualism: Schwenckfeld and Franck and their Early Modern Resonances," in *A Companion to Anabaptism and Spiritualism, 1521–1700* (Leiden: E.J. Brill, 2007), 119–61. Ulrich Bubenheimer, "Schwarzer Buchmarkt in Tübingen und Frankfurt:

audience lived strictly underground.[72] Both Franck and Schwenckfeld advocated an idea that they developed in the 1530's. Physical and spiritual realms, they said, are utterly distinct. The physical is external and a deceiving shadow of the internal and real. Both Protestants and Catholics, they said, were locked into an external deception. We live in "double worlds," said Franck, an external world of war and violence and an internal world of spiritual conflict.[73]

4 Michael Servetus and Philip Melanchthon

Spirit was more commonly seen as physical, even among theological writers unbound by conventional orthodoxies. Michael Servetus, whom Franck and Schwenkfeld encountered at Strasbourg in 1531 and who probably contributed to

---

Zur Rezeption nonkonformer Literatur in der Vorgeschichte des Pietismus," *Rottenburger Jahrbuch für Kirchengeschichte* 13 (1994): 149–63. Franz Michael Weber, *Kaspar Schwenckfeld und seine Anhänger in den freybergischen Herrschaften Justingen und Öpfingen* (Stuttgart: W. Kohlhammer, 1962). Donald Spaeth, *The Church in an Age of Danger: Parsons and Parishioners* (Cambridge University Press, 2000), 155–72. Maarten Roy Prak, *The Dutch Republic in the Seventeenth Century: the Golden Age* (trans. Diane Webb; Cambridge University Press, 2005), 210–21. Alistair Hamilton, *The Family of Love, I: Hendrik Niclaes* (Baden-Baden: Valentin Koerner, 2003). Jean Dietz Moss, *"Godded with God": Hendrik Niclaes and His Family of Love* (Philadelphia: American Philosophical Society, 1981), 22–69. David R. Como, *Blown by the Spirit: Puritanism and the Emergence of an Antinomian Underground in Pre-Civil-War England* (Stanford University Press, 2004), chapter 7. Alexandre Koyré, *Mystiques, spirituels, alchimistes: Schwenckfeld, Sébastien Franck, Weigel, Paracelse* (Paris: Gallimard, 1971). Patrick Hayden-Roy, *The Inner Word and the Outer World: A Biography of Sebastian Franck* (New York: Peter Lang, 1994), 168–71.

72 For the campaign against Franck, Alfred Hegler, ed., *Beiträge zur Geschichte der Mystik in der Reformationszeit, Archiv für Reformationsgeschicte, Texte und Untersuchungen*, Ergänzungsband 1, (Berlin: C. A. Schwetschke, 1906), 215–16; Patrick Hayden-Roy, "Sebastian Franck and the Reformation in Ulm: Heterodoxy, Tolerance and the Struggle for Reform," in *Beiträge zum 500. Geburtstag von Sebastian Franck (1499–1542)* (ed. Siegfried Wollgast; Berlin: Weidler, 1999), 127–58; Marc Venard, "Les formes personnelles de la vie religieuse," *Histoire du christianisme*, 8:991–1028, here 1014–18. For Schwenckfeld, McLaughlin, *Caspar Schwenckfeld*, 221–22.

73 Sebastian Franck, *Chronica zeitbuch und Geschichtbibell von angebyn bis in dis gegenwertig MDXXXVI. iar verlengt* (n pl: n pub, 1536)= British Library 9007 I 3 vol. 2, third part (Ketzerchronik), *Die drit Chronica der Bapst unnd Geystlichen Ha[e]ndel von Petro biß auf Clementem den sibenden, des glaubens und allerley geystlichen, Ka[e]tzereyen, o[e]rden Concilien und Ba[e]psten, betreffende*, On the "doppel welt": [Aa ii(v)-Aa iii] "Nunbey diser meyscherischen hinderlistigen doppel welt, ho[e]ret man nitt vil von kriegen, mo[e]rden (dann yhn gezimpt niemand zu[e]to[e]dten) rauben, etc. sunder diß geschieht als geystlich, innerlich verschlagen mitt der seel, wie die eüsserlich welt mit dem leißlichen schwert offenlich wider den lieb ist gericht. Souil gefa[e]rer ist nun dise geystliche doppel welt dann ihene, wiewil heimischer."

their views of the distinction between physical and spiritual realms,[74] studied medicine with Johannes Winter von Andernach, an attentive reader of Galen who ranked Servetus second to his other best student and assistant in dissections, the more famous Andreas Vesalius.[75] Servetus was the semi-anonymous, infamous author of anti-Trinitarian books, whom John Calvin (through Guillaume de Trye) betrayed to the general inquisitor of Lyons in 1552,[76] where he was jailed, where he escaped, and from which he fled for Italy by way of Geneva, there to be captured, tried, and executed in 1553. By then he had spent more than two decades hoping to understand what Jerome Friedman has called a "diminishing continuum," a continuum that regresses from divine nature to the world.[77] He was also a biblical humanist and a physician. He began to study the bible while he learned to work philologically as a law student at Toulouse, the way Calvin had learned to study texts philologically as a law student at Orléans and Bourges.[78] In his final book, written shortly before his downfall, he tried to reconcile medical and theological sensibilities, saying that the Holy Spirit enters the body through the nostrils, is conveyed by the lungs to the heart (for which he correctly alleged pulmonary circulation of blood), and ignites the spirit-vapour that fuels corporeal motion.[79] Servetus, ever the humanist, embedded this claim within a prolonged historical and exegetical discussion of spirit in Hebrew, Greek, and Persian antiquity and in a biblical theology of Christ's person. There was, to him, no apparent tension between spirit considered in the rhetorical-biblical or the medical manner, no absolute differentiation of spirit and nature. As in the general consensus, spirit was to him a physical entity bridging internal and external realms, establishing their continuity. This was not merely an idea but a particular way of deploying humanistic practice.

It is strange to find Philip Melanchthon *mutatis mutandis* sharing this conviction in his *De anima* commentary of 1553, the year of Servetus' condemnation.

---

74 McLaughlin linked Schwenckfeld's dualism to Servetus' Christology. McLaughlin, *Caspar Schwenckfeld*, 213–14.

75 Earl Morse Wilbur, *The Two Treatises of Servetus on the Trinity* (Cambridge: Harvard University Press, 1932), xxii. Joannes Guinterius Andernacus, *Anatomicarum institutionum ex Galeni, sententia libri IIII* (Basil: Robert Winter, 1539), preface, sig. a5 recto – a5 verso.

76 O'Malley, *Michael Servetus*, 9–14.

77 Jerome Friedman, *Michael Servetus: A Case Study in Total Heresy* (Geneva: Droz, 1978), 45–74.

78 Gordon, *John Calvin*, 18–29. Olivier Millet, *Calvin et la dynamique de la parole* (Geneva: Éditions Slatkine, 1992), 35–55.

79 O'Malley, *Michael Servetus*, 195–208. Michael Servetus, *The Restoration of Christianity* (trans. Christopher A. Hoffman and Marian Hillar; Lewiston: Edwin Mellon, 2006), 231–83.

After reviewing the role of bodily spirit in physical motion and emotion, Melanchthon marveled at the Holy Spirit in the body.[80]

> Of course, attentive students should ponder this wonderous work of God in a human being. By vital and animal spirit actions are principally executed: the conservation, nutrition, generation of life, then sensation, motion, cogitation, and feeling in the heart. Some say those vital and animal spirits or little flames are the soul. Galen says, concerning the soul of the human being, these spirits are the soul or the immediate tool of the soul. That is definitely true, and by their own light they outshine the light of the sun and all the stars. And what is more remarkable, divine Spirit himself mingles with these spirits in a human being, and it produces their stronger gleaming in divine light, so that there might be a brighter recognition of God and a more firm assent and more fiery passion toward God.
>
> On the other hand, where devils occupy hearts, the spirits in the heart and in the brain whirl about in their own turbulence, obstructing judgement, causing the furies that have been exposed, and pressing hearts and other body parts toward the fiercest motions, such that Medea should kill her newborns and Judas should kill himself.
>
> Therefore, let us regard our nature and rule it carefully and know to prepare our spirits to be homes of the Holy Spirit, and let us pray to the Son of God, that he drive the demons from us and transfuse divine spirit into our spirits.

Melanchthon knew there were questions about the distinction of soul and spirit ("these spirits are the soul or the immediate tool of the soul"), but these didn't

80 Philip Melanchthon, *Liber de anima* (1553), CR 13:88–89: "Iam cogitent studiosi hoc mirandum Dei opus in homine. Spiritu vitali et animali actiones praecipuae efficiuntur, vitae conservatio, nutritio, generatio, deinde sensus, motus, cogitatio, adfectus in eorde. Ideo aliqui dixerunt, animam esse hos spiritus seu flammulas vitales et animales. Galenus inquit de anima hominis, hos spiritus aut animam esse, aut immediatum instrumentum animae. Quod certe verum est, et sua luce superant solis et omnium stellarum lucem. Et, quod mirabilius est, his ipsis spiritibus in hominibus piis miscetur ipse divinus spiritus, et efficit magis fulgentes divina luce, ut agnitio Dei sit illustrior, et adsensio firmior, et motus sint ardentiores erga Deum. Econtra uhi diaholi occupant corda, suo adflatu turbant spiritus in corde et in cerebro, impediuut iudicia, et manifestos furores efficiunt, et impellunt corda et alia membra ad crudelissimos motus, ut. Medea interficit natos. Iudas sibi ipsi consciscit mortem. Aspiciamus igitur naturam nostram, et diligenter eam regamus, et sciamus, oportere spiritus nostros esse domicilium Spiritus sancti, et oremus filium Dei, ut ipse depellat a nobis diabolos, et spiritum divinum in nostros spiritus transfundat." Salatowsky stresses the distinction between physiological and psychological dimensions of this passage, the physiological referring to the production of human spirits and the psychological referring to the purification of the heart from evil affects. Salatowsky, *De Anima*, 116. Jürgen Helm, by contrast, stresses the synergy of divine and human spirits and sees here a "physiology of the effect of spirit." Helm, "Die 'spiritus' in der medizinischen Tradition," 236. Salatowsky, following Günter Frank, outlines the "substantial relationship between divine and human spirit" in Melanchthon's description of innate, pre-empirical knowledge, again stressing a "theologization" of epistemology. Salatowsky, *De Anima*, 121–22. Günter Frank, "Philipp Melanchthons Idee von der Unsterblichkeit der menschlichen Seele," *Theologie und Philosophie* 3 (1993): 349–67, here 363.

really matter. *Miscetur ipse divinus spiritus*, divine spirit itself mingles with spirits in a human being to his or her benefit: Melanchthon wanted his reader to think of human spirit as not merely analogous to divine spirit but substantially akin to it.

This spiritual realism enhanced Melanchthon's enthusiasm for nature's metaphors. Biology is full of useful allegories that confirm the God-nature continuum. While Melanchthon was finishing his second edition of the *Loci communes* in the early 1530's, he first turned to Aristotle's and Galen's writings on the soul. His subsequent *De anima* and natural-philosophical writings reflected the commonplace Aristotelian-Galenic hybrid. In them, he stressed the figuration of divine things in nature. The place of *spiritus* as a figuration of God in the human body appeared in the second edition of his *Loci communes* (1535), two years after the first evidence of Melanchthon's interest in *De temperamentis* and three years before adding a preface to the Lutheran humanist Joachim Camerarius' new Greek edition of Galen's works (Basel 1538).[81] Divine traces in the body illustrate how the church, through its discipline and ministry, nurtures the pious. So, for example, the process of coagulation and sorting in foetal gestation is a figure of the church, said Melanchthon, relishing the technical sound of Greek medical terms.

> The belly is like the church. Veins go into it all over, whose orifices, that they might embrace the foetus, are just like cotylidon polyps. A skin surrounds the foetus, which is called a chorion, which the cotylidons embrace, so that the foetus will be held in the uterus. And fibrils turn from the umbilical cord, arisen from the chorion to the orifices of veins, which draw blood from the veins, by which the foetus is fed. First the liver is made from coagulated blood, from a seed in the venal cavity of the liver comes next the heart from warmer blood, and vital spirit, and from a seed in the artery, thence from a most excellent part of seed, the brain and nerves, [and] from blood drawn, flesh. Because, therefore, the veins feed the foetus, they are an image of the ministry divinely ordained.[82]

81 Melancthon to Camerarius, Ep. 1145 (5 December 1533), CR 2:686–87, here 687. "Praefatio in Galenum ad Regem Galliae Franciscum," Ep. 1652 (13 February 1538), CR 3:489–95. Cf. Salatowsky, *De Anima*, 112–13.

82 CR 21:555–56. Alvus velut ecclesia est, venae undique in alvum deductae sunt, quarum orificia, ut amplecti foetum possint, sunt velut polypi cotylidones. Foetum autem pellicula curcumdat, quae χόριον vocatur, quam amplectuntur cotylidones, ut retineri foetus in utero possit. Et fibrae ex umbilico ortae per chorion ad venarum orificia tendunt,quae attrahunt sanguinem ex venis, quo foetus alitur. Ac primum quidem ex coagulato sanguine fit epar, et ex semine vena cava in epate, deinde cor ex calidiore sanguine, et spiritus vitalis, et ex semine arteriae, deinde ex praestantissima seminis parte cerebrum ac nervi, ex sanguine, qui attrahitur, caro. Cum igitur venae alant foetum, image sunt mininsterii divnitus ordinati.

It is possible, of course, for a body to be made of pure spirit, without bones and flesh, such as angels: *Substantia [angelorum] est spiritualis, quia vocat* [Heb 1:14] *eos spiritus. Discernit autem scriptura spiritus a corporibus, cum inquit: spiritus carnem et ossa non habet.*[83] Angels are not disembodied but have a particular kind of body. They are all fuel, bodies of pure fuel.

Melanchthon discussed the external sources of vital spirit in his *Initia doctrinae physicae*, first published in 1549. There, applying Aristotle's theory of physical change as a result of shifting proportions of qualities (he names heat, frigidity, humidity, dryness, condensation, thin texture, coagulation, liquefaction, hardness, and softness), he explained how heat and humidity transform food and air into the vital spirit that makes the body warm.[84] It is a process of bodily "cooking" (*coctio*) or digestion. The stomach boils food, where humid heat turns it into chyle and passes it on to the liver, where it is boiled and baked some more, reducing the chyle to a bloody mass, part of which is baked and converted into yellow bile, one of the four humors governing the body's health. Too much heat in the liver burns the substance and infects it with putrefying and poisonous discharges. These cause disease, such as scabies and leprosy. Through baking, some of the bloody mass is converted into bone matter.[85] The process begins before birth, with the "root moisture" (*humidum radicale*) in the "root component parts (*membris radicalibus*) of the foetus. It is a marvelous construction, Melanchthon thought, full of the marks of a divine creator.

> There is no other reason to seek for this than that divinity has so constructed the nature of animals, so that life be like a flame, thereupon taking food from the humid thing. As wax nurtures flames in a lamp, so heat, and vital spirit, which is the principle instrument of life and motion, takes food from that moisture. [...][86]

So the body feeds and refines food into fluids by God's design. Nature, in short, is a figure of the divine, because spirit fuels bodies.

The figure is based upon a *substantial* link between God and nature expressed in the human biology of vital spirit. This factum rooted moral pedagogy in nature. The *Initiae doctrinae physicae* (Wittenberg lectures of 1549) says,

83 CR 21:557.

84 CR 13:400–402.

85 CR 13:402–403.

86 CR 13:406: nominatur autem humidum radicale, quod per generationem et primam foetus formationem inest membris radicalibus, ut calor naturalis eo alatur et conservetur. Nec causa alia quaerenda est, nisi quia divinitus ita condita est natura animantium, ut vita similis sit flammae, subinde rapienti ex humido alimentum. Ut enim in lychno flamma alitur cera, sic calor, seu spiritus vitalis, qui praecipuum est vitae et motus instrumentum, rapit ex illo humido alimentum.

> Therefore heat or vital spirit, which is the work of God, is dominated by another spirit, namely the divine, and signifies that this concrete moral nature in the human being is ignited from the elements, that it might be made immortal. The nature of bodies and the causes of life and motions cannot be examined entirely, but there is no doubt that many shadows of eternal things are implanted in us. And God wants us to watch over the order established by him. Nature is snuffed out by immoderate heat or immoderate moisture. Just as the flame of a lamp is fed by the right amount of oil, when immoderate oil has been poured into it, it is extinguished. No other causes are to be sought, except that God so constructed nature, that active and passive things should come together in a certain way.[87]

His philosophy of the soul expresses the starting point of a moral philosophy, as Sachiko Kusukawa has said of the *De anima* commentary.[88] This belongs to a reworking of Aristotle through the lens of Galen within the framework of a Lutheran distinction of law and gospel: the commentary falls within the frame of law, not grace; nature, not revelation, Sachiko Kusukawa argues. But the analogy of natural spirit and moral nature is based upon a physical link between God and the human self as a body-soul composite, which impinges, therefore, on the powers of growth, physical movement, and reason, as well as all the psychic shifts that comprised human emotion.[89] God is spirit, and human beings are spiritual in a physical-moral sense.

In 1550, Melanchthon wrote an academic oration for Jacob Milichius on the anatomy of the heart, recited upon Milichius' promotion to the doctorate in medicine on 6 November 1550. In it, Melanchthon described "the parts and motions of the heart" in a typical arrangement of Galenic components and emphasized the structures associated with spirit.[90] The heart's thick, compact flesh (*disimilis carni in reliquo corpore, spissa et bene compacta*) is shaped in a flame-like pyramid, positioned in the center of the chest cavity, with its tip pointed to the left, ad-

---

87 CR 13:406–7: Dominatur ergo calor seu spiritus vitalis, qui est Dei opus, et significat, alio spiritu, divino scilicet, hanc mortalem naturam in homine concretam ex elementis accendi, ut fiat immortalis. Perspici penitus natura corporum, et causae vitae et motuum non possunt, sed umbras multas rerum aeternarum nohis inditas esse non est dubium. Et vult Deus nos tueri ordinem a se institutum. Extinguitur natura immodico calore et immodica humiditate, ut mediocri oleo alitur lychni flamma, immodico oleo infuso extinguitur. Nec alia causa quaerenda est, nisi quia Deus ita condidit naturam, ut conveniant agentia et patientia certo modo.

88 Sachiko Kusukawa, *The Transformation of Natural Philosophy* (Cambridge University Press, 1995), 75–123. Juan Luis Vives' *De anima et vita* also recognized the overlap between Galen's medical description of the passions and Aristotle's "psychological" one, trying, in effect, to coordinate Galen and Aristotle. Juan Luis Vives, *The Passions of the Soul: the Third Book of De anima et vita* (trans. Carlos G. Noreña; Lewiston: Edwin Mellen, 1990).

89 Kusukawa, *Transformation*, 100–101.

90 CR 11:947–54.

ding heat to that side of body, compensating for the heat feverishly produced on the right side by the liver.[91] The right cavity of the heart takes blood flowing into it from the vena cava, prepares and diverts it, with one part going to nourish the lungs (no pulmonary circulation here) and from another part extruding the thinner element into the left cavity, where it is converted into vital spirit. The arteries distribute this vital spirit throughout the body pulse by pulse, spreading heat and fueling the operation of the whole, while the heat generated by the production of vital spirit is cooled by the lungs through the pulmonary vein (*arteria venosa*), again, with every pulse.[92] The spirit produced in the heart is "the proximate instrument of the actions in the brain and nerves, and it drives the thought, sensation, and motion of what otherwise would be a life without sense, movement, and thought."[93] Pulse is one of the heart's two motions. The other is affect, "which follows thought and ignites notional ideas" (*qui cognitionem sequitur, et accenditur noticiis*).

> How this is done, whether the energy of the thrusting spirits be at the brain and at the heart, such that the various movements are driven, I cannot say, except that nature is so constructed that there should be agreement and [he digresses to Greek] sympathy between brain and heart. God wanted to shine beams of his own wisdom into our brain, and he wanted hearts to agree with these beams of wisdom, in a gladdening recognition of God, and he wanted to be present in our hearts as though on his own throne, to drench us with his light and joyfulness. We understand these things less, because the first harmony of brain and heart, which God created, has been disturbed. So now they argue that feelings commandeer knowledge, [feelings] such as anger, conflagrations of loves, happiness, hope, dread, in the way to be aroused, because the heart is struck by spirit dispatched from the brain. But there is an easier explanation, by those who say that the heart is the proper home of the substance of the soul. Yet we should be content with any explanation for the coupling of brain and heart, as long as the heart either desires or repells the things presented by cogitation ..."[94]

91 CR 11:949.

92 CR 11:949–52.

93 This is the second of three functions of the heart (the other two are to heat the body and to cause the affects, which is its principal function). CR 11:951: Secunda utilitas, quod spiritus geniti in corde, cum ostea cerebri vi temperantur, fiunt instrumenta proxima actionum in cerebro et in nervis, et cient cogitationem, sensum et motum, quid autem esset vita sine sensu, motu et coitatione.

94 CR 11:952: "Id vero quomodo fiat, aut quae vis sit cerebri et spirituum ferientium corda, ut tam varii motus cieantur, dicere non possum, nisi quia sic natura condita est, ut cerebri et cordis talis sit consensus et συμπάθεια. Voluit Deus lucere suae sapientiae radios in cerebro nostro, cum his et corda congruere voluit, laetantia agnitione Dei, et ipse adesse in cordibus nostris tanquam in sede sua voluit, et perfundere nos sua luce et laeticia. Haec minus intelligimus, quia prima cerebri et cordis harmonia, quam Deus condidit, turbata est. Nunc igitur ita disputant, adfectus comitantes noticiam, ut iram, incendia amorum, laeticiam, spem, metus, hoc modo excitari, quia cor feritur spiritu a cerebro misso. Sed facilior est explicatio iis qui dicunt, cor domicilium esse

Heart, in this text, is not a figure of speech but an organ. The distributor of bodily spirit, the heart, is God's throne in the body because its biology is the product of divine agency.[95] The study of biology proves this.

A final example of Melanchthon's natural spirituality comes from a speech in praise of the foundation of schools by the Saxon dukes (presumably, the editor speculates, the schools of Pforta and Meißen founded in 1543 and the school of Grimma founded in 1550 by dukes Heinrich the Pious and Moritz). In this speech there was an *argumentum a necessitate*: "As the coupling of veins and arteries in the human body is necessary, so is the conjoining of schools and churches. For as veins supplement the blood in arteries, by which the vital spirit is nourished, so the gardens of the church are watered by rivers of schools." The point may be further amplified by *antithesis*. "If in 30 years no one learns letters and piety, there would follow barbarity worthy of the Cyclops, a contempt of religion, ignorance of necessary learning, a total lack of discipline. Unending barbarity and confusion would follow everywhere."[96] Galen's neurology becomes a figure of the social body. Churches and schools quite literally nourish the spirit of society.

5 Martin Luther and John Calvin

Historians of religion in late medieval and early modern Europe have taught us to pay close attention to how indebted sixteenth-century anti-papal reformers were to late medieval mystical spiritualities, particularly in Germany and France; late medieval mystical concepts and theological debates expressed paradoxical atti-

---

proprium substantiae animae. Sed contenti simus hac qualicunque expositione, talem esse copulationem cerebri et cordis, ut corda vel appetant vel fugiant res oblata cognitatione ..."

95 The epistemology and the role of spirit in it is outlined by Salatowsky, as a modification of going Aristotelian doctrine of agent intellect, Melanchthon even expressing sympathy for Averroes' identification of agent intellect with God. Salatowsky, *De Anima*, 116–28, 125–26 for Melanchthon and Averroes.

96 *Supplementa Melanchthoniana. Werke Philipp Melanchthons die im Corpus Reforatorum vermisst Werden*, 2. Abteilung, Teil 1 (Leipzig: Rudolf Haupt, 1911), 166: "A necessitate: Quam necessaria est in corpore humano copulatio venarum et arteriarum, tam necessaria est coniunctio scholarum et ecclesiarum. Ut enim venae suppeditant arteriis sanguinem, quo alitur spiritus vitalis, ita hortuli ecclesiae rivulis scholarum irrigantur. Amplificatio sumitur ex antithesi: si intra annos triginta nemo disceret literas aut pietatem, sequeretur Cyclopica barbaries, contemtus religionis, ignoratio necessariae doctrinae, interitus disciplinae; denique infinita barbaries et confusio sequeretur." For the Cyclops as a figure of an uncivilized, religionless life, see Erasmus' *Adagia*, in Erasmus, *Opera omnia*, 10 vols. (Louvain: Vander, 1703–6, reprinted London: Gregg Press, 1962), 2:153A, 385F, 1132D, and Aristotle's *Nicomachean Ethics*, where (x.9, 1180a, lines 24–34).

tudes about spiritual reality and embodiment, producing, Carolyn Walker Bynum argues, "a crisis of confidence in Christian materiality."[97] Reformers also presupposed a general medical consensus about the physical nature of spirit. They presupposed a continuum of God and nature. But was there, among Reformation theologians, an *implicit* "functional differentiation" of natural and divine realms, human and divine spirit?

Martin Luther, no friend of natural-philosophical speculation in theology, at least after the Heidelberg Disputation of 1518,[98] after which he noisily avoided the vocabulary of Aristotle, Galen, or any other philosopher, could suggest such a functional differentiation. But he presupposed the common idea of vital spirit, for example, in his lectures on Genesis, which he delivered in Wittenberg from 1538 to 1542. When he explained Isaac's dream-vision in Genesis 26, he digressed to a discussion of sleeping visions and sleep. To Luther, sleepers were "senselesss" and "quasi-dead."[99] Yet in a dream, one does think and know, sometimes with tremendous insight. Luther described sleep as a state of peculiar acuity, caused by the restoration of vital spirit in the body while sleeping (*recte igitur dixerimus nos, dum dormimus et morimur, vivere maxime: quia spiritus vitalis tum maxime est efficax*).[100] More commonly, the restoration of vital spirit was attributed to the completion of digestion during sleep, and sleep was normally compared to epilepsy rather than death, yet Luther, in this late work, clearly presupposed a physiology of spirit.[101] However, as to the connection of vital spirit to God and the universe, Luther appears to have had nothing to say.[102]

---

97 Volker Leppin, "Transformationen spätmittelalterlicher Mystik bei Luther," in *Gottes Nähe unmittelbar erfahren*, (ed. Berndt Hamm and Volker Leppin; Tübingen: Mohr Siebeck, 2007), 165–85. Berndt Hamm, "Wie mystisch war der Glaube Luthers?," in *Gottes Nähe*, 237–87. Heather M. Vose, "More Light on Sixteenth-Century *Evangélisme*: A Study in Cross and Spirit," *Journal of Religious History* 14(1987): 256–67. Carolyn Walker Bynum, *Christian Materiality: An Essay on Religion in Late Medieval Europe* (New York: Zone, 2011), 269–73, 272 for the quotation.

98 Speaking of the Heidelberg Disputation, after a careful examination of Luther's somewhat free but genuine engagement with late medieval discussions of the soul, Theodor Dieter concludes, "Es ist höchst überraschend, Luther als einen Theologen kennenzulernen, der mit großer Intensität philosophische Probleme philosophisch erörtert." Theodor Dieter, *Der junge Luther und Aristoteles: Eine historisch-systematische Untersuchung zum Verhältnis von Theologie und Philosophie* (Berlin: De Gruyter, 2001), 627.

99 From Genesisvorlesung (1538/1542), WA 43:480, in the expostion of Ge. 26:24–25, and the term Elohim in 26:24: "Inspice homines raptos aut dormientes, de illis nemo potest dicere, quid sint, etiam cum dormiunt corporaliter. Sunt enim sine sensu et quasi mortui."

100 WA 43:480.

101 Karl Dannenfeldt, "Sleep: Theory and Practice in the Late Renaissance," *Journal of the History of Medicine and Allied Sciences* 41 (1986): 415–41.

102 I base this on a search of cognate terms for *spiritus vitalis* in *Luthers Werke im WWW*.

Calvin was another matter. In his first book, a commentary on Seneca's *De Clementia* of 1532, John Calvin displays a strong, rudimentary grasp of Galenic neuroanatomy.[103] It was occassioned by Seneca's description of the Roman Emperor Nero's position in the social body: the ruler is the head, his people are the body, and the people are utterly dependent on the head, serve him, would sacrifice anything for him. In fact, their "vital spirit" flows together to strengthen the ruler, Seneca said. Calvin commented upon the phrase *spiritus vitalis*. He recorded parallel uses of the ruler-social body figure in Quintus Curtius Rufus' *Life of Alexander the Great* and others, and he explained the figure's biological basis.[104]

> Vital spirit] It is another metaphor, by which it is signified that the people live and breath in their rulers, hang from the life of one as though by a thread ... Curtius in fact uses the metaphor more literally in the person of Philippus the physician to Alexander: my spirit always hung from you, but now, I swear, it is carried to your sacred and venerable mouth. And Erasmus imitated it in the panegyric of Philippus. This was taken up by the philosophers, who said that the life of a human being consists principally in it [vital spirit], that one breaths and receives air through the wind artery, which Celsus calls the wind pipe, and Lactantius

---

103 *De Clementia* (1532), chapter iv, CR 33:82 (= CO 5:82, and *De Clem.* 1.4.1).

104 John Calvin, *De Clementia* 1.4.1. Joannes Calvinus, *Opera quae supersunt omnia*, 59 vols. (Braunschweig: C.A. Schwetschke et Filius, 1863–1900) 5:82 (hereafter CO): Spiritus vitalis] Altera est metaphora, qua significatur in suis ducibus vivere ac spirare populos: ab unius vita quasi de filo pendere: sicut illa Lucani apostrophe ad Caesarem libro quinto: Quum tot in hac anima populorum vita salusque Pendeat, et tantus caput hoc sibi fecerit orbis. Curtius lib. IX. de Alexandro loquens: Toto eo die, et nocte quae sequuta est, armatus exercitus regiam obsedit, confessus omnes unius spiritu vivere. Verum Senecae metaphoram magis ad verbum expressit Curtius in persona Philippi medici ad Alexandrum: Rex, semper quidem spiritus meus ex te pependit: sed nunc vero, arbitror, sacro et venerabili ore tuo trahitur. Et imitatus est Erasmus in panegyrico Philippi. Porro hoc a philosophis sumptum est, qui vitam hominis in eo praecipue consistere affirmant, quod aerem hauriat et recipiat per asperam arteriam, quam Celsus asperam fistulam vocat, et Lactantius gurgulionem: et quae animae aestuantis, ut ait Gellius, iter est: de qua satis multa Cicero lib. IL de Natura deorum. Causam autem cur spirare necesse habeamus, vide apud Aristotelem, problematum sectione XXXIV, problemat. XII.: Quamobrem sunt qui opinantur vitam nihil aliud esse, quam spiritum, seu animam. Servius in illud Vergilii, Vitam exhalantem, secundum eos, inquit, loquutus est, qui vitam ventum volunt. Et idem in IV. commentar. Aeneidos quum Vergilius dixisset: Atque in ventos vita recessit, Eos, inquit, sequitur, qui vitam aerem esse dicunt. Verius tamen est ex quatuor elementis et divino spiritu constare omnia animalia. Cuius sententiae fuisse Aristotelem constat. Trahunt enim a terra carnem, ab aqua humorem, ab aere anhelitum, ab igne fervorem, a divino spiritu ingenium. Quamquam aliter astrologi: putant enim nos, quum nascimur, sortiri a Sole spiritum, a Luna corpus, a Marte sanguinem, [pag. 37] a Mercurio ingenium, a Iove desiderium, a Venere cupiditates, a Saturno humorem. Non abs re igitur spiritus dictus est a Seneca epitheto vitalis. Nam, ut ait Quintilianus lib. V., illud retrorsus valet, et spirare hominem qui vivit, et vivere qui spirat: ut spiritus pro vita, et spirans pro vivente interdum sine adiecto reperiantur, Eege incolumi] Haec duo hemistichia transtulit ...

> the gullet: and which is the passage of "the roiling soul," as Gellius says: about which enough is said by Cicero, book 49, *De natura deorum*. For why we must breath, see [Pseudo-]Aritstotle, *Problematum* section 34, problemat. 12: who are they who think life is nothing other than spirit and soul? Servius on that passage of Vergil, exhaling life, "according to them," he says, "it was said, those who lack wind lack life." And again in the Aeneid commentary iv, when Vergil said: "those," he says, "follow who say life is air." Yet it is true that all animals are constituted from four elements and divine spirit, which was consistent with Aristotle. For they [all animals] draw flesh from earth, humor from water, deep breath from air, heat from fire, and capacity [*ingenium*] from divine spirit. Although the astrologers have it otherwise. For they think that, when we are born, spirit exits from the sun, body from the moon, blood from Mars, capacity [*ingenium*] from Mercury, desire from Jove, cupidity from Venus, humor from Saturn. Therefore the spirit mentioned by Seneca by the epithet "vital" is not vital without the king. For as Quintillian says in book 5, "he returned" signifies that, and anyone lives to breathe and breathes to live, so that spirit is for life, ...

This tapestry of classical commentary testifies to hard work done, scouring ancient sources, all to establish the meaning of Seneca's metaphor. The point of it all is not biological but rhetorical, the interpretation of a verbal figure. Seneca's medical knowledge, or classical medical knowledge in general, sheds light on the anatomy of a historical metaphor of "vital spirit." Calvin followed this hermeneutical stratagem for the rest of his life, as one can observe on those other occasions when he wrote about vital spirit.

Of course, he presupposed a God-nature continuum. He could describe it in strong terms, *imo ne id quidem ipsum quod sumus aliud esse quam in uno Deo subsistentiam*: to be is to subsist in God.[105] "Wherever you cast your eyes," *quoquaversum oculos coniicias*, divine glory is seen, such that even the slightest denial of complete dependence on God and divine will, for example by setting the effect of a human choice above the providential divine agency, counts as nothing but temerity, which justly deserves unrelenting punishment forever.[106] Yet from early on he also perceived a barrier to stand between theological (or biblical) discourse and any other discourse about anything. This kind of differentiation, as a habit of thinking rather than idea as such, appears in the *Psychopannychia* (1534), his second book. There Calvin took on a recently published claim that the soul becomes temporarily inoperative at death, until the resurrection of the body. This mistaken idea, he claimed, is due to a confusion of *anima* and *spiritus*.

> The disagreement between us concerns the human soul. Some admit that it really exists, but think it sleeps, without memory, without understanding, without sensation, from death until the day of judgement, when it will be made to be aroused from its sleep. Others con-

105 John Calvin, *Institutes* (1559), 1.1.1. CO 2:31.
106 Calvin, *Institutes* (1539), 1.11. CO 1:286. Calvin, *Institutes* (1559), 1.5.1. CO 2:41–42.

> ceded that it is nothing less than a substance, but they say it is merely the energy (*vis*) of life, which is conducted by agitation of the lungs from spirit in artery, and because it cannot subsist without being affixed to a body, therefore it perishes and vanishes together with the body, until the entire human being is revived.[107]

Calvin then treated this as a textual problem. These opinions, he said, arise from confusion over biblical language, namely the failure to recognize the correct range of meanings attributed to "spirit" and "soul" in the bible. Reviewing a variety of biblical passages, he argued that both terms may refer to life or the condition of being alive, while spirit sometimes refers to the soul and sometimes has a narrower reference to intellect. By the same token, soul sometimes has a narrower reference to the will, and it can even refer to "the breath by which human beings breath, in which the motion of the vital body resides," a function more typically attributed to *spiritus*.[108] Both terms, therefore, comprise a scriptural figure signifying the immortal essence that causes human life, and both terms contrast the spiritual nature of a human being with the body as meat.[109] The remainder of the treatise argues the post-mortem consciousness of the soul from the rhetorical analysis of biblical examples.

Later in life, when prompted by a biblical text to address the biology of spirit, Calvin still restricted himself to knowledge derived from the rhetorical criticism of biblical literature. 1 Corinthians 15:44 says, "[the human body] is sown a physical body, it is raised a spiritual body. If there is a physical body, there is also a spiritual body." Calvin wrote,

> *It is sown an animal body*. Because [the apostle Paul] cannot express each part [of the body] one by one, the whole [body] is covered by one word, saying that what is an animal body now will be spiritual in the future. In turn, he calls the body molded from the soul (*anima*) animal (*animale*), and the body molded from the spirit (*spiritus*) spiritual (*spirituale*). Now the soul is what vivifies the body, lest it be a dead cadaver: that is why he uses the word [animal, a word derived from 'soul', *anima*]. After the resurrection that vivifying energy will be

---

107 CO 5:178: "De hominis ergo anima nobis certamen est, quam alii fatentur quidem esse aliquid: sed a morte, ad iudicii usque diem, quo e somno suo expergefiet, sine memoria, sine intelligentia, sine sensu dormire putant. Alii nihil minus quam substantiam esse concedunt: sed vim duntaxat vitae esse aiunt, quae ex spiritu arteriae, aut pulmonum agitatione ducitur: et quia sine corpore subiecto subsistere nequit, ideo una cum corpore interit et evanescit, 2) donec totus homo suscitetur."

108 CO 5:179: Nonunquam et flatum vocari, quo spirant ac respirant homines: in quo vitalis corporis motus residet.

109 CO 5:180: Verum quum utrumque plurimis locis essentiam immortalem, quae in homine vitae causae est, significet, non rixandi causas captent ex niminibus, sed rem ipsam percipiant, quocunque significetur nomine.

> more present, as it receives [this vivifying energy] from spirit. We must always remember what was seen beforehand [i.e. before the resurrection] is the unified substance of a body, and such a body here and now is driven by a 'quality'. The present quality of the body is called, by way of explanation, animation (*animatio*), and the future quality is called inspiration (*inspiratio*). For what now vivifies the body by the soul is done by many interposed props: we need drink, food, clothing, sleep, and other similar things; whence the infirmity of animation is exposed. The energy of spirit for vivifying will be much fuller, and free of any kind of necessity. This is the simple and natural mind of the apostle: lest someone philosophizing at greater length ramble in the air, as they do who think the substance of the body will be spiritual: here he makes no mention of substance, nor could there be any change of substance in the future.[110]

On the backdrop of a basically Galenic consensus over the physiology of *spiritus* Calvin's concluding dismissal of natural philosophy suggests the confidence he felt in knowledge derived from by a rhetorical method. In biblical discourse soul and spirit describe "qualities" of vivification. The presupposition, which we find, for example, in the last Latin edition of Calvin's *Institutes*, a handbook for the study of biblical literature, is that *anima* and *spiritus* are usually synonyms, and their distinctions are determined purely by context.[111] So here, the *anima* and *spiritus* are differentiated by the implication of the body and its dependence on the natural environment. A resurrected body is animated directly by *spiritus* and should therefore be called spiritual.

In another famous context of debate about spirit, Calvin exercises again a hermeneutical strategy that seems, functionally, to separate biological and theological explanation even while appealing to biology. In November 1548, in the exchange between Calvin and Bullinger on the sacraments, Calvin defended the

---

110 CO 49:557–58: *Seminatur corpus animale.* Quia singulas partes enumeratione exprimere non poterat, summam uno verbo complectitur, corpus nunc animale esse dicens, tunc futurum spirituale. Porro vocatur animale, quod ab anima: spirituale, quod a spiritu informatur. Nunc anima est quae corpus vivificat, ne sit mortuum cadaver: ergo ab ea iure denominationem sumit. Post resurrectionem vero praestantior erit vis illa vivifica, quam a spiritu accipiet. Semper autem meminerimus quod ante visum est, unam esse substantiam corporis: ac tantum hic agi de qualitate. Praesens corporis qualitas vocetur, docendi gratia, animatur, futura vocetur inspiratio. Nam quod anima nunc corpus vivificat, id fit multis adminiculis intercedentibus: indigemus enim potu, cibo, vestitu, somno, et aliis similibus: unde convincitur animationis infirmitas. Energia autem spiritus ad vivificandum multo erit plenior, ideoque exempta eiusmodi necessitatibus. Haec simplex est ac genuina mens apostoli: ne quis longius philosophando, in aere vagetur. Quemadmodum faciunt qui substantiam corporis putant fore spiritualem: quum nulla hic fiat mentio substantiae, nec ulla futura sit eius mutatio.

111 Calvin, *Institutes* (1559) 1.15.2. CO 2:135–36. Cf. also his commentary on 1 Thess. 5:23, *et integer spiritus.* CO 52:178–79. Richard Muller, *The Unaccommodated Calvin: Studies in the Foundation of a Theological Tradition* (Oxford: Oxford University Press, 2000), 21–38.

idea that Christ is really present in the eucharist "spiritually." Responding to Bullinger, who said, "we do not transfer the power or office of the Holy Spirit to the sacraments," Calvin opted for a stronger union between divine agent and physical medium:[112]

> The power and office of the Holy Spirit is to unite us to Christ, to make us participants of Christ and of all the heavenly gifts. Note that passage of the apostle, "and through this we know that he remains in us, from the Spirit he gave to us" (1 Jn. 3:24). And again, "From this we know that we remain in him and he in us, since he gave from his Spirit to us (Jn. 4:13). This vital spirit is that juice which is transferred from the vine into the branches and makes them fertile. If you do not recognize the virtue and office of the Holy Spirit, how can you say that through the 'perception' of the sacraments, it is effected that Christ dwell in us, and we in Christ, and by that reason we enjoy all the good things of Christ?

Calvin's appeal to a living body's spirit-fuel or "juice" serves to ground his description of the Holy Spirit's activity, with no necessary implication of *physical* kinship between bio-spirit and divine spirit. Rather, his point was to emphasize the instrumentality of sacraments in the activity of Holy Spirit. Calvin added a notation on this point:[113]

> I acknowledge the office of the Spirit to be to make us participants in Christ and all his good things. But it's least absurd [to say] that, because he works in us by his own power, he may work through sacraments no less, as instruments. The Holy Spirit is the σφραγίς [seal] which sets as a seal the promises of God on our hearts. Paul attributes the same title to circumcision (Rom 4:11), without removing Spirit. For the things which are subordinated do not contradict. The Spirit is the author. The sacrament is the instrument that he uses.

112 CO7:693–94: [Bullinger] II. Ad sacramenta non transferimus spiritus sancti virtutem aut officium. [Calvin] Virtus et officium spiritus sancti est coniungere nos Christo, participes nos facere Christi et omnium donorum coelestium. Nota enim est illa Apostoli sententia: Et per hoc scimus quod manet in nobis, e spiritu quem dedit nobis (1 Ioann. 3:24). Et iterum: Ex hoc cognoscimus quod in eo manemus, et ipse in nobis, quoniam de spiritu suo dedit nobis (ib. 4:13). Hic spiritus vitalis ille succus est qui e vite in palmites transfunditur et frugiferos reddit Quod si sacramentis non tribuitis virtutem et officium spiritus sancti, quomodo dicitis perceptione sacramentorum effici ut Christus in nobis habitet, et nos in Christo, et ea ratione universis Christi bonis fruamur?

113 CO 7:701–2: Officium spiritus esse fateor, Christi et omnium eius bonorum nos facere participes. Sed minime absurdum est, ut, quod propria virtute in nobis efficit, per sacramenta quoque, velut instrumenta, efficiat. Spiritus sanctus est σφραγίς quae Dei promissiones in cordibus nostris obsignat. Eundem titulum Paulus circumcisioni tribuit (Rom. 4, 11), neque tamen quidquam spiritui derogat. Nam quae subordinantur non pugnant. Spiritus autor est, sacramentum vero instrumentum quo utitur.

Bullinger's reply to this was brief, emphasizing his preferred diction:[114]

> The proper office of the Spirit is to make us participants in all the good things of Christ. We do not attribute this office to the sacraments, except by sacramentary reason and by the manner proper to sacraments. For God properly and truly exhibets his gifts to us through the Holy Spirit. He offers the sacraments themselves to us sacramentally, to the end that they represent and seal.

Although Bullinger placed more distance between the Holy Spirit and the physical signs of the sacrament, both he and Calvin agreed that the agency of divine Spirit makes something spiritual. This much could be agreed within a universe of biblical discourse, which in itself may suggest an incidental fissure of religious and natural-philosophical thinking communicated unintentionally by these two preachers. Near the end of his life, in his response to the Heidelberg theologian Tileman Heshusius (1561), borrowing a definition made by Jan Łaski, better known as John Lasco, five years before, Calvin said this about the communication of the body and blood of Christ in the eucharist:

> Our definition is, the body of Christ is eaten because it is spiritual food for the soul. Again it is called food for us in this sense: because by an incomprehensible energy of spirit he breaths into us his life, so that he might be shared with us, no less than the vital juice spreads itself from the roots of a tree into the branches, or the vigor flows from the head into every limb. In this definition there is nothing deceptive, nothing obscure, nothing ambiguous or equivocal.[115]

Vital spirit is analogous to, not an explanation of, the spirituality of the sacrament. But to call the presence of Christ spiritual in the sixteenth century was nevertheless likely to be understood as a physical claim.

In 1558, Calvin explained a passage in the Minor Prophets, Hos 10:8, where the people are condemned for idolatry. He relied on a biblical vocabulary to fix

---

114 CO 7:709–10, Bullinger's response to Calvin's notation: II. Proprium officium spiritus est omnium bonorum Christi nos facere participes. Sacramentis hoc ipsum non tribuimus, nisi ratione sacramentaria et modo sacramentis proprio. Deus enim proprie et revera per spiritum suum dona sua nobis exhibet. Sacramenta eadem nobis offerunt sacramentaliter, adeoque repraesentant et obsignant.

115 CO 9:519: Nostra autem definitio est, corpus Christi comedi, quia spirituale est animae alimentum. Rursus alimentum a nobis vocatur hoc sensu, quia incomprehensibili spiritus virtute nobis vitam suam inspirat, ut sit nobis communis, non secus atque a radice arboris vitalis succus in ramos se diffundit, vel a capite in singula membra manat vigor. In hac definitione nihil captiosum, nihil obscurum, nihil ambiguum vel flexiloquum. For the same definition in a Lasco's *Declaratio de Coena*, a brief he prepared for his colloquy with the Lutheran Johannes Brenz in 1556, CO 16:152 no. 2459.

the meaning of terms. The prophet says that thorns and thistle should grow over the altars of idolaters. According to Calvin, the condemnation applies to the idolaters' entire manner of life, infected as it is by their humanly invented forms of worship and their failure to confine themselves to the temple worship ordained by God. According to Hos 10:8, "they will say to the mountains, fall on us, and to the hills, cover us." Calvin explains:[116]

> This is a sign of ultimate desperation, when people should freely seek the abyss, plunged into which they drive away the sight of God, where God's presence has been annihilated. And therefore Christ referred to this passage as ultimate destruction, about which he declared, "they will say this to the mountains, cover us, and to the hills, fall over us" [Matt 17:20, Mark 11:23]: that is, again will it be fulfilled what was once said by the prophet, that namely the reprobate people should prefer a hundred deaths to one life, because light and vital spirit will be odious and despicable to them, because they know the horrible hand of God is upon them.

Vital spirit means nothing more here than being alive. Elsewhere Calvin defines the Hebrew נפש ("soul") as being alive, "although we translate it as soul, it means nothing other than vital spirit to the Hebrews, and life itself."[117]

Literary knowledge displaced natural philosophy in Calvin's theological imagination. This allowed him to describe spirit without expounding Renaissance medicine. How should we evaluate the importance of this practice in the context of the controversy over traditional religion, the Reformation?

---

116 CR 70:217: His loquendi formulis propheta exprimere voluit horribilem Dei vindictam: ac si diceret, tam gravem fore cladem, quae iam instabat, ut satius esset centies perire, quam illo modo esse superstites. Quum enim dicunt collibus, cadite super nos, et montibus, tegite nos, certe appetunt interitum dictu horribilem. Sed perinde est ac si diceret propheta, vitam illis, et hanc lucem, et conspectum solis, et communem spiritum fore horrori, quia sentient manum Dei sibi adversam. Denique hoc signum est ultimae desperationis, quam homines libenter quaererent abyssos, in quibus demersi fugerent Dei conspectum, et interitum praesentem. Et ideo etiam Christus transtulit locum hunc ad ultimam cladem, de qua concionatur, Dicent hoc montibus, operite nos, et collibus, cadite super nos: hoc est, iterum tunc implebitur quod semel dictum fuit a propheta, ut scilicet reprobi homines praeferant centum mortes uni vitae, quia et lux et spiritus vitalis illis erunt odio et detestationi, propterea quod sentient instare sibi horribilem Dei manum.
117 On Ps 16:10 (he began the Pss lectures in 1552), "because you will not abandon my soul in the grave," CO 31:157: נפש autem, licet latine anima vertamus, Hebraeis tamen nihil aliud est quam vitalis spiritus, vel ipsa vita.

6 Conclusion

We should evaluate a practical, functional differentiation of theology from medicine on the backdrop of a consensus about the continuity between living, expressive, passionate, socialized bodies and the being of God. The basis of this conviction of divine-animal continuity, the entity that made such continuity an essential component of interpersonal judgements, was spirit, the physical thing described in authoritative medical literature and tested by physicians willing to improve Galen's physiology. The physiology of spirit was assimilated by polymath theologians such as Michael Servetus and Philip Melanchthon and presupposed by most if not all learned people. Physiological debates and natural-philosophical concepts of spirit belonged to the background noise of the literate environment that eventually gave enduring political and social shapes to reform programs of the 1530's. The general consensus over the physicality of spirit suggests how strong the interface betweeen natural philosophy, medicine, and theology remained in this crucial phase of the religious controversy. A functional separation of theological and natural reasoning among some, such as Luther or Calvin, or their ideological separation by Franck and Schwenckfeld, points us to the ambivalent position of the Reformation in European cultural change, a position evident in the peculiar "spirituality" I am trying to describe here.

Seen retrospectively, from the vantage of the mid-seventeeth century and the biological reordering to follow, the strongest challenges to medical consensus and the most reluctant users of natural philosophy in theology loom large.[118] Francis Bacon (d. 1626) said it was time to study spirit empirically,

> one must ask of every body how much spirit there is in it, and how much tangible essence; and of the spirit itself ask whether it is abundant and swelling, or weak and sparse; thinner or denser; tending to air or fire; sharp or sluggish; feeble or robust; advancing or retreating; broken or continuous; at home or at odds with the surrounding environment, etc.[119]

And so they would: Boyle, Mayow, Willis, and others searched for a chemical spirit in blood and dispensed with the idea of some transcorporeal sub-

---

118 For the mid-seventeenth century as the end point of humanistic medicine, Nancy Siraisi, *History, Medicine, and the Traditions of Renaissance Learning* (Ann Arbor: University of Michigan, 2007), 263.

119 Francis Bacon, *Novum organum*, ii.7 (first published 1520, ed. Lisa Jardin and Michael Silverthorne; Cambridge: Cambridge University Press, 2000), 108. See also Bacon, *Novum organum*, ii.40, 173–74.

stance.[120] Bioelectricity, discovered by Luigi Galvani at the end of the 18th century, would eventually replace bodily spirit altogether, while spirit became a non-physical quality, attached to the soul's "spirituality," "personality," and "intellectual substance"; although, when it did, there were others who still insisted on the reality of an unseen world.[121] No one could have imagined Cartesian, Kantian, or Romantic conundrums in the Reformation. Looking backward, Calvin's studious avoidance of natural philosophy, his exploration of spirit purely in a context of a religious-literary source, might seem prescient, compatible with a kind of poetics of spirit and modern "functional differentiations" separating religious from medical ways of thinking and talking. Yet in his generation, he could only have been understood as Melanchthon or even Servetus were, on the backdrop of a medical consensus which said that spirit is the fuel of bodies and somehow akin to ghosts, angels, and God.

If I am right, there is much more to do than can be done in an exploratory essay such as this. Spirit belonged both to "an order of bodies" and "an order of communication," two crucial spheres of social construction in a "society of presence."[122] Put another way, it was a fundamental component of the "social stock of knowledge" and the "communicative budget" of early modern society, while theological debates may be seen within narrower "communicative genres" restricted to certain contexts of interaction.[123] It requires ethnolinguistic study. Those contexts also included formal debates between theologians, such as debates over corporeal versus spiritual presence in the eucharist. In the light of the character of spirit in the social stock of knowledge in the 1530's and 1540's, eucharistic debates may have involved, not physical versus semi and non-physical alternatives, but competing forms of *physical* presence – and alternative methods

---

120 Antonio Clericuzio, "The Internal Laboratory: The Chemical Reinterpretation of Medical Spirits in England (1650–1680)," in *Alchemy and Chemistry in the Sixteenth and Seventeenth Centuries* (ed. Piyo Rattansi; Dordrecht: Kluwer, 1994), 51–84, here 72.

121 Kant, *Critique of Pure Reason*, A:342–43, B:405–6; Müller, trans., 250. "In all his occult writings – particularly in *The Political history of the Devil, as well Ancient as Modern* (1726), *A System of Magick, or a History of the Black Art* (1726), and in the *Essay on the History and Reality of Apparitions* (1727) – Defoe, like Meric Casaubon, Henry More, and Joseph Glanvill in the previous century, was striving in an age of sensuous epistemology to reestablish the reality of an unseen world. This serious concern of writers on apparitions became increasingly urgent after about 1660, for waning of belief in witchcrft removed the most striking manifestation of man's immortality." Rodney M. Baine, "Daniel Defoe and 'The History and Reality of Apparitions,'" *Proceedings of the American Philosophical Society* 106 (1962): 335–47, here 335.

122 Schlögl, *Die Stadt in der europäischen Vormoderne*, 11.

123 Thomas Luckmann, "Prolegommena to a Social Theory of Communicative Genres," *Slovene Studies* 11 (1989): 159–66.

and social aptitudes to detect them. Future research in this direction could shed light on the coincidence of arguments about the eucharist and social discipline in this crucial period, the 1530's and 1540's, since the eucharist was not merely a matter of ritual and its mythical framework, but also of the distribution of divine substance, while discipline involved the observation of its effects on living human flesh.

Consider a final example from the German-speaking lands, where the religious controversy began. The most cataclysmic, large-scale "Reformation" in Martin Luther's lifetime occurred in the duchy of Württemberg in 1534–1535, when Duke Ulrich, removed from the duchy by the Swabian League in 1519, returned as a Protestant and, with the help of the Landgrave of Hesse and with support from the French king, drove out the Austrian Habsburgs, to whom the Emperor Charles V had given the duchy. Then, in a mere two years, Duke Ulrich confiscated virtually all the church lands and other properties in his territory, including whatever liturgical gear his officers could gather. He drove out priests, monks, and nuns, and he imposed a Lutheran church order.[124]

The documents recording Duke Ulrich's secularization of cloisters in the state archive in Stuttgart include charters, registers, memoranda, briefs from Ulrich's court, and a note written in Early High German by an anonymous eyewitness. The eyewitness tells us that on the feast of Candlemas (2 February) 1535, in the Church of the Holy Cross,

> Duke Ulrich did away with the mass, but before that, three offices were sung. Many people were in the church, and many lamps and candles were burning, and the people wept and there was a great offering of devotion. And then all the priests beneficed by his royal majesty [Ferdinand] or his government were demanded of their benefices, [that they] should renounce [them] and so [let them] fall to [Ulrich's] hands. And then they must all leave the land, but it has not yet happened.[125]

124 Christopher Ocker, *Church Robbers and Reformers in Germany, 1525–1547* (Leiden: E.J. Brill, 2006), 90–94. Werner-Ulrich Deetjen, *Studien zur Württembergischen Kirchenordnung Herzog Ulrichs 1534–1550* (Stuttgart: Calwer Verlag, 1981), passim.

125 Stuttgart, Baden-Württembergisches Hauptstaatsarchiv, A 63 Bü 4 (the entire text): "Herzog Ulrich hat auff nechst zÿnstag zue studgarten die mess hinweg thon unnd hat man vorhin dreie ampter gesungen unnd vil volckss in der kierchen gewesen unnd vil liechter und kerzen gebrannt unnd das volck her gewaynet unnd ayn gross opffer gewesen. Unnd darbeÿ allen priestern so von kun.[r] mt. oder der regierung belechent seynd irer pfruonden mitkomt und sullt abkündt unnd zuo seynen handen genomen. Unnd ist die sag sy muossen all auss dem land. Ist aber noch nit geschehen." I am grateful to Judith Bolsinger of the Hauptstaatsarchiv for providing me with a copy of the document. See also Oliver Auge, *Stiftsbiographien: Die Kleriker des Stuttgarter Heilig-Kreuz-Stifts (1250–1552)* (Leinfelden-Echterdingen: DRW-Verlag, 2002), 97 and

Duke Ulrich's ancestors were buried here, and the church's chapter, long occupied by the ruling family's relatives and friends, had always been conspicuous at court – in its ritual life, in culture more broadly, and in official deputations.[126] The canons now staged a final outpouring of Catholic devotion, on a major feast, one of four principal celebrations of the Blessed Virgin spread across the seasons of the year: candlemas completed the Christmas cycle by commemorating Mary's purification in the temple and Christ's presentation there. The people were to feel a wintery longing for Spring, as St. Simeon longed for the new dispensation in the New Testament, in a passage associated with this feast, where he takes up the Christchild and sings about the transition from the tedious age of expectation to the rebirth of promise and joy.[127] A redemptive, penitential sorrow was prescribed for this day, and happiness.[128] When people entered church, they were to chant Simeon's story, feeling privileged to own the divine mercy promised by Jewish prophets and saying, "we receive your mercy, O God," as candles were distributed.[129] Here, in the Church of the Holy Cross, the people wept, which involved, medically speaking, an extrusion of humors heated by the body's produc-

Gustav Bossert, *Zur Geschichte Stuttgarts in der ersten Hälfte des sechzehnten Jahrhunderts* (Württembergische Jahrbücher für Statistik und Landeskunde 1914), 138–81, 183–243, here 175.

126 For the foundation's role in *memoria* of members of the ruling house of Württemberg and in service at court, Auge, *Die Kleriker des Stuttgarter Heilig-Kreuz-Stifts*, 51–55, 167–207.

127 The *Nunc dimittis* (Luke 2:29–32), a staple canticle of the Divine Office, or numerous chants recounting the story of Simeon (Luke 2:25–35) were assigned for this feast and communicated this emotion. For a contemporary Benedictine example, *Analecta Hymnica medii Aevi*, 55 vols. (New York: Johnson Reprint Co., 1961, reprint of the edition of Leipzig, 1886–1922), 55:337–38 nr. 306. For the chants, Rene-Jean Hesbert, *Corpus antiphonalium officii* 6 vols. (Rome: Herder, 1963–79), 3:444 nr. 4639, 4:382 nr. 7537. A search for the *Nunc dimittis* restricted by the feast of the purification of Mary in the Cantus database (http://publish.uwo.ca/~cantus/) quickly demonstrates its ubiquity as antiphon, responsory, and versicle in the divine office for the feast.

128 The other three principal Marian Feasts were: Annunciation (25 March), Assumption (15 August), Nativity (3 September). Guillelmus Durandus, *Rationale officiorum divinorum (libri I–VIII)* VII.vii.2, 8–17; 3 vols., ed. A. Davril, T.M. Thibodeau, B.G. Guyot, *Corpus Christianorum Continuatio Mediaevalis* (hereafter CCCM), vols. 140, 140A, 140B, (Turnhout: Brepols, 1995–2000), 140B:35, 38–43, and Jacobus de Voragine, *The Golden Legend* 2 vols. (trans. William Granger Ryan; Princeton University Press, 1993), 1:148–151, for this and the following. A year before this, Martin Luther used the occasion of this feast to preach a macaronic sermon on baptism, the New Testament sacrament that 'fulfills' circumcision, defending infant baptism against the Anabaptists. Luther, WA 37:278–84. Sermons for the feast in 1538 and 1539 lacked this polemic and emphasized the characteristically Lutheran themes of original sin and forgiveness in Christ, against a backdrop of Mary's submission to the law, its prefigurement of the New Testament, and the intimacy of mother and child. WA 46:156–61; 47:659–66.

129 According to the influential *Rationale officiorum divinorum* of Durand, VII.vii.12, CCCM 140B:41.

tion of fire-like *spiritus*. Soon after, the church's affiliated officers (forty canons, vicars, chaplains, and priests) were reduced to two preachers and two deacons. Of the seventeen or eighteen altars honoring dozens of named saints, most were gone by summer.[130] Reformers gloated, and the liturgical challenges of such rapid change increased pressures among Swiss and German Protestants to confront sacramental disagreements, a debate not over the actuality of spiritual "presence" of Christ in the eucharist, but the manner in which it truly occurs and whether it is Christ's resurrected body or representative of it.[131] To be sure, embedded in the duchy's religious cataclysm, signalled by an anonymous author's handwritten note, were debates about sacraments, a technology of the Holy Spirit

130 Auge, *Stiftsbiographien*, 73–74, 76, 97. Most canons received some kind of pension from the duke, which means that they retained a relationship to the duchy and easily maintained a sense of entitlement to their former office in Stuttgart's church. Some stayed in the city. Some who moved away sued for damages or fought for better terms. See Auge, *Stiftsbiographien*, 399–401 nr. 191; 269–72 nr. 23; 454 nr. 248; 269 nr. 20; 557 nr. 329; 457–60 nr. 253; 484–84 nr. 282; 549–51 nr. 317; 445–46 nr. 237; 352 nr. 133; 368–69 nr. 149; 398 nr. 190; 303–7 nr. 53. Christoph Nollau, "Theologie in Zwiefalten zwischen 1540 und 1551," *Blätter für württembergische Kirchengeschichte* 90 (1990): 169–92. Only two of the church's vicars became evangelicals. Auge, *Stiftsbiographien*, 472 nr. 265; 554–55 nr. 325. A little over a decade later, under the Augsburg Interim, the old Catholic canons were asked to return. Most declined, but sued for incomes lost during Ulrich's reign. Auge, *Stiftsbiographien*, 554 nr. 324; 98–102.

131 For example the Tübingen theologian, Ambrosius Blaurer, the veteran reformer of southwest cities, in a letter to Heinrich Bullinger, who was supplying some of the duchy's new preachers from Zürich, "The Word of God races on and is gloried here!" (*hic currit et glorificatur sermo dei*), while in Stuttgart, Cannstatt, and Herrenberg "the papistic mass is already snuffed out" (*missa papistica prorsum extincta est*)! *Briefwechsel der Brüder Ambrosius und Thomas Blauerer 1509–1548*, 3 vols. (ed. Traugott Schieß; Freiburg: Friedrich Ernst Fehsenfeld, 1908–1912), 1:653–655 nr. 534 (15 February 1535). Pollutions had been purged – priestly vestments, the idolatrous elevation of host and cup – and the Church of the Holy Cross in Stuttgart resounded with Psalm-singing and a doxology at least sometimes performed in the German vernacular. *Briefwechsel der Brüder Ambrosius und Thomas Blauerer*, 1:654 nr. 534. Bucer had counseled Ambrosius Blaurer, in his earlier negotiations over rites, to make three points non-negotiable: ending intercessions of the Virgin Mary and the saints, the celebrant's wearing a simple choir robe in the vernacular mass, and no elevating the Eucharist in the ritual. The precendent had already been established, Bucer noted, in Schwäbisch Hall, Heilbronn, and Reutlingen. Ibid., 1:584–585 nr. 477. Consider also the territorial church order that was published in 1536 and probably written by Schnepf (and not followed by Blarer). Brecht, Ehmer, *Südwestdeutsche Reformationsgeschichte*, 225–27. For background to the Eucharistic controversy, Thomas Kaufmann, *Die Abendmahlstheologie der Strassburger Reformatoren bis 1528* (Tübingen: J.C.B. Mohr, 1992); for Luther's position at this time, *Glossae D. Martini Lutheri super sententias patrum de controversia coenae exhibitas ipsi a D. Philippo Melanchthone* (1534), WA 38:294–300. For this phase of Eucharistic controversy in general, Ernst F. Bizer, *Studien zur Geschichte des Abendmahlsstreits im 16. Jahrhunderts* (Darmstadt: Wissenschaftliche Buchgesellschaft, 1962), 65–130.

linked to confession-defining, theological arguments about priestly power and human redemption. Implicit to the record of tears was, of course, emotion, and with emotion, as everyone knew, came the physiology of spirit.

III Politics of Miracle Stories

Sharon V. Betcher

Disability and the Terror of the Miracle Tradition

The movie *Avatar* – with its multi-million dollar budget and computer-generated graphics – has become one of North American culture's most well known ecological myths. And embedded there, so expected as to be unremarkable and therefore unnoticed, sits yet again one of our culture's favored miracle stories – specifically, the remediation of disability to wholeness. Wheelchair-using Jake Sully – carried through an overtly imitative Christological passage from grave to pietà (on the lap of the Na'avi woman, Neytiri) – resurrects into wholeness by transmitting his consciousness into the hybrid Na'avi body.[1] Even as the movie overtly problematizes technology, miraculous remediation of disability makes the story work by delivering on the culturally assumed, Edenic promise of restoration to the garden and, implicitly, to somatic wholesomeness – in this case, the garden of Na'avi, of ideal, ecologically wise natives.[2] Disability works symbolically here: appearing so tangibly intractable, unsettling and, therefore, apparently unlivable, it must be – presumably, compassionately, sympathetically – remediated, overcome. This myth of ecological recuperation rides upon the stock feature of disablement, which always immediately signals cure as resolution – whether in terms of miraculous remediation (as depicted in *Avatar*) or, as in liberal humanitarianism, the transposition of miracle to conspicuous compassion.[3] Enlightenment incredulity has evidently not impeded the ways in which the miraculous re-

---

1 This appears to be a very Athanasian notion of hybridic wholeness, wherein the body is miraculously "resurrected" into an eternal realm (now nativist), which is "more real" than the finite world.

2 "The paradise themes of the gospels come into focus when we read the miracle stories ... through the lens of Genesis 1–2," observe Rebecca Ann Parker and Rita Nakashima Brock, though without troubling the notion of miracle or therefore paradisaical themes. See their *Saving Paradise: How Christianity Traded Love of This World for Crucifixion and Empire* (Boston: Beacon, 2008), 28.

3 "The novel as a form relies on cure as a narrative technique," observes Lennard Davis, suggesting how we have become habituated toimplicitly consume, and so metabolize this notion of disability as pathology to be remediated by cure. See his *Bending Over Backwards: Disability, Dismodernism and Other Difficult Positions* (New York: New York University Press, 2002), 98.

mediation of disablement continues to inform Western cultural horizons and morphological expectations. I suspect that means we will need equally to examine the role played by disability in relation to the miracle stories.

If, as I will come to argue, the miracle accounts of "the blind see, the deaf hear, the lame walk" (Isa 35:5–6, Luke 7:22, Matt 11:4–5), when worked through theological anthropology and postcolonial-disability analysis, serve rather as metonyms for resisting empire, we today will be challenged to read miracle stories in such a way as to reverse the assumed normalization of bodies, which makes them complicit with cultural horizons of labour and consumer value. In this era of biopolitics, when the command to be healthy is everywhere,[4] the populace at large has been trained in pathology analysis (for which "disability" serves as primer), finding in each of ourselves more and more imperfection – fatigue, stress, depression, manias, weight gain, or hearing loss, etc. – to be resolved through product supplementation – whether diuretics, remedies for impotency or indigestion, or mobility aids. "This late capitalist litany of bodily frailties, imperfections and incapacities gluts advertising networks … [so that] disability rapidly becomes synonymous with a humanity that we are all seeking to overcome."[5] In other words, continuing to circulate these stories as accounts of miraculous remediation, or even simply as "healing," contributes today to the scaling of the body for "empire," for globalizing capitalism, for making bodies complicit with consumer capitalism. A failure to identify our own sociocultural horizon overloads the interpretation of these texts in such a way that it conjoins us with an unwitting moralization implicit in neoliberal "responsibilization" policies.[6]

After establishing the relationship between miracle and disability in Western cultural narratives, I proceed towards this argument by way of considering the role of miracle stories within the most recent accounts of the Historical Jesus scholars, especially Marcus Borg and John Dominic Crossan. Following this brief exposé of liberal relations to the miracle tradition, exposing epistemological lenses related to the scaling of our own still most modern bodies, I undertake an anthropological consideration of "disability" – that condition which seems so obvious it remains unquestioned. While I will hint at ways in which a disability studies informed, postcolonial lens might explicate the miracle accounts, I will

4 Ian Buchanan, *Deleuzism: A Metacommentary* (Edinburgh: Edinburgh University Press, 2000), 110.

5 David T. Mitchell and Sharon L. Snyder, "Disability as Multitude: Re-Working Non-Productive Labor Power," *JLCDS* 4.2 (2010): 190–91.

6 Regarding neoliberal responsibilization of the self, see Nickolas Rose, *Governing the Soul: The Shaping of the Private Self* (2nd ed.; New York: Free Association Books, c1989/1999).

conclude by suggesting ways, given our despair at/of the world, we might today read miracle without being "contrary to nature" (Spinoza) and still amenable to the locus of the experience of disability.

Miraculous Remediation of Disablement as Cultural Prosthesis

Western Christian culture uses miraculous remediation of disability as its utopian horizon of health, of spiritual care, of its ideals of nature – as it has learned from the gospels and theological tradition. Since biblical theology's credulity in the miraculous has given way before the Enlightenment and resultant demythologization, science, medicine, and technology have assumed the rhetorical force of these supernatural miracles – for selling cochlear implants and sensate prostheses, for example. And just as *Avatar* did, ecological activist and theologian Cynthia Moe-Lobeda builds her critique of Christian response to globalization, i.e., *Healing a Broken World: Globalization and God* (2002), around a covertly embedded miracle story. Her book, neatly divided into Part I, which "explores … the disabling of moral agency," and Part II, which "explores … the enabling of moral agency by relationship with God indwelling creation," rides upon the miraculous healing of the paralytic to represent the remediation of Christianity's spiritual incapacity in the face of globalization.[7] She writes, echoing Jesus' command to the paralytic in Matt 9 and Mark 2, "The moral crisis … is the failure to get up and walk."[8] And again, "The purpose of all that I have said is … that we might rise up and walk away from compliance with economic violence …"[9] Unwittingly, Moe-Lobeda, as also *Avatar*, conflate their justifiable ecological and economic concerns with the desire for miraculous wholesomeness with which globalization, including its biotechnoscientific tributary, mobilizes itself.

This culturally broad and contemporary pattern recalls expectations reaching back as far in Christian thought as Irenaeus (2nd century) and Augustine (4th–5th century). Despite the gospels of Luke (ch. 24:38–9) and John (ch. 20) presenting Jesus' resurrected body as recognizably scarred from nails and spear, thus corporeally consistent with his somatic history, Christian theological tradition by

7 Cynthia Moe-Lobeda, *Healing a Broken World: Globalization and God* (Minneapolis: Fortress, 2002), 1.
8 Moe-Lobeda, *Healing a Broken World*, 4.
9 Moe-Lobeda, *Healing a Broken World*, 133.

the second century treated the resurrection of bodies as continuous with the interpretation of miraculous remediation: miracles on earth stood as promises of the remediation to wholeness at the resurrection as, inversely, the promised heavenly body served as photo negative in relation to the miraculous healing of disablements, even if disabled bodies had to wait until time beyond time. In the words of Pseudo-Justin, Irenaeus' predecessor, "'If on earth He healed the sicknesses of the flesh, and made the body whole, much more will He do this in the resurrection, so that the flesh shall rise perfect and entire.'"[10] Even as Pseudo-Justin's position could have worked socially to value disabled persons (Since all bodies rise glorious, why should one allow the ancient disgust with deformity to stand in the way of relationship here on earth?), disability was yoked with the corruptibility of the flesh – and, hence, to sin or "brokenness" – for which the only resolution in Christian thought was remediation to wholeness – again, either through miracle on earth or resurrection to perfectibility. Comparably, while "Irenaeus stands at the beginning of a highly materialistic western tradition, which locates personal identity in the body's materiality, ... disability ... is not a part of that identity," but signals rather "God's handiwork impaired by wickedness."[11] Likewise Augustine's confidence in heaven's perfectibility of the body allowed him to see the disabled body as a photo negative of the wonder-working power of God:

> The name "monster" evidently comes from *monstrare*, "to show" ... Now these signs are, apparently, contrary to nature ... For us, however, they have a message. These "monsters," "signs," "portents" and "prodigies" ... "show" us ... that God is to do what he prophesied that he would do with the bodies of the dead, with no difficulty to hinder him, no law of nature to debar him from so doing.[12]

As Christian theology in these centuries authorized the image of the perfect heavenly body, this contributes to "the systematic removal of disability from the Kingdom of God" on earth, allowing the Platonic valuation of symmetry and proportionality, these ancient notions of beauty, to overlay Christianity's materialist disposition and its social orientation to the difference of disablement.[13]

Because consequently disability has been "inherently understood as a problem in need of a solution," it can serve as what disabilities scholar David Mitchell calls a "narrative prosthesis." Variously said, disability serves as a metonym within literature that works effectively, even without articulation, to deliver a

10 Pseudo-Justin, cited in Candida Moss, "Heavenly Healing," *JAAR* 79.4 (2011): 1005.
11 Moss, "Heavenly Healing," 1008.
12 Augustine, *City of God* Book XXI, chapter 8, 982–83.
13 Moss, 995, 992.

story, especially a story for bringing chaoid, presumably recalcitrant matter/s under control, remediation, normalization.[14] This depreciation of variable morphology within implicated orders, set in a world of becoming, contributes still today to the West's wishful socio-cultural imaginary, even its biotechnoscientific agenda, promising the eradication of somatic variation, of difference, of asymmetry. Miracle stories – when the reader presumes them to be something like a "narrative prosthesis" – religiously sanction the way we metabolize redemption or hope as cure. Equally, though, these stories contribute to socially positing disability as deficient matter, as requiring remediation.

Miracle stories have, perhaps not surprisingly then, often been used by Christians to throw supposedly good wishes for an extreme makeover at disabled bodies – even likely, as in *Avatar*, with respect to the bodies we all fear as the blowback of ecological decimation. The summary refrain of the miracle tradition, i.e., "The blind see, the lame walk, the deaf hear," carried from Isa 35:5–6 to Matt 11:4–5 and Luke 7:22, became the drumbeat of Christian advent liturgies and hymns, setting the horizon of Christian expectation answered by Easter's resurrection of the body all glorious. But notice this: despite Christianity's decided materialism, observable already in the writings of Irenaeus, and its insistent attention to bodies, the difference of disability has been consistently "disappeared." Disabled bodies on pallets – whether carried before Jesus or, as now, into the medical theatre – are not allowed to speak up for ourselves, to interpret ourselves or to express our own needs. Ever and again the horizon of hope has been set for us, even as that horizon supersedes what we know of flesh and rains down upon persons living with disabilities a formulation of transcendence (social expectations hiding themselves within notions of "divine power") that, far from compassionate, proves punishing, moralizing, dismissive, judgmental. Because these stories performatively engender the objectification of persons living with disabilities, miracle stories constitute – for persons living with disabilities – "texts of terror."[15]

---

14 David T. Mitchell, "Narrative Prosthesis and the Materiality of Metaphor," in *Disability Studies: Enabling the Humanities* (eds. Sharon L. Snyder, Brenda Jo Brueggemann, and Rosemarie Garland-Thomson; New York: The Modern Language Association of America, 2002), 15. Mitchell explains that "the repair of deviance may involve an obliteration of the difference through a cure, the rescue of the despised object from social censure, the extermination of the deviant as a purification of the social body, or the revaluation of an alternative mode of experience" (20). One easily recognizes how liberal readings of miracle accounts have simply moved from "repair of deviance ... through cure" to "rescue ... from social censure," as I'll detail shortly. Disability appears completely naturalized for both of these and so cannot be revalued.

15 Phyllis Trible coined the term "texts of terror" to describe the rape of Tamar and the sacrifice of Jephthah's daughter in the Hebrew testament. See her book of this title, i.e., *Texts of Terror: Literary-Feminist Readings of Biblical Narratives* (Minneapolis: Fortress, 1984).

When preached as accounts of healing, the miracle stories marginalize persons living with disabilities because of the screaming incongruity between our lived experience of the body and what these stories seem, on the surface, both to see, i.e., deficiency (persons living with disabilities don't necessarily experience our bodies in this way), and to promise, i.e., the hope of miraculous remediation to normalcy – as if that were desired, even desirable, and as if flesh were so amenable. Further, miracle accounts performatively authorize a "Pick up your bed and walk" mentality that circulates in Western culture as the ethos of morality (notice the erect scaling of the body that has been coordinated with sound moral disposition) and intact economic resource, i.e., labour power. Even for feminist biblical interpreters the miracle stories hold promise of empowerment as wholesomeness – as, for example, "standing straight," no longer bent.[16] Understood through the lens of historical realism, these stories are incredible: they don't appreciate our experience of the limits and finitude, if equally the exquisite wonder, of the human body. Miracles as "metaphysical demonstrations," as philosophical theologian John Caputo puts it, "prove too much – they make light of the *tehom* and the *tohu wa-bohu*, the formless void, with which we must all cope."[17]

Even the more liberally modified accounts of miracle as healing or compassionate inclusion still include us by calibrating the difference of disablement as deficit, whereas for any number of us living with disabilities, these bodies are what they are: our exquisite chance of a lifetime. Put another way, liberal notions of compassionate inclusion have tended still to transcendentally leap over disabled persons, that desired "transcendence" apparently inflated by fear and resentment of pain. Simply then, there appears to be no way in which disabled bodies can ever participate in the theo-logic of a Christian community that circulates these texts as stories of miraculous remediation to normalcy – even where supernatural calibration has yielded to the realist notions of liberal healing and compassionate inclusion. Because those liberal readings appear to be our most "reasonable" accounts, especially in the broadly popular Historical Jesus materials, I turn now to explicate those.

---

16 Bernd Kollmann, "Images of Hope: Towards an Understanding of New Testament Miracle Stories," in *Wonders Never Cease: The Purpose of Narrating Miracle Stories in the New Testament and its Religious Environment* (eds. Michael Labahn and Bert Jan Lietaert Peerbolte; New York: T&T Clark, 2006), 256–58.

17 John D. Caputo, *The Weakness of God: A Theology of the Event* (Bloomington: Indiana University Press, 2006), 240.

The Miracle Tradition and the Historical Jesus as Healer

In the wake of the Enlightenment and intellectual incredulity regarding miraculous remediation, modernism transmuted the supernaturalist transcendence of the miracle tradition into the "higher consciousness" of "the man of reason"[18] – superior, broad-minded, and God-like. Consistent with the demands of rationalism, this transcendental, self-sufficient consciousness "stands above life," apart from natural feeling, and was, therefore, as context-free and as expansive as the colonial landscape – like God, compassionately overseeing all.[19] In this perspective, Jesus – as 18th century theologian Friedrich Schleiermacher suggested – was "the founder of a new religion who had an extraordinary awareness of the presence of God, resulting from his unique religious consciousness, [... and] served in that way as an *Urbild* [prototype] for humanity, introducing the possibility for all humanity of a closeness to God."[20] "Jesus' consciousness" – essentially "de-Judaized,"[21] observes philosopher Susannah Heschel of this modernist turn – "marks a new beginning for humanity. His divinity is constituted by the veritable existence of God in him, as proven by his own God-consciousness."[22] Within the tradition of rationalism, wherein transcendence has been translated into higher consciousness, Jesus appears chiefly as a teacher of wisdom and as a healer, including of socio-relational justice, given his supposed boundary-breaking inclusivity. If biblical scholar Adolph von Harnack set the course for this vision of Jesus, the most well known of the Historical Jesus scholars today, Marcus Borg and John Dominic Crossan, continue to expound the model and, thus, this notion of superior – if colonial, as decolonizing theorist Franz Fanon insisted – consciousness, which borrows upon the normal versus abnormal, and wholeness versus degeneracy, schemas of modernism. Espying bodies through such optics, persons always readily recognize "the disabled," degenerate, or otherwise deficient in need of healing.

In von Harnack's early 20th century reconstruction of Christian origins, Christianity "deliberately and consciously ... assumed the form of 'the religion of ...

---

18 Genevieve Lloyd, *The Man of Reason: 'Male' and 'Female' in Western Philosophy* (2nd ed., 3rd print.; Minneapolis: University of Minnesota Press, c1984/1998).

19 Lloyd, *The Man of Reason*, 90.

20 Susannah Heschel, *Abraham Geiger and the Jewish Jesus* (Chicago: University of Chicago Press, 1998), 144.

21 Heschel, *Abraham Geiger and the Jewish Jesus*, 234.

22 Heschel, *Abraham Geiger and the Jewish Jesus*, 144.

healing.'" Christianity appeared expressly as "a religion for the sick" and, while supported by an impressive philosophy of religion, won over the ancient world on the basis of its healing praxis. Yes, "Jesus proclaimed a new message," but von Harnack qualifies, he "appeared among his people as a physician." He "did his work as the Savior or healer of [persons]." Imagining Jesus' bedside manner, von Harnack observes that "Jesus says very little about sickness; he cures it ... [Jesus] sees himself surrounded by crowds of sick folk; he attracts them, and his one impulse is to help them ... No sickness of the soul repels him ... Nor is any bodily disease too loathsome for Jesus. In this world of wailing, misery, filth and profligacy, which pressed upon him every day, he kept himself invariably vital, pure, and busy."[23] Jesus, as modern consciousness assumed, brought to bear – as von Harnack detailed – a suprasensible God-consciousness, untouched and untrammeled by the determinacies of the mundane world.

By the time Marcus Borg enters the roundtable of the Historical Jesus Seminar in the latter part of the 20th century more attention is given over to sociological constituents, even as Christianity effectively remains, in Borg's view, a "religion of healing." While Borg has recognized and allows for a discrepancy between Jesus' worldview and our own, thus re-inserting Jesus into a world full of spirits, Jesus was still principally a healer and exorcist. Jesus was "a channel for the power of the other realm," such that his "healings were the result of 'power'" – that is, the power of Spirit.[24] Recognizing that miracles, healings and exorcisms were common to Jesus' world, Borg is driven by Christological claims regarding the uniqueness of Jesus to look elsewhere. And by that route, Borg lands on what he calls Jesus' "politics of compassion."[25] "The stories of his healings," Borg writes, referring to the miracle tradition, "shatter the purity boundaries of his social world. He touched lepers and hemorrhaging women."[26] Jesus' exuberant compassion exposed him to impure people, to "'dirty' people," as for example "women, the untouchables, the poor, the maimed, and the marginalized."[27] In Borg's hands, Jesus' healing ministry becomes a conscious politics of boundary subverting inclusiveness, as he extends a touch across social boundaries, essentially moving – as von Harnack had earlier also surmised – from the vital, clean

23 Adolph von Harnack, *The Mission and Expansion of Christianity in the First Three Centuries*, vol I (trans. James Moffatt; New York: G. P. Putnam's Sons, 1908), 101–9.

24 Marcus Borg, *Jesus, A New Vision: Spirit, Culture and the Life of Discipleship* (San Francisco: HarperSanFrancisco, 1987), 70–71.

25 Borg, *Jesus, A New Vision*, 100–102, 130–42.

26 Marcus Borg, *Jesus in Contemporary Scholarship* (Valley Forge, Penn: Trinity International, 1994), 53.

27 Borg, *Jesus in Contemporary Scholarship*, 55–56.

and pure Jesus towards "the miserable wash" of humanity, all effectively "disabled."[28]

John Dominic Crossan's "historical Jesus" appears as cynic philosopher, hippie peasant, and healer among grassroots people, who shares comparably in the energies and ethos of "open commensality and healing." Contrary to Borg, Crossan – with his infinitely low Christology – undercuts Jesus as a mediator of the divine, insisting that "He was neither broker nor mediator but, somewhat paradoxically, the announcer that neither [broker nor mediator] should exist between humanity and divinity or between humanity and itself. Miracle and parable, healing and eating were calculated to force individuals into unmediated physical and spiritual contact with God ... and ... with one another."[29] Yet, as inconspicuous as he tries to make Jesus, Crossan promotes a socially ingenious Jesus with a unique "religiopolitically subversive" touch, a touch that reaches across so as to dismantle caste boundaries, to overturn spiritual and social hierarchies, to erase somatic distinctions.[30]

If Borg and Crossan, both here following the lead of Adolf von Harnack, each emerge with a portrait of Jesus as healer, I would suggest that their Jesus portraits have emerged through the optics of modern realism. In their various propositions, Crossan and Borg have swept bodies differing into a pool of permanent social outcasts – namely (here in Borg's words), "women, the untouchables, the poor, the maimed, and the marginalized."[31] Yet this sociological categorization of the marginal suspiciously resembles modernity's designation of the degenerate types – "those groups whom Foucault describes as the 'internal enemies' of the bourgeois male" (namely, "women, racial others, the working class, people with disabilities, in short all those who would weaken the vigorous bourgeois body and state").[32] The constituting of "the disabled" as also "The Wretched of the Earth" (Frantz Fanon) was an outcropping of modern rationalist consciousness and the utopian, scientific hope of normalcy.

More troublingly, both scholars intend their constructed portraits of "the historical Jesus" to become, in turn, broader communal or ecclesial strategies –

28 Von Harnack, *Mission and Expansion of Christianity* ..., 109.
29 John Dominic Crossan, *Jesus: A Revolutionary Biography* (New York: HarperCollins, 1994), 31–32, 37, 198.
30 John Dominic Crossan, *The Historical Jesus: The Life of a Mediterranean Jewish Peasant* (New York: HarperCollins, 1992), 304, 323–24.
31 Marcus Borg, *Meeting Jesus Again for the First Time* (New York: HarperCollins, 1994), 51, 56.
32 Sherene Razack, "Gendered Racial Violence and Spatialized Justice: The Murder of Pamela George," *CJLS* 15.2 (2000): 94n7.

hence, Crossan's "open commensality" and Borg's "politics of compassion." "Miracles" become, within liberalism, "healing" stories that still use our disabled bodies as silent stage props, and that's what we then become within a Christian community – silent stage props, if not for miraculous remediation (faith healing), then for the liberal display of that community's compassion. Consequently, what is being effected as Christian compassion moves from a presumably God-like consciousness on the clean, intact and superior side so as to touch upon the apparently mutilated and dirty body of another. Performatively reading the normal, as set over against the abnormal – as liberal traditions have read into the miracle tradition – even so as to counter-suggest inclusiveness, does not disperse social dominance. Rather, it retains as central the hegemony of normalcy within which the different is paternalistically accommodated; it sets up a logic of control, or, among liberals, conspicuous compassion, which is not far distant from presuming an omniscience of insight. Transcendental consciousness here maintains "a partition of the sensible" between enspirited consciousness and recalcitrant matter and, consequently, ignores "the vitality of ... the lively powers of material formations"[33] – the liveliness of persons living with disability, for example. Compassion, still ruled by the norms and laws of the able, arrives riddled with the murderous love of the self-same, of the normal, of the merely identical. Integration, hardly a modern phenomenon, most easily hides from itself its aggression towards difference.[34]

At the historical moment when medicine presumes to step forward as a more reasonable, if "lay carbon copy" of the Church,[35] theology recovers Jesus as healer. Not surprisingly, these share epistemological lenses. The binary of "normal vs. abnormal" – which Borg and Crossan have unconsciously used presumably to work liberative inclusion of "the maimed and marginalized" – belongs not to the ancient world but to modernity. Defect – and the compensatory compulsion toward normalcy – got caught in the eye of the modern West. The notion of degeneracy, from which was generated cultural race and gender theory – i.e., black was seen as degenerate in relation to white, just as woman was seen as a degenerate in relation to man – operates in tandem with modern science, anthropology and, hence, political colonialism. So as to bring humanity to the dark continents, to civilize, to cure, the template of normalcy and its contrary – lack,

33 Jane Bennett, *Vibrant Matter: A Political Ecology of Things* (Durham: Duke University Press, 2009), vii.

34 Henri-Jacques Stiker, *A History of Disability* (trans. William Sayers; Ann Arbor: University of Michigan, c1999, 2009 print), 9–15.

35 Michel Foucault, *The Birth of the Clinic: An Archaeology of Medical Perception* (New York: Vintage, 1994), 31–32.

deficit, deformation, deviation, degeneracy, disability – were deployed as maps of the West's and of Christianity's social mission in the 19th and 20th centuries. As anthropologist Jean Comaroff observed in this regard, as "colonial relations found an alibi in the ailing human body,"[36] so "metaphors of healing ... have justified 'humane imperialism.'"[37] Because disability, like the colonial notion of degeneracy, emerges via the optics of modernism, it should not be surprising that persons living with disability find that the "politics of compassion" can be as terrifying as notions of supernatural miraculous remediation.

Disability has caught modernity's eye because of economic demands for a fit body and ideological notions of self-sovereignty. Even compassion, the liberal spirituality affectively crystallized by the miracle tradition in the wake of historical-critical biblical methodologies, aggressively wishes away what it views as the "deficit" of disablement. Only in this way can one like von Harnack speak of the "vital, pure and busy" Jesus, while ignoring the biblical interpretation of Jesus with Isa 53, i.e., the Song of the Suffering Servant, one of the most important intertexts for crafting the figure of Jesus in the Synoptics. Shaped through Isaianic imagery, Jesus appears grotesque – "despised, rejected, a man of suffering, acquainted with infirmity, one from whom others hide their faces" (Isa 53:3). We might then suspect psychological projection of modern consciousness as that which allows an incandescent Jesus to emerge within Historical Jesus scholarship. Assuming epistemological privilege, the eye to measure deficit and to scale the body for productivity and public appearance and health, the modern self also unconsciously presumes as health the values most conducive to capitalism. Even as black civil rights and the feminist movement challenged those optics in the late twentieth century, disability – seemingly so self-evident – has remained the undeconstructed "degenerate" type and may as such act like a keystone holding modern optics – and their related economic and neo-colonial systems – in place.

---

36 Jean Comaroff, "The Diseased Heart of Africa: Medicine, Colonialism, and the Black Body," in *Knowledge, Power, and Practice: The Anthropology of Medicine and Everyday Life* (ed. Shirley Lindenbaum and Margaret Lock; Berkeley: University of California Press, 1993), 307.

37 Comaroff, "The Diseased Heart of Africa," 313. Comparably, postcolonial-disabilities theorist Clare Barker observes: "Colonized identities were variously depicted in terms of physical degeneracy, psychological dysfunction, behavioural disorder and/or limited intellectual capacity ... Ableist discourse ... was, in fact, pivotal to such ideologies and it continually bolstered western colonial cultural and racial domination." See her *Postcolonial Fiction and Disability: Exceptional Children, Metaphor and Materiality* (New York: Palgrave MacMillan, 2011), 8. This way of reading the other as deficient continues to characterize discourse related to poverty, wherein the assumption is made that "If you're needy, you must be in need of correction." Poverty is, in other words, seen as a character flaw, not the shortage of money. See Barbara Ehrenreich, "How I Discovered the Truth about Poverty," http://www.alternet.org/module/printversion154571 (March 26, 2012).

Postcolonial-Disability Inflections of The Miracle Tradition

Indisputably, in terms of Gospel texts and also early Christian icons and reliefs, miracles – the multiplication of the loaves of bread, the resurrection of Lazarus, the blind man healed by clay, the cure of the paralytic, etc – appear to be "the core, the mainstay of Early Christian imagery," in contradistinction to today's life of Jesus, for example. These images of miracle, in story and art, were, "like advertising slogans, ... repeated to the point of saturation," observes art historian Thomas Mathew.[38] On everything from dinner plates to rings, from textiles (especially the hems of tunics) to tombs, from amulets to iconography, appeared images from one miracle story or another. Stylized miracle lists were also transmitted as lore and carried by rumor. Yet, "a convincing argument for inferring miracle working activity from miracle stories has been difficult to find," biblical scholar Burton Mack confesses.[39] So if the preponderance of miracles does not imply miraculous remediation or, even perhaps, conspicuous compassion (itself challenged not only by disabilities scholars like myself, but by Jewish Talmudic scholars), what shall we make of their historical profusion? Reading the stories at the intersection of disability and postcolonial studies suggests another possibility.

In the same way that Karen King insightfully quipped that "men use women to think with,"[40] Christianity and Judaism have analogically engaged disabled bodies. Refractions of the metaphor have never been narrowly monological: Pharisees were criticized as more blind than the blind, while Jacob's limp signified an intimacy with God marked precisely by impairment. Paul knows a ratcheting up of insight and resilience by using "disability" as something like a training harness, such that he with the residually annoying "thorn in the flesh" (2 Cor 12:7) is made "perfect in weakness" (2 Cor 12:9).[41] Within Western contemporary culture, disability – that is, the deficient or "in-valid" body – emerges at the intersection of modern notions of subjectivity (namely, self-mastery, the supremacy of reason, and individualism), economics (given the modern demands to

38 Thomas F. Mathews, *The Clash of Gods: A Reinterpretation of Early Christian Art* (Princeton: Princeton University Press, 1993), 62, 65.

39 Burton L. Mack, *A Myth of Innocence: Mark and Christian Origins* (Minneapolis: Fortress, 1988), 209.

40 Karen King, cited by Elizabeth Castelli, "Romans," in *Searching the Scriptures: Volume 2: A Feminist Commentary* (ed. Elisabeth Schussler Fiorenza; New York: Crossroad, 1994).

41 The West's relationship with pain, and how persons understand the construction of soul as gymnastically worked out in relation thereto, has been changed by the introduction of anesthetics and aspirin.

sell our labor as our natural reserve), and the development of the norm within modern science and mathematics. Contrarily, "the Bible," Yvonne Sherwood reminds us, "is in some respects radically other to the modern project of the care and growth of the self."[42] Sherwood's conclusion evolves from her reading of the *Akedah*, the story of the binding of Isaac (Gen 22), as "simply the most famous of a series of tableaux ..."[43] Reading this as a series of tableaux, beginning with the night wrestler, "crip" hero Jacob, and the "limping nation" bearing his name,[44] allows also for the possibility that Israel and then the Jesus movements might not have been in a superior relation to cripped bodies, but might well have identified themselves with just such cripped iconography. Moving back to the early decades of the common era and our gospel traditions, we must now take account of two significant insights related to the use of the metaphor of disability: 1) the grotesque was a signifier of the people, of common life;[45] and, 2) slavery, not disability as we today construe it, may have been more precisely that which was signified by bodies blind, maimed, lame and deaf.

In our contemporary reading of the miracle stories, Christian theologians have often overlooked the possibility that these stories may have been told by those who themselves were less than whole, those who knew the wisdom, "better torn life from limb than wholesome and without savor," and those, including Jesus, who found best medical practice in amputation, i.e., "If your hand, your foot, etc., causes you to sin, cut it off" (Mark 9:42ff, Matt 18:8). Somatic intactness, the fit body, has been much more important to the contemporary Western world as a symbol of well-being than it was to the ancients. Amputation was simply basic medicinal wisdom and best practice. Further, disablement from disease, war and malnutrition were, quite unlike today, culturally pervasive, given limited medical remediation, the state of war technology, and the nature of physical labor. Quite simply, "a physically handicapped person earning a living would not have been a remarkable sight."[46] Whatever then was the intent of miracle stories,

---

42 Yvonne Sherwood, "Passion-Binding-Passion," in *Toward a Theology of Eros: Transfiguring Passion at the Limits of Discipline* (ed. Virginia Burrus and Catherine Keller; New York: Fordham University Press, 2006), 188.

43 Sherwood, "Passion-Binding-Passion," 178.

44 Holmes Rolston III, "Does Nature Need to be Redeemed?," *Zygon* 29 (1994): 220.

45 Lennard Davis, "Constructing Normalcy: The Bell Curve, the Novel, and the Invention of the Disabled Body in the Nineteenth Century," in *The Disability Studies Reader* (ed. Lennard Davis; New York: Routledge 1997), 10–11.

46 Martha Edwards, "Constructions of Physical Disability in the Ancient Greek World," in *Body and Physical Difference* (ed. David Mitchell and Sharon Snyder; Ann Arbor: University of Michigan Press, 1997), 38.

their tellers did not find them as starkly opposed to the ancient, if brutal medicinal wisdom of guillotine amputations as we do. But that leaves us rationalists in the 21st century with something that resembles a Zen koan: If the life that speaks miracle has known the salt and fire of experiences tearing life from limb, why would they tell them?

The miracle tradition, as Burton Mack already observed, seems to reprise "the miracles of the ten plagues" effected before Pharaoh by Moses,[47] "the Jewish figure through whom the greatest miracles were worked."[48] "This insistence on a 'face-off' between Moses and Pharaoh," explains art historian Thomas Mathews, "is the one constant in all of the Early Christian representations of the miracle." Ironically, Pharaoh was now, however, iconically garbed in the military tunic of the Roman emperor – with requisite beard and hair bound up with a diadem. In other words, the iconography of the miracle scenes present us with a "hidden transcript,"[49] a subversive history subtly "spoken" below the level of understanding of the imperial colonizers, recalling the Exodus from empire and the promissory hope it loosed yet again. The message, Mathews insists, is inescapable: "Salvation is represented as a deliverance from the power of the Roman emperor."[50]

"Disability" – blindness, lameness, deafness – then plays metaphorically as a condensed symbol of the history of the people of Israel, who well remember that empires enslave – whether by instilling the tastes for another life, e.g., "We remember the fish we ate in Egypt for nothing, the cucumbers, melons, leeks, onions and garlic!" (Num 11:5), or, literally, by the strategies and tactics of political, colonial enslavement. The biblical story of the blinding of King Zedekiah (2 Kgs 24:16–25:7) records the imperial practice of mutilation so as to prevent the flight of prisoners of war and/or slaves. Similarly, historical documents report the punching out of eardrums and the hobbling of the body to prevent slaves from seeking their own freedom. In Kirghiz practice, "an incision [was made] in the sole of a captive's foot" and "a horse's hair [was inserted], so that after the wound is completely healed walking is very painful.[51] Citing sources like Seneca, Jewish scholar Shemuel Rubinstein explains the amputation of various appendages, including of a slave's ears, among slave-control practices in the ancient world: "For some wrongdoing in his work, or for breaking some vessel, the slave's fingers or

47 Mack, *A Myth of Innocence*, 217.

48 Eric Eve, *The Jewish Context of Jesus' Miracles* (London: Sheffield Academic, 2002), 196.

49 James C. Scott, *Domination and the Arts of Resistance: Hidden Transcripts* (New Haven: Yale University Press, 1990).

50 Mathews, *The Clash of Gods*, 76.

51 K. Neumann, *Die Hellen im Skythenlande* (Berlin 1855), cited in Stephanie West, "Introducing the Scythians: Herodotus on Koumiss (4.2)," *Museum Helviticum* 56 (1999): 78n10.

hands could be cut off ... The amputation of a slave's ears was so commonly practiced that it was established as a punishment for slaves. The Hammurabi Code stipulates: 'If a slave strikes a free person on the cheek, his ear is to be cut off.'[52] Slavery, not disability (as we know it today, i.e., the presumed deficient, impaired and invalid body), was the historical problematic of the body extending from Egypt through life within the Roman Empire. And the rumor of miracles may not, then, have had so much to do with supernatural remediation to wholeness as with the destabilization and leveling of empire – or, at the least, with socio-psychological recuperation from dominant culture (that is, interrupting and/or resisting the prevailing, imperial definitions of a life).

Even among persons who might have economically benefitted from empire, as certain merchant classes of persons may have within the Roman as also the Babylonian empires, the Isaianic refrain calls an unwilling people out of the imperial mindset. The summary refrain of the miracle tradition, i.e., "The blind see, the lame walk, the deaf hear," may then have acted something like a prophetic call to conscientization, a call to awaken to the ideological, if not sociopolitical, powers in the hands of which people found themselves. In unfolding eras, people might have found ways, using this metaphorically loaded refrain, to remind themselves that they were but "docile bodies" (Foucault), socially constructed by regimes not resonant with their own cultural sense of life and well-being, constructed by regimes that hobbled their flourishing. In this vein, Gerd Theißen's insights regarding miracles verge upon, without quite seeing, the postcolonial development: "One factor in the increase of belief in miracles [within "primitive Christianity"] ... was the tension between country and city culture, between Jews and Gentiles, and between traditional and new cultural forms of life ... [O]rdinary people pluck up courage in the face of concrete emergencies by telling miracle stories."[53]

Yet it is to be admitted that, on another level, empires are, as biblical scholar Warren Carter has put it, bad for your health.[54] Given warfare, population displacement, socio-political trauma consistent with mental illness, and forced ur-

---

52 Shemuel Rubinstein, cited in Rav Elchanan Samet, "Parashat Mishpatim" in "The Israel Koschitzky virtual Beit Midrash," 8–9. Accessed November 28, 2004. Online: http://www.vbm-torah.org/parsha.63/18.

53 Gerd Theißen, "Jesus as Healer: The Miracles of Jesus," in *The Historical Jesus: A Comprehensive Guide* (ed. Gerd Theißen and Annette Merz; Minneapolis: Fortress, 1998), 290–91, emphasis added.

54 Warren Carter, "'The blind, lame and paralyzed' (John 5:3): John's Gospel, Disability Studies and Postcolonial Perspectives," in *The Bible and Disability* (ed. Jeremy Schipper et al.; New York: Palgrave, forthcoming).

banization occasioning poverty and consequent malnutrition, "disability" likely functions both metaphorically and materially. Again, Theißen verged upon such insights when he insisted that "[miracle stories] contain a protest against human distress." "Wherever these stories are related," he continues, "people are not content that there is too little bread for many, that there is no healing for many who are sick, and that there is no home in our world for many who are hurt ... The miracle stories need always to be read 'from below' as a protest against human suffering." However, Theißen, like most moderns (as well as contemporary Christians wishing to extend compassion), tends to treat suffering as an individual phenomenon, not admitting the over-determination of socio-political forces – like empires – on health, illness, or alienation.[55]

That "disability" functions both metaphorically and materially in the contestation of neo-imperial forces as much today as it did in the ancient world can be seen in the deployment of disability within postcolonial art and literature. Frida Kahlo, in her painting "Roots 1943," already imagistically identified her fractured body with the colonially fractured land, with the traumatized state – in her case, Mexico. Likewise, from Salman Rushdie's *Midnight's Children* and Anosh Irani's *A Cripple and His Talisman* to Indra Sinha's *Animal's People*, Barbara Kingsolver's *Poisonwood Bible* and J.M. Coetzee's *Slow Man*, disabled characters, especially children, "feature ... prominently as the protagonists and narrators of postcolonial texts."[56] Disability serves as one of the most "persistent postcolonial narrative tropes employed by creative writers and critics alike" insomuch as it "becomes an embodied marker of the 'damage' experienced by postcolonial nations and communities," even as it "remains an unspoken and under-theorized term in postcolonial textual analysis."[57] These differently enabled bodies, "through their 'differences and transgressions,'" create "'cracks' in hegemonic ... renderings of 'nation', 'power' and 'normalcy' ..."[58]

If "disability" within the Gospel traditions might register such meanings as identification with the history of Israel, that "limping" or Crip Nation, and its protest against empire, then, in a horribly ironic twist, a biblical metaphor celebrating decolonization has been – within "transcendentalist" or supernaturally enthused readings of the miracle tradition – reversed to serve empire. Read with

55 Gerd Theißen, *The Miracle Stories of the Early Christian Tradition* (ed. J. Riches, trans. F. McDonagh; New York: T&T Clark, 1983), 231–32.

56 Barker, *Postcolonial Fiction and Disability*, 2, emphasis added.

57 Clare Barker, "Interdisciplinary Dialogues: Disability and Postcolonial Studies," *RDS* 6.13 (2010): 17.

58 Barker, *Postcolonial Fiction and Disability*, 14.

enlightened eyes, fitted with modernist optics, which sort the normal from the abnormal, the able from the degenerate, the miracle tradition has effected a measure of imperial control – normalcy, the fit body for industrial, now consumerist capitalism. Given postcolonial-disability insights regarding the primacy of "disability" within texts of those protesting colonization, what might we now rather make of that bastard child born to the Crip Nation at midnight hour?

"Poetics of the Impossible" (Caputo)[59]: Throwing Wonder in the face of Empire

From a postcolonial-disabilities perspective, miracles are not quite the same kind of problem as they have been for rationalists.[60] "In the case of postcolonial literature ..., the primary thing we need to bear in mind is that there is no ... place where truth is bare and universal ... This should not forestall critical effort, but should work recurrently to qualify judgments as cultural instead of true."[61] One of the criteria for interpreting the miracle tradition must then be anthropological attention to bodies, even then to "disability," especially as disability has been metaphorically at the crux of anti-colonial discourses, ancient to contemporary. Disability has been, during modernity, invariably seen as so surely the occlusion it appears to be, i.e., deficiency in need of a cure, that it lifts the best intentioned of scholars out of the historical-critical mode, and out of anthropological attention to cultural contexts, otherwise carefully attended within biblical scholarship. Working with a postcolonial-disabilities lens, I have suggested that we arrive rather at an alternative incredulity regarding miraculous remediation to normalcy; as if the gospels were interested in generating bodies to serve the epitome of Empire! In the age of biopolitics, when the imperative to "be well" is everywhere, we should, as readers of the gospel, be suspicious of any demand for whole(some)ness.[62] Further, we'll need to remind ourselves ever and again of the Western Christian tendency to hide our resentment of pain, transience, and other aspects of mortality

59 Caputo, *The Weakness of God*, 102

60 See Gerd Theißen's synopsis of the rationalist interpretation of miracles in his "Jesus as Healer: The Miracles of Jesus," 285ff.

61 John Rothfork, "Zen Comedy in Postcolonial Literature: Kazuo Ishiguro's 'The Remains of the Day,' *Mosaic* 29.1 (1996): 80–81.

62 Buchanan, *Deleuzism*, 110. Also see Charles Edgley and Dennis Brissett, "Health Nazis and the Cult of the Perfect Body: Some Polemical Observations," *Symbolic Interaction* 13.2 (1990): 257–79.

by over-reaching the flesh through one or another form of transcendentalization, whether miraculous remediation or modern consciousness, and its conspicuous politics of compassion.

That said, this postcolonial-disabilities critique is not then yet one more contribution to demythologization, an invitation to set aside the mood-mode of the miraculous. Admitting the openness of every view of the world, miracles will – even as rumor, yearning, innuendo – challenge the proscriptive imperial or normative view of reality. After all, in the early stages of the Jesus movements, persons, their bodies hobbled by slavery and not expecting to be reconditioned by biotechnology, nevertheless began assaulting the Roman empire, its military legions and its socio-politically habituated realism, with rumors of miracle. Up against aristocratic rule, foreign occupation, the monetizing of the agrarian economy, the innovation of property rights, heavy taxation and dislocating urbanization, Christians took heart. The real world for them had somehow just admitted a psychic supplement to the Roman economy – had admitted a sense of wonder, a life enchantment apparently not so delusional as Rome's free market felt to them.

Miracle might have to do then, as philosopher Ernst Bloch earlier in the 20th century put it, with "blasting apart ... the accustomed status quo."[63] Likewise, Spirit, as the energy of miracle, may be said, in a Hegelian sense, to "absolve" – that is, to loosen the ties and constraints which buckle us into the whims of sovereign power.[64] In this sense, miracle disrupts the realist option, the values which bind a life into its daily, sometimes enslaving, syntax. As we catch the glimmers of a generosity, an abundance, a resplendent emptiness into which we truly rest, something miraculous then transpires as we, longing to become otherwise than merely undead and resolute, cross into this other economy without absenting ourselves from the midst of life for fear of pain. Miracles – far from being a visitation of the fantastic – clear away "the fantasies that confine our energies within an ultimately defensive ... existence, that keep us at a distance from our answerability within everyday life ..., from the possibilities for new possibilities that are all the time breaking out within it."[65] That said, Spirit – this energy of miracle – may sometimes, especially in relation to ego, occasion that unhinging which can only be compared to a guillotine amputation of life from limb.

More than ever, given the way in which despair occasions our immunization of self from community and commons, we in the 21st century need a worldview

---

63 Ernst Bloch, *The Principle of Hope* (trans. Neville Plaice, Stephen Plaice and Paul Knight; Cambridge, Mass.: MIT Press, 1986), 1306.

64 Hent de Vries as cited by Bennett, *Vibrant Matter*, 3.

65 Eric Santner, *On the Psychotheology of Everyday Life* (Chicago: University of Chicago Press, 2001), 101.

that can respect such wonder, the "miracula."[66] "The affective force of moments [of enchantment]," philosopher Jane Bennett observes, "inspire deep attachment," as well as "nurture the spirit of generosity that must suffuse ethical codes."[67] Warning that "ontological cynicism feeds political cynicism," she concludes that "Presumptive generosity, as well as the will to social justice, are sustained by periodic bouts of being enamored with existence ..."[68] If miracles challenged the staleness and oppression of life within the mixed strata of the *Pax Romana* (rather than returning life to normal), this mood of wonder might yet again open out upon a religious view that challenges the sterility of rationalism as well as the "banal occultism" and "hair raising sorcery" occasioned by supernatural notions of transcendence,[69] which but engender the colonial and authoritarian superstructure already carefully analyzed by postcolonial Latina theologian Mayra Rivera, among others.[70] As I've shown, miracle need not be aversive to bodies differently abled; the miracle tradition need not be the terror it has been to persons living with disabilities. Rather, as Bloch suggested, the miraculous might better be related to "the Christian-advental imagination" and its "sudden flashing" or "opening up ... of the new world,"[71] an insight which was picked up, directly or not, by mid-twentieth century philosopher Franz Rosenzweig for whom miracle marks the openness of time's flow,[72] and by Jacques Derrida in the sense of deconstruction as opening out the "to come," as the mood of advent.[73]

The vitalist materialism of Deleuzean thought – more simply, of "a world of becoming," that is, of an open pluriverse with "a bumpy, twisting flow reducible to neither linear causality nor providential design" and wherein we are subject to "'competing serial time systems derived from different families of duration'"[74] – proves more conversant with readings of miracle, if as event. "Every moment must be ready to receive the plenitude of eternity," Rosenzweig, the mid-twen-

66 Jane Bennett, *The Enchantment of Modern Life: Attachments, Crossings, and Ethics* (Princeton: Princeton University Press, 2001), 5.

67 Bennett, *Enchantment of Modern Life*, 3–4.

68 Bennett, *Enchantment of Modern Life*, 12, 34.

69 Bloch, *Principle of Hope*, 1307–8.

70 Mayra Rivera, *The Touch of Transcendence: A Postcolonial Theology of God* (Louisville, Ky.: Westminster John Knox, 2007).

71 Bloch, *Principle of Hope*, 1308.

72 Virginia Burrus, "Augustine, Rosenzweig, and the Possibility of Experiencing Miracle," in *Material Spirit* (ed. Carl Good, Manvel Asensi and Gregory Stallings; New York: Fordham University Press, forthcoming), [6].

73 John Caputo, "The Messianic: Waiting for the Future" (Chapter 6) in *Deconstruction in a Nutshell: A Conversation with Jacques Derrida* (New York: Fordham University Press, 1997).

74 William E. Connolly, *A World of Becoming* (Durham: Duke University Press, 2011), 149.

tieth century Jewish philosopher, advised us.[75] Miracle, "the timelessness of ... communion occurring at 'the border of life' where eternity impinges on time ...," then appears, concludes scholar Virginia Burrus, Rosenzweig's contemporary reader, as something "like a scar." As a "thickening within time, its density draws our attention like a scar."[76] Comparably reversing the signification of miracle from "nothing left to see" to this dense historical fold, Mary-Jane Rubenstein speaks of wonder "as an unsuturable gash that both constitutes and deconstitutes thinking ...," a gash whose eclipse is related but to "a certain will toward mastery."[77] Miracles, as philosophical theologian John Caputo more simply concludes, warning us away from holding miracle as an excuse for thinking disincarnately, "belong to the sphere of a theology of the event, not to a mythology of magical occurrences."[78]

In a world of becoming, the socio-cultural world would cease "invalid/ating" persons living with disabilities, since "difference [is] the law of the real" and "the real is only a succession of disparities and mutations."[79] Disability, but a variation within folds of flesh, stands out only as an indicator of a culture's sociality – or lack thereof – regarding certain differences.[80] Disability, as we now know it, is a socially created structure of exclusion, generated amidst industrial capitalism and aggravated by the "cult of public appearance" within this latter stage of consumer capitalism. If "the miraculous is the flash of light [... within] which nothing alienated exists any more and in which subject and object have simultaneously ceased to be separated," as Bloch put it,[81] from a disabilities perspective this might be enacted as the utopian seaming of social flesh – of finally stitching the truth of flesh "as everything that is vulnerable, able to be wounded, which means bent, cut, lacerated, ulcerated, withered, inflamed, paralyzed, numbed, killed"[82] into the becoming of the world – without metaphysical refusal of disability (which amounts to resentment of the becoming of the world) and its off-shoot, objectification and alienation of persons living with disability. The Gospel of John remembers Jesus' wounds as an integral part of Jesus' identity, even in relation to his resurrection. Comparably, the differences marked as "disability" remain an

---

75 Burrus, "Augustine, Rosenzweig, and the Possibility of Experiencing Miracle," [6].

76 Burrus, "Augustine, Rosenzweig and the Possibility of Experiencing Miracle," [15, 18].

77 Mary-Jane Rubenstein, *Strange Wonder: The Closure of Metaphysics and the Opening of Awe* (New York: Columbia University Press, 2008), 10, 16.

78 Caputo, *Weakness of God*, 238.

79 Stiker, *History of Disability*, 12.

80 Stiker, *History of Disability*, 14–15.

81 Bloch, *Principle of Hope*, 1311.

82 Caputo, *Weakness of God*, 131.

integral part of the identity of those of us living with them. Such a world wherein our differences are not disappeared, either by miraculous remediation (presumed of "faith healing" as of biotechnoscience) or conspicuous compassion, remains unknown only because of our resentment and despair of flesh, historically hidden in the notion of "miracle."

James A. Noel

Miracle & Eschatology in Two African American Slave Narratives & the Spirituals: From 'Orality' to Text

Abstract: In this article I implicate the nature of miracles in the New Testament by theorizing backward from two African American slave narratives [Eli Whitney and Nat Turner] and the African American spirituals. I argue that miracle must be comprehended as one of the experiential components of the African American slave community's eschatology. I then explore the implications of this claim for understanding miracle and eschatology in the New Testament through the mediation the Jewish scholar Jacob Taubes writings on eschatology and apocalypticism and the insights of my colleague and conversation partner Matthew V. Johnson's work on "the tragic." This situates the phenomenon simultaneously within the present realm of its witnesses and the future realm it invokes and anticipates. Miracle, therefore, has as much to do with how a community experiences itself situated in time and space as how it apprehends nature. Because the end never fully arrives in the present, miracle does not remove failure and defeat from the slave and former slave community's experience and requires a hermeneutic of its non-reoccurrence as well as the event itself.

I Introduction to Jackson Whitney's Narrative

On March 18, 1859, an escaped slave named Jackson Whitney who had made his way to Canada wrote his former master named William Riley (John W. Blassingame, 114–15). This letter was published in the newspaper published by Frederick Douglass, Douglass' Monthly in August of that year.

> Sir: I take this opportunity to dictate a few lines to you, supposing you might be curious to know my whereabouts. I am happy to inform you that I am in Canada, in good health, and have been here several days.

Further along in the letter Jackson Whitney explained why he decided to escape. He said to his former owner that if he

> … could not by any entreaty or permission be induced to do as you promised you would, which was to let me go with my family for $800 – but contended for $1,000, when you had promised to take the same you gave for me (which was $660) at the time you bought me, and let me go with my dear wife and children! But instead would render me miserable, and lie to me, and to your neighbors … and when you was at Louisville trying to sell me! Then I thought it was time for me to make my feet for Canada, and let you conscience feel in your pocket.

Jackson Whitney then elaborated on how he came to his decision to make his escape to Canada.

> You know, too, that you proved a traitor to me … But I rejoice to say that an unseen, kind spirit appeared for the oppressed, and bade me take up my bed and walk – the result of which is that I am victorious and you are defeated.

He then offers his former master an opportunity for repentance.

> I wish you could realize the contrast between Freedom and Slavery; but it is not likely that we shall ever meet again on this earth. But if you want to go to the next world and meet a God of love, mercy, and justice, in peace; who says, 'Inasmuch as you did it to the least of my little ones, you did it unto me' – making the professions that you do, pretending to be a follower of Christ, and tormenting me and my little ones as you have done – had better repair the breaches you have made among us in this world, by sending my wife and my children to me; thus preparing to meet your God in peace; for, if God don't punish you for inflicting such distress on the poorest of his poor, then there is no use in *having any* God, or *talking* about one.

After some additional remarks Jackson Whitney ended his letter saying:

> You must not consider that it is a slave talking to "massa" now, but one as free as yourself.
>
> I subscribe myself one of the *abused* of America, but one of the *justified* and *honored* in Canada.

II Discussion

The phrase "from orality to text" in this article title refers to the mode of reception through which Jackson Whitney engaged in a hermeneutical praxis of the biblical text (s). He was not reading the bible. He wrote: "An unseen, kind spirit appeared for the oppressed, and bade me take up my bed and walk." It is unclear whether the unseen, kind spirit was invoking the Synoptic story of the paralytic let down into Jesus' mists through the roof or the crippled man sitting beside the Pool at Bethsaida in the Gospel according to John. What is remarkable in the interpretation of whatever miracle story was being referenced is that it was conveyed to Jackson Whitney by an "unseen spirit." Hence, in this narrative the miracle is not only located in the biblical text but, also, both in its mode of transmission to the interpreter and the outcome of its interpretation. To put it another way: the miracle is located both in the text, its mode of transmission which we might term "revelation," and its replication suggested in the text's interpretation. This in turn was conveyed to other readers through the letter Jackson Whitney wrote to his former master which serves as text in this article. Jackson Whitney would probably not have identified any particular event in his saga as a miracle. He is writing his narrative in such a way that its entirety be seen as miraculous – something whose outcome can only be comprehended as due to Devine intervention. In viewing Jackson Whitney's letter in this light it raises the question of how many other slave narratives might also be read as miracle stories. It depends upon how we understand the term.

Intercourse with unseen entities was not unusual at all within the African American slave community and was a characteristic feature of their cultures of origin in West Africa whose cosmos was comprised of humans in interaction with each other, the material world, and the unseen world populated by forces of nature, animal spirits, deceased ancestors, gods, and the Creator. These unseen forces were ubiquitous and discerned through cultural distinctions between things sacred and profane, divination practices, and rituals that facilitated spirit possession that effected communication between the human and spiritual realms. Although distinction between the sacred and profane pertained, the boundary between these two spheres of existence was porous and entailed sometimes maintaining the boundary through taboo and, at other times, bridging over its borders through ritual. African slaves brought to the Americas maintained this cosmology with various degrees of intensity and … depending upon a number of complex factors we need not specify in this paper. This can be observed in Haitian Voodou, Cuban and Puerto Rican Santeria, Brazilian Candomble, and Hoodoo in the American South. Suffice it to say that within this cosmological orientation the phenomenon we term "miracle" would have an entirely different meaning among them than it does for us. Miracle would occasion wonder and instigate the necessity for interpretation as a "sign" but it would not be responded to with incredulity as it is in the case of us moderns.

In a number of West African societies from which the vast majority of African slaves originated, sickness and disease was understood as the result of malevolent forces which had to be warded off, exorcised, propriated, etc. through a combination of varied herbal remedies and ritualistic practices orchestrated or performed by a religious specialist. In some areas the healing process has been termed by anthropologists as "affliction cults." A person cured from a particular disease – small pox, for instance – is understood to then have a special relationship with the small pox spirit. This qualifies that person to become an initiate in the healing cult and learn how to heal other's suffering the same affliction. The healer is one who has suffered from the same disease for which a cure is sought. The healer is a person who was formerly afflicted with the disease for which a cure is sought. But one has to be careful in describing such cures as miracles because the boundary between the natural and spiritual realms was much more porous than ours in which the existence of spiritual entities is questionable. For Africans on both sides of the Atlantic the cosmos included manifestations of spiritual power resulting in beneficial or harmful individual or communal outcomes. In Central West Africa human persons, nature, and carved objects contained various degrees of spiritual power and were referred to as "nkisi." The king for instance was a "nkisi" (James A. Noel). When Christianity was introduced to the Ki-Kongo kingdom the priests, churches, crosses, and Jesus were classed under this category. Both disease and its cure involved spiritual forces mediated through various "nkisi" but this was not necessarily conceptualized as miracle in the sense of which we speak today. Our discussion of miracles originates in a different epistemological framework. This is relevant to our discussion insofar as the African American slave community imagined Jesus both as one who had shared their affliction in his crucifixion and been delivered from it in his resurrection, thereby qualifying him as the agent of their "miraculous" deliverance. The "nkisi" or agent could also be "De Lord" as in the spiritual "Didn't the Lord Deliver Daniel," or Moses as in, "Go Down Moses," or nature as in, "Steal Away" wherein thunder and lightning are agents of deliverance. The phenomenal and noumenal realms were porous. In the NT what we term "miracle" is referred to and conceptualized as manifestations of Divine power.

> If the Bible sees as direct divine actions events that are not outside the realm of nature or history, then we must recognize that the elements of the marvelous, which is so much a part of the traditional understanding of miracle, is not overly prominent in the Bible. This is seen in the terms used for miracles ... In the NT the Syn word for miracle is *dynamis* "act of power" and Jn uses *semeion*, "sign," or *ergon*, "work." *Teras*, "wonder," is never used alone to refer to a miracle of Jesus (Raymond Brown, "The Gospel Miracles").

The entry on miracles in *Encyclopedia of Religion and Ethics* (1915), edited by James Hastings, give us an idea of what I am talking about. After a brief introduction, the next short section is sub-titled "miracles in the lower culture." The obvious paradigm is one of human progress and conveys the impression that miracles are credible in lower, primitive cultures but lose their credibility as peoples evolve. We read the following:

> Why magic should have come to be believed in, why some men should have been thought to possess magical power, is not clear, though various causes might be suggested. One of these is the unexplained phenomena of ... telepathy, hypnotism, and cure by suggestion, clairvoyance, and inspirational possession. These exist among the sages, and would be regarded as magical, as to us they are supernormal ... Magic or thaumaturgic miracle belongs to a primitive stage of thought but many of the miracles attributed to the shaman are ascribed to Lao-tse, Buddha, Muhammad, or to ethnic and Christian saints (677).

One of the problems with the above is the confusion it evidences between magic, psychic powers, shamanism and miracle. The other problem is that it fell into the trap of attempting to itemize in an objective fashion various types of events and occurrences that fall under the category of miracle. This tends to isolate the phenomenon from its epistemological and cultural modes of apprehension. Here, I am perhaps being influenced by my very scant knowledge of sub-atomic particle physics where the same phenomenon can appear as either a wave or particle depending upon how it is observed. Hence, the issue we are confronted with in Jackson Whitney's letter is what notion of miracle are we imposing on the text? And even if that notion of miracle is valid, we must ask where the miracle located in Whitney's account – in the NT miracle ... in his account of the kind, unseen spirit ... in his successful escape from slavery ... in what is indicated at the close of his letter where he wrote, "You must not consider that it is a slave talking to "massa" now, but one as free as yourself, I subscribe myself one of the *abused* of America, but one of the *justified* and *honored* in Canada" – or, all of these?

We should note that Whitney does not himself employ the term miracle. I am the one responsible for bringing him into this conversation. And I must confess that when I first approached this topic I naively thought I knew where the miracle was located in his account. I was thinking the miracle occurred when the "kind, unseen spirit" spoke to Whitney. I am now convinced that "miracle," if the term has any meaning at all, has a much broader scope than I initially thought. I hope to further substantiate this assertion in my discussion of Nat Turner's *Confession*. But for the present, let us stick to the text of Whitney's letter.

At one point in his letter Whitney explains to his former master: "I did all that was honorable and right while I was with you, although I was a slave. I pretended all the time that I thought you, or someone else had a better right to me than I had to myself, which you know is rather hard thinking." In this regard – to use the term in the vernacular sense – it is, indeed, a miracle that after having been almost thoroughly accommodated to servitude he could write defiantly to his former owner: "You must not consider that it is a slave talking to "massa" now, but one as free as yourself ..." This is not the consequence of the miracle – this is the miracle.

So, what does this mean for an understanding of miracles in the NT text or, more particularly, the stories of the paralytic and the man beside the pool of Bethsaida? My assumption is that Whitney, like many of his enslaved counterparts, received these texts orally and not by literary access to a written bible. Moreover, I will speculate that he was probably unaware of there being two different stories in the NT about someone being healed and commanded to take up his bed and walk. Or, let me say, he was aware of this it did not matter for the purposes of his hermeneutic. In his situation of having been relegated to an item of property, any type of healing that he might of experienced that was confined to his physical body would not have benefited him at all because he did not own his body. Therefore, under those circumstances, the beneficiary of such a healing would not have been Whitney but his master. And his master was endeavoring to sell Whitney to another party. Thus, when Whitney heard the "kind, unseen spirit" say "take up thy bed and walk" he knew it meant he was to take ownership of his own body and walk to freedom. Short of leading to Whitney's freedom, healing would not have been gospel or "Good New." This leads me the conclusion my colleague Annette Weissenrieder has already made in her paper – every healing story is not a miracle and every miracle does not entail healing narrowly conceived. So what does it entail?

In reading Whitney's letter I am now compelled to view miracle in the NT this sense: Miracle is the communal hermeneutical act wherein the sacred and profane intersect in such a way as to facilitate individual and social transformation and liberation. In other words, it is not something that can be verified through criteria extraneous to the interpretive framework of the community's narrative. In Whitney's case he was transformed from a commodity or property into a human. This posited a possibility for other slaves who encountered his story. The miracle is not just in the biblical text, or in its supernatural mode of reception, or in its interpretation – these are not distinct, linear items. In the hermeneutical act the biblical text became contemporaneous with the interpreter's – Whitney's – context. The miracle is in the two overlapping narratives taken as a whole. Note as well that Whitney graciously offers his former master an opportunity to voluntarily participate in the miracle through repentance and conversion where he wrote: "But, in this letter, I have said enough to cause you to do all that is necessary for you to do, providing you are any part of the man you pretend to be. So I will close by saying that, if you see proper to reply to my letter, either condemning or justifying the course you have taken with me, I will again write you." This suggests to us that miracle also occasions judgment within a Hegelian "master-slave dialectic."

III Nat Turner's Narrative

This way of understanding miracle is substantiated in another slave narrative – that of Nat Turner. Since I have already stated my perspective on miracles, we can dive right into Nat Turner's Confession and see if it is further substantiated.

Nat Turner led one of the most violent slave insurrections in U. S. history in Southhampton County, Virginia in 1831 in which ten men, thirty five children and fourteen women were killed. I should add that many more black people who had nothing to do with Turner in reaction to his insurrection. The details of his insurrection were narrated by Turner to a lawyer named T.R. Gray in what is now known as *The Confession of Nat Turner*. Turner begins his narrative by addressing Gray, "Sir, you have asked me to give a history of the motives which induced me to undertake the late *insurrection, as* you call it. To do so, I must go back to the days of my infancy, and even before I was born."

Now, in terms of what I have said thus far, I am viewing Turner's entire narrative as a miracle story and not merely individual items in the narrative that may seem miraculous to the modern gaze. Nat Turner seems to have intuited that he would encounter the same difficulty at the point in his narrative where he, while in the midst of saying "knowing the influence I had obtained over the minds of my fellow servants," interjects the parenthetical caveat (not by the means of conjuring and such like tricks, for to them I always spoke of such things with contempt,), but by the communion of the Spirit, whose revelation I often communicated to them, and they believed and said my wisdom came from God. The African practices of conjuring, divination, witchcraft, etc. are things that would not have come to the mind of the contemporary reader had Nat Turner not mentioned it Thus, the brief reference he makes to "conjuring and such like tricks" would indicate that he wants to set himself apart from slaves who were engaged in these practices and that there at least were some who must have suspected that this was the secret behind his method. In other words, Turner does not want the miracles associated with him to be understood as magic – "conjuring and such tricks." In defending himself against the accusation that he was a conjurer, Turner is telling the truth but it is a truth which is not unmixed with error. This becomes clear when we ask ourselves the question of what similarity there might be between conjuring (and its related practice of divination) and any act of discursive interpretation.

It is interesting to note here that Turner was refused baptism at the local white church and so he and a white man whom he had healed of boils and converted to Christianity "went down into the water together; in the sight of many who reviled us, and were baptized by the Spirit." This shows that the source of Turner's inspiration and the methodology behind his interpretive scheme was suspect among some in and near his plantation. The local white church in refusing baptism to Turner and his white friend was also refusing to recognize the miraculous in Turner's ministry. If miracle could happen in and through the life of a slave independent of the church controlled by slave owners then the locus of God's activity would have shifted from the oppressor to the oppressed with obvious consequences for the system that established the difference in their respective status. The content of Turner's visions, as reported by him, is quite bizarre and impervious to our understanding; that they occurred to him does not provide us a clue as to the hermeneutic principle he used in their interpretation. Turner only tells us that he did not employ the method of conjuring. Yet for the practitioner of divination cowrie shells thrown on the ground elicit from him the same complex task as words written on the page for the modern biblical scholar – discerning a pattern from some visual configuration whose interpretation produces meaning and transformation.

Turner explained that as early as three or four years of age while playing with other children, he began to relate incidents that occurred on the plantation prior to his birth and when these things were verified by the older slaves it so impressed them that they remarked: "He surely would be a prophet," as "the Lord had shown me things that had happened before my birth." Additionally, the way Nat Turner learned to read and write was equally miraculous. He says, "It not only had a great influence on my mind, (as I had acquired it with the most perfect ease, so much so, that I have no recollection whatever of learning the alphabet,) but to the astonishment of the family, one day when a book was shown me to keep me from crying, I began spelling the names of the different objects." Turner says that after this incident his learning constantly improved. Whenever he was not working he spent his time in prayer "or in making experiments in casting differing things in molds made of earth; in attempting to make paper, gunpowder, and many other experiments ..."

After reaching adulthood, while listening to a sermon, Turner was struck by the passage saying, "Seek ye the Kingdom of Heaven and all things shall be added unto you." After praying daily for the interpretation of this passage, one day at his plough, the Spirit spoke to him and quoted this same passage. When asked by Gray what he meant by the Spirit, Turner said, "The Spirit that spoke to the prophets in former days." After this occurrence Turner prayed consistently for two years and then had the same revelation. More years passed during which he was given additional revelations and confirmations that he was ordained for a special task. At one time Turner says:

> I saw white spirits and black spirits engaged in battle, and the sun was darkened – the thunder rolled in the Heavens, and blood flowed in streams – and I heard a voice saying, "Such is your luck, such you are called to see, and let it come rough or smooth, you must surely bear it.

We notice that Turner's visions are obviously drawn from his acquaintance with the Book of Daniel. That is the text being signified in the narrative. But as in Whitney's letter, "orality" is integral to his hermeneutic in the "voice" which simultaneously points to the vision he is having and those he will receive later. After this vision he stopped interacting with his fellow slaves as much as the plantation schedule would allow in order to devote himself more fully to the Spirit.

> ... and it appeared to me and reminded me of the things it had already shown me, and that it would then reveal to me the knowledge of the elements, the revolution of the planets, the operation of the tides, and the change of the seasons ... The knowledge of the elements being made known to me, I sought more than ever to obtain true holiness before the great Day of Judgment should appear; and then I began to receive the true knowledge of faith.

The reason Turner was instructed in the knowledge of the elements, revolution of the planets and operation of the tides was connected with what we learn elsewhere in his narrative. This knowledge was necessary for him to determine the precise timing of his revolt. Turner's hermeneutic pertained not only to the biblical text and his visions but also nature. Nature, in turn, was constantly being transfigured before his vision into the Bible's apocalyptic imagery.

> And on the 12th of May, 1828, I heard a loud noise in the heavens, and the Spirit instantly appeared to me and said the Serpent was loosened, and Christ had laid down the yoke he had borne for the sins of men, and that I should take it on and fight against the Serpent, for the time was fast approaching when the first should be last and the last should be first. *Question.* Do you not find yourself mistaken now? *Ans.* Was not Christ crucified. And by signs in the heavens that it would make known to me when I should commence the great work – and until the first sign appeared, I should conceal it from the knowledge of men – And on the appearance of the sign, (the eclipse of the sun last February) I should arise and prepare myself, and slay my enemies with their own weapons. And immediately on the sign appearing in the heavens, the seal was removed from my lips, and I communicated the great work laid out for me to do, to four in whom I had the greatest confidence, (Henry, Hark, Nelson, and Sam) – It was intended by us to have begun the work of death on the 4th July last – Many were the plans formed and rejected by us, and it affected my mind to such a degree, that I fell sick, and the time passed without our coming to any determination how to commence – Still forming new schemes and rejecting them, when the sign appeared again, which determined me not to wait longer.

Let me point out the obvious and say that oppressed communities cannot depend solely upon a literary text for revelation and miracle because literacy, the text and its interpretation are withheld from them as part of the power dynamic. Revelation itself is miraculous in this context. There are numerous stories of slaves acquiring the ability to read without any prior instruction. After Turner's rebellion it became a crime in Virginia to teach slave to read and any slave who could read was suspect because that meant he could think or, in other words, come up with an independent interpretation of reality. Whites, therefore, endeavored by killing Turner and his co-conspirators to eliminate what they viewed as the source of the other insurrections they imagined all around them. [The war on terror in America originated with the terror inflicted on native Americans and African slaves – it is not new for us. In fact, it has never ended.] So, Gray asked Turner during his interview if Turner had other cells on adjacent plantations. Turner answered in the negative but warned Gray that more such rebellions were certain because slaves on other plantations would also be interpreting the signs that were appearing right before their eyes in the heavens. The white plantation owners were incapable of interpreting nature or in seeing in nature the apocalyptic imagery found in Daniel and Revelation. To have done so would have confronted them with the judgment of God which they could only escape through repentance – by freeing their slaves. Turner regarded his rebellion as God's judgment upon America's plantocracy. When Turner uses the term "miracle" it is in reference to his visions in which nature was being transfigured into imagery based on that of Daniel and revelation. He said:

> And I wondered greatly at these miracles, and prayed to be informed of a certainty of the meaning thereof – and shortly afterwards, while laboring in the field, I discovered drops of blood on the corn as though it were dew from heaven – and I communicated it to many, both white and black, in the neighborhood – and I then found on the leaves in the woods hieroglyphic characters, and numbers, with the forms of men in different attitudes, portrayed in blood, and representing the figures I had seen before in the heavens. And now the Holy Ghost had revealed itself to me, and made plain the miracles it had shown me – For as the blood of Christ had been shed on this earth, and had ascended to heaven for the salvation of sinners, and was now returning to earth again in the form of dew – and as the leaves on the trees bore the impression of the figures I had seen in the heavens, it was plain to me that the Savior was about to lay down the yoke he had borne for the sins of men ...

And while Turner was making his confession from his jail cell, slaves elsewhere were gathered in the catacombs of their brush arbor meetings singing: "My Lord, he calls me ... he calls me by the thunder ... the trumpet sounds within my soul ... I ain't got long to stay here ... green trees are bending ... poor sinner stand a-trembling ... the trumpet sounds within my soul ... I ain't got long to stay here."

IV The Spirituals

In the 1845 edition of his autobiography, Frederick Douglass wrote in *My Bondage and My Freedom* of the spirituals he heard in his youth as a slave: "They told a tale which was altogether beyond my feeble comprehension; there were tones loud, long and deep, breathing the prayer and complaint of souls boiling over with the bitterest anguish. Every tone was a testimony against slavery and a prayer to God for deliverance from chains" (p. 31). In one of the most thorough studies of African American spirituals, *Black Song: The Forge and the Flame*, John Lovell, Jr. wrote: "The fundamental theme, though perhaps not the greatest, that pervades the spiritual is the need for a change in the existing order" (223). Lovell employed the discipline of Anthropology in his examination of approximately two thousand spirituals taken from all over the South and treated them as folksongs. As such they are to be studied as communal creations which articulate the fears, concerns, aspirations, and religious orientation and experience of the people who created, preserved and transmitted them from plantation to plantation and generation.

According to Lovell the slave's "reading of the Bible had conditioned him to miracles and mighty feats of power." What the slave expected from making contact with these powers of which he heard of in the bible was "a radical change in the existing order" which were heralded by his songs." The kind of miracle longed for is quite evident in the spirituals and make sense in terms of the slave's situation. "Since he was in bondage, the key concept of the change he sang about was deliverance." In song after song it is difficult to find one "without some evidence of this sense of powerful deliverance and the slave's reliance on it. In refrain or verses the recurrence of the symbols of power, Jesus, the Lord, God, the angels, and various inanimate things, is so great that a comprehensive list of examples would be little less than a dozen volumes of poems and poetic phrases" (230). Heaven was the spatial symbol of where the slaves wanted to go. It posited a place that was the antithesis of slavery. One could "walk all over heaven." Death was one means of getting there – getting to the other side, reaching the "promise land." But death was also conceived cosmically in terms of God's destruction of the entire earthly order so that the heavenly city could appear and welcome God's children. Apocalypse was the vehicle for the slave community reaching the spatial and temporal realm of freedom. This is the most important miracle hoped for in the slave community and it relativizes all other miracles. It also happens to be the miracle that still has not occurred. Hence, we have the sorry, pathetic, parody of African American Christianity in the prosperity gospel.

African American slaves invented hundreds of spirituals which meditated and sought to invoke the apocalypse such as; "In that Great Getting-Up Morning;" "And de Moon Will Turn to Blood;" "O Rocks, Don't Fall on Me:"

When every stars refuse to shine,
Rocks and mountains don't fall on me;
I know that King Jesus will-a be mine,
Rocks and mountains don't fall on me.
The trumpet shall sound and the dead shall rise,
Rocks and mountains don't fall on me;
And go to the mansions in-a the skies,
Rocks and mountains don't fall on me
(Eileen Southern, *The Music of Black Americans: A History*, Norton Press; 1982, 174–75)

And also belonging to this class of spirituals is "My Lord What a Morning."

My Lord, what a morning ...
When the stars begin to fall
You'll hear the trumphet sound,
To wake the nations underground,
Looking to my God's right hand.
When the stars begin to fall

In one of the spirituals, "Ride On King Jesus," notice the connection between individual healing and social transformation

When I was blind and could not see,
King Jesus brought the light to me
He built his throne up in the air ...
And called his saints from everywhere
He pitched his tents on Canaan's ground
And broke the Roman kingdom down (231).

In these spirituals we can see how intensely vivid was the African American slave community's eschatology. In their situation wherein human agency was futile in overcoming the might of the political, societal, and military forces arrayed against their emancipation, their only hope was in the intervention of some spiritual power(s)-God, Jesus, the Lord, Abraham, Moses, John the Baptist, Gabriel, or whomever. There were at least one hundred and fifty instances, however, when slaves were motivated to participate in what they perceived as God's intervention on behalf of their deliverance. Nat Turner was one such slave. In Nat Turner's narrative we were able to see his sense of the future pressing upon and breaking into the present. In his visions, Nat Turner apprehended what his slave counterparts were singing of.

V Implications for Miracle & Eschatology in the New Testament

In their quest for the so-called historical Jesus biblical scholars were confronted with the apocalyptic core of Jesus and his followers. Both Jesus and the early church were consumed by an intense expectation and longing for a dramatic and violent disruption of time through the sudden in-breaking of God's Kingdom through the "Son of Man" whom the early church identified with the resurrected Christ. It seems, however, that biblical scholars and theologians were reluctant to ponder the implications of their discovery for understanding the nature the faith and its "founder." Eschatology never became the starting point for Christian theology from which its other items could be coordinated but ever remained an option which one could decide either to discuss or not discuss. This, at least, was my experience studying in the United States where course offerings in Christology, Pneumatology, Soteriology, Atonement Theory, etc. have little to do with Eschatology – that of Jesus and his early followers. Protestants look quite ridiculous in this regard because it legitimates itself through a narrative of returning to the "Apostolic faith" through Paul. But in that the Pauline corpus is quite earlier than the Synoptic Gospels, John, the Catholic Epistles and Revelation we should expect to encounter in it the same apocalyptic core discovered in the historical Jesus quest. At least, if Paul is not read through a Lutheran lens this become apparent. Perhaps there was the tendency within the diverse population of people who followed Jesus during his brief ministry and throughout the first one hundred and fifty years after his execution to deny the eschatological core of his message. This is why it does not leap out at us from the books of the NT until one sees it. The eschatological and apocalyptic content of Jesus message was problematic even during Jesus ministry. Subsequently, "one of the principal problems confronting the theologians of the apostolic age was the meaning of the period of history between the first and second coming of Jesus Christ. The tension between the already and not yet is felt continually throughout the NT" (Raymond E. Brown). The tension caused by the tendency of NT texts to try to have it both ways – affirm and deny the world – enables the reader to see what he/she wants to see in the NT What one sees is determined by ones location or where one intentionally locates oneself. A bourgeois culture will not readily attend to eschatology. The slave master is not likely to see what her slaves see in the text. Scholars such as Jacob Taubes who finally brought biblical scholars back to this base line established posthumously (1778) by Reimarus (1694–1768) (*On the Intention of Jesus and His Disciples*) and reinforced by Albert Schweitzer's *Quest of the Historical Jesus* (German, 1906/English 1910). Quoting Reimarus, Taubes wrote: "Jesus is not the initiator of something new, but is to be regarded as a phenomenon within the apocalyptic movement in Israel. Jesus fits in a wider sense into a succession of eschatological itinerant preachers ..." *Occidental Eschatology*, 48).

I have chosen in this article to locate myself within the context of a nineteenth century slave community in the United States whose descendants are known as African Americans. This community had, by virtue of its social location, the phenomenological frame of reference to have perceived what biblical scholars and theologians are rediscovering in the twenty-first century – the eschatological character and apocalyptic dimension of the early churches. Like the slaves in the United States in the nineteenth-century, first century Christians were waiting for the present world to end and a new world to begin. This means that for them too, the big miracle they imagined occurring was for the eschaton's arrival with Jesus' return. All other miracles would be interpreted in relation and relegated to that. Let us view this in terms of the classical perspective employed in Renaissance art. The artist established a relationship between all the various objects in a painting through a vanishing point. All objects in the painting grew smaller as they approached this point on the horizon and eventually vanished. The vanishing point is not seen but structured the relationship between all the other objects to achieve depth. In terms of our discussion on miracle, the eschaton is the vanishing point. A specific miracle can be depicted in the foreground or background but it only has coherence to other objects depicted through its relationship to the eschatological vanishing point that is not seen usually. Not only in the Gospel of John but in the Synoptics as well can we now read the miracle accounts as "signs." As with Jackson Whitney, early first-century Christians would not have been completely content with an experience of individual healing while the history continued apace. Whatever experiences of individual or even corporate healing they experiences would not have abated their yearning for what was signified in Jesus' return. Moving in this fashion from a study of miracle in nineteenth-century African American slave communities to the early first-century Christian community [need I mention that at least one third of the population in the Roman Empire were slaves?] it is easy to see in almost every new testament text the problem of coping with the delay of Jesus' return. The big miracle did not happen. It did not happen for African American slaves and it did not happen for first-century Christians. According to Jacob Taubes, Christian theologians have assiduously avoided the implication. So too have black theologians save for Matthew V. Johnson who discerned a "tragic vision" within the phenomenological field of the African American religious experience. Taubes even located the crisis earlier than the post-resurrection period but during Jesus ministry-when he sent the disciples out to preach with the promise they would see the Son of man descending from heaven.

> If the whole history of Christendom is founded upon the delayed Second Coming ... then the first date in Christian history can be taken to be the non fulfillment of the prophecy of Jesus. This non occurring event ... marks the decisive otherwise inexplicable turn of events in the work of Jesus (*Occidental Eschatology*, 56).

Although interpreted as miraculous, the individual and corporate deliverance of African American slaves from bondage did not signal the eschaton's arrival. It moved the African American community into the phase of its history termed Jim Crow which consisted of segregation, lynching, and all manner of dehumanizion and degredation. This is where Matthew V. Johnson's work on "the tragic" is so crucial and demands what he terms the "recalibration" of all of Christian Theology's primary symbols. In "The Middle Passage, Trauma and The Tragic: Re-Imagination of African American Theology," Johnson wrote:

> When we consider the primary symbols of the Christian faith in the context of African American Christian consciousness I am lead to de-center the resurrection replacing it with a polarity established by the paradigmatic events of crucifixion and Second Coming, with the Second Coming replacing the resurrection as the primary Christological moment and focus of faith. The persistent longing, the chronic desire characteristic of Dasein's infinalitute, looks out of the horror of Calvary (the finality of infinalitude) past the resurrection (relegated to, at most, penultimate theological significance) to the Second Coming. It sublates the resurrection which secures only the determination of desire, a determination captured in the familiar phrase 'keep on keeping on.' Promise sustains desire. It does not end, foreclose or fulfill it. Therefore only in the unfulfilled promise of the Second Coming does desire come to rest or more accurately locate, albeit uneasily, as its most adequate symbolic representation ... The Second Coming, however, is deeply problematized because it is an unfulfilled promise, perhaps, even as I prefer to see it, a broken promise – a cracked symbol (558).

VI Conclusion

The above understanding of miracle problematizes the various Liberation theologies of which I am intimate. One of the items on the agenda of Black Theology, in particular, was to counter what it deemed the black church's "otherworldliness." In light of my assertions in this article, it can be said that, Black Theology is not sufficiently other worldly. It must posit a goal beyond the mere ending of racism because that has no structural or temporal impact on the present empire's political-economy. There is no warrant for Black Theology to recruit an Eli Whitney or a Nat Turner into a progressive Civil rights narrative but situate their narrative within the above paradigm of miracle and eschatology.

In this article I have argued for the necessity of comprehending NT miracles in relation to Jesus' and the early Christian community's eschatology. I have also pointed out that no individual miracle fulfills that eschatology. I posited the eschatological religious consciousness of the nineteenth-century African American slave community in the US as paradigmatic for understanding the nature of miracle in the NT as a component of the NT community's narrative about its relationship to earthly power being destroyed or overcome through the in-breaking of Divine power. In discussing the phenomenon of miracle as it appears in the narratives of Jackson Whitney and Nat Turner, I claim it must be understood within the hermeneutical framework of its witnesses. This framework is eschatological in both the African American slave community and the early Christian community (Whitney, Turner, Taubes). The eschatological framework establishes a built-in contention between the miracle and its historical context. Miracle does not belong to the present age but announces one that never fully arrives. This is the temporal structure and existential framework wherein the African American Christian community elaborated its tragic sensibility (Johnson). When miracle is domesticated in ordinary time – when it severed from the future (it vanishing point) – it is no longer miracle in the NT sense.

Miracle is the communal hermeneutical act wherein the sacred and profane are understood by its witnesses to intersect in facilitating individual and social liberation. Insofar as the phenomenon of miracle is historical and transformative of oppressive social structures, repentance is called for from those whom the social structure benefits. Those oppressed by the social structure will imagine and long for the arrival of reality wherein they are no longer exploited, degraded and dehumanized. In this regard, miracle is eschatological and anticipated in apocalyptic texts, images and vocalizations. The sense that such a future is revealing itself in an individual life of one of the oppressed or in its corporate praxis is interpreted by them as miracle – as God being with them in their struggle. This is always partial. Events are interpreted thusly even if their cause suffers setback and defeat. In viewing the entirety of the narratives of Whitney and Turner as miracle stories – not stories containing miracles – I recommend returning to the NT gospels and reading them similarly. They become miracle when our hermeneutic and praxis make them contemporaneous with ourselves. In the African American slave narratives I discussed, miracle is accompanied with judgment – so too in the gospels. The Word that became flesh seeks contemporaneity in our own narratives (personal, social, historical). The extent to which miracle remains hermetically and hermeneutically sealed within the text as something representing a world-view no longer credible to our modern epistemological orientation is the extent to which human transformation and liberation elude us. Miracle is not the suspension of natural law but the suspension of injustice which is unnatural.

Bibliography

Blassingame, John W., ed. *Slave Testimony: Two Centuries of Letters, Speeches, Interviews, and Autobiographies.* Baton Rouge: Louisiana State University, 1977.

Brown, Raymond E. "The Gospel Miracles," p. 785; and "New Testament Eschatology," p. 779, in *Jerome Biblical Commentary.* Englewood Cliffs, N.J.: Prentice-Hall, 1968.

Douglass, Frederick. *My Bondage and My Freedom.* CreateSpace Publisher, 2011.

Gray, Thomas R., ed. *The Confessions of Nat Turner.* Baltimore: Thomas R. Gray, 1831 http://docsouth.unc.edu/neh/turner/turner.html.

Hastings, James, ed. *Encyclopedia of Religion and Ethics.* Edinburgh: T. & T. Clark/New York: Charles Scribner, 1915, v.8.

Johnson, Matthew V. "The Middle Passage, Trauma and The Tragic: Re-Imagination of African American Theology," *Pastoral Psychology*, vol. 53, No. 6 (July 2005) 541–61. Also: *The Tragic Vision in African American Religion.* Palgrave: 2010.

Lovell Jr., John. *Black Song: The Forge and the Flame.* Paragone press, 1986.

Noel, James A. "African American Art and Biblical Interpretation," in *True To Our Native Land: An African American New Testament Commentary.* Edited by Brian K. Blount. Fortress Press, 2007, 76–77.

Southern, Eileen. *The Music of Black Americans: A History.* Norton Press, 1982.

Taubes, Jacob. *Occidental Eschatology.* Stanford Press, 2009.

Annette Weissenrieder

Cultural Translation: The Fig Tree and Politics of Representation under Nero in Rome (Mark 11:13–15, 19–20; Matthew 21:18–19; Luke 13:1–9)

Rarely does an interpretation of the New Testament story of the fig tree avoid referring to the history of religion background in antiquity, even if this approach is not normally reflected upon within the interpretation itself. The reason for this reliance on historical religious material is easily found: since as is commonly believed the story of the fig tree is the only miracle of punishment in the New Testament, its significance cannot be explained by the New Testament alone.[1] Even Augustine, for instance, asks, "Quod arbor fecerat fructum non afferendo? Quae culpa arboris infecunditas?"[2] by which he means the connection between the fig tree's offense in failing to bear fruit and the subsequent curse, stating that no fruit should grow on it "henceforward forever" (Mark 11:14; Matt 21:19). At least by the time of Augustine, then, the question was widespread as to whether the curse was to be interpreted as a punishment, and the story thus as a miracle of punishment (or norm miracle). And at least from this time on, scholars have tried to understand this curse in terms of translations taken from the Hebrew and the Aramaic into Greek and therefore as a cultural translation not only from one language into another but also into a different discourse. In translating the image of the fig tree, the goal was to delineate equivalences or similarities in the image that can help us interpret the non-intelligibility of the text.[3]

A story's semantic field allows us to determine whether it belongs to the genre of punishment miracles, so it is noteworthy that the story of the fig tree lacks an explicit, formulaic curse such as ἐπικατάρατος – accursed.[4] Even the

---

1 This is the interpretation supported by most scholars, in any case. In his book *Wunder und Wirklichkeit in den Briefen des Apostels Paulus: Ein Beitrag zu einem Wunderverständnis jenseits von Entmythologisierung* (WUNT 134; Tübingen: Mohr Siebeck, 2001), Stefan Alkier attempted to make the genre of the punishment miracle plausible for the Corpus Paulinum as well. In his paper in this volume Michael Rydryck argues in a similar way although with a different theoretical framework.

2 Augustine *PL* 38.592–93. See also PSJoh Chrys. *PG* 59.587.

3 Here, as below, I use the concept of cultural translation not just in the literal sense, as in translating from one language to another. This concept of translation places less emphasis on similar characteristics than it does on foreignness.

4 Only in Gen 3:14 LXX and Gal 3:10, 13.

semantic field of verbs, that are often associated with miracles of punishment, collected by Stefan Alkier, – such as deliver up/ surrender, destroy, ruin, cover, judge and finally correct (παραδίδωμι, φθείρω, ἀπόλλυμι, καταστρώνυμι, κρίνω or παιδεύω) – is entirely lacking from our text. Nor is there any mention of a miraculous power (often δύναμις – power, πνεῦμα – spirit).[5] Only καταράομαι – to curse (*kataraomai*; Mark 11:21), a *hapax legomenon* in New Testament, could be interpreted in this way. Thus simply referring to the term "curse" is not helpful here if we want to interpret the story as a miracle of punishment.[6]

It is also possible to classify stories as miracles of punishment using a theoretical concept. A survey of the more recent interpretations of the fig tree story shows an indisputable connection with G. Theißen's interpretation, which treats the story as a "norm miracle" (*Normenwunder*) – a category that includes Sabbath healings as well as the only miracle of punishment in the NT, the story of the fig tree. Miracles, according to Theißen, "cross the boundary of concrete need;" in "norm miracles," he says, "the hidden nature of divine being and will" constitutes the "central boundary."[7] Thus it is only logical to emphasize the authority of God's messenger over obstacles in order to underline the power of his word. The cursing of the fig tree should be interpreted as a miracle of punishment: a transfer of power is taking place.[8] Alkier presents a similar definition of the genre "miracle of punishment" while focusing on Pauline miracle stories, defining it as "the perceivable manifestation of divine power, namely that of the identifiable God."[9]

5 Alkier, *Wunder und Wirklichkeit in den Briefen des Apostels Paulus.*

6 See the argument below.

7 Gerd Theißen, *Urchristliche Wundergeschichten: Ein Beitrag zur formgeschichtlichen Erforschung der synoptischen Evangelien* (StNT 8; Gütersloh: Gütersloher Verlagshaus, 6th ed. 1990), 123; see also Gerd Theißen, Annette Merz, *Der historische Jesus: Ein Lehrbuch* (Göttingen: Vandenhoeck & Ruprecht, 1996), 266. With this interpretation, Theißen follows in the footsteps of Rudolf Bultmann, who classifies the story of the fig tree, in his *Geschichte der synoptischen Tradition* (FRLANT 12; Göttingen: Vandenhoeck & Ruprecht, 7th ed., 1967), 234, as a natural miracle; cf. Ernst Lohmeyer, *Das Evangelium des Markus* (KEK I/2; Göttingen: Vandenhoeck & Ruprecht, 1937); Peter Dschulnigg, *Das Markusevangelium* (ThKNT 2; Stuttgart: Kohlhammer, 2008), 299. Other scholars define the story as a prophetic symbolic action: Rudolf Schnackenburg, *Matthäusevangelium 16,21–28,20* (NEB 1; Würzburg: Echter, 1987), 199; Craig Blomberg, "The Miracles as Parables," in *Gospel Perspectives VI: The Miracles of Jesus* (Sheffield: JSOT Press, 1986), 327–59, here 332. Adela Yarbro Collins, *Mark: A Commentary* (Hermeneia; Minneapolis: Fortress, 2007), 525 argues for a "metaphorical narrative."

8 Cf. Petra von Gemünden, "Die Verfluchung des Feigenbaums Mk 11,13f.20f.," *WuD* 22 (1993): 39–50.

9 Alkier, *Wunder und Wirklichkeit*, 290. It is surely significant that Alkier attempts to make his interpretations of the punitive miracles in the Corpus Paulinum plausible solely based on the discursive universe of the text. In doing so, he applies a concept of reality that is related to the text:

However, here too the narrative of the fig tree cannot be clearly designated as a miracle of punishment, since the need is not characterized, nor is the scene prepared for the miraculous act. The miraculous act is even confusing – the tree will no longer bear any fruit, but neither is there any indication that the tree itself will wither. Even if we follow Bultmann, who places norm miracles in the broader category of object miracles[10] and states that the point of the story is not to punish the fig tree or nature, but to establish a new norm, certain questions remain: What constitutes the "concrete need" that is expressed by the curse? Why is divine power manifested toward a fig tree, and what does this punishment actually represent?[11] And which norm is being redefined?

The story in the versions of Matthew and Mark does not provide any answers to these questions, so we are reliant on other materials for comparison. But in their rhetoric they assume that the image of "the cursed fig tree" is directly meaningful to the audience. In light of these aspects, one can start with the current scholarship:[12]

"Die semiotische Formulierung der Wunderfrage geht von der Theorie aus, dass die Welt, in der wir leben, mittels Zeichenprozessen kommunikativ erschlossen wird. Was als Wirklichkeit gelten soll, ja sogar in welche ontologischen Modalitäten die Welt gegliedert ist und wer sie bewohnt, wird mittels Zeichenprozessen kommunikativ und konfliktreich erarbeitet. *Formal* muß daher die semiotische Wunderfrage lauten: Welche Zeichenprozesse ermöglicht der Signifikant/ WUNDER/ oder eines seiner Äquivalente innerhalb einer gegebenen Welt?" (p. 86–87).

10 Bultmann, *Geschichte der Synoptischen Tradition*, 14. 233.

11 For more on the New Testament understanding of the fig tree pericope, see William R. Telford, *The Barren Temple and the Withered Tree: A Redaction-Critical Analysis of the Cursing of the Fig-Tree Pericope in Mark's Gospel and its Relation to the Cleansing of the Temple Tradition* (JSNT.S 1; Sheffield: JSOP, 1980); idem, "More Fruit from the Withered Tree: Temple and Fig-Tree in Mark from Greco-Roman Perspective," in *Templum Amicitiae. Essays on the Second Temple presented to E. Bammel* (JSNT.S 48; Sheffield: JSOT, 1991), 264–304; Wendy J. Cotter, "'For It was Not the Season for Figs'," *CBQ* 48 (1986): 62–66; Maria Trautmann, *Zeichenhafte Handlungen Jesu: Ein Beitrag zur Frage nach dem geschichtlichen Jesus* (fzb 37; Würzburg: Echter, 1980), 319–46; Beate von Kienle, "Mk 11,12–14.20–25: Der verdorrte Feigenbaum," *BN* 57 (1991): 17–25; M. Woijciechowski, "Mark 11.14 et Tg.Gn. 3.22: Les fruits de la loi enlevés à Israel," *NTS* 33 (1987): 287–89.

12 Previously, I have written on the fig tree in Mark, although with an emphasis on iconography: cf. Annette Weissenrieder, "The Didactics of Images: The Fig tree in Mark 11:12–14 and 20–21," in *The Interface of Orality and the Written Text* (ed. A. Weissenrieder and R. Coote; Tübingen: Mohr Siebeck, 2010).

1 The image of the fig tree in the history of interpretation

Generally, interpretation of the image of the fig tree takes one of three approaches: The fig tree is either understood *literally*, in which case the image reflects the actual landscape of Palestine, or it is understood *pedagogically* as an Old Testament woe word which is then later translated and interpreted as a curse or finally *intertextually*, so that we must determine its meaning from the stock of images in the traditions available at that time.

In principle, the *literal interpretation* is possible. Along with olive trees, there were fig trees in the countryside of Palestine and Syria. Thus the image of the fig tree in Mark 11 and Matt 21, as numerous scholars since Jülicher suggest, is oriented toward the *obvious* and *simple rural world of images* drawn from the realities of the land.[13] Thus some scholars presume that the tree in question was a winter fig that does not ripen until spring.[14] In this way they attempt to deal with the problem that otherwise it would have been completely senseless for Jesus to have looked for figs to be in season. A second interpretation links this analysis with the feast of booths, a time when one could indeed expect figs. This would point toward an interest in the temple as well as the relationship to the Gentiles. In the context of the feast of booths, one interpreter sees the following symbolism: In Jesus, the king comes into the city and the Lord comes into his temple.[15]

In my opinion both interpretations are unsatisfactory. In view of the comment, "For it was not time season for figs," it is unlikely that the appearance of the "(withered) fig tree" had to do exclusively with the realities of the Palestinian environment. This comment makes Jesus' expectation appear unreasonable.[16] The

---

13 Adolf Jülicher, *Die Gleichnisreden Jesu* vol. I (Tübingen: Mohr Siebeck, 1920; repr. Darmstadt: WBG 1969), 118. See also *Die Gleichnisreden Jesu 1899–1999: Beiträge zum Dialog mit Adolf Jülicher* (ed. U. Mell; Beih. ZNW 103; Berlin/New York: de Gruyter, 1999).

14 On this see for example E. Hirsch, *Die Frühgeschichte des Evangeliums* vol. I (2nd ed.; Tübingen: Mohr Siebeck. 1951), 124 f.; Hermann L. Strack and Paul Billerbeck, *Kommentar zum Neuen Testament aus Talmud und Midrasch* vol. I (Munich: C.H. Beck, 1922), 857.

15 Especially C.W. Smith, "No Time for Figs," *JBL* 79 (1960): 315–27, esp. 327.

16 In his 2010 dissertation, *Wege des Heils: Erzählstrukturen und Rezeptionskontexte des Markusevangeliums* (Göttingen: Vandenhoeck & Ruprecht, 2010), 357, Karl Matthias Schmidt writes: "How closely the temple and fruit, agricultural area and sanctum were related can be seen from coins dating to the first Jewish War, documenting the iconographic relationship between temple artifacts, tree fruit and fruits of the field, particularly between the sanctum and the vine [...] While Haggai's prophecies called for the sanctum to be rebuilt, the Evangelist was already looking back at the destruction of the second Temple. The Temple was dead, the tree of Israel had died; Mark could no longer hope for a reconstruction, and this tree would never again bear fruit."

problem is that we transfer our knowledge about the realities of Palestine and the land into the texts. The result is a failure to appreciate the force of images for Mark 11 and Matt 21. The question remains open, not least, why Jesus noticed the fig tree on the way to the temple, or to say this in another way: Why does the fig tree in Mark 11 and Matt 21 play such a central role whereas it is not central in this context in Luke or John? Are we dealing here with a piece of local color that was known only to the authors of Mark's and Matthew's Gospel? In any case, it should be considered that the Gospel texts do not reflect only the local color of Jerusalem and Galilee, but that they could also be located in other parts of the Imperium Romanum. Thus the local is also global.

Early on, the form of a punitive miracle was called into question, since such an event would not only have been unique in the synoptic tradition. In addition, the story itself does not provide any illuminating reasons for a punishment.[17] Even in the late 19th century, scholars referred to Old Testament research showing that the mode of the curse can be expressed using a formula that varies between a wish and a statement. Willy Schottroff convincingly showed that the curse's original tendency was as a magical proclamation; it was later subjected to religious faith and thus became a request for a curse.[18] Curses beginning with αὐσαί (*ausai*) are related to the woe words, but in general they are lamenting a loss that has already taken place. A woe word should be understood more as a *pedagogical word* that expresses a warning about consequences. Some scholars thus posit that the reader's attention was originally meant to be directed toward a regret and a lament by Jesus, which Jesus would have spoken in Aramaic;[19] the origins in Mark are read as words of lament, which then moves the story more solidly into the realm of the Passion. The curse reflects the perspective of the post-Easter community, which includes the woe word in the Passion story and then translates it as a curse.[20] Although researchers view this approach with a certain degree of skepticism, I do find it interesting that it relies on a text that pursues a story told in another language and in a non-Greek context. Thus it defines the performative character of the translation from one culture to another. The translation includes the experiences gained in the first language, thus in a sense transferring the narrative processes of traditional oral literature along with the text.

---

17 Peter Fiedler, *Das Matthäusevangelium* (ThKNT 1; Stuttgart: Kohlhammer, 2006), 327.

18 Willy Schottroff, *Der altisraelitische Fluchspruch* (Neukirchen-Vluyn: Neukirchener Verlag, 1969), 112–20.

19 Hans-Werner Bartsch, "Die 'Verfluchung' des Feigenbaums," *ZNW* 53 (1962): 256–60; Ludger Schenke, *Die Wundererzählungen des Markusevangeliums* (Stuttgart: Kohlhammer, 1974), 158–66.

20 Christoph Böttrich, "Jesus und der Feigenbaum: Mk 11:12–14, 20–25 in der Diskussion," *NT* 39 (1997): 328–59, here 348.

Hence again and again interpreters have searched for traditions that would offer an *intertextual interpretation* of the withered fig tree. The most obvious possibility is the Old Testament background. The fig tree symbolizes Israel or Jerusalem, which did not produce fruit and therefore lost all privileges as God's people. In contrast, faith in God is central. The majority of scholars draw on Mic 7:1–6,[21] Jer 7 and 8. Thus, Gerhard Münderlein[22] or Wilfried Eckey[23] attempt to make the motif of the fig tree understandable on the basis of a series of Old Testament passages, in particular Jer 8:13ff. This passage is located in the context of Jeremiah's laments over the temple: "When I would gather them, says the Lord, there are no grapes on the vine, nor figs (σῦκα LXX) on the fig trees (pl. ἐν ταῖς συκαῖς LXX); even the leaves are withered (κατερρύηκεν LXX)."[24] The combination of motifs – the search in vain for figs and the withered fig tree together with explicit connection with the temple – strongly suggests an association with Jeremiah. Giesen even dared to take another step when he connected also the motif of hunger for figs with Jeremiah.[25]

But the linguistic agreements are less impressive than these scholars would have us believe. Thus in Mark 11:13, Matt. 21:19 καὶ ἰδῶν συκῆν (and seeing a fig tree) refers to ὁ ἰδὼν αὐτό in Jer 8, but the withering of the root of the tree, which in the Septuagint is described with κατερρύηκεν, is depicted by the verb ξηραίνω (both translated to wither).[26] This interpretation assumes that the Old Testament tradition of prophetic speech about Israel as a whole is preserved in the story of the fig tree. However, it must be asked why the New Testament authors did not keep the word for "wither" (κατερρύηκεν) in the text. Should we assume a transcription

---

21 A. De Q. Robin, "The Cursing of the Fig Tree in Mark XI: A Hypothesis," *NTS* 8 (1961/62): 276–81, here 280, and Walter Klaiber, *Das Markusevangelium* (Die Botschaft des Evangeliums; Neukirchen-Vluyn: Neukirchner, 2010), 214.

22 Gerhard Münderlein, "Die Verfluchung des Feigenbaums," *NTS* 10 (1963/64): 89–104. See also Jan W. Doeve, "Purification du Temple et Desséchement du Figuier: Sur la Structure du 21eme Chapître de Matthieu et Paralléles (Marc XI. 1-XII.12; Luc XIX.28-XX.19)," *NTS* 1 (1954/55): 297–308, esp. 303–4, 306.

23 Wilfried Eckey, *Das Markusevangelium. Orientierung am Weg: Ein Kommentar* (Neukirchen-Vlyun: Neukirchener, 1998), 287; Heinz Giesen, "Der verdorrte Feigenbaum – Eine symbolische Aussage? Zu Mk 11,12–14.20f.," *Biblische Zeitschrift* 20 (1976): 95–111.

24 According to Telford, *The Barren Temple and the Withered Tree,* Mark 11 refers to B.Meg. 31b and B.Ta'an. 29a–30b where a day of fasting is described, which the destruction of the first temple is mourned. C.H. Dodd refers to the trove of sayings in Jeremiah, which is picked up in the destruction of Jerusalem in the New Testament, but especially in Mark (C.H. Dodd, *According to the Scriptures: The Sub-structure of New Testament Theology* [London: Nisbet, 1952], 86–87).

25 Giesen, *Der verdorrte Feigenbaum*, 104.

26 One may argue that this substitution is insignificant if we take the conditions of oral tradition into consideration: Specific words would not be that important.

oversight or a translation error in this case, or do the two verbs have different connotations?

Accordingly, should the "withered fig tree" be understood as an image of judgment which Mark 11 and Matt 21 simply updated? If so, the following interpretation suggests itself: The disciples would thereby emerge as partly responsible for the catastrophe indicated by the symbolic withering of the fig tree. This is hardly conceivable since at least Mark explicitly emphasizes their hearing – ἀκούειν (*akouein*).

Although the three excerpts described here could not be more different, they are linked by a central question: the question of cultural translation, whether it is from one language to another such as from Aramaic or Hebrew into Greek; from one genre to another such as from woe words to a curse; or from one cultural space to another. Each of these levels thematizes a transformation.

Theoretically, these materials can be anchored by the question of cultural translation, which here I am basing entirely on Homi K. Bhabha's concept.

2 Cultural translation, or the performative character of translation

In his essay *On Language as Such and Language of Man*, Walter Benjamin deals with the always-already-translated nature of languages, writing, "Translation attains its full meaning in the realization that every evolved language (with the exception of the word of God) can be considered a translation of all the others."[27] Benjamin goes on to say that translation "passes through continua of transformation, not abstract areas of identity and similarity," meaning that the performative nature of translation is foregrounded. This is probably the idea that makes Benjamin the inspiration for Homi K. Bhabha's essay *How Newness Enters the World*.[28] But what exactly does this concept of "cultural translation" mean for Bhabha?

By looking at three very different texts, Bhabha develops various facets of the concept. He opens the sequence with Joseph Conrad's short novel *Heart of Darkness*, which was published in 1902. Conrad, he says, describes the colony as a place of non-intelligibility and radical cultural foreignness. But Conrad narrates the experience of foreignness in a special "poetic translation," as Bhabha refers

27 Walter Benjamin, *Medienästhetische Schriften* (Frankfurt a.M.: Suhrkamp, 2002), 76.
28 Homi K. Bhabha, "How Newness Enters the World. Postmodern space, postcolonial times and the trials of cultural translation," in *The Location of Culture* (London/ New York: Routledge, 1994), chap. 11, 212–35. In addition, Routledge has published the *Translation Studies* journal since 2008.

to it, by integrating the foreign into the personal. This also includes the experience of fear: The main character mirrors his experiences with the foreignness of culture, and thus with the dark side of a culture, in his own body – in this case in his heart. In this sense, Benjamin's interpretation of the "continua of transformation" that measure a translation also inspires fear. The first aspect of a culture of translation thus involves dealing with the uncanny, in other words with fear, as Bhabha also says.

This dealing with uncanny fears is taken a step further when Frederic Jameson, a postmodern theorist, is ultimately challenged to develop forms of perception in order to perceive of the global – a process that Jameson describes as "incommensurability-vision."[29] By this, Jameson means a way of seeing in which various historical moments are present simultaneously.[30] This ultimately "reveals the anxiety of enjoining the global and the local."[31] Bhabha supports this idea when he discusses the category of space before the category of time.[32] He arrives at the following formulation: "To revise the problem of global space from the postcolonial perspective is to move the location of cultural difference away from the space of demographic plurality to the borderline negotiations of cultural translation."[33] This finding leads Bhabha to the following dichotomy: demographic plurality vs. borders as places of negotiation and hybridization. Or, in other words: a parallel existence of cultures that is misunderstood as multiculturalism vs. a transforming procedural basis that includes everyone and everything and is not directed solely toward individual marginal groups. It is my impression that this transforming procedural basis is the second aspect of cultural translation as Bhabha understands it. If we see his main focus as being this aspect, then the culture of translation has a positive effect and is distinct from the culture of the uncanny or of fear.

While Bhabha understands the concept of cultural translation to this point metaphorically, in his further observations he also arrives at the literal significance – the process-based concept of cultural translation is applied to the experiential world of migrants when he writes, "Walter Benjamin has described as the irresolution, or liminality, of 'translation', the *element of resistance* in the process of transformation, 'that element in a translation which does not lend itself to

---

29 Bhabha, "How Newness Enters the World," 218.

30 Bhabha, "How Newness Enters the World," 218 cites Jameson: "Different moments in historical time [...] jumps back and forth."

31 Bhabha, "How Newness Enters the World," 216.

32 It is only natural that he draws on Foucault here, when we consider that nearly all post-colonialists take Foucault as their starting point.

33 Bhabha, "How Newness Enters the World," 333.

translation'."[34] In turn, this statement requires him to address Walter Benjamin's concept of translation: There is only one aspect of language that cannot be translated, and that is the Word of God. Only from a messianic perspective is the multiplicity of God's Word revealed.[35]

Still, it is to some extent noteworthy that Bhabha does not refer to this context; instead he writes, "The liminality of migrant experience is no less a transitional phenomenon than a translational one [...]."[36] With this, we come to the most difficult point in Bhabha's argument: In contrast to Benjamin, he is talking about cultures here and not languages, and the migrant experience is now described as a "translating" experience – while at the same time, migrant culture is described as being untranslatable.[37] At this point, it is not just the references to Benjamin that begin to founder, but also Bhabha's own metaphorical and literal interpretation.

As a result, however, he is able to make up for this weakness by describing translation as a performative practice, using the example of Rushdie's *The Satanic Verses*. Cultural translation does something to a text by transferring it into a foreign context; this necessarily changes the text. Thus he focuses on the transfer of contexts into other, foreign contexts: "it is a moment when the subject-matter or the content of a cultural tradition is being overwhelmed, or alienated in the act of translation."[38]

Thus we come to the third aspect of cultural translation, which not only preserves traditions, but also creates the new. "The newness of cultural translation is akin to what Walter Benjamin describes as the 'foreignness of languages' – that problem of representation native to representation itself."[39] Although Bhabha

34 Bhabha, "How Newness Enters the World," 224.

35 Walter Benjamin, "Die Aufgabe des Übersetzers," *Gesamte Schriften* vol IV,1 (Frankfurt a. M.: suhrkamp), 9–22, here 14: 2 "But if these [languages] continue to grow in this way till the messianic end of their history, then it is translation which takes fire in the eternal continuing life of the works and in their ceaseless renewal, again and again testing the holy growth of language – how far distant the hidden may be from revelation, how conscious the awareness of this distance may be." [trans. James Hynd and E.M. Valk, 1968]

36 Bhabha, "How Newness Enters the World," 224.

37 Bhabha, "How Newness Enters the World," 224 who writes, "This space of translation of cultural difference *at the interstices* is infused with that Benjaminian temporality of the present which makes graphic a moment of transition, not merely the continuum of history."

38 Bhabha, "How Newness Enters the World," 225.

39 Bhabha, "How Newness Enters the World," 227. Here, too, the fairly free interpretation of Benjamin's text should not be ignored: In Benjamin, the foreignness of languages is discussed in the context of Biblical linguistic confusion, and is considered an imperfection in the individual human languages.

once again goes beyond the metaphorical and literal interpretation of cultural translation with this analysis, the idea can be productive in terms of further work on the New Testament. I would like to illustrate this using one more quotation from Bhabha: "With the concept of 'foreignness' Benjamin comes closest to describing the performativity of translation as the staging of cultural difference."[40] Or, in other words: Giving space to cultural difference means making it visible in its foreignness, and coming closer to intelligibility and translatability by way of this making-visible. The fact that this translatability can also subvert intelligibility, however, is the uncanny aspect of cultural translation.

The following will show that the image of the fig tree is central not only in the Old Testament texts, but also particularly in the Roman Empire during the first century C.E. Thus the image of the fig tree allows imagery to be transferred from one culture to another; in other words, various historical moments and spaces are present simultaneously in the image of the fig tree. The performative character of cultural translation makes it possible to integrate the foreign into personal experience. The image of the withered fig tree is meant to be explained in the context of the foundation myth of Romulus and Remus, to whom the story may be referring. The New Testament texts will be used to show that the foreign culture is made visible in its foreignness.

3 The fig tree as an emblem for the founding of Rome, its founding fathers, and the war goddess Roma

Romans had special appreciation for the fig tree.[41] One aspect of this connection is its convergence with persons and divinities of the time whose essential characteristics were associated with the fig tree.[42]

40 Bhabha, "How Newness Enters the World," 227.

41 Timothy P. Wiseman, *The Myths of Rome* (Exeter: University of Exeter Press, 2004), 52 points to the ten Sibyls, "Bronze statues of Sibyl and of Attus Navius stood at the Comitium. Close by was a sacred enclosure where the stone and razor were buried, and 'Navius' fig-tree', evidence of another of his miracles, was carefully preserved as a guarantee of the freedom of the Roman People."

42 Davina C. Lopez, *Apostle to the Conquered: Reimagining Paul's Mission* (Minneapolis: Fortress, 2008) tries to relate the topic of "nation" – *gens* with the myth of Romulus and Remus; see also the article of Harry O. Maier "Barbarians, Scythians and Imperial Iconography in the Epistle to the Colossians," in *Picturing the New Testament: Studies in Ancient Visual Images* (ed. A. Weissenrieder, F. Wendt and P. v. Gemünden; Tübingen: Mohr Siebeck, 2005), 385–407.

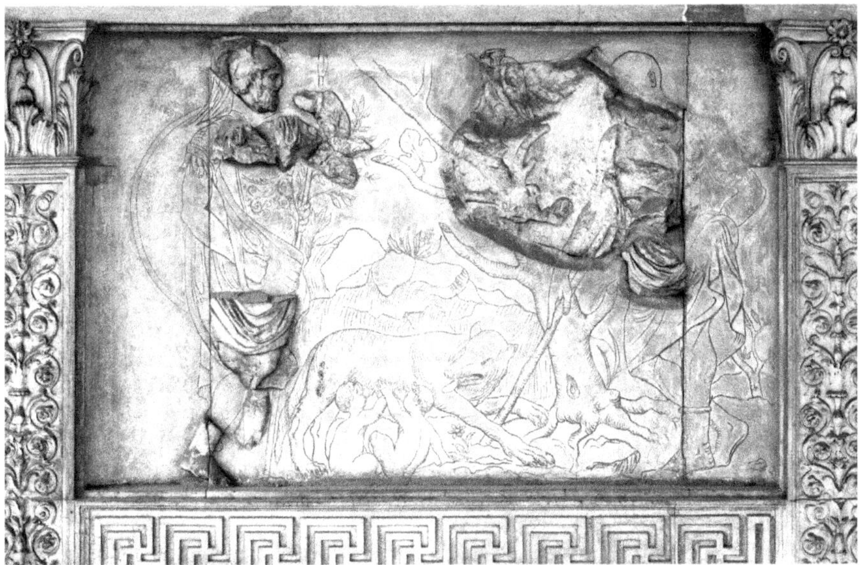

Ara Pacis © DAI Cologne.

It may be a trivial observation that since the second century B.C.E. the entire Mediterranean world was part of the history of an empire ruled from Rome, the extent of which was considerably extended by Pompey, Caesar, Augustus, and finally Trajan. And by the first century C.E. the city of Rome had become the political and social center of the empire. So it is no wonder that anyone even partially involved in domestic political situations, situations which culminated both in excesses like civil wars and in simultaneous successes in external politics, reflected on the supposed founding figures of the city. The city did not lack founders. With the beginning of the Augustan reign only two of these founders were selected from the myths, namely Aeneas and Romulus:[43] While Aeneas stands as an image for grief, Romulus appears as an image of triumph. Architecturally, on the altar in the *campus martius*, the so-called *Ara Pacis*. the group in the statuette is the center of the representational complex. A small frieze portraying a festival procession is carved around the entire altar, likely depicting the entry of the emperor after his victories in the East; further reliefs of various personifications are found on it.

Divine providence is picked as a central theme, as Romulus and Remus are saved by the fig tree and are nursed by the *Lupa Romana*. The shepherd Faustulus

43 See Livius 1. 3. 10–4.3; different: Dionysius 1.77.1f.

and the god Mars frame the scene with Romulus. On behalf of the viewer both are surprised at the bounty of the providence under whose protection Rome stood. At the exit of the altar one meets as the reverse of the nursing Lupa Romana the goddess Roma, who is connected with the picture of the triumph. The goddess Roma appears as a youthful warrior dressed with a short garment with helmet, seated on spears and signs one of which shows the nursing Lupa. On the left knee she balances a sword, symbol of the military power over life and death.

So from the middle of the fourth century or the beginning of the third century B.C.E., in both writing and images, we encounter the twins Romulus and Remus under the fig tree, the *ficus ruminalis*, sitting as they are suckled by the mother wolf.[44] This constellation of motifs is especially frequently documented for us on coins.[45]

---

44 Theodor Mommsen [*Gesammelte Schriften* V, Berlin: Weidmannsche Buchhandlung, 1908] writes on the she-wolf: "Die Wölfin vom Capitol ist als Wahrzeichen Roms mit einer solchen Bedeutungsintensität ausgestattet, wie man dies von keinem anderen Wahrzeichen der Stadt sagen kann. Weder die attische Eule noch der Berliner Bär sind im Bewußtsein der Menschen so sehr das Symbol dieser Städte, wie die Bronzestatue im Konservatorenpalast es für Rom geworden ist. Die Bedingung hierfür ist zunächst die hohe schöpferische Qualität der Bronzeplastik. [...] Als entscheidendes Element kam aber die Wirkung des Mythos hinzu, der sich um das Bildwerk rankt." See also *Social Struggles in Archaic Rome* (ed. K.A. Raaflaub; Oxford: Blackwell, 2005); idem, "Born to be Wolves? Origins of Roman Imperialism," in *Transitions to Empire* (ed. R.W. Wallace and E.M. Harris; Norman, Okla.: University of Oklahoma Press, 1996), 273–314; idem, "Epic and History," in *The Blackwell Companion to Ancient Epic* (ed. John M. Foley; Oxford: Blackwell Publishing, 2005), 55–70; J. Vansina, *Oral Tradition as History* (Madison: University of Wisconsin Press, 1985); J. von Ungern-Sternberg, "Romulus Bilder: Die Begründung der Republik im Mythos," in *Mythen in mythenloser Gesellschaft, Das Paradigma Roms* (ed. J. Graf; Stuttgart/ Leipzig: Teubner, 1993), 88–127; *Vergangenheit in mündlicher Überlieferung* (ed. idem and H.J. Reinau; Colloquium Rauricum; Stuttgart: Teubner, 1988), and T.P. Wiseman, *Remus* (Cambridge: Cambridge University Press, 1995).

45 See e.g. Herbert C. Grueber, *Coins of the Roman Republic in the British Museum*, 3 vols. (London: British Museum, 1910; repr. London: British Museum, 1970), vol. 1,145,1; 284, 562; 514–17; 926–27; 3208–9; 4018; 4023; Harold Mattingly and Robert A.G. Carson, *Coins of the Roman Empire in the British Museum*, 6 vols. (London: British Museum, 1932–62; repr. London: British Museum, 1962), II, 223–24; III, LXXIV, 9; Edward A. Sydenham, *The Coinage of the Roman Republic* (New York: American Numismatic Society, 1976), 95, table 14; 297, b-d; 530; 781a table 22; 965; Michael H. Crawford, *Roman Republican Coinage*, 2 vols. (Cambridge: Cambridge University Press, 1974), 20,1; 21,2; 183,1; 183,3–4; 235, table XXXVI,1; 388,1a,1b table XLIX,10 e11; 472,2; Harold Mattingly, Edward A. Sydenham, C.H.V. Sutherland, Robert A.G. Carson, *The Roman Imperial Coinage*, 10 vols. (London: British Museum, 1923–94), II, 193, table XIII, 249; II, 194 table I,12; III, 649; III, 734; IV, 15 table 6,9; VII, Thessalonica 187, 229; VII, Cizico, 71; VII, Roma 354; Robert A.G. Carson, *Coins of the Roman Empire* (London and New York: Routledge, 1990), table 41, 607; Laura Breglia, *La prima fase della coniazione romana dell'argento* (Rome: P&P Santamaria, 1952); Peter Thompsen, *Early Roman Coinage: A Study of Chronology*, 3 vols. (Copenhagen: Nationalmuseets Skrifter, 1957–61; repr. vol. 1 1974), 50,4, p. 51, fig. 7, p.101.

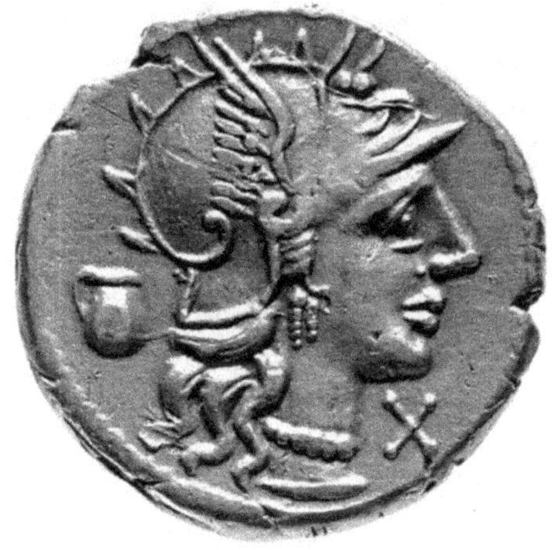

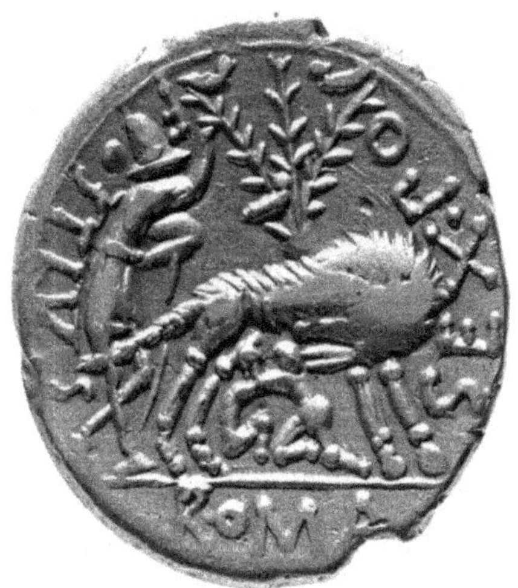

Denarius of Sestio Pompeio Festulo, 135–126 B.C.; RRC 235/1; ©ANS 1999.13.1[46]

In addition, the prevalence of statues or bas-reliefs of the mother wolf with the children positioned under a fig tree gives us a notion of the familiarity with this story. The combination of the nursing mother wolf, rescued twins, and the fig tree is so prominent that all subsequent combinations of these images evoke the same idea. This holds to a special degree also for the fig tree, which in the first century B.C.E. had impacted the Forum Romanum and its surroundings.

46 See e.g. Eugenio La Rocca, "La memoria delle origini: le immagini della lupa con I gemilli in età romana," in *La Lupa Capitolina di Claudio Parisi Presicce* (ed. Eu. La Rocca and A. Mura Sommella et al.; Rome: Elemond Editiori Associati, 2000), 21–33.

The nourishing aspect stands at the center of this imagistic tradition and is represented visually by the mother wolf and the fig tree. The name of the fig tree, *ficus Ruminalis*, is etymologically connected with *Ruminalis* or *rumis*, which stands for the female breast,[47] or with the toponymic connection with the Etruscan *Rum*, that is, the goddess Roma.[48] Thus the veneration of the fig tree combines the story of the saving of the twins and the story of the goddess Roma. The connection between the city of Rome and its legendary founder is made apparent on coins on which a leaf of the fig tree is represented on the reverse together with the she-wolf, Romulus and Remus and Roma. Especially typical, of course, is the inscription: ROMA. This title, accordingly, designates both the goddess as well as those in the engraved group with the fig tree. Although a nourishing function is attributed to the fig tree, it is striking that nowhere in the visual images are the fruits of the tree also displayed. Moreover, it is noteworthy that the cultic veneration of Rome might externally have relied more readily on Roma, whereas the veneration of the foundation of Rome might internally have been molded by Romulus and the fig tree. Thus numerous cults and monuments in honor of Rome which are dedicated to the goddess Roma are found in Greece. But also in Palestine, Syria, and Caesarea, coins were minted with the Roman goddess adorning the obverse.

So far we have taken our bearings from images that point to Romulus the child as the foundation figure. However, alongside these, numerous images are found depicting the adult Romulus, who like Mars, is bellicose, erects the holy walls around the city, and consequently strengthens the security of its inhabitants and potently extends Roman imperial territory, until finally he is deified by Mars as he is carried away and enters into the heaven of the gods as Quirinius.

Caesar had already set himself the task of rehabilitating the myth of Romulus. Of his successor Dio Cassius reports that the senators "wished to call him by some distinctive title, and men were proposing one title and another and urging its selection, [Octavian] was exceedingly desirous of being called Romulus [...]."[49] Moreover, Suetonius calls him the second founder of the city of Rome and of the Roman Empire.[50]

Besides images of the fig tree, numerous ancient textual sources can be found with somewhat perplexing descriptions of multiple fig trees. Four different fig trees,

47 At this point it is to be connected to the goddess "Rumina" who is often connected with the fig tree and the tradition around Romulus and Remus. Cf. also Ph.C. Robert, "Art. Rumina," *DNP online*, Brill, 2009.

48 Cf. Robert, "Art. Rumina," *DNP online.*

49 Dio Cass. 53.16.7–8 (LCL E. Cary).

50 Suet. *Aug.* 7; see also Florus 2.34.

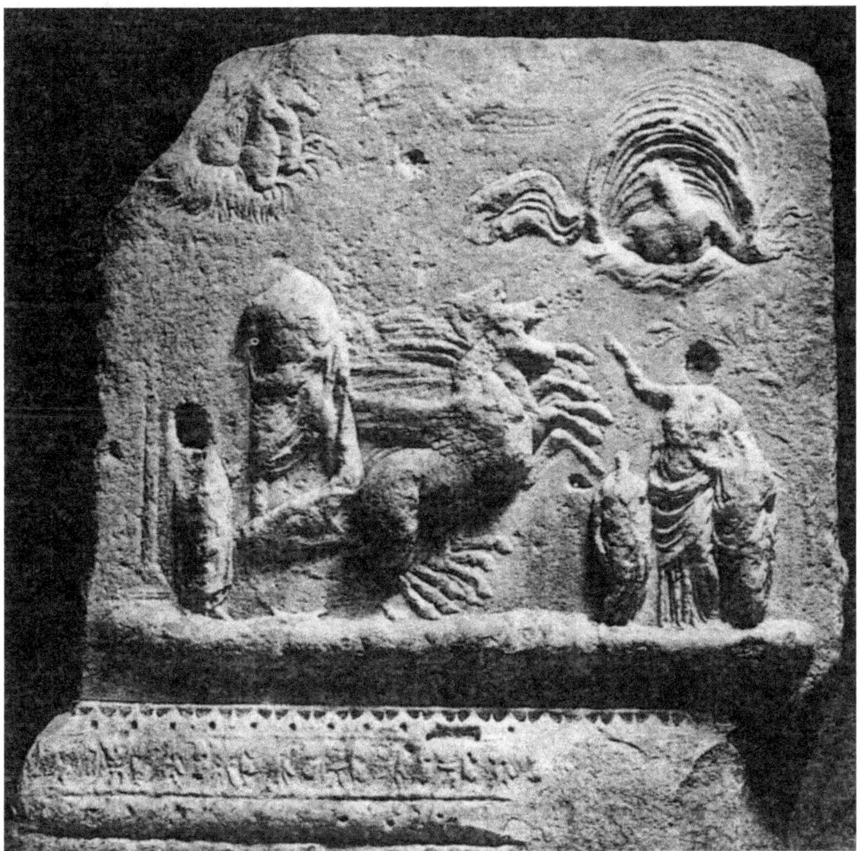

Belvedere Altar, Vatican Museum: apotheosis DAIR 75.1289

which were positioned in central locations in the Forum Romanum and which played a central role in the cultic observances of the inhabitants, are mentioned.[51] All ancient sources known to me are in agreement with respect to one sacred fig tree. It is the *ficus ruminalis* or *ficus Romularis* (Livy and Ovid), which was named for *rumis* – the breast of the goddess Rumina or the teat of the animal.[52] Livy,[53]

51 See Weissenrieder, "The Didactics of Images: The Fig tree in Mark 11:12–14 and 20–21," 271.
52 Ch. Huenemoerder, "Feige," NP, Brill 2009/ Brill online.
53 Livius 1.4.5: "So they made shift to discharge the king's command, by exposing the babes at the nearest point of the overflow, where the fig tree Ruminalis – formerly, they say, called Romularis – now stands. – *ita, velut defuncti regis imperio, in proxima alluvie ubi nunc ficus Ruminalis est – Romularem vocatam ferunt – pueros exponunt.*"

Ovid,[54] Pliny,[55] Plutarch,[56] Servius,[57] and finally Varro[58] connect the tree with the place where the twins were rescued and nursed on the palatine near Lupercal. Hence it is certainly significant that Augustus moved his residence to a location directly beside that of the founding father Romulus.

This message about the identification of the fig tree with Rome could be understood by everyone, as is particularly demonstrated by the fact that historians like Tacitus find it worth mentioning that even this holy *ficus Ruminalis* suddenly lost its leaves in the year 58 and so was cut down. Tacitus says: "In the same year, the tree in the Comitium, known as the Ruminalis, which eight hundred and thirty years earlier had sheltered the infancy of Remus and Romulus, through the death of its boughs and the withering of its stem, reached a stage of decrepitude which was regarded as a portent [...]. *Eodem anno ruminalem arborem in comitio, uae octingentos et triginta ante annos Remi Romulique infantiam texerat, mortuis ramalibus et, arescente trunco deminutam prodigii loco habitum est* [...]."[59] This was evidently perceived as a worrisome sign not only by the simple folk. Subsequently the fig tree in the Forum, the *ficus Curtia*, became the object of reverence and in this move then also received a change in name. Other sources re-

54 Ovid *Fast.* 2.411 ff.

55 Cf. Plinius *Nat.Hist.* 15.77.

56 *Rom.* 4.1 "Now there was a wild fig tree hard by, which they called Ruminalis, either from Romulus, as is generally thought, or because cud-chewing, or ruminating, animals spent the noontide there for the sake of the shade, or best of all, from the suckling of the babes there; for the ancient Romans called the teat 'ruma,' and a certain goddess, who is thought to preside over the rearing of young children, is still called Rumilia, in sacrificing to whom no wine is used, and libations of milk are poured over her victims" (LCL); *De fort. Rom.* 320 C-E.

57 Servius *Ad Aen.* 8.90: "*rumore secundo hoc est bona fama, cum neminem laederent: aut certe dicit eos ante venisse, quam fama nuntiaret venturos. aut 'rumore' pro 'Rumone' posuit; nam, ut supra diximus, Rumon dictus est: unde et ficus ruminalis, ad quam eiecti sunt Remus et Romulus. quae fuit ubi nunc est lupercal in circo: hac enim labebatur Tiberis, antequam Vertumno factis sacrificiis averteretur. quamvis ficum ruminalem alii a Romulo velint dictam, quasi Romularem, alii a lacte infantibus dato: nam pars gutturis ruma dicitur. ergo si fuerit 'Rumone secundo', favente fluvio intellegimus.*"

58 Varro *L.L.* 5.54.

59 Tac. *Ann. 13.58* (LCL V). Pliny *Nat.Hist.* 15.77 "*Colitur ficus arbor in foro ipso ac comitio Romae nata, sacra fulguribus ibi conditis magisque ob memoriam eius quae, nutrix Romuli ac Remi, conditores imperii in Lupercali prima protexit, ruminalis appellata, quoniam sub ea inventa est lupa infantibus praebens rumim, (ita vocabant mammam), miraculo ex aere iuxta dicato, tamquam in comitium sponte transisset Atto Navio augurante. nec sine praesagio aliquo arescit rursusque cura sacerdotum seritur. fuit et ante Saturni aedem, urbis anno* [...] *sublata sacro a Vestalibus facto, cum Silvani simulacrum subverteret.*" Cf. also W.R. Telford "More Fruit from the Withered Tree: Temple and Fig-Tree in Mark from a Graeco-Roman Perspective," 264–304.

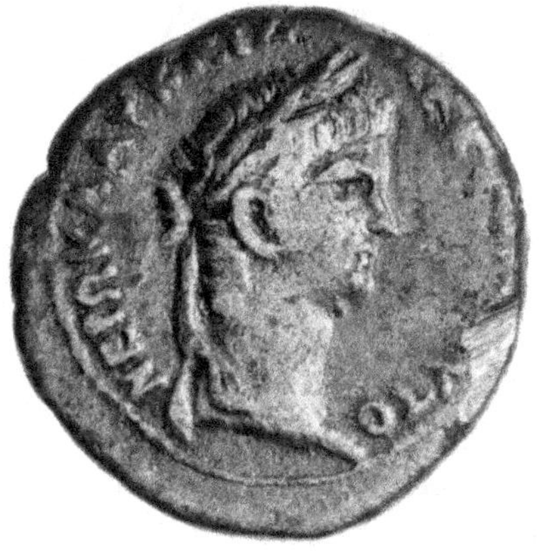

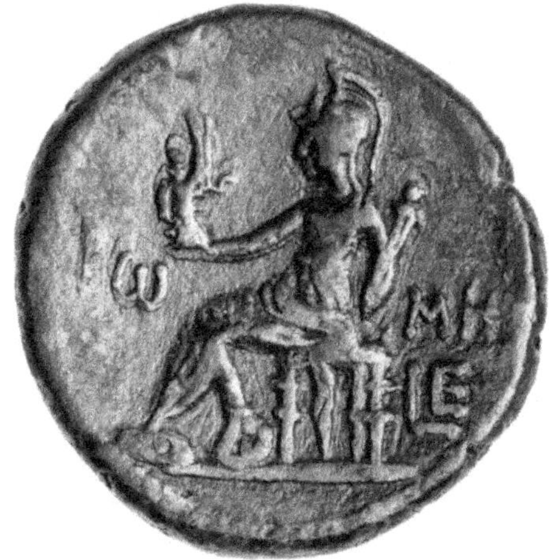

Obverse: NERO KLAV KAIS SEBA GER AVTO; Head Nero laur. r.; reverse: Roma std. l. holding Victory, legend: ROME; © ANS 1974.26.2116

port that the tree had once again borne fruit, which is almost certainly a legend.[60] According to Hartmann, these varying interpretations primarily make one thing clear: that it was possible for a legend to be created within just a few years.[61] So it is finally not coincidental that, using a model that was already in circulation under Caligula, Nero had a new coin minted that emphasizes the special position of the fig tree as an emblem for Rome. While Aeneas is shown as *pius* Aeneas on

60 In this regard, Pliny describes a new planting by the priests in the era of Nero Pliny. *Nat.Hist.* 15.77: *nec sine praesagio aliquo arescit rursusque cura sacerdotum seritur.* Tacitus says that the tree later bore fruit again (Tac. *Ann.* 13.58)

61 See Andreas Hartmann, *Zwischen Relikt und Reliquienpraxis: Objektbezogene Erinnerungspraktiken in Antiken Gesellschaften* (Berlin: Verlag Antike, 2010), 518 f.

Caligula's coin, on Nero's Romulus was the warrior-king and he is shown as Romulus *triumphans*. The propaganda embodied in Romulus as the Romulus *triumphans* highlighted Augustus', Caligula's, and later also Nero's own role with their triumphs.[62] Caligula's numismatic message is picked up by Nero and sharpened. A relief of a pediment of the Temple of Quirinus is very interesting: In the middle stands Augustus with Roma and Fortuna. The figures adorning the ornamental gable area: in the middle appear Romulus with the fig tree and Mars Ultor, who was Romulus' adopted father. Now Nero draws the parallel between Augustus and the founder of the city Romulus. Here the role of the second founder of the city and of the deified human being falls to Augustus. In this context, a coin from the year 58 is remarkable: Nero's head is pictured on the obverse. On the reverse a representation of Roma is found as an allegory of bellicose Rome and the allegory of peace and triumph in the image of a woman. However, inasmuch as Nero associates this with the representation of his bust on the obverse, he makes one thing clear: the Roman Empire interprets the representation of the fig tree not as a bad omen, but relates it to the long positive tradition. And it is noteworthy that this coin was not only minted as a city coin for Rome but widespread in the Roman Empire. It is therefore plausible that the news of the fig tree which symbolized the foundational myth of the Roman Empire and especially the Roman triumph was well-known at that time.

A noteworthy development can also be noted in Galilee, where evidence of the Roman motif of the sacred fig tree and the suckling she-wolf has shown up not only on coinage but also recently on another archaeological find. Two researchers, Richard A. Freund and Rami Arav, leaders of the Bethsaida Excavation Project,[63] discovered the motif of the nursing she-wolf on a small basalt originally in a first-century C.E. Roman Imperial cult temple built by Herod Philip in honor of Livia Julia in Bethsaida, across the Jordan from Chorazin, where it is now in the gable of the synagogue.[64]

The two threads of motifs, the withering of the fig tree together with the renaming of the *ficus Curtia* to *ficus Ruminalis* as it is documented for us by some authors, and the minting of the coin of Nero, intersect in the year 58 C.E. This dat-

62 Cf. Weissenrieder, "The Didactics of Images. The Fig tree in Mark 11:12–14 and 20–21."

63 See in Weissenrieder, "The Didactics of Images: The Fig tree in Mark 11:12–14 and 20–21," 278–79.

64 Cf. E.R. Goodenough's work, *Jewish Symbols in the Greco-Roman Period*, vol. 1 (New York: Pantheon Books, 1953), page 194–95, it is figure 492, from the Chorazin synagogue. He did not think to associate it with Romulus and Remus. It is obviously a hybrid version made to look like the classical view but with slight differences. He simply says: "Fig. 492 shows an animal suckling her young."

ing offers us a concrete clue to the historical context of the passage about the fig tree. The tradition of the fig tree in Rome can, therefore, just like the Old Testament passages, convey the punishing action of God, but it also has the advantage of explaining the proximity of the fig tree to the temple in Mark and Matthew. Through it we can see the meaning of the fig tree for the 1st century C.E. in a specific locale, as well as the background of the story in the legends about Rome's founding fathers. From this, the story of the withered fig tree might have been located in Rome rather than in Palestine.

4 The cultural translation of the fig tree in Matthew, Mark and Luke

We have seen that the fig tree appears on coins as well as in reliefs as an allegory for the founding of Rome and for the founding figures of Romulus and Augustus. But is it also evident from the Synoptic gospels that the fig tree refers to Rome and the founding fathers, and what repercussions do these political dimensions then have in connection with the miracle of the fig tree? Did the visual images on coins and state reliefs have an effect on the Gospel text?

It is interesting to examine Mark's and Matthew's terminology for withering: ἐξηραμμένην ἐκ ῥιζῶν (*exērammenēn ek rizōn*) Mark 11:20; καὶ ἐξηράνθη παραχρῆμα ἡ συκῆ (*kai exēranthē parachrēma hē sukē*) Matt 21:19. Especially striking is the participle ἐξηραμμένην, because the Septuagint and also numerous ancient sources instead use the verb κατερρύηκεν for the withering of a plant. Now it is surely notable that except for the reference to this passage in the writings of the church fathers Gregory of Nyssa and Clement and the continuing historical explanations of the Christian historian Oribasius, the concept of withering is found mostly in medical sources. It is especially abundant in writings that investigate the way nourishment affects the human body, e.g. the Pseud-Hippocratic text *De diaeta*[65] or Galen's *Locis Affectis* or *De Simplicium Medicamentorum Temperamentis ac Facultatibus*.[66] There are also numerous references in the *Epitomae Medicae Libri Septem* of Paul of Aegina.[67] Interestingly, these passages speak not of drying up leading to the death of the whole body, but rather of an occasional loss of liquid from a single organ or body limb. Thus *De mulieribus* cites the drying up of

65 CH *Vict* XXI,7.

66 Galen *Loc. Aff.* VIII,172 (K.); *Meth. Med.* X,410 (K.); *Simpl. Med. Temp. Ac Fac.* XII, 146. 147. 294 (K.); *Thrasyb. Med.* V,852 (K.); *De Usu Part.* III, 471 (K.).

67 Paulus *Epit.* VII.3.1; VII.3.8; VII.3.12; VII.3.16; VII.3.20.

the milk in the breast of a breastfeeding mother and *De victu* I mentions the "driest water [in the body], [...] because the fire has the moisture from the water, and the water the dryness from the fire"[68] and in the Epidemics we find the commentary "may the body dry up in the sickbed [...]."[69] According to these references, the concept ξηραίνω marks not the complete demise of a body part, but a temporary state of the body which can absolutely be changed back.

The New Testament also has reports of drying up in the body ἐξηραμμένην (*exērammenēn*), namely with the healing of the "withered hand" on the Sabbath (Luke 6:8) and the healing of the woman with the flow of blood (Mark 5:29 parr.). In addition the term ξηραίνω (*xērainō*) is also used in the parable of the sower: In three stories the drama is told *in the parable* about sowing and the failure of the seed, and three criteria are central, namely place, time and opponent: the unfavorable places cause the sowing not to grow at all (κατέφαγεν *katefagen* v.4d), or to sprout early (ἐκαυμάτισεν αὐτό *ekaumatisen auto* v.6a) or too late (ἐξηράνθη *exēranthē* 4,6b; ἀνέβησαν *anebēsan* vv.4,7c). The birds, the sun and the thorns as opponents do the rest. The inability of the plant to grow is the result of unfavorable conditions. This example is especially important because Jesus personifies here the seed as different persons. Therefore, the use of the concept ξηραίνω could point to the fact that Jesus appeals here to the tree as a human body and personifies it. And from these examples it is clear that Mark, Matthew and Luke must have been aware of withering as the physiological meaning of ἐξηραμμένην (*exērammenēn*).

Nevertheless, this makes sense only if the fig tree is also a personification of the goddess Roma in connection with the entry into the temple in the 1st cent. C.E. The personified fig tree in this sense is a figure for Roma as the seed personifies different persons. Therefore it is important that ἐξηραμμένην (*exērammenēn*) is used as withering related to persons and not plants.

In this context, we must once again ask: who is receiving the punishment? Could it be that the fig tree in the Synoptic gospels does not refer to Jerusalem but rather to Rome by personifying the city's founders and refounders – Romulus, Augustus, Caligula and most recently Nero? And who are the addresses in each of the Gospels? In order to answer this question, we must also include the context of the narration.

---

68 CH *Vict.* I 35.
69 CH *Epid.* VII. 222.

4.1 Mark's version 11:12–15, 19–20

While Matthew's story of the fig tree focuses on the city, Mark mentions Bethany, the starting point of the journey for Jesus and his disciples (v. 12), rather than the destination. While references to Jerusalem are found in two obvious places in the story of the temple purification (vv. 15, 19), it is not mentioned in the story of the fig tree. No destination is named in the story of the fig tree. Instead, the emphasis is on the fact that Jesus and his disciples are traveling; this is marked by a series of verbs indicating movement, such as ἐξελθόντων, ἦλθεν, and παραπορευόμενοι (*exelthontōn*, *ēlthen* and *paraporeuomenoi* vv. 12, 13, 20), which further emphasize the act of leaving (ἐξ- *ex-*) a place. This much is clear: the curse laid upon the fig tree is not associated with a place. The only central issue is that the tree is in an exposed location. While the location is only vaguely named, Mark describes various facets of time that share a certain aspect: it is time! The chronological sequence of two days is described using the terms τῇ ἐπαύριον and πρωΐ (*tē epaurion; prōí* the following day; the early morning).[70] The fact that the fig tree has leaves (ἔχουσαν φύλλα *echousan phylla*) can be understood as a seasonal indication. The story takes place in the spring, and it is supposed to be the time shortly before Passover, which also marks the beginning of Jesus' suffering. Since fig trees are deciduous, they lose their leaves in the winter and sprout new leaves in the spring; the spring figs continue to mature, but the first figs cannot be expected at least until May.[71] Jesus' expectation of finding fruit also includes a chronological component. The term εἰ ἄρα (*ei ara*) and the future tense εὑρήσει (*heurēsei* v.13 whether he would find [something on it]) show a sense of expectation that is again emphasized by καιρός (*kairos* time).[72] In the exegesis, καιρός is often interpreted as an indication of the season.[73] As Delling demonstrated, however, in non-Biblical usage καιρός can also refer to a point in time when a god acts as a creator. In contrast to χρόνος (*chronos*), which is understood to mean quickly pas-

70 The story of the fig tree is part of a three-day structure. Is this evidence of a pre-Marcan tradition, or should this structure be understood as an editorial decision? In my opinion, the latter interpretation, which has already been suggested by R. Bultmann and M. Dibelius, is to be preferred. In other words, the story of the fig tree would have been built into the three-day scheme retroactively.

71 For a detailed, more recent account, see Böttrich on Mark ("Jesus und der Feigenbaum," 337 ff.)

72 E.g. Pesch, *Markusevangelium*, 193 and many other scholars after him; see Matt 13:20; 21:34; Mark 12:2; Luke 20:10.

73 By contrast, Cotter, "For it was not the Season for Figs," attempts to show that v.13 can be interpreted as a stylistic feature in Mark ("misplaced order"). The time aspect, he says, refers to Jesus' expectation. It indicates not the failure, but the reason for the search.

sing time, καιρός (*kairos*) more often stands for a point in time that an individual person or a group must use, or that the gods use. Philostratus e.g. uses *kairos* to describe the appearance of Nux in a painting. That is, Nux appears not in a body *sōma* but as *kairos*. The term is always used for a qualitative interpretation of the encounter between God and people, when the "right point in time" is therefore decisive.[74] In the New Testament, too, καιρός (*kairos*) has become established as a salvific term: It is God who sets the time. In Mark's Gospel, καιρός (*kairos*) is given a special position because the term mentions the "fulfillment of time" at the start of the Gospel (Mark 1:15), which is accelerated with the Passion of Jesus in that Mark 10:30 speaks of the end times. This salvific period, directed toward fulfillment, is contrasted with the period of the fig tree's curse: μηκέτι (*mēketi*), never again, and εἰς τὸν αἰῶνα (*eis ton aiōna*), in eternity. The fig tree's curse is thus not limited to a specific point in time, and it characterizes the opposite of καιρός.

In Mark's Gospel, the story's special narrative profile comes from nesting the two parts of the narrative within the story of the cleansing of the temple (vv.12–14.15–19.20–21). Grammatically speaking, at first glance the two stories seem to be consistent; they are characterized by hypotaxes in vv. 13b, 16, 18b, parataxes with καί (vv. 13c, 18c and d) and direct speech (vv. 14, 17bc, 21b). However, four points suggest that the two stories should not be seen as a single narrative unit: (1) first of all, it is interesting that numerous terms are either *hapax legomena* in the New Testament or only appear in Mark's Gospel as part of this story, such as ἐπαύριον (*epaurion*, on the following day v. 12), πεινάω (*peinaō* hungry, exhausted, also in Mark 2:25), ἀναμνήσθεις (*anamnēstheis*, the only place it is seen in the synoptic Gospels and in Mark 14:72, also in connection with Peter) and καταράομαι (*kataraomai* Mark 11:21; *hapax legomenon*). (2) The intent of the high priests and scribes to kill Jesus is mentioned at three central points in Mark's Gospel (3:6; 11:18; 12:2; 14:1). This murderous intent generally forms the conclusion of a pericope, as in 3:6 and 12:2, or the start of a new textual unit, as in 14:1. In this context, it makes sense to read 11:18 as the end of the pericope of the temple cleansing. Thus the narrative is not understood to continue with the story of the fig tree. (3) In addition, Jesus' entry into Jerusalem and into the temple, described in v. 11a (καὶ εἰσελθὼν εἰς τὸ ἱερὸν ἤρξατο ... ἐν τῷ ἱερῷ) is repeated in v.15b. It is also worth noting that the context refers to the significance of the temple at central points, such as 14:49; 14:58 and 15:29. This is the main focus of the text. Furthermore, the high priests and scribes (v. 18) and the crowd (v. 18d) are actors who will play an important role in the following stories as well. (4) Fin-

74 H.C. Hahn and W. Kraus, "*kairos*," *ThBNT* 2, 2003 ff. In the OT, trusting in the right time is particularly anchored in the experiences of the people of Israel (ἐν τῷ καιρῷ εἰκείνῳ).

ally, it is noteworthy that the temple-cleansing pericope cites Isa 56:7 and Jer 7:11, but the story of the fig tree lacks any such biblical reference.[75] These observations suggest that the nesting of the two stories is the result of an editorial revision.[76] For whom, then, is the curse intended? If these observations are correct, then the story of the fig tree is not addressed toward the temple in Jerusalem, nor Jerusalem itself, nor Israel. None of these addressees is named in the story.

There remain only two direct addressees: the disciples and the tree. First of all, it is significant that the disciples are hearing, ἀκούειν (*akouein*, v.14), and that this hearing is not further specified by an object. The word ἀκούειν (*akouein*) expresses a direct perception at this point; in other words, the fact of the disciples' hearing is the main focus here.[77] The disciples hear the curse that Jesus speaks to the fig tree, which also implies understanding: "these words do not mean merely that they heard Jesus curse the fig tree but imply as well that the words penetrated them."[78] Hearing is the first path of perception in order to understand the curse.

Ἀκούειν (*akouein* hearing) is often found at the beginning of a story, and is then the starting point for further actions, as is seen here. It is certainly noteworthy that Mark tells the story of the fig tree's curse before the temple cleansing, but only presents Peter's confirmation of its effect after the temple cleansing. This shows us, firstly, a conscious separation of the curse and Peter's confirmation. The verb ἀναμιμνήσκειν in v. 21 stands out (*anamimnēskein*, remembering again; to recollect);[79] in the other Gospels, this is only seen in Mark 14:72 – also in the context of the Peter tradition. But why must Peter remember it "again"?

---

75 Telford, *The Barren Temple and the Withered Tree*, 39–59, referred explicitly to the editorial tendency of verses 22–26, which I will not repeat again here.

76 Different: Rudolf Pesch, *Das Markusevangelium II. Teil. Kommentar zu Kap. 8,27–16,20* (Freiburg: Herder, 1977), 190f.

77 The differentiation between direct and indirect perception is taken from Kristina Dronsch, *Bedeutung als Grundbegriff neutestamentlicher Wissenschaft: Texttheoretische und semiotische Entwürfe zur Kritik der Semantik dargelegt anhand einer Analyse zu ἀκεύειν in Mk 4* (Tübingen: Francke, 2010), 266–72. This text also includes a list of all the passages in Mark's Gospel relating to direct and indirect perception. While Ernst, *Markus*, 324, speaks of a "'deplacierte' Bemerkung über das Hören der Jünger," Hans F. Bayer, *Das Evangelium des Markus* (HTA; Giessen: Brockhaus, 2008), 398 mentions the importance of hearing.

78 R.M. Fowler, *Let the Reader Understand: Reader-Response Criticism and the Gospel of Mark* (Augsburg, MN: 1991), 121.

79 That Peter remembers is interpreted as a typical motif of recognition that a miracle occurred; see Theißen, *Miracle Stories*, 65–66; Yabro Collins, *Mark*, 534. However, ἀναμιμνήσκειν never occurred before.

Chronological marking is essential to understanding ἀναμιμνήσκειν (*anamimnēskein*).[80] Memory exists "when time has passed"[81]; it is a perception (*aisthesis*) that assumes a before and an after. According to Aristotle, we perceive time when we can perceive and differentiate movement (κίνησις – μετανολή).[82] The chronological dimension is also expressed in a second aspect:[83] the quality of the memory or remembering depends on people's varying personalities. While memory is associated with slowness, remembering implies quickness and action. Do both refer to experiences that have already taken place? The double title *Memoria et reminiscentia* takes this into account: as the continued existence of a memory on the one hand, and as remembering "again" in the sense of a creative "recollection,"[84] a kind of search. Although the two terms describe a similar subject, the prefix ἀνα- (*ana-*) in ἀνάμνησις does indicate a difference. What is this difference, precisely?

Recollection is differentiated from memory work, and clearly defined, when Aristotle says, "But with ἀλλ', when one retrieves knowledge that was (already) known earlier, or an earlier perception or mental image whose retention we have defined as memory, this constitutes recollecting – ἀναμιμνήσκεσθαι (*anamimnēskesthai*) – one of the aforementioned affections."[85] Recollections thus reactivate mental images. The act of recollection attempts to retrieve what has been lost after a period of time has passed, when the impression of the perception or thought is no longer, or not currently, present. Whether or not the impression has been stored in the memory is irrelevant. As a result, one thing is clear: according to Aristotle, there is no causal relationship between remembering and memory. *Recollecting* refers *exclusively* to the impression of the perception or thought and ask for achian. However, when this impression is reactivated though the act of remembering, a memory *can* result. Still, recollection and memory, which both follow the impression of a perception or thought, never coincide. Recollection requires the ability to recover a forgotten object *of one's own accord*. While someone who is learning requires another person to help him or her find the object again, someone who recollects must possess the power of movement.[86] In other

80 Arist. *De mem.* 449b15.

81 Arist. *De mem.* 449b26. (Translation: King)

82 Arist. *Phys.* 221a 5–7.

83 Victor Caston, "Aristotle and the Problem of Intentionality," *Philosophy and Phenomenological Research* 58 (1998): 249–98, here 258.

84 The translation of ἀνάμνησις is a matter of debate. Richard Sorabij, in his translation and commentary for *Aristotle on Memory*, suggested "recollection," while King suggests "remembering" in *Aristoteles. Memoria et reminiscentia*.

85 Arist. *Mem.* 451b4ff.

86 Arist. *De mem.* 452a10f.

words, a person in the process of recollecting performs a series of internal motions so that, "if successful, he will ultimately find the motion that retrieves the object he has been seeking."[87]

Thus ἀναμιμνῄσκειν – recollect/ remember again – is dependent upon listening, ἀκούειν (*akouein*). In this case, listening has a dual function: it describes the act of listening to Jesus' words, but it also means listening to the written text, which is being heard again.[88] These two events – listening to the words of Jesus and listening to the spoken text once again – are separated by a period of time that is indicated in the text by its nesting within the story of the temple cleansing. Seeing the now-withered tree sparks Peter's recollection. As they walk by the tree (παραπορευόμενοι *paraporeuomenoi*; 3rd person plural "they", v. 20), only Peter remembers the curse. This is especially plausible in Mark 16:8 (καὶ οὐδενὶ οὐδὲν εἶπαν): Mark's readers are asked to become listening witnesses to the written Gospel. The disciples as listening witnesses, and not the tree, are thus the main addressee of the Marcan version of the text.

Still, the tree is also treated as an addressee. This suggestion is strengthened even more if we factor in verses 13 and 14 of Mark 11. After Jesus first ascertains that, contrary to his expectation, the fig tree bears nothing but leaves, he addresses the fig tree personally with the pronoun αὐτῇ, which is further reinforced by ἐκ σοῦ ("from you"). Here, as in Matthew's Gospel, the tree can be interpreted as a personification of Rome, which must wither.

We can conclude: the Marcan version focuses on the disciples' listening, which makes them the main addressees of the text. Mark thus reflects the transition between the oral and written versions of the fig tree story. It is likely that not much time has passed between the telling of the story and possibly the historical event – the withering of the *ficus ruminalis* in the Forum Romanum – since according to Mark Peter sees the withered tree himself. Therefore, this story might be connected the local color of Rome.[89] Some might have had knowledge about the local Roman color of this text, which is accessible to us only with difficulty.

---

87 Cf. Wiesner, *Aristoteles*, 130.

88 Dronsch, *Bedeutung als Grundbegriff neutestamentlicher Wissenschaft*.

89 And it is certainly significant that church fathers such as Irenaeus name the place of origin for Mark's Gospel as Rome. Iren. *Contra Haer.* 3.1.1 "After their departure (their deaths), Mark, the disciple and interpreter of Peter, did also hand down to us in writing what had been proclaimed by Peter." C. Clifton Black, *Mark: Images of an Apostolic Interpreter* (Studies on Personalities of the New Testament; Columbia: University of South Carolina Press, 1994), 119 mentions an introductory note in some manuscripts of the Latin version: He [Mark] was Peter's interpreter. After the departure of Peter himself [his death], the same man wrote this Gospel in the regions of Italy." See also Hippol. *Refutatio Omnium Haeresium* 7.18.

In this case, the coin which was minted in 58 C.E. and was widespread in the Roman Empire could have also functioned as a kind of newspaper making this news available.

4.2 The story of the fig tree in Matthew 21:18–22

The story is given a special narrative profile by its two-phase narration as a double pericope: As in 21:1–11 (preparation and entry into Jerusalem) and 21:12–17 (temple cleansing with healings, reactions by the high priests and elders), the vv. 18–22 also contains a double pericope – the cursing of the fig tree (18f.) and the subsequent conversation with the disciples about faith (20–22). And as in the previous pericopes, which contain a miraculous element through healings, for example, this story contains aspects of a miracle narrative.[90] However, it is different from other miracle stories in Matt in that it does not include a metaphysical dimension.[91] While the two preceding stories are given their theological shape by a Biblical quotation, such clear references are lacking in verses 18–22. These differences suggest that the story was not originally included in this context. In addition, Matthew uses the term "immediately," *parachrēma*, which is a hapax legomenon in Matthew, where normally he uses *euthys*, "fast"; this may be because *parachrēma* tends to express the immediacy of an action (right away!).[92]

In the first part of the story, Jesus curses the fig tree ("Never again shall you bear fruit [...]" 19c), with the result that the fig tree "immediately withers" (19d). This immediate withering is repeated verbatim by the disciples, and is associated with a question about the cause; for Jesus' curse only stated that the tree should never again bear fruit, not that it should wither. In other parts of his Gospel, Matthew also shows particular interest in the idea of bearing fruit (Matt 3:8.10; 7:16–20; 12:33; 21:19ff., and Matt 21:43), and describes fruits as being good (Matt 3:10; 7:17.18.19; 12:43), bad (7:17) or foul (12:33). The idea of justice also depends upon the motif of fruit-bearing (Matt 3:10; 7:16; 12:34; 15:13; 21:41), which in the context of the fig tree refers to its never bearing fruit again for all of eternity. Thus it is "no more" (οὐ μηκέτι *ou mēketi*) and "in eternity" (εἰς τὸν αἰῶνα *eis ton aiōna*), the aorist subjunctive is used (*genētai*; instead of the optative in Mark 11:14). In addition it is no surprise when Matthew emphasizes the fact that

90 "Miraculous word, notice, demonstration, admiraton" G. Theißen and A. Merz, *Der historische Jesus: Ein Lehrbuch* (Göttingen: Vandenhoeck & Ruprecht, 3. ed., 2001) 266: "Strafwunder".
91 Ulrich Luz, *Das Evangelium nach Matthäus* (Neukirchen-Vluyn: Benzinger/ Neukirchener, 1992), 23.
92 Telford, *The Barren Temple and the Withered Tree.*

the tree *only* has leaves (*monon*; Matt 21:18). Jesus does not address the hyperbolic concretization of his curse at all, but rather emphasizes the curse by saying that faith can remove mountains (21b). Does this indicate an attempt to top the other miracle stories, in the sense of more "minor" and "major" miracles?[93] And toward whom is the curse directed? Toward Israel, the city, the people or individual Jewish opponents?

First, it is a matter of scholarly debate whether the reader is being directed toward Israel in this section,[94] or whether it is limited to the disciples. In addition to the disciples, the fig tree story also mentions crowds of people (21:8) who support Jesus, as well as blind and lame people whom Jesus had healed, and cheering children (21:15). The opponents mentioned in the context of the story are high priests, scribes and Pharisees (21:15.23.45). Thus individual religious groups and their leaders are mentioned, but never Israel as a whole. Moreover, the crowds of people are characterized as "sheep without a shepherd" (9:36).[95] In any case, there is no explicit mention of salvation for Israel through Jesus and the church. By contrast, Jesus and the disciples are named multiple times in this section as actors. Two aspects undermine the thesis that the reader's attention is directed solely toward the disciples: (1) the stories in Mark and Matthew (Mark 11:12–14; Matt 21:18–19; and in Luke 13:6.9) contain the same verb sequence to the extent that Jesus was hungry, came, found nothing and declared (indicative in Matt). However, while the disciples are the subject of the sentence in Mark's Gospel, in that they listened (ἤκουον *ēkouon*), Matthew's Gospel makes the tree the subject of the sentence: it withered (ἐξηράνθη *exēranthē*, aorist passive). (2) Jesus speaks not only to the disciples, but also to the tree ("from you" ἐκ σου *ek sou*). Thus the disciples are present, but his conversation partner is the tree. Indeed the reader's attention is directed toward the tree, and the tree is what draws the reader's attention. It is addressed. As a result, one can assume that the fig tree is being addressed as a personified emblem of the founding father of Rome. This assumption is confirmed by an additional observation: only in Matthew, in 21:15, is there a reference to Jesus as the son of David, which in turn refers to the family tree and the birth of Jesus, 1:17.20, and 2:2 ("newborn King of the Jews"). Rome's foundation myth is called into question with a new foundation myth: Jesus, the son of David. The mission commandment may even reinforce this argument, in that it applies to "all people," *panta ta ethnē*. According to Bhabha, however, it is

93 Fiedler, *Matthäusevangelium*, 327.

94 Luz, *Matthäus*, 23.

95 Hubert Frankemölle, *Das Matthäusevangelium neu übersetzt, vol 2* (Düsseldorf: Patmos Verlag, 1997), 303.

entirely possible to call a national symbol into question. Thus the story of the fig tree's curse could be read as a political story that does not in fact condemn Israel, but instead the power of Rome. In this context, Bhabha speaks of national counter-stories that shatter the unity-based concept of Rome.[96] Thus it makes sense to interpret the tree not as Jerusalem or Israel, but as Roma, the personified Goddess of War, who bears no fruit and therefore withers. However, one significant argument can be made against this interpretation: the connection with Jerusalem.

Matthew's Gospel shows a particular interest in Jerusalem, which is not just seen cataphorically through the death of Jesus on the cross in Jerusalem, but is also developed with references throughout the entire Gospel (2:1f.; 3:5; 4:25; 5:35; 15:1; 16:21; 17:22f.; 20:17f.). We see a particular concentration of references to Jerusalem in ch. 21. In 21:1, for instance, we learn that Jesus "approaches" Jerusalem, and in 21:10 he "enters into" Jerusalem; in 21:18a, he "went up to the city," and in 21:23 he once again visits the temple. The reference in v. 18 is even more noteworthy because Mark, unlike Matthew, associates the departure with Bethany. The "city" is mentioned, but Jerusalem itself is not mentioned by name. Does the word "city" refer to Jerusalem? The lack of a city name makes it possible to interpret the story as referring to Rome.

We can see that Matthew found the story of the withered fig tree elsewhere and inserted it into his sketch of the Passion narrative. The aforementioned characteristics of the Matthew version suggest that he was aware of the historical context of the withered fig tree in the *Forum Romanum*, and that this might have been the reason he chose the fig tree as a conversation partner.

4.3 Luke's version in 13:1–9

Luke differs significantly from the versions given by Mark and Matthew. While Luke does give the same version as Mark 11:1–12:44, he leaves out the story of the fig tree. Instead, he inserts a complaint about Jerusalem in Chapter 19, which immediately precedes the temple cleansing. In the following, I would thus like to briefly argue that the two pericopes in Mark 11:12–14.20–21par and Luke 13:6–9 are different critiques of the same recollection, but that in Luke they lead into a parable.[97]

---

96 Bhabha, *The Location of Culture*, 205–44.

97 See also François Bovon, *Das Evangelium nach Lukas (Lk 9,51–14,35)* (EKK III,2; Neukirchen-Vluyn: Neukirchener, 1996), 373.

There are numerous obvious similarities between the fig tree story according to Mark/ Matthew and the comparison of the barren fig tree according to Luke: walking to the fig tree, unsuccessfully searching for figs and the complete destruction of the tree, as well as numerous lexical matches such as συκή, ἦλθεν, καρπόν, ἐν αὐτῇ καὶ ... οὐχ οὐδὲν εὗρεν. These form the foundational structure for every story about the fig tree. Luke adopts this structure as well, though with a new twist: the Lucan interpretation is not based on the historical reference to the *ficus Ruminalis* in Rome, but rather on the reference to Pilate's attack on Jewish pilgrims in Rome – mixing human blood with the blood of animals. The massacre may have taken place in the area around the temple. Scholars have noted that this story, like the fig tree pericope in Mark and Matthew, takes place during Passover.[98] Josephus mentions numerous attacks by the Roman ruler, but none of the actions he mentions match the Lucan version.[99] The fig tree episode is in fact connected with Jerusalem here, but it has lost its irreversible character. According to Luke, God's plan for salvation does not abandon the people of Israel and the city of Jerusalem.

This concern can also be seen in the lament for Jerusalem, which precedes the temple cleansing (19:41–44): while the rapidly approaching fate of Jerusalem and the temple is expressed, this is done in the indicative case, which demonstrates the inability to fulfill this wish. One thing, after all, is clear for Luke as well: wishing cannot change the coming judgment of the city and the temple, so this wish falls within the category of the Old Testament prophets' lament.[100] For them, however, as for Jesus, God's renewed care for His people and His city were always certain.

5 Conclusion

The image of the withered fig tree is the subject of broad exegetical debate. It contains a concrete lesson and thus has to be interpreted.

The more specific question is: how can the image of the withered fig tree be explained in such a way that Jesus' reaction to the empty tree does not seem pitiable at best? As we have seen, the earlier references to extra-textual codes of the ancient world, particularly with regard to agriculture in Palestine or Old Testa-

98 See e.g. J. Binzler, "Die Niedermetzelung von Galiläern durch Pilatus," *NT* 2 (1957/58): 24–49, here 29–31.
99 Binzler, "Niedermetzelung," 32–37.
100 Cf. Böttrich, "Jesus und der Feigenbaum," 358.

ment imagery, do not help us much on their own. Instead, we looked at visual materials as ancient extra-textual codes, which are reinforced by references in numerous texts to the withered *ficus ruminalis* in the Forum Romanum. The numismatic materials and the texts, which mainly come from 58 C.E., demonstrate that the image of the withered tree in Rome was well known around 58 C.E. under Nero and that it referred to Roman rule, but particularly to the foundation myth of Rome. The Emperor, according to the coins dating to 58 C.E., is causing Rome to flourish as a world power. The withering of the tree does not by any means indicate a pending downfall. Read in this context, the narrative of the fig tree in Mark and Matthew tells a contrasting story: the symbol for Rome's global power is withered down to the root and will not bear any more fruit. And just as the coins remind us of the foundation myth, the story of the withered tree may remind us of the coming downfall of Rome.

Seen in the context of political propaganda, Jesus' hunger also makes more sense. He concretizes the population's suffering without losing himself in the imagery, although an act of identification is at the forefront here.

We have been able to show that the image of the withered fig tree was not associated directly with the city of Rome or with Jerusalem in either Mark's or Matthew's Gospel. Thus the story is open to transferring the imagery from one culture to the other, from Rome to Jerusalem; in other words, the image of the fig tree simultaneously contains a variety of historical moments and locations. Just as one could connect the image of the withered tree with the historical event in Rome, the image could also be interpreted as referring to the destroyed temple in Jerusalem and to Israel as a whole. This transfer takes place through the criticism of the temple, which is also found in Jeremiah. The performative nature of the cultural translation makes it possible to integrate the foreign into the familiar. The image of the withered fig tree can be explained just as well by the foundation myth of Romulus and Remus as it can by the later event of the destroyed temple, to which the story may be referring. The New Testament texts showed that the foreign culture is made visible in its foreignness: Jesus' hunger and his unsuccessful search for fruit at a time when the tree would not yet have been producing fruit, along with the participle ἐξηραμμένην (withering of a human body part) instead of the verb κατερρύηκεν (withering of a plant in LXX), emphasizes this foreignness.

Should the story thus be interpreted as a miracle of punishment that introduces a new norm? If the interpretation provided here is correct, then it reflects a historical event, namely the withering of the foundation myth of Rome – the *ficus Ruminalis* in the Forum Romanum – which was the subject of wide debate in the ancient texts of Pliny, Tacitus and Plutarch after 58 C.E. There is no doubt that the withered fig tree can be interpreted as a sign from God indicating the coming downfall of Rome. The fact that Peter's recollection plays a central role in both

Mark 11:21 and Mark 14 suggests that the story was inserted later, in the context of the Passion narrative. This would make sense both in Mark and in Matthew.

Because the story in both Mark's and Matthew's versions only includes vague references to the semantic field of curses, because the familiar motifs of miracle stories are barely in evidence here, because a "transfer of power" seems questionable here and because no groundwork is laid for a new norm either, I do not consider it very convincing to assign the story of the fig tree to the genre of the "norm" or "punishment" miracle.

This narrow investigation was accompanied by a more general investigation of cultural translation as a methodological way of deepening the history of religion method.

The starting point was Bhabha's methodological argument about cultural translation. His argument is based on the idea that a text undergoes a transformation when it is immersed in a foreign context. Thus the translated text has a performative character, in which the experience of the foreign is integrated into the familiar, the global into the local. At this point I would like to come back to the concept of cultural translation, particularly the last aspect of the essay, entitled *Community Matters*. Bhabha includes a minority counter-discourse within the concept of community: community is "the territory of the minority, threatening the claims of civility; in the transnational world it becomes the border-problem of the disaporic, the migrant, the refugee."[101] And it is community that determines the place and time of this cultural translation, which thus indicates the place and time of collective identifications.[102] In referring back to Benjamin again, Bhabha describes this historical time as present time, a "present which is not in transition, but in which time stands still and has come to a stop."[103] This, then, is the fourth aspect of the cultural translation concept: cultural difference is represented in a performative way and is reflected in the narrative of the fig tree in Mark, Matthew, and Luke in diverse ways which all mirror varying geographical and time perspectives.

101 Bhabha, "How Newness Enters the World," 231.

102 Bhabha, "How Newness Enters the World," 231: "Binary divisions of social space neglect the profound temporal disjunction – the translational time and space – through which minority communities negotiate their collective identifications."

103 Bhabha, "How Newness Enters the World," 231.

Hartmut Leppin

Imperial Miracles and Elitist Discourses*

It is difficult to work in a field where a classic work already exists. Marc Blochs's exciting thesis *Les rois thaumaturges* (*The Royal Touch: Monarchy and Miracles in France and England*) from 1924 dealt with the phenomenon of rulers working wonders in medieval France and England and remains the primary reference in this field.[1] Bloch collected and interpreted narratives about kings who after their anointment worked wonders on a regular basis, regardless of their personal sanctity, thus testifying to the sanctity of their office. The author himself was struck by the high degree of acceptance of this phenomenon over the centuries. Bloch's main theme is medieval, Christian rulership. Imperial wonders in pagan contexts are mentioned only in passing and as a marginal phenomenon. In my paper, I would like to argue in the first part that imperial wonders were much more important in pagan antiquity than Bloch surmised. Secondly, I will discuss the difference that Christianization made in this regard.[2] It is self-evident that I cannot claim to be complete, but I hope to show the fruitfulness of the pursuit of this question.

There is no doubt that the Roman emperor was regarded as a sacral figure by contemporaries. Many revered him as a god while others prayed to his *numen* or *genius*. Temples for the imperial cult were erected in many public places and the religious rituals of the troops included the celebration of the emperors, but the imperial cult was also fostered in private. Stories about *prodigia* announcing the emperors' rule circulated; their births were often highlighted by miraculous events. The military and political successes of an emperor were regarded as the expressions of divine favor, although, in contrast to China, failure was not enough to dethrone an emperor. There could be coincidences between the *adventus* of an emperor and natural wonders, allowing them to be interpreted as signs of the em-

---

* I am grateful to Paul Boles (Tufts University) for improving my English and Jan Rüdiger (Frankfurt / Main) for comments from the standpoint of a medievalist.

1 Consider also the sceptical remarks scattered in Joachim Ehlers, "Der wundertätige König in der monarchischen Theorie des Früh- und Hochmittelalters," in *Reich, Regionen und Europa in Mittelalter und Neuzeit: Festschrift für Peter Moraw* (ed. Paul-Joachim Heinig, Sigrid Jahns et al.; Historische Forschungen 67; Berlin 2000), 3–19. Continuity between antiquity and medieval history is regarded as possible in Manfred Clauss, *Kaiser und Gott: Herrscherkult im römischen Reich* (Stuttgart 1999), 113–15, 346 s.

2 Cf. the famous article by Ramsay MacMullen, "What Difference Did Christianity Make?" *Historia* 35 (1986): 322–43.

peror's divine character, such as rain after a long period of drought. Generally speaking, the prayers of emperors could bring about miraculous changes in nature and also during battles. What I am now going to discuss, however, is not the sacredness of the Roman emperor in general, but, in conformance with the concept of this volume, a much more restricted theme: their capacity to work healing wonders, especially through their healing touch.[3] This is much more difficult to grasp.

Let us begin with an episode in the life of Emperor Vespasian.[4] After Nero's death in 68 CE, several imperial pretenders arose. Whereas Galba and Otho soon perished, Vitellius, the commander of the troops who had been stationed in Germania, established himself in Rome. Opposing him was Vespasian, a Roman ex-consul and successful military commander of equestrian background, who was acclaimed by his troops. He had no dynastic ties to the Julio-Claudian dynasty and thus no right to the throne except by way of his military prowess. When the commanders of the troops in the Danube region declared for him, his military superiority became obvious. His allies marched to Rome, whilst the pretender himself secured the rich province of Egypt which was of central importance for the grain supply of the capital. In Alexandria, where he arrived in the end of 69, Vespasian received notice of his rival's defeat and subsequent death in Rome. Nevertheless, he probably felt uneasy in Egypt because tax increases were provoking protests. Generally, his legitimacy was easily contested, as he in fact was nothing more than a commander who had successfully grabbed the throne. Therefore various stories were circulated with the clear intention of supporting the view that Vespasian's rule was providential. A series of *omina* which allegedly had taken place at the time of his birth, and throughout various stages of his career until his time in Judaea, were disseminated.[5] He was even acclaimed as New Serapis in Alexandria.[6] This is the Egyptian context to which the anecdotes about Vespasian's healing miracles belong.

---

3 Trevor Stacy Luke, "A Healing Touch for Empire: Vespasian's Wonders in Domitianic Rome," *Greece & Rome* 57 (2010): 77–106, 77 s. has a larger concept of miracles. He includes *omina* for future rule and the emperor's influence on nature, as for example the famous rain miracle in the time of Marcus Aurelius.

4 For Vespasian: Barbara Mary Levick, *Vespasian* (Oxford 1999); M. Gwyn Morgan, *69 A.D.: The Year of Four Emperors* (Oxford 2006), 170–255; Filippo Coarelli (ed.), *Divus Vespasianus: Il bimillenario dei Flavi* (Rome 2009).

5 Cf. the impressive list in Suet. *Ves.* 4 s.

6 For the religious veneration of Vespasian in Egypt: SB XVI 12255 (P. Fouad 1.8) with Orsolina Montevecchi, "Vespasiano acclamato dagli Alessandrini – ancora su P. Fouad 1.8," *Aegyptus* 61 (1981): 155–70; cf. the divergent interpretations in Philippe Derchain, "La visite de Vespasian au Serapeum d'Alexandrie," *ChrEg* 56 (1953): 261–79 (Vespasian was not formally enthroned, but

However, it is neither this problem nor the clear political or propaganda dimensions in which I am interested. I propose to read the evidence as a source for the perception of the possibility of imperial wonders in Roman society, and as evidence for discussions among the elite about this subject. This calls for a close reading of some passages from the relevant texts; our most significant source is Tacitus, who writes in his *Histories* about Vespasian's accession to the imperial throne. Tacitus is well-known as an imposing representative of senatorial historiography. Rationality and detestation for bigotry seem to imbue every sentence of his work. Thus, the 81st chapter of the fourth book, which deals with miracles worked by Vespasian, has always worried his friends among classicists.[7] This

underwent a certain royal ritual); Albert Henrichs, "Vespasian's Visit to Alexandria," *ZPE* 3 (1968): 51–80, esp. 65–72; Jean Gagé, *"Basiléia": Les Césars, les rois d'orient et les "Mages"* (Paris 1968), 130–35; for the Egyptian background with the *veneratio* of Serapis: Sarolta Anna Takács, "Vespasian as New Serapius," in *Isis and Sarapis in the Roman World* (Leiden 1995), 96–98 (Vespasian was to be interpreted as a god against the Egyptian background); Lothar Spahlinger, "Sueton-Studien II: Der wundertätige Kaiser Vespasian (Sueton, Vesp. 7, 2–3)," *Philologus* 148 (2004): 325–46, esp. 340; Stefan Pfeiffer, "Ägypten in der Selbstdarstellung der Flavier, *Tradition und Erneuerung," in Mediale Strategien in der Zeit der Flavier* (ed. Norbert Kramer, Christiane Reitz; Beiträge zur Altertumskunde 285; Berlin/New York 2010), 273–88 underlines that Vespasian was not regarded as Pharaoh.

7 *Per eos menses quibus Vespasianus Alexandriae statos aestivis flatibus dies et certa maris opperiebatur, multa miracula evenere, quis caelitim favor et quaedam in Vespasianum inclinatio numinum ostenderetur. e plebe Alexandrina quidam oculorum tabe notus genua eius advolvitur, remedium caecitatis exposcens gemitu, monitu Serapidis dei, quem dedita superstitionibus gens ante alios colit; precabaturque principem ut genas et oculorum orbes dignaretur respergere oris excremento. alius manum aeger eodem deo auctore ut pede ac vestigio Caesaris calcaretur orabat. Vespasianus primo inridere, aspernari; atque illis instantibus modo famam vanitatis metuere, modo obsecratione ipsorum et vocibus adulantium in spem induci: postremo aestimari a medicis iubet an talis caecitas ac debilitas ope humana superabiles forent. medici varie disserere: huic non exesam vim luminis et redituram si pellerentur obstantia; illi elapsos in pravum artus, si salubris vis adhibeatur, posse integrari. id fortasse cordi deis et divino ministerio principem electum; denique patrati remedii gloriam penes Caesarem, inriti ludibrium penes miseros fore. igitur Vespasianus cuncta fortunae suae patere ratus nec quicquam ultra incredibile, laeto ipse voltu, erecta quae adstabat multitudine, iussa exsequitur. statim conversa ad usum manus, ac caeco reluxit dies. utrumque qui interfuere nunc quoque memorant, postquam nullum mendacio pretium.* I am quoting the translation by Alfred John Church and William Jackson Brodribb for this passage. Dorit Engster, "Der Kaiser als Wundertäter – Kaiserheil als neue Form der Legitimation," in *Tradition und Erneuerung: Mediale Strategien in der Zeit der Flavier* (ed. Norbert Kramer, Christiane Reitz; Beiträge zur Altertumskunde 285; Berlin/New York 2010), 289–309 is fundamental for the importance of the miracles for Flavian representation and for their addressee. Luke, "A Healing Touch for Empire," offers a sophisticated approach: he puts the narrations of the wonders as the results of Domitianic interpretation of history which underlined the divinity of the emperor. If he is correct, this would not change my argument that even Roman elites accepted wonders to a certain degree;

makes going through the text phrase by phrase even more important. *In the months during which Vespasian was waiting at Alexandria for the periodical return of the summer gales and settled weather at sea, many wonders (*miracula*) occurred which seemed (*ostenderetur*) to point him out as the object of the favor of heaven and of the partiality of the Gods.* From the beginning, Tacitus makes the connection between divine authorization and wonders clear. The main philological problem is how to understand *ostenderetur* within this context, which has been translated with 'seemed.' Does it, as a conjunctive, give an ironic twist to the text, as Ronald Syme supposed,[8] referring to a sort of staged miracles? This would presuppose that the word would have the sense of *ostentaretur*, which is possible. Or is it used in a neutral way, with the meaning 'to make evident,' which would be the normal use of this verb and therefore might be the more convincing interpretation? The conjunctive could be explained by the modal implication of the sentence.[9] In any case, the interpretation of *ostenderetur* only refers to the historian's intention, which is less important to my interpretation than his description of the attitude of the persons involved. It is clear that Tacitus presupposes that there were people who believed that miracles of this kind showed the favor of the gods or the divine character of the emperor as a New Serapis.[10] And even if, as some rationalizing interpretations suggest,[11] adulatory Egyptian priests manipulated the scene, it is undisputable that there was a receptive public for imperial miracles in Alexandria. Tacitus continues his report with the following: *One of the common people of Alexandria, well known for his blindness, threw himself at the Emperor's knees, and implored him with groans to heal his infirmity. This he did by*

Gregor Weber, *Kaiser, Träume und Visionen in Prinzipat und Spätantike* (Historia ES 143; Stuttgart 2000), 382–86; Spahlinger, "Sueton-Studien II," for the narrative structure; see moreover Lisa Palmirani, "Vespasiano: Uomo degli dei?," *Rivista Storica dell' Antichità 29* (1999): 177–98, 188–98; Ulrike Riemer, "Wundergeschichten und ihre Erzählabsicht im Kontext antiker Herrscherverehrung," *Klio 86* (2004): 218–34 and "Miracle Stories and their Narrative Intent in the Context of the Ruler Cult of Classical Antiquity," *The Wonders Never Cease: The Purpose of Narrating Miracle Stories in the New Testament and its Religious Environment* (ed. Michael Labahn and Bert J. L. Peerbolte; London 2006), 32–47 (40–44 for imperial healing miracles) argues that Christian miracle stories adopted pagan *topoi*.

8 Ronald Syme, *Tacitus* vol. 2 (Oxford 1963), I 206.

9 See Raphael Kühner and Carl Stegmann, *Ausführliche Grammatik der lateinischen Sprache* vol. II 2 (reprint Darmstadt 1982 [1976]), 296; this interpretation is contested apodictically by Heinz Heubner, *P. Cornelius Tacitus, Die Historien 4. Viertes Buch: Mit einem Beitrag über Vespasian in Alexandria und Sarapis* (Heidelberg 1976), add. l.

10 Henrichs, "Vespasian's Visit to Alexandria," 71; Luke, "A Healing Touch for Empire," 103.

11 For example Albrecht Dieterich, "Griechische und römische Religion," *Archiv für Religionswissenschaft* 8 (1905): 475–510, esp. 500, n. 1.

the advice of the God Serapis, whom this nation, devoted as it is to many superstitions, worships more than any other divinity. He begged Vespasian that he would deign to moisten his cheeks and eye-balls with his spittle. Another with a diseased hand, at the counsel of the same God, prayed that the limb might feel the print of a Caesar's foot. Readers of Tacitus stumble over this passage, whereas scholars accustomed to miracle stories will not be surprised by it; the literary structure is well known – Christian theologians especially will know about the healing power of saliva.[12] Putting a foot on a diseased limb is also a healing practice attested to elsewhere.[13] In those phrases we encounter people who are typical beneficiaries of wonders: men who suffer from infirmities that cannot be cured in a normal way and who ask for the intervention of supernatural powers. Tacitus introduces the name of Serapis, whose cult is numbered among the *superstitiones* of the Egyptians. In fact, one of the most popular stereotypes about Egyptians in antiquity was their superstitiousness. Tacitus seems to demonstrate his uneasiness with what happened to Vespasian in Alexandria. On the other hand, some chapters later Tacitus' histories offer a long excursus about the origin of the cult of Serapis in Egypt. This is based on the accounts of Egyptian priests and contains some bewildered remarks, presupposing that this god can be the source of miracles.[14]

But once again: my aim is not to reconstruct the author's intention as most philologists set out to do, but his reflection of the attitude of Roman elites to imperial miracles. In this regard, Vespasian's conduct is extremely illuminating because of his skepticism. There were other thaumaturges who sometimes refused to work a wonder, but usually the thaumaturges of the ancient world trusted in their own power. Vespasian, on the other hand, is obviously embarrassed by the whole situation:[15] *At first Vespasian ridiculed and repulsed them. They persisted;*

12 Mark 8:22–26 (cf. 7:31–37); John 9:1–7; Engster, "Der Kaiser als Wundertäter," 296; Palmirani, "Vespasiano: Uomo degli dei?," 191 suggests Christian influence. But miracles of this kind were not specifically Christian, cf. Spahlinger, "Sueton-Studien II," 333.

13 Plu. *Pyrrh.* 3; Otto Weinreich, *Antike Heilungswunder: Untersuchungen zum Wunderglauben der Griechen und Römer* (Gießen 1909), 67.

14 Tac. *Hist.* 4.83.

15 Lellia Cracco Ruggini, "Imperatori romani e uomini divini (I–VI secolo d.C.)," in *Governanti e intellettuali, popolo di Roma e popolo di Dio (I–VI sec.)* (ed. Peter Brown; Turin 1982), 9–91 makes clear that the capacity to work wonders was not inherent to the emperor's personality, but expression of his high dignity (s. 12–14 for Vespasian); Paolo Frassinetti, "I resoconti dei miracoli di Vespasiano," in *La struttura di Fabulazione antica* (Genua 1979), 115–27 convincingly argues on p. 125 that Vespasian is not described as a holy man since he is doubtful of his capacities. For a different view, Bernd Kollmann, *Jesus und die Christen als Wundertäter: Studien zu Magie, Medizin und Schamanismus in Antike und Christentum* (FRLANT 170; Göttingen 1996), 106–9 on Vespasian, who has a rather broad concept of *theioi andres*.

and he, though on the one hand he feared the scandal of a fruitless attempt, yet, on the other, was induced by the entreaties of the men and by the language of his flatterers to hope for success. At first, Vespasian reacts in a deprecatory way, but then becomes ambivalent about the matter. Interestingly, he is not afraid of making a fool of himself if he accepts the role of wonder-worker – this seems to be something which is compatible with the imperial role. Vespasian in fact struggles with another problem. Tacitus uses a complex phrase: the emperor was anxious about the *fama vanitatis*, the rumor of *vanitas*. *Vanitas* certainly means 'failure, futility' in this passage. But *vanitas* has another connotation, too, 'vanity.' Perhaps Tacitus alludes to the vanity on the part of the alleged possessor of supernatural powers. Vespasian is disquieted about the prospect that he could be shown to be unable to perform miracles which, probably, would raise serious doubts about the divine character of his rule. On the other hand, there were people surrounding him who encouraged him to give it a try, obviously hoping precisely for a sign of divine favor for an emperor whose legitimacy could still be contested.

In general, Vespasian is regarded by modern historians as a pragmatic, sober personality, which is also the picture Tacitus draws. Yet, there seems to be no contradiction between soberness and the interest in miracles in Tacitus' view. This could be an indication that imperial miracles were far better accepted by the Roman elites than is generally believed.

But Tacitus' Vespasian remains hesitant: *At last he ordered that the opinion of physicians should be taken, as to whether such blindness and infirmity were within the reach of human skill. They discussed the matter from different points of view. "In the one case," they said, "the faculty of sight was not wholly destroyed, and might return, if the obstacles were removed; in the other case, the limb, which had fallen into a diseased condition, might be restored, if a healing influence were applied; such, perhaps, might be the pleasure of the Gods, and the Emperor might be chosen to be the minister of the divine will; at any rate, all the glory of a successful remedy would be Caesar's, while the ridicule of failure would fall on the sufferers."* The Alexandrian doctors whom we meet here are excellent diplomats. They do not treat the sufferers as medical cases; they even endorse the possibility of healing if divine power interferes, which they also ascribe to Vespasian. Their assertion that the emperor can only profit from the situation is strange, but effective. Perhaps the idea is that, if Vespasian fails, the assertion of the sufferers to have been admonished by Serapis to implore the emperor must be wrong. Let us again follow Tacitus' narrative: *And so Vespasian, supposing that all things were possible to his good fortune, and that nothing was any longer past belief, with a joyful countenance, amid the intense expectation of the multitude of bystanders, accomplished what was required. The hand was instantly restored to its use, and the light of day again shone upon the blind. Persons actually present attest both facts, even now when nothing is to be gained by falsehood.* Trusting in his good fortune, Vespasian does what he is asked and is successful. Tacitus, our rational Tacitus, does not ascribe the success to Egyptian superstition, but takes it as a credible story. In one of his beloved sarcastic phrases, he states that nobody would have gained an advantage from telling lies at the time when he is writing, after the end of the Flavian dynasty established by Vespasian. While this is not a whole-hearted endorsement, Tacitus does not regard a miracle of this kind as impossible and thus does not deride the testimonies.

In the next chapter the historian deals with a vision had by the emperor. While visiting a temple without attendants, he catches sight of a certain Egyptian called Basilides who, as other people attest, is far away from Alexandria at this time and whose name "Kingly" is reminiscent of the Greek form of the imperial title *basileús*. Tacitus comments neither positively nor negatively on the reality of this vision.

These intriguing passages show that even members of the Roman elite who were committed to traditional Roman values might take the possibility of imperial miracles for granted. This clearly shows that the belief in miracles was not restricted to the lower classes. Vespasian abhors the form of the miracle proper he is asked to perform, afraid that he may fail, but neither he nor the historiographer regard miracles merely as an expression of popular superstition.

Tacitus is not the only author to speak of the miracles worked by Vespasian in Alexandria. Suetonius, an equestrian who was an important figure in the imperial administration under Trajan and Hadrian, is best known as a prolific author who profited from his privileged access to the imperial archives. Among his *Twelve Caesars* we also meet Vespasian working wonders, but Suetonius differs from Tacitus' account in various details.[16] Like Tacitus, he explicitly connects the miracles to Vespasian's accession, though he stresses the uncertainty of his final success in his bid for the imperial throne to a far greater extent. In contrast to Tacitus,

---

16 Suet. *Ves.* 7: *Suscepto igitur civili bello ac ducibus copiisque in Italiam praemissis interim Alexandriam transiit, ut claustra Aegypti optineret. Hic cum de firmitate imperii capturus auspicium aedem Serapidis summotis omnibus solus intrasset, ac propitiato multum deo tandem se convertisset, verbenas coronasque et panificia, ut illic assolet, Basilides libertus obtulisse ei visus est; quem neque admissum a quoquam et iam pridem propter nervorum valitudinem vix ingredi longeque abesse constabat. Ac statim advenere litterae fusas apud Cremonam Vitelli copias ipsum in urbe interemptum nuntiantes. Auctoritas et quasi maiestas quaedam ut scilicet inopinato et adhuc novo principi deerat; haec quoque accessit. E plebe quidam luminibus orbatus, item alius debili crure sedentem pro tribunali pariter adierunt orantes opem valitudini demonstratam a Serapide per quietem: restituturum oculos, si inspuisset; confirmaturum crus, si dignaretur calce contingere. Cum vix fides esset ullo modo rem successuram ideoque ne experiri quidem auderet, extremo hortantibus amicis palam pro contione utrumque temptavit, nec eventus defuit.* Translations by J. C. Rolfe.

Suetonius first reports the vision of Basilides, which in his account is the result of a fervent prayer of the pretender, and is followed by the news of the victory of Vespasian's troops in the second battle of Bedriacum, a victory that would decide the civil war. He then continues with an important sentence introducing the miracles: *Vespasian as yet lacked prestige (*auctoritas*) and a certain divinity, so to speak* (quasi maiestas quaedam), *since he was an unexpected and still new-made emperor; but these also were given him.* In contrast to Tacitus, Suetonius considers a sign of divine favor which might be reflected in miracles as necessary for the imperial role. The use of *auctoritas* is revealing. *Auctoritas* was a central concept of imperial representation during the principate. Augustus famously used it in his *res gestae* (34) to mark the difference between himself and other functionaries who relied on their *potestas*.[17] But for Augustus his *auctoritas* was the result of his former offices, his priestly functions and his deeds for the republic, whereas Suetonius sees in it a sign of divine favor, one which may compensate for the lack of *auctoritas* of the family of Vespasian, who was a *homo novus*.[18] The numinous character of *auctoritas* is underlined in this way as a foundation of imperial sacredness. *Maiestas* is translated with 'divinity' here, which gives a one-sided interpretation of this word, which has a broad sense of sublimity and grandeur.[19] The narration of what the sufferers do is similar to that of Tacitus, although here the ailing man is lame, whereas Tacitus spoke of a defective hand. *A man of the people who was blind, and another who was lame, came to him together as he sat on the tribunal, begging for the help for their disorders which Serapis had promised in a dream; for the god declared that Vespasian would restore the eyes, if he would spit upon them, and give strength to the leg, if he would deign to touch it with his heel.* But the reaction of Suetonius' Vespasian differs fundamentally from the tactical deliberations which Tacitus ascribes to him: *Though he had hardly any faith (*fides*) that this could possibly succeed, and therefore shrank even from making the attempt, he was at last prevailed upon by his friends and tried both things in public before a large crowd; and with success.* Suetonius underlines that the emperor feels uneasy about the possibility of these miracles although the doctors do not play any role in his account. Eventually, his attendants convince Vespasian to give it a try. Suetonius adds no comment, neither on Vespasian's lack of trust or on the success of his working. It is not even clear what Vespasian's lack of *fides*

---

17 For the extensive literature see Dietmar Kienast, *Augustus: Prinzeps und Monarch* (Darmstadt 2009), 84.

18 For this interpretation, Palmirani, "Vespasiano: Uomo degli dei?," 177; more extensively Spahlinger, "Sueton-Studien II," 336–40; for this problem in the reign of Vespasian, David Shotter, "Vespasian, Auctoritas and Britain," *Britannia* 35 (2004): 1–8.

19 Cf. Chiara d'Aloja, *Sensi e attribuzioni del concetto di maiestas* (Lecce 2011), esp. 163.

refers to. Does Suetonius' emperor question the possibility of miracles as a matter of principle, or does he doubt his personal capability to work wonders? In the end, it becomes clear that imperial miracles are possible and yes, Vespasian could perform them.

The third author to mention these miracles is Dio Cassius, a senatorial author writing in the early third century, about a century after Tacitus and Suetonius.[20] He very briefly mentions the miracles among other portents that attest to the divine favor for Vespasian. The reaction of the Emperor and his attendants is not discussed at all. The whole episode, which, however, may have been abridged by Byzantine–Christian editors, seems to be unproblematic; there is no expression of doubt with regard to their veracity. On the other hand, the continuation is sobering: despite the miracles, the Alexandrians turn away from Vespasian because they are not compensated for their loyalty and even have to pay higher taxes. Dio Cassius does not seem to be truly persuaded about the legitimating power of miracles.

Josephus, by the way, ignores this episode entirely, perhaps because he wanted to put the stress on his own prophecy of Vespasian's rule or because he, as a Jew, did not accept miracles of this kind.[21]

Vespasian's miracles are the most extensively attested imperial miracles in antiquity. Mostly, they have been treated as something exceptional connected to the specific situation in Alexandria; sometimes the orientalist paradigm prevails and the wonders are regarded as a specificity of Egypt.[22] This, however, is not true, although the passages do have an Egyptian flair. If wonders of this kind were something oriental, one would expect such miracles to have been mentioned under Hellenistic rulers. Yet, as far as I can see, only one case of healing miracles worked by a Hellenistic king is mentioned in our sources. The wonder-worker in this case is not even an Egyptian king, but Pyrrhus of Epirus, the famous enemy of Rome, who, in contrast to Vespasian did the miracles regularly.[23] There are a few similar cases: Alexander is said to have had dreams which gave him advice on

20 D.C. *68.1.1.*
21 J., *BJ* 4, 656; e.g. Henrichs, "Vespasian's Visit to Alexandria," 76–80; Raban von Haehling, "Der römische Kaiser – ein Wunderheiler?" in *Jesus als Bote des Heils: Heilsverkündigung und Heilserfahrung in frühchristlicher Zeit* (ed. Linus Hauser et al.; Stuttgarter Biblische Beiträge 60; Stuttgart 2008), 226–36, 230; Luke, "A Healing Touch for Empire," 81; Philostr. *V. A.* 5.27 does not mention Vespasian's miracle either, which is not really surprising as the text is focused on Apollonius' importance.
22 Cf. Siegfried Morenz, "Vespasian, Heiland der Kranken: Persönliche Frömmigkeit im antiken Herrscherkult?" *WJA* 4 (1949/50): 370–78.
23 Plu. *Pyrrh.* 3.7–9.

how to heal his comrades.[24] In a similar way, Pericles, not a king, but a leading politician in Classical Athens, allegedly cured an artisan, seemingly mortally injured, after a dream which revealed him the necessary healing herb.[25] Interestingly, all three anecdotes are transmitted by Plutarch, who worked at a time when miraculous powers were ascribed to the Roman emperor. More importantly, all of our sources about Vespasian are deeply steeped in a Roman tradition; nevertheless, neither Tacitus, who exhibits his traditionalism on every page of his work, Suetonius or Dio Cassius questions the reality of the miracles. Imperial miracles were possible in Roman eyes, even in the eyes of members of the Roman elite.[26]

There is further evidence to confirm this thesis. The *vita Hadriani* of the *Historia Augusta* mentions miracles which are worked by Hadrian's touch: *About this time there came a certain woman, who said that she had been warned in a dream to coax Hadrian to refrain from killing himself, for he was destined to recover entirely, but that she had failed to do this and had become blind; she had nevertheless been ordered a second time to give the same message to Hadrian and to kiss his knees, and was assured of the recovery of her sight if she did so. The woman then carried out the command of the dream, and received her sight after she had bathed her eyes with the water in the temple from which she had come. Also a blind old man from Pannonia came to Hadrian when he was ill with fever, and touched him; whereupon the man received his sight, and the fever left Hadrian.* The anecdotes confirm that there were people who believed in the miraculous power of the emperor, although the miracles themselves are different from those worked by Vespasian. Hadrian does not have to become active; they cannot be imputed to him in person. It seems to be enough that he is near the water for it to cure the suffering woman while in the other case the blind man is healed by touching the Emperor. Interestingly, Hadrian himself recovers from fever when touched by this man. This aspect is entirely missing in the accounts about Vespasian.

There is a third point that is important to note with regard to our interest in the attitude of the Roman elite. After narrating the miracles, the author of the *Historia Augusta* makes a poignant remark: *All these things, however, Marius Maxi-*

24 Plu. *Alex.* 41.6 (Craterus); Cic. *Div.* 2.66.135; D.S. 19.103.7; Strab. *15.2.7*; Curt. *9. 8. 20–27*; Iust. *Epit.* 12.10.3 (Ptolemaeus); Weber, *Kaiser, Träume und Visionen*, 368–70.

25 Plu. Per. 13.12 s.; Plin. Nat. 22. 20. 44 (herb); cf. Hieronym. Rhod. Frg. 19 (Wehrli); s. Weber, *Kaiser, Träume und Visionen*, 366–68 who argues plausibly that this anecdote was generated after Pericles' time.

26 Gabriele Ziethen,"Heilung und römischer Kaiserkult," *Sudhoffs Archiv: Zeitschrift für Wissenschaftsgeschichte* 78 (1994): 171–91 (182–85 on Vespasian) underlines that the emperor was often described as the healer (*sotér*) of the problems in the empire; this might have facilitated the acceptance of miracles.

mus declares were done as a hoax.[27] Marius Maximus, a contemporary of Dio Cassius, was often adduced as an authority by the author of the *Historia Augusta*. He obviously was skeptical about all of this miraculous stuff. Admittedly, the author of the *Historia Augusta* is a very difficult case. He wrote a pagan text in a Christian world – the Roman Empire of the fourth century. His work is notorious for its untrustworthiness although the *vita Hadriani* is generally regarded as a relatively reliable text.

One could ask whether the remarks on Hadrian's miracles contain anti-Christian polemic, as is often the case in the *Historia Augusta*. I think that this possibility can be dismissed: we will see that Christian emperors were very hesitant in working miracles; in addition, Hadrian's miracles cannot be read as paratexts to biblical wonder-stories. Therefore, these passages from the *Historia Augusta* can be understood most convincingly as documents of a tradition from the second century connected to the name of Marius Maximus.

Our third attestation does not come from historiography, but from a panegyrical text; I refer to Pliny's panegyric of Trajan. When he describes the emperor's *adventus* in Rome, he depicts the people flooding together to greet the emperor, among them the sick: *They disregarded their doctors' orders and dragged themselves out for a glimpse of you as if this could restore their health.*[28] Since panegyrics set out to paint a positive image of the events described, suffering people who believed they have the chance to be healed by the emperor's presence are painted into the impressive scenery. Those people were obviously not despised, although the Latin word *quasi*, which has been translated with 'as if' here, leaves open whether their expectations were valid. While Pliny does not mention any-

---

27 *Hist. Aug. Hadr.* 25: *1 Ea tempestate supervenit quaedam mulier, quae diceret somnio se monitam, ut insinuaret Hadriano, ne se occideret, quod esset bene valiturus. Quod cum non fecisset, esse[t] caecatam. iussam tamen iterum Hadriano eadem dicere atque genua eius osculare ⟨oculos⟩ receptura⟨m⟩, si id fecisset. 2 Quod cum ex somnio implesset, oculos recepit, cum a⟨qua⟩, quae in fano erat, ex quo venerat, oculos abluisset. 3 Venit et de Pannonia quidam vetus caecus ad febrientem Hadrianum eumque conti[n]git. 4 Quo facto et ipse oculos recepit, et Hadrianum febris reliquit. Quamvis Marius Maximus haec per simulationem facta commemoret.* Translation by David Magie. Weber, *Kaiser, Träume und Visionen*, 386–88; Peter Kuhlmann, *Religion und Erinnerung: Die Religionspolitik Kaiser Hadrians und ihre Rezeption in der antiken Literatur* (Formen der Erinnerung 12; Göttingen 2002), 139–42, who thinks that the author wants to characterize Hadrian, who in fact appears to be weak, in a negative way; Jörg Fündling, *Kommentar zur Vita Hadriani der Historia Augusta* vol. 2 (Antiquitas 4.3; Bonn 2006), 2, 1097–1102 who suggests that this anecdote was an anti-Christian construction – as always in interpreting the *Historia Augusta* it is difficult to determine how subtle the allusions might have been.

28 Plin. *Pan.* 22.3: *aegri quoque neglecto medentium imperio ad conspectum tui quasi ad salutem sanitatemque prorepere.* Translation by Bethy Radice.

body who was actually healed, this should not be interpreted as criticism of the emperor. For the orator the most important point seems to have been the trust of his subjects in the emperor as part of the celebrations of his *adventus*.

To draw a first conclusion: it is clear that imperial miracles were regarded as possible by many Romans, at least in the time of the Flavians and the early second century. The prominence of attestations from this time is perhaps due to the hazards of transmitting the tradition, but might also be linked with the necessity of legitimizing new emperors, evident in the most spectacular sense with Vespasian. Perhaps trust in imperial miracles was fading at the time around 200 CE, which would be reflected in the comments of Dio Cassius and Marius Maximus. Secondly, when the concept of imperial miracles became popular, a belief in them was not restricted to people of the lower classes or from the East, but was shared by members of the elite and even by a traditionalist, sober historiographer such as Tacitus. But imperial wonders were not an everyday occurrence. Emperors did not offer their healing powers spontaneously. It seems to have been necessary that the rulers were asked to work wonders by people who had been admonished by divine powers to access the emperor. Among the sick who asked the emperor for help, no member of the elite is mentioned. Miracles occurred on the rare occasions when weak people could get in contact with the emperor. Thus, the scarcity of the attestation of imperial miracles is not surprising; they were connected to very special circumstances such as the imperial *adventus*. As regards imperial representation, miracles seem to have been conceived of as an expression of *laetitia*, a climate of exultation which occurred during public festivities, namely when the emperor met his subjects.[29] Even if the miracles were in general regarded as possible events, they were not an experience one had every day.

Christianization profoundly changed the context of miracles; however, they remained important signs attesting to God's rule of the world and to the deep relationship between God and the respective wonder-worker. During Late Antiquity, though fewer wonders occurred, as contemporary Christians observed, certain groups, such as holy men, were still seen to be able to perform miracles.[30] Under such circumstances, it comes as no surprise that imperial miracles were

---

29 Cf. Pliny, 22.1 (*laetum*), and *laetus vultus* in Tac. *Hist*. 4.81; for *laetitia*, Heinz-Joachim Schulzki, *Laetitia*, LIMC VI (1992), 181–84; Hans von Kamptz, s.v. laetitia, ThLL 7.2. (1970–79), 874–79 (esp. 2b). Suet. *Tit*. 8.4 might hint at attempts to work wonders on the side of Titus, (see Luke, "A Healing Touch for Empire," 85) but the hints are weak.

30 Christoph Kleine, Winfried Thiel, Michael Becker, Bernd Kollmann, Martin Ohst, Jan Štefan, Thomas Klie, "Wunder," *TRE* 36 (2004): 378–415, 398–400.

rare during Christian times.[31] Christian emperors demonstrated their piety by supporting the church and by humiliating themselves. Sometimes the appearance of the emperor was accompanied by miraculous events, but while these were coincidences which might have been worked by God and which might show God's favor towards the emperor, they were only loosely connected and thus attributed to acts of the emperor himself. There is a strange exception in the case of Justinian (527–565). Emperor Justinian is known to have been a ruler for whom it was important to present himself as one who was near to God. One of many ways he sought to do this was by imitation of holy men. There is, as far as I can see, no record of a wonder worked by Justinian in person, but the idea of the imperial touch, which we came across in the case of Hadrian, is palpable. The source which hands down the relevant episode is the book *De aedificiis* by Procopius of Caesarea. This text, which is written in classical style, praises the buildings erected by Emperor Justinian with lavish words. In the first book the author deals with the church of the martyr Eirene. During its construction the relics of the Forty Martyrs were found, which already demonstrated God's favor towards Justinian. Very illuminating is the continuation of this passage. Procopius describes a malady of the knee which tortured Justinian and which drove physicians to despair: *But during this time he heard about the relics which had been brought to light, and abandoning human skill, he gave the case over to them, seeking to recover his health through faith in them, and in a moment of direst necessity he won the reward of the true belief. For as soon as the priests laid the reliquary on the Emperor's knee, the ailment disappeared instantly, driven out by the bodies of men who had been dedicated to the service of God. And God did not permit this to be a matter of dispute, for he shewed a great sign of what was being done. For oil suddenly flowed out from these holy relics, and flooding the chest poured out over the Emperor's feet and his whole garment, which was purple. So this tunic, thus saturated, is preserved in the Palace, partly as testimony to what occurred at that time, and also as a source of healing for those who in future are assailed by any incurable disease.*[32] It is not Jus-

31 Ramsay MacMullen, "Constantine and the Miraculous," *GRBS* 9 (1968): 81–96 rightly underlines that the belief in miracles (in a large meaning) was a common feature of pagan and Christian mindsets in late antiquity; nevertheless the working of miracles was perceived differently. Lellia Cracco Ruggini, "The Ecclesiastical Histories and Pagan Historiography: Providence and Miracles," *Athenaeum* 55 (1977): 107–26 includes miracles which follow the prayers of the emperors (esp. 109–13).

32 Procop. *Aed.* 1.7.6–16, esp. 13–16: μεταξὺ δὲ τὰ περὶ τῶν δεδηλωμένων λειψάνων ἀκούσας, τῆς ἀνθρωπείας ἀφέμενος τέχνης, ἐπὶ ταῦτα τὸ πρᾶγμα ἦγε, τὴν ὑγιείαν ἐπισπώμενος τῇ ἐς αὐτὰ πίστει, καὶ δόξης τῆς ἀληθοῦς ἐν τοῖς ἀναγκαιοτάτοις ἀπώνατο. οἱ μὲν γὰρ ἱ ερεῖς τὸν δίσκον ἐπὶ τὸ τοῦ βασιλέως ἐτίθεντο γόνυ, ἀφανίζεται δὲ τὸ πάθος εὐθύς, σώμασι δεδουλωμένοις θεῷ

tinian himself who works the wonder, but rather it is the tunic soaked in holy oil which heals the emperor. However, it is a relic that is connected to the emperor. The healing of the emperor makes possible the healing of the believers. Interestingly, this episode is described by Procopius, a classicizing author of the sixth century, in a book on Justinian's buildings. The readership of this work, which praises many church buildings, must have been Christian; on the other hand the work contains several allusions to classical authors, which presupposes a well educated audience; again, an imperial wonder is inscribed into an elitist discourse.

Another early case is a near-contemporary of Justinian, Guntram (c. 561–592), the Merovingian king of Burgundy, who is mainly known from his description by Gregory of Tours.[33] Guntram is the *exemplum* of a good Christian king, who had committed sins but then repented and turned to a better life. Gregory describes at length how Guntram acts when a plague swept across southern Gaul. Gregory, the episcopal historiographer himself, says that Guntram acted like a bishop and he even goes a step further with the following anecdote: *It was then commonly told among the faithful that a woman whose son was suffering from a four-day fever and was lying in bed very ill, approached the king's back in the throng of people and secretly broke off the fringe of the royal garment and put it in water and gave to her son to drink, and at once the fever died down and he was cured. I do not regard this as doubtful since I have myself heard persons possessed by demons in their furies call on his name and admit their ill deeds, recognizing his power.*[34] Again it is not the

βιασθέν. ὅπερ ἀμφίλεκτον ὁ θεὸς οὐ ξυγχωρῶν εἶναι, σημεῖον τῶν πραττομένων ἐνδέδεικται μέγα. ἔλαιον γὰρ ἐξαπιναίως ἐπιρρεῦσαν μὲν ἐκ τούτων δὴ τῶν ἁγίων λειψάνων, ὑπερβλύσαν δὲ τὸ κιβώτιον, τώ τε πόδε καὶ τὴν ἐσθῆτα τοῦ βασιλέως κατέκλυσεν ὅλην ἁλουργὸν οὖσαν. διὸ δὴ ὁ χιτὼν οὕτω καταβεβρεγμένος διασώζεται ἐν τοῖς βασιλείοις, μαρτύριον μὲν τῶν τηνικάδε γεγενημένων, σωτήριον δὲ τοῖς ἐς τὸ ἔπειτα πάθεσι περιπεσουμένοις τισὶν ἀνηκέστοις. Translation by H. B. Dewing. Cf. Mischa Meier, *Das andere Zeitalter Justinians* (Göttingen 2003), 623–26; Hartmut Leppin, *Justinian: Das christliche Experiment* (Stuttgart 2011), 287.

33 Maximilian Diesenberger, Helmut Reimitz, "Zwischen Vergangenheit und Zukunft: Momente des Königtums in der merowingischen Historiographie," in *Das frühmittelalterliche Königtum: Ideelle und religiöse Grundlagen* (ed. Franz-Reiner Erkens; Ergänzungsbände zum Reallexikon der Germanischen Altertumskunde 49, Berlin 2005), 214–69, 216–19 for the exceptionality of this figure and esp. 224–29 for Gregory's literary construction in describing Gunthram's reign; Martin Heinzelmann, *Gregor von Tours: (538–594); "Zehn Bücher Geschichte" – Historiographie und Gesellschaftskonzept im 6. Jahrhundert* (Darmstadt 1994), 49–69 (esp. 64 s.), 158–67 (for the role of Gunthram within Gregory's concept of history); Régine Le Jan, "Die Sakralität der Merowinger: Oder Mehrdeutigkeiten der Geschichtsschreibung," in *Staat im frühen Mittelalter* (ed. Stuart Airlie et al.; Wien 2006), 73–92 from an anthropological perspective.

34 Greg. Tur. *Hist. Franc.* 9.21 (MGH SS rer. Mer. I/1, ed. Bruno Krusch, Wilhelm Levison, Hannover 1951, 441): *Nam caelebre tunc a fidelibus ferebatur, quod mulier quaedam, cuius filius quart-*

king himself who works the wonder, but it is a piece of his garment that is used to cure the woman's son. But this should not be regarded as a factor that reduces the king's sanctity. Readers versed in the New Testament would be reminded of Matthew 9.20–22, where a woman was healed because she touched Jesus' garment. It is interesting that Gregory, as a bishop and a member of the church elite, accepts the miraculous power of the king despite the sanctity of a king having the potential to challenge the priest in his sacral role. But in contrast to what Tacitus and Suetonius say about Vespasian, the healing power of the Merovingian ruler is not the expression of the ruler's position. It does not serve as a confirmation of Guntram's royal position. Guntram's personal holiness is at stake in this case, not his office. Gregory does not sanctify the king's office, but the incumbent – who was, by the way, a penitent sinner. He had not always been the perfect model of a king, but provides an example for a conversion to Christian life and the possibility for a king to obtain holiness. Both the wonders of these Christian rulers have in common that they are not worked intentionally. They emerge from the holiness of the emperors and are transferred to objects connected with them. They cannot be imputed to their will, but are the result of their personal quality – quite a contrast to Vespasian, who perhaps hesitantly, but intentionally worked the wonder.

To conclude: *rois thaumaturges*, wonder-working kings, are a phenomenon well-known in antiquity. Emperors were able to work miracles in the perception of pagan people. This perception was neither restricted to members of the lower classes nor the Orient, but was shared by members of the Roman elite, even by traditionalists such as Tacitus. People like him were, however, not interested in stressing the importance of miracles since they enhanced the sacredness of the emperor, whereas Roman senators preferred to stress the human character of the emperor. In contrast to our enlightened times, miracles did not have a provocative character in antiquity, which might be a reason for their rare attestation. They could allude to a power that transgressed the boundaries that normal human beings had to accept, but they were not necessarily the expression of a

---

ano tibo gravabatur et in strato anxius decubabat, accessit inter turbas populi usque ad tergum Regis, abruptisque clam regalis indumenti fimbriis, in aqua posuit filioque bibendum dedit; statimque, restincta febre, sanatus est. Quod non habetur a me dubium, cum ego ipse saepius larvas inergia famulante nomen eius invocantes audieram ac criminum propriorum gesta, virtute ipsius discernente, fatere. Translation by Earnest Brehaut. Ehlers, "Der wundertätige König," 7; Franz-Reiner Erkens, *Die Herrschersakralität im Mittelalter: Von den Anfängen bis zum Investiturstreit* (Stuttgart 2006), 17; Gernot Kirchner, "Heilungswunder im Frühmittelalter: Überlegungen zum Kontext des vir Dei-Konzeptes Gregor von Tours," in *Gesundheit – Krankheit. Kulturtransfer medizinischen Wissens von der Spätantike bis in die Frühe Neuzeit* (ed. Florian Steger and Kay Peter Jankrift; Cologne 2004), 41–76, 50 in the context of the hagiographical tradition.

good agent, as is made clear by the ambiguity of miracles in the New Testament.[35] Vespasian, in his way of working wonders, has similarities to the Jesus of the gospels, probably because a common literary tradition existed about how miracles used to occur. But he is not a predecessor of the medieval *rois thaumaturges*. Quite the contrary: the Christianization of the Roman Empire interrupted this tradition, since the connection between holiness and the ability to work wonders was strict, and kings were typically not holy men. Even the most devout kings such as Theodosius were themselves not able to perform miracles. His prayers, however, were capable of successfully invoking the aid of God – most famously in the battle of the river Frigidus – but nothing more.[36] When however, during the sixth century the pretensions of rulers both in the East and in the West rose to be like holy men, miracles connected with the personality of certain rulers became more prominent. In those cases, the capacity to work miracles remained the expression of personal holiness, not of the office. This still holds true for kings such as Robert the Pious (996–1031) in France and Edward the Confessor (1041/2–1066) in England.[37] But from the thirteenth century onwards, medieval French and English kings used to cure scrofula, the King's Evil as it was called, by touching the sufferers. This became part of the crowning ceremony and was regarded as the result of the anointment of kings. To a certain degree, this was a return to the role of pagan emperors. It is clear that Tacitus and Suetonius see Vespasian's healing power as a confirmation of the divine favor towards his rule, independent of his personal behavior, just as the medieval interpreters assumed for their kings – but within a completely different religious frame. Christianization had made it more difficult for rulers to perform wonders. It was a long way from Late Antiquity to the sacredness of the imperial or royal office which was the base of the royal touch that had the power to cure scrofula.

35 Cf. the relevant contributions in this volume; for an introduction Kleine et al., "Wunder."

36 Cf. Socr. *H.e.* 6.23.1–6 on Arcadius.

37 Fundamental: Erkens, *Die Herrschersakralität im Mittelalter*; cf. for Scandinavia, Erich Hoffmann, *Die heiligen Könige bei den Angelsachsen und den skandinavischen Völkern: Königsheiliger und Königshaus* (Quellen und Forschungen zur Geschichte Schleswig-Holsteins 69; Neumünster 1975).

IV Media of Miracles

Norbert Zimmermann

The healing Christ in early Christian funeral art: the example of the frescoes at Domitilla catacomb/Rome[1]

The biblical representations of the Roman catacombs have often been studied from their rediscovery in the 16th century onwards, since they document the first Christian images in Western art. Therefore much attention has already been paid by scholars on the images of New Testament miracle stories and the different ways Jesus is represented in such scenes in context with the grave, mostly for their theological meaning. Nevertheless, by summarizing the research carried out until now and by focusing on the question how and why New Testament miracles appear in this private art, some new aspects can be added and new conclusions can be reached, especially regarding the concept of reality which these images express. This last point, a focal point of the conference, brings much clearer results when considered in contrast to the concept of reality expressed in the funeral art of the pagan world around the early Christians who were buried in the catacombs. Consequently, in the final section of this paper, the reality of myth and the biblical reality in funerary art will be compared; here one may find the most important conceptual difference. As a first step however, a short introduction will examine the general nature of the catacomb art. The main part is dedicated to the analysis of the miracles of the New Testament in catacomb painting, especially in the Domitilla catacomb. Since we are looking at images, our approach is iconographical and the method is generally formed by the theory of the images[2].

---

1 First of all, I want to express my warmest thanks to the organizers for inviting me to the conference on healing stories and the concepts of realities, and to accept my paper for the acts. I am grateful for the possibility to contribute some aspects of Roman catacomb painting, and especially on paintings of the catacomb of Domitilla. This catacomb is the aim of a START-project of the Austrian science-foundation FWF (Y282-G02), installed at the Institute for Studies of Ancient Culture at the Austrian Academy of Sciences, and conducted in a national cooperation with the Institute of History of Art, Building Archaeology and Restoration at the Vienna University of Technology. We are grateful to the responsible of the PCAS (Rome) for the possibility to get familiar with the monument for the preparation of the repertory of its paintings, which is nearly ready for print.

2 This is important, not because texts could not be helpful for an understanding, which they indeed are, but only in a second step. In a first viewing, all these images communicate directly through their visual expression, and it seems unnecessary to look for sophisticated meanings be-

The Roman catacombs are the cemeteries of the early Christian community at Rome[3]. They were in use for burials for almost 200 years, from the early 3rd century onwards. Nearly 70 catacombs were found outside of the Roman city walls, and a grid of more than 150 kilometers of catacomb galleries extended under the earth, with certainly hundreds of thousands of buried persons. Compared with these large numbers, about 400 known painted units, entire rooms or single graves in the galleries form a relatively small group of monuments: statistically, only two paintings were created every year[4]. Even though there are so few, not all of them have been published appropriately[5]. In any case, they document the origin and the first development of Christian iconography in the West: while other monuments *sub divo* have been destroyed, they form the missing link in art history from AD 200–400.

From the early 3rd century onwards, Christians started to decorate the graves of their deceased with images of their faith and hope for salvation, depicting for the first time biblical scenes as part of a private sepulchral art around the tomb. On the one hand, three traditional pagan motives were directly included into the Christian repertory of images: the bucolic shepherd, becoming the Good Shepherd of John's parable, the orant, a personification of piety to men and gods, becoming a Christian *pietas* or prayer, and the banquet scene, becoming both a *refrigerium* for/with the bereaved and an eternal meal[6]. On the other hand, completely new iconographies were invented for a group of over 20 biblical scenes, illustrating intense moments of salvation, healing or revelation, such as Noah in his ark, Moses striking the rock, Abraham offering his son Isaac and Daniel with the lions, all from the Old Testament, and, from the New Testament, Christ healing the blind and the lame, the multiplication of bread and the transformation of water into wine or calling Lazarus back to life, which is the most natural scene in

tween the lines if the meaning is clearly visible anyway. For the methodological approach see Engemann 1997.

3 As a general introduction to the Roman catacomb, their origin, development and study see Fiocchi Nicolai – Bisconti – Mazzoleni 1998; and Fiocchi Nicolai 2004.

4 For a complete list with the actual numbering of all catacomb paintings and an overview on their iconographical content see Nestori 1993; for the statistics see Zimmermann 2002, 41–44. The iconographical themes and their development are discussed in Bisconti 2000.

5 The largest collection of catacomb paintings is still Wilpert 1903. Complete repertories of their paintings exist for the catacombs of Ss. Marcellino e Pietro, Anapo, and Commodilla, see Deckers – Seeliger – Mietke 1987, Deckers – Mietke – Weiland 1991, and Deckers – Mietke – Weiland 1994. All the paintings of the via Latina catacomb are available in Ferrua 1991 and the repertory of Domitilla will appear soon, Zimmermann – Tsamakda, forthcoming.

6 Engemann 1997, 111–20.

the sepulchral context[7]. Christian sarcophagi generally report a similar repertory, however a generation later[8]. While in the 3rd century, more scenes from the Old Testament are depicted, at the time of Constantine the attention slightly focused on the New Testament. At the same time, Christ changed from a young philosopher to a long haired and bearded Father God, depicted with all honors of imperial iconography, such as the throne or the nimbus[9]. Private, personal representation became, from the late 3rd century onwards, one of the major aspects of imagery and the painters invented different ways to connect private portraits with the scenes of biblical salvation[10]. Nearly everywhere orants were depicted, which very often were images of the buried persons, but also real portraits in frames or tondos, representations of professions of their employers or the whole family of the owner of a tomb. And, as will be examined later, sometimes the private representations were directly integrated into the biblical scenes. With the creation of Christian churches from the middle of the 4th century onwards, Roman catacomb painting became less innovative but more reflexive, copying the theological images found in the apses, such as Christ between his twelve apostles, and now generally ordering the scenes into lateral friezes. Christian images without a direct biblical source became more common such as Christ appearing on a globe, sometimes between Peter and Paul. With pope Damasus (366–384), the martyrs became mediators and patrons of the hope of salvation in the imagery, but only at the end of the 4th century did theological paintings with the character of official ecclesiastical monuments occur in the subterranean cult centers of the martyrs. Fortunately, at the same time as the last catacomb paintings occurred in the early 5th century, the monumental tradition *sub divo* began[11]. Generally, the largest part of the catacomb paintings arose as private funeral art and the importance of these mostly private monuments is based on their content and iconography and not so much on their artistic level. One can assume that the *fossores*, the diggers of the subterranean galleries and graves and the undertakers of the dead, were often the painters as well. Therefore, it is not surprising to often see these *fossores* represented from the beginning to the end of the catacomb paintings, maybe even as owners or protectors of the tombs. A last scene should be mentioned here, as it will be discussed later: Orpheus, the mythical singer who was equalized with Christ from the middle of the 3rd century onwards, singing and playing the *lyra*,

7 See Nestori 1993, 189–218.

8 Koch 2000.

9 Deckers 1996.

10 On portraits in catacomb painting see Zimmermann 2007.

11 Ihm 1960.

becalming the wild animals and giving a paradisiacal peace[12]. To summarize, catacomb painting as private sepulchral art had two main topics: the self-representation of the deceased and the illustration of his hope for salvation and Christian afterlife. All single paintings are unique and individual and are the output of single contacts between a private client or applicant and the executor, who may be called an artist or a craftsman[13].

After this short introduction, as the next step we will try to understand the reason for selecting a biblical story for an image and the way the story is pictured. Both the content of a story and the kind of representation give an important input for the interpretation of a scene and, of course, of the combination of scenes. Generally, one can foreclose that more or less all scenes respect a common semantic line. They all illustrate moments of dense salvific history: they report stories from salvation of danger to life, like Daniel between the lions, the three Hebrews in the fire, or Moses striking the rock for water. Some tell miracles of healings of an illness, like the paralytic or the blind, or they relate miracles of immediate salvation from death, like Lazarus. Finally, they can also document moments of a direct contact between God and men during a salvific act, speech or lesson, such as Moses receiving the law, or the Samaritan woman at the well. In any case, the repertory is quite limited. We find about 11 scenes from the entire Old Testament[14], here in order of their statistical occurrence: Moses striking the rock (Exod 17:1–6, Num 20:1–11), Jonah' story (Jonah 1–4), Daniel between the lions (Dan 14), Noah in the ark (Gen 7–8), Adam and Eve (Gen 3), Abraham offering Isaac (Gen 22:1–18), the three Hebrews in the fire (Dan 3:1–97), Job (Job 2:7–8), Moses doffing his sandals (Exod 3), Moses receiving the law (Exod 24), Susanna with the old men (Dan 13) and finally Balaam indicating the star (Num 24:17). The concept of this selection is quite clear, as the plot of each story is directly salvific: however, the images do not tell a story, but shed light on the salvific content. The narration is always reduced to one emblematic moment and is restricted to the most important persons, normally only one or two. For example, the lions usually were not shown while attacking Daniel, but they only assist to identify the scene, like attributes. Because of the static character, the images were commonly classified as symbolic, concentrating on the most important part of the story in order for it to be readable. In only one case, Adam and Eve, the purpose at first view of its selec-

12 Bisconti 2000, 236–37.

13 Zimmermann 2002, 260–64.

14 Scenes with uncertain interpretation or only one single appearance were not listed here; for the absolute numbers see Zimmermann 2007, 156–57.

tion is somehow unclear[15]. Sometimes the images are even more clearly connected to the grave context than the biblical story was: while the text of the story of Jonah focuses on the people of Nineveh and their behavior, the images of the cycle with three and later four scenes of Jonah accents a secondary aspect of the story; the resting Jonah, saved from the fish, lying under his pergola like the sleeping Endymion[16]. In this case, it becomes very clear that the motivation, why the story was chosen and why that iconography was invented, was at the most only partly the biblical content of that narration. Nevertheless, it still follows the same salvific line.

One can observe the same minimalistic reduction in the 12 scenes from the New Testament, which are worth a closer look, first again in order of their statistical value[17]. It is not surprising to find Lazarus' rising (John 11:1–24) as the statistically most important scene, with 66 appearances. His recall back to life offers the best plot to be near the grave, as it is full of hope of personal salvation; Christ personally calls his three days gone and already foul-smelling friend Lazarus back to life, an incomparable act of salvation and a wonderful demonstration of his power over the death. The illustration of the story is concentrated on the most important moment and is limited to the most necessary persons: Christ and Lazarus. In the first known representation of the scene from the early 3rd century at the S.Callisto catacomb[18], Jesus is standing on the right, in front of the tomb aedicula, holding a virga in his left hand. With the right hand he is enacting the gesture of speech (Redegestus), calling Lazarus (fig. 1). The miracle has just happened, and as a response Lazarus comes walking out of his tomb. A little later, the miracle found its standard iconography, with Lazarus standing as a mummy in the entrance of his grave and Christ touching Lazarus' head with the top of the virga in his hand (fig. 2). The biblical text is much more extended and tells more details, such as the presence of the entire family and some talks between the family members and Jesus, but the redactor of the images was strictly minimalist and reinforced the most important members and action. To change the walking Lazarus to a mummy is reasonable as well, since the deceased were buried in the form of mummies, so they could directly and visibly take part in the hopeful as-

15 Only Adam and Eve in the moment of the original sin do not offer a simple explanation in the funeral context. In this case, the interpretation from patristic literature seems to be helpful, as the progenitors were interpreted to be not only the first sinners, but also the first to be saved after the final judgment; they are both, at the beginning of the history and at the beginning of the salvation, see Dassmann 1973, 232–58.

16 See Speigl 1978; and Engemann 1997, 110.

17 See Zimmermann 2007, 156–58.

18 Callisto no. 25, Nestori 1993, 125: Wilpert 1903, Taf. 46,2; Bisconti 2009, 26.

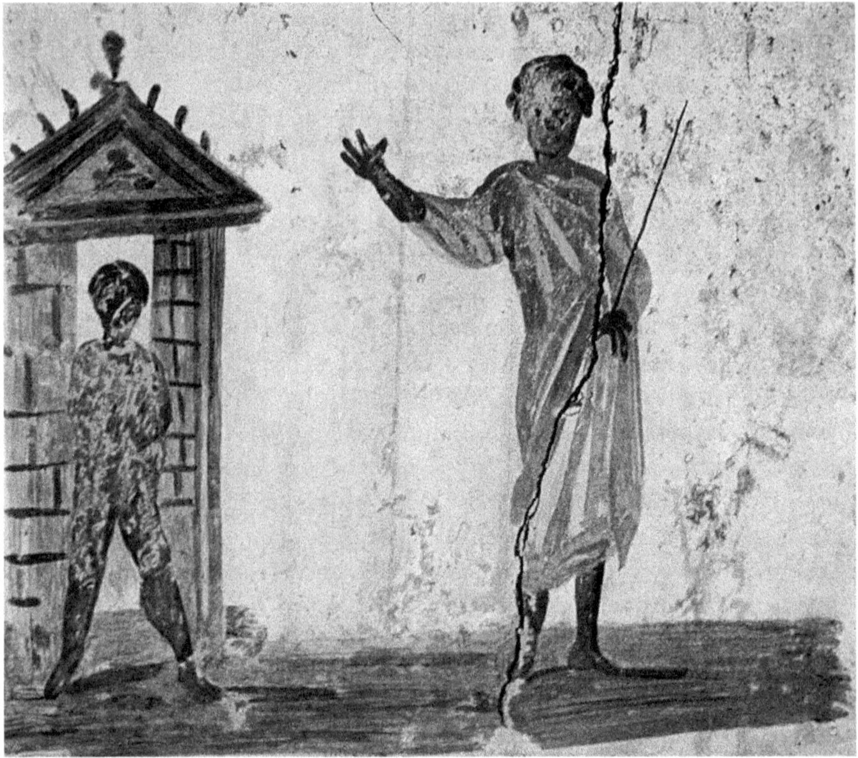

Fig. 1: S. Callisto catacomb, no. 25, Lazarus, after Wilpert 1903, Taf. 46,2.

pect of the miracle. A very important detail is one addition made by the redactor of the image, which is lacking in the text sources: the virga. Its crucial significance will be considered later.

The second most often scene, with 37 images, is the multiplication of bread (Matt 15:32–39). Jesus as a young man is standing in the center or beside usually seven chests of bread and is enacting the miracle with a virga in his hand (fig. 3). Again he is isolated and the story is regressed to a symbol, which becomes even clearer when Christ transforms into a sheep, as can be seen in a symbolic image at the Commodilla catacomb[19].

The next scene is the healing of the paralytic (John 5; Matt 9:5; Mark 2,9; Luke 5:23) with 24 occurrences. Here, the story is mostly restricted to the pure re-

19 See Commodilla catacomb, painting no. 5, Nestori 1993, 143; Deckers – Mietke – Weiland 1994, 97.

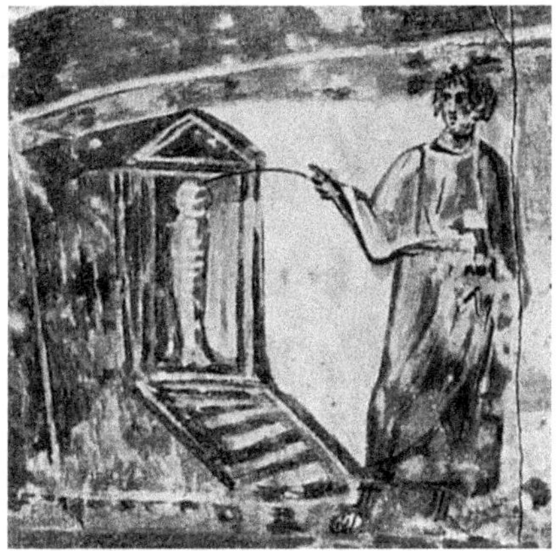

Fig. 2: Domitilla catacomb, no. 73, Lazarus, after Wilpert 1903, Taf. 192.

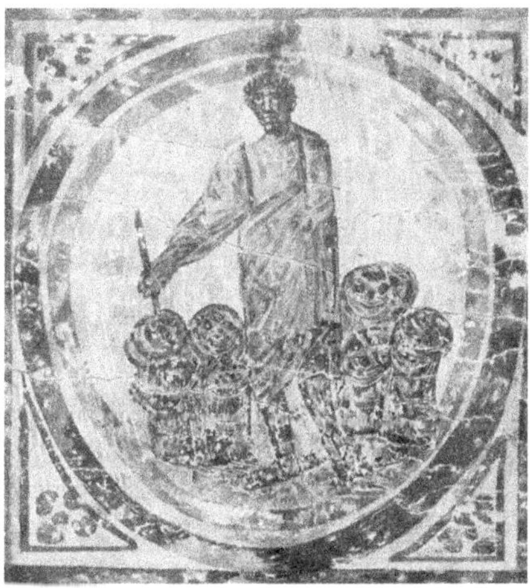

Fig. 3: Domitilla catacomb, no. 77, multiplication of bread, after Wilpert 1903, Taf. 240,1.

sult of the miracle: the healed paralytic carries his bed away; Jesus is not even required to be present (fig. 4).

With 18 images, the adoration of the three magi is also depicted quite often (Matt 2). Normally centralized with two or four symmetrical magicians, but also with Mary holding Jesus on her knees on one side and three magicians arriving with their gifts from the other, the plot is the moment of adoration itself. It seems to be impossible that this scene, which very much reflects imperial images, was created before the time of Constantine[20].

20 Deckers 1982.

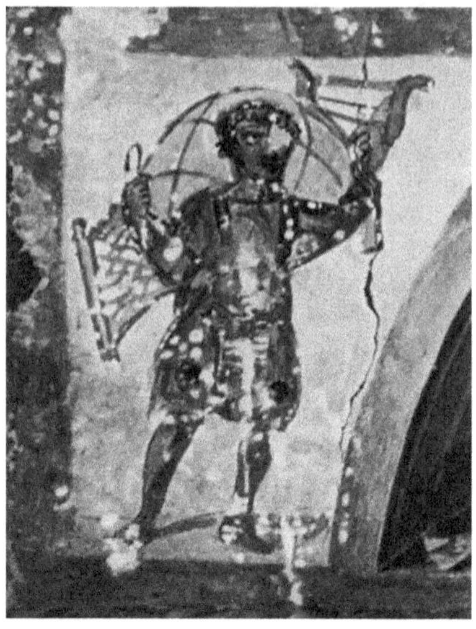

Fig. 4: Domitilla catacomb, no. 77, The paralytic man, after Wilpert 1903, Taf. 239.

A baptism is depicted 12 times (Matt 3:13–17; Mark 1:1–9; Luke 3:21). Only if the dove and John appear is it called the baptism of Christ. Again, even if there is water and some kind of waterside, the scene is reduced and symbolic. It is interesting to see that, as once at Domitilla, even John can be missing, and the scene is restricted to the water falling from the sky and the figure of Christ[21].

The healing of a blind person is shown nine times in the catacombs (Luke 18:35–43; Mark 10:46–52; John 9:1–7). Usually, Jesus is taller than the blind in the images and enacts the healing by touching his front, his head or his eyes. The paintings are often not well-conserved, but the reason why one cannot decide which one of the biblical stories (after Mark or John) is being depicted, is, again, the reduced way of illustration.

Also quite often, eight times, Jesus with the Samaritan woman (John 4) is shown. The reason to represent this story nearby the grave is obviously the content of Jesus' speech about the water of salvation. The Samaritan woman was, in the example from the via Latina catacomb, depicted with earrings and a modern haircut and serves as an example for a portrait of the deceased brought into direct contact with Jesus in a meaningful context[22].

Seven times, in a lucky conjunction with the multiplication of bread, the first public miracle of Jesus at Kana, the transformation of water to wine (John 2) is

21 Zimmermann – Tsamakda 2009, 418 with Abb. 20–21.
22 Zimmermann 2007, 176.

represented. The components are Jesus, the wine amphora and his virga, which is the sign of his power. Direct Eucharistic representations are missing[23], but it is logical that the context of both miracles, with bread and wine, was interpreted in a salvific, and more specific, in a Eucharistic way.

The healing of the bleeding woman (Matt 9:18–22; Mark 5:25–34; Luke 8:43–48) was detected six times. It is characterized by a woman kneeling beside Jesus and touching his tunica. Jesus usually enacts the miracle with a virga in his hand or, more seldom, with only his hand. For the context of the image there seems to be no difference.

The next scenes are present less than five times, and due to their rare presence one could not find a standard iconography. The annunciation shows Mary sitting, with the angel gesturing to her (Luke 1); this is the starting moment of salvation. It is difficult to identify the healing of the obsessed (Matt 8:28–34; Mark 5:1–20; Luke 8:26–40) and the healing of the leprous (Matt 8:1–4; Mark 1:40–45). Both healings, and also the healings of the lame and the bleeding woman, are very similar in their iconography. Some scenes are hard to identify due to their state of conservation, but again we seem to become aware of another problem: the important point was the image of the miracle, the healing, and not always the doubtless identification of a specific miracle. Of course it would have been possible to be more precise in the iconographic expression, but the lack of interest in this indicates that we have lost some information: maybe for the family of the deceased there was no question what miracle was intended or we simply are more interested in details today than the ancient viewers were. The paintings of cubiculum 65 at Marcellino e Pietro[24] may be helpful here: The main lunette shows three "female miracles", enacted for women, and one has rightly asked if this fact is not due to the circumstance that a woman was buried here. So, sometimes, one can assume personal reasons and very personal motivations for choosing a story and illustrating the content in a certain way. Finally, two images refer to the parable of the prudent virgins and show five virgins with burning torches (Matt 25); this is also a clear salvific content.

To summarize the motivation for the illustration of the analyzed scenes, there are some clear common grounds: the content is directly salvific, a miracle, a divine epiphany or a manifestation. Jesus is often present in person (fig. 1, 2), but he can also be absent, as in the miracle of the paralytic (fig. 3). If he is present, he can talk or act with his hand or, more often, with his virga, a non-biblical attribute of his divine power. The biblical stories chosen to adorn the graves were illustrated

23 See Zimmermann 2010, 1124–27.

24 Deckers 1987, 314–15; see Zimmermann 2002, 200.

in the simplest way. They are not narrations and they do not intend to tell a whole story. On the contrary, they symbolically remind the viewer of their most important content. The personnel are reduced to the main protagonists and one can assume that a private and individual detail was more important for the iconographical setting than textual literacy was. Yet, no attention was paid in specifying a miracle, if more than one literary source exists within the synoptic texts. One can imagine that not necessarily a literal source was illustrated in the redaction process for the images, but moreover an oral tradition of the biblical narration has to be considered[25].

As a next step, the context of the images painted around the graves will be considered, hereby focusing on the New Testament healings and exemplary at a specific catacomb: Domitilla. Due to factors such as the state of conservation or the distinct historical development, every catacomb has its own slightly different character and specific layout[26]. The Domitilla catacomb has been chosen here, because it is currently being examined in order for the repertory of its paintings to be prepared[27]. Domitilla is the largest catacomb of Rome, with 12 kilometers of subterranean galleries and more than 80 preserved paintings, stemming mostly from two important periods: the early 3rd century, with a few pagan paintings in some formerly isolated hypogea, which are not of interest here, and, with many paintings, the 4th century, when Domitilla was greatly extended as a Christian catacomb. The task here is to analyze how the miracle scenes from the New Testament were used and distributed in the context of different rooms and scenes.

To start with, here are again some statistics: of the 84 painted units at Domitilla[28], 36 are pagan or neutral without specific Christian images. Some are very poorly conserved and a substantial group has Christian paintings without scenes from the New Testament. The examination group of interest here contains 20 paintings, generally consisting of more than one scene. From all the New Testament

---

25 At least it seems to be unnecessary to construct an addition of the paintings from only the written biblical text and the patristic writings.

26 For example S. Callisto is most important for the early paintings from the 3rd century as well as Marcellino e Pietro for the paintings of the Constantine period.

27 Zimmermann – Tsamakda, forthcoming. Since 2006, a team of archaeologists of the Austrian Academy of Sciences and architects from the Technical University Vienna has been working, under concession of the PCAS, at the Domitilla project, preparing the repertory of its paintings and a 3D-documentation, based for the first time on laser-scanner data of the entire catacomb; see Zimmermann-Tsamakda 2007.

28 Nestori 1993, 120–36, listed 77 painted units; the complete list with a detailed description, images, and bibliography in Zimmermann – Tsamakda, forthcoming. The main research on the Domitilla catacomb in the last decades was carried out by Philippe Pergola, see Pergola 2004, with bibliography.

scenes cited before, only eight can be detected at Domitilla. The most frequent one is the raising of Lazarus with 13 images[29], followed by 12 representations of a central Christ[30], standing alone (four times) between the 12 apostles (eight times) or between Peter and Paul (two times). The multiplication of bread is depicted ten times[31] and the baptism five times[32]. Four healings of the paralytic[33] are followed by one healing of the blind man[34], and at least one image exists with Jesus and the Samaritarian woman[35]. Only four scenes are miracles: the raising of Lazarus, the multiplication of bread and the healings of the paralytic and the blind. All these scenes were part of 20 painted units of three types[36]: two loculi walls (no. 28, 29), 11 arcosolia (no. 19, 36, 42, 43, 46, 50, 67, 70, 73, 75, 77), and seven cubicula (no. 31, 33, 40, 45, 62, 69, 74)[37]. All three groups shall be examined exemplarily.

The simplest type is a loculus wall, consisting of one loculus or a line of loculi, one over the other, decorated with paintings. No. 28[38] is a good example to begin with: it has a succession of four Christian scenes above the central loculus, a bird on each side and a line of garlands underneath the loculus (fig. 5). The four scenes are, from left to right: Daniel between the lions, Moses striking the rock, the revival of Lazarus, and the deceased as an orant between two men, usually interpreted as two saints or as the deceased turning into Susanna, situated between the old men. If the deceased is meant to be Susanna, then we may assume that her family or her husband wanted to praise the woman's quality, her virtue and her pudicity. The compact composition does not offer much space for a development or an interaction between the scenes, but the three-person-group at the right occupies more space, with the effect that Christ in the second scene from the right comes to be in the center of all four scenes. Of course this might not be accidental, even if one could imagine a more elegant division for a centralized composition. However, in a simple succession the hope for eternal life of a deceased woman is told in images that express the faith in Christian salvation, with personally selected and modified scenes of both the Old and the New Testament.

---

29 Domitilla no. 19, 28, 31, 33, 43, 45, 46, 50, 70, 73, 75, 77, and the mosaic arcosol.

30 Domitilla no. 18, 19, 33, 38, 39, 45, 46, 47, 54, 69, 74 and 80.

31 Domitilla no 29, 31, 36, 42, 46, 62, 69, 71, 74, and 77.

32 Domitilla no. 37, 42, 52, 62, and 77.

33 Domitilla no. 31, 40, 69, and 77.

34 Domitilla no. 31.

35 Domitilla no. 31.

36 On the different types of grave architecture in the Roman catacombs in general see Nuzzo 2000, and especially for Domitilla Nuzzo 2000, 44–62.

37 Cubiculum 52 certainly has some scenes from the New Testament as well, but it was never restored or cleaned after its excavation, so they remain unreadable, see Nestori 1993, 128.

38 Nestori 1993, 124; Wilpert 1903, Taf. 219,2.

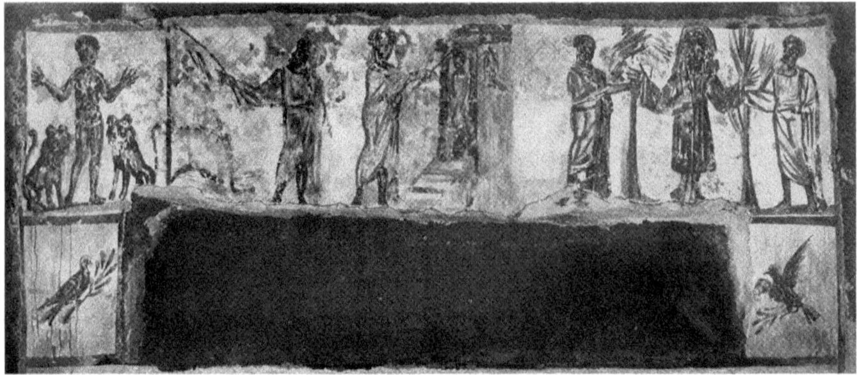

Fig. 5: Domitilla catacomb, loculus wall no. 28, after Wilpert 1903, Taf. 219,2.

More complex are the compositions of paintings for arcosolia. Their arches occupy more space and were therefore more expensive; as an architectural symbol they mark the owner's dignity and offer more space for images in the lunette and the arch itself. At Domitilla, the painted arcosols mainly stem from the second half of the 4th century and some include New Testament miracles: No. 36[39] has figural paintings only at the front. On the left hand side, Jonah is thrown out of the ship, and on the right hand, the multiplication of bread is depicted; here, the proportion of Old and New Testament scenes is therefore 1:1. In contrast, no. 42[40] is more complex: the female deceased is depicted as an orant on the left side of the front; in the center above the arch is a *tabula ansata*, which formerly had an inscription. On the right side the scene is destroyed, but one could expect a male orant, her husband, here. Jesus the Good Shepherd is shown on the top of the arch. On his left there is the multiplication of bread (without a virga?) and on the right a scene of baptism. Here, the front is dedicated to self-representation and inside the arch all scenes are from the New Testament. In contrast, at no. 43[41] only the front was painted with four scenes (fig. 6): from left to right one recognizes the raising of Lazarus, Adam and Eve, Noah in the ark and Moses striking the rock. Certainly, the larger Jesus and Moses, who are both striking with the virga, create a schematic and an iconological brace and make best use of the larger space at the sides of the front[42]. Anyway, the inner scenes do not offer any visual or iconological

39 Nestori 1993, 125; Wilpert 1903, Taf. 226,3.

40 Nestori 1993, 126; Wilpert 1903, Taf. 228,1–2.

41 Nestori 1993, 126–127; Wilpert 1903, Taf. 227.

42 Dinkler 1939, 21, spoke of "formale Bedingtheit", that means the formal ability of both scenes to build the outer limits of a sequence of images.

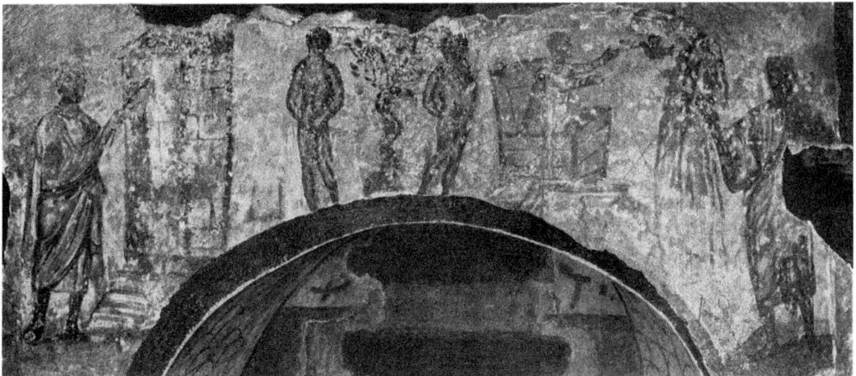

Fig. 6: Domitilla catacomb, arcosol no. 43, after Wilpert 1903, Taf. 227.

help for a more programmatic reading – they 'only' repeat and multiply the common salvific aspect. With only three images, arcosol no. 46[43] seems to be less rich but not less concise. Here, the front is adorned only with garlands, while the top of the arch shows one of the earliest portraits of Christ, bearded as a father god, but unfortunately poorly conserved. On his left side the multiplication of bread is depicted, on his right side is the raising of Lazarus – thus, only scenes from the New Testament exist here. It is not clearly visible whether Christ multiplies the bread without a virga in this image, which would be very unusual. No. 50[44] is the beautiful and famous so-called red arcosol: Only few traces of Christ on a globe or throne remain in the lunette and while Paul is missing on the right, Peter on the left side attests a scene of the type of the so called *traditio legis*. On the front one can see Lazarus' rising on the left side and, again, on the right Moses striking the rock. Therefore, the scenes from the Old and the New Testament were completed by the timeless *traditio legis* and while there is only one scene from each theological era, much emphasis was placed on the strong colors and the unusual and beautiful decorative ornaments. No. 67[45] is however more individualized: the lunette shows the portrait of a young man. At the top of the arch he is accompanied by the Good Shepherd; on the left side is Daniel between the lions, and on the right Lazarus' rising. The décor of the front socle evokes a garden fence, and may allude to a paradisiacal garden. Finally, in the same area no. 70[46] is situated,

43 Nestori 1993, 127; Wilpert 1903, Taf. 127,1; 228,3–4.
44 Nestori 1993, 128; Wilpert 1903, Taf. 182,1; 248.
45 Nestori 1993, 129–130; Wilpert 1903, Taf. 200,1–3.
46 Nestori 1993, 130; Wilpert 1903, Taf. 190; 191,2.

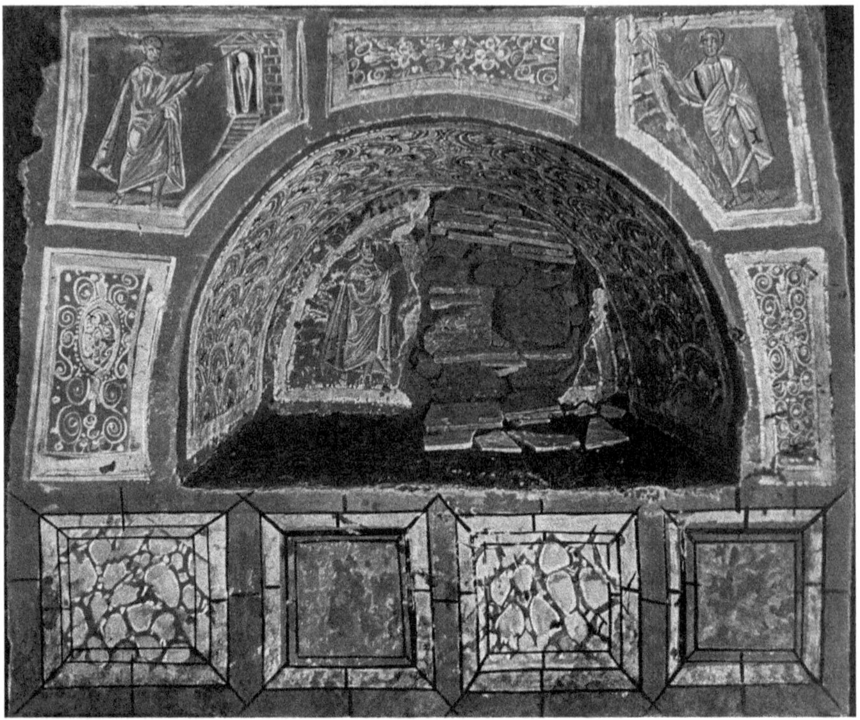

Fig. 7: Domitilla catacomb, arcosol no. 50, after Wilpert 1903, Taf. 248.

which is a typical arcosol of this region, formed as a conch (fig. 8). Its painter was one of the best catacomb painters: in the center we see the Good Shepherd and at his feet the deceased couple as orants. They are incorporated into a flock of sheep, and especially the woman is directly praying to the Good Shepherd. On the left, Moses is striking the rock and, obviously, on the right, Jesus reanimates Lazarus. Once more, self-representation and direct access to the eternal sphere were put together with only a few, but well composed scenes.

All these arcosols belong to the second half of the 4th century. More or less they all use the very common iconographic repertory and repeat, nearly without alternations, the standard scenes. But they all combine the scenes in a different and always individual way. To summarize the scenes and their position: the appearance of Christ as a portrait or Good Shepherd allocates him a central position. A certain concurrence exists with the private portraits of the deceased, which can also take a very important position, with all other scenes subordinated to the side or, if more than two existed, in a scattered arrangement. New Testament miracles are part of the salvific illustrations and exist in addition or contra-part to Old Tes-

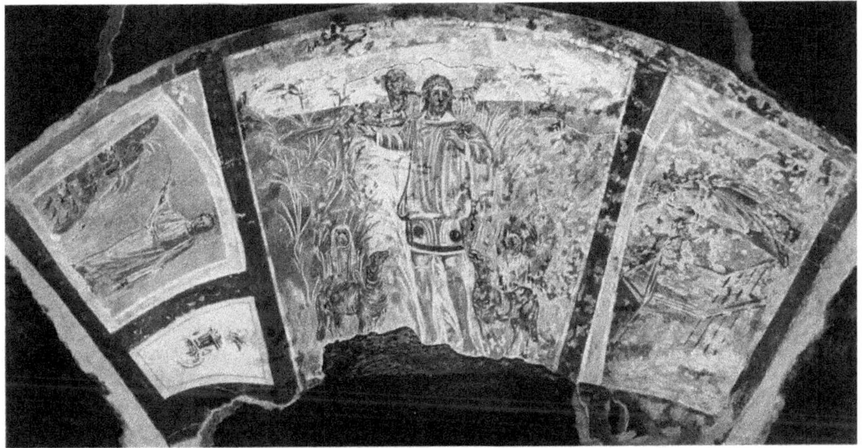

Fig. 8: Domitilla catacomb, arcosol no. 73, after Wilpert 1903, Taf. 190.

tament scenes. Certainly Lazarus and Moses striking the rock are a preferred combination and appear very often. But generally, all scenes seem to be inter-changeable with each other and one hardly finds a meaningful and readable order in that eclecticism, if not the already analyzed common salvific line. "Redaction work" is done, if one can use this term here, not in iconographical details inside the repertory of biblical stories, but in the way they were combined with the personalized image of self representations. Subsequently, the scenes do not differ in the respective meaning, but they always have the same meaning, however are individualized for different deceased.

This becomes even clearer when considering two of the cubicula with the most complex and even more individual situations from both the architectural and painted viewpoints. No. 31[47], called "King David", is the only one belonging to the ending of the 3rd or beginning of the 4th century. It has four sides, two of which, the main- and the right wall, have deep arcosols. The ceiling is semi-destroyed, but was engraved by Antonio Bosio[48]: In the central field Christ as Orpheus between the wild animals is depicted. Four biblical scenes were ordered around him: Daniel between the lions, Lazarus, David with the catapult[49], and Moses striking the rock, bringing about a relation of 3:1 between the Old and the

47 Nestori 1993, 125; Wilpert 1903, Taf. 40,2; 54,1–2; 55.

48 Bosio 1632, 239.

49 This scene is singular in early Christian art, but one may interpret David with the catapult as a kind of savior for the elect people and therefore again in the same salvific line.

New Testament. On the main wall, the three Hebrew in the fire take the central field between two philosophers. The deep arch had a combination of only Old Testament scenes as well: Noah in his ark in the center, with four scenes of Jonah around him. All other biblical scenes are healings from the New Testament. The right wall is partly destroyed today, but is also documented by Bosio's engravings[50]. The multiplication of bread was depicted in the central position, with Christ on the left and the Samaritan woman on the right; this is a very unusual disposition of the scene. While underneath the arch of the arcosol only a philosopher remains, two healings are depicted on the entrance wall: to the left the healing of the blind and on the right a very unusual scene, probably the healing of the lame. Jesus clearly holds a virga in his hand, enacting a healing for a person on his knees to his left[51]. Once more, whichever miracle was exactly meant is secondary or was probably clearer for the ancient viewer.

A last example to be examined is no. 45[52], the so-called cubiculum of Orpheus, a cubic room with three arcosols on the sides: This beautiful cubiculum with four columns in the corners shows a portrait of Christ in the center of the ceiling and Orpheus with the animals in the arcosol of the main wall (fig. 9). Above, in the central field of the front, was the adoration of the three magicians, now no longer preserved. The scenes of Thekla and Paul to the left[53] and Moses striking the rock to the right are still there. The left wall shows Jonah resting and Moses opening his sandals. In the lunette, Antonio Bosio drew Daniel between the lions[54]. The right wall is adorned with the deceased as a female orant on the left side, Noah in his ark in the center and Lazarus on the right. The lunette shows Elijah rising to the sky. Finally, the entrance wall shows Job on the low left and three more scenes which have been destroyed. All in all, there are 14 scenes and three destroyed ones, three are from the New, seven from the Old Testament, one is apocryphal and one is a mythological image: it is however impossible to recognize a distinct program. Indeed, a real program in an academic sense does not exist; it rather seems as if all scenes were put together without any interest to create a meaningful content out of a plausible succession of images. Nevertheless, it is a beautiful compilation of meaningful salvific images, clearly expressing the Christian hope of afterlife. Again, not the scenes became personalized by 'editorial' changes of their iconography, but their salvific content was personalized

50 Bosio 1632, 245.

51 See Tsamakda 2007, 32–33.

52 Nestori 1993, 127; Wilpert 1903, Taf. 187,3; 226,2; 229; 230,1–2.

53 This is the only example for this scene at Rome, see Zimmermann – Tsamakda 2009, 420–21.

54 Bosio 1632, 259.

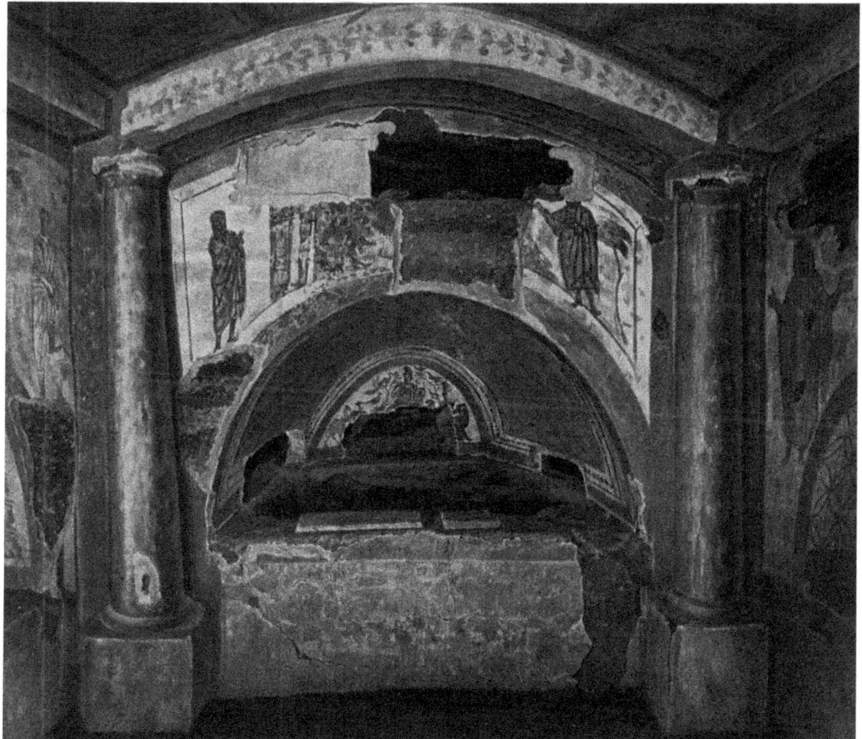

Fig. 9: Domitilla catacomb, cubiculum no. 45 "Orpheus", after Wilpert 1903, Taf. 229.

by adding them particularly for the special deceased or the special group of deceased[55].

One can summarize the same observation as before within the arcosols: there was a strong will to form an individual room and an individual succession of images, often with personal details and personal images mixed with the common biblical scenes. But again, the scenes themselves were repeated without a change.

So, before focusing on the question of the concept of reality in the New Testament miracles, one more painting shall be analyzed, a lunette of the polygonal cubiculum no. 40[56]. It shows a very unusual version of the healing of the paralytic man, with Christ enacting the healing with his virga (fig. 10). As Vasiliki Tsa-

55 This is valid also for the even more complex cubicula, such as the so-called cubiculum of the mensores, no. 74, see Zimmermann 2002, 129–35.
56 Nestori 1993, 126; Wilpert 1903, Taf. 127,2.

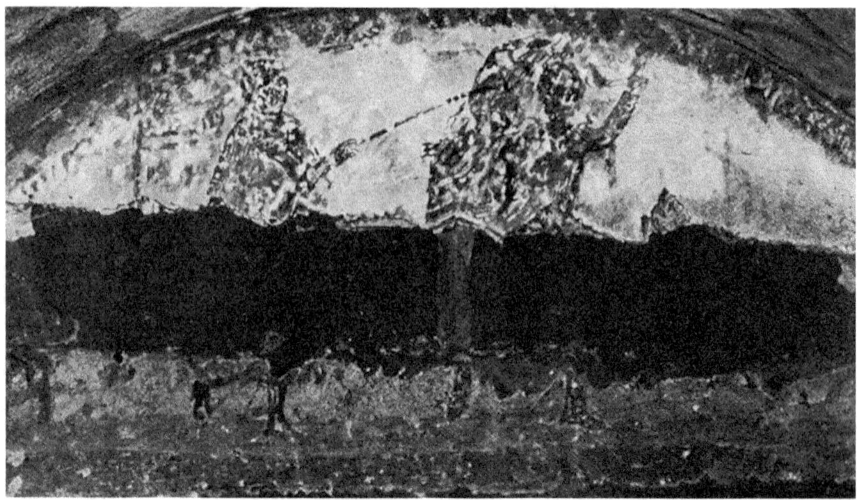

Fig. 10: Domitilla catacomb, cubiculum no. 40, after Wilpert 1903, Taf. 127,2.

makda, who recently identified the scene correctly, pointed out, the virga is not only an unbiblical magical instrument, but it is also most unusual in ancient art[57]. There was no direct tradition for representations of such a magical wand before the Christian scenes and it is impossible to identify an iconographic development from pagan to biblical miracles, as was assumed beforehand[58]. This virga appears nearly exclusively in the Christian sepulchral art, mostly catacomb painting and sarcophagi, and only in connection with Jesus and Moses. While Moses has at least a wand in the biblical source or, more precisely, a kind of walking-stick to enact his miracle of striking water out of the rock, no word mentions the virga in Christ's hand. Iconographs have tried to apply the virga to certain miracles only, such as the wine or the bread and Lazarus, but as can be seen at Domitilla, it also appears in the catacomb art with the lame or leprous and the paralytic. Vasiliki Tsamakda underlined that with the appearance of the same biblical scenes in monumental art, for example as part of biblical friezes in the churches from the 5th century onwards, the virga disappeared[59]. This is the same moment that theologians became the patrons of the artists. It seems reasonable, therefore, to sup-

57 Tsamakda 2007. It is Tsamakda's merit to clear this very important position against the elder studies, namely De Bruyne 1943, Dulaey 1973 and Dulaey 1989, Nauerth 1980 and Nauerth 1983.
58 See the detailed discussion of literary and iconographical sources in Tsamakda 2007, 38–43.
59 Tsamakda 2009, 44.

pose that the non-biblical wand was erased when the now doubtless triumphant Christian scenes were chosen to adorn the cult buildings[60]. In fact, there are very good reasons to interpret the virga of the catacomb art as the most important visualization of the eternal power of the new Christian god. It is connected, but not only, to Jesus, when he is enacting his powerful, salvific miracles, i.e. when he is acting beyond the natural order. And he does it in the same way as his antecessor of the Old Testament, Moses, did. Both scenes, the raising of Lazarus and the striking of the rock, appeared at S. Callisto at the same time[61]. The virga represents a new kind of salvific reality that is inherent to the new religion, the new god, who is stronger than the old pagan gods before. Jesus, or Moses, can even hold both a virga and a rotulus, as symbols of power and magisterium or doctrine[62]. Already in the 4th century, in a room in a catacomb at Naples, Christ was shown, standing alone, in the center of the ceiling, with virga and role: the real magister and powerful god (fig. 11)[63].

To show this last aspect, we finally compare the biblical representations of sepulchral art with the pagan scenes and here mostly with the mythological ones. Only a few examples shall suffice here, but they can stand as general samples of the Roman pagan world: In the via Latina catacomb, a succession of 4th century private cemetery rooms in Rome, scenes from the myth of Heracles (cubiculum N), and Christian images (cubiculum O) exist side by side in neighboring rooms[64]. If one looks at the scenes chosen from the pagan myth, one can see Heracles victorious over an enemy and over the Hydra, with the apples of the Hesperids offering eternal youth, in direct contact with his patron-divinity Athena and last but not least, coming back out of the underworld and bringing her husband King Admetos Alcestis back to life, against the Cerberus who guards the entrance of the Hades. This is, in short, the same semantic selection as one could already see in the new "Christian myth" – the Bible[65]. At first view, there seems to be no difference in the concept of reality, but of course there is and this difference contains the difference between the pagan and Christian era. On behalf of the Roman sepulchral art and the use of the myth, Paul Zanker recently summarized the two

---

60 Anyway, this remains a hypothesis.

61 Nestori 1993, 107: Domitilla no. 25, the so-called capella dei sacramenti A 6, see Bisconti 2009, 26.

62 For Moses striking the rock with virga and roll see in the via Latina catacomb, cubiculo C, Ferrua 1990, fig. 72, and in Marcellino e Pietro, cubiculo 67, Deckers – Seeliger – Mietke 1987, 323.

63 Fasola 1974, Fig. 47.

64 For the via Latina catacomb see Ferrua 1990, for the program of the paintings Zimmermann 2002, 61–125.

65 Zimmermann 2002, 100–103.

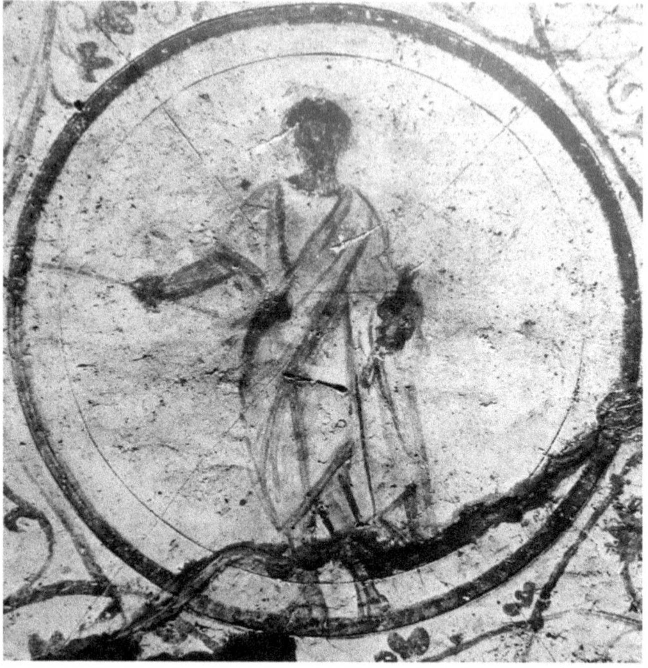

Fig. 11: Naples, San Gennaro catacomb, Christ with roll and virga, after Fasola 1974, fig. 47.

main aspects of use in his important book on the mythological sarcophagi: the praise of the deceased and the comfort of the bereaved[66]. The myth's role is, generally, to reflect the most important, deep human feelings such as pain and love as well as to present the stories of the gods or the stories of gods and men for this reflection[67]. Death, suffering parents, suffering children, painful moments, praise of love, farewell, war, fidelity and infidelity: everyday-life moments were put in contrast with the gods' stories. The usual method of illustration to apply divine virtues to private persons and to equalize the divine with the private person is to mount the portrait of this person on the shoulders of the god[68]. This technique is widely common, and it is sufficient to give only a very few examples: On sarcophagi, as a usual technique to underlie the *virtus*, Heracles with the private portrait

66 Zanker – Ewald 2004, 42–43.

67 On the role of myth see for example Zanker – Ewald 2004, 37–42, or, more generally, Griffin 1986, and De Angelis 1999.

68 See, especially on this concept, Wrede 1981.

of the deceased is shown, or Dionysus, or, for equalizing beauty and *virtus*, a female divinity with the portrait of the deceased woman as praise of her Aphrodite-like qualities, sometimes however with doubtful success[69]. But of course, since nobody believed the deceased would become a god or be a god, the mounting of the portrait was not a reconstruction of reality and nobody believed that Heracles would bring back the deceased or preached in his name for eternity. The manner to use the language of myth is not an aspect of reality, but a kind of psychological expression of the ancient Roman culture[70].

Very different is the Christian imagery and belief, even if the iconographical technique uses the same background: in no single case does a representation of Jesus show assimilation to a private portrait[71]. Never is the image of God mixed in the same traditional way[72]. The reason is very simple: the beliefs were real and not a cultural mannerism or a psychological expression or reflection of consolation[73]. In this, we can secure what one could call a clear and distinct concept of reality: the Christian god offered, in the Roman world, a new and much more powerful promise of eternal life; he promised a precise paradise and the biblical stories report another 'historical' reality that the old pagan myths did not. In addition, the images around the grave show not only another history, but promise another

69 The examples from sarcophagi are listed in Wrede 1981, the special value and use of the portraits in the different myths is discussed in Zanker – Ewald 2004; see also Deckers 1996, 140.

70 Of course, in pagan religious life, the apotheosis exists as concept for good imperators see Zanker 2004. On the concept and imagery of "Glücksvisionen" in the pagan Roman art, see Zanker – Ewald 2004, 116–77. In any case, the Christian meaning of paradise and how to get there was completely different.

71 Zimmermann 2007, 160; Koch 2000, 108. Manuela Studer-Karlen, in her recent work on portraits of deceased on early Christian sarcophagi, points out the same observation for the funeral sculpture: the deceased are introduced as near as possible to Christ or the salvific scenes, Studer-Karlen 2012, 221. However, they never overlap with the Christian goodness.

72 A singular case is the painting of arcosolium no. 22 at Maius catacomb, where it seems to be reasonable that the deceased, a young mother with a child, has been portrayed in a similar way as Mary with the child was usually shown. Here, her parents might have chosen the Mary-like appearance to underlie – in a traditional way of illustration – the qualities of her daughter/wife. For a portrait of Mary, the clothing and jewelry of a rich Roman matron seems inappropriate, see Zimmermann 2007, 177.

73 The Christians were of course not the only ones to believe in the reality of their afterlife, as is best documented in the success of oriental cults of salvation, like Sarapis. Meaningful in this sense are the paintings of the late 4th century catacomb of Vibia: here, a priest of Sabazius named Vincentius, prepared for his wife Vibia a tomb adorned with paintings that show Vibia's death as the rupture of Proserpina, her final judgment, her entrance to the paradise garden, and finally the eternal meal of Vincentius, his priests and Vibia, as a concrete and hopeful expectation of what will happen after her death, see Engemann 1997, 116–22.

future. This difference did not detain the Christians to better explain Christ's nature with a traditional, mythical example, which is the image of Orpheus. But no private person would express his wish for salvation by merging his portrait on God's image.

It is in this context that the sepulchral and mostly the catacomb art invents a new instrument, the virga, to express a new kind of eternal power, some kind of magic wand. In all super-natural events or acts, the virga symbolizes the divine power. One may analyze that, of course, this was only another level of psychological reflection. And of course, for some parts of the ancient society there might have been no difference between magical belief and the new religion. However, the early Christians who chose these images were certainly full of hope to have another truth and that this truth was real. We might see the lack of scenes dealing with the sorrow for the dead of the loved ones, generally in the Christian world and especially in the catacomb art, as confirmation of that interpretation[74]. The New Testament miracles are only one part of the salvific context of Roman catacomb painting, but they visibly attest the reality of the new religion.

Bibliography

Bisconti, Fabrizio, ed., 2000: *Temi di iconografia paleocristiana*. Città del Vaticano: Mancini.

Bisconti, Fabrizio 2009: L1–L2, A1–A6, X–Y, C–E. Relitti iconografici e nuovi tracciati figurativi alle origini della pittura catacombale romana. *Rivista di Archeologia Cristiana* 85:7–54.

Dassmann, Ernst 1973: Sündenvergebung durch Taufe, Buße und Martyrerfürbitte in den Zeugnissen frühchristlicher Frömmigkeit und Kunst. Münsterische Beiträge zur Theologie 36. Münster: Aschendorff.

De Angelis, Francesco, ed. 1999: Im Spiegel des Mythos. Bilderwelt und Lebenswelt. Symposion 19.–20. Februar 1998 DAI Rom. Palilia 6. Wiesbaden: Reichert.

De Bruyne, Lucien 1943: L'imposition des mains dans l'art chrétien ancien. Contribution iconologique à l'histoire du geste. *Rivista di Archeologia Cristiana* 20:132–140.

Deckers, Johannes Georg; Seeliger, Hans Reinhard; Mietke, Gabriele 1987: *Die Katakombe "Santi Marcellino e Pietro". Repertorium der Malereien*. Roma sotterranea cristiana 6. Città del Vaticano – Münster: Aschendorff.

Deckers, Johannes Georg; Mietke, Gabriele; Weiland, Albrecht 1991: *Die Katakombe "Anonima di via Anapo". Repertorium der Malereien*. Roma sotterranea cristiana 9. Città del Vaticano: Pontificio Istituto di Archeologia Cristiana.

74 For one of only a very few examples for expressions of sorrow in the catacombs, two Erots with dropped torches, flanking and holding the panel with the portraits of the deceased couple, in cubiculum no. 39, at Domitilla, see Zimmermann 2007, 165, and complementary, for the Christian grave inscriptions, Jutta Dresken-Weiland's observations, Dresken-Weiland 2006.

Deckers, Johannes Georg; Mietke, Gabriele; Weiland, Albrecht 1994: *Die Katakombe "Commodilla". Repertorium der Malereiein.* Roma sotterranea cristiana 10. Città del Vaticano: Pontificio Istituto di Archeologia Cristiana.

Deckers, Johannes Georg 1982: Die Huldigung der Magier in der Kunst der Spätantike. *Die Heiligen Drei Könige – Darstellung und Verehrung. Katalog zur Ausstellung des Wallraf-Richartz-Museums in der Josef-Haubrich-Kunsthalle Köln 01. Dez. 1982 – 30. Jan. 1983.* Köln, 20–32.

Deckers, Johannes Georg 1996: Vom Denker zum Diener. Bemerkungen zu den Folgen der Konstantinischen Wende im Spiegel der Sarkophagplastik. Brenk, Beat, ed., Innovation in der Spätantike, Kolloquium Basel 1994, Wiesbaden: Reichert, 137–72.

Dinkler, Erich 1939: *Die ersten Petrusdarstellungen.* Sonderheft Marburger Jahrbuch für Kunstwissenschaft 11. Marburg.

Dulaey, Martine 1973: Le symbole de la baguette dans l'art paléochrétien. *Revue d'Études Augustiennes et Patristiques* 19/1–2:3–38.

Dulaey, Martine 1989: Virga virtutis tuae, virga oris tuae. Le bâton du Christ dans le christianisme ancien. *"Quaeritur inventus colitur". Miscellanea in onore di Padre U. M. Fasola.* Studi di Antichità Cristiane 40. Città del Vaticano: Pontificio Istituto di Archeologia Cristiana, 235–245.

Engemann, Josef 1997: *Deutung und Bedeutung frühchristlicher Bildwerke*, Darmstadt: Wissenschaftliche Buchgesellschaft.

Fasola, Umberto Maria 1974: *Le catacombe di S. Gennaro a Capodimonte*, Roma: Editalia.

Ferrua, Antonio 1900: *Catacombe sconosciute. Una pinacoteca sotto terra*, Firenze: Nardini.

Fiocchi Nicolai, Vincenzo; Bisconti, Fabrizio; Mazzoleni, Danilo 1998: *Roms frühchristliche Katakomben*, Regensburg: Schnell & Steiner.

Fiocchi Nicolai, Vincenzo 2001: *Strutture funerarie ed edifici di culto paleocristiani di Roma dal IV al VI secolo*, Città del Vaticano: IGER.

Fiocchi Nicolai, Vincenzo 2004: Art. Katakombe (Hypogäum). *Reallexikon für Antike und Christentum* 20:342–422.

Griffin, Jasper 1986: *The mirror of the myth*, London: Faber and Faber.

Ihm, Christa 1960: *Die Programme der christlichen Apsismalerei vom 4. Jahrhundert bis zur Mitte des 8. Jahrhunderts.* Wiesbaden: Steiner.

Koch, Guntram 2000: *Frühchristliche Sarkophage*, München: Beck.

Nauerth, Claudia 1980: *Vom Tod zum Leben. Die christliche Totenerweckung in der spätantiken Kunst.* Göttinger Orientforschungen 2/1. Wiesbaden: Harrassowitz.

Nauerth, Claudia 1983: Heilungswunder in der frühchristlichen Kunst. Stutzinger, Dagmar, ed., *Spätantike und frühes Christentum.* Ausstellung im Liebieghaus in Frankfurt am Main, 16. Dezember 1983 bis 11. März 1984. Frankfurt: Liebighaus, 339–346.

Nestori, Aldo 1993: *Repertorio topografico delle pitture delle catacombe romane.* Roma sotterranea cristiana 5. [2]Città del Vaticano: Pontificio Istituto di Archeologia Cristiana.

Nuzzo, Donatella 2000: *Tipologia sepolcrale delle catacombe romane. I cimiteri ipogei delle vie Ostiense, Ardeatina e Appia.* BAR Int. Ser. 905. Oxford: Archeopress.

Pergola, Philippe 2004: s.v. Domitillae coemeterium. *Lexicon Topographicum Urbis Romae. Suburbium* II, Roma 203–207.

Speigl, Jakob 1978: Das Bildprogramm des Jonahmotivs in den Malereien der römischen Katakomben. *Römische Quartalsschrift für Altertumskunde und Kirchengeschichte* 73:1–15.

Tsamakda, Vasiliki 2009: Eine ungewöhnliche Darstellung der Heilung des Paralytikers in der Domitilla-Katakombe: Zur Verwendung des Wunderstabes in der frühchristlichen Kunst. *Mitteilungen zur Christlichen Archäologie* 15:25–49.

Wilpert, Joseph 1903: *Die Malereien der Katakomben Roms*, Freiburg i.Br.: Herder.
Wrede, Henning 1991: *Consecratio in formam deorum. Vergöttlichte Privatpersonen in der römischen Kaiserzeit.* Mainz: Philipp von Zabern.
Zanker, Paul; Ewald, Björn 2004: *Leben mit Mythen: die Bilderwelt der römischen Sarkophage.* München: Hirmer.
Zanker, Paul 2004: *Die Apotheose der römischen Kaiser. Ritual und städtische Bühne.* München: Carl Friedrich von Siemens Stiftung.
Zimmermann, Norbert 2001: Beobachtungen zu Ausstattungspraxis und Aussageabsicht römischer Katakombenmalerei. *Mitteilungen zur Christlichen Archäologie* 7:43–59.
Zimmermann, Norbert 2002: *Werkstattgruppen römischer Katakombenmalerei.* Jahrbuch für Antike und Christentum Erg.-Bd. 35. Münster: Aschendorff.
Zimmermann, Norbert 2007: Verstorbene im Bild. *Jahrbuch für Antike und Christentum* 50:154–179.
Zimmermann, Norbert 2012: Zur Deutung spätantiker Mahlszenen: Totenmahl im Bild. Danek, Georg – Hellerschmid, Irmtraud (eds.), Rituale – Identitätsstiftende Handlungskomplexe. Akten der 2. Tagung des ZAA, 2.–3. November 2009. Origines, Schriften des Zentrums Archäologie und Altertumswissenschaften Band 2. Wien: Verlag der ÖAW, 171–185.

Rossitza Schroeder

The Rhetoric of Violence and Healing in the Church of Prophites Elias in Thessaloniki

The healing ministry of Christ occupies a special place in late Byzantine monumental art (1261–1453).[1] The popularity of this subject reflects the theological realities of the late thirteenth and fourteenth centuries, characterized by the restoration of Constantinople to the Byzantines in 1261, the consequent 'healing' of the Orthodox Church, and the renewal of the miraculous powers of its shrines and icons.[2] The rising interest in composing new and elaborating on old miracle stories[3] is paralleled by the proliferation of representations of Christ's healing miracles in churches in Byzantine Macedonia, Constantinople, and Mistra. Frequently, ministry cycles occupy the subsidiary spaces – nartheces and ambulatories – of urban monastic churches, and the number and choice of scenes included in them varies widely. In this paper, I will consider the healing ministry in the narthex of the fourteenth-century church of Prophites Elias in Thessaloniki, while concentrating on the prominent but little known fresco of the Healing of the

1 For late Byzantine images of Christ's healing ministry, see R. Etzeoglou, "The Cult of the Virgin Zoodochos Pege at Mistra," in *Images of the Mother of God: Perceptions of the Theotokos in Byzantium* (ed. M. Vassilaki; Aldershot, 2005), 239–49; T. Gouma-Peterson, "Christ as Ministrant and the Priest as Ministrant of Christ in a Palaeologan Cycle of 1303," *Dumbarton Oaks Papers* 32 (1978): 199–216; K. Kirchheiner, "Die Bildausstattung des südlichen Annex der Nikolauskirche in Thessaloniki: Überlegungen zum Verhältnis von Bildauswahl und Funktion eines Seitenraumes," in *Byzantinische Malerei: Bildprogramme – Iconographie – Stil*, (ed. G. Koch; Wiesbaden, 2001), 147–61; R. Schroeder, "Healing the Body, Saving the Soul: Christ's Healing Ministry in Byzantium," in *Holistic Healing in Byzantium* (ed. J. Chirban; Brookline, 2010), 253–79; P. Underwood, "Some Problems in Programs and Iconography of Ministry Cycles," in *The Kariye Djami*, 4 vols. (New York, 1966–1975), 4:245–302.

2 S. Efthymiadis, "Late Byzantine Collections of Miracles and Their Implications," in *The Heroes of the Orthodox Church: the New Saints, 8th–16th c.* (ed. E. Kountoura-Galake; Athens, 2004), 239–50; A. M. Talbot, "Epigrams of Manuel Philes on the Theotokos tes Peges and Its Art," *Dumbarton Oaks Papers* 48 (1994): 135–65; eadem, "Healing Shrines in Late Byzantine Constantinople," in *Women and Religious Life in Byzantium* (ed. eadem; Aldershot, 1996), 1–26; eadem, "Pilgrimage to Healing Shrines: The Evidence of Miracle Accounts," *Dumbarton Oaks Papers* 56 (2002): 165–65; eadem, "Two Accounts of Miracles at the Pege Shrine in Constantinople," *Travaux et mémoires* 14 (2002): 605–15.

3 A. M. Talbot, "Old Wine in New Bottles: The Rewriting of Saints' Lives in the Palaeologan Period," in *The Twilight of Byzantium: Aspects of Cultural and Religious History in the Late Byzantine Empire* (ed. S. Ćurčić and D. Mouriki; Princeton, 1991), 15–26.

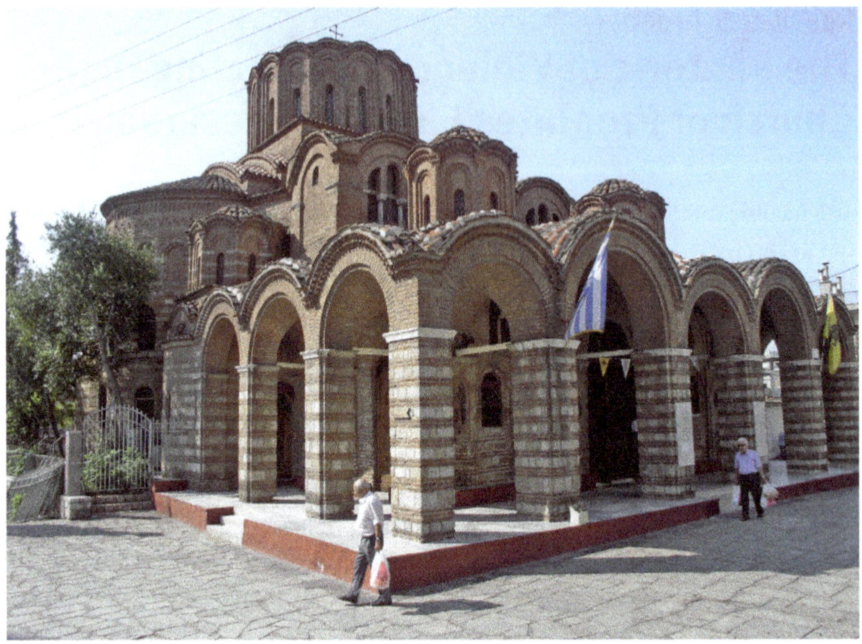

Figure 1: Church of Prophites Elias, Exterior, View of Porch from the West. Second Half of Fourteenth Century. Thessaloniki, Greece.

Multitude.[4] As one of the many healing miracles performed by Christ in the context of the liti, the image participates in a visual network of associations that highlights the relationship between the healing of body and soul through confession and sincere penance.[5] Through the healing scene's distinct pairing with the Massacre of the Innocents, it acquires an additional dimension that uncovers contemporary attitudes to senseless violence and its potential to be a destructive as well as a generative force.

Perched on a hill above the basilica of Hagios Demetrios and accessed through a rather steep street, Prophites Elias commands a spectacular view of Thessaloniki and its bay (Figure 1). It was founded ca. 1360 by Makarios Choum-

4 In Thessaloniki five other Palaeologan churches similarly contain extensive Ministry cycles. These are the chapel of St Euthymios, Holy Apostles, St Catherine, Nicholas Orphanos, and the katholikon of the Vlatadon Monastery.

5 For Christ's healing miracles as metaphors for spiritual healing, see M. Evangelatou, "Virtuous Soul, Healthy Body: The Holistic Concept of Health in Byzantine Representations of Christ's Healing Miracles," in *Holistic Healing in Byzantium* (ed. J. Chirban; Brookline, 2010), 173–241; Schroeder, "Healing the Body, Saving the Soul," 258–64.

nos and was once a katholikon of a monastery dedicated to the Virgin commonly referred to as Nea Moni.[6] Architecturally the church belongs to the so-called Athonite type which is characterized by a spacious narthex, liti, and side apses, choroi, which together with the altar apse, when looked at from above, form a massive trefoil.[7] While most late Byzantine churches in Thessaloniki were built with prominent nartheces and ambulatories, none of them display the uninterrupted wide space of Prophites Elias' vestibule (Figure 2).[8] It remains unclear whether this specific, and unique to Thessaloniki, architectural type was intended to accommodate new rituals, a different type of audience that extended beyond the monastic community, or to signal symbolic affiliations with Mount Athos.

The vaults and upper walls of the liti were extensively frescoed with images from the childhood and ministry of Christ, while individual sainted figures, mostly monks, line up the lower portion of the space. Jesus' healings and teaching form the lengthiest surviving cycle in Thessaloniki. The events from the Nativity cycle were once painted on the north wall and conclude on the east wall with the Massacre of the Innocents. Fortunately, most of the frescoes at the easternmost vaults have survived allowing us to trace a clear narrative thread initiated by the Temptation and followed by scenes from the ministry that reiterate Christ's miraculous powers on earth. The episodes included immediately relevant to our discussion are the Healing of the Demoniac at Capernaum, the Raising of the Widow's Son at Nain, the Healing of Peter's Mother-in-Law, the Healing of the Multitude, and the Healing of the Two Gadarene Demoniacs on the south wall. Generic, yet prominent, cityscapes and luxurious interiors must have cued the audience into perceiving the frescoed events as happening within an urban context, perhaps even their own city where Christ continuously and mercifully intervenes in the lives of humans of various stations and walks of life. Preserved throughout the liti are other scenes from Christ's ministry among which clearly discernable are the Healing of the Leper at Nazareth, the Healing of the Nobleman's Son, the Healing of the Archon's Demoniac Son, the Healing of the Ten

---

6 J. Thomas and A. C. Hero, eds., *Byzantine Monastic Foundation Documents*, 5 vols. (Washington, D.C., 2000), 4:1433–54. For an alternative identification, see T. Papazotos, "The Identification of the Church of 'Profitis Elias' in Thessaloniki," *Dumbarton Oaks Papers* 45 (1991): 121–27.

7 For a discussion of the Athonite type church with extensive bibliography, see most recently S. Mamaloukos, "A Contribution of the Study of 'Athonite' Church Type of Byzantine Architecture," *Zograf* 35 (2011): 39–50; A. Tantsis, "The so-called 'Athonite' Type of Church and Two Shrines of the Theotokos in Constantinople," *Zograf* 34 (2010): 3–11.

8 For subsidiary spaces in late Byzantine churches in Thessaloniki, see E. K. Hatzitryphonos, *To peristoō stēn hysterobyzantinē ekklēsiastikē architektonikē: schediasmos – leitourgia* (Thessaloniki, 2004), 269–96.

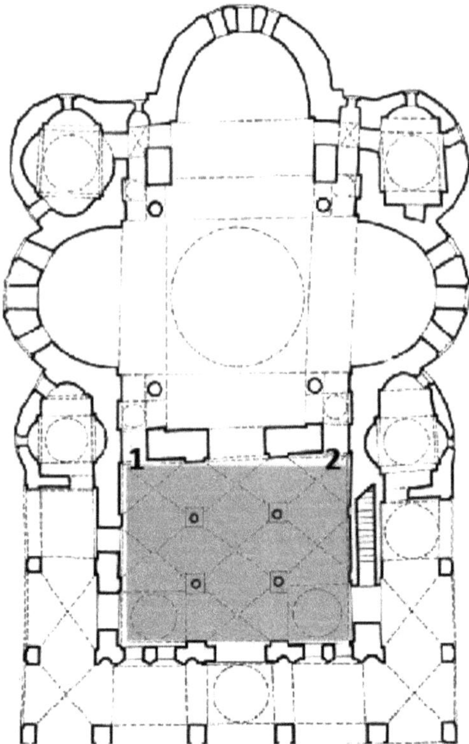

Figure 2: Church of Prophites Elias, Ground Plan with Shaded Area Showing the Liti. Number 1 Indicates the Placement of the Massacre of the Innocents and Number 2 Indicates the Placement of the Healing of the Multitude. Second Half of Fourteenth Century. Thessaloniki, Greece.

Lepers, the Healing of the Man with a Withered Hand, the Blessing of Little Children, the Parable of the Royal Feast and the Calling of Matthew. Within the fragmentary program two types of people are prominently present: demoniacs and children. It is my contention that the emphasis on these particular groups was determined by the function of the narthex as a site of spiritual cleansing where one could be freed from sin through confession and penance and returned to a child-like innocence.[9]

9 For the narthex as a place for confessions, see V. Marinis, "Tombs and Burials in the Monastery *tou Libos* in Constantinople," *Dumbarton Oaks Papers* 63 (2009): 154–55 and n.42; V. Milanović, "Narteks kao mesto pokajnika i katihumena. Podatsi iz vizantijskog pisanog nasleča i nihova re-

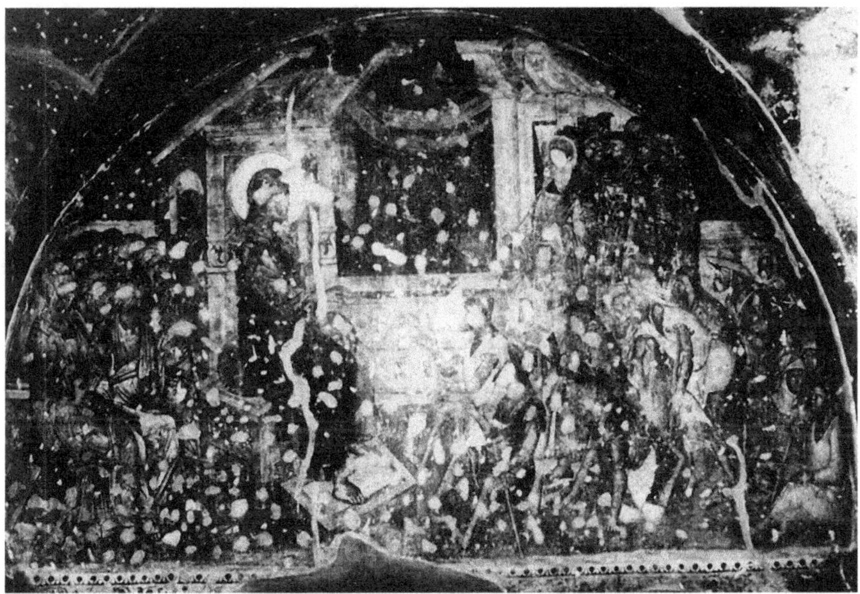

Figure 3: Healing of the Multitude and Two Prophets with Scrolls. Church of Prophites Elias, Liti, Lunette over South Entrance into the Naos. Second Half of Fourteenth Century. Thessaloniki, Greece.

The Healing of the Multitude is represented on the east wall of the narthex (Figure 3). The image is very rarely brought into scholarly discussions, perhaps because the church and the fresco program of its narthex have yet to receive a thorough treatment by conservators and art historians. Only the spectacular and rather gruesome fresco of the Massacre of the Innocents has been considered in greater detail as it captures the eye with its bright and saturated colors and stirs the imagination with its chaotic brutality (Figure 4).[10] By means of its placement

cepcija u naučnoj literaturi," in *Na tragovima Vojislava J. Djuriča*, ed. D. Medaković and Grozdanov (Belgrade, 2011), 109–34. R. Schroeder, "Prayer and Penance in the South Bay of the Chora Esonarthex," *Gesta* 48 (2009): 37–53. That repentance was one of the main themes of the visual program of Profites Elias' liti is confirmed by the epigram inscribed in the scroll of the Virgin on the north wall. See I. M. Djordjević and M. Marković, "On the Dialogue Relationship between the Virgin and Christ in East Christian Art. Apropos the Discovery of the Figures of the Virgin Mediatrix and Christ in the Naos in Lesnovo," *Zograf* 28 (2000–2001): 24; A. Rhoby, *Byzantinische Epigramme auf Fresken und Mosaiken* (Vienna, 2009), 336.

10 S. Gerstel, "Civic and Monastic Influences on Church Decoration in Late Byzantine Thessalonike," *Dumbarton Oaks Papers* 57 (2003): 227–28; M. Kambá-Voulgaráki, "Les fresques de la lite

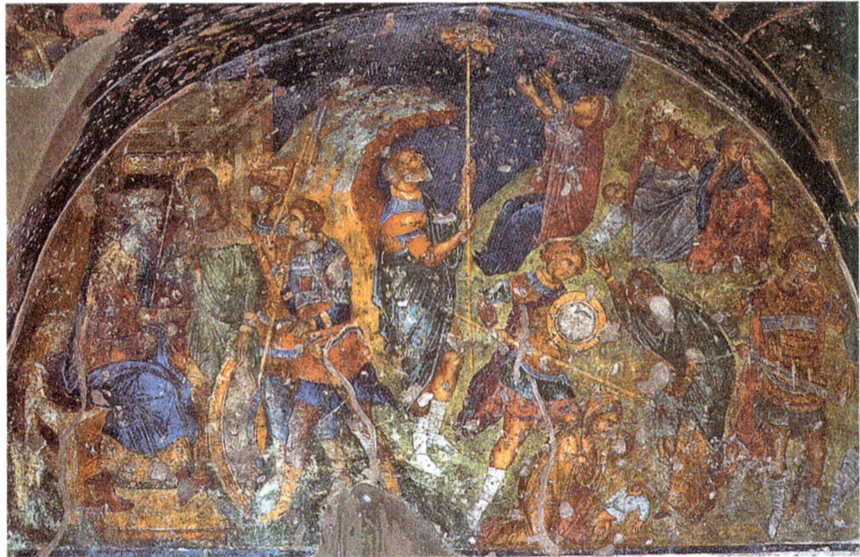

Figure 4: Massacre of the Innocents. Church of Prophites Elias, Liti, Lunette over North Entrance into the Naos. Second Half of Fourteenth Century. Thessaloniki, Greece.

on the lunette over the north side entrance into the naos, the Massacre appears to be purposefully juxtaposed with the Healing of the Multitude which occupies an analogous position on the southern end of the narthex's east wall (see Figure 2). It is clear that the two images were intentionally paired to form the visual equivalent of the rhetorical figure of synkrisis or comparison.[11] The healing miracle can be understood only in relation to the Massacre and vice versa.

The Massacre of the Innocents is the only surviving scene from the Infancy cycle which once occupied portions of the north wall of the liti. The composition lacks coherence and symmetry, its violent movement spilling over onto the vaulted ceiling and the neighboring wall. Herod is represented to the left giving orders. Above him rises a beautiful red ciborium with an empty altar underneath it, an architectural frame that provides a proper setting for Herod's royal presence or possibly indicates the site of the prophet Zechariah's

du Prophete Elie de Thessalonique: Une approche iconographique," *Paterikē-Byzantinē Epitheōrises/The Patristic and Byzantine Review* 25 (2007): 131; Ch. Mavropoulou-Tsioume, "Hē mnemeiakē zōgraphikē stē Thessalonikē sto deutero miso tou 14ou aiōna," in *Euphrosynon: Aphierōma ston Manolē Chatzēdakē*, 2 vols. (Athens, 1992), 2:663.

11 On synkrisis in Byzantine visual culture, see H. Maguire, "The Art of Comparing in Byzantium," *Art Bulletin* 70 (1988): 88–103.

murder.[12] The king, dressed in full imperial regalia, sits on a backless throne and gestures agitatedly in the direction of three soldiers who listen to him attentively. His feet are represented in motion as if he is about to get up and become an active participant in the children's slaughter; he seems to be in the throes of destructive passions as some of the literary texts about the Massacre attest.[13] Herod's agitation stands in stark contrast to the enemy against whom he wages war – the one- and two-year old children of Bethlehem – a point which was mentioned in Matthew's Gospel (2:16), and which was continuously elaborated on and rehearsed in homilies and poetic compositions.[14] About two thirds of the fresco relates the murder, with the soldiers purposefully engaged in the massacre of young children. The event unfolds on the backdrop of a barren mountainous landscape, carried over into the neighboring scene of the Temptation where Christ is visible perched on a high hill turning his head in direction of a winged demonic figure.[15] At the foreground of the Massacre composition is the distinct figure of a balding gray-haired elderly man additionally framed by a rock formation which precariously curves above him. He is holding a spear with an impaled baby on its tip visually dividing the composition in the middle; the child's mother desperately raises her arms toward the lifeless corpse. A younger soldier, also on the foreground, has skewered a boy as his mother vigorously tries to pro-

---

12 For a similar use of a ciborium to frame Herod, see a twelfth-century icon with a Christmas cycle in St. Catherine's on Mount Sinai or the fourteenth-century Bulgarian *tetraevangelion* in the British library (Add. 3627), fol. 11 (L. Zhivkova, *Das Tetraevangeliar des Zaren Ivan Alexander* [Recklinghausen, 1977], fig. 15). The murder of Zachariah was painted in one of the domes of the south gallery of the Hodegetria church at Mistra as well as in the building near the Chalkoprateia church at Constantinople. See, J. Lafontaine-Dosogne, "Iconography of the Cycle of the Infancy of Christ," in *The Kariye Djami*, 4 vols. (ed. P. Underwood; New York and Princeton, 1966–1975), 4:231, and fig. 59.
13 For a discussion of Byzantine literary descriptions of Herod's behavior during the Massacre and their influence on the scene's iconography, see E. D. Maguire and H. Maguire, *Other Icons: Art and Power in Byzantine Secular Culture* (Princeton, 2007), 144; H. Maguire, *Art and Eloquence in Byzantium* (Princeton, 1981), 25–27; G. Millet, *Recherches sur l'iconographie de l'Évangile aux XIVe, XVe et XVIe siècles* (Paris, 1916; rpt. 1960), 159.
14 F. Scorza Barcellona, "La celebrazione dei Santi Innocenti nell'omiletica greca I," *Bollettino della Badia Greca di Grottaferrata* 29 (1975): 112–15, 123–24. In the fourteenth-century mosaic with the Massacre in the Constantinopolitan church of the Chora (P. Underwood, *The Kariye Djami*, 4 vols. [New York and Princeton, 1966–1975], 2:184–85) Herod is even dressed as a general, furthering the paradox of him warring against children. See M. Parani, *Reconstructing the Reality of Images: Byzantine Material Culture and Religious Iconography (11th–15th Centuries)* (Leiden and Boston, 2003), 149.
15 Christ assumes similar posture in the mosaic of the healing of the woman with an issue of blood in the esonarthex of the Constantinopolitan Chora church (Underwood, *Kariye Djami*, 2:268) and in an unpublished fourteenth-century fresco of the healing of the two blind men (Matt 9:27–31) in the exonarthex of the Thessalonikan church of the Holy Apostles.

tect him and pull him away. At this soldier's feet is a seated woman who weeps over the beheaded body of a young child. Another armed man in the lower right corner has just cut off the head of a swaddled infant, and blood gushes out of the fresh wound. Two women sitting on the ground in the upper right end of the composition pull their hair as a sign of grief; their wailing hovers over the dead children who lie before them. The scene is not only startlingly polychromatic, it is also noisy – one could easily imagine the clatter of weapons and chainmail, children's screams as they are torn away from their mothers, and women's cries over their unbearable loss. It visualizes ataxia, a lack of order typical for barbarians and religious dissidents.[16] Unlike the slightly earlier expansive narrative in the exonarthex Constantinopolitan Chora church which stands out with its classicizing beauty and golden mosaic glitter,[17] the Massacre in Prophites Elias is compressed, busy and chaotic, poignantly juxtaposing flashes of brutal force with helpless innocence and heartbreaking grief. The possibility that its iconography might have something to do with an actual mass killing which took place during an uprising in 1345 in Thessaloniki makes it that much more likely that the audience would have been especially sensitive to the subject matter, distant past and immediate present easily overlapping.[18] Indeed, some scholars

---

16 Maguire and Maguire, *Other Icons*, 135.

17 Lafontaine-Dosogne, "Iconography of the Cycle of the Infancy of Christ," 4:233; Maguire, *Art and Eloquence*, 32; for beautifully rendered scenes with gruesome subject matter and their effect on the audience, see U. R. D'Elia, *The Poetics of Titian's Religious Paintings* (Cambridge, 2005), 63–83; H. Hendrix, "The Repulsive Body: Images of Torture in Seventeenth-Century Naples," in *Bodily Extremities: Preoccupations with the Human Body in Early Modern European Culture* (ed. F. Egmond and R. Zwijnenberg; Aldershot, 2003), 68–91.

18 Gerstel, "Civic and Monastic Influences," 227–28; H. Maguire, "Rhetoric and Reality in the Art of the Kariye Camii," in *The Kariye Camii Reconsidered*, (ed. H. A. Klein et al.; Istanbul, 2011), 66. A. Semoglou, "L'éloquence au service d'archéologie: Les 'enfants aimés' de Theodore Métochite et sa bibliothèque dans le monastère de Chora," *Series Byzantina* 8 (2010): 54. The Thessalonikan massacre was described by Demetrios Kydones in a literary lament translated and discussed by J. W. Barker, "The 'Monody' of Demetrios Kydones on the Zealot Rising of 1345 in Thessaloniki," in *Meletēmata stē mnēmē Vasileiou Laourda/ Essays in Memory of Basil Laourdas* (Thessaloniki, 1975), 285–300. On the ways in which images of the Massacre of the Innocents might relate to certain historic events, see B. Fricke, "'... Humanizing What Was Monstrous'? A Remark on the Reception and Aesthetic of the Massacre of the Innocents by Nicola and Giovanni Pisano," unpublished paper delivered at *Beautiful Martyrs: Aesthetics and Violence* colloquium, University of California, Berkeley and Graduate Theological Union, March 2011; D. Kunzle, "Spanish Herod, Dutch Innocents: Bruegel's *Massacres of the Innocents* in Their Sixteenth-Century Political Contexts," *Art History* 24 (2001): 51–82; R. Nelson, "Taxation with Representation: Visual Field and the Political Field of the Kariye Camii," *Art History* 22 (1999): 75; Semoglou, "L'éloquence au service d'archéologie," 54.

have commented on the fact that in comparison with other fourteenth-century monumental images of the Massacre in the Chora[19] and the Virgin Hodegetria in Mistra,[20] the image in Prophites Elias appears to be strikingly realistic, allowing the viewers to more immediately and no doubt more effectively relate to the figures involved in the events represented.[21] It could be, of course, that the image reflects the violence that accompanies the monastic lifestyle. This idea was poignantly articulated by John Klimakos in his popular manual for monastic behavior, *The Heavenly Ladder*:

> Violence and unending pain are the lot of those who aim to ascend to heaven with the body, and this especially at the early stages of the enterprise, when our pleasure-loving disposition and our unfeeling hearts must travel through overwhelming grief toward the love of God and holiness.[22]

The Healing of the Multitude, unlike the Massacre, is well ordered and serene. Judging from the lavish textile flung between the two massive stone piers that frame the image the event is partially unfolding in an interior space. Christ is represented seated on a backless throne with a red pillow and rests his feet on a footstool. A somewhat unrealistic architectural structure rises above him, additionally emphasizing his figure. With one hand he blesses the crowd which has gathered before him and with the other clutches a scroll. In the left corner of the fresco Jesus' disciples are represented clustered behind him. A group of sick people balance the composition to the right some of them barely standing supporting themselves on crutches and sticks and others sitting on a verdant ground. Those placed to the front gesture toward Christ, engaging him in a wordless conversation. They exhibit their infirmities without shame, their bent bodies, immo-

---

19 Underwood, *Kariye Djami*, 2:184–96.

20 Maguire, *Art and Eloquence*, figs. 15–16.

21 On the realistic tendencies in the frescoes of Prophites Elias, see E. Kourkoutidou-Nikolaidou and A. Tourta, *Wandering in Byzantine Thessaloniki* (Athens, 1997), 116. Ch. Mavropoulou-Tsioumi, "Hē mnēmeiakē zōgraphikē stē Makedonia kata to 14o aiōna," in *Hē Makedonia kata tēn epochē tōn Palaiologōn* (Thessaloniki, 2002), 403. For the shift in late Byzantine art in emphasizing the horror rather than the beauty of martyrodom, see M. Hatzaki, *Beauty and the Male Body in Byzantium. Perceptions and Representations in Art and Text* (New York, 2009), 84–85. Hatzaki argues that by the thirteenth and fourteenth centuries the audience needed to see the suffering of the martyrs in order to be affected by the images.

22 John Climacus, *The Ladder of Divine Ascent* (trans. C. Luibheid and N. Russell; New York, Ramsey, Toronto, 1982), 75. On monastic violence in the West, see K. Ambrose, *The Nave Sculpture of Vézelay: The Art of Monastic Viewing* (Toronto, 2006), 73–86; M. B. Pranger, *The Artificiality of Christianity: Essays of the Poetics of Monasticism* (Palo Alto, 2003), 17–95.

bile limbs, and spotted skin on display for Christ and the audience to see and perhaps even diagnose.[23] Only two women can be distinguished amongst the sick, and they are tucked in the right corner of the image; one of them seems to be distracted and conspicuously turns her face toward the viewer, becoming a Byzantine festaiuola, inviting and drawing the audience into the picture. A group of Pharisees is painted in the upper right observing the interaction. Only one child is distinguishable in the fresco, even though they figure prominently in other fourteenth-century representations of the miracle.[24] The fresco can be interpreted not only as healing but also as a teaching scene. The symmetrical arrangement with the apostles behind Christ on the right and the group of sick people on the left recalls images of instruction.

On the vault immediately above the miracle two older men dressed in light-colored antique garments hold scrolls that unfold unnaturally up. The identifying inscriptions of the two figures and those on their scrolls are not visible and we can only imagine that their texts once related to the narrative image below. It is very likely that these are prophets, who occasionally appear in close proximity to New Testament scenes in manuscripts and monumental paintings holding scrolls inscribed with relevant prefigurative passages.[25]

The late Byzantine representations of the Healing of the Multitude were inspired by different Gospel passages: the image in the Metropolis at Mistra by Luke 4:40–41 and in the Kariye Djami by Matt 15:29–31.[26] In two fourteenth-cen-

---

23 For the late Byzantine interest in the aetiology of various illnesses, see Talbot, "Healing Shrines," 17–19; eadem, "*The Miracles of Gregory Palamas* by Philotheos Kokkinos," in *The Byzantine World* (ed. P. Stephenson; London and New York, 2010), 242.

24 The single child is being carried in a basket strapped in the back of his father and is visible in a detail published in Mavropoulou-Tsioumi, "Hē mnēmeiakē zōgraphikē ," fig. 18; cf. the Healing of the Multitude in the Chora church (Underwood, *Kariye Djami*, 2:277) and in the main church of the Serbian monastery in Dečani (http://www.srpskoblago.org/Archives/Decani/exhibits/Frescoes/Altar/Apse/CX4K3047_l.html).

25 R. Etzeoglou, "Keimeno kai eikona: Parastaseis ston narthēka tou naou tēs Odēgētrias ston Mystra," in *Psēfides. Meletes istorias, archaiologias kai tehnēs stē mnēmē tēs Stellas Papadakē-Oekland*, (ed. O. Gratziou and Ch. Loukos; Haraklion, 2009), 133–44; S. Pelekanides, *Kaliergēs. Olēs Thettalias aristos zōgraphos* (Athens, 1973; repr. 1994), 75, 137; I. Rapti, "Gloses prophétiques sur l'évangile: À propos a quelques manuscrits arméniens enluminés en Cicilie dans les années 1260," *Dumbarton Oaks Papers* 58 (2004): 119–54.

26 S. Pasi, "La scena della guarigione di diverse malattie nella pittura monumentale tardo-bizantina" *Corsi di cultura sull'arte ravennate e bizantina* 42 (1995): 694, 697. In the Metropolis church at Mistra, as in Prophites Elias, the Healing of the Multitude follows the Healing of Peter's Mother-in-Law, and unfolds in an interior space as indicated by the draped architecture in the background. In Mistra Christ, however, is not represented seated. See S. Dufrenne, *Les programmes iconographiques des églises byzantines de Mistra* (Paris, 1970), pl. 7, fig. 10.

tury Thessalonikan churches that only slightly predate Prophites Elias – St Nicholas Orphanos and St Catherine – one finds an abbreviated version of the miracle with only two crippled man (κυλλοὺς) who are explicitly mentioned only in Matthew's account of the healing (15:30).[27] In Prophites Elias, the artist more or less seems to have followed Mark 1:32–34 which, while relating the same story as Luke 4:40–41 about how after relieving Peter's mother-in-law of her fever Christ healed a number of sick people, is the only text that specifies that the crowd had gathered at the door of the house:

> That evening after sunset the people brought to Jesus all the sick and demon-possessed. The whole town gathered at the door, and Jesus healed many who had various diseases. He also drove out many demons, but he would not let the demons speak because they knew who he was.

In some middle Byzantine manuscript illumination a difference was made between Luke's and Mark's narratives. Thus the artist of the late eleventh- or early twelfth-century Gospel book, Florence, Biblioteca Laurenziana, VI.23, fol. 64v followed Mark faithfully and represented Christ in a manner similar to that seen in Prophites Elias, seated within an architectural structure with two apostles behind him and a group of sick people in front.[28] The illustration of the same episode in Luke differs: on fol. 111r Christ is depicted standing and no sign of enveloping interior space is discernable.[29]

The issue with the textual source for the fresco in Prophites Elias is additionally complicated by the images of the two prophets painted in the vault. In reporting the incident of healing Peter's mother-in-law, only Matt 8:17 uses prefigurative references invoking Isa 53:4: "He took up our infirmities and carried our diseases." It is indeed possible that one of the figures in the vault is Isaiah, yet Matthew's text is not very helpful in establishing the identity of the other individual. In the end, the image would appear to reflect at least two if not all three Gospel accounts about the Healing of the Multitude at the gate of Peter's house. The choice to represent Christ and the apostles in an interior space and the crowd in the exterior, which seemingly reflects Mark's text, might have been additionally prompted by the placement of the scene over one of the three actual entrances into the church's naos.

A different text, the monastery's foundational document, or typikon, offers another dimension to our understanding of the message of the healing miracle

---

27 A. Tsitouridou, *Ho zōgraphikos diakosmos tou Hagiou Nikolaou Orphanou stē Thessalonikē: Symbolē stē meletē tēs Palaiologeias zōgraphikēs kata ton prōimo 14º aiōna* (Thessaloniki, 1986), 133–34.
28 T. Velmans, *Le Tétraèvangile de la Laurentienne, Florence, Laur. VI. 23* (Paris, 1971), figs. 130–31.
29 Ibid., fig. 195.

and how it might relate to life in fourteenth-century Thessaloniki. In it the monastery's founder Makarios Choumnos insisted on a special form of institutional philanthropy – catechetical instructions and accommodations – for outsiders:

> Receive with graciousness and much kindness all who love us on account of the Lord and who come to us in piety for the sake of their salvation and improvement ... Do not in any way avoid looking at or talking with these people, but if they need something from you, to the best of your ability, do not neglect them for the sake of the [divine] commandment, but put yourself completely at their service.[30]

He continued:

> As for the brethren who visit you often, either out of physical necessity or for spiritual improvement, look upon them and do unto them as unto yourselves, remembering the One who said "Love thy neighbor as thyself" (Matt. 19.19) and "Whatever you wish that men would do to you, do so to them" (Matt. 7.12), and [the apostle] who said, "Do not neglect to show hospitality to strangers, for thereby some have entertained angels unawares" (Heb. 13.2).[31]

We might suspect, and with good reason, that monks and laity actually met in the church's spacious liti of the monastery's katholikon. Indeed, the visualization of the Healing of the Multitude indicates that the interaction between Christ and the sick people is occurring between the inside and outside, matching in a way the liminal nature of the church vestibule. In general, the nartheces of monastic churches seem to have been especially permeable allowing laity to visit monasteries without interfering with the brethren's routine.[32] The Healing just like the Massacre thus seems to illustrate an actual event that would have been happening within the monastery. The difference, of course, is that while the Massacre of the Innocents alludes to the singular quelling of the zealot revolt in 1345, the healing miracle illustrates the encounter between monks and laity which would have been a common and continuous occurrence.

---

30 Thomas and Hero, *Byzantine Monastic Foundation Documents*, 4:1444.

31 Ibid., 1450.

32 Tombs of lay people as well as commemorative services could happen in the narthex. See, for example, F. Bache, "La fonction funéraire du narthex dans les églises byzantines du XIIe au XIVe siècle," *Histoire de l'Art* 7 (1989): 25–33; S. T. Brooks, *Commemoration of the Dead: Late Byzantine Tomb Decoration (Mid-Thirteenth to Mid-Fifteenth Centuries)* (PhD Dissertation, New York University, 2002), 300–12; S. Ćurčić, "The Twin-domed Narthex in Palaeologan Architecture," *Zbornik Radova Vizantološkog Instituta* 13 (1971): 333–44; S. E.J. Gerstel, "Painted Sources for Female Piety in Medieval Byzantium," *Dumbarton Oaks Papers* 52 (1998): 98–102; Marinis, "Tombs and Burials"; R. Ousterhout, *The Architecture of the Kariye Camii in Istanbul* (Washington, D.C., 1987), 98–110.

The Massacre of the Innocents and the Healing of the Multitude are connected in several other ways mutually informing one another's meaning. The two scenes occupy the lunettes of the north and south entrances into the naos. Both are related to multitudes, one of the children saved by sacrifice and one of the afflicted saved by grace. Herod kills innocents while Christ saves sinners. The violence in one scene is, however, supplanted with benevolence in the other. The seated figure of Herod in the left half of the Massacre is echoed by the seated Christ in the left half of the healing. Different symbols of royal authority were employed: Herod is dressed as an emperor, while Christ is seated on an improvised throne. The two also have a specific entourage: Herod is surrounded by soldiers, and Christ by apostles. The chaotic and disorderly composition of the Massacre is juxtaposed with the symmetrical and ordered composition of the Healing. The violent action and exaggerated movements are balanced with the peaceful picture of Christ enthroned amidst his disciples and before the afflicted people. In the Massacre the mothers occupy as important position as the soldiers do, their grief palpable and perhaps even audible, in the healing scene women are hardly noticeable tucked in the corner, their male counterparts actively engaged in a dialogue with the seated Jesus. The viewer is offered a glimpse into two different worlds of violence and compassion. Herod's kingship is juxtaposed with Christ's. Jesus is a benevolent and charitable king, not formidable and judgmental. By comparison with Herod's violent and irrational acts, Christ's mercy appears greater.

In a sermon entitled *In Herodem et innocentes*, known from a limited number of manuscripts dated between the tenth and seventeenth centuries, the author Pseudo-Chrysostom, provides the closest textual parallel for the pairing of the images of the Massacre and the Healing. In it the author extols Christ's power and specifically recalls his healing of paralytics.[33] Indeed, paralytics predominate amongst the afflicted in the Healing of the Multitude in Prophites Elias, and one wonders if the painters were not drawing on imagery and juxtapositions similar to those found in the homily.

A striking feature of the liti's program is the importance of scenes related to children and family. The familial imagery in the church is further expanded through the fresco icons in the porch, where St Anna with Mary and the Virgin with the Child Christ model exemplary maternity.[34] The ideas of motherhood are carried on in the representation of the Massacre, where the grief of the mothers is

33 F. Scorza Barcellona, "La celebrazione dei Santi Innocenti nell'omiletica greca II," *Bollettino della Badia Greca di Grottaferrata* 30 (1976): 79–80.

34 The images are unpublished. On Anna's exemplary motherhood, see E. Panou, *Aspects of St Anna's Cult in Byzantium* (PhD Dissertation, University of Birmingham, 2011), 235–36, 274–78.

as important as the actions of the soldiers who slaughter their young sons.[35] Furthermore, several other scenes such as the healing of the Archon's Demoniac Son, the Raising of the Widow's Son at Nain, and the Blessing of Little Children are directly connected to parenthood and children. The audience was apparently prompted to ponder the relationship between parents and their offspring and it is worth considering the possible reasons for this.

The Palaeologan period, when the church of the Prophites Elias was built and frescoed, witnessed a rising interest in children. In contemporary hagiography saints' childhoods were described in greater detail than ever before, and frequent mention is made of children miraculously cured from various afflictions.[36] Visual images of children similarly proliferated as seen in depictions of Christ's Baptism in several early Palaeologan monuments in Byzantine Macedonia, Mount Athos, and Mystra.[37]

The population of late Byzantine Thessaloniki and the monks who lived in Nea Moni would have been familiar on a local level with the importance of children. The latter seem to have been particularly relevant to the cult of the city's protector saint Demetrios. Both male and female children were prominently represented among the donors of the homonymous church indicating that the city's sainted protector fostered special relationship with them.[38] This connection would have been further strengthened by the likely existence of a hospital nearby which specialized in treating children.[39] When in 1303 Michael Tarcha-

35 The grief of the mothers is given special prominence in the early fourteenth-century mosaics in the Constantinopolitan Chora church where they are represented mourning over the dead bodies of their children in a separate scene in the fifth bay of the exonarthex. See Underwood, *Kariye Djami*, 1:102–3; 2:194–96. The grief of the mothers was similarly emphasized in contemporary thirteenth- and fourteenth-century images of the Massacre in the West. See L. Jacobs, "Motherhood and Massacre: The Massacre of the Innocents in Late Medieval Art and Drama," in *The Massacre in History* (ed. M. Levene and P. Roberts; New York, 1999), 39–54.

36 A. M. Talbot, "Children, Healing Miracles, Holy Fools: Highlights from the Hagiographical Works of Philotheos Kokkinos (1300–ca. 1379)," *Bysantinska Sällskapet Bulletin* 24 (2006): 48–64.

37 V. Katsaros, "Hē parastasē tēs Baptisēs stēn Palaia Mētropolē Beroias," *Deltion tēs Christianikēs Archaiologikēs Hetaireias* (2006): 169–80; D. Mouriki, "Revival Themes with Elements of Daily Life in Two Palaeologan Frescoes Depicting the Baptism," *Harvard Ukrainian Studies* 7 (1983): 458–74 (rpt. in eadem, *Studies in Late Byzantine Painting* [London, 1995], 310–40).

38 C. Hennesy, "Iconic Images of Children in the Church of St Demetrios, Thessaloniki," in *Icon and Word: The Power of Images in Byzantium. Studies Presented to Robin Cormack* (eds. A. Eastmond and L. James; Aldershot, 2003), 157–72; eadem, *Images of Children in Byzantium* (Farnham and Burlington, 2008), 88–91, 112–16.

39 M. Parani, "Review of C. Hennesy, *Images of Children in Byzantium* (Farnham, 2008)," *The Medieval Review*. https://scholarworks.ui.edu/dspace/bitstream/handle/2022/3784/09.10.07.html?sequence=1

niotes and his wife Maria renovated the chapel of St Euthymios, which is attached to the eastern end of the basilica of St Demetrios, the couple seemed to have been hoping to conceive their own progeny.[40] While scholars have identified Euthymios as particularly appropriate saint for this purpose, I wonder if it was not Demetrios and his steady relationship with children that inspired Michael and Maria to seek a close connection with the saint and as a result to patronize the small chapel.

Although Byzantine monks were continuously encouraged to sever the connections with their relatives, familial relationships akin to those in the outside world were built anew within the monastery. The abbot became the principal parent and could be perceived as both mother and father, while the monks were considered his children.[41] Indeed in the rule and testament of Nea Moni, the founder Makarios Choumnos spoke of the monastic community as a family, and encouraged the monks to maintain loving brotherly relationships. In one passage he explicitly identified them as his children:

> I beg of you, grant me this last favor, my beloved young saplings, my inheritance beloved even more than that of heaven, my spiritual children, the brethren beloved by my worthless self, but one who is your exceedingly beloved father, as am persuaded, by time and great testing on your behalf ... Everything which you observed for me, loyalty and faith and love and true obedience, observe also for him, whom I enjoin as a father and entreat as a brother to associate with you as he knows I lived with you ...[42]

Choumnos represented himself as the spiritual mother of one of the monks: "As for Joseph, to whom I gave spiritual birth, with great expectations, conceiving and enduring labor pains with much toil and words."[43] Toward the end of the rule Makarios spoke of spiritual formation within the community utilizing conception metaphors:

---

40 Th. Gouma-Peterson, *The Frescoes of the Parecclesion of St Euthymios in Thessalonica: An Iconographic and Stylistic Analysis* (PhD Dissertation, University of Wisconsin, 1964), 6.

41 A.-M. Talbot, "The Byzantine Family and the Monastery," *Dumbarton Oaks Papers* 44 (1990): 119–29 (rpt. in eadem, *Women and Religious Life in Byzantium* [Aldershot and Burlington, VT, 2001], XIII). See also, C. W. Bynum, "Jesus as Mother and Abbot as Mother: Some Themes in Twelfth-Century Cistercian Writing," *The Harvard Theological Review* 70 (1977): 257–84; eadem, *Jesus as Mother: Studies in the Spirituality of the High Middle Ages* (Berkeley and Los Angeles, 1982, rpt. 1984), 110–69. On the presence of children in Byzantine monasteries, see R. Greenfield, "Children in Byzantine Monasteries: Innocents Hearts or Vessels in the Harbor of the Devil," in *Becoming Byzantine: Children and Childhood in Byzantium* (ed. A. Papaconstantinou and A.-M. Talbot; Washington, D.C., 2009), 253–82.

42 Thomas and Hero, *Byzantine Monastic Foundation Documents*, 4:1446.

43 Ibid, 1445.

> For I have no confidence in my own actions, even though I am mindful of the words of the apostle: "Yes woman will be saved through bearing children" (I Tim. 2:15). For I say that true childbearing is that of the spirit. For if the former [brings salvation], then the latter [saves] to an even greater extent.[44]

The importance assigned to children in Palaeologan visual and literary sources, the relationship that the patron saint of Thessaloniki Demetrios maintained with them and the language of parenthood attested in monastic literature in general, and the writings of Nea Moni's founder in particular, provide a context that allows us to better understand the emphasis on children in the visual program of Prophites Elias' narthex. It is hard to imagine that the audience of the frescoes in the church's liti would not have been able to detect and mentally elaborate on the relationship between parents and their offspring. The emotional nature of this relationship where mothers and fathers grief or supplicate on behalf of their children, would have had a special effect on the inhabitants of Nea Moni.[45] A passage from John Klimakos's manual for monastic behavior, *The Ladder of Divine Ascent*, encapsulates how the imagery of loss could be utilized by monks:

> The man turning away from the world in order to shake off the burden of his sins should imitate those who sit by the tombs outside the city. Let him not desist from ardent raging tears, from the wordless moans of the heart ...[46]

Here grief for the death of a loved one and grief for one's own sinfulness are equated. The violent severing of the relationship between mothers and children in the Massacre of the Innocents and the visual language of grief employed throughout, invite the monks to become participants in the temporally distant event and develop an affective relationship with the image and its subject matter.[47]

In order to understand the peculiar relationship between violence and healing in the liti of Prophites Elias, it is important to look at the larger picture of late medieval European Christianity, which in the thirteenth and fourteenth centuries appears to have grown similarly violent in its literary and visual expressions. Violent imagery became prominent in Italian altarpieces of the fourteenth century,[48] and

44 Ibid, 1450.

45 For the ways in which Byzantines perceived the death of children, see A.-M. Talbot, "The Death and Commemoration of Byzantine Children," in *Becoming Byzantine: Children and Childhood in Byzantium* (ed. A. Papaconstantinou and A.-M. Talbot; Washington, D.C., 2009), 283–308.

46 Climacus, *Ladder of Divine Ascent*, 74–75.

47 For the iconography of grief in Byzantium, see H. Maguire, "The Depiction of Sorrow in Middle Byzantine Art," *Dumbarton Oaks Papers* 31 (1977): 123–74.

48 D'Elia, *The Poetics of Titian's Religious Paintings*, 63.

the body and blood of Christ were parceled out, chopped into pieces, and made available to a multitude of faithful Christians all over Western Europe.[49] Interestingly enough, scholars such as Caroline Walker Bynum and Jody Enders have given a somewhat positive spin to this violence. I tend to agree with Enders' discussion of the productive, generative nature of medieval violence; according to her violence reconfigures "images of destruction and dismemberment as creational, persuasive, salubrious, curative, civilizing, edifying, instructive ..."[50] It is Bynum's conclusions, however, that seem even more fitting and relevant for the purposes of this study. Unlike what one might expect she does not interpret late medieval violent imagery as gratuitous or a mere reflection of the prevailing violence in contemporary society. She suggests instead that the shedding of blood and disfiguring of the body is more about incorporation, love and oneness with God, rather than separation.[51]

In Byzantium, the only positive image of a child's body torn to pieces is the liturgical sacrifice or melismos (from the Greek for dismembering or dividing) which since late twelfth century could be represented as a young boy with the identification Jesus Christ.[52] In several gruesome hagiographic stories people who doubted the reality of the Eucharist would eventually see the young Child being slaughtered and parceled out in order to be offered as the true liturgical sacrifice.[53] When considered in relation to the Healing of the Multitude, the Massacre

---

49 See for example, C. W. Bynum, "Violent Imagery in Late Medieval Piety," *Bulletin of the German Historical Institute* 30 (2002): 1–36; eadem, *Wonderful Blood: Theology and Practice in Late Medieval Northern Germany and Beyond* (Philadelphia, 2007); E. Cohen, *The Modulated Scream: Pain in Late Medieval Culture* (Chicago, 2009); V. Groebner, *Defaced: The Visual Culture of Violence in the Late Middle Ages* (trans. P. Selwyn; New York, 2004).

50 J. Enders, *The Medieval Theater of Cruelty: Rhetoric, Memory, Violence* (Ithaca, 1999), 67.

51 Bynum, "Violent Imagery," 31.

52 G. Babić, "Hristološke raspre u XII veku i pojava novih stsena u apsidalnom dekoru vizantijskih tsrkava: Arhijereji služe pred Hetimasijon i arhijereji služe pred Agnetsom," *Zbornik za likovne umetnosti* 2 (1966): 9–31; S. E. J. Gerstel, *Beholding the Sacred Mysteries: Programs of the Byzantine Sanctuary* (Seattle and London, 1999), 40–47.

53 For literary and visual images of the Child Christ fragmented into pieces, see M-H. Gongourdeau, "L'enfant immolé. Hyper-réalisme et symbolique sacrificielle à Byzance," in *Pratiques de l'eucharistie dans les Églises d'Orient et d'Occident (Antiquité et Moyen Age): actes du séminaire denu à Paris, Institut catholique (1997–2004)*, (ed. N. Bériou et al.; 2 vols.; Paris, 2009), 1:291–307, M. Garidis, "Approche réaliste dans la representation du Melismos," *Jahrbuch der Österreichischen Byzantinistik* 32.5 (1982): 495–502; I. Rapti, "Un Melismos arménien et la politique de l'image de Lewon (Léon) II (1271–1289)," *Cahiers archéologiques* 50 (2002): 161–74; C. Walter, "The Christ Child on the Altar in the Radoslav Narthex: a Learned or a Popular Theme," in *Studenica i vizantijska umetnost oko 1200 godine: Međunarodni naučni skup povodom 800 godina manastira Studenice i stogodišnijce SANU* (ed. V Korać; Belgrade, 1988), 219–41 (rpt. in idem, *Pictures as Language: How the Byzantines Exploited Them* [London, 2000]).

of the Innocents appears to be about incorporation in the community rather that about segregation or separation from it. Language does not disappear as a result of violence, as Elaine Scarry would argue, but rather is born from it.[54] In the same way in which the slaughter of the young boys prefigures and in a way necessitates the Crucifixion, the wailing of the mothers and the cries of the children are inseparable part of Jesus' healing verbal rhetoric. Christ does not mix water and mud to anoint the blind, not does he touch or is being touched by the inflicted people; it is instead through his words that he heals the multitude gathered before him. The two prophets who 'oversee' the miracle from the vault above comment with their inscribed scroll on the event, confirming the efficacy of words as healing agents. The visual rhetoric of incorporation is further strengthened by the invitation that the founder Makarios Choumnos extended to the resident monks to be hospitable and cater to the needs of the people who come to the monastery seeking physical and spiritual relief.[55]

The artist of the frescoes cleverly employed the rhetorical device of synkrisis in order to both underscore and amplify the seemingly disparate but in fact associated messages of the Massacre of the Innocents and the Healing of the Multitude. The placement and formal characteristics of the two representations provided the monks with an opportunity to meditate on the similarities and differences between the two compositions, thus keeping their minds occupied and alert in a search for individual as well as combined meanings.[56] The astute monk will have recognized that the two images, when contemplated as a pair, results in a visual encomium of Christ whose peaceful benevolence, through the poignant juxtaposition with Herod's murderous actions, appears that much more effective, compassionate, and worthy of emulation. That same astute monk, in his quest to be as Christ-like as possible, might then have recalled the above quoted injunction of the founder Makarios to aid the needy who came to the monastery "to the best of your ability ... put yourself completely at their service."[57]

---

54 E. Scarry, *The Body in Pain: The Making and Unmaking of the World* (New York, 1985), 4; E. Smith, "'The Body in Pain': An Interview with Elaine Scarry," *Concentric: Literary and Cultural Studies* 32 (2006): 224–26. Cf. Enders, *Medieval Theater of Cruelty*, 26.

55 See n. 30 and 31 above.

56 In speeches comparisons were thought to relieve boredom in the listeners. See Maguire, "Art of Comparing," 89.

57 See p. 283 above.

Stefan Alkier

The Wondrous World of the Cinema: Types of Depictions of the Miraculous in Jesus Films

I The Temptation of Ryker

Suddenly the Q creature stands once more on the bridge, this time in the form of a magician. Commander Ryker, the highest-ranking officer after Captain Picard, the "Number 1" on board the new Starship Enterprise, was taken with thoughts of employing the powers Q has given him. Indeed, with their help he could have saved a girl who died in his arms, and she could even have been brought back to life. Therefore, he wants to leave the starship and, as a parting gift, he would like to fulfill a wish impossible with mere human powers for each of his comrades gathered there on the bridge. Since he has already given Captain Picard his promise that he will not use his Q powers and since he would like to remain (yet) loyal, he works his first wonder only after the Captain grants him permission. Picard, however, strictly refuses for himself a parting gift made from Q's power. He has seen through Q's game. Q, who appears to possess immeasurable power, needs Ryker, a mortal. Therefore he lets him participate in Q's power and the miraculous power conferred upon Ryker begins to corrupt him.

Those to whom a miracle would be given do not need to ask for it. Ryker's Q-power knows what everyone wants most. In a split second the youth Wesley becomes a grown man with the superb figure of a body builder. The blind Jordy, who is only able to see with a highly complex visor, can now remove this crutch, since he has received new eyes. Data, the artificial man, refuses the fulfillment of his wish of becoming a real human. Data, the artificial man, argues for letting things take their natural course and not manipulating them with miraculous powers.

Picard's wise equanimity overcomes Q's diabolical attempt and even restores their prior forms to those who had already received their wondrous gifts. When even Wesley asks Commander Ryker to make him a lanky youth once more so that he might mature in human ways, Ryker finally notices the Q creature's attempt to corrupt him and sides with his human captain. The attempt fails; the Q creature departs from the starship with howls of pain. The message of the episode: humans should remain human and not let themselves be corrupted through superhuman power.

A reader well-versed in the Bible will have perceived the echoes of the Temptation narrative told in the Gospels (Matt 4:1–11 par.). Luke's version in particular speaks about the central concern of the scene described above from *Star Trek: The Next Generation*: "And the devil said to him, 'To you I will give their glory and all this authority; for it has been given over to me, and I give it to anyone I please. If you, then, will worship me, it will all be yours'" (Luke 4:6–7).

It would be an interesting undertaking to compare the staging of the Temptation narrative in different Jesus films with the portrayal of the scene in the Starship Enterprise, and with its source in the biblical text, in order to highlight their similarities and differences. Here, however, I will not go further into the question, but rather deal with the depiction of miracles in Jesus films.

A weak point of the medium of a Jesus film is its depiction of the miraculous. This problem is perceived not only by the ecclesiastically-controlled *Schwalbacher Entschließung* but also by film critics not associated with the church and especially by enlightened directors like Pier Paolo Pasolini. Pasolini renders judgment on his own film, *The First Gospel: Matthew*, which was highly praised in church circles, as follows: "There are some horrible moments of which I am ashamed, which are almost counter-Reformation Baroque, repulsive: the miracles."[1]

The *Schwalbacher Entschließung*, a publication in operation to this day, in June 1950 utterly denied that film was a suitable medium for "the representation of divine revelation:" "We must also request that the cinematic representation of divine revelation (the life of Christ, miraculous events, celebration of the sacraments) be avoided. Film can only make the reality of the Holy Spirit perceptible in the mirror of human destiny." (Evangelischer Filmbeobachter [Protestant Film Observer], 1. 7. 1950, 90)

How does it happen, however, that there is next to no criticism of the representation of the miraculous in science fiction, fantasy, and other films – indeed the same viewers appreciate miraculous scenes in science fiction – while they find such things inappropriate or even simply embarrassing in a Jesus film? The answer can hardly lie in the material, for the temptation of Ryker, for example, works with the same plot as the Temptation of Jesus in Jesus films.

Films construe worlds. The stories they tell maintain their logic through reference to the world so construed, which we would name the universe of discourse of a given film. In the same way that the cover and paratexts of a book signals to the reader, prior to the reading of the book, how it should be received – novel, autobiography, nonfiction, dictionary, scientific treatment, etc. – so also do the opening credits and end titles have the same function for a film. As the text of a

1 Hans-Klaus Jungheinrich, "Überhöhung und Zurücknahme: Musik in den Filmen Pasolinis," in *Pier Paolo Pasolini* (ed. Peter W. Jansen and Wolfram Schütte; Reihe Film 12; Munich 1977), 123.

book sets its paratexts in brackets, so a film sets its paratexts in opening credits and end titles. The paratexts steer our reception expectations precisely toward the universe of discourse envisioned for the film. Advertising campaigns announcing a new book or film are also to be counted among these paratexts. Before one reads the first sentence, before the viewing of the first frame, the universe of discourse one should expect is already sketched out, and a reception-expectation is awakened.

The plot depicted is indebted to and draws its plausibility from the universe of discourse. In a fantasy film we expect the intervention of a good fairy who, with her miraculous powers, saves the hero or the threatened lovers, and we are quite happy even though we expected nothing else. If a fairy were to appear at the end of the film *Titanic* and conjure the sinking vessel up on land and spare the viewer the pleasure of mourning for the lovers we would not be happy, for the fairy would have violated the laws of the universe of discourse of the film *Titanic* and thus also its plausibility – and consequently would have robbed the film of its emotional effect. The miracles of a fairy are not regarded as plausible in and of themselves, but rather are meaningful or nonsensical only within the framework of a given universe of discourse. The universe of discourse of the film must be construed in such a way that fairies belong to this world; otherwise they destroy its plausibility and effect.

Even what can be regarded as a miracle is dependent upon the foundational universe of discourse. It would certainly be a miracle for the universe of discourse of a daily paper in our present, if a man could cover the distance from Hamburg to Goslar in three seconds. Not so for the universe of discourse of the Starship Enterprise, for here there is the technology of *beaming*. But even in the world of *Star Trek*, it is a miracle when someone like the Q creature can cover immeasurable distances in seconds without using the technology of beaming.

The problem of the depiction of the miraculous in Jesus films therefore is to keep the relationship between the universe of discourse and the plot in view, in order to make sound judgments about the staging of miracles. A sweeping judgment such as the *Schwalbacher Entschließung* offers is to be rejected on theological grounds as well as on grounds pertaining to the semiotics of film.

As regards the semiotics of film, it must be pointed out that there is no such thing as *the* Jesus film, but a multiplicity of Jesus films, each of which depicts its own respective universe of discourse, within which the plot realizes its meaning. The film-semiotic question must therefore be phrased as follows: does the staging of a miracle fit within the universe of discourse of a given Jesus film?

As regards theology, the Schwalbacher explanation is to be rejected because it suggests that there are appropriate and inappropriate media for "the representation of divine revelation." Every representation, however, is directed to signs and every sign system has its own opportunities and problems. The theological defamation of images has a long, sad history, which Georg Seeßlen fittingly points out: “The image in itself is a fundamental problem of all religion – all the more 24 images per second.”[2] The theological questions are, how does the film stage the representation of a miracle within the universe of discourse it sets forth, and what theology of the miraculous does it present to its viewers?

II Types of Depictions of the Miraculous in Jesus Films

The wide effect of Jesus films is certainly greater than the effect of specialized exegetical works and, while we’re at it, probably also greater than the effect of the New Testament texts themselves. The workmanship and quality of Jesus films is as divergent as those of expert exegetical contributions. Jesus films should be taken seriously as narrative commentaries on biblical (and apocryphal) texts. As such, they are an object of New Testament studies, since they understand themselves as a theory of reading early Christian texts. In what follows, I will sketch this with reference to selected examples of the staging of miracles in Jesus films.

A The Miracle of Film – Miracles in Film, or: The Desire of Cinematic Narration

That motion pictures were received as a miracle of technology at the time of their first appearance, nowadays people of Western industrial nations can hardly comprehend. The new technology at first produced films no longer than 15 minutes. Frequently only one scene was depicted. In order to proceed under these conditions, one had to be certain that viewers would be able to contextualize the scene on the basis of their own fund of encyclopedic knowledge in order to understand it. Since biblical stories were still widely known in all levels of society at the turn of the century, they were a preferred subject for early filmmakers. Often scenes were taken from religious paintings, or passion plays were simply filmed.

One notices rather quickly, however, that filmmakers were eager to experiment with the possibilities of the new technology. Biblical miracle stories were superbly suited for that. How should the scene of Jesus’ walking on the water be

2 Georg Seeßlen, “Sakralität und Blasphemie,” in *Film und Theologie: Diskussionen, Kontroversen, Analysen* (ed. Wilhelm Roth and Bettina Thienhaus; epd Texte 20; Stuttgart 1989), 96.

depicted? The new technology made it possible. Méliès "brought out the sensational elements of the cinematic genre such as the life of Jesus in the miracle report 'Christ walking on the waves.' The attraction of such cinematic staging culminated in the double question: 'How did the filmmaker do that? And how did it happen in reality?'"[3]

Cecil B. de Mille's monumental film *The King of Kings* (USA 1926/27) is also shaped by this desire for cinematic narration, with its new technological possibilities. The film decisively helped develop Hollywood cinema as we know it even today, aimed at a wide public. *The King of Kings* displayed the narrative-visual joy of miracle stories imaginatively, creatively, and in a manner well worth seeing.

While the single-scene presentations of the first short films left it almost entirely to viewers to locate the scene(s) within a virtual universe of discourse on the basis of their own encyclopedic knowledge, de Mille's longer film construed a universe of discourse formed by the wondrous action of God on the basis of the reproduction and dramaturgical function of the staging of miracles. While the film is in constant danger of veering into naive historicizing, it succeeds in narrating the miracle stories as stories that permit the freedom of viewing them either as *historical reports* or as *religious fiction*. De Mille achieves this openness precisely by not problematizing the miracle stories, but by developing their narrative effects. He does not want to display any problem-oriented theology of the miraculous. Rather, he wishes to use the *action* of miracle stories to please his public.

B Miracle as Psychotherapy, or: The Staging of the Miraculous under the Sign of Rationalism

The title of George Stevens' 1963 film about Jesus, *The Greatest Story Ever Told*, is programmatic. The film is based on Fulton Oursler's book of the same name, the writings of Henry Denker, and biblical texts. It offers the viewer a closed universe of discourse by opening the film with a painting depicting Jesus in the style of medieval ecclesiastical painting; the film closes with the same image. But it is actually a simulated picture for which Max von Sydow, who played Jesus in Stevens' film, served as a model. Stevens thus simultaneously signals the fictional connections of his film in two directions; showing that he respects the ecclesiastical-religious orientation of the material content of the film; and that he endeavors to

3 Gerd Albrecht, "Jesus – eine Filmkarriere: Entwicklungslinien des Jesus-Films und seiner Rezeption," in *Jesus in der Hauptrolle: Zur Geschichte und Ästhetik der Jesusfilme* (ed. Katholisches Institut für Medieninformation e. V.; film-dienst extra. Kino – Fernsehen – Video; Köln 1992), 9.

respect church tradition in an appropriate way. But his film thus emphasizes the claim to transform medieval religious art into the technical art of the age of film, something at which he succeeds in places, and not least because of the dramatic achievement of Max von Sydow as an actor. The film therefore employs fewer spectacular effects and celebrates the solemnity of its content in a much more deliberate manner.

The title also signals the intent of the film to *narrate* a *story* and not to report history. The film advances these auspicious reception signals above all through its kitschy representation of women's roles; through its just as kitschy exaggerated coloration; through its clichéd musical score; through its antiquated language; and not least through its indecision in the staging of miracles – which swerves between pious rehistoricizing and rationalist psychologizing on one hand, and erotic fantasy on the other.

In what follows I would like to depict the rehistoricizing-psychologizing type of staging, with help from a scene from Stevens' film, in order to present the magical type of staging (with the help of another scene from the same film) in the subsequent section.

Jesus answered: "In God's sight, no one is crippled, except in his soul." The lame man (quiet and sad): "That's easy for you to say. I can't walk." Jesus (inspiring awe): "Stand up and you will walk." The lame man: "Do you want to mock me? I say to you, I can't walk." Jesus: "You only haven't tried, because your faith is weaker than your legs." The lame man (self-consciously): "I pray to God and my faith is strong." Jesus: "Then stand up and walk!" The lame man thinks for a moment, reaches for his crutches, pauses, and looks at Jesus, who looks back with encouragement. The lame man throws his crutches away and raises himself up slowly, trembling. He takes his first tentative steps. His naked feet are shown in fade-ins to close-ups several times in order to demonstrate the progress of the healing. While his feet are at first severely turned inward, at the end of the healing they point forward in a normal way. [After the story of Lazarus, this lame man is later faded in running, and employed as a witness to the Messiahship of Jesus.] The almost four-minute scene has no background music and an impressive exchange of voices and silence. The lame man now says: "Look, I can walk!" Turning to Jesus he says, "Look at me, I can walk. You, Jesus of Nazareth, you've healed me." Music with brass horns now starts. Jesus responds (with background music): "No, your faith has healed you. There are many who cannot walk and still more who can walk but don't want to." The lame man repeats, "I can walk." Violins begin playing. The lame man repeats again, "I can walk." The violins take over. Jesus leaves the synagogue; an old man nods at him benevolently. Jesus reclines for a moment on the synagogue wall; the event has drained him of his strength. He goes his way resolutely; the violins accompany him with celebration, supported by woodwinds.

The scene attempts to connect desire for healing with healing itself. The healing is thoroughly misplaced within faith itself in a psychologizing manner, and then mislocated even in the will of the lame man, and thus rationalized. The staging departs from the biblical "Your faith has helped you" and puts forth the will as the acting subject of the healing. Jesus steps into the role of the psychotherapist who listens to the patient and encourages him to use his own powers. The message to the sick is that they can actually be healed, but they don't really want to – a message that for its part often can lead to religiously-motivated psychosomatic or even psychotic illnesses.

On the other hand, this psychologizing staging of the miracle is thwarted through the fading in of two feet made healthy in a mere two minutes, a successful healing that no psychoanalyst can reproduce. The fading in of the healed feet rehistoricizes the miracle story by making the viewer an eyewitness of the wondrous event. By wanting to do both things with the scene – making the healing psychologically plausible for twentieth-century viewers and at the same time, in a way bound to tradition, showing the healing as a miracle not humanly possible – the staging fails and the viewer does not know whether the formerly lame man is correct when he says, "Jesus of Nazareth, you have healed me," or whether Jesus is right when he responds, "No, your faith has healed you." In any event the brief moment of weakness Jesus displays at the end of the scene signifies that the event has cost Jesus power as he successfully completes the miracle. This, however, implies that he was lying in maintaining that not he, but the faith of the lame man, is responsible for the miraculous event. The viewer remains confused.

The ecclesiastical-religious universe of discourse of the film, established by the traditional painting at the beginning, could have allowed a traditional conception of the miracle to appear more plausibly. The anachronistic, rationalistic conception of the miraculous, present not only in this scene but also interspersed in much of the film's dialogue, works like an alien body – as if, in a film adaptation of *Alice in Wonderland*, a debate about whether tea kettles and teacups could sing and dance would suddenly break out.

C Miracles as Wizardry, or: The Staging of the Miraculous under the Sign of Fantasy Film

The film *The Greatest Story Ever Told* sets the scene of the story of Lazarus effectively as the story of a miracle that actually awakens faith by proceeding from a dirge on the occasion of the death of Lazarus, to the beginning voices of Handel's Hallelujah Chorus.

After Jesus' silent arrival in the house of Lazarus, which lasts 90 seconds of the 11-minute Lazarus sequence, accompanied only by a tonally creepy alienated dirge, Mary rebukes Jesus severely, saying that as a declared doer of miracles, he could still have saved Lazarus. Jesus speaks the words of John 11:25–26: "I am the resurrection and the life. Whoever believes in me will live, even though he dies, and everyone who lives and believes in me will not die forever. Do you believe this?" In place of Martha's confession of Jesus as Messiah, which presents the answer to Jesus' question in the Johannine story of Lazarus, in Stevens' film Mary and Martha remain silent, and put no faith in him – upon which Jesus, weeping but with a resolute expression, goes alone to the grave of Lazarus, visible from the sisters' house. There Jesus takes on a cramped and strained posture and speaks with a menacing voice, uttering spells in incongruous phrases misquoted from Second and Third Isaiah: "Who is like you, O Father in heaven? Who is like you, radiant in holiness, fearful in glorious deeds, working wonders? No one can take me from your hand. You wound and bind up again. You kill and make alive. [Pause] Come from the four winds, O Spirit, and breathe upon this dead man, that he may live again." Jesus opens the door and calls Lazarus forth with an alien voice of a technical echo. Choir music and violins begin to play. One sees the horrified and expectant faces of those viewing the event from afar. Then one sees the tomb and Lazarus in front of it, but dimly. The reactions of the witnesses follow, several of which are emphasized. Again and again the camera shows the lame man who had been healed earlier in the film, as well as the blind man given his sight. The witness shown most frequently calls out: "I've seen it with my own eyes. Lazarus was dead, but he now lives again." Handel's Hallelujah Chorus now begins. The eyewitness runs to the city gate of Jerusalem, followed by the formerly lame man and formerly blind man. He calls to the city gate: "The Messiah has come. The Messiah has come. A man was dead, now he's alive again." The formerly lame man, who has arrived at the same time, adds: "I was lame, now I can walk again." And the formerly blind man calls out: "I was blind, now I can see again." A sonorous voice asks from the city gate, "Who has done this?" The witness answers: "A man by the name of Jesus."

Compared to medieval paintings and the Jesus films of the first 50 years of cinematic history, Stevens is relatively sparing in portraying the miraculous in images. The decisive thing for him is the reaction of people, which, however, are not related in the Gospel of John. Stevens shapes the scene for his film in such a way that the indubitable miracle leads the eyewitnesses to a necessary confession of the Messiahship of Jesus.

Through his posture and his vocal tremolo when he calls upon the Spirit, the Messiah appears as a wizard; the whole of the scene is creepy. Contemporary viewers can easily make associations with zombie films.

With the image of Lazarus before the tomb (briefly shown in a fade-in, in long shot), which a viewer in any event quickly passes over, and with the eyewitnesses, the staging offers a realistic presentation of a miracle. But in contrast to the Gospel of John, that presentation nowhere makes this faith in miracles a thematic element, but rather displays it in an unbroken manner. The fact of the respectively divergent encyclopedias of the Gospel of John on one hand, and that of the viewers of the film on the other, is simply ignored, which again and again leads to the unwanted effect of laughter.

Even the wholly other, psychologizing conception of the miraculous, as the story of the healing of the lame man sketched above relates, plays no more role here. These unbalanced contradictions hurt the film as a whole and cause its project of telling a coherent, comprehensive presentation of the story of Jesus to fail in both theological and narrative terms.

D Miracle as Miracle: The Staging of the Miraculous as Literary Filming

The staging of a miracle in a Jesus film, attempting to represent the story of Jesus in a narrative fashion that is probably most faithful to the biblical text, is seen in Pier Paolo Pasolini's 1964 film *The First Gospel.*

Pasolini's film is a composition combining music, sounds, imagery, language, stories, lighting, and editing in an impressive way. Each of the sign systems employed, as well as their ordering, is effectively and meaningfully arranged.

"The music accompanying the opening credits, sounds from a Creole Mass and excerpts from Bach's St. Matthew Passion, delimit the framework of the film's meaning. Thus the Creole mass connotes the popular and universal, peoples-binding significance of the Gospel as Pasolini understands it, an understanding determinative for the whole film,"[4] while the St. Matthew Passion frames the emphasis on solemnity and the theological dimension of what follows. With the media-conscious "recourse to musical 'cultural goods' at hand Pasolini underscores that he does not wish to colonize the story of the life of Jesus in an ahistorical territory and thus tell that story in a way immediately naïve. [...] The music strengthens the connection to tradition."[5]

4 Hans-Klaus Jungheinrich, "Überhöhung und Zurücknahme: Musik in den Filmen Pasolinis," in *Pier Paolo Pasolini* (ed. Peter W. Jansen and Wolfram Schütte; Reihe Film 12; München 1977), 39.

5 Ibid., 40.

The film's opening credits sequence displays only tablets and lasts 100 seconds. The music ends and a sequence of 3 minutes and 25 seconds, staging Matt 1:18–25, begins. The first image already disappoints the expectations of Hollywood cinema and connotes, with black and white takes, the difference between cinematic and extra-cinematic reality.

It is precisely the reception-references, pointing to the artistic character of the medium, that open up the possibility of a literary filming without kitschy effects, which narrowly but not timidly gives space to its source and indeed permits something new to come into being. This has a wonderful effect upon the staging of miracles. The universe of discourse of the film sets itself up to be perceived as a narrated world throughout the film, in which the laws of its literary sources are regarded as valid. Therefore the miracle stories can be staged in a naïve manner without having naïve, sanctimonious, or grotesque effects.

After Jesus healed a demoniac in a silent scene by means of a silent prayer (this event finds expression through the posture of the demoniac who, in a scene accompanied by the undertones of cacophonous strings, first wails and rolls on the ground and then after a cut is shown making no noise in a posture worthy of a human being), a cut combined with a new musical signal transitions to the healing of a leper (cf. Matthew 8:1–4). The leper is seen at first in a midrange shot, and then in a close-up showing his horribly disfigured face. Accompanied by string music evoking woe and lamentation he walks to Jesus, who is seen first in a long distance shot far away. After they look at each other, Jesus walks to the leper. A smile on the disfigured face of the leper shows his trust in Jesus. As they stand opposite each other the leper says, seen in a close-up: "Lord, if you are willing, you can make me clean." After a cutaway, Jesus is seen in a closeup. He says: "I am willing! You are clean." The camera remains focused on Jesus. Meanwhile the joyous Gloria Dei *of the Creole mass begins. All viewers believe the words of Jesus without having seen! Then a cut follows quickly and the man now healed is seen in a close-up. After one sees the close-up of Jesus once more, Jesus says, "Look, say nothing to anyone, but go to the priest and show yourself and offer the sacrifice which Moses prescribed as a witness for each." After a cut the healed man is again in the picture. He takes hold of his face and after determining that the pustules have disappeared from his face, he trots happily toward people, now fading in in a long shot, and calls, "I am healed."*

Throughout the entire staging, in which dialogue is sparing, the words of Jesus bear special weight. Since Jesus did not speak in the preceding scene (in which the healing of the demoniac was staged), the words "I am willing! You are clean" are the first vocal expression after several minutes of silence.

The Jesus of Pasolini's film adaptation of Matthew utters no superfluous words. The utterances of Jesus therefore have an even greater effect. Within the universe of discourse Pasolini has created, they bear such power that to them is given divine miraculous power beyond all magic or sorcery shrouded in mystery. Thus Pasolini can refrain from using Matthew's stage direction, "Jesus stretched out his hand and touched him" (Matt 8:3a).

Pasolini's staging of the miraculous represents an impressive theology of the word, which can refrain from spectacle and dazzle just as much as from psychologizing, rationalizing, and rehistoricizing. The effects of Jesus' words are not shouted monumentally into the public domain through pseudohistorical sounds of fanfare and sappy Technicolor mass images, but are shown all the more impressively through the countenances and bodies of their addressees. The reception of the body corresponds to the theology of the word. What learned theology frequently missed – connecting a theology of the word to a comprehensive attitude of reception ordered to the body – the director succeeds in doing, knowing how to connect both semiotically.

E Miracle as History, or: The Staging of the Miraculous under the Sign of Documentary Films

While Pasolini's Gospel of Matthew presents a preponderance of close-ups, Rossellini favors long-distance shots, knee shots, and medium-range shots. Rossellini's preferred approach is not interested in individual faces and visages, but in the interaction of different actors and their historical settings. Neither does Rossellini attempt any unusual camera perspectives. Rather, he strives to leave the impression of a documentary. Images as clear and colorfast as possible attempt to simulate a normal human perspective. Rossellini's film *The Messiah*, appearing in France and Italy in 1975, came into being "after he made a memorial to the Sun King Louis XVI, Socrates, Augustine, Pascal, and Descartes in a heavily-financed TV-encyclopedia." The universe of discourse of his Jesus film generates the claim to historical, reproducible reality.

The extraordinarily sparing use of music corresponds to the documentary style. Only in a few places does a simple, melancholy flute melody fade in, underscoring the simplicity and clarity of the images. In still fewer places, for instance at the Slaughter of the Innocents in Bethlehem, there are synthetic sound effects accompanying the events. Natural flute melodies (attached to the protagonists) and synthetic sound effects (attached to the antagonists) connect the sequences involving both. Both the images simulating documentary realism and the flute music connoting simplicity harmonize with the ways in which the Kingdom of God is announced, the proclamation of which stands in the center of the film. The verbal expressions concerning this are characterized by a quiet and even cadence, and non-solemn tones. Above all, those who speak forth parables concerning the Kingdom of God – not only Jesus, but also Mary and several disciples – are engaged in simple manual tasks. The content of verbal expressions is determined by the staging of those verbal expressions: it concerns a simple, unaffected, everyday truth comprehensible by all and unambiguous to all, a truth standing in opposition to all religious and political ideologies of domination.

In this documentary universe of discourse, representations of the miraculous work like a contaminant. Rossellini consequently abstains. Only the story of the feeding of the 5000 is represented, but it is integrated into the documentary universe of discourse. After the Sermon on the Mount, without words Jesus distributes loaves to the disciples, who in turn distribute them to the crowd. Viewers expert in the Bible recognize the miracle story of the feeding of the 5000, which, however, in Rossellini's staging can be received simply as a story of sharing.

Other miracles are not shown but discussed, such as the healing of the man born blind. The blind man asserts before the Sanhedrin that he was healed by Jesus. He is the sole witness of the event, offering viewers his witness alongside the witness of the New Testament writings. They all recount the miracle as an event that happened. Rossellini does not force viewers into the undesired role of witnesses through his manner of staging the miraculous, but leaves them in their role as addressees of a narrative.

Thanks to the thoroughgoing abstention from miracle stories, Jesus stands at the center of the story as a wise teacher who stands against oppression and for harmonious coexistence among men, and he goes heroically to death for his convictions. The resurrection is thus almost out of place, since there is hardly any preparation for it through other miracle stories. Rossellini's film unintentionally makes one conscious of what is surrendered when miracle stories are virtually edited out of the plot of the story of Jesus: the story becomes a biography of a wise philosopher executed unjustly. One can make a similar memorial for Socrates, Augustine, Pascal, and Descartes, and one can make such a memorial for Jesus, but just a mere *memorial* for a dead man. That might suffice for most contemporaries. Compared to the Gospels, however, it is a truncation. That even Rossellini's documentary style cannot fully suppress the resurrection of Jesus, and that this together with the few miracle scenes in the film undermines the historical biographical project, points at least to the narrative power of miracle stories to throw assumptions about what is plausible and what is real into question.

F Miracle as Symbol, or: The Staging of the Miraculous beyond Narrative Grammars

Derek Jarman's film *The Garden* (Great Britain/West Germany 1989) breaks with the conventions of narrative cinema. He delegitimizes the great narrative and offers a sequence of images proceeding without any narrative grammar, but rather following associative laws. He organizes his film using strong fadeouts followed by subsequent empty images lasting up to three seconds, as well as original music composed for the film by Simon Fisher. The individual music pieces comprise the continuum of the quick succession of images. The endings and beginnings of the music pieces on the one hand, and picture sequences on the other hand, do not run together totally in sync. They are displaced by a few seconds, with which Jarman achieves the macrosyntactic connection.

Jarman's film demands that the viewer does the work of connection himself, and it is thus possible to go in different ways and directions with one's visual and auditory impressions. Jarman ties together coded images from religious and secular tradition with coded images of the present; with nature shots; with fuzzy images difficult to decipher; with detail shots; and with abstract lighting, all of which do not generate denotation but rather the connotation of the act of perception itself. Moreover, Jarman's use of repetition of images, varying cinematographical techniques, and different color schemes, as well as further texts and sounds, [and] idiolexical coding, would require a precise film analysis to decipher. Images from diverging and different connections and times are routinely bound together in a collage.

Jarman cites the narrated life of Jesus in various ways. In the first film sequence the resurrection image of Piero della Francesca is shown together with a crucifix. In addition, details of the image are faded in, and a resurrected Christ, played by Roger Cook, is shown in a desolate industrial landscape. This medial reproduction of the image of Christ, inside another image, and inside a series of images, shows at the outset the problem of the medial appropriation of perception and thus the problem of perception in general, which runs throughout the entire film.

The citation of the story of Jesus is no return to a religious, otherworldly utopia, but a medial sign of protest against socially-legitimated violence against others. The role of Christ in the passion scenes is played by a homosexual couple of our time and stands "in the long tradition of the *self-identification of marginalized groups with the suffering Jesus* – comparable to the familiar image of the crucified Campesino in Latin American liberation theology.[6]"

6 Zwick, Reinhold, "[...] Die Jesusfigur [...]" *HerKorr* 49 (1995): 616–20, here: 618.

With and near the visual plane, Jarman evokes narrative knowledge with reference to the canonical Gospels and contemporary cultural knowledge of the world's threatened state. He demands that the viewer supplies the context of the Bible scenes himself, in a way similar to the first silent films. He blocks every possibility of a sanctimonious flight into a religious world of appearances, however, since he connects the biblical scenes syntagmatically with images of the present as surreal scenes. He withdraws from viewers the certainty of a universe of discourse which always functions according to the same rules, and requires us to be constantly confused and reoriented.

Jarman contrasts images of destruction and violence with images of intact nature. In light of this background, these beautiful shots of nature receive the ascription of a miracle. The nature miracles of Jarman admittedly have nothing supernatural. On the contrary: it is precisely the natural that becomes a miracle in light of destroyed, ugly creation. This staging of the miraculous can be designated as symbolic. Individual elements of nature become symbols of an intact and beautiful life, praised not as something taken for granted but as something wonderful.

Jarman does stage one episode, however, based on Jesus walking on the water (Mark 6:45–52 par), which is designated as a nature miracle according to the canons of classical form criticism. He has a man on the shore of the rolling sea take a walk in the evening twilight, so that in several places it looks as if he is strolling on the sea. Jarman concentrates his scene on Jesus walking on the water alone; he leaves the other elements of the story to the intertextual knowledge of the viewer. He dissolves the narrative grammar in order to concentrate wholly on a single point. The scene of Jesus walking on the water maintains an enormous intensity of rest thereby. It has the effect of a miracle when set against the choppiness of the subsequent and previous surreal scenes, but above all in contrast to the hectic images of violence and destruction.

For the biblically-literate viewer of Jarman's staging of Jesus walking on the water, the transfer of the miraculous character of the scene results from the literary source of the scene. The viewer reads the miracle of the biblical scene of Jesus walking on the water into Jarman's staging thereof, and thus transfers the miraculous conception of the evangelists, which places the breakthrough of that which is otherwise impossible in the foreground, to the commonplace event of a walk along the sea. This in the universe of discourse of Jarman's film, has the effect of a wondrous breach and breaking of the activity, destruction, and violence, with symbolic power as a miracle.

G The Representation of Representation, or: The Staging of the Miraculous as Deconstruction of Faith in Miracles

Herbert Achternbusch's film *Das Gespenst* [*The Ghost*] without doubt belongs to the category of scandalous Jesus films. That precipitating scandal and offense need not necessarily involve speaking against a thing, is something those familiar with the Bible should know from experience. Whoever dismisses Achternbusch's film solely as a blasphemous botch, and refuses a theological confrontation with this film, has not paid sufficient attention to the film or even seen it.

The encyclopedia *Religion im Film* provides a fitting summary of Achternbusch's film: "A life-size Christ figure in a cloister climbs down from the cross at the lamentation of a disappointed abbess [Oberin] in order as an abbot [Ober] to come into conflict with the police, a bishop, and Munich pedestrians. An aesthetically and theoretically tragicomedy by and with Herbert Achternbusch who from an extremely subjective perspective poses the question of what Jesus would do if he came to Bavaria today. Under the blasphemous surface of the film and behind the clown mask of the main actor are concealed deep consternation and profound skepticism in view of the petrified political-cultural relationships within West Germany. Achternbusch's provocative attacks on church and state precipitated a heavy counter-reaction from the German Bishops, state prosecutors, and the Federal Ministry of the Interior." (ibid., 94–95)

In the discussion of Achternbusch's *Ghost* few observed that this film poses a radical Christological question: does the divine nature of Christ leave any room at all for the human nature of Christ? Achternbusch's thesis in response to that question is a clear no. Achternbusch becomes a defender of the man, of the individual Jesus of Nazareth, beyond all Christological claims about him. Against the "greatest story ever told," against the "King of kings," Achternbusch demands Jesus have a small, insignificant but private life of his own. The postmodern grammar of Achternbusch's film, which employs the associative connections between visual and linguistic signs in order to construe its own narrative logic, traces the ideological principles of both the construction of Christological discourse, and also at the same time the narrative grammar of Hollywood cinema, and reveals them as such.

Independently of each other, the literary theorist Paul de Man and the philosopher Jacques Derrida first developed this procedure of not simply negating ideological constructions and replacing them with another construction, but rather showing their nature as constructs in order to undermine their absolutizing claims. Both named this procedure *deconstruction*. Deconstruction cannot be reduced to destruction or negation. Deconstructive reading is much more concerned with tracing "the complexities, the aporias, the blind spots of a given stance or position or text, in the interest of a more thorough examination of our theoretical claims and our ethical practices."[7]

Achternbusch deconstructs a crucial issue of theological and cinematic Christological discourse – the miracle stories – by means of a new staging of the story of Jesus walking on the water, which I would now like to sketch.

Walking along together in animated conversation, the abbess and the Christ-figure encounter a pool in which frogs are to be seen.

Jesus: Do you see the frogs? It's too bad that they never come into my bar, I'd readily serve them.

Abbess: I'll catch some for you. Will you help me?

Jesus: Will they come on land?

Abbess: We'll go to them in the water.

Jesus: I can't do that. I can only walk on water.

While the abbess walks into the water, the Christ figure tramps around on the surface of the water without help.

Abbess: Come on, step on in.

Jesus: It doesn't work.

Abbess: You have to walk alongside, then.

Jesus: Where alongside? Then I'd be on land again.

It is instructive to compare Achternbusch's staging with its biblical source.

The Gospel of Matthew relates, "Immediately he made the disciples get into the boat and go on ahead to the other side, while he dismissed the crowds. And after he had dismissed the crowds, he went up the mountain by himself to pray. When evening came, he was there alone, but by this time the boat, battered by the waves, was far from the land, for the wind was against them. And early in the morning he came walking toward them on the sea. But when the disciples saw him walking on the sea, they were terrified, saying, 'It is a ghost!' And they cried out in fear. But immediately Jesus spoke to them and said, 'Take heart, it is I; do not be afraid.' Peter answered him, 'Lord, if it is you, command me to come to you on the water.' He said, 'Come.' So Peter got out of the boat, started walking on the water, and came toward Jesus. But when he noticed the strong wind, he became frightened, and beginning to sink, he cried out, 'Lord, save me!' Jesus immediately reached out his hand and caught him, saying to him, 'You of little faith, why did you doubt?' When they got into the boat, the wind ceased. And those in the boat worshiped him, saying, 'Truly you are the Son of God.'" (Matt 14:22–33)

---

7 A.K.M. Adam, "Deconstruction and Exegesis," in *Exegese und Methodendiskussion* (ed. Stefan Alkier and Ralph Brucker; Tübingen/Basel 1998), 101.

The disciples think that the Jesus who walks on the water is a ghost and are terrified. The supposed ghost reveals to the disciples that he is actually Jesus. In order to examine the self-identification of the supposed ghost, Peter requests that Jesus commands him to walk upon the water to him. The act succeeds only half-way because of Peter's little faith. Peter's fear, however, drives out his doubts about the identity of the One who walks upon the water: "Lord, save me!" – one does not address a ghost in this way. Peter surrenders his arrogant position as the one who would examine Jesus' identity. Peter's little faith gives Jesus the opportunity to step forth as the savior of the sinking apostle.

After Peter and Jesus have climbed into the boat, the wind dies. Jesus has shown himself to be no ghost but a wonderfully powerful savior whom even wind and wave obey. This wondrous power, shown forth several times over, leads the disciples from their error of seeing a ghost to a new confession: "Truly you are the Son of God."

In the title of his film Achternbusch takes up the first impression of the disciples: the Christ figure in Achternbusch's film is a ghost, and – in contrast to the synoptic sources – he remains a ghost. Achternbusch's ghost shocks no one, however, but is a sad and often farcical figure. Achternbusch does not negate the miraculous power of Jesus in the pathos of enlightenment, however. Rather, he uses the tradition of the miraculous power of Jesus in order to deconstruct the messianic claims of Christological discourse, as well as the ideological stagings of miracles in Hollywood cinema: from Jesus' mighty ability to work the wonder of walking *on* the water comes the inability of the ghost to walk *in* the water. The "greatest story ever told" has ideologically absorbed the little story of the human Jesus and made it inaccessible.

The abbess is therefore both wholly and not at all influenced by the Christ figure's walking on the water and does not demand that he do it right away to prove his divine identity. She calls him into the water, and indeed with a tone (chant?) that underscores the ridiculousness of Jesus' inability to tread into the water. The abbess gives the Christ figure no opportunity to act as a savior. Rather, she herself takes over the role of the helper, and gives the one walking on the water instructions on how he can actually get into the water. But her help fails. The Christ figure cannot do that most human of all things: walk into the water.

By leaving the Christ figure with his miraculous powers staged not as a spectacular capability but as a hindrance to true humanity, Achternbusch deconstructs the Christological claim that Jesus is the savior of humanity, as well as the ideologically-laden monumental stagings of Hollywood cinema. How can a klutz, who can't even walk into water, save humanity? Wouldn't that be ghastly?

3 Looking Back, or: Cinema as Reading Aid

In this superficial analysis of several cinematic stagings of miracles, it has already been made clear just how much those who make films endeavor to stage miracle stories in accord with their own understanding. Thanks to the interplay of different sign systems and their technological possibilities, the medium of film offers a sheer unlimited spectrum of possible ways to stage a miracle. Its theological appeal lies precisely in the fact that directors are generally not expert theologians. They are therefore not so very constrained by theological traditions of interpretation, noted and handed down in the footnotes and bibliographies of academic works. A theologically-grounded criticism of Jesus films, and films in general, is so very necessary because films portray humanity's great longings and hopes for redemption, and play with them. Therefore they always touch on theological themes and it is productive to use films as reading aids.

Every reader is a director who stages the text in an act of reading. On the basis of this insight, the New Testament scholar Reinhold Zwick has even developed his own very productive academic process of reading, which he has named "exegesis in view of film." In several essays, and in an especially influential way in his work *Montage im Markusevangelium. Studien zur narrativen Organisation der ältesten Jesuserzählung (SBS 18, Stuttgart 1989; Montage in Mark's Gospel: Studies on the Narrative Organization of the Oldest Story of Jesus)*, Zwick has verified the thesis that analysis of Jesus films can sharpen the view of their sources.

"Filming biblical text means interpreting them in a new, multidimensional context. As such interpretations, adaptations can then shed light back upon the understanding of the text of departure. [...] In spite of enormous difficulties, with which a Bible film appears especially confronted, new dimensions of the source's meaning can unfold as part of the medial exchange in a film [...] What makes film production so interesting in this connection is its polyphonic structure, in which all conceivable forms of the literary, visual, and musical reworking of the Bible flow into each other. Pursuing how iconographic traditions and sociocultural conditioning, theological interpretation and dramaturgical calculus here pervade each other is anything but a self-purposeful endeavor. Rather, with film rich in moments productive of meaning, much more does an enormous number of possibilities open up for initiating (where possible) new encounters with its literary sources, new processes of communication and understanding valid for it." (Zwick, ibid., 53–54)

The diversity of cinematic stagings of miracles discloses a view of the diversity and differentiation of biblical miracle stories, and possibilities for their reading. They show us that it is not a question of two rigid perspectives standing opposed to each other – that of an ancient conception of miracles over against a contemporary conception of miracles – but rather an enormous spectrum of various narrative possibilities and narrative organizations which correspond to a spectrum, at least as large, of various ways of reading miracle stories.

At the end of an encounter with miracles in film, the question should therefore not be, “What did the director wish to say to us?” but rather, “What miracle story would you wish to stage and how would the staging look?” With this question, one reads differently and may perceive familiar texts in new ways.

Commander Ryker overcame the temptation of Q’s magical power only with the help of his comrades. We will not master the magical power of the mass media through condemning them, but only through reflection on the ways they work, their limitations, and their possibilities. As an individual Commander Ryker had no chance against Q’s temptation. Viewing film requires an exchange among a critical community of viewers in order to deprive them of their magical force. If critically productive exposure to the new media succeeds, then the exegesis of biblical texts can discover new worlds and “*boldly go where no man has gone before*” ...

V Rethinking the Miraculous

Stefan Alkier and David M. Moffitt

Miracles Revisited. A Short Theological and Historical Survey[1]

1 Tracing the Changing Conceptions of Miracles from Early Christianity through the Form Critical Methodology of the 20th Century

Arguments over texts of the New Testament that mention signs, wonders, and powerful deeds, as well as over statements that claim for early Christianity and its founding figure the ability to act in ways that exceed the limits of human possibilities, have accompanied Christianity through the ages and will no doubt continue to do so. Yet, the particular points of contention that give rise to these disputes change according to the cultural, historical, and individual assumptions that drive the notions of plausibility and possibility that are in play for those who engage in the discussions.

Jesus' Jewish opponents, at least as they are described in the New Testament, do not deny that he and his Apostles could do miraculous deeds. They dispute whether or not these miracles ought to be attributed to the power of God (cf. Mark 3:22–27; Acts 4:7). They recognize that if the power of God is truly responsible for the miracles done by Jesus and his followers, then this very fact would prove that Jesus' message really was legitimated by God. That is to say, if the power of God were the source of the miracles, this would serve as a clear sign of the divine commission of Jesus and his followers. In that case the message of Jesus and his emissaries would obviously need to be obeyed. For this reason the Jewish opponents of Jesus one finds in the Gospels associate these miracles with the effective power of Satan. Jesus and his companions are not only characterized by their enemies as clever charlatans, but – particularly because the fact of these miracles is not in dispute – as those who must be in league with Satan. They clearly cannot be – as their Jewish antagonists claim for themselves – those who are truly in covenant with God. It is hard to imagine a harsher attack on Jesus and his disciples, for this claim asserts that they stand outside the covenant God made

1 See also Stefan Alkier, *Wunder und Wirklichkeit in den Briefen des Apostels Paulus: Ein Beitrag zu einem Wunderverständnis jenseits von Entmythologisierung und Rehistorisierung* (WUNT 134; Tübingen: Mohr Siebeck, 2001), 1–54.

with Abraham. In fact, they have exchanged this covenant for one with Satan instead (cf. Mark 3:22–27 and parallels).

The conflict described in the Gospels concerning Jesus' miracles occurs between Jesus, a Jew, and his Jewish followers on the one hand, and his Jewish antagonists on the other. In other words, this is an intra-Jewish, theological argument. The parties involved therefore conditioned by exactly the same historical and cultural assumptions about reality. There is no question in this dispute about the possibility of miracles or about how they can be made to cohere with the natural world. The real issue in question concerns whose power is on display in these amazing events. Thus it is a question of what *theo*-logical status they can be said to have. Are they signs of God's covenant, or are they signs indicative of a covenant with Satan?

By way of contrast, the *question* concerning miracles has in the modern period changed multiple times. In the 18th century, given the influence in the context of scientific reasoning, miracles were put in the dock of criticism. The biblical miracles, which had up this point commonly been viewed as proof *for the spirit and power* of Christianity, now came under categorical attack from critical thinkers.

Already in 1670 the Jewish philosopher Baruch de Spinoza (1632–1677) had come out against the biblical miracle stories. In the sixth chapter of his *Tractatus Theologico-Politicus*, a chapter dedicated to the problem of miracles, he stated that "everything related in Scripture as having truly happened came to pass necessarily according to the laws of Nature, as everything does."[2] Since God himself issued the eternal laws of nature, the notion that they could be broken would amount to God contradicting himself and this even leads finally to "atheism."[3]

A number of Enlightenment philosophers of the 18th century worked to make the ideas of biblical criticism acceptable to the wider society. Voltaire (1694–1778) in his hugely influential *Essais sur les mœurs et l'esprit des nations* (1756) issued the categorical judgment that "miracles cannot be believed."[4]

David Hume (1711–1776) in his essay *An Enquiry Concerning Human Understanding* (1748/58) defined a miracle as follows: "A miracle is a violation of the laws of nature; and as a firm and unalterable experience has established these laws, the proof against a miracle, from the very nature of the fact, is as entire as

2 Baruch Spinoza, *Tractatus Theologico-Politicus* (trans. Samuel Shirley; Leiden: Brill, 1989), 134.

3 Ibid., 130.

4 Voltaire, *Essais sur les mœurs et l'esprit des nations, introduction et notes par Jacqueline.Marchand* (Paris: Eìditions sociales, 1962), 147.

any argument from experience can possibly be imagined."[5] Hume combined this theorem, that empirical observation proves that natural laws are inviolate, with a series of associations that continues to influence exegetical studies on miracles even today. Specifically, he linked belief in miracles with the superstitious perspectives embraced by the uneducated. Thus he established the following series of negative associations: miracles – fiction – superstition – anxiety – uneducated – lower social class. These associations, together with the aforementioned theorem, formed the corner stone of Hume's argument for the 10th section of his *Enquiry*, entitled *On Miracles*, and for his psychologized conception of the structure of religious history, which he presents in his *Natural History of Religion*.

The Enlightenment reduced the prevailing structures of the world. By so doing, the various available options for attributing truth values and for making judgments about the acceptability, or plausibility, of worlds was greatly narrowed. A new cultural encyclopedia of conventional, socially acceptable knowledge was produced. Accordingly, miracles were not factual, but were instead self-evidently fictional. Neither the narrator, nor the reader, nor the style, nor any other textual category could be counted on to guarantee the truthfulness of a story. The laws of nature alone became the arbiters of fact and fiction. The roll of the miracle worker, whether it was filled by the Saints, or Jesus, or God, was relegated to the world of fantasy. In this way the critical study of miracles targeted, among other things, the social and political power of the Church. The attack was effective because the Church had ideologically committed itself to the assertion of the truth of miracles as a means to undergirding its assertion of the truth of Christianity.

Although late to the party, theological discourse eventually accepted the foundational assumptions of scientific reasoning. As a result, a number of strategies for interpreting miracles were devised. One finds, for example, theories of accommodation, rationalistic explanations, and even early attempts to demythologize miracles. Admittedly the language of demythologizing is, strictly speaking, anachronistic. The fact remains, however, that the basic interpretive approach that Rudolf Butlmann dubbed "demythologizing" has clear Enlightenment precursors.

According to Johann Salomo Semler's (1725–1791) theory of accommodation, Jesus and the Evangelists belonged to an earlier, more primitive stage of hu-

5 David Hume, *An Enquiry Concerning Human Understanding and Other Writings* (ed. Stephen Buckle; Cambridge Texts in the History of Philosophy; Cambridge: Cambridge University Press, 2007), 100. Cf. also the discussion of Hume's conception of miracles in Heiko Schulz, "Das Ende des *Common Sense*: Kritische Überlegungen zur Wunderkritik David Humes," ZNThG 3 (1996): 1–38.

manity. At this stage in human history people still believed that miracles could happen. Miracles were for them a way of adapting or accommodating eternal truths and conveying them in a manner understandable to their primitive minds. This approach helped Semler counter the rationalistic explanation of miracles advanced in the *Wolfenbüttel Fragments* (Reimarus), a document that accused Jesus' disciples of intentionally perpetrating outright fraud when they proclaimed such miraculous events as the resurrection.

The leading advocate for a rationalistic approach to explaining miracles was Heinrich Eberhard Gottlob Paulus (1761–1851). In general rationalists sought to explain miracles as naturally occurring events that, for some perfectly reasonable cause, were misunderstood by those who witnessed them. Such a theory was, of course, already anticipated by Spinoza in 1670 when he claimed the miracles, if they were real events, had to have natural causes and natural, scientific explanations. Thus the event of Jesus' resurrection could be explained by recognizing that Jesus had only appeared to die. Similarly, the account of Jesus walking on water can be attributed to an optical allusion, etc.

Demythologizing approaches to the question of miracles from those of Johann Gottfried Eichhorn (1752–1827) and Johann Philipp Gabler (1753–1826) through David Friedrich Strauss (1808–1874) and up to Rudolf Bultmann (1884–1976) and Gerd Theißen regard miracle stories as an aspect of a primitive and outmoded mythological conception of the world. Such an understanding of reality is an artifact from humanity's childhood. Nevertheless, "behind" this now dead mythology there is "a still deeper meaning which is concealed under the cover of mythology."[6] Demythologizing wants to "remove the mythological conception precisely because we want to retain its deeper meaning."[7] Therefore, the goal is to peel away the miraculous elements of the miracle story as a kind of mythological husk in the story in order to expose the real message it contains. This goal varies a bit according the particular underlying philosophy driving it. For some it is the essential "doctrine" (Gabler).[8] Others seek to expose the "idea" (Strauss).[9] Still others look for an account's underlying "understanding of human existence,"[10] or rather "self-understanding"[11] (Bultmann). In every case these in-

6 Rudolf Bultmann, *Jesus Christ and Mythology* (New York: Charles Scribner's Sons, 1958), 18.
7 Ibid., 19.
8 For additional discussion of Gabler see Otto Merk, *Biblische Theologie des Neuen Testaments in ihrer Anfangszeit: Ihre methodischen Probleme bei Johann Philipp Gabler und Georg Lorenz Bauer und deren Nachwirkungen* (MThSt 9; Marburg, 1972), 29–140, esp. 52–81.
9 David Friedrich Strauss, *The Life of Jesus Critically Examined* (ed. Peter C. Hodgson; trans. George Eliot; Philadelphia: Fortress, 1972), 76–77.
10 So Bultmann, *Jesus Christ, 19.*

terpreters try to free and *make understandable* for their contemporaries the actual message that has been hidden in story through the ages. Thus, this method explicitly understood itself during the 19th century as engaged in the task of translation. Strauss puts the point well when he states that the Scriptures are writings that are,

> [T]he production of an infant and unscientific age; and treat, without reserve of divine interventions, in accordance with the conceptions and phraseology of that early period. So that, in point of fact, we have neither miracles to wonder at, on the one hand, nor deceptions to unmask on the other; but simply the language of a former age to translate into that of our own day.[12]

This translation work rests, therefore, solely on the conviction expressed by Bultmann that, "For modern man the mythological conception of the world ... [is] *over and done with.*"[13]

Theories of accommodation, rationalism, and demythologizing posit different strategies for explaining the miraculous element of miracle stories. Nevertheless, they come together at this point – they agree with the scientific perspective regarding the possibility, or better, impossibility, of miracles. They do not, however, want to exclude them from the canon. They try instead to understand the miracle stories as theological messages that have to be decoded. The question, therefore, shifts from a scientific discussion to one of hermeneutics. The real issue for these interpreters becomes how one can *understand* miracle accounts as *stories*. Their goal is to produce readings of these (embarrassing) biblical narratives that can justifiably and simultaneously be held as true within the modern scientific and philosophical worldview, and as true for the Christian faith, which is based upon biblical texts.

This hermeneutical conundrum is solved by appealing to a particular philosophical theory of history – the theory of *development*. People from a lower or earlier, child-like stage of human development were not able to think as abstractly as people who live in a higher or later stage of development. Belief in miracles belongs, almost self-evidently, to an earlier, outmoded understanding of the world, an understanding that could believe miracle stories because of its naïve assumptions about reality. Bultmann draws the categorical conclusion,

---

11 Rudolf Bultmann, "On the Problem of Demythologizng," in *New Testament and Mythology and Other Basic Writings* (ed. and trans. Schubert M. Ogden; Philadelphia: Fortress, 1984), 157.

12 Strauss, *Life of Jesus*, 48.

13 Bultmann, *Jesus Christ*, 17 (Emphasis added).

> Therefore, in any discussion, the 'wonders [i.e., miracles] of Jesus' are entirely open to critical investigation. It should be most strongly emphasized that Christian faith is not concerned with proving the possibility or the actuality of the [miracles] of Jesus as events of the past. On the contrary, such concern would be wrong.[14]

He says at another point, "The idea of miracle has, therefore, become untenable and it must be abandoned."[15]

Nevertheless, a significant difference between discussions about miracles in the 19th and 20th centuries should be noted. With the rise of form criticism in the last twenty years of the 19th century, texts were classified as miracle texts based solely on the form-critical features of a miracle *story*. Because of this, however, a significant number of texts that were previously considered under the theme of *miracle*, no longer qualified as such. A comparison of the article entitled "Wunder" ("Miracle") in Zedler's *Universallexikon* from the first half of the 18th century with Bultmann's section on miracles in his *History of the Synoptic Tradition* will illustrate the point. First, as a result of the form-critical restrictions on the exegesis of miracles, the New Testament's epistolary literature falls out of view. Second, in the 19th century the question of miracles was always bound up with the question of the resurrection of Jesus. Even this question, however, was gradually moved out of the discussion of miracles because of the establishment of form criticism.

This applies even to Gerd Theißen's influential form-critical study *The Miracle Stories of the Early Christian Tradition*. By differentiating his examination into synchronic, diachronic and functional approaches to miracle stories, Theißen offers a wide variety of fascinating perspectives. His "functional approach" provides some especially important new directions that expand form criticism's myopic approach to miracles by way of help from sociological research. In particular, his illuminating discussion of the healing function of miracle *stories*, which calls attention to the energizing power of language, has enriched research in the field.[16] On closer examination, however, one can see that Theißen's study remains beholden to the history of religions school, traditional form criticism and Rudolf Otto's religious phenomenology. With his psychological rationalism he even falls back upon the well-articulated positions of Baur and Bultmann. The problem of the interconnectedness of language, conceptions of reality and historical evaluations of the phenomena of miracles is completely ignored in

---

14 Rudolf Bultmann, *Faith and Understanding* I (ed. Robert W. Funk; trans. Louise Pettibone Smith; New York: Harper & Row, 1969), 260.

15 Ibid., 249.

16 Theißen further developed this idea in his essay "Synoptische Wundergeschichten im Lichte unseres Sprachverhältnisses," WPKG 65 (1976): 289–308.

Theißen's exegetical assessments of miracles. In spite of its dominance, form-critical work has, at least in terms of the problem of the *miraculous* in miracle accounts, lead to a dead end.[17]

2 "New" Solutions in the Study of Miracles: Between Rehistoricizing and Neorationalism

Recent rehistoricizing approaches to miracle accounts can be considered a countermove to the marginalization of the miraculous just discussed. Because Bultmann had so adamantly stressed "that Christian faith is not concerned with proving the possibility or the actuality of the [miracles] of Jesus as events of the past,"[18] some went in search of "new" solutions in the study of miracles. These solutions move principally between the poles of rehistoricizing and neorationalism. Their goal is to do exactly what Bultmann said could no longer be done – to prove the "actuality of the [miracles] of Jesus as events of the past."[19]

This shift marks a fundamental about-face in the assessment of what can be held to be historically possible. In his 1957 essay entitles "Is the Gospel Objective?," Ernst Käsemann described the exegetical consensus around the problem of miracles. He declared, "We may say that today the battle is over, not perhaps as yet in the arena of church life, but certainly in the field of theological science. It has ended in the defeat of the concept of miracle which has been traditional in the Church."[20]

---

17 Just as form critical work does not delve into the theme of the *miracles* from the perspective of the *phenomena* of the miraculous, so also redaction-critical work shows little methodological interest in the questions of the miraculous element in miracle accounts and the relationship between language and notions of reality. Vgl. D.-A. Koch, *Die Bedeutung der Wundererzählungen für die Christologie des Markusevangeliums* (BZNW 42; Berlin/New York: DeGruyter, 1975); Karl Kertelge, *Die Wunder Jesu im Markusevangelium: Eine redaktionsgeschichtliche Untersuchung* (StANT 23; Munich: Kösel, 1970); Ludger Schenke, *Die Wundererzählungen des Markusevangeliums* (SBB 33; Stuttgart: Katholisches Bibelwerk, 1974); H. J. Held, "Matthäus als Interpret der Wundergeschichten," in *Überlieferung und Auslegung im Matthäusevangelium* (ed. G. Bornkamm, G. Barth, and H. J. Held; WMANT 1; Neukirchen: Neudirchen, 1960), 155–287; Ulrich Busse, *Die Wunder des Propheten Jesu: Die Rezeption, Komposition und Integration der Wundertradition im Evangelium des Lukas* (FzB 24; Stuttgart: Katholisches Bibelwerk, 1977); Stefan Schreiber, *Paulus als Wundertäter: Redaktionsgeschichtliche Untersuchungen zur Apostelgeschichte und den authentischen Paulusbriefen* (BZNW 79; Berlin/New York: De Gruyter, 1996).

18 Bultmann, *Faith and Understanding* I, 260.

19 Ibid.

20 Ernst Käsemann, "Is the Gospel Objective?" in *Essays on New Testament Themes* (trans. W. J. Montague; SBT 41; London: SCM Press, 1964), 48.

If this consensus really ever did exist, there would be no more conversation on the topic today. Instead, though, culturally conventionalized knowledge about miracles today, particularly the validity of assumptions about their reality, is undergoing a remarkable change.

This shift in the cultural encyclopedia is apparent in recent discussions of miracles. In 1989 no fewer than three studies appeared that specifically addressed the problem of *miracles*.[21] In January of that year an editorial in the *Internationalen katholischen Zeitschrift* could even joyfully declare, "People are longing for the miraculous and once again believe in 'miracles'."

Among other things a rising anti-rationalism has paved the way for this change of popular opinion. This anti-rationalism advocates for the possibility of the facticity of the New Testament's miracles in a crypto-rationalist fashion and with help from psychosomatic and parapsychological "evidence." Thus Otto Betz and Werner Grimm claim in their book *Wesen und Wirklichkeit der Wunder Jesu*,

> After the knowledge of the incompleteness of the world has won space in the natural sciences themselves, and after the openness of the world is being reported by boundary crossing experiences in the fields of parapsychology, meditation, and near-death experiences, things that point to the effects of a transcendent reality, the only possible intellectual approach is to remain open.[22]

The short-circuit-like logic that fuels ever increasing demands for events such as healing services suggests a reversal of conclusions that are based on the principle of historical analogy. The practitioners of these healing services also hold the view that miracles are still a realistic possibility today. They believe this in large part because such events are attested in the earliest Christian texts. At the same time, however, the purveyors of these ideas generally fail to realize how dependent they are on a contemporary, capitalist theology of power. This is especially true when they imply that the intercessory prayer of the Sunday service is not sufficient for the worshippers, and when they arrogantly put the focus on themselves and prey upon the hopes of desperate people by playing at being divine healers.

In his own exegetical research on miracles, Hans Weder cautiously affirms the possibility of the New Testament's miracles should not be excluded from his-

---

21 *Theologia Practica* 24 (1989); *Internationale katholische Zeitschrift* 18 (1989); and, *Katechetische Blätter* 114 (1989).

22 Otto Betz and Werner Grimm, *Wesen und Wirklichkeit der Wunder Jesu: Heilungen – Rettungen – Zeichen – Aufleuchtungen* (ANTI 2; Frankfurt a.M.: Peter Lang, 1977), 5f. Along these same lines see Klaus Berger's short book *Darf man an Wunder glauben?* (Stuttgart: Gütersloher, 1996).

torical consideration. He even posits "that the miraculous deeds of Jesus, especially his miraculous healings and exorcisms (possibly also his resuscitations of the dead) cannot be denied historically (cf. Theißen, 274 [ET: 277])."[23]

The larger section that Weder here cites from Gerd Theißen's monograph, *The Miracle Stories of the Early Christian Tradition*, needs, however, to be brought into the discussion. Theißen writes, "There is no doubt that Jesus worked miracles, healed the sick and cast out demons, but the miracle stories reproduce these historical events in intensified form."[24]

While Hans Weder's statement regarding the historicity of Jesus' resurrection of the dead only provokes headshaking from critical historians, Theißen's argumentation is more palatable because he follows a dual strategy. The first sentence from Theißen's study cited above by Weder makes a historical claim about miracles – that they are factual events. The second quotation, however, qualifies this claim by combining it with social-psychological, psychosomatic, and finally, neorationalistic explanations of miracles. Such explanations can look back to a long exegetical tradition.

H.E.G. Paulus' rationalistic explanation of miracles had already allowed for the historicity of the healings and exorcisms. Paulus and Theißen agree with each other that Jesus' exorcisms of demons did not really involve the expulsion of *demons*. Rather, these were cases of healings of mental illness, which Theißen explains primarily as instances of socio-culturally generated mass depressions. In his words, "Within a society which can express its problems and intentions in mythical language, social and political pressure can be expressed as the rule of demons. Or, to put it more carefully, political control by a foreign power and the resulting socio-cultural pressure can intensify the experience expressed in belief in demons and lead to the spread of possession on the vast scale which we must assume existed in the world of primitive Christianity."[25] For Theißen, as for Paulus, there are no real *demons*. There is only the now outmoded belief in demons and devils, a belief that according to Theißen's demythologized account can be understood as "a very human interpretation of negative phenomena."[26]

---

23 Hans Weder, "Wunder Jesu und Wundergeschichten," Verkündigung und Forschung 29 (1984): 25–49, here 28.

24 Gerd Theißen, *The Miracle Stories of the Early Christian Tradition* (ed. John Riches; trans. Fancis McDonagh; Philadelphia: Fortress, 1983), 277.

25 Ibid., 256. For an opposing view see P. Brown's work on late antiquity, *The Cult of the Saints: Its Rise and Function in Latin Christianity* (Chicago: University of Chicago Press, 1981).

26 Gerd Theißen, *Argumente für einen kritischen Glauben oder: Was hält der Religionskritik stand?* (TEH 202; Munich: Kaiser, 1978), 14. See also, ibid., 45, 48f., 90f., 103.

Thus Theißen also does not think that any *demons* were actually sent by Jesus into a herd of swine (cf. Mark 5:13). The story more likely presents a coded message about the Romans (note that the demon's name is "legion"). Because of their "aggressive desire" for political possession, which is not to be confused with demon possession, the "story symbolically satisfies the desire to drive them into the sea like pigs."[27]

Even David Friedrich Strauss thought that the New Testament healing stories and exorcism accounts had a basis in historical fact. He argued, in rationalistic fashion, that these stories could be explained as the healing of psychosomatic illnesses. This is remarkable for two reasons. First, Strauss was generally a fierce critic of rationalistic explanations of miraculous accounts. Second, his demythologizing approach led him to regard most of the New Testament's miracle stories as unhistorical myths. Many of these stories, he thought, were produced through the transfer of motifs and themes from the Elijah-Elisha tradition and through the messianic reception of Isa 35:5f.[28] Nevertheless, in some of the case of Jesus' exorcisms and healings Strauss held the view "that Jesus cured many persons who suffered from supposed demoniacal insanity or nervous disorder, in a psychical manner, by the ascendancy of his manner and words."[29]

Many others (e.g., Rudolf Otto, one of Theißen's main influences) could also be located within this tradition of rationalistic explanations for the so-called healing "miracles" and "demon" exorcisms. It is almost a distinguishing feature of rationalistic and crypto-rationalistic explanations of miracles that they only consider Jesus' exorcisms and healing miracles to be historically "indisputable." One can see that "in a similar fashion it is relatively easy today, given our current understanding of the world, to countenance paranormal phenomena," as a quick glance at contemporary text books that deal with the theme of miracles will show.[30]

---

27 Theißen, *Miracle Stories*, 255.

28 Cf. Bernd Kollmann, *Jesus und die Christen als Wundertäter: Studien zu Magie, Medizin, und Schamanismus in Antike und Christentum* (FRLANT 170; Göttingen: Vandenhoeck & Ruprecht, 1996), 22.

29 Strauss, *Life of Jesus*, 436.

30 Stefan Alkier and Bernhard Dressler, "Wundergeschichten als fremde Welten lesen lernen: Didaktische Überlegungen zu Mk 4,35–41," in *Religion zeigen: Religionspädagogik und Semiotik* (ed. Bernhard Dressler and Michael Meyer-Blanck; Grundlegungen 4; Münster: LIT, 1998), 163–87, here 173.

3 Some Remarks on the Debate over Miracles in English Language Scholarship during the 20th Century

Thus far this essay has focused largely on discussions surrounding miracles in German academic circles. Naturally no impermeable boundary exists between Continental European scholarship and the conversations happening in other parts of the world such as Great Britain and North America. In many ways the debates that went on in these circles involved appropriations and rejections of the views of German thinkers. Nevertheless, within these appropriations and rejections there were some significant and distinctive conversations that occurred in English language scholarship during the 20th century. Too much literature was produced during this period to be comprehensively assayed here. We will, however, attempt to identify some of the major categories or responses to the question of the reality of miracles. At least four different approaches may be identified: 1) Fideistic approaches, 2) Presuppositional or Neo-Augustinian approaches, 3) Demythologizing approaches, and 4) Neo-Humean approaches.

One response to the question of miracles that has been especially distinctive in some forms of American Christianity can accurately be called fideism. A great number of books, essays and articles, however, were also penned by North American and British scholars during the 20th century that took more presuppositional than fideistic approaches to the question of miracles. These are not mutually exclusive or even unique approaches. They do, however, illustrate the tenacity of religious belief. That is to say, in spite of (and often in direct response to) the growing influence of accounts of reality that ruled out *a priori* the possibility of the miraculous, many Christian scholars have continued to assert their reality on the basis of their more fundamental faith in the existence of the God attested in the Bible.

In the English speaking world, and particularly in North America, arguments over the reality of miracles played a significant role in the so-called Fundamentalist-Modernist Controversy. Between 1910 and 1915 several essays were published in a series of 12 volumes entitled *The Fundamentals: A Testimony to the Truth.*[31]

31 For a more detailed discussions see D. G. Hart, "Evangelicals, Biblical Scholarship, and the Politics of the Modern American Academy," in *Evangelicals and Science in Historical Perspective* (ed. David N. Livingstone, D. G. Hart, and Mark A. Noll; Oxford: Oxford University Press, 1999), 306–26, esp. 309–12; Mark Hutchinson and John Wolffe, *A Short History of Global Evangelicalism* (Cambridge: Cambridge University Press, 2012), 156–60; and, George M. Marsden, *Fundamentalism and American Culture* (2nd ed.; Oxford: Oxford University Press, 2006), 118–23.

Written by an internationally and denominationally diverse group of broadly evangelical scholars and pastors, these essays expressed some of the basic points of disagreement that conservative believers had against the influence of "modernism" and "higher criticism" in theological discourse. The possibility of the miraculous was a major emphasis throughout these articles, several of which directly addressed issues such as the reality of prophecy, the virgin birth, the incarnation and the bodily resurrection of Jesus. The title and much of the content of these essays was the inspiration for the moniker of one of the movements that grew out these circles and became known as "Fundamentalism."

In his essay "Science and the Christian Faith," James Orr cuts to the chase when, precisely reversing Spinoza's view, he argues that those who would use the scientific understanding of the uniformity of nature to dismiss the supernatural and miracles ultimately deny the existence of Theism, which he defined as the belief that God is both immanent in the world and in infinite ways transcendent.[32] Orr stated,

> What the scientific man needs to prove to establish his objection to miracle is, not simply that natural causes operate uniformly, but that no other than natural causes exist; that natural causes exhaust all the causation in the universe. ... [T]he real question at issue in miracle is not natural law, but *Theism*.[33]

Thus for Orr the debate over miracles is reducible to a more fundamental and ultimate question – is there a God who exists apart from the "natural" world or not?

This same idea was espoused by J. Gresham Machen, the New Testament professor who left Princeton Theological Seminary to help found Westminster Theological Seminary. Machen argued that belief in the reality of miracles depended upon two presuppositions: "1) [T]he existence of a personal God, and 2) the existence of a real order of nature."[34] Yet belief that the creator God is a personal God, which like Orr Machen referred to as "Theism," was the essential point. This belief implied that a miracle "is not wrought by an arbitrary and fantastic despot, but by the very God to whom the regularity of nature itself is due – by the God, moreover, whose character is known through the Bible."[35] Because the real issue for Machen was whether or not one believed in a personal God, one's position on

32 James Orr, "Science and the Christian Faith" in *The Fundamentals: A Testimony to the Truth*, 4 vols. (ed. R.A. Torrey, A.C. Dixon et al; 1917; repr., Grand Rapids: Baker, 1972), 1:339.
33 Ibid. (emphasis original).
34 J. Gresham Machen, *Christianity and Liberalism* (1923; repr., Grand Rapids: Eerdmans, 1996), 99.
35 Ibid., 102.

miracles signaled for him whether or not one was truly a Christian. Reject the miracles and one rejected the God of the Bible. For such a person Jesus became only "the fairest flower of humanity."[36] Accept the miracles and Jesus was known to be "a Saviour who came voluntarily into this world for our salvation, suffered for our sins upon the Cross, rose again from the dead by the power of God, and ever lives to make intercession for us."[37] Machen continued, "The difference between these two views is the difference between two totally diverse religions."[38]

As the views of Orr and Machen suggest, this approach to the debate over miracles is not one of hermeneutics, nor even ultimately about the significance of miraculous events (though there are numerous instances of fundamentalist and evangelical apologists who appeal to the Bible's miracles as a ground for believing in Christianity). Rather, the debate boils down to whether or not one believes in a personal God who created and sustains the world – specifically, God as they think the Bible presents him.[39]

The following assessment will no doubt present an oversimplified account, but at least two different appropriations of this "theistic" conviction can be seen within the circles that produced, were influenced by, and/or were otherwise sympathetic to the positions stated in *The Fundamentals*. One was a fideistic withdrawal from the larger endeavors of philosophical and scientific discourse. The other consists of more Augustinian "faith seeking understanding" or presuppositional attempts at engagement.

The post-1930's Christian Fundamentalist movement coupled the approach expressed by Orr and Machen with a kind of militant pursuit of doctrinal and ecclesiastical purity and independence. It is not difficult to understand how this tended in the direction of the separatist stance that became the hallmark of this later Fundamentalism.[40] Indeed, as Fundamentalism grew, an alternate culture necessarily developed around it with its own independent educational institutions and its own idiosyncratic assessments of scientific evidence and claims.

---

36 Ibid., 109.

37 Ibid.

38 Ibid.

39 Machen comments, "The English word 'God' has no particular virtue in itself; it is not more beautiful than other words. Its importance depends altogether upon the meaning which is attached to it." Ibid., 110.

40 For an insider's account of the differences between Fundamentalism before and after the 1930's and between later Fundamentalism and Evangelicalism, see David O. Beale, *In Pursuit of Purity: American Fundamentalism Since 1850* (Greenville, S. C.: Unusual Publications, 1986), esp. 3–12, 353–56.

A similar, though more irenic and broadly oriented approach was (and continues to be) widespread among the diverse group of evangelical and/or more conservative English speaking scholars. This group is hugely varied and diverse but shares the conviction that faith and reason are mutually compatible. One thinks here especially of the influential apologist C. S. Lewis and of his book *Miracles* in particular. In the latter work Lewis framed the discussion in terms of naturalism (where nature is a closed system) and supernaturalism (where there is a transcendent, creator God).[41] Lewis argued that only the existence of such a God can assure the kind of consistency that naturalists observe and (incorrectly) elevate to the level of uniformity. In Lewis's words,

> The philosophy which forbids you to make uniformity absolute [i.e. supernaturalism] is also the philosophy which offers you solid grounds for believing it [i.e., uniformity] to be general, to be *almost* absolute. The Being who threatens Nature's claim to omnipotence confirms her in her lawful occasions. Try to make Nature absolute and you find that her uniformity is not even probable.[42]

In other words, for Lewis the fact of rationale inquiry makes the most sense on the assumption of the existence of a creator God.

Among biblical scholars this more presuppositional approach tended to be characterized by varying levels of critical engagement with the biblical texts that sought to bring together the confession of a creator God and the ways in which the miracle stories might be understood in their ancient context. By so doing the essential integrity and trustworthiness of the accounts could be plausibly affirmed.

The well-known form critic Vincent Taylor, for example, rigorously applied form-critical methodology to the miracle stories. He notes, however, that such study "brings us only to the threshold of the historical problem."[43] Taylor continued,

> This problem does not admit of any solution which can be called scientific, for our decision includes a personal element which cannot be removed; it depends on our world-view, our estimate of the Person of Christ, and our use of the principles of Higher Criticism. ... The importance of a true estimate of the Person of Christ cannot be over-emphasized.[44]

---

41 C. S. Lewis, *Miracles: A Preliminary Study* (1947; repr. San Francisco: HarperSanFrancisco, 2001), 5–15.
42 Ibid., 169.
43 Vincent Taylor, *The Formation of the Gospel Tradition: Eight Lectures* (2nd ed.; London: Macmillan, 1935), 134.
44 Ibid., 134–35.

In Taylor's own view, "[I]f Jesus is divine, as I believe He is; if, that is to say, the divine was revealed in his humanity in a way to which history offers no parallel."[45] Because of this presupposition he was "ready to accept the healing miracles, and to recognize that they are more than cures by 'suggestion'."[46] On this supposition, "The stories of raising from the dead would also be easier of acceptance, for there is no reason why One such as He should not be able to recall the spirit of a man from the very gates of death."[47]

His Christology, however, also led him to a highly nuanced approach to other miracles attested in the Gospels. He found the nature miracles in particular harder to accept. He appears to be worried about the problem of Docetism and the full humanity of Jesus. "The best Christian thinking has always repudiated the idea that Jesus was a demi-god in human form; it has recognized ... that the Incarnation imposed limitations both of knowledge and power."[48] Here, then, Taylor leaves only a question mark:

> If we are honest with ourselves we have to say that we do not know [the extent of the Incarnation's limitations]; and this admission means that the full recognition of the divinity of Christ does not settle the problem of the nature-miracles. To deny that they happened is not to deny that 'the Word became flesh and dwelt among us'; it might even be consistent with a fuller appreciation of the wonder of the Incarnation.[49]

Such a nuanced approach attempts to bring theological presupposition together with higher critical methodology and for Taylor no easy decision can be made and both acceptance and denial are theologically respectable positions. "Those of us who think that the incidents were natural events ought to keep an open mind, since we may have misread the limitations of the Incarnation."[50] But, he went on to add, "those who accept the stories should ask if they do not rob the Incarnation of its grace and infinite condescension."[51]

C. F. D. Moule's circumspect marshaling of arguments for the possibility of the resurrection provides another salient example.[52] Moule highlighted the empty tomb tradition and noted that it is hard to imagine Jews of the time claiming the

45 Ibid., 135–36.
46 Ibid., 136.
47 Ibid.
48 Ibid.
49 Ibid.
50 Ibid., 140.
51 Ibid.
52 C. F. D. Moule, ed., *The Significance of the Message of the Resurrection for Faith in Jesus Christ* (SBT 2/8; London: SCM Press, 1968), 8–11.

tomb was empty without them all assuming Jesus' bodily resurrection. This claim, though, should have been easy to refute by producing a body. Moreover, those who announced Jesus' resurrection knew of resuscitations and apparitions, but their claims about Jesus do not cohere with either of these modes of life after death. Instead, they make the historically unanticipated claim that Jesus had received the kind of permanent life that apocalyptic Jews believed would be granted *en masse* and only on the Last Day. For Moule such a claim "was a preposterously novel idea – indeed, clearly unthinkable, for any Jew who had not been compelled to it by experience – it is hardly logical to assume that the whole story is a tissue of materials moulded on a standard pattern."[53] In that case Jesus' resurrection would be an act of new creation that transformed Jesus' body "into a different mode of existence."[54] Such a view, Moule averred, "is certainly congruous with a God who never creates without a purpose."[55]

In another place Moule commented that the most tenable view that a consistent theist can hold is that "the only ultimate regularity is to be looked for not within the material realm itself but in the character of a personal God. It is of his character that the material realm is a manifestation."[56] He continued, "[W]hat is possible and probable in [the material realm] is better measured by what is known of the character of God than by what is observed on the much narrower scale of the purely mechanistic."[57] Moule used this approach as a criterion to test accounts of miracles, both within and outside of the Bible. The story of God making the sun stand still for Joshua can be dismissed in part because "there is no evidence that this is the kind of way in which a personal God helps and trains his children."[58] Given Jesus' "absolute obedience to the will of God," Moule asks, "Why should we not allow that [Jesus' resurrection] seems consistent with all we know of God ...?"[59] For the theist the trans-material realm "is personal and includes the material" which means that "the ultimate consistency is in the character of the God and Father of our Lord Jesus Christ."[60]

When speaking of the virgin birth N. T. Wright expressed the point even more forcefully when he wrote,

53 Ibid., 9.
54 Ibid., 10.
55 Ibid.
56 C. F. D. Moule, ed., *Miracles: Cambridge Studies in Their Philosophy and History* (London: A. R. Mowbray, 1965), 16.
57 Ibid.
58 Ibid., 17.
59 Ibid.
60 Ibid.

> There are indeed more things in heaven and earth than are dreamed of in post-Enlightenment metaphysics. The 'closed continuum' of cause and effect is a modernist myth. The God who does not intervene from outside is always present and active within the world, sometimes shockingly, may well have been thus active on this occasion.[61]

For Wright the assumption of a creator God who is involved in his creation makes the reality of miracles such as the virgin birth possible. The evangelical scholar Craig Blomberg has well summarized this basic position when he stated, "Despite a long tradition in Christian apologetics of arguing from miracles to the existence of God, it seems rather that God's existence needs to be either demonstrated or presupposed before the miracles can be believed."[62]

At the same time, however, variations on the approaches to the problem of miracles already discussed in sections 1 and 2 above were well represented in 20th century English language scholarship. The demythologizing approach and the influence of figures such as Strauss and Bultmann are especially evident. In general, the scholars who endorsed such hermeneutical strategies would sharply dispute the charge of Orr and Machen that they are not "Theists" or, indeed, Christians. The interpretive project for many of these scholars has a theological concern at its core – to show how the Christian religion can continue to be practiced and remain relevant in the modern world. There are so many instances of these sorts of approaches that only a few will be here presented by way of example.

The Anglican theologian John Macquarrie provides an especially thoughtful example of one who strove to reinterpret Christian convictions in view of the changes in science and cosmology that occurred in the 20th century. Macquarrie, while critical of Bultmann at points, was impressed by the potential that the recognition of the category of myth in Scripture held for communicating what he considered to be the essential truth of Christianity to modern people. Thus, on the issue of miracles he noted the importance of distinguishing between miracles of healing and so-called "nature miracles." The former were understood by the New Testament writers and by Jesus himself as exorcisms, but this very fact testifies "to the genuine humanity of Jesus, whose understanding of the world and of nature was that of his contemporaries."[63] We may not fully understand yet how the mind, body, and illness are interrelated, but such healings "still occur within our experience, and so reports of such happenings from the past have to be treated

61 Marcus J. Borg and N. T. Wright, *The Meaning of Jesus: Two Visions* (San Francisco: HarperSanFrancisco, 1999), 172–23.

62 Craig L. Blomberg, *The Historical Reliability of the Gospels* (Downers Grove, Ill.: InterVarsity Press, 1987), 111.

63 John Macquarrie, *Jesus Christ in Modern Thought* (London: SCM, 1990), 79.

with respect."[64] These events, moreover, illustrate the concrete benefits of the salvation Jesus offered.

The nature miracles, however, "apart from their legendary character, do not have the significance of fuller life attaching to the healing miracles, but seem to act only as impressive evidence of supernatural power."[65] Nevertheless, at least some of the incredible events that surround the accounts of Jesus in the Gospels can be recognized as "true legend."[66] The nativity stories of Matthew and Luke, for example, are clearly legendary but they are nonetheless "true theologically, in fact, very near to that transvaluation of all values which ... lies at the very core of Christianity."[67] That is to say, some of the legendary elements express the true, essential values and message of the Christian faith and are therefore theologically valuable, even if the particulars of these accounts must be dismissed by modern Christians.

With respect to Jesus' miracles, George Wesley Buchanan's volume *Jesus: The King and His Kingdom* bears many similarities to the approach of Strauss already summarized above. Like Strauss (and Theißen), he also appealed to psychological explanations for Jesus' exorcisms and "emotional healings."[68] Jesus other miracles, however, can be explained by way of the early church writing them back into Jesus' lifetime on the basis of types and expectations they had from their Scriptures (esp. types based on the prophets Elijah and Elisha). Unlike Strauss, Buchanan did not feel the need to attempt a comprehensive study of Jesus miracles. Rather, he discussed some key categories (e.g., Jesus' power over water, provision of food, healing of gentiles), showed how these categories are analogous to deeds done by Elijah and Elisha, and concluded, "There is enough evidence to cast doubt on some, if not all, of the miracles attributed to Jesus."[69] Concerning the authors of the Gospels he went on to clarify,

> They were not malicious fiction writers. They presented what they believed were the normal conclusions of their beliefs on the basis of scripture, typology, and accepted methods of exegesis. They searched the scriptures and when they found two supporting proof texts or typologies they believed they proved that the item involved was fact. They had only to record it.

64 Ibid.
65 Ibid.
66 Ibid., 89.
67 Ibid., 95.
68 George Wesley Buchanan, *Jesus: The King and His Kingdom* (Macon, Ga.: Mercer University Press, 1984), 301.
69 Ibid., 309 (remarkably, he states in a footnote that he intends this statement to be directed against Bultmann).

Jesus' miracles are mostly, if not entirely, the result of this kind of historicizing of biblical types and prophecies.

Yet another approach to the question of miracles has been dubbed "Neo-Humean." The philosopher Antony Flew argued strenuously for this position suggesting that Hume's basic argument needed to be strengthened because Hume did not make "the crucially necessary distinction between the merely marvelous and the genuinely miraculous."[70] Flew emphasized the epistemological problem of miracles more than the ontological one. He wrote,

> The heart of the matter is that the criteria by which we must assess historical testimony, and the general presumptions that alone make it possible for us to construe the detritus of the past as historical evidence, must inevitably rule out any possibility of establishing, on purely historical grounds, that some genuinely miraculous event has indeed occurred.[71]

This follows, according to Flew, because the interpretation of evidence from the past requires the assumptions of regularity and of the historian's reliance on his or her own understanding of what is possible or impossible.[72] Apart from these assumptions, one could not interpret artifacts from the past. In the case of the claim that a miracle happened one must weigh a claim regarding a one-time, unrepeatable event that runs contrary to the principles of regularity and what is probable. Since one can no longer directly confirm or disconfirm the alleged miracle, the issue is that of weighing evidence in terms of what is, at least in principle, verifiable. The laws of nature are, in principle, testable. Thus historical reasoning must depend on the principle that the laws of nature (because they are verifiable) indicate what is probable.[73] An event can, therefore, be recognized to be a marvel (i.e., to be an event that appears to be contrary to our understanding of the laws of nature), but it cannot be known to be a miracle because such events are not historically intelligible.

This limited survey of some of the approaches to the problem of miracles in English language scholarship during the 20th century illustrates the extent of disagreement on the issue. It is clear that in the English speaking world there were (and continue to be) substantive differences concerning the nature of reality, what can and cannot happen, and how we can know it.

---

70 Antony Flew, "Neo-Humean Arguments about the Miraculous" in *In Defense of Miracles: A Comprehensive Case for God's Action in History* (ed. R. Douglas Geivett and Gary Habermas; Downers Grove, Ill.: InterVarsity Press, 1997), 45–57, here 49.

71 Ibid. See also Flew's 1967 essay "Miracles" *EP* 5:346–53.

72 Ibid.

73 Ibid., 50–51.

4 The Debate over Miracles and the Necessary Problematizing of Concepts of Reality

Biblical scholarship is faced with the task of clarifying its concept of reality in view of the ongoing interdisciplinary theological and philosophical discourse. When considering the question of the "historicity" of miracles, what exegesis takes to be dispensable or disputable elements does not actually depend on the exegetical details of a given story. These determinations are really based on prior assumptions about what is plausible, assumptions that are always already in play before one looks at any particular exegetical detail. If one begins, as Bultmann did, by assuming that the so-called "laws of nature" are always consistent and unbreakable, a view beholden to the mechanistic understanding of physics popular in the 18th century, then no account of an event that is inconsistent with these "laws of nature" can ever be accepted as "historical." If one works as, for example, Theißen does, with a psychosomatic model when explaining miracles, then one can interpret any reported case of a healing miracle or an exorcism as an instance of a psychosomatic healing of a physical and psychological ailment. If one opts instead for a fundamentalistic, authoritarian view of God and withdraws from or simply denies the wider endeavor of society to develop a common conception of reality, then one can, without batting an eyelash, accept not only that Jesus walked on water, but also that the entire Egyptian army was drowned. Yet such an approach takes an overly cynical view of our abilities both to comprehend reality and to understand the wisdom of the biblical witness.

There is no simple "solution" to the problem of miracles. Indeed, it is not the "solution" to the question of miracles that offers us a promising historiographical, philosophical, exegetical, or theological way forward, but rather the openness that the question demands. This latter approach exposes fundamental questions and problems that scientific discourse can only dismiss or reduce to its own detriment and to the detriment of society. The problem of miracles must be addressed in new ways, and indeed in ways that move beyond the demythologizing and rehistoricizing methodologies. Only exegetical approaches that work within the dominant conceptions of reality are able to support both learned and pious miracle discourse in our pluralistic societies.

In his seminal essay of 1972 entitled "'Text' und 'Geschichte' als Grundkategorien der Generativen Poetik," Erhardt Güttgemanns addressed the controversy over the reality of Jesus' resurrection. He problematized the traditional approaches to the relationship between the text and reality, or better, between the text and history, by appealing to recent work in the field of semiotics. He made the point that reality/history can only be experienced when it is vested with "significance."[74] That which is experienced as reality is, therefore, dependent upon the context or meaningful connections that are created by the text in which it is located. Güttgemanns states, "'Text' and 'history' are not static facts. Rather, they are relational factors within a semiotic system. They can, therefore, only be adequately analyzed within their semiotic relationships."[75]

The open question, before which the problem of miracles now stands, is this: How shall we then proceed given the fact of the diversity of worldviews we face today? Should we adopt the radical pluralism of the postmodern project that considers any singular position and any one claim to truth to be an act of violence that excludes the other? Or, should we try, along the lines of the categorical semiotics of Charles Sanders Peirce, to work out a concept of reality that can make the qualified plurality of meanings intelligible without having to surrender the claim to truth? A great deal depends on finding a way to work through these questions, not only for biblical scholarship and theological discourse as a whole, but also for the larger project of finding ways to live and work together within a pluralistic society.

74 Erhardt Güttgemanns, "'Text' und 'Geschichte' als Grundkategorien der Generativen Poetik: Thesen zur aktuellen Diskussion um die 'Wirklichkeit' der Auferstehungstexte," LingBib 11 (1972): 1–12, here 8.
75 Ibid., 10.

Werner Kahl

New Testament Healing Narratives and the Category of Numinous Power

1 The Numinous – an unpredictable career of a category

Rudolf Otto forcefully introduced the category 'das Numinose' – the numinous – into the fields of theology and religious studies. According to Otto, the numinous is the *essence* of all religion. The term denotes "holiness minus moralistic and rationalistic aspects".[1] Not only did Otto identify and write about this new category, the expressionistic writing style of his influential work Das Heilige, 1917, seems shaped by the author's own encounter with numinous realities. After a few decades of thriving amongst some phenomenologists of religion (including van Leuw, Heiler, and Eliade), the term was categorically rejected in Germany. Around the middle of the 20th century, the term lost appeal amongst international scholars of theology and of *Religionswissenschaft*, the critical study of religion.[2] According to critics from the field of the study of religion, Otto's work demonstrated "the radical decontextualisation and deprocessualization of religious data"[3]; it came to be regarded as an expression of 'anti-historicism'. On the one hand, the numinous appeared devoid of any concern for questions of religious identity and the role of social contexts favouring an irrational emotional dimension of religious experience; on the other hand, it was indicted for its ontologized transcendence.[4] For these reasons, and more, the category became increasingly stigmatised as un-scientific in the study of religion field. Most scholars abandoned the category numinous. Nevertheless, even theologians – many of whom were representatives of Karl Barth's version of *Dialectical Theology* – likewise disregarded the category as being problematic.

---

1 Rudolf Otto, *Das Heilige: Über das Irrationale in der Idee des Göttlichen und sein Verhältnis zum Rationalen* (Munich: C.H. Beck, 1963), 6: "(…) das Heilige *minus* seines sittlichen Momentes und (…) minus seines rationalen Momentes überhaupt".

2 For an overview on the history of the category on which I rely here, cf. Dirk Johannsen, *Das Numinose als kulturwissenschaftliche Kategorie* (Stuttgart: Kohlhammer, 2008), 11–96.

3 Christiano Grotanelli and Bruce Lincoln, "A brief note on (future) research in the history of religions," *Method & Theory in the Study of Religion* 10 (1998): 311–25, 317.

4 Hans G. Kippenberg and Kocku von Stuckrad, *Einführung in die Religionswissenschaft: Gegenstände und Begriffe* (Munich: C.H. Beck, 2003), 142–43.

The logic behind this rejection is quite telling. I quote from Friedrich Feigel's critique of Otto's work: "Otto's Numinosum erweist sich für die Begründung der *Wahrheit* der Religion als ungeeignet, weil es noch nicht einmal eine Möglichkeit an die Hand gibt, Gott vom Teufel zu unterscheiden."[5] Ironically, it is this very ambivalence of the term *Das Numinose* which might account for its value as a means to compare religious narratives in rather "neutral" terms.[6] This comforted researchers like Robert Levy, Jeanette Mageo, and Alan Howard who shied away from referring to the 'spiritual', 'supernatural' or 'to a non-empirical reality' because such vocabulary tended to reinforce ethno-centricism. It is therefore no coincidence that Otto's category survived in the fields of ethnology, folklore studies, and comparative literature. In their methodological introduction, the editors of the volume *Spirits in Culture, History, and Mind* – a collection of ethnological papers from 1996[7] – defended their preference for the term 'numinous'. 'Numinous' from this perspective denotes a realm different from everyday experiences within the visible world, without superimposing the interpretation of reality dominant in a particular culture; instead of using the term 'spiritual beings' transculturally, they prefer the term *numinals* as more neutral category.

2 'Numinous power' as useful category

When I wrote my Emory dissertation on a *religionsgeschichtliche* comparison of New Testament miracle healing stories from a structuralist perspective exactly twenty years ago,[8] I had no idea of the academic debate on the problem of the term 'numinous'. In fact, I had not even read Otto's work. It never featured in my theological studies back at Göttingen university, and we now know what accounts for this silence: In theology, 'das Heilige' had long been buried together with 'the Numinous', primarily for theological but also for methodological reasons.

---

5 Friedrich K. Feigel, *"Das Heilige", Kritische Abhandlung über Rudolf Ottos gleichnamiges Buch* (Tübingen: J.C.B. Mohr, [2]1948), 133; (engl. translation: W.K.): "Otto's Numinosum is useless for establishing the *truth* of religion, since it does not even allow to distinguish God from the devil."

6 Cf. Johannsen, *Das Numinose*, 90.

7 Robert Levy, Jeannette M. Mageo and Alan Howard, "Gods, Spirits, and History: A Theoretical Perspective." In *Spirits in Culture, History, and Mind* (ed. Jeannette M. Mageo and Alan Howard; New York: Routledge, 1996), 11–28, 13.

8 Werner Kahl, *New Testament Miracle Stories in their Religious-Historical Setting: A Religionsgeschichtliche Comparison from a Structural Perspective* (FRLANT 163; Göttingen: Vandenhoeck & Ruprecht, 1994).

Going through the PhD program at Emory I *was* made aware of the problematic of terminology in New Testament studies: Just remember the terms 'Spätjudentum' (late Judaism), 'Jewish legalism', and the like. After reading Rudolf Bultmann's work on miracles, including his *New Testament and Mythology*, it became obvious that he regarded them as 'mirakulös'. According to him, the belief in miracles is due to a magical understanding of the world; they are an expression of a primitive faith. A faith which is dependent on the word of God in Christ alone represents the proper Christian attitude. This faith constitutes, for Bultmann, the real Christian miracle.

I also did not believe in miracles but that was not the issue here. The issue was: How can we do justice to religious expressions – and to those expressing them – even though they appear to be strange to us? Since I had wanted to compare New Testament healing narratives with narratives of the same theme in the *Tanakh* (תנ״ך), Qumran literature, writings of Hellenistic and Rabbinic Judaism, as well as with narratives from Greco-Roman traditions, how could I avoid *methodologically* the ever luring temptation of elevating the New Testament narratives over against those of other traditions, as had been common in some of New Testament scholarship?[9] Searching for a solution I turned to the study of method with respect to the analysis and comparison of narratives from different cultures: methods that had been developed and tested in the fields of folklore studies, ethnology, and semiotics, esp. structuralism. I adopted the *Narrative Schema* derived from Algirdas J. Greimas' reorganization[10] of Vladimir Propp's thirty one narrative functions[11] which had been introduced into the field of New Testament studies by Hendrikus Boers[12] and I applied it to the analysis and comparison of approximately 150 narratives of miracle healing stories from Mediterranean antiquity.[13]

---

9 Cf. the overview in Kahl, *Miracle Stories*, 19 ff.

10 Cf. Algirdas J. Greimas and Joseph Courtés, *Sémiotique: Dictionnaire raisonné de la théorie du langage* (Paris: Hachette, 1993), 244–47.

11 Vladimir Propp, *Morphology of the Folktale*, (Austin: University of Texas Press, ²1968).

12 Hendrikus Boers, "Introduction" in Wilhelm Egger, *How to Read the New Testament: An Introduction to Linguistic and Historical-Crititical Methodology* (Peabody: Hendrickson, 1996), xxxvii–lxix, lxv; H. Boers, *Neither on This Mountain Nor in Jerusalem: A Study of John 4* (Atlanta: Society of Biblical Literature, 1988), 9–14.

13 Kahl, *Miracle Stories*, 44–62.

The Narrative Schema

A. NEED	B. PREPAREDNESS	C. PERFORMANCE	D. SANCTION
A subject of a circumstance disjoined from a desirable object or conjoined with an undesirable object.	An active subject, willing or obliged, and able (having the power) to overcome the need, specified in A, by a performance.	The active subject performing the action to transform the circumstance specified in A into the opposite.	Recognition of the success or failure of the performance, or of the achievement of a desired value.

This model proved useful in reducing the risk of favouring one tradition over the other. I simply analysed the sequence of narrative moves, strictly confined to the syntagmatic unfolding of events, in order to distinguish structural features from the level of motif. In so doing, I arrived at the following structuralistically informed description of miracle healing stories:

A miracle healing story shares the same morphology with other narratives. It describes the move from a need to the fulfilment of that need by means of a performance of an active subject specially prepared for the task. The difference of *miracle healing* stories from other narratives is constituted by the way structural features ('motifemic slots') are realised, i.e. the difference is located on the level of *motif*: The initial need belongs to the topic of *health*. This need can only be fulfilled by the involvement of a *bearer of numinous power* in the phase of the preparedness and / or performance, either directly or through a mediator. The reversal of the initial circumstance depends on the involvement of some numinous power, since – from the perspective of normal human ability – the initial lack is irreversible: "Consequently, the involvement of a *bearer of numinous power* (BNP) in the narrative process, its activation for and its engagement in a NP (narrative program, W.K.) aimed at the reversal of the initial circumstance, plays a crucial role in miracle stories."[14]

Comparing about 150 miracle healing stories and analysing the functions of active subjects, I realized that the widely used term *miracle worker* was misleading when it was applied to figures like Abraham, Moses, Elijah, Elisha, Tobit, Hanina ben Dosa, Jesus of Nazareth, Peter, Paul, Asclepios, the God of Israel, Vespasian, Apollonius of Tyana, and others, alike. Those figures function in *different roles* within miracle healing narratives. Therefore I introduced three types of figures which are actively involved in the miracle healing performance: *bearer of nu-*

14 Kahl, *Miracle Stories*, 63–64.

minous power (BNP: like the God of Israel, Jesus, Asclepios, and Apollonius), *petitioner of numinous power* (PNP: like Moses, Hanina ben Dosa, Peter, and Paul), and *mediator of numinous power* (MNP: like Tobit and Vespasian). Figures of the latter two types do *not incorporate constantly* numinous healing power. Often PNPs can also function as MNPs in one and the same narrative, as is the case with Moses, Elijah, Elisha, Peter, and Paul. This distinction has proved useful and quite a number of colleagues in the field of New Testament studies work with it.

How did I come up with the category 'numinous power'? I am not entirely certain, but I hope the following scenario was at play: In analysing narratives from Mediterranean antiquity I *was* aware that I was engaged in an activity of cross-cultural understanding. (This should not become just another exercise in cultural domination and distortion.) At the same time, I had gathered material from *various* distinct traditions of antiquity. How could I do justice to each and every one of them? Terms like magical, miraculous, supernatural, occult, or mythical had problematic and derogatory undertones. 'Numinous' as an attribute of 'power' sounded like a neutral and broad enough term to denote the competence and activity of such diverse figures as gods, angels, unclean spirits, demons, ancestors, Satan, and so on. In Latin, 'numen' at times denotes a deity, and at times the effects of its activity. I could use 'numinous' in a more general sense, and give the following definition of 'numinous power': It denotes a power effecting changes beyond human ability which is attributed to the competence and activity of spiritual or divine beings.

The involvement of such figures clearly comes to expression in miracle healing narratives. It should be noted that 'numinous power' in the above definition is considered neutral – simply signifying the activities of figures connected to a numinous sphere. Only in actual healing narratives are the involved powers qualified as good or evil, life enhancing or destructive – depending on the value system of the narrator. It should also be noted that in the New Testament, God and Christ's power can also cause death and destruction, miracles can be attributed to Satan (Rev 13:11–15; 2 Thess 2:3–10; Matt 24:24), and critics ascribed Jesus' healing activity to demonic forces (cf. Mark 3:22).

As for the presentation of Jesus in the Synoptic Gospels, the records describe the Holy Spirit descending into (Mark 1:10: εἰς) or onto him (Matt 3:16 and Luke 3:22: ἐπ' αὐτόν). For example, this happens at the occasion of his baptism when the Spirit bestows Jesus with *constant* divine power (cf. Mark 1:22: ὡς ἐξουσίαν ἔχων; 1:27: διδαχὴ καινὴ κατ' ἐξουσίαν; Luke 4:36: ἐν ἐξουσίᾳ καὶ δυνάμει; cf. 4:14: ἐν τῇ δυνάμει τοῦ πνεύματος). Due to this divine preparedness he is enabled to overcome Satan resp. the Devil and to drive out 'unclean spirits' from people, healing them, and restoring their personal and communal integrity. While 'unclean spirits' or demons belong to the numinous sphere, they remain *embedded* within the visible world.

Due to their numinous power, the unclean spirits can overpower human beings, causing illness and social ostracism among other circumstances that are not desired from a regular human perspective. These spirits recognize that the numinous power of Jesus surpasses theirs. Within the Markan narrative they, and only they, know who Jesus is immediately upon encountering him: Jesus as the Holy one of God: οἶδά σε τίς εἶ, ὁ ἅγιος τοῦ θεοῦ (Mark 1:24; cf. 5:7: Τί ἐμοὶ καὶ σοί, Ἰησοῦ υἱὲ τοῦ θεοῦ τοῦ ὑψίστου). As such, Jesus was declared by a heavenly voice after the spirit had descended into him as: You are my beloved son (1:11: Σὺ εἶ ὁ υἱός μου ὁ ἀγαπητός). By implication, the narrative informs its readers that Jesus is the 'son of God'. Whatever the precise meaning of the designation 'son of God' might have been in the matrix of ancient Judaism within which the term has to be located,[15] it implies that Jesus is different from OT prophets, certain rabbinic figures, Early Christian apostles, or shamans past and present: He *constantly incorporates divine power* by means of which he is able to restore health and life. This is brought to expression in the numerous miracle healing stories of all the Gospels: God's healing power extends to Jesus. He, as an *innerworldy* figure, is presented as a constant *bearer of numinous power*. This is – apart from the historically later figure of Apollonios of Tyana – a unique attribution in ancient miracle healing stories. Other figures indiscriminately designated as 'miracle workers' in New Testament scholarship, are either transcendent gods that might appear on earth for a particular performance, or they are human beings who are being used by a god or who might be bestowed temporarily with numinous ability for a particular performance. The latter might function as *mediators of numinous power* or they appear as figures that are able to motivate, persuade, or force a transcendent being to engage in a miracle healing. As such they function as *petitioners of numinous power* like Hanina ben Dosa who in Rabbinic literature is portrayed as a rabbi with the special ability to successfully reach God with prayer requests. But he is *not* a miracle worker in the strict sense of the word. The same applies to Paul according to Acts and according to his epistles.[16] With respect to Rabbinic literature, the miracle worker is *God* as transcendent *bearer of numinous power*.

---

15 Cf. the recent study by Daniel Boyarin, *The Jewish Gospels: The Story of the Jewish Christ* (New York: The New Press, 2012).

16 With respect to the Pauline epistles, this has been convincingly pointed out by Alkier, *Wunder und Wirklichkeit in den Briefen des Apostels Paulus* (WUNT 134; Tübingen: Mohr-Siebeck, 2000).

3 Numinous power and concepts of reality

We try to make sense of the ambiguities of life as members of communities within distinct cultures. We cannot escape being bound to traditions within which we experience and conceptualize, communicate, manipulate, and forecast reality. This also holds true for discourses on concepts of reality. The very terms 'reality' and 'existence' open up whole universes of meaning, and at the same time, they also limit our understanding.

In the early 2000s, I spent three years in West-Africa doing field research on the interpretation of the Bible in Ghana. I had wanted to understand the cultural frame of reference – the encyclopaedia in and through which people make sense of the world and of the Bible in West-Africa. My experiences and reflections in Ghana allowed for a fresh view on the miracle healing stories of the New Testament, and I became aware of meaning dimensions in these narratives previously hidden from me that were enormously different from the European interpretation.

Classicists working in West-Africa in the fifties and sixties of the last century had already observed that a West-African cultural perspective might be helpful in gaining insides with respect to life in antiquity, as e.g. John Ferguson claimed 1967 while teaching in Nigeria:

> "Our Classics department is set in one of the few parts of the world where you can still consult oracles, where there are tonal languages (as Classical Greek was tonal), where there is a living tradition of religious dance-drama (what is Greek tragedy in origin but that?), where sacrifice is understood, where contemporary society offers many fascinating parallels to ancient Greek and Roman society. Nigerian scholars, if they will look at the classics with Nigerian and not European eyes, can interpret the classics to us in ways no European scholar can do."[17]

A note of caution is in order here: It would be problematic to *identify* concepts of reality or cultural features of contemporary West-Africa with corresponding concepts of societies in Mediterranean antiquity, but certainly the former often exhibit certain degrees of closeness to the latter, esp. when compared with perspectives of the modern West.[18] With respect for our concern here – New Testament Healing Narratives and the Category of Numinous Power – it is obvious that cer-

---

17 Quoted in Kwame Bediako, *Christianity in Africa: The renewal of a Non-Western Religion* (Edinburgh: Orbis Books, 1995), 252.

18 Cf. the references to African examples in Meyer Fortes, *Oedipus and Job in West African Religion* (Cambridge: Cambridge University Press, 1959); Walter Burkert, *Creation of the Sacred: Tacks of Biology in Early Religions* (Cambridge: Harvard University Press, 1996).

tain affinities do exist between West-African and ancient Mediterranean experiences of life and the construction of reality. This applies first and foremost to the ever present reality of untimely death and the unpredictable occurrence of disease, and secondly to sickness aetiologies which reckon with the possibility of the involvement of evil spirits as root-cause for the predicament of an individual. At the same time, quite a number of people interpret and communicate an experienced healing in terms of miracle. The realities of ever threatening incurable diseases, of disease causing spirits and of miracle healings are to be presupposed as self-evident in antiquity in general and in Early Christianity in particular. Against this background, Martin Dibelius' rationalistic and romanticized verdict that New Testament miracle healing stories were an expression of a 'Lust am Mirakel' – a delight taken in miraculous events – totally misses the point:[19] New Testament healing stories elucidate the struggle of survival or the struggle to (re)gain health in life-threatening circumstances that were common in antiquity. These stories contain a narrative expression of the Early Christian belief that God might assist them in overcoming sickness and help ward off potentially fatal attacks of evil spirits. The Lord's Prayer asks to deliver us from evil, which could refer to saving and protecting from evil forces. What is at stake in the miracle healing traditions is a matter of life and death. According to the general concept of reality in antiquity, an individual is *not* the master of his or her life and death; he or she is rather *sub-iectus* to both the family or the community and to the powers of the numinous sphere. According to the latter, the visible world is experienced and thought of as embedded in a wider net of activities of various spiritual beings including gods, angels, demons, ancestors, etc. belonging to the invisible, numinous sphere.

With this orientation to the world, it was of utmost importance to avoid the wrath of gods or fall prey to the spell of an evil spirit in order to avoid disasters such as grave illness. This can only be achieved by securing the help of a friendly numinous power. Taking this conception into account, I arrived at a more radical understanding of the significance of the numinous sphere in antiquity compared with positions long taken for granted in New Testament scholarship, according to which numinous powers or evil spirits in antiquity played a less dramatic role. Even Susan Garrett in a recent publication speaks of a mere "influence of invisible powers in affairs of the visible world".[20] I propose the notion that this 'influence' was perceived in antiquity as *all-pervasive* and ever threatening should be taken seriously. In this scenario, it is human beings who hope to counter and 'influence'

19 Martin Dibelius, *Die Formgeschichte des Evangeliums* (Tübingen: Mohr-Siebeck, [6]1971), 171.
20 Susan R. Garrett, "Jesus als Befreier vom Satan und den Mächten" *ZNT* 28 (2011): 14–23, 19.

Ancient Mediterranean World Knowledge System

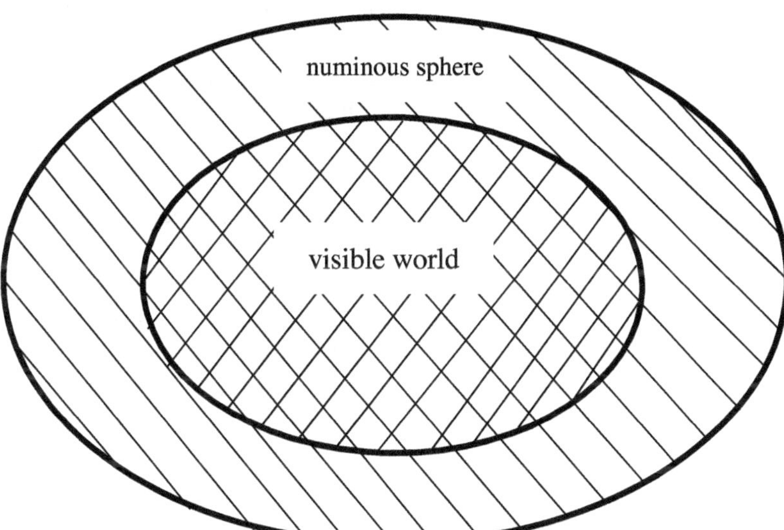

the invisible powers. Thus, humans tried to exercise power through their behaviour, by performing sacrifices or magic, or through intermediaries like priests, healers, or shamans.

It should be noted that this ancient concept of reality is *not* irrational and it was also *not* an expression of simple minded and uneducated populations, even though such judgment has been passed by exegetes – a typical attitude that frequently occurs in cross-cultural studies:

> "People of one nation (or class or society, etc.) may sometimes appear to another to be 'illogical' or 'stupid' or 'incomprehensible' simply because the observer is over a long period of time taking an alien standpoint from which to view their activity, instead to learn their emic patterns of overt and covert behaviour."[21]

This system of world-knowledge was shared by the educated strata of ancient societies. As we learn from Plutarch, there were varying degrees or intensities in reckoning with numinous powers, and only the extremes seemed problematic to

21 Kenneth L. Pike, *Language in Relation to a Unified Theory of the Structure of Human Behavior* (The Hague: Mouton, ²1967), 51. With respect to exegetes like Rudolf Bultmann or Gerd Theißen declaring people who believe in miracles as naïve, primitive, or psychologically instable, cf. Alkier, *Wunder und Wirklichkeit*, 4 and 28.

Plutarch.[22] The reality of the potential involvement of numinous powers in everyday life affairs was self-evident to philosophers from Socrates via Aristotle to Plutarch. Reality was perceived to be more than its reduction to the visible and measurable world. Ancient concepts of the world *extended* reality into the invisible sphere of potent numinous powers or spiritual beings. Their activities could be regarded as spiritual root causes of experiences in the visible world interpreted as direct effects of these activities.

In order to come to a more appropriate, i.e. *emic* understanding of New Testament miracle healing stories, it is necessary to constantly keep in mind the implications of ancient knowledge systems when interpreting these narratives. Since an understanding of the world in terms of the numinous was regarded as self-evident, its implications are at times only presupposed or alluded to in miracle stories, so that the modern reader might have difficulty in grasping what is actually at stake in a particular story. The American anthropologist and linguist Edwar Sapir described this dilemma in cross-cultural communication back in 1927 when he maintained that untrained observers in a foreign culture are constantly tempted to attribute weight to cultural items which might be of rather secondary importance to the cultural insiders while he or she might totally fail to notice or ignore the essential significance of, let us say, a ritual:

> "Let anyone who doubts this try the experiment of making a painstaking report [i.e. an etic one] of the actions of a group of natives engaged in some activity, say religious, to which he has not the cultural key [i.e. a knowledge of the emic system]. If he is a skilful writer, he may succeed in giving a picturesque account of what he sees and hears, or thinks he sees and hears, but the chances of his being able to give a relation of what happens, in terms that would be intelligible and acceptable to the natives themselves, are practically nil. He will be guilty of all manner of distortion; his emphasis will be constantly askew. *He will find interesting what the natives take for granted as a casual kind of behaviour worthy of no particular comment, and he will utterly fail to observe the crucial turning points* in the course of action that give formal significance to the whole in the minds of those who do possess the key to its understanding."[23]

Sapir's research prepared the emic-etic or insider-outsider debate in ethnology and folklore studies in the USA which was developed by his student Kenneth Pike in the fifties, and from the sixties onward, by Pike's protégé Allen Dundes.[24] The

---

22 Plutarch, *Moralia*, 171E-F; cf. Xenophon, *Memorabilia*, 1,1,6–9.

23 Pike, *Language*, 39 (italics: W.K.).

24 Edward Sapir, "The Meaning of Religion" in *The Collected Works of Edward Sapir*, vol. 3, (ed. Regna Darnell; Berlin and New York: de Gruyter, 1999), 134–45; Edward Sapir, "The Unconscious Patterning of Behavior in Society" in *Collected Works* 3, 156–72; Pike, *Language*; Pike, "On

same dynamics described here are at play in the cross-cultural encounter of exegetes and classicists with ancient texts.

One example is the interpretation of Mark 1:29–31 (The mother-in-law of Simon is lying down feverish): "After Jesus approached her he raised her up after he took her hand. And the fever left her, and she served them" (v. 31). A modern reader might overlook the implication of the following phrase: καὶ ἀφῆκεν αὐτὴν ὁ πυρετός. The fever functions grammatically as active subject of the narrative move that immediately brings about healing, or to put it in terms of the Narrative Schema: The activity of the fever *effectuates* the disjunction from the undesirable object that the woman was previously conjoined with – undesirable from the perspective of the woman and her relatives. It seems to be implied that the fever is actually forced out of the woman by the physical connection brought about by Jesus: he takes her by the hand. In short, this is an *exorcism story*. Luke's rendering of the story in 4:38–39 strongly reinforces the presupposition of a numinous power struggle in this case. Here we have Jesus ἐπετίμησεν τῷ πυρετῷ (v. 39) resulting in the fever's withdrawal from the woman. ἐπιτιμάω is a *terminus technicus* in ancient exorcism stories, and we also find the expression in other New Testament exorcism stories such as in Mark 1:25 where Jesus commands an unclean spirit to leave a person, or in Mark 4:39 where Jesus commands the storm to calm down. I realize that it might not be obvious to a modern reader that an *exorcism* is being narrated in the storm stilling episode, with the storm as a numinous spirit being.

Concerning Mark 1:29–31 it should be noted that Simon's mother-in-law, after being liberated from the fever, engages in the activity of "serving them", i.e. the visitors. What was the function of this activity? From a form-critical perspective, this performance would solely signal the *success* of the miracle performance of Jesus. This is certainly one function of this motif, but there is more to it: If "serving them" implies here – in line with general gender expectations in the Mediterranean world of antiquity – that the woman prepares food, then numinous as well as social-communal dimensions are involved, as would be self-evident e.g. to the

the emics and etics of Pike and Harris" in *Emics and Etics: The Insider/Outsider Debate* (ed. Thomas Headland, Kenneth L. Pike and Marvin Harris; Newbury Park: Sage Publications, 1990), 28–47; Pike and Carol V. McKinney, "Understanding Misunderstanding as cross-cultural emic clash" in *The mystery of culture contacts, historical reconstruction, and text analysis: An emic approach* (ed. Kurt R. Jankowsky; Washington: Georgetown University Press, 1996), 39–64; Thomas Headland, "Introduction: A Dialogue Between Kenneth Pike and Marvin Harris on Emics and Etics" in: *Emics and Etics*, 13–27; Alan Dundes, "From Etic to Emic Units in the Structural Study of Folktales," *Journal of American Folktales* 75 (1962): 95–105; Dundes, *The Morphology of North American Indian Folktales* (Helsinki: Suomalainen Tiedeakatemia, 1964).

average West-African reader of the story: In traditional society nobody would take food from a person regarded as polluted by an evil, i.e. sickness causing spirit. People would be afraid to get contaminated, not only with the sickness but – even more dangerous – with the sickness-spirit. Against this background it is remarkable that Jesus establishes *physical* contact with the feverish woman. By means of this touch causing the withdrawal of the fever, the narrator brings out the conviction that *Jesus' purity or divinely bestowed holiness is more contagious and stronger than the impurity of adverse spirits.*[25] At the same time, his very touching and raising the woman up signify the *reintegration* of the woman into her regular communal and family affairs, so we can come to a deeper understanding of what is being communicated in this short passage: *Jesus' integrative purity overrules the disintegrative impurity of adverse spirits.* From here, we can confirm the results of an anthropological study on Jas 5:13–16 by M.C. Albl who concludes that in Early Christian healing rituals, the levels of the individual, the communal, and the spiritual intermingle.[26]

4 Conclusion: The theological significance of New Testament miracle healing stories

It has long been recognized in New Testament studies that the healing and exorcism stories of the Gospels function as narrative expressions of the closeness of God's kingdom. This is certainly correct, but more can be said – here I come back to an insight shared by Rudolf Otto. According to him, the announcement of the kingdom by Jesus was first and foremost a "proclamation of the most numinous object of all, that is, the good news of the kingdom (...). The kingdom however is the *absolute* miracle".[27] Inherent in this statement is a polemic against the reduction of Jesus to a moral teacher and preacher, as was widespread in liberal theology of that time.[28] The kingdom is of utmost *numinous* significance because it is an *extension of God*. According to the Synoptic Gospels, in and through Jesus' per-

25 Cf. Robert R. Beck, *Nonviolent Story: Narrative Conflict Resolution in the Gospel of Mark* (Maryknoll: Orbis Books, 1996).

26 M.C. Albl, "'Are any among you sick?' The health care system in the Letter of James." *JBL* 121/1 (2002): 123–43.

27 Otto, *Das Heilige*, 102.

28 Cf. Adolf v. Harnack, *Das Wesen des Christentums* (Leibzig: J.C. Hinrichs'sche Buchhandlung, 1900); v. Harnack, *Sprüche und Reden Jesu: Die zweite Quelle des Matthäus und Lukas* (Leipzig: J.C. Hinrichs'sche Buchhandlung 1907), especially 173.

formances, the kingdom of God began to spread on earth, pushing away destructive and life threatening spirits working in this world. As we have seen, the miracle healings of Jesus aim at restoring individuals in terms of health, but at the same time affecting communal reintegration and affirming a relationship with God to those stigmatized as spirit possessed. As such, the miracle healing stories can be read as paradigmatic narratives communicating manifestations within the parameters of this world of the all inclusive salvation of God. This, according to Paul, is the basic meaning of the resurrection of the crucified one by God, who identifies 'himself' with Jesus who suffered the most shameful death and God resurrects him. Paul interprets this *divine miracle* in terms of its universal and social significance: God selects the despised ones – the sick and powerless – "that which is not": τὰ μὴ ὄντα (1 Cor 1:28). God establishes 'his' good order of things, overcoming disintegrative and life-threatening forces. Salvation is de-limited and universalized while identity markers causing the separation of people and peoples have been declared invalid as *exclusive* signs of salvation.[29] This constitutes δικαιοσύνη θεοῦ, aiming at the realization of an all inclusive שלום devoid of separation and suffering (cf. Isa 65:17–25; Rev 21:1–4).

---

29 This is the most important insight of *The New Perspective on Paul*, cf. Hendrikus Boers, *The Justification of the Gentiles: Paul's Letters to the Galatians and Romans* (Peabody: Hendrickson 1994); Daniel Boyarin, *A Radical Jew: Paul and the Politics of Identity* (Berkeley and Los Angeles: University of California Press, 1994). Markus Barth was one of the first scholars to recognize the socio-political implications and relevance of Paul's rejection of any notion of justification by works, favoring justification by grace, cf. his almost forgotten article "Jews and Gentiles: The social character of justification in Paul," *Journal of Ecumenical Studies* 5/2 (1968): 241–67, 251: "Thus fellow-man and community with him are not secondary but integral to 'my' acquittal in the process of justification. Justification by Christ, is, therefore, an event which ties man and man together. It is a social happening. Justification by works is, correspondingly, to be identified with anti-social behavior." Barth brings out this meaning dimension of the Pauline figure of justification much clearer in the English version compared with the German original, cf. M. Barth, "Gottes und des Nächsten Recht (Eine Studie über den sozialen Charakter der Rechtfertigung bei Paulus)," in *ΠΑΡΡΗΣΙΑ: Karl Barth zum achtzigsten Geburtstag am 10. Mai 1966* (ed. Eberhard Busch; Zürich: EVZ-Verlag, 1966), 447–69, especially 454.

Heiko Schulz

The Concept of Miracle and the Concepts of Reality

Some Provisional Remarks

> *A naturalist came from a great distance to see the Baal Shem and said: "My investigations show that in the course of nature the Red Sea had to divide at the very hour the children of Israel passed through it. Now what about that famous miracle!" The Baal Shem answered: "Don't you know that God created nature? And he created it so, that at the hour the children of Israel passed through the Red Sea, it had to divide. That is the great and famous miracle!"*
>
> Martin Buber[1]

What I would like to present in the following is primarily, though not exclusively, part of a work in progress. The project I am currently involved in is a book on miracles and the part I have been working on recently – and which in fact I am still struggling with – is a chapter on the *notion* of miracle. If you look at it from an analytic perspective you might want to say that the chapter aims at an exercise in conceptual analysis and clarification. Such a judgment would not be unjustified or beside the point, as I am of the opinion, indeed, that the conceptual issue is of fundamental importance, not only in and as itself, but also to adequately tackle all other pertinent aspects of the subject. Moreover, it seems to me that within current research the conceptual side of the problem has been unduly neglected. This notwithstanding, I often find the existing examples of conceptual analysis overly abstract and technical at best, simplistic or occasionally even dull at worst. Therefore I have taken great pains to also be and remain attentive and sensitive to the purportedly rather marginal aspects of the phenomenon, in order eventually to arrive at something like a genuine, and hopefully also comprehensive, phenomenology of miracles.

Now, even full-fledged phenomenologies tend to be hopelessly ahistorical, due to their more or less stubbornly clinging to the underlying premise of an 'immutable essence' of given phenomena, as these are purportedly manifest as and for themselves within conscious human experience. In light of this difficulty, I was more than pleased some time ago to be challenged by my friend and colleague Stefan Alkier who suggested I should work out an article about the ways in which historically shifting and materially differing conceptions of reality might

1 Buber 1947, 71.

have, and actually have had, a theoretical and/or practical bearing on the issue at hand. Accordingly, I will try in the following to do justice both to his suggestion and to my own current research perspective. First I will present what I take to be provisional results of my conceptual and/or phenomenological efforts (I./II.). Second, I will – albeit very briefly – tackle the question of whether these purely systematical, and thus seemingly free-floating, efforts can be confirmed or at least maintained, once they are historically and dogmatically contextualized by a genuinely biblical (here: New Testament-)perspective on miracles (III.). Finally, and on purely philosophical grounds I will – no less provisionally, as I hasten to add – try to determine if, in which ways, and to what extent different notions of reality might have a bearing upon both the phenomenologically descriptive and epistemically normative dimension of our theme (IV./V.).

I

1. David Corner has recently suggested a useful distinction between three basic types of approaching the miraculous (see Corner 2007, 6–14 and *passim*). *Supernaturalistic* approaches conceive of miracles as supernaturally caused events, which as such cannot be accounted for by drawing on natural (in particular causal) laws alone. A famous case in point is David Hume's definition of miracles as a "violation of the laws of nature" (Hume 1992, 68). *Teleological* approaches conceive of miracles primarily as expressions of divine agency and as such as involving certain divine purposes. Here we may quote Richard Purtill, who maintains that a miracle is "an event in which God temporarily makes an exception to the natural order of things, to show that God is acting" (Purtill 1997, 64).[2] Finally, *contextual* approaches conceive of miracles as events, which can be called miraculous only in a particular context, which as such admits of reacting to them in a contextually appropriate way (e.g., via admiration, awe, gratitude etc.). Thus, for instance, John Hick notes that in order "to be miraculous, an event must be experienced as religiously significant" (Hick 1973, 51).

Corner rightly hastens to add that the three conceptions are not to be considered "mutually exclusive" (ibid., 6), but that they rather accentuate basic – and in fact one-sided[3] – approaches to describe and account for the phenomenon

---

2 See also Woodward's definition of miracles, from a biblical perspective, as "extraordinary acts of God ... by which God reveals His power and His will for His people" (Woodward 2001, 23).

3 In the case of supernaturalism even: flawed, see Corner 2007, 2f., 16; in addition, ibid., chapters 3 and 4.

in question. Accordingly, he himself insists that a miracle must not only refer to something "extraordinary, it must also express divine agency, and possess religious significance of a sort that will allow it to play some role in theistic religious practice" (ibid., 16). Corner does *not* address the question, however, why he takes it for granted that there are just *three* – and in particular *these* three – conceptual types. I suggest that this is all but accidental. Note, for instance, that these conceptualizations seem to be dependent upon, and in fact tacitly repeat, the three fundamental dimensions and themes of modern metaphysics: world (= supernaturalistic type), God (= teleological type) and man (= contextual type). Precisely for this reason, I will in the following replace Corner's categories by more general, fundamental and as such, in my opinion, more appropriate terms; I will thus speak of a *cosmological, theological* and *psychological* (or phenomenological) approach – in short: CA, TA, PA – to miracles instead.

A second reason why Corner's trichotomy can hardly be chosen at random is that all three conceptual types have at least one thing in common: They conceive of miracles as *events*.[4] And closer scrutiny would reveal that events must equally be analyzed in terms of the three basic dimensions or properties sketched out before. Due to space restrictions I cannot dwell on this point,[5] but in paving the way for the following I will at least have to take a brief look at the connectedness of events, in relation to human experience and its uniformity-conditions. The uniformity of human experience requires at least three principles to obtain – I call these the *conceivability* principle, the *regularity* principle and the *similarity* principle. Human experience is capable of uniformity only if it conforms to all three of them at the same time, in a certain way: whatever happens (either as an event *simpliciter* or as an act) must, in order to become part of a uniform experience, be capable of being conceived, grasped or understood – at least roughly or in parts (for instance, with regard to its causal antecedents). This first requirement can only be met, if two further conditions are fulfilled: on the one hand, both the genesis or constitution of an event and its consequences must follow and be capable of being spelled out according to certain (e.g. causal) laws or rules. Now, since no event is completely identical with any other (due, first and foremost, to spatio-temporal differences), this second requirement can only be met if there is at least a basic similarity or analogy to be found between events – *nota bene*, a similarity, which admits of *applying* pertinent laws and rules to any individual case or in-

---

4 This includes the teleological approach, since (here: divine) action can be spelled out as a *type* of event. Thus we may distinguish between an *event simpliciter* and *action* as a special, namely teleological or intentional kind or type of event – though I have to ignore the details and issues concerning that distinction; see Casati/ Varzi 2006, 5f.; Swinburne 1986, 86; Corner 2007, 103f.
5 I have dealt with the issue elsewhere: see Schulz 2013.

stantiated event, either by explaining it backwards or by predicting it. This being said, the category *miracle* would be applicable to all and only those events which suspend or violate or destroy the uniformity of experience, in at least one of the respects just mentioned.

2. Now, if and as long as we consider causality a chief principle of regularity within human experience and understanding of the world, three fundamental definitions of miracle suggest themselves as possible and *prima facie* plausible. I take these to be fundamental, because they roughly correspond not only to the three principles of uniform experience just described, but also to the three key dimensions of events mentioned above.[6]

(1) Event E is a miracle, if and only if it is apparently impossible, due to its *having no cause.*
(2) Event E is a miracle, if and only if it is apparently impossible, due to its *cause being unknowable and / or unknown.*
(3) Event E is a miracle, if and only if it is apparently impossible, due to its *cause being supernatural or transcendent* (= radically different from any natural or immanent cause, which as such conforms to the principles of uniform human experience).

It is plain to see that a miracle defined along the lines of option number (1) violates the regularity, number (2) the conceivability, and number (3) the similarity principle. Moreover, option (1) defines miracles by putting a special emphasis on the (oddity of the) event itself, option (2) on its witness – the human subject and its awareness and interpretation of the respective event –, whereas option (3) accentuates its unique origin and cause. Aesthetically speaking, we might as well say that the first definition is product-, the second recipient- and the third producer-oriented. Likewise, option one is, metaphysically considered, world-, option two is man- and option three is God-centered. Combining these triads we yield the following matrix:

6 Please note again that each of the following notions merely brings to the fore a special accent or a particular emphasis on one of the aspects in question; each of them functions as a mere abstraction for analytical purposes, rather than as designations of ontologically distinct and independent entities.

Definition	Uniformity-principle affected	Event-theoretical aspect	Metaphysical aspect	Aesthetical aspect
1. Event E is a miracle, if and only if it is apparently impossible, due to its *having no cause.*	Principle of regularity	Ontological: the event itself	World	Product
2. Event E is a miracle, if and only if it is apparently impossible, due to its *cause being unknowable and / or unknown.*	Principle of conceivability	Phenomenological: the self-givenness of the event in the conscious experience of its addressee and/or witness	Man	Recipient
3. Event E is a miracle, if and only if it is apparently impossible, due to its *cause being transcendent.*	Principle of similarity	Causal: the relation of event and cause	God	Producer

It is worth noting that my previous event-account requires that all three of the latter's dimensions and properties must be given and actualized somehow, in order for (any understanding of) an event to be possible at all; however, the account does *not* require, preclude or necessitate any specific *way* in which such actualization has to take place. Likewise, no concept of *miracle* (as a certain kind of event) will be sufficient and convincing as an explanation, unless it proves capable of drawing on and actually incorporating all three fundamental event-dimensions described above. This notwithstanding, no such concept requires, precludes or necessitates any specific way in which these dimensions have to be engaged. Hence, some of the definitions suggested above may be compatible with or even supplementary to each other, whereas others are incompatible. *In concreto*, definition one is obviously incompatible with both two and three, whereas three (provided it is true) runs counter to one. By contrast, definition two precludes one, but not three – at least in some weaker or more liberal reading: the fact that some person (let us call him Peter) does not and cannot *know* the cause of event E does not in principle rule out the possibility of E to be caused by some *transcendent entity* (e.g. God). Thus, option two can, but need not be combined with option three.[7]

7 For example, a notion of miracle along the lines of definition number two above is to be found in Augustine already: a miracle "is not against nature, but against the most common order of nature" (Augustine 1947, vol. 2, 329 = XXI/ 8). That miracles do in fact have a cause, though a super-

Finally, option three can be spelled out as a variant of two and it is fairly easy to see why. All known and/or knowable causes must meet at least three requirements: First, they must be immanent *qua natural* causes; secondly, they must be necessary and sufficient for causally explaining backwards, and predicting forwards, *particular* events as a consequence and effect. Finally, in order for the latter to be possible they must admit of *repeatedly* doing their job and thus of repeatedly being found successful in fulfilling their explanatory and predictive function. Now, it is plain to see that transcendent and as such supernatural causes do not and cannot meet any of these requirements. Therefore, if we claim that 'the cause of event E is transcendent' instead of just claiming 'it is unknown and/or unknowable,' the only difference[8] will be that the former claim is contrary, the latter contradictory in relation to the claim 'the cause of event E is known and/or knowable.' Now, denying the truth of some judgment ('A is B') by claiming the contrary ('A is C') *implies* a contradiction ('A is not B'), but not *vice versa*. From which follows that the judgment, 'the cause of event E is transcendent,' ends up being no more than a stronger, more specific and at the same time epistemically riskier way of saying, 'the cause of event E is unknown and/or unknowable.'

Moreover, the idea of 'violating' a natural law in a stricter, namely ontological – instead of merely a descriptive or statistical (see Gregersen 2005, 1725ff.) – sense is bound up with and entailed in definition number one only. If we conceive of a miracle as an event, which happens to *have* no cause, we are saying in effect that such an event 'violates' the principle of regularity, and this by lacking or suspending any causal connectedness with other events. If, by contrast, we subscribe to either definition two or three, we are no longer compelled to take refuge in the violation-idea, at least not in this stronger sense. In both cases we admit that we simply do not (and perhaps also cannot) know the particular natural cause of a given event – due, for instance, to the latter's dissimilarity to any known causal nexus – and thus leave room for the possibility that eventually there might *be* some immediate (as in two) or mediating (as in three) natural cause for the event in question. Miracles described along the lines of definitions

natural and/or transcendent one (see above, definition number three) is emphasized, for instance by C.S. Lewis (see Lewis 1947, 5 and 60). As to a cumulative view, more exactly a combination of definitions two and three see, e.g., Thomas Aquinas, STh I,105,7 (Aquinas 1951, 67f.). An interesting attempt to show that miracles may be acts of God, while simultaneously being considered events *lacking* any cause, is made and defended by Corner (2007, 88–91); see, for instance, ibid., 89 (my emphasis): "Saying that the water's turning into wine [see John 2:1–10] *has* no cause is entirely compatible with saying God [miraculously] turned the water into wine, where this refers to an action on the part of God."

8 More exactly: the only *de re*-difference, for *de dicto* things may be otherwise.

two and three are therefore violations in a considerably weaker, primarily epistemic sense, as opposed to those which are taken to suspend the principle of regularity, ontologically conceived.

II

1. So far I have restricted my account to some familiar and at least *prima facie* plausible attempts to define miracles, namely by invoking the idea of causality and its violation. To be sure, the notion of causality is intricate enough in its own right, even more so in relation to the miracle-issue,[9] and as such we should definitely not take it lightly. This notwithstanding, I find it useful to expand on it in our present context, and this in particular for heuristic reasons. On the one hand the causal notion of miracles confronts us with an extremely one-sided, yet at the same time historically influential approach to the problem of miracles – in particular, within the context of post-enlightenment Western culture. On the other hand, even the most uncompromising defender cannot but admit that the approach willy-nilly confirms the obvious irreducibility of the three fundamental dimensions of miracles sketched out above. In that sense the account is heuristically illuminating to the extent that it involuntarily, as it were, speaks the truth. Finally, the causal account also (and again: more or less tacitly) testifies to a deep-seated, apparently ineradicable intuition underlying any notion of miracle: the intuition, namely, that the latter must be something seemingly impossible by natural standards, such that to understand and realize its possibility is, in any case, way beyond human capacity.

Despite these (at least heuristic) merits, a purely causal account of miracles must be deemed seriously flawed, and this in particular, because it fails to capture the properly religious nuances of the phenomenon (see also Corner 2007, 11). Sure enough, any event apparently having no (or at least: no natural or otherwise known) cause may elicit surprise and astonishment on the part of its addressee and/or witness, and as such it may be capable of meeting an essential requirement of miracles, according to the psychological account.[10] But this alone will hardly qualify as sufficient. George Schlesinger (1997, 362f.) relates the story of a church choir in Beatrice (Nebraska), which met once every week for practicing;

9 See Evers 2007 for a detailed historical and systematical account of the relation between (the belief in) miracles and (the notion of) causality as a natural law; see also Corner 2007, chapters 1 and 2; Levine 2005; Gregersen 2005; Hughes 1992 and Adams 1992.
10 Remember that the term 'miracle' is derived from the Latin verb *mirari*, to wonder.

on March 1, 1950 all choir members happened to be ten minutes late – fortunately enough, as it turned out, because shortly before they arrived, the building where they regularly met was destroyed by an explosion. This strange and fortunate coincidence, resting, among other things, upon the absolute improbability of *all* members being late on the same occasion, might at least generally lend itself to being explained within a causal framework; however, *as* a coincidence – that is, as a singular, absolutely improbable constellation of factors – it lacks the conditions of adequately being accounted for in terms of the various requirements for such explanations as specified above. We might say that even though this coincidence probably *had* a cause (and a *particular* one at that), we do not and perhaps cannot ever *know* it. Even so, the decisive fact remains that unless we invoke at least the third variant of a causal miracle-account, which as such requires that the event in question be couched in terms of a *transcendent* (for instance, divine) cause, we will in all probability refuse to call the unexpected rescue of the choir members a miracle in the proper sense; and this holds true even if we admit that the latter may have been personally highly significant for the people involved.

If, by contrast, we adopt beforehand a genuinely religious or at least metaphysical view of miraculous causality (along the lines of definition three above), it turns out quickly that we can *in toto* do away with the idea of a miracle *qua* violation. Thus conceived, this latter idea seems not even sufficient, much less necessary, but in fact merely accidental for the possibility of a miracle in the stricter sense. Just one example may suffice in order to substantiate my claim. As is well known, Martin Luther had a strong bias towards an apocalyptic interpretation of eschatology, such that he expected an immediately imminent end of the world as we know it. In light of this eschatology he maintained that the proper miracle in the realm of nature is to be found in its *conservatio* – the divine act of sustaining the world despite and *vis à vis* its radical sinfulness.[11] Thus, for Luther the continuous existence of the world, depending every minute on God's gracious act of re-establishing and preserving it, appeared to be completely improbable and inexplicable in the first place, and for both reasons Luther saw it as a constant source of awe and gratitude. Sure enough, a miracle thus conceived was still taken by him to refer to something *extraordinary* (and also as religiously highly significant, of course[12]); however, its extraordinary character was not at all coex-

---

11 See, for instance, Luther 1964, 356: "Ja, wunder ists, das uns die Erde tregt und die Sonne noch leuchtet, So doch für unser undankbarkeit billich der ganz himel solt schwarz und die Erde versalzen werden."

12 Note that the former does not *imply* the latter, nor the latter the former: an event may be, and may be experienced, as extraordinary without necessarily being, and taken to be, religiously significant – and *vice versa* (see Corner 2007, 132).

tensive with or reducible to its being irregular in a scientific sense, and thus tantamount to any violation of the causal nexus. Rather, it was bound up with the surprising fact of regularity itself – a regularity defying all attempts at sufficiently explaining its possibility in mundane terms.[13]

Luther's view is noteworthy in yet another respect, for it leads to the conclusion that astonishment, admiration and awe (on the part of an event's addressee and/or witness) can simply be considered a logical and psychological *implication* of perceiving the respective event as an instance of divine action. Regardless of whether Peter tends to believe that some event or state of affairs lends itself to being accounted for in purely immanent (e.g. causal) terms or not, he will in any case be susceptible to perceiving and interpreting it as a miracle, as soon and as long as he believes it to be a manifestation of divine action. By contrast, many things may strike us as surprising, astonishing, significant or even awe-inspiring *without* as such qualifying as miracles in the proper sense of the word – and this regardless of whether the respective event should be or is in fact perceived by its recipient as open to immanent causal explanation. Consider, for instance, Philo's arithmetical observation (related in Hume's *Dialogues*, part IX) that, surprisingly enough, "the products of 9 compose always either 9 or some lesser product of 9" (Hume 1992, 253). Philo comments that to "a superficial observer, so wonderful a regularity may be admired as the effect either of chance or design: but a skilful algebraist immediately concludes it to be the work of necessity, and demonstrates, that it must for ever result from the nature of these numbers" (ibid.). Chiefly important here is the fact that even if it were *not* possible to transform the purported 'miracle of regularity' into mathematical necessity and thus to dissolve it, the phenomenon in question would still hardly qualify as a miracle. More exactly: it would not count as such, unless the surprise and astonishment elicited by its discovery would be accounted for, by its recipient, in terms of a genuinely *religious* or at least metaphysical interpretation, according to which this strange arithmetical coincidence calls for being traced back to some pre-established harmony, in particular to divine purpose and design. And such 'pious' interpretation does not invariably emerge from the former experience.

This notwithstanding, I am far from denying the irreducible and indispensable function of wonder for the discovery and identification of miracles as such.[14] In fact, wonder (coming in a variety of forms, such as surprise, astonishment,

---

13 For a related idea in Jewish thought see, for instance, Buber 1990, 186; see also Corner's account of the Exodus-miracle (the parting of the Red Sea): Corner 2007, 15f.

14 Thomas Aquinas has repeatedly emphasized the point; see, for instance, Aquinas 1951, 67f. (STh I,105,7).

amazement, admiration, awe etc.) dissolves actuality into possibility, as it were, thus giving rise to the question if, and how, that which immediately appeared to be so and so, could have ever become what it appeared to be in the first place. Although still remaining on this side of reflection and doubt, a person in wonder or amazement discovers something deeply ambiguous: how was E (= a particular event or state of affairs) possible? And yet: how was it possible that *not*-E? In wonder, awe or surprise the wondrous event appears to be equally and simultaneously possible (for it is experienced as actual, and whatever is actual must have been possible in some way) and impossible (for one cannot imagine and grasp the conditions of its possibility). This paradoxical ambiguity is experienced as strange, or even repelling, and fascinating at the same time; therefore Kierkegaard considers wonder itself a deeply ambivalent state of consciousness (see, e.g., SKS 5, 399 / TD, 18) – a sympathetic antipathy and an antipathetic sympathy, if you will.[15] A full-fledged account of the nature and function(s) of wonder in the context of our present topic cannot be given here; suffice it to say that wonder is obviously necessary, but not sufficient for a miracle to be possible.

5. Now, if we express the upshot of my previous analysis in a genuinely theological (instead of just a generically metaphysical) fashion, we might put it like this: a miracle is an act of God, perceived as such, period. On the one hand, if any such perception is missing, we will never arrive at something truly worthy of being called miraculous; on the other hand, wherever it is present (that is, wherever we see God at work), we perceive miracles. God can only do, what *only* God can do; and miracles can only be done by *God* (or at least some divine power). Thus, everything done by God is and must be perceivable as a *miracle*. Kierkegaard puts it this way: “God can appear to man *only* in the miracle, i.e., *as soon* as he sees God he sees a miracle.” (JJ:270, SKS 18, 226 / JP 1, 6; my emphasis) In other words, perceiving God is not only necessary (see above), but also sufficient for perceiving a miracle, whereas perceiving the latter – which in turn presupposes faith (see Kierkegaard, SKS 4, 290 f. / PF, 93) – is necessary for the former.

Now, compared to this genuinely *theological* approach, the *cosmological* view suggesting, at least in its strongest version, that every miraculous event must *per se* entail some violation of a law of nature, has only a minor conceptual role to

---

15 As such it also accentuates the *subject* of wonder, triggering the latter’s awareness of him- or herself as the sole and decisive instance of determining how to dissolve the ambiguity: ‘How shall *I* relate to and cope with such ambiguity – and why and for what purpose am I addressed or struck by it in the first place?’ As to an in-depth-analysis of wonder and its far-reaching philosophical implications, see Verhoeven 1972.

play; for any such violation has shown to be accidental at best.[16] Finally, the *psychological* (or more exactly: the phenomenological) account just adds another necessary, albeit not a sufficient condition to the mix. And here it is of vital importance, namely in terms of avoiding possible misunderstandings, to give due credit to the idea that any miracle, conceived in the way described, must be – and must be conceivable as – an *extraordinary* event: not necessarily in the sense of a causal irregularity *qua* violation of a law of nature, but definitely as an astonishing, wondrous or awe-inspiring event, which indicates that it exceeds any human cognitive and practical capacity, and as such prompts the idea of a divine purpose and/or cause. This being said, I would even go so far as to maintain that either what we are talking about is to be conceived of as humanly possible – or we are talking about miracles. *Tertium non datur.* With these restrictions and specifications in mind we may sum up the foregoing analysis in schematic form as follows:

Miracle-Condition	According to the PA	According to the CA	According to the TA
Accidental	–	X	–
Sufficient	–	–	–
Necessary	X	–	–
Necessary and Sufficient	–	–	X

III

I pointed out at the beginning of my paper that the account presented so far may evoke the impression of a more or less free-floating endeavor, due chiefly to the fact that I relied throughout on certain basic intuitions, combined with a phenomenologically flavored attempt at conceptual analysis and clarification. Moreover, one might suspect that my account can hardly claim to stand on solid ground, as long as it fails to determine if, and to what extent, it is either in full agreement or at least principally compatible with the pertinent testimony of any specific religious tradition. Hence, what I intend to do in the following – if only very briefly and in

16 In a forthcoming article (see Schulz 2013) I argue that in Kierkegaard's view an ontological (i.e. strictly deterministic) account of causality cannot even be deemed *accidental* for a coherent concept of miracle to be possible, but rather as a sufficient condition of the latter's *impossibility*. The reason is that (a) miracles are to be considered a kind of event, (b) events are possible only, if freedom is (not only logically, but also) metaphysically possible, and (c) strict determinism denies and in fact precludes the latter.

passing – is to check whether the conceptual analysis defended so far meshes with a genuinely Christian – or more exactly: a New Testament – view of miracles. I argue that it does, indeed.

To begin with, it can hardly be denied that the miracle-theme is of major importance for the New Testament as a whole, in particular, but by no means exclusively, within the context of the four gospels.[17] Not only do we find an intricate, if tacit, typology of miracles ranging from epiphanies to exorcisms; healing; punitive; gift; deliverance miracles; resuscitations and so forth (see Alkier 2001, 296–301; Alkier 2005, 1719) – but we also encounter sophisticated accounts of who does and who can perform miracles (Jesus, demons, disciples etc.), as well as who is and can be considered a possible addressee, witness and/or medium of miraculous events or actions (again, Jesus, demons, apostles, also nonhuman beings: see, e.g., Matt 21:18–22). Moreover, the relation of miracle and faith – in terms of specifying the conditions of performing, mediating, identifying and appropriating a miracle – is a recurrent, albeit tricky theme, especially in the gospels (see Grimmlinger 1963, 62–74). We also find hints as to a critical assessment of the human quest for and dependence upon miracles and signs (see, for instance, Mark 8:11f.). Finally, scholars have rightly pointed out that the miracle-topic receives varying, and in fact at times divergent, treatments in the New Testament sources, depending on the overall theological perspective and intention of the respective author(s), plus the significance and function of the former topic within this overarching frame of reference.[18]

This variety notwithstanding, it seems hardly far-fetched to maintain that a careful exegetical analysis will yield not only a comprehensive, but also a fairly coherent, picture of the New Testament view of miracles. One problem looms large, though: the biblical concept of miracle itself. Sure enough, many stories related in the texts, such as the virgin birth of Jesus, his walking on water or stilling of the storms, his healing of the ten lepers, feeding of the 5000 or resuscitation of Lazarus will easily pass for miracle stories – and have in fact always done so – for unbiased readers past and present. And yet, it is not easy to see if, in which sense, and to what extent the New Testament authors actually intend to tell or re-tell these stories *as* miracle-stories. For on the one hand this is not normally part of the narratives as such;[19] and on the other hand the texts operate with a whole array of different, if semantically closely related and functionally subsidiary ex-

---

17 As to the latter, see the comparative matrix in Bowden 2005, 759.

18 See Alkier 2005, 1720ff.; Grimmlinger 1963, 52–74; Woodward 2001, 98–136.

19 It is worth noting, however, that there are also discursive and thus non-narrative treatments of the topic to be found in the New Testament writings, in particular in the letters of the *Corpus Paulinum*; see Alkier 2001 and 2005, 1720.

pressions, yet without ever making any attempt at explicitly defining the term miracle itself. Now let me, as a starting-point, simply list what I take to be key expressions in this regard (see also Alkier 2005, 1719; Grimmlinger 1963, 60 ff.), and this by utilizing three already familiar rubrics:

Event (= CA)	**Cause (= TA)**	**Effect (= PA)**
Thaúma	*Dýnamis/ dynámeis*	*[Thaúma]*
[Parádoxon]	*Érgon*	*Parádoxon*
Téras		*[Téras]*
Semeíon		*[Semeíon]*

The first column contains four basic categories accentuating key characteristics of the miraculous event itself. Column two refers to God and/or the numinous power or powers, which are said to be capable of and responsible for those events, whereas the last column reflects actual or possible effects on the recipient – that is, the addressee and/or witness of a miraculous event. One may notice also that, for instance, the term *semeíon* is listed under two rubrics. The simple reason is that (not only) in the present context a sign has to be spelled out *both* as characterizing the respective event or action itself (for instance, Jesus' miraculous healings as signs of the presence of the Kingdom of God), *and* the recipient who interprets the events in question as eschatological signs in the way described. In general, the appearance of one and the same term under different rubrics is meant to point to an analogous, yet semiotically different function of the respective term under more than one rubric. The brackets, on the other hand, simply indicate a derivative usage, so that a term without brackets is to be considered primary. It goes without saying that here, like in all other cases, we are neither dealing with semantically identical nor mutually exclusive, but rather complementary aspects of one and the same phenomenon under varying descriptions, accents and rubrics.[20]

Now, whereas *thaúma* (normally in verbal form: *thaumázein*) refers to any event prompting wonder or amazement, *semeíon* points to the signifying nature and function of those events. Frequently the events themselves are said to evoke an overwhelming, at times even violent and terrifying, impression; in these cases the term *téras* is used, normally in syntagmatical form (*semeía kaì térata*). Moreover, *any* miraculous event narrated in the New Testament is to be interpreted, according to its authors, as a divine or numinous act, an *érgon*, which in turn must be conceived of as being rooted in certain numinous and as such transhuman

20 Here and in the following I rely more or less on Alkier 2005, 1719 f.

powers, *dynámeis*. Finally, the addressee and/or witness of such events is often presented in such a way as to experience these as unexpected, amazing, extraordinary, at times even absurd or inconsistent – in short: as *parádoxa*.

Now, in the present context it is not so much the usage of these terms and/or their respective meaning which appears to be of specific interest, but the fact, rather, that they mesh perfectly with the three basic dimensions or properties of miracles (and *a fortiori* of events *simpliciter*) sketched out above. I take this as a first piece of evidence for the truth, at least for the contextual and exegetical adequacy, of my conceptual account. More important is a second observation: throughout the New Testament writings we do not find, to the best of my knowledge, any hints as to what I have coined the causal account of miracles. On the one hand this does not at all come as a surprise, since, as is well known, the obsession with causality as a paradigm of natural laws and correspondingly, the concept of miracle as a violation of the latter, does not proliferate prior to the Enlightenment-period. On the other hand it strikes me as remarkable that although we certainly have no reason to imply that the people of the first and second centuries were lacking in any notion of cause and effect,[21] they nevertheless do not invoke such a notion, much less that of a natural law, when it comes to dealing with the nature and meaning of miracles. What appears to be of chief importance for them instead is that the uniformity of their ordinary experience admits of being momentarily suspended or 'interrupted'[22] by extraordinary events, which as such testify to the presence of some divine and/or numinous, but in any case strictly transhuman, power. Thus explained, however, the biblical notion of miracle seems to me to harmonize perfectly with, and in fact supports, my earlier proposal to conceive of miraculous events as divine or numinous acts perceived as such.

IV

In his detailed comparison of miracle stories and their meaning in Christianity, Judaism, Buddhism, Hinduism, and Islam, Kenneth Woodward notes that what "constitutes a miracle within each religious tradition is defined to a great extent

21 As to the Hellenistic background of and impact on Christian thought with regard to the ideas of nature, natural law, necessity, fate etc. see, for instance, Bultmann 1986, 128–33, 147 f. and 158–64; cf. also Keener 2011, 867 ff.

22 I am following Alkier's terminology here: "Das W. ist im NT Friktion, eine Unterbrechung der Alltagserfahrung durch das Wirken einer Kraft, die menschliche Möglichkeiten übersteigt." (Alkier 2005, 1721)

by the tradition itself" (Woodward 2001, 24). Here the author seems to suggest that a miracle-definition, which as such would have to be universally valid and thus also across the boundaries of each positive religion, is simply not to be had. And as we can never hope to arrive at the standpoint of such universality in the matter at hand, our search for a *concept* of miracle will be in vain, except for the irreducibly particular and historically varying accounts provided by each religious tradition itself. Thus conceived, miracles appear, for instance, as "signs of the continuing power and presence of God in this world (for Jews, Christians and Muslims), of the continuing power of the diverse gods and goddesses (in Hinduism), and of the continuing power of the Dharma, or teachings, of the Buddha – and in some Buddhist traditions, of the enduring presence of the Buddha himself" (ibid.). Now, if Woodward indeed subscribed to conceptual relativism or historicism, he would simply contradict himself. For one thing, there is still a common essential trait to be found in all of the descriptions just quoted: according to Woodward, a miracle is generally to be conceived of as a sign, and more specifically a sign of the continuing power and presence of the divine, or at least of something numinous, in this world. Secondly, the author provides, although reluctantly, a definition himself – a definition which in turn specifies what such divine manifestation of continuing power and presence actually consists in.[23]

Now in my opinion, this somewhat ambivalent result suggests that we have to take seriously both the irreducible universality *and* particularity of religious and non-religious worldviews – at any rate, if what we strive for is to fully do justice to their respective view of miracles. Such two-dimensional sensitivity seems also and in particular advisable, when it comes to investigating and assessing the impact of what may be coined a 'conception of reality' within a given worldview. The idea behind this notion is not so much that individuals (and in fact also larger social, historical and cultural unities) are operating on the basis of an – either explicit or tacit – ontology, meaning a theory of *reality as such* (*realitas*). What is meant, rather, is that they operate on the basis of certain underlying assumptions about what *counts as real* (*reale*). What is at stake here, therefore, is an extensional rather than an intensional view, and a largely tacit one at that. What counts as real is and appears, in turn, as invariably bound up with certain equally tacit assumptions about the presuppositions, scope and limits of reason, rationality and science; about the nature, form and function (both epistemic and moral) of

23 "*A miracle is an unusual or extraordinary event that is in principle perceivable by others, that finds no reasonable explanation in ordinary human abilities or in other known forces that operate in the world of time and space, and that is the result of a special act of God or the gods or of human beings transformed by efforts of their own through asceticism and meditation.*" (Woodward 2001, 28.)

emotions and attitudes; about standards of conduct and behavior; about personal and cultural values; about the content of and (in-)compatibility between worldviews, and so forth. Following Stefan Alkier (who in turn draws on Umberto Eco's terminology), we may say that the overarching unities, in which such conceptions of reality appear as an integral part, may be called *encyclopedias*; they are defined as the whole of a conventionalized cultural knowledge within particular social entities (see Alkier 2001, 74) – for example, the Roman empire, the early church, the French Enlightenment and so forth.

Of special hermeneutical importance is the fact that within each encyclopedia we find an endless array of 'universes of discourse:' texts, games, conversational conventions etc., each with their own principles, rules and the corresponding ontological and practical commitments. Now, since the encyclopedias, along with their respective conceptions of reality, are subject to (sometimes radical) historical change, we have to expect and to cope with considerable hermeneutical difficulties when it comes to understanding, explaining and adjudicating other conceptions of reality, and the respective encyclopedia of which they are a part. For instance, we do not share with the writers and the addressees of the biblical texts a common universe of discourse, and probably not their deepest ontological commitments either (see Alkier 2001, 77), so the stakes for misinterpreting them are high. We have to reckon with their world as a world of strangers, before we can ever hope to achieve a deeper and more adequate understanding of it.

Now, taken as a regulative hypothesis (see Alkier 2001, 72f.), the idea of historically varying encyclopedias and conceptions of reality seems to me to be of considerable hermeneutical value, and this also in our present context. Successfully applied, the idea may help us better understand certain descriptive implications of our theme and thus guide our attempts at answering questions like the following: how do other religions (or Christianity within other encyclopedias) conceive of miracles – and why so? How do they specify the extension of the term? How do they describe the function of miracles or of miracle narratives, and why in this particular way? How do they conceive of the possibility of miracles and what reasons do they give for or against it? Who can perform miracles according to their view, and why? How do they account for the relation between miracle and rationality? Which role do they ascribe to faith in the matter at hand? How do they specify the identifiability-conditions of miracles? Finally, and in particular: does their respective view of miracles express an underlying conception of reality (in the sense described above), and if so, which one?

V

1. As I said before, the idea of historically, socially and probably also geographically varying encyclopedias, including among other things certain tacit conceptions of reality (viz. conceptions of what counts as real), seems to me to be hermeneutically fruitful. At any rate it appears to be fruitful in a heuristic way, namely as sort of a regulative idea. If, for instance, we try to make sense of the seemingly outlandish beliefs of some other individual, group or culture as a whole, we should withstand the rash conclusion that these are simply false and/or irrational; instead, we are well advised for the time being to look at them as possibly consistent, and perhaps unavoidable, expressions of an encyclopedia apparently at odds with our own. For in that case (and perhaps only so) a deeper understanding of these beliefs, together with their connectedness and proper function within an overarching worldview, in which they occupy a well-defined place by serving the coherence of the whole, becomes possible. And yet, understanding is not explaining, any more than describing is judging, or pardoning forgiving. Accordingly, a deeper *understanding* (in terms of the idea of differing encyclopedias) does not save us from the separate and unique task of *assessing the truth and viability* of the views in question. And if I am not mistaken, the encyclopedia-idea as such is and cannot be of much help here.

Let me expand on the point by invoking a helpful distinction, introduced by Wayne Proudfoot, between *descriptive* and *explanatory reductionism* (Proudfoot 1985, 196ff.). Suppose, for instance, Peter is running from what he takes to be a bear – erroneously, as it turns out, for in reality it is just a tree which he mistook for a bear. If we *described* Peter's conduct by saying 'Peter is running from a tree,' such description would be reductionist – and as such inappropriate. Adequately describing Peter's behavior requires understanding it, and understanding it is in turn dependent upon the ability and willingness to make sense of it in terms of the description and interpretation (actually or at least hypothetically) provided by Peter himself. We deprive ourselves of the chance to understand his behavior if, and as long as, we impose a reductionist description upon it, in other words a description which substantially deviates from the one he himself would be prepared to give and rightly be willing to accept as adequate.

This notwithstanding, it seems perfectly possible and also legitimate to *explain* Peter's behavior in a manner *deviating* from his own (description and) explanation, namely by 'reducing' it to what in effect has, *ex hypothesi*, turned out to be the one and only true account: Peter is running from a tree, which he mistook for a bear. Note that such an explanation does justice both to his own experience and interpretation of the situation – plus the behavior to which the latter gave rise – and to the actual truth about the matter at hand. Strictly speaking, what is at our disposal, both in the case at hand and in general, are four options, two of which have to be deemed adequate and two inadequate. In the present case the following picture emerges:

	Description	**Explanation**
Reductionist	Peter is running from a tree. [= inadequate]	Peter is running from a tree, which he mistook for a bear. [= adequate]
Non-Reductionist	Peter is running from what he took to be a bear. [= adequate]	Peter is running from a bear. [= inadequate]

2. This table can easily be transferred to the miracle-issue, or more exactly, to the problem of miracle-reports. Suppose Peter claims to have perceived a miraculous event, for instance the resuscitation of a deceased person. Given the four options above we might then try to explain and/or describe his perception (plus the corresponding report) in the following manner:

	Description	**Explanation**
Reductionist	Peter perceived an outward projection of his own wishful thinking. [= inadequate]	Peter perceived an outward projection of his own wishful thinking, which he mistook for a miracle. [= ?]
Non-Reductionist	Peter perceived what he took to be a miracle. [= adequate]	Peter perceived a miracle. [= ?]

The first thing to note (apart from the two question marks, to which I will return shortly) is that we have here on the descriptive level an obvious analogy to Proudfoot's bear-example: as opposed to the second description, the first description of Peter's perception is obviously a rationalistically flavored version of reductionism, which as such has to be considered inadequate. In general we might say that in order not to misunderstand or radically misrepresent miracle-narratives, it is of vital importance to withstand the temptation of describing these reports – or the beliefs which gave rise to them – in such reductionist (in particular: rationalist) fashion. Of course, the danger of misrepresentation looms large, whenever and as soon as we are confronted with someone relating rather outlandish perceptions, beliefs or experiences, as in the case of Peter's miracle-report. Here the ideas of varying encyclopedias may serve as a useful heuristic reminder not to give in to rash conclusions within the explanatory, much less the purely descriptive, realm of enquiry.

This need to abstain from rash conclusions becomes even more apparent when certain ontological assumptions (= tacit conceptions of what counts as real) are part and parcel of the respective views, such that ignoring these assumptions even makes us fail to discover and acknowledge basic *similarities or parallels* between our own encyclopedia and the one seemingly at odds with it. Thus, for instance, Stefan Alkier has rightly pointed out that the New Testament-conception of reality implies that a miracle can only fulfill its *symbolic* function of bearing witness to the presence of the Kingdom of God if, and as long as, it is rightly to be conceived of as *actually having happened* (see Alkier 2005, 1721). As an example underscoring Alkier's point, we might refer to Matthew's testimony of Jesus' answer to the question raised by John's disciples, if Jesus was in fact 'the one who is to come' (Matt 11:3). As a reply, Matthew has Jesus simply point to his miraculous deeds: "[T]he blind see again, and the lame walk, those suffering from virulent skin-diseases are cleansed, and the deaf hear, the dead are raised to life and the good news is proclaimed to the poor; and blessed is anyone who does not find me a cause of falling." (Matt 11:4–5) In my opinion, Alkier makes an important hermeneutical observation here, which as such testifies both to Matthew's view of miracles in general and to a corresponding (if tacit) notion of reality and its theological and epistemic implications, in particular. But his point is noteworthy in yet another respect, as it admits of building an epistemic bridge between the encyclopedia of early Christianity and that of modernity. Provided we can make sense of the symbolic function of miracles (as salvific signs of the impending and yet also already present Kingdom of God) at all, we will in all probability be able to do so only by virtue of some tacit ontological assumption that we, not (?) surprisingly, *share* with the New Testament authors, at least with the gospel of Matthew: the assumption that such function can only be realized – in fact, it can only make sense – if that which is supposed to fulfill that function (the miraculous event) has actually taken place.

3. This being said *in favor* of the encyclopedia-idea it is time now for a *caveat*: we should not dismiss or take all too lightly the fact that the previous deliberation is located on a purely descriptive level. As such it leaves the *epistemic* question largely unaffected, and thus also the issue of explanatory reductionism versus non-reductionism. To be sure, there is an important epistemic and/or explanatory difference between the two examples sketched out above. Whereas, in the case of Peter's flight from the purported bear we presuppose (and rightly so) that there is a third-person-perspective available, admitting of a definite and objective decision as to the correct explanation of Peter's behavior, no such overarching perspective is available in the case of the miracle-report: we simply do not and

cannot know for sure – at least not for the time being – which explanation must be considered correct.[24]

This notwithstanding, I am hesitant with regard to the epistemic scope, or more exactly the actual and/or possible apologetic cash-value, of such a (temporary?) stalemate. By contrast, there is at least one thing I am pretty sure about: the idea of differing encyclopedias, plus the notion of varying conceptions of reality as an integral part of the former, will not and cannot be of much help in addressing these issues. To begin with, in the biblical example mentioned above it would surely be rash to conclude, without any further ado, that Matthew himself *believed* in the facticity of the miracles which he related to his readers as actually having taken place (and as symbolizing the Kingdom of God). More importantly though, even *if* he did, we are still left with merely being entitled to infer that, in his opinion, these miracles *must* have actually happened, if and as long as they are supposed to fulfill their semiotic and eschatological function; we are *not* entitled to infer, however, that the events in question *have* actually happened.[25] In that sense there is and always remains a serious epistemic gap between testimony and fact.

But there is yet another and even more substantial gap to be bridged, pertaining in general to the nature and truth-conditions of experience and as such also to Proudfoot's distinction: it is obviously one thing to perceive someone apparently resuscitating a deceased person; it is quite another to believe – let alone: rightly to believe – this to be a miracle; and yet another to believe (and rightly so) that as such it was and had to be done by a god-man. Sure enough, in any such situation at least three aspects stand as phenomenologically and epistemically undisputed, as far as the first person-perspective of the respective subject of experience is concerned: (a) Peter has indubitably *experienced* something (= experiential aspect); (b) Peter has indubitably experienced *something* (= referential aspect); and (c) Peter has indubitably experienced something *as* something – namely: as somebody (here: a god-man) resuscitating a deceased person and thereby performing a miracle (= symbolic aspect). Still dubious, however, is and remains (d), the genuinely epistemic aspect: is the experience, qualified and structured in the way described, in fact *veridical*? In other words, is what undoubtedly appears to be the divinely performed miracle of resuscitat-

---

24 For the time being I simply take this for granted as a well-founded claim. I am justified in doing so, since my point is purely consequential: even *if* the claim is well-founded, we are in for serious epistemic problems, the possible solution of which remains essentially unaffected (for better or for worse) by the encyclopedia-idea.

25 Likewise St. Paul does not (in 1Cor 15:6) present five hundred eye-witnesses for the facticity of the risen Christ; rather he presents one witness – himself – for the facticity of the five hundred.

ing someone *in fact* a divinely performed miracle, in particular, the miracle just described?[26]

Moreover, and for the sake of sharpening the point, let us compare the previous epistemic situation to that of someone who is not subject of a direct, but rather and exclusively of an indirect (viz. a testimonially mediated) experience of an alleged miracle.[27] Under such circumstances the epistemic question takes on a quite different form: is what *ex hypothesi* indubitably appears to be a credible[28] witness of a divinely performed miracle *in fact* a credible witness? What is at issue in this latter case, other than in the former, is – as I would prefer to put it – not only ideality, but also facticity. In other words: the account of the witness may appear dubitable not only in terms of *what* happened, but also in terms of something to have happened *at all*! Therefore, we might not only ask: is what has been witnessed to as the divinely performed miracle of resuscitating a deceased person *in fact* what is being witnessed to? Rather, it is possible and in fact mandatory also to ask: has anything, which happened to appear as a divinely performed miracle, taken place at all? Has there *been* any such event which gave rise to its interpretation as a divine miracle? And yet, the situation thus qualified is exactly *our* situation, and as we have seen, it is somewhat different from someone directly experiencing something as miraculous (although, as I am quick to admit, analogous epistemic problems loom large in the latter case also).

Given these situational circumstances, conditions and constraints, there are in my opinion precisely four options at our disposal, when it comes to assessing the facticity in relation to the ideality of events, which have been witnessed to as a miracle:

---

26 Accordingly, we may of course say that the resurrection of Jesus is *real* (in Peircean terms: as an instance of categorical thirdness) and that as such it has something *existent* (in Peircean terms: as an instance of categorical secondness) as its objective correlate (see Alkier 2006, 354, 355, 357). But this will not get us off the hook epistemically, for the crucial problem still looms large: is the objective correlate of a reality, in which some existing entity *appears* to be the resurrection of Jesus, *in fact* the resurrection of Jesus, or is it rather to be explained reductively, namely as some other, perhaps as of yet unidentified correlate?

27 Of course, every indirect experience is also a direct experience – if only in terms of directly experiencing (something or someone as) the witness of some other purported direct experience, as such. Moreover, one should not confuse direct and *immediate* experience, for the former is equally mediated (just like indirect experience): either I believe my own senses or I believe some *other* witness!

28 I take the credibility of a witness to imply at least two things: (a) honesty (= the witness intends to communicate to her addressee what she herself believes in the issue at hand) and (b) expertise or knowledgeability (= the witness does in fact know what her addressee does not and cannot know about the issue at hand).

	Supernaturalism	Rationalism	Skepticism	Naturalism
Facticity	*Some* of those events, which have been witnessed to as a miracle, have actually *happened.*	*Some* of those events, which have been witnessed to as a miracle, have actually *happened.*	*None* of those events, which have been witnessed to as a miracle, have actually *happened.*	*None* of those events, which have been witnessed to as a miracle, have actually *happened.*
Ideality (extension)	*Some* of those events, which have been witnessed to as a miracle, are actually *miraculous.*	*None* of those events, which have been witnessed to as a miracle, are actually *miraculous.*	*Some* of those events, which have been witnessed to as a miracle, are actually *miraculous.*	*None* of those events, which have been witnessed to as a miracle, are actually *miraculous.*

Now, remember that the conceptual account I argued for earlier has led to a complete disjunction: either an event lends itself to being conceived of as possible, or we are talking about a miracle. *Tertium non datur*. Hence, the more we might gain apologetically (by making the respective event appear probable or at least possible), the more we are about to lose conceptually (namely by betraying the ideality or true nature of miracles) and *vice versa*. However, if that holds true, then every Christian (and every religious person, for that matter) must be a supernaturalist – *nota bene*: as long as he or she wants to cling to a belief in miracles.[29] And even if we rightly insist that a genuinely Christian realm has to be situated beyond both the vocabulary of naturalism *and* supernaturalism[30] – so that, following Rudolf Bultmann, we are to speak of miracles as eschatological events instead – this may at best affect the extension,[31] but not the concept of miracle itself, much less the rationality-issue.

Frankly, I will not even begin to pursue the project of discussing the evidential and/or pragmatical conditions and requirements which have to be met in

29 For otherwise one may also be and remain consistently skeptical.

30 This seems to me to be the point in Wilhelm Herrmann's argument: We must "verlangen, daß in unserer Kirche die Versuche, den Gedanken des Wunders, der wirklich zum Glauben gehört, abzuschwächen, bekämpft werden. Zu diesen Versuchen müssen wir das Unternehmen rechnen, an dem Wundergedanken seine Kollision mit dem Gedanken der Natur in Abrede zu stellen ... Wenn uns das, was der Glaube ein Wunder nennt, nämlich das Wirken der speziellen Fürsorge Gottes auf uns selbst, gewiß ist, so haben wir eine Wirklichkeit vor Augen, die sich in Naturbegriffen überhaupt nicht fassen läßt." (Herrmann 1967, 204 f.)

31 To the effect that now faith and revelation must primarily (if not exclusively) be categorized as miracles: see Bultmann 1972, 222–25 (note that Bultmann insists on speaking of 'wonder' ['Wunder'] as opposed to 'miracle' ['Mirakel'] here).

order for any actual belief in miracles – and thus also, any kind of religious supernaturalism – to be true and/or rationally justified. All I want to emphasize in conclusion is that, as far as I see, the idea of differing encyclopedias and their underlying reality-conceptions does not and cannot have any crucial bearing upon the conceptual and epistemic issues discussed here. At any rate, the theoretical tools provided by the idea are[32] hardly sufficient for successfully guiding our search for a rationally grounded decision between the four options mentioned above. In light of the previous analysis this somewhat skeptical conclusion will hardly come as a surprise, much less pass for miraculous.

Bibliography

Adams, Robert M.: "Miracles, Laws and Natural Causation (II)." *Proceedings of the Aristotelian Society* 66 (1992): 207–24.

Alkier, Stefan: *Wunder und Wirklichkeit in den Briefen des Apostels Paulus: Ein Beitrag zu einem Wunderverständnis jenseits von Entmythologisierung und Rehistorisierung*. Tübingen 2001.

Alkier, Stefan: "Wunder III. Neues Testament/ IV. Kirchengeschichtlich" in *RGG*[4], vol. 8. Tübingen 2005, 1719–25.

Alkier, Stefan: "Die Realität der Auferstehung" in *Theologie zwischen Pragmatismus und Existenzdenken: Festschrift für Hermann Deuser zum 60. Geburtstag*. Edited by G. Linde et al. Marburg 2006, 339–59.

Aquin, Thomas von: *Summa Theologica*, dt.-lat. Ausgabe, vol. 8. Heidelberg 1951.

Augustine: *The City of God (De civitate dei)*, 2 vols. Translated by J. Healey. Edited by R.V.G. Tasker, London/New York 1947[2].

Austin, J.L.: "A Plea for Excuses" in *Classics of Analytic Philosophy*. Edited by R.R. Ammermann. New York 1965, 379–98.

Bowden, John: "Miracle," *Encyclopedia of Christianity*. Edited by J. Bowden. Oxford 2005, 757–61.

Buber, Martin: *Tales of the Hasidim: The Early Masters*. New York 1947.

---

32 Apart from other, more general or principle epistemic problems; here is one of them: no one ever speaks or thinks as a mere or immediate *representative* of encyclopedia A, but rather and inevitably as a representative simultaneously *relating* to his own representative function, namely in relation to some representation of encyclopedia B. He does so not only from a descriptive, but also from a genuinely normative perspective or stance. However, if and as soon as Peter is (a) *normatively* motivated, and this to the extent that (b) he perceives A and B as *incompatible*, he needs (and in fact always engages) some standpoint, perspective, standard or measure C as being valid both in and beyond A *and* B, in order, namely, to adjudicate between A and B. (Note that in the case of miracle-reports the incompatibility takes on the form of either one of the four standpoints mentioned above.)

Bultmann, Rudolf: "Zur Frage des Wunders," in *Glauben und Verstehen*, vol. 1. Tübingen 1972[7], 214–28.
Bultmann, Rudolf: *Das Urchristentum im Rahmen der antiken Religionen.* Darmstadt 1986[5].
Casati, Roberto; Varzi, Achille: "Events," *The Stanford Encyclopedia of Philosophy*, 2006 (http://plato.stanford.edu/archives/entries/events; accessed 03. 11. 2011).
Corner, David: *The Philosophy of Miracles.* London/ New York 2007.
Evers, Dirk: "Wunder und Naturgesetze" in *Zeichen und Wunder*. Edited by W.H. Ritter and M. Albrecht. Göttingen 2007, 66–87.
Gregersen, Niels Henrik: "Wunder V. Religionsphilosophisch," *RGG*[4], vol. 8. Tübingen 2005, 1725f.
Herrmann, Wilhelm: "Der Christ und das Wunder" in W. Hermann, *Schriften zur Grundlegung der Theologie*, vol. 2. Edited by P. Fischer-Appelt, Munich 1967, 170–205.
Hick, John: *God and the Universe of Faiths.* Oxford 1973.
Hughes, Christopher: "Miracles, Laws and Natural Causation (I)" in *Proceedings of the Aristotelian Society* 66 (1992): 179–205.
Hume, David: *Eine Untersuchung über den menschlichen Verstand.* Translated and edited by H. Herring. Stuttgart 1979.
Hume, David: *Writings on Religion*. Edited by A. Flew. La Salle 1992.
Kierkegaard, Søren: *Søren Kierkegaards Skrifter*, vols. 1–28, K1-K28. Edited by Niels Jørgen Cappelørn et al. Copenhagen 1997ff. (quoted as: (a) SKS + vol. + page-number [= works]; (b) entry-number + SKS + vol. + page-number [= journals]).
Kierkegaard, Søren: *Philosophical Fragments.* Translated by Howard V. Hong and Edna H. Hong. Princeton 1987[2] (quoted as PF + page-number).
Kierkegaard, Søren: *Three Discourses on Imagined Occasions.* Translated by Howard V. Hong and Edna H. Hong. Princeton 1993 (quoted as TD + page-number).
Kierkegaard, Søren: *Journals and Papers.* Edited and translated by Howard V. Hong and Edna H. Hong, assisted by Gregor Malantschuk, vol. 1–6, vol. 7 Index and Composite Collation, Bloomington and London 1967–78 (quoted as JP + vol. + entry-number).
Keener, Craig S.: *Miracles: The Credibility of the New Testament Accounts*, vols. 1–2. Grand Rapids 2011.
Levine, Michael: "Miracles," *The Stanford Encyclopedia of Philosophy*, 1996, revisited 2005 (http://plato.stanford.edu/archives/2005/entries/miracles; accessed 03. 11. 2011).
Lewis, Clive S.: *Miracles.* New York 1947.
Luther, Martin: *Werke: Kritische Gesamtausgabe* (Weimarer Ausgabe), vol. 22. Weimar/ Graz 1964.
Proudfoot, Wayne: *Religious Experience.* Berkeley/ Los Angeles 1985.
Purtill, Richard: "Defining Miracles" in *In Defense of Miracles.* Edited by R.D. Geivett and G.R. Habermas. Downers Grove 1997, 61–72.
Schlesinger, George: "Miracles," *A Companion to Philosophy of Religion.* Edited by Ph.L. Quinn and Ch. Taliaferro, Cambridge 1997, 360–66.
Schulz, Heiko: "Das Ende des common sense: Kritische Überlegungen zur Wunderkritik David Humes," *Zeitschrift für neuere Theologiegeschichte* 3 (1996): 1–38.
Schulz, Heiko: *Theorie des Glaubens*. Tübingen 2001.
Schulz, Heiko: "*Eines* wollen können: Überlegungen zum Verhältnis von Christentum und intellektueller Redlichkeit im Anschluss an D.F. Strauß und S. Kierkegaard" in *Instinkt Redlichkeit Glaube. Zum Verhältnis von Subjektivität und Religion*. Edited by H. Schulz. Frankfurt a.M. 2011, 45–88 [2011a].

Schulz, Heiko: *Aneignung und Reflexion I: Studien zur Rezeption Søren Kierkegaards*. Berlin/ Boston 2011 [2011b].
Schulz, Heiko: "Kierkegaard and the Problem of Miracles" in *Aneignung und Reflexion II: Studien zur Theologie und Philosophie Søren Kierkegaards*, Berlin/ Boston 2013 (forthcoming).
Swinburne, Richard: *The Evolution of the Soul*. Oxford 1986.
Verhoeven, Cornelis: *The Philosophy of Wonder*. New York 1972.
Woodward, Kenneth L.: *The Book of Miracles: The Meaning of the Miracle Stories in Christianity, Judaism, Buddhism, Hinduism and Islam*. New York et al. 2001[2].

Hermann Deuser

Marvels, Miracles, Signs and the Real: Peirce's Semiotics in Religion and Art

I

Are miracles nothing more than illusionary elements of an unenlightened religious mind set? Or should they still be accorded a function today in dealing with reality, even if they are transformed into aesthetic and psychological phenomena? These questions briefly sketch the public, subjectively perceived and scientific debate in the twentieth century, and certainly not only in Germany. The point here is not to come to a decisive conclusion for one of the two alternatives. Syntheses are possible. For example, the fictional content of alleged miracles can be appealing when seen aesthetically, psychologically, in terms of the history of mentalities, etc. Moreover, between reality and illusion, the boundaries can run differently from those determined by the empirical sciences. However, the notion that religions, especially Christianity, are true because they are founded on miracles is hardly recognized any more as a communicative and rationally justifiable assertion. In any case, viewed in this way, the original question seems compelling in one respect. Empirical reality in the narrow (natural-scientific) sense is no longer intended (assuming it ever was) when the factuality of miracles is to be discussed, and its claim of validity judged in accordance with the spirit of modernism – and not only in terms of the history of religion. Does this do away with the problem of the miracle altogether? Does it not represent, in all religious criticism, an expanded sense of reality that unlocks the processes of self- and world-comprehension, in a way that is completely different than the restrictive question about empirical or historical factuality?

II

It is notable that the appeal of Marxist and atheistic philosopher Ernst Bloch in the second half of the twentieth century, against the demythologizing interpretation of miracles by the theologian and exegete Rudolf Bultmann, was already quite inconsistent with the spirit of modernism. In referring to the Bible's obviously outdated worldview, and taking the viewpoint of modern science, Bultmann designated miracles to be no-longer-comprehensible 'marvels' (*Mira-*

kel).[1] With its angels and devils, the old cosmology supposedly enables the other world to shine through into this world, that is, it permits a marvellous, magical and mythical view of reality upon which the Christian faith is not absolutely dependent, and from which, taken methodically in the program of *demythologizing*,[2] it must absolutely be freed. In the place of unscientific cosmologies, then, a modern analytics of existence and anthropology recommends itself, which construes faith as a call from God in terms of real life and, at the same time, has no reservations about reading Biblical texts in an historical-critical manner. Existential messages and scientific views no longer compete with, but rather complement, each other.[3]

By contrast, Ernst Bloch argued that this adaptation to science is done at the cost of losing worldliness. What disappears is the rebellious and cosmic-apocalyptic character of the myth – the "historical and cosmic blast chamber" and the "the highly explosive Christ who is let into it."[4] Miracles and myths, especially the resurrection of Jesus and the Kingdom of God, contain images of hope that stand in opposition to death. For these to be more than mere illusions, a real-utopian world process must be implied, in which the possibility of surviving death emerges and comes to light. This is exactly what happens to the degree that literary and religious pictures, stories and symbols have worldly transformative power: "[Jesus'] miracles are the *signs* of the coming end," and thus signs of the cosmic turning point and the radically new, the "*interruption*" and the "*absolutely good content*."[5]

The accusation that demythologizing is privatistic, politically naive, and existentialist and that it entirely loses, along with the aspect of the cosmic, a sense of world responsibility[6] – appears, at least to Bultmann, unfounded.[7] The

---

1 Rudolf Bultmann, "Zur Frage des Wunders" (1933) in *Neues Testament und christliche Existenz: Theologische Aufsätze* (ed. A. Lindemann; Tübingen 2002), 84–98; here, 84 f. Regarding the place of Bultmann's theology in intellectual history Robert C. Neville, *Religion in Late Modernity* (Albany: SUNY 2002), 112; Idem, *Realism in Religion: A Pragmatist's Perspective* (Albany: SUNY 2009), 26, 64 f.

2 Cf. D. Fergusson, "Entmythologisierung," *RGG*[4] 2 (1999): 1328–30.

3 Cf. H. Deuser, "Elektrisches Licht und/oder die Geister- und Wunderwelt des Neuen Testaments? Rudolf Bultmanns Redlichkeitsforderung als Kritik der Weltbilder," in *Religiosität und intellektuelle Redlichkeit* (ed. G. Hartung and M. Schlette; Tübingen 2012).

4 Ernst Bloch, *Atheismus im Christentum: Zur Religion des Exodus und des Reichs* (Frankfurt am Main 1968), 70.

5 Ernst Bloch, *Das Prinzip Hoffnung*, 3 vols. (Frankfurt am Main 1967, 1542 and 1544) (in the context of chapters 52 and 53).

6 Cf. Bloch, *Atheismus*, loc. cit. 69.

7 This is evidenced not least by Bultmann's lucid and forthright approach in 1933, see Deuser, "Bultmann and Heidegger" in *Philosophische Rundschau* 56 (2009): 258–66.

crucial question remains, however, as to what is expressed that is worldly (i.e. real) via miracles and specifically through them, how and why they must be understood as 'signs' and what therefore differentiates them from superstition. The 'interruption' of the ordinary and the 'leap' in the guise of every determinism[8] represent what still has no place, yet announce its presence – that which is vicariously experienced in the empirical and world process, precisely because it is hidden. For example, faith, hope and love are instances for miracles that belong to the type of experience in which they create indirect, figurative forms of expression: worlds of meaning in pictures, stories and symbols. On this point, Bultmann's hermeneutics of existence and Bloch's theory of hope can also agree.

III

In the twenty-first century, such a tentative constructive approach to the miracle problem appears to be gaining more and more acceptance. From the perspective of world politics, this is due first of all to the powerful emergence of religions in acute conflict areas. There is little doubt that religion should be taken seriously as an element of development and/or disruption.[9] Another factor – at least for the consumer and media worlds of industrial nations – is the late (post-) modern acceptance and intermingling of difference in the process of cultural exchange, where reverence is given to even the most exotic religious practices and the most abstruse artistic intentions. Along with this, surprising access is again proclaimed to the miraculous. The most recent example of this is the Hamburg exhibition, *Wunder*,[10] the miracles on display here epitomizing the unusual, mysterious and world-overturning (not just scientifically). What the artworks imagine and portray at once seems to be in agreement with religious miracles and with the scientifically elusive: comics, pictures of the Virgin Mary, random combinations, disasters, cosmic lights, ghost-like things, technical artefacts, art-historical objects, etc. What do all these have in common? One might say, the game that deals with 'the signs of the marvellous.'[11] Just as Bultmann already made a distinction

8 Cf. Bloch, *Prinzip Hoffnung*, loc. cit. 1545.

9 On the negative effects of religion's newly political dimension, see Stefan Alkier et al., eds., *Religiöser Fundamentalismus: Analysen und Kritiken* (Tübingen 2005).

10 D. Tyradellis, B. Hentschel and D. Luckow, eds., *Wunder: Kunst, Wissenschaft und Religion vom 4. Jahrhundert bis zur Gegenwart* (Exhibition catalog of Deichtorhallen Hamburg and the Siemens Foundation; Hamburg/Cologne 2011).

11 D. Haas, "Ich weiß, es wird einmal ein Wunder gesehen," *FAZ 300* (24. 12. 2011), 37.

between the incomprehensible marvel and the productive miraculous, the negative assessment here is apparent. The exhibition's wide-ranging writings, however, try to present a context that aims to do more than play with the incomprehensible: our – thoroughly scientific and technically oriented – reality has something fragile about it, which can produce a creative effect when brought together with works of art. That which does not conform to the rules not only gives rise to subjective *wonder*, but to an objective *opening* of perception.[12] The existence of the miraculous must therefore be due to the way the world itself is composed! However, this conclusion seems to go too far. The aesthetic interpretation which exemplifies the opening and the wonder (*Öffnung* and *Staunen*) predominates, without asking about the miraculous reality itself. Quite the reverse; the conclusion that could be drawn here is, 'Miracles happen to those who believe in miracles.'[13] This is all well and good from the standpoint of religious and ideological criticism, but it glosses over the question of the reality in which the miraculous is precisely not a superstitious marvel, but rather reflects an opening to an experience that gives rise to wonder.

The same reorientation occurs more easily when it is put into aesthetic terms. If the spellbinding effect of Christian images may be allowed – e.g. regarding their power to directly confirm biblical stories and content – then, even though a reorientation away from the Church's interpretative authority may occur with increasing secularization, this does not also imply that there is a loss in the peculiar power of images.[14] These have the ability to achieve 'reality' "at the interface between humans and their (surrounding) world, the visible and invisible, the present and the absent." An art exhibition, moreover, can succeed in making the necessary affective media available for such experiences. What the narrativity of biblical miracle stories in the pre-modern era promised – namely, to explode the opening to the world's restrictive conditions – is now a task for works of art. And the binding framework for art's world concept is provided today by the natural sciences, and their narrativistic and visually expressive cosmologies and evolutionary ideas. One might say that the miraculous is hibernating in the art galleries.

But what does this then mean for the critique of religion? Of course, superstition and authoritarian manipulation must be distinguished from marvellous realities on the one hand, and the reality-disclosing significance of the miraculous on

12 See the essays from R. Pfaller, "Die Erschwernisse des Staunens; D. Tyradellis: Das Wunder ist eine Öffnung in der Welt," in *Wunder*, loc. cit. 237–45, 13–19.

13 Z. Bauman, "Gebrauch und Missbrauch der Wunder," in *Wunder*, loc. cit. 281–88; here, 288.

14 E. Blumenstein, "Denken im Affekt: Warum die zeitgenössische Kunst ein guter Ort für die Wunder ist," in *Wunder*, loc. cit. 51–59; here, 51ff.; in the following, 53f.

the other. This, however, is nothing new to internal religious debates.[15] It is precisely at the periphery or rationalizing centre of the accepted, scientific and material conditions for understanding that the special disclosing power of art and religion is called upon. In this regard, the current cosmologies are no different from the old ones. We rely on the Big Bang theory as much as people in Biblical times trusted in their creation myths. First, the miracle suddenly appears in this act of creation as such. (What else might be 'explanatory' here?) Second, it exists in the recurring presence of the novel and the non-derivable processual reality which contains its own possibilities. On the other hand, superstition is at hand – in science, art and religion – whenever, contrary to the applicable conditions of knowledge, a special reality of manipulative empirical effects is left to be demonstrated and proven, such that the otherwise valid standards for empirical evidence must be suspended.

The salutary exception to each of these familiar circumstances is the miraculous, which may be justifiably included in the image on either aesthetic or religious grounds, inasmuch as it can appear as an affective and potent symbolic promise. By contrast, reifying points of view which capture, record and empirically demonstrate miracles always have a tendency toward a belief in marvels. This, however, proceeds from entirely different, authoritative-manipulative intentions and therefore can be sustained before a tribunal neither of knowledge nor of belief.

Ultimately, the question is justified about why the miraculous can be defined positively in one particular case, whereas catastrophes have the same experiential structure.[16] The answer is twofold. On the one hand, due to its deep grammatical roots, it must be remarked that *miracle* is usually understood as a rescue. That is, it is understood positively against the background of negative events and is only properly used in this dialectic.[17] On the other hand, from a cosmological standpoint, it is also true that miracles and catastrophes stem from the same unforeseen 'causes' which no longer have any real explanatory value. They remain unexplained as *accidents* that are to be considered as signs of basic contingency. It is precisely at this point that the issue of the miracle arises. The fact that the 'miracle of technology' can be spoken of secularly, and completely apart from

15 Cf. E. Schüttpelz, "Die Folklorisierung des Wunders," in *Wunder*, loc. cit. 209–16; here, 209f.

16 On this question, whereby disasters are noted to be apocalyptic 'signs of miracles,' see M. Frye, "Das Wunder in der Katastrophe: Von frühneuzeitlichen Wunderzeichen bis zu Jonathan Horowitz' Apokalypto Now," in *Wunder*, loc. cit. 31–40.

17 Ibid., loc. cit. 31.

works of art,[18] only shows the undeniable correspondence of the miracle (here as it relates to technology) to catastrophes, while allowing the encounter with contingency to remain untreated.

IV

Nonetheless, to establish miracles of this kind under new conditions – and to grant them a key function in original wonder, the opening of the unfamiliar, the disruption of rules and the promise of success and salvation – requires a precise determination of their reality status. This is especially true if the aim is to do more than merely take note of an interesting aestheticization of religious traditions. Therefore, the question is: in what sense is the miraculous part of our world of experience? Moreover, can it be imagined today in such a manner that the constitutive aspects of original wonder, an experimentally accessible reality and an overall (intellectual, rational) determination of real life can be said to apply in the same way? The answer is that such thinking began to take root for various historical reasons in American pragmatism at the end of the nineteenth century. Its special character, particularly in the work of its founder C.S. Peirce, lies in its novel and productive way of communicating the practical values of the humanities and natural sciences. The reason why religiosity also 'counts' in this kind of scientific approach is best demonstrated by the example of Peirce's *categorical semiotics*, which is representative of his pragmatism.[19]

> This new conceptual link refers to a tendentially unified epistemological (i.e. semiotic) and categorical (i.e. ontological) scientific attitude, which elucidates the tripartism previously illustrated as an equally logical, phenomenologically plausible and clearly defined theoretical model of a processual reality. The term *category* here – purposely derived and delineated from Aristotle and Kant – is conceived as an at once phenomenally proximate and structurally formalizable tripartite structure.[20] In the first instance, there is the always perceptually intense, passive imaginational presence of a non-derivable preceding quality (*firstness*); in the second instance, there is a distinct determination of an object reference of empirical character (*secondness*); thirdly, there is an interpretive behaviour that contains, but also independently expresses the two preceding categories in a vital expression (*third-*

18 L=Ibid., loc. cit. 36.

19 The following paragraph utilizes the outline of the philosophical theory of signs from H. Deuser, "Geistesgegenwart: Pneumatologie und kategoriale Semiotik," *Zeitschrift für Neues Testament 13* (2010): 78–85; here, 79 (in the context used illustratively for the interpretation of the Emmaus pericope [Luke 24, 13–34]).

20 Cf. H. Deuser, *Religionsphilosophie* (Berlin/New York 2009), § 1, note 44; § 10.2.

ness). This categorical structure now corresponds to the triadic foundation of Peircean semiotics, whereby a *sign*, as qualitatively first in a sign event (be it empirical, text-mediated or a purely ideal perception), implies an *object* relation (a definable second). These two determinations are, in turn, discharged in the effectiveness of an *interpretant*, that is, in the mental activity or formation of consequences or behaviour in the third position. The basic idealized structure of categorical semiotics described here for analytical purposes actually only arises in very complex interrelations, series, gradations, etc. The former, however, can be recognized in the latter and used to interpret experiential reality without having to posit metaphysical assumptions (e.g. substance ontology as in the Christian Middle Ages or materialistic or idealistic ontology as in the modern age of Europe).

If all experience and recognition must be imagined in sign processes, then the same is true for art and religion, the arrangement of art exhibits and also, of course, for miracles and the reporting of miracles. Peirce further remained firm on three points in his discussion of David Hume's classic miracle critique. First, Hume's criticism of the reliability of reports about miracles should (with qualification) be upheld. Second, that objection is however invalid because the supposition about revelations and the 'existence of a benevolent God' argues about probabilities. A divine miracle is just as special or unique as an ingenious artwork![21] Third, this does not mean of course that – from a modern viewpoint – God's existence might be merely accepted, whereas miracles belong to "real religion,"[22] or that today or with regard to the history of religion miracles are not simply assumed to be valid but their real status needs to first be demonstrated. From Peirce's perspective, that is, from the modern non-deterministic view of science, Hume in his critique of the belief in miracles "... has completely mistaken the nature of the true logic of abduction."[23] For Peirce's part, this status of the logic of abduction can now be elucidated by categorical semiotics.

How can religious phenomena such as miracles or revelations even be expressed? Semiotically speaking, it may occur by means of certain representational forms of *iconicity*, *indexicality* and *symbolicity*. The microsemiotic distinctions of individual sign forms from Peirce's classification will not be used here, but instead the rather broad, phenomenologically more accessible triadic re-

21 C.S. Peirce, *Religionsphilosophische Schriften* (ed. H. Deuser; Hamburg (1995) 2000), 272–74, 308. See for a detailed analysis of Hume's position, H. Schulz, "Das Ende des *common sense*: Kritische Überlegungen zur Wunderkritik David Humes," *Journal for the History of Modern Theology 3* (1996): 1–38.

22 Peirce, loc. cit. 217.

23 C.S. Peirce, *Collected Papers [CP]*, vol. 6 (Cambridge [1935] 1978), CP 6.537. See H. Schulz, loc. cit. 37 (note 122); on Peirce's Hume manuscripts in general: *Religionsphilosophische Schriften*, loc. cit. 493f. (note *).

lation which corresponds to the basic structure of the sign and the following three categories: *firstness* as primary quality and iconicity; *secondness* as object relation and indexicality; *thirdness* as interpretant and symbolicity. These structural terms have nothing in themselves that are specifically religious, but they can show where the significance of religiosity lies – and quite appropriately, in a parallel comparison to art or aesthetic signs and life forms.

Iconicity encompasses the mediation of all signs that express a qualitative representational relationship. The most immediate examples are "colours and sounds,"[24] for there is no longer anything distancing, so to speak, between perception and what is perceived. Of course, such emotionally imbued qualities become themselves the subject of further and more complex sign processes. Their qualitative core, however, does not disappear as a result, but is rather articulated further and in different ways (in respectively different signs). In his fourth lecture on pragmatism, Peirce gives an aesthetic and religious answer to the question of what "role" such "qualities can play in the economy of the universe."[25] It may serve as an interpretative basis in the question about the miraculous:

> 'The universe is a vast representamen, a great symbol of God's purpose, working out its conclusions in living realities. Now every symbol must have, organically attached to it, its Indices of Reactions and its Icons of Qualities; and such part as these reactions and these qualities play in an argument, that they of course play in the Universe, that Universe being precisely an argument. [...] Those premisses of nature, however, though they are not the *perceptual facts* that are premisses to us, nevertheless must resemble them in being premisses. [...] As premisses they must involve Qualities.'[26]
>
> 'The Universe as an argument is necessarily a great work of art, a great poem, – for every fine argument is a poem and a symphony, – just as every true poem is a sound argument. But let us compare it rather with a painting, – with an impressionist seashore piece, – then every Quality in a premiss is one of the elementary colored particles of the painting; they are all meant to go together to make up the intended Quality that belongs to the whole as a whole. That total effect is beyond our ken; but we can appreciate in some measure the resultant Quality of parts of the whole, – which Qualities result from the combinations of elementary Qualities that belong to the premisses.'[27]

---

24 Cf. Peirce's *IV. Pragmatismusvorlesung*, ed. E. Walther; Hamburg 1991 77/78; *The Essential Peirce*, vol. 2 (1998), [*EP 2*], 192. The text edition of the lectures in EP 2 was done on the basis of Peirce's manuscripts and is therefore preferable to the body of texts in the German edition, which relies on the idiosyncratic arrangements of *Collected Papers*.

25 Peirce, loc. cit. 78, *EP 2* 193.

26 loc. cit. 78, *EP 2* 193/194.

27 Ibid., loc. cit. 78/79; EP 2, 194.

(1) At first glance, the two passages seem to be as magnificent as they are mysterious! They are magnificent because a scientifically based cosmology and philosophically elaborated categorical semiotics mutually interpret each other. Thus is everything included in one sweep that has been forbidden by the exact sciences, on the one hand, and the hermeneutical humanistic sciences since Kant and Kantianism (or corresponding epistemologies), on the other. They are mysterious because the linkages that Peirce briefly centers on in these lectures – between cosmology, the philosophy of science, semiotics, pragmaticistic realism, aesthetic perception theory, and, along with all this, the philosophy of religion! – cannot be elaborated upon so quickly. What happens here is certainly revolutionary in view of the main currents of modern philosophy, even though, according to Peirce, it only provides a concept for what any of the true natural sciences know from the experience of their own scientific work, for what corresponds to the material basis of their trust and, consequently, for what must also be a shared product of their philosophical attitude.

(2) As a scientific cosmology, a three-fold dimension of the 'universe' is to be understood here that completely accords with the contemporary evolutionary sense, extending from the Big Bang to the cultural consciousness of the human intellect. The universe, as it is accessible to empirical and experimental experience (*secondness*), must in any case always be seen in connection with the facilitation of experience in "qualities of feeling"[28] (*firstness*) and with the real effectiveness of "general principles,"[29] that is, the uniformity and regularity in nature (*thirdness*). If this intellectual commonality – always understood to be as real as the effectiveness of the natural laws – is seen together with the irrefutable, forceful singularity of qualitative perceptions, empiricist determinism is ruled out and the way is opened to the real meaning of the miraculous. Because the laws of nature do not apply absolutely, miracles are not to be interpreted as their 'interruption,' but as their correlate in coming into being, in the novel, in the primary quality of perception generally – in short, in the miraculous ("mirabile"[30]) in a fundamental sense that can no longer be surpassed by anything.

(3) In the two passages, semiotic explanation is required for the interpretative structure, which, as the form of representation, also has self-referential character and is therefore as ontological-existential as it is aesthetic and religious. Human beings (their experiences of feeling, desiring and thinking) are sign processes in

28 Ibid. EP 2, 190; dt. loc. cit. 74f. translated with "quality of sensation."

29 Ibid.EP 2, 183; dt. loc. cit. 68.

30 See the three possible interpretations of miracles in relation to the natural laws: N.H. Gregersen, "Wunder V. Religionsphilosophisch," *Religion in Geschichte und Gegenwart 4*, vol. 8 (2005): 1725f.

which the structures of the universe are represented, experienced and partially understood. This is exactly what art and religion demonstrate, along with the miraculous that is in them. In its relatedness of exclusive *firstness*, the miracle is irreplaceable and fundamental. The task of art and religion is precisely to deal with the miraculous, with processing the qualitatively first *as such*.

(4) What the two passages have in common is their semiotic terminology. The *thirdness*-related sign form *symbol* is certainly a freely agreed upon sign (like all linguistic signs), but it also has an implied object reference (index) and the intrinsic emotional quality of the icon. At a higher level of reflection about the knowledge of *thirdness*-related connections as an intellectual process of conclusion, a symbol can thus be understood as an *argument* that moreover effectively implements the inference relation of iconicity, indexicality and symbolicity. Now, if the universe – from a cosmological perspective – can be described as an argument, this implies that an *abductive* conclusion about 'God's purpose' may be drawn from 'quality' (premise 1) and real 'reactions' in the empirical world (premise 2) precisely because the present perception can be sensibly explained (insofar it is abduction and not deduction or induction) in a spontaneous, situational and convincing way. Characteristic of this basic model of religious semiotics, then, is the 'role' of the original qualities in the developmental process of the universe or the "universes of experience,"[31] as the argument for the existence of God will put it. And the 'role' lies in the perceived 'intention,' which can then only be received in this perspective of qualitative *firstness* religiously – that is, in human terms, passively, but also as a creative enabling. To this extent, religious faith is the miraculous itself. Indeed, between human primary perception and the primary perception that is a process of nature, there remains a distinction – that is, the human perspective remains passive with respect to the "premises of the nature." The basic semiotic structure, however, may be attributed to both, such that with the justification of an abductively derived hypothesis nature shows "God's purpose."

(5) The argument concerning God's reality (1908) then discusses, in more detail, how the abduction comes to be a fundamentally convincing material and scientific hypothesis. This involves certain conditions, which, fully in accordance with the aesthetic attitude, amount to eliminating prejudices, and persuasively suggest a posture of open engagement. Three aspects should be emphasized: the final form of abduction is not arbitrary, but guided by "instinctive reason" or

31 Cf. Peirce, "Ein vernachlässigtes Argument für die Realität Gottes/A Neglected Argument for the Reality of God" (1908) in *Religionsphilosophische Schriften [RS]* (Hamburg [1995] 2000), 330ff.; *EP* 2, 435.

"consciousness of divining."[32] The integration and embeddedness of human thought in the universes of experience, and their evolution, is what then interconnects nature and culture. This alone assures the discovery of the unfamiliar in the expansion of nature, as well as the sciences. If we can keep our understanding from being blocked by obscure scientistic (Peirce: nominalistic) perspectives which do not allow for any thoughts about the reality of the three universes of experience, then "the very bedrock of logical truth"[33] discovers itself by virtue of instinctive reason: in the God-hypothesis and the epitome of the creative, "purposed"[34] understanding of the universes of experience. The lecture on pragmatism[35] and the argument about God's reality are thus formulated entirely analogously in this regard. It is this 'intention' which, in religious semiotics, is genuinely expressed in the miraculous – in the religious imagery of the original creation, in the historical creation myths and in the (culturally mediated) God symbol.

The God-hypothesis also has the characteristic of being highly persuasive and hard to resist.[36] This is true of signs that have the quality reference of *firstness* as regards the basic conditions of instinctive reason disclosed here, and which are now comprehended in terms of the authentic attitude[37] of "musement." Literary persuasiveness, and the rhetoric of the role model and the imitation, run throughout these sections of the argument on God's existence, as the integrity, meaning and power of hypothesis formation rest on this idiosyncratic approach. Expressed negatively and, again, using a natural scientific example:

> One who sits down with the purpose of becoming convinced of the truth of religion is plainly not inquiring in scientific singleness of heart [...] So, he can never attain the entirety even of a physicist's belief in electrons [...]. But let religious meditation be allowed to grow up spontaneously out of PURE PLAY without any breach of continuity; and the MUSER will retain the perfect candor proper to MUSEMENT.[38]

Finally, it is this mood state of "pure play" which exists as the condition of musement under the paradoxical motto, "no rules" are needed except for the "law of

32 Cf. *RS*, 347f; *EP 2*, 443.

33 *RS*, 349; *EP 2*, 444.

34 *RS*, 340; *EP 2*, 439f.

35 See in the seventh lecture, loc. cit.129, EP 2, 231: the final form of abduction with the emphasis on the "surprising fact" (P 1) and the suddenly present "matter of course" of its explanation (P 2) in the abductive conclusion.

36 *RS*, 353: "a hypothesis of the very highest PLAUSIBILITY," *EP 2*, 446.

37 *RS*, 333; *EP 2*, 436.

38 *RS*, 333; *EP 2*, 436.

liberty"![39] Restrictions thus cannot be imposed. Openness and the liberation of the natural processes are to be practiced, as they are presented in the sign universes to which the human perceptual capabilities actually already belong. What then appears is what must appear: the "idea of GOD'S REALITY" as an "attractive fancy" – the "explained wonder" that only has one explanation![40]

(6) In the second portion of text that responds to the question about what role "function [i.e. the qualities] plays in the economy of the universe", the focal point is not the universal and evolutionary processes, but rather the representation of the qualities themselves. Here the signs used in the *argument* determine the possibilities of a suitable symbolicity: the work of art. As qualities, its ideograms, colours or tones are poem, picture or symphony. In the case of an impressionistic picture, Peirce shows in detail how the generalizing perceptual judgment enables the iconicity-representing perspective to come about. Each of the elements of the artwork has its own quality, and their sum total creates a whole. Here too, as in the case of the semiotics of religion earlier, it needs to be indicated that while human beings do not have access to the whole as such, they can approach the whole through the 'combination' of perceptual premises. The purpose that is identified (the "intended quality") thus belongs to the genuine interest of the artwork, whose configuration the original creativity of perception attempts to repeat. This is also a 'reasonable' conclusion here, but with the attitude that Peirce already recommended earlier in the same lecture as a specific *naiveté*.[41] It has a moment that is questioning and receptive, but is also always active: works of art make the miraculous surprising, and the surprising seem miraculous.

(7) Religious and aesthetic abduction do not differ formally, and the *argument* in both cases is such that, with regard to the quality of *firstness*, an involuntary perceptual judgment can hardly be distinguished any longer from the abductive form of conclusion. Miracles are overwhelming! This is also the reason for the much-quoted tag line in the 'third cotary proposition' of the seventh lecture on pragmatism: "The abductive suggestion comes to us like a flash."[42] A distinction, in any case, is made between religious and aesthetic semiotics in view of the perceptual premises of reigning sign forms. In emphasizing the musement and pure play in the case of religious belief formation, the focus is on symbols of creation, bestowal, and entrustment. In the case of aesthetic perception, what is at issue is the object-forming restoration of the original. Both attitudes, however, concern

39 *RS*, 332; *EP* 2, 436.
40 *RS*, 339, 343; *EP* 2, 439, 441
41 Cf. *Pragmatismusvorlesungen*, loc. cit. 73; *EP* 2, 189.
42 *Pragmatismusvorlesungen*, loc. cit. 123; *EP* 2, 227.

"homogeneity," "continuity," "growth" and "beauty" in the three universes of experience and their correlation.[43] Here the miracle is grounded in its possibility – in the astounding creativity which, in response to the question of the experiential correlation, is abductively deduced and made representable. Scientifically speaking, there is no reason to want to exclude miracles from the perception of reality. On the contrary, the miracle of the creatively new is already inherent to all processes of becoming. In this respect, one can say: miracles are signs of reality.

Certain miracles belong to certain religions; the miraculous, rather, to works of art. Still, every difference that is emphasized between art and religion assumes, in particular, the autonomous development of the arts in modern times, whereas they were likely seamlessly linked in their cultural origin.[44] Consequently, the categorical-semiotic difference cannot demonstrate a fundamental separation, but rather the shift in emphasis and – increasingly in the modern era – the alternate focus on the idiosyncratic, autonomously active *naiveté* (in Peirce's sense of this term), which dominates the aesthetic attitude and finds expression and representation in the paradoxical "making" of an original quality. The first perception of quality is also irresistible for the "aesthetic state of mind," but this, moreover, is what is specifically at stake: a return "back into such a pure naïve state."[45] In contrast to religious perception, this is what must not be primarily distinguished as creative-passive, but rather as creative-naive-active. In the paradoxical situation for works of art, there is the simultaneous desire to get as close as possible to the original quality of perception, while also giving form to precisely this. Perhaps one should instead refer to artworks' continually fractured naiveté. The same would also hold true for the miraculous.

The relationship between works of art and religion gets even trickier when traditional religious symbolic systems today become more self-critical and have a desire for a new and different kind of representation. While they need works of art, they must accept the art's specific situation of fracturedness. Similarly, if contemporary art consciously and critically wants to adopt, reference or re-use religious situations (rituals, myths, miracles), it also requires the respective religious traditions and must therefore, in a certain sense, take the specific perceptual approach seriously. On both sides it might be a useful criterion for (religious or aesthetic) kitsch to be able to determine whether, in this reciprocal usage, each understands what it is doing – whether or not each knows how to correctly assess

43 *RS*, 337–339; *EP* 2, 438f. While the key (mathematical) concept for Peirce's cosmology of *continuity* is not itself explicated here in the argument on God's existence, it is referenced in various ways (here, *RS*, 339, "continuously tending to define itself").

44 Deuser, *Religionsphilosophie*, loc. cit. § 10.2.3.

45 *Pragmatismusvorlesungen*, loc. cit. 73; *EP* 2, 189.

the challenge of the creative-passive side, and the creative-naive-active side. Not knowing in the case of a miracle and the miraculous leads to superstition, intentional deception and illusion: in short, to kitsch, which results from the violation of the conditions and limitations of the sign-mediated – fractured – representational capacity of original creativity. However, sensitive religious and aesthetic respect for the perception of quality is both the very first and the most difficult aim for all of its representational forms. If successful, then the miracle of the universe is "a symbol of God's purpose" and, together with this argument, "a great work of art."

[Text translated by Christopher Reid; sponsored by the Kolleg-Forschergruppe, Max-Weber-Kolleg, University of Erfurt.]

List of Contributors

Stefan Alkier
1961
Professor of New Testament and History of the Early Church at Fachbereich Evangelische Theologie, Johann Wolfgang Goethe Universität, Frankfurt / Main
Dr. theol., Habilitation
Miracles, Resurrection; Numismatics, Ancient economy; Paul, Revelation, Mark; History of Research; Semiotics, Intertextuality, Hermeneutics, Methodology; History and Theology of the Biblical Canon

Sharon V. Betcher
1956
Independent Scholar and Affiliate Professor of Theology, Vancouver School of Theology (Vancouver, BC CA)
BA, MDiv, MPhil, PhD
Research involves critical and cultural studies intersections with constructive theology, primarily in the venues of disability, postcolonial, ecology and comparative religions

Hermann Deuser
1946
Institution: Prof. em. at Goethe University Frankfurt am Main (Systematische Theologie und Religionsphilosophie) / Fellow at the Max Weber Center for Advanced Cultural and Social Studies, University of Erfurt
Degrees: Dr. theol. (1973, Tübingen), Habilitation (1978, Tübingen), Dr. theol. h.c. (2003, University of Copenhagen)
Areas of Research: S. Kierkegaard, C.S. Peirce, American Pragmatism, Semiotics

Philip Erwin
1983
Graduate Theological Union
Doctoral Student (GTU); Master of Theological Studies (Garrett Evangelical-Theological Seminary); Bachelor of Arts (Calvin College)
Letters of Paul; Epiphany in the New Testament; Reading the New Testament in relation to ancient Greco-Roman texts and images

Werner Kahl

1962
Institution: Missionsakademie at the University of Hamburg / Protestant Faculty, Frankfurt University
Degrees held: PhD (Emory University, 1992); Dr. theol. habil. (Frankfurt University, 2004)
Main areas of research: Miracle Stories past and present; West-African Biblical Interpretation; Synoptic Gospels; intercultural theology; interreligious dialogue

Hartmut Leppin

1963
Institution Goethe-Universität Frankfurt / Main, Historisches Seminar, Abteilung für Alte Geschichte
Degrees held: Dr. phil. (Marburg) 1990, Dr. habil. (Berlin) 1995
Main areas of research: Ancient Christianity; ancient historiography

David M. Moffitt

1974
Institution: Campbell University Divinity School (Current position is Assistant Professor of New Testament and Greek)
Degrees: B.A. Grove City College; M.Div. Trinity Evangelical Divinity School; Th.M. Duke Divinity School; Ph.D. Duke University Graduate School
Main Areas of Research: Epistle to the Hebrews, Gospel of Matthew, Jewish Apocalypticism, Theories of Sacrifice and Atonement

James Anthony Noel

1948
Professor of American Religion & H. Eugene Farlough Chair of African American Christianity at San Francisco Theological Seminary; Convener, Black Church/Africana Studies Certificate at The Graduate Theological Union, Berkeley, Ca.
BA, UC Berkeley; M.Div., San Francisco Theological Seminary; Ph.D., The Graduate Theological Union.
American Religion; African American Religious Studies and African Diaspora History

Christopher Ocker

1958
San Francisco Theological Seminary and the Graduate Theological Union at Berkeley
Ph.D. Princeton Theological Seminary
Late medieval and early modern Christianity

Michael Rydryck
1980
Assistant for New Testament and History of the Early Church at Goethe-University, Frankfurt / Main
M.A., Dipl. Theol.
Miracles in Luke-Acts, Ancient History and History of Religion, Biblical Hermeneutics

Rossitza Schroeder
1970
Institutional Affiliation: Pacific School of Religion/Graduate Theological Union
Degree: PhD in art history and archaeology
Main areas of research: Byzantine art and archaeology, Monastic contemplative practices and visual arts, East-West interactions

Heiko Schulz
1959
Institution: Goethe University Frankfurt
Degrees held: Dr. phil. (1993)
Main areas of research: Sören Kierkegaard, modern (analytical) philosophy of religion, protestant 19th century theology, general ethics

Teun Tieleman
1960
Institution: Utrecht University
Degrees held: MA, PhD
Main areas of research: Ancient Philosophy, Ancient Medicine

Elaine M. Wainwright
1948
Institution: School of Theology, University of Auckland, New Zealand
Degrees held: BAHons (Queensland); MA (Theol) (CTU Chicago); Eleve Diplome (Jerusalem); BSS (Rome); PhD (Queensland)
Main areas of research: Biblical Hermeneutics; Critical Theory; Feminist, Postcolonial and Ecological Hermeneutics and reading; Socio-Rhetorical interpretation

Annette Weissenrieder

1967
Associate professor of New Testament at San Francisco Theological Seminary and member of Core doctoral faculty at the Graduate Theological Union;
Dr. theol. (University of Heidelberg);
main areas of research: Theology of Paul and the Synoptic Gospels, Greco-roman medicine and philosophy, New Testament anthropology, pneumatology, theories of the history of religion, Roman domestic art, numismatic, and architecture

Norbert Zimmermann

1968
Institut für Kulturgeschichte der Antike der österreichischen Akademie der Wissenschaften, Wien
Institute for the Study of Ancient Culture, Austrian Academy of Sciences, Vienna
M.A., Dr. phil., START-Prize (2005)
Römische Wandmalerei, Spätantikes Sepulkralwesen, Wohnbauforschung, Ikonographie

Index of Subjects and Persons

Index of Biblical Sources

Index of Authors

www.ingramcontent.com/pod-product-compliance
Lightning Source LLC
LaVergne TN
LVHW010851110826
845149LV00005B/1385